NEW TESTAMENT MASCULINITIES

Society of Biblical Literature

Semeia Studies

Number 45

NEW TESTAMENT MASCULINITIES

NEW TESTAMENT
MASCULINITIES

Edited by
Stephen D. Moore
and
Janice Capel Anderson

Society of Biblical Literature
Atlanta

NEW TESTAMENT MASCULINITIES

Library of Congress Cataloging-in-Publication Data

New Testament masculinities / edited by Stephen D. Moore and Janice Capel Anderson.
     p. cm. — (Society of Biblical Literature Semeia studies, no. 45)
   Includes bibliographical references.
   ISBN 1-58983-109-8 (pbk. bdg. : alk. paper)
   1. Men in the Bible. 2. Bible. N.T.—Criticism, interpretation, etc. 3. Men (Christian theology)—History of doctrines—Early church, ca. 30–600. 4. Masculinity—Religious aspects—Christianity—History of doctrines—Early church, ca. 30–600. I. Moore, Stephen D., 1954– II. Anderson, Janice Capel, 1952– III. Series: Semeia studies ; no. 45.
   BS2545.M39 N49 2003
225.8'30531—dc22   2003020054

11 10 09 08 07 06 05 04 03   5 4 3 2 1

Printed in the United States of America on acid-free, recycled paper conforming to ANSI/NISO Z39.48-1992 (R1997) and ISO 9706:1994 standards for paper permanence.

CONTENTS

ABBREVIATIONS

ANCIENT SOURCES

	Full Greek/Latin title	English title
1. En.		*1 Enoch*
1QM		*War Scroll*
1QS		*Rule of the Community/ Manual of Discipline*
4 Macc		4 Maccabees
4Q286		*Blessings*
4Q491		*War Scroll* (fragment)
Aeschines		
Tim.	*In Timarchum*	*Against Timarchus*
Ambrosiaster (Pseudo-Ambrose)		
Com. Ep. Paul	*Commentaria in Epistulam ad Romanos*	*Commentary on the Epistle to the Romans*
Apuleius		
Metam.	*Metamorphoses*	*The Golden Ass*
Aristophanes		
Eccl.	*Ecclesiazusae*	*Women of the Assembly*
Aristotle		
An. post.	*Analytica posteriora*	*Posterior Analytics*
Eth. nic.	*Ethica nichomachea*	*Nichomachean Ethics*
Gen. an.	*De generatione anamalium*	*Generation of Animals*
Oec.	*Oeconomica*	*Economics*
Poet.	*Poetica*	*Poetics*
Probl.	*Problemata*	*Problems*
Rhet.	*Rhetorica*	*Rhetoric*
Artemidorus of Daldis		
Oneir.	*Oneirocritica*	*Dream Analysis*
Athenaeus		
Deipn.	*Deipnosophistae*	*Deipnosophists*
Augustine of Hippo		
Civ.	*De civitate Dei*	*The City of God*

Conf.	Confessiones	Confessions
Exp. prop. Rom.	Expositio quarumdam proposi- tionum ex Epistola ad Romanos	Exposition of Certain Pro- positions from the Epistle to the Romans
Nupt.	De nuptiis et concupiscentia ad Valerium comitem	Marriage and Concupis- cence
CD		Damascus Document
Cercidas		
Meliamb.	Meliambi	
Cicero		
Fin.	De finibus	On Ends
Inv.	De inventione rhetorica	On Invention
Leg.	De legibus	On the Laws
Nat. d.	De natura deorum	On the Nature of the Gods
Off.	De officiis	On Duties
Rep.	De republica	On the Republic
Tusc.	Tusculanae disputationes	Tusculan Disputations
Clement of Alexandria		
Paed.	Paedagogus	Christ the Educator
Strom.	Stromateis	Miscellanies
Demosthenes		
Cor. trier.	De corona trierarchiae	On the Trierarchic Crown
Tim.	Contra Timotheum	Against Timotheus
Dio Chrysostom		
Or.	Orationes	Orations
Dio Halicarnassus		
Ant. Rom.	Antiquitates romanae	Roman Antiquities
Diogenes Laertius		
Vit. Phil.	De clarorum philosophorum vitis	Lives of Eminent Philo- sophers
Epictetus		
Diss.	Dissertationes	Discourses
Euripides		
Andr.	Andromache	
Eusebius		
Hist. Eccl.	Historia ecclesiastica	Ecclesiastical History
Gellius, Aulus		
Noct. Att.	Noctes Atticae	Attic Nights
Gennadius of Constantinople		
Ep. Rom.	Fragmenta in Epistulam ad Romanos	Fragments on the Epistle to the Romans
Gos. Naz.		Gospel of the Nazarenes
Gos. Thom.		Gospel of Thomas

Homer
  Il.   *Ilias*   *Iliad*
Horace
  Ep.   *Epistulae*   *Epistles*
Ignatius
  Pol.   *Pros Polykarpon*   *Letter to Polycarp*
  Smyrn.   *Pros Smyrnaiois*   *Letter to the Smyrnaeans*
John Chrysostom
  Hom. Rom. *Homiliae in epistulam ad*   *Homilies on the Epistle*
               Romanos   *to the Romans*
Josephus
  Ant.   *Antiquitates Judaicae*   *Jewish Antiquities*
  J.W.   *Bellum Judaicum*   *Jewish War*
Jub.   *Jubilees*
Justin Martyr
  1 Apol.   *Apologia 1*   *First Apology*
  2 Apol.   *Apologia 2*   *Second Apology*
Juvenal
  Sat.   *Satirae*   *Satires*
Lactantius
  Inst.   *Divinarum institutionum*   *The Divine Institutes*
Lucian
  Fug.   *Fugitivi*   *The Runaways*
  Nigr.   *Nigrinus*
  Peregr.   *De morte Peregrini*   *The Passing of Peregrinus*
  Vit. auct.   *Vitarum auctio*   *Lives at Auction*
Lucretius
  Rer. nat.   *De rerum natura*   *On the Nature of Things*
Macrobius
  Sat.   *Saturnalia*
Martial
  Epigr.   *Epigrammata*   *Epigrams*
  Spect.   *Spectacula*   *Spectacles*
Musonius Rufus
  Diss.   *Disserationum*   *Discourses*
Origen
  Cels.   *Contra Celsum*   *Against Celsus*
Ovid
  Metam.   *Metamorphoses*
  Trist.   *Tristia*
Pelagius
  PCR   *Commentaria in Epistolam* *Commentary on the Epistle*
               ad Romanos   *to the Romans*

Persius
   Sat.   *Satirae*   *Satires*
Philo
   Abr.   *De Abrahamo*   *On the Life of Abraham*
   Contempl.   *De vita contemplativa*   *On the Contemplative Life*
   Ebr.   *De ebrietate*   *On Drunkenness*
   Fug.   *De fuga et inventione*   *On Flight and Finding*
   Legat.   *Legum allegoriae*   *Allegorical Interpretation*
   Mos.   *De vita Mosis*   *On the Life of Moses*
   Opif.   *De opificio mundi*   *On the Creation of the World*
   QE   *Quaestiones et solutiones in Exodum*   *Questions and Answers on Exodus*
   QG   *Quaestiones et solutiones in Genesin*   *Questions and Answers on Genesis*
   Somn.   *De somniis*   *On Dreams*
   Spec.   *De specialibus legibus*   *On the Special Laws*
   Virt.   *De virtutibus*   *On the Virtues*
Plato
   Gorg.   *Gorgias*
   Hipp. maj.   *Hippias major*   *Greater Hippias*
   Lach.   *Laches*
   Phaedr.   *Phaedrus*
   Resp.   *Respublica*   *Republic*
   Symp.   *Symposium*
   Theaet.   *Theaetetus*
   Tim.   *Timaeus*
Pliny the Elder
   Nat.   *Naturalis historia*   *Natural History*
Pliny the Younger
   Ep.   *Epistulae*   *Epistles*
   Pan.   *Panegyricus*   *Panegyric*
Plutarch
   Alex.   *Alexander*
   Caes.   *Caesar*
   Conj. praec. *Conjugalia Praecepta*   *Advice to Bride and Groom*
   Lyc.   *Lycurgus*
   Mor.   *Moralia*
   Tranq. an.   *De tranquillitate animi*   *Tranquillity*
Pseudo-Aristotle
   Physiog.   *Physiognomenica*   *Physiognomy*
Quintilian
   Inst. orat.   *Institutio oratoria*   *The Orator's Education*

Seneca the Elder
    Contr.   *Controversiae*   *Disputes*
Seneca the Younger
    Ben.   *De beneficiis*   *On Favors / On Benefits*
    Clem.   *De clementia*   *On Clemency*
    Ep.   *Epistulae morales*   *Moral Epistles*
    Herc. fur.   *Hercules furens*
    Ira   *De ira*   *On Anger*
    Nat.   *Naturales quaestiones*   *Natural Questions*
    Vit. beat.   *De vita beata*   *On the Good Life*
Shenute of Atripe
    Vit. mon.   *De vita monachorum*   *On the Monastic Life*
Shepherd of Hermas
    Man.   *Mandate*
    Sim.   *Similitude*
    Vis.   *Vision*
Sir   Sirach
Suetonius
    Aug.   *Divus Augustus*   *The Deified Augustus*
    Cal.   *Gaius Caligula*   *Gaius Caligula*
    Claud.   *Divus Claudius*   *The Deified Claudius*
    Dom.   *Domitianus*   *Domitian*
    Gal.   *Galba*   *Galba*
    Gramm.   *De grammaticis*   *On Grammarians*
    Jul.   *Divus Julius*   *The Deified Julius*
    Ner.   *Nero*   *Nero*
T. Ash.   *Testament of Asher*
T. Dan   *Testament of Dan*
Tacitus
    Ann.   *Annales*   *Annals*
Tertullian
    Apol.   *Apologeticus*   *Apology*
    Spect.   *De spectaculis*   *The Shows*
Wis   Wisdom of Solomon
Xenophon
    Ages.   *Agesilaus*
    Mem.   *Memorabilia*   *Remarkable Things*
    Oec.   *Oeconomicus*   *Economics*

MODERN SOURCES

AA   *American Anthropologist*
AB   Anchor Bible

ABR   *Australian Biblical Review*
ABRL   Anchor Bible Reference Library
ANF   *Ante-Nicene Fathers*
AJP   *American Journal of Philology*
ANTC   Abingdon New Testament Commentaries
BAGD   Bauer, W., W. F. Arndt, F. W. Gingrich, and F. W. Danker. *A Greek-English Lexicon of the New Testament and Other Early Christian Literature.* 3d ed. Chicago: University of Chicago Press, 2000.
BibInt   *Biblical Interpretation*
BNTC   Black's New Testament Commentaries;
BR   *Biblical Research*
BTB   *Biblical Theology Bulletin*
BZ   *Biblische Zeitschrift*
BZNW   Beihefte zur Zeitschrift für die neutestamentliche Wissen-schaft
CBQ   *Catholic Biblical Quarterly*
CER   Origen. *Commentarii in epistulam ad Romanos.* Edited by T. Heither. 5 vols. Freiburg: Herder, 1990–95.
CSEL   Corpus scriptorum ecclesiasticorum latinorum
CTM   *Currents in Theology and Mission*
ENPK   *Ein neuer Paulustext und Kommentar.* Edited by H. J. Frede. Freiburg: Herder, 1974.
FC   Fathers of the Church
FCNTECW   Feminist Companion to the New Testament and Early Christian Writings
HBT   *Horizons in Biblical Theology*
HDR   Harvard Dissertations in Religion
HTR   *Harvard Theological Review*
ICC   International Critical Commentary
IESS   *International Encyclopedia of the Social Sciences.* Edited by D. L. Sills. 19 vols. New York: Macmillan, 1968–.
JAAR   *Journal of the American Academy of Religion*
JBL   *Journal of Biblical Literature*
JEA   *Journal of Egyptian Archaeology*
JECS   *Journal of Early Christian Studies*
JETS   *Journal of the Evangelical Theological Society*
JFSR   *Journal of Feminist Studies in Religion*
JJS   *Journal of Jewish Studies*
JRE   *Journal of Religious Ethics*
JRS   *Journal of Roman Studies*
JSJ   *Journal for the Study of Judaism in the Persian, Hellenistic, and Roman Periods*

JSNT	*Journal for the Study of the New Testament*
JSNTSup	Journal for the Study of the New Testament Supplement Series
JSOT	*Journal for the Study of the Old Testament*
JSOTSup	Journal for the Study of the Old Testament Supplement Series
JTSA	*Journal of Theology for South Africa*
LCL	Loeb Classical Library
LEC	Library of Early Christianity
LS	*Louvain Studies*
LSJ	Liddell, H. G., R. Scott, H. S. Jones, *A Greek-English Lexicon.* 9th ed. with revised supplement. Oxford: Oxford University Press, 1996.
NCB	New Century Bible
NICNT	New International Commentary on the New Testament
NovT	*Novum Testamentum*
NPNF[1]	*Nicene and Post-Nicene Fathers,* Series 1
NTS	*New Testament Studies*
PCR	*Pelagius's Commenatry on St. Paul's Epistle to the Romans.* Edited by T. De Bruyn. New York: Oxford University Press, 1993.
PG	Patrologia graeca [= Patrologiae cursus completus: Series graeca]. Edited by J.-P. Migne. 162 vols. Paris: Migne, 1857–86.
PL	Patrologia latina [= Patrologiae cursus completus: Series latina]. Edited by J.-P. Migne. 217 vols. Paris: Migne, 1844–64.
PRSt	*Perspectives in Religious Studies*
RAC	*Reallexikon für Antike und Christentum.* Edited by T. Kluser et al. Stuttgart: Klauser, 1950–.
RelEd	*Religious Education*
ResQ	*Restoration Quarterly*
RevQ	*Revue de Qumran*
SBEC	Studies in the Bible and Early Chrisianity
SBLDS	Society of Biblical Literature Dissertation Series
SBLWGRW	Society of Biblical Literature Writings from the Greco-Roman World
SPhilo	*Studia philonica*
SR	*Studies in Religion*
StPatr	*Studia patristica*
SVF	*Stoicorum veterum fragmenta.* H. von Arnim. 4 vols. Leipzig: Teubner, 1903–24.
SymBU	Symbolae biblicae upsalienses

TDNT	*Theological Dictionary of the New Testament.* Edited by G. Kittel and G. Friedrich. Translated by G. W. Bromiley. 10 vols. Grand Rapids: Eerdmans, 1964–76.
TNTC	Tyndale New Testament Commentaries
TS	*Theological Studies*
WBC	Word Biblical Commentary
VC	*Vigiliae Christianae*
ZNW	*Zeitschrift für die neutestamentliche Wissenschaft und die Kunde der älteren Kirche*

"O Man, Who Art Thou...?":
Masculinity Studies and New Testament Studies

Stephen D. Moore
Drew University

> *Nay but, O man, who art thou that repliest against God? Shall the thing formed say to him that formed it, Why hast thou made me thus?*
> Romans 9:20

Masculinity, Masculinism, Feminism

> *If this ... work be of men, it will come to nought.*
>
> Acts 5:38

What does masculinity have to do with biblical studies? Almost nothing—and nearly everything: *almost nothing* until relatively recently, when studies specifically analyzing the construction of masculinity in biblical and cognate texts began to appear (about which studies I shall have much to say below); but *nearly everything* throughout most of the history of critical biblical scholarship, when men, and men alone, almost without exception, constituted the rank and file of the discipline. Masculinity was, at once, everywhere and nowhere in the discipline, so ubiquitous as to be ordinarily invisible, and possessed, too, of the omnipotence that omnipresence confers. As significant numbers of women scholars, however—feminist scholars in particular—began to achieve hard-won visibility in the field, gender finally stirred itself and emerged into plain view. For feminist biblical critics, the long-repressed realms of femininity and women's experience in biblical texts and biblical interpretation were paramount; the study of masculinity per se did not figure significantly in their research or teaching, there being more immediate and more important fish to fry. To elaborate the point, although

---

* I am indebted to Janice Capel Anderson for a close, critical reading of an earlier draft of this article.

critiques of hegemonic masculinities *were* a standard, even constitutive, component of feminist biblical scholarship from the outset, studies dedicated solely or primarily to critical reflection on masculinity per se did not figure in such scholarship during the 1970s or 1980s. As an index of the general state of gender studies within biblical studies by the beginning of the 1990s, consider the multivolume *Anchor Bible Dictionary* (Freedman), which appeared in 1992 and, in unsurprising contrast to the *Interpreter's Dictionary of the Bible* (Buttrick) of thirty years earlier that it superseded, included an entry on "Feminist Hermeneutics." One searches *ABD* in vain, however, for an article on masculinity or even on gender in general, among the myriad of other articles, from "Aaron" to "Zuzim," that the industrious editors and their distinguished advisory board (themselves all males, as it happens) deemed appropriate for a comprehensive topical survey of the Bible and the field(s) of biblical studies.

Meanwhile, a Men's Studies in Religion program unit had been launched at the 1990 annual meeting of the American Academy of Religion, a development made explicable, if not rendered inevitable, by the fact that "men's studies" was by then an established presence in a number of other contiguous academic disciplines and professional organizations, the latter ranging from the American Psychological Association and the British Sociological Association to the Modern Language Association. Men's studies had also infiltrated the college classroom: "By 1991, approximately four hundred courses were being taught in North American institutions of higher education that had men's studies ... as a major component," Stephen Boyd claims (265). In common with many other practitioners of men's studies, Boyd credits its emergence to the massive impetus provided by women's studies and feminist studies to construe and analyze human existence as fundamentally and ineluctably *gendered* existence (ibid.).

To conceive of men's studies, however—now also (and increasingly) known as masculinity studies—as a province solely of males, many of whom look to (female) practitioners of feminism for inspiration, attempting to appropriate feminist strategies of interpretation and redeploy them for the critical study of masculinity, would be a gross oversimplification of a complex terrain, for several reasons. First, much of the work that falls under the rubric of masculinity studies itself invites description simply as a further exercise in feminist studies rather than as an attempt to hijack, or even "appropriate," certain features of feminist analysis and utilize them for other, nonfeminist ends.[1] Second, many of the practitioners of masculinity studies themselves happen to be female. This circumstance,

---

[1] I am indebted to my colleague Virginia Burrus for originally enabling me to see this.

too, is by no means invariably a secondary phenomenon, a case of certain women critics leaping aboard an accelerating bandwagon originally set in motion by men. In literary studies, for instance, a field responsible for a high percentage of the multifaceted work on masculinity now flooding forth across the humanities and social sciences,[2] Eve Kosofsky Sedgwick's 1985 monograph, *Between Men*, is frequently seen as a kind of charter document of an amplified feminist studies that invites the label "gender studies" because of the highly productive (and resolutely nonreductive) symbiosis that it stages between feminist studies and gay-male studies, in the process yielding an exceptionally challenging model for masculinity studies.

All that being said, however, it would be fanciful in the extreme to imagine that the interface between feminist and masculinity studies is a friction-free zone (see Gardiner 2002b). On the contrary, many feminists have been, and continue to be, suspicious of "men's studies" (for the spectrum of suspicion, see Hagan), and not without reason. Sedgwick gives incisive expression to such reasoning:

> To figure gender studies as a mere sum of women's studies plus something called "men's studies" ... reduces both women's studies and the supposedly symmetrical men's studies to static denominations of subject matter and reduces any understanding of relations between genders to something equally static and additive. That genders are constituted as such, not only in dialectical relation to each other but in relation to the oppression historically exercised by one over the other, is a knowledge repressed by this impulse toward the separate but equal. Things get even worse when the rationale for an additive gender studies agenda involves not a nominally depoliticized and positivist study of women as women and men as men but rather the conscious promotion of masculinist viewpoints (under the men's studies rubrics) as a remedial "balance" against feminist ones. (Sedgwick 1992: 272)

Fanning the flames of suspicion, for many feminists, is the fact that outside the hallowed halls of academe, the term "men's studies," coupled with the more general notion of attending to masculinity as a problem for men as well as for women (the "crisis of masculinity," so-called; see Horrocks; S. Robinson; Traister; Gardiner 2002a: 6–11), readily conjures up, in North America at any rate, the idea not merely of a "counterbalance" to women's studies and feminism but an outright backlash against them. The more common label for this groundswell of extra-academic attention

---

2 See the "General" section in the classified bibliography (pages 23–42 in the present volume) for representative works.

to the problem of masculinity is, of course, "the men's movement." The semantic shift from "studies" to "movement" is not an insignificant one, for although we are still in the realm of books, more or less, we are also in the realm of glossy media coverage, weekend workshops and retreats, football stadiums packed with Promise Keepers, and Million Man Marches on Washington—all now receding into the muted hubbub of history, to be sure, but not without having left a livid mark on American ideologies of gender.[3] And while books *have* featured in the men's movement, these are books that have sold more than enough copies, and hence carried enough commercial clout, to accost the reader boldly by the door of Borders or Barnes & Noble (as opposed to lurking in the little-visited literary criticism section, say), books such as Robert Bly's *Iron John: A Book about Men,* Sam Keen's *Fire in the Belly: On Being a Man,* or (stretching the category somewhat) Susan Faludi's *Stiffed: The Betrayal of the American Man.* In contrast to the *critical interrogation* of traditional masculinites that, to a greater or lesser extent, and impelled by feminism and women's studies, together with queer studies, has tended to characterize academic writings on masculinity, works such as *Iron John* have tended to amount instead to an *uncritical celebration* of traditional masculinities conducted, to a greater or lesser extent, in reaction to the erosive effects on them of feminism and women's studies.[4]

MASCULINITY STUDIES AS NEW TESTAMENT STUDIES

I knew a man in Christ...

2 Corinthians 12:2

At the time of writing, only a tiny handful of published works have dealt with the manifold ways in which masculinities are constructed or performed in New Testament texts. I review four such studies below.[5]

---

3 For analysis of the Promise Keepers phenomenon and the Million Man March, see Messner: 24–35, 64–66, 70–71. The workshops and retreats mentioned above are especially associated with the "mythopoetic men's movement," which I discuss later.

4 Not that all popularly-pitched works on masculinity share this reactionary agenda. Susan Bordo's *The Male Body* is one example of a popular book on men whose critical edge is directed elsewhere than at feminism.

5 The principal remaining examples (that I know of) are Eilberg-Schwartz: 223–37 (on the Gospel infancy narratives); Neyrey 1998a: 29–32, 148–51, 180–222 passim (on Matthew); D'Angelo 2002 and A. Smith (both on Luke-Acts); Kahl (on Galatians); Moore 1996: 75–138 (on selected texts from the Hebrew Bible, the Gospels, and Revelation); and Moore 2001: 133–99 (on Romans and Revelation). For further studies in masculinity dealing with the literature of the Hebrew Bible or extracanonical Jewish or Christian texts, see §§5–7 of the classified bibliography in this volume.

Among other things, I shall be interested in seeing how each study positions itself in relation to feminism and in noting the (other) practical, critical, or theoretical resources that inform or infuse its analysis of masculinity. These four studies have been selected, not for their similarity to the bulk of the studies contained in the present volume, but for their dissimilarity. Taken as a whole, the present collection very likely conveys the impression that the study of New Testament masculinities, and early Christian masculinities more generally, is characterized by a relatively high degree of methodological and theoretical uniformity. (I shall elaborate upon this observation in my concluding section.) The four earlier studies here selected for review, each very different not only from most of the essays collected in the present volume but also from its three companions, perhaps serve to complicate that impression of homogeneity and indicate other avenues of approach—while exposing certain of the pitfalls that attend these approaches.

Jennifer Glancy's "Unveiling Masculinity" takes as its text Mark's account of the execution of John the Baptist (6:17–29). Glancy's stated aim is twofold: first, she will attempt "to unveil assumptions about gender, especially masculinity," that inform the narrative itself (1994: 34); second, she will attempt to single out "tendencies in late nineteenth and twentieth century thinking about gender" that have "overdetermined" certain modern interpretations of the narrative (ibid.), interpretations enshrined in artistic representations of it, on the one hand, most notably Oscar Wilde's Salome, and in scholarly representations of it, on the other. Glancy does not explicitly label her own interpretation of these assorted interpretations a feminist one, but it could hardly be construed in any other way. The closest she comes to articulating her relationship to feminism occurs as something of an aside: having remarked that "[c]ritics have approached this tale as though 'the head of John the Baptist' were a plausible answer to Freud's question, '*Was will das Weib?*'," she suggests that a survey of the modern reception history of the tale is more likely to provide clues to a rather different question, "What do (some) men fear?", adding: "I have framed the question this way in part to redress a tendency in both feminist and non-feminist writings to conflate gender issues with women's issues" (34 n. 2). Although this last sentence occurs in a footnote, it is tempting to frame Glancy's article in terms of it as an "early" example of feminist biblical criticism turning its analytic attention fully to the problem of masculinity—and, in the process, reenacting in miniature the transition from feminist studies to gender studies that had already occurred in literary studies (on which see Schor).

Of what theoretical armature does Glancy avail herself for her study? The reference to Freud, however critical, is no throwaway, for Glancy does draw heavily upon the psychoanalytic tradition as represented especially by Joan Riviere and Karen Horney. Taking her cue from Riviere's (proto-Butlerian) suggestion that femininity is a "masquerade," Glancy asks why masculinity might not be similarly understood, and further asks what might ensue were we to approach Mark 6:17–29 "with the assumption that masculinity is a front to disguise vulnerability and weakness" (36). Glancy then invokes Horney's argument that men's anxieties about their own masculinity are routinely externalized by being projected onto women, who are thereby transformed into appropriate objects of male dread, a perception spectacularly epitomized by the male creation of an infamous set of emasculating female monsters: the Sirens, the Sphinx, Kali, Delilah, Judith—and Salome (Horney: 135; Glancy 1994: 37). Pushing off from Horney's hypothesis, Glancy then turns to an analysis of the complex relationships in the Baptist execution narrative between the anonymous girl (whom tradition has dubbed "Salome"), Herodias, Herod, and the Baptist himself. Among her conclusions is the (Laura Mulveyesque) suggestion that the representation of gender in the episode is informed by "assumptions that 'to-be-looked-at-ness' defines femininity, and that active voyeurism is a prerogative of masculinity; that masculinity is vulnerable before the expression of female desire...; and perhaps that the bond between a mother and her daughter is threatening to men who encounter them" (42). She immediately adds, however, that "Herodias herself is not represented as a monster" in the tale (ibid.): this characterization of her, along with the concomitant characterization of "Salome" as epitomizing deadly femininity, is a product, rather, of the tale's reception history, including its modern scholarly reception, as she then attempts to demonstrate, arguing that "modern critics have not attempted to disentangle Mark's representation of masculinity and femininity from their own presumptions about gender" (38).

But does Glancy herself fall prey to her own critique? Does her psychoanalytic methodology, however tempered by her historical sensibilities, enable her in the end to separate out Mark's own representations of gender from the sedimented layers of interpretation laid down by Mark's innumerable other readers (if such separation is, indeed, ever possible, a conundrum that Stanley Fish long ago taught us to ponder)? That Glancy herself is not unaware of the problem is signaled by a sentence in the abstract printed at the end of her article that is curiously at odds with the unflinchingly confident pronouncements on Mark in the article itself: "Whether or not Mark demonizes women and their capacity for power may be an undecidable question; we can more certainly establish that modern readers have offered interpretations molded by their own fears about female subjectivity" (50). Viewed "vertically," so to speak, through the intricately layered history of interpretation, Mark's own representations of femininity, as well as of masculinity, in this episode may indeed be so deeply buried as to be all but undecidable, especially when the primary excavating tool—in this case, psychoanalytic criticism—is so ineluctably modern in its manufacture. But what if the episode were viewed "horizontally" instead, as it were, side-by-side with the predominant stereotypes of masculinity and femininity in ancient Mediterranean culture? Close attention to the differential matrix of ancient Mediterranean gender protocols and prohibitions in which Mark's own gender ideology is embedded—or rather of which it is the product—might serve to bring that ideology into sharper focus (albeit without avoiding the vicissitudes of interpretation). This, as it happens, is the avenue of approach to early Christian masculinities adopted by most of the contributors to the present volume—Glancy herself included.

A second "early" study in New Testament masculinity, David Clines's "*Ecce Vir*, or, Gendering the Son of Man," is disarmingly frank about its relationship to feminism: "I am writing this paper because one day, feeling a little marginalized by the impact of feminist biblical criticism, I asked Cheryl Exum, in the words of Peter, What shall this 'man' do?, feeling sure that feminist criticism could be no business of mine. I got a one-word answer: Masculinity; and I have gone in the strength of that word forty days and forty nights" (1998: 353). Whether Clines's plaintive question to Exum harbored the simple assumption that feminist criticism could be no business of his, specifically, or, rather, the more sweeping assumption that it could be no business of men in general, and whether Exum's prophetic response to Clines in turn harbored the simple assumption that the analysis of masculinity was something to which Clines, specifically, could plausibly and profitably turn his hand, or, rather, the more sweeping assumption that the analysis of masculinity is properly a male preserve, are matters about which we can only speculate.[6] What seems certain, in any case, is that Clines has, to date, produced more work on biblical masculinity than any other biblical scholar, the bulk of it on texts of the Hebrew Bible, Clines being a Hebrew Bible specialist.[7]

"*Ecce Vir*" bears a symbiotic relationship to Clines's earlier studies in biblical masculinity (see especially Clines 1995a), in which he identified

---

6 The proper and possible roles of men in relation to feminism has been a topic of vigorous debate in other fields; see, for example, Jardine and Smith; Porter; Digby; Schacht and Ewing; Newton.

7 At the time of writing, Clines's personal Web page, http://www.shef.ac.uk/uni/academic/A-C/biblst/DJACcurrres/PlayMan.html, provides the complete text of seven papers on biblical masculinity, four as yet unpublished. (The three published papers are Clines 1995a; 1998; and his contribution to this volume.) These papers are part of a work in progress, he informs us, provisionally entitled *Play the Man! The Masculine Imperative in the Bible.*

the components of masculinity in the Hebrew Bible as "strength, violence, bonding, womanlessness, solitariness, musicality, beauty, persuasive speech, honour, binary thinking, objectifying" (1998: 354). Clines confesses his predisposition to probe the Gospel Jesus for these same indices of masculinity, although he also intends to "work inductively" from the evidence of the Gospels themselves (ibid.; the prospect of a musical Jesus, fleetingly conjured up, is thus cruelly dashed!). His specific object of investigation will be the masculinity of the Jesus who emerges from the composite portrait of the canonical Gospels, as distinct either from the masculinity of the historical Jesus or the Jesuses of the individual Gospels. One might add that the composite Jesus has been an oddly neglected figure even in "postmodern" Gospel studies, given that this Jesus is precisely the one who has towered over Western history and culture. It is hardly coincidental that this last and most intractable taboo in Gospel studies—the one that prohibits reading across the borders between the Gospels (borders tirelessly policed by the great mass of New Testament scholars)—should be infringed by an interloper from Hebrew Bible studies.[8]

The central section of *"Ecce Vir"* is entitled, appropriately enough, "The Masculinity of Jesus," and falls into six subsections: "Jesus the Strong"; "Jesus the Violent"; "Jesus the Powerful and Persuasive Speaker"; "Jesus the Male Bonder"; "Jesus the Womanless"; and "Jesus the Binary Thinker." "It is fundamental for the traditional male to be strong," states Clines (1998: 355), and the Gospel Jesus is indeed strong, on Clines's reading, a doer of mighty deeds and a binder of "the strong man," although his strength is never described in physical terms (ibid.). Clines pithily remarks: "The name for strength in action, in traditional male terms, is violence. And the name for the violent action of men in groups is war" (356). But whereas physical warfare abounds in the David story, say, it is in rather short supply in the Jesus story. As evidence for "Jesus the Violent," Clines is able to adduce only Jesus' injunction to his disciples to sell their garments to purchase arms (Luke 22:36); his rough handling of the money changers in the temple; and the occasional violence of his language, notably his curses and "woes." For "Jesus the Powerful and Persuasive Speaker," in contrast, evidence abounds. "To be master of persuasion is to have another form of power," argues Clines, "which is not an alternative to, and far less a denatured version of, physical strength, but part of the repertory of the powerful male" (358). Introducing "Jesus the Male Bonder," Clines remarks: "Male bonding is a

---

8 Clines perpetrates a similar infraction in his study of Paul's masculinity in the present volume, refusing to keep the Paul of the seven "undisputed" letters separate from the Paul of the disputed six.

feature of male behaviour that has been attested throughout history but that has only recently been given a name" (362). On the one hand, the concept of "male bonding" enables Clines to reflect provocatively on the incontrovertible fact that Jesus does surround himself with other males in the Gospels (a series of observations further elaborated in the ensuing subsection, "Jesus the Womanless"). On the other hand, the employment of a concept and term so characteristically late-twentieth-century (the term appears to have been coined by Lionel Tiger in 1969, as Clines himself notes) to analyze relationships between males in texts from antiquity might be expected to set many a historian's teeth on edge, disposed as she or he might be to construe "male bonding" as a discursive construct specific to a certain historical moment, as distinct from something that long preexisted the contingencies of its naming (although to mount such objections and posit such distinctions may, in the end, amount to no more than a Promethean contestation of the ineradicable anachronism of historiography itself).

Clines's final category, "Jesus the Binary Thinker," raises problems of another sort. The question is not whether the Gospel Jesus tends to think in binary terms—Clines has little trouble demonstrating that he does, while acknowledging that it is also characteristic of this Jesus to blur binary categories on occasion ("Love your enemies" would be a prime example)—but rather whether binary thinking is an authentic index of masculinity. "I am arguing that binary or oppositional thinking is a typically male mode of thought," asserts Clines (367), appealing to Derrida, while attempting to exceed him:

> Derrida has shown, and it would be a brave person who denied it now, that the whole edifice of Western intellectual thought has been built upon a set of binary categories, such as nature/nurture, mind/body.... If now we add that the construction of binaries has been an essentially male project—like the Western intellectual tradition in general—we can contemplate the future emergence of a different conceptuality that is more representatively human. (367–68)

The problem with this assertion, however, notwithstanding the commendable sentiments that it enshrines, is that one can hardly help suspecting that even outside the predominantly male bastions of the Western intellectual tradition, the tendency to think in binary terms has been endemic and no respecter of gender and that the step beyond binarism is not nearly as simple as Clines would seem to suppose (the extraordinary difficulty of that step, indeed, being a recurrent theme in Derrida's early oeuvre).

"The Displaced Body of Jesus Christ," by theologian Graham Ward, likewise turns its analytic attention to "the presentation of the male

Jesus in the Gospels and its representation in the life of the Church"
(1999: 163), not as an end in itself, however, but in the interests of for-
mulating a "nascent theology of the ascension" (ibid.).[9] Further
complicating Ward's examination of the Gospel Jesus' masculinity is the
fact that the essay is his own contribution to the manifesto-like collection *Radical Orthodoxy: A New Theology* that he co-edited (see Milbank,
Pickstock, and Ward), so that Ward has various theological fish to fry
whose aroma pervades his essay even when they are not visibly sizzling
on its surface. Stir into the mix Ward's unusual intellectual reach (he is
that rarest of theologians who appears equally at home in the classics of
the theological tradition and the most arcane regions of contemporary
critical theory), and an adequate summary of his densely argued essay
becomes all but impossible.

A truncated version of Ward's argument as it bears on the masculinity of the Gospel Jesus might run as follows. The ascension of Jesus
represents, for Ward, the final "displacement" of his male body, a body
that, from the patristic period onward at least, is never simply or unam-
biguously material to begin with, pointing backward to the Adamic
perfection of prelapsarian corporeality, on the one hand, yet forward to
the no-less-idealized corporeality of resurrection, on the other. Ward is
especially interested, therefore, in those Gospel episodes in which Jesus'
physical body is subject to explicit displacement, enabling "the divine [to
be] manifested in the sexed and corporeal" (165): the transfiguration, the
eucharist, the crucifixion, the resurrection, and, of course, the ascension.
In the transfiguration, Jesus' physical body is displaced by becoming an
icon of what shimmers dimly beyond it, namely, the divine. In the
eucharist, this displacement is yet more pronounced, as Jesus' body
"begins its withdrawal from the narrative" (167). "A certain metonymic
substitution is enacted," whereby Jesus' male physique is resituated
"within the neuter materiality of bread (*to arton*)" (167). As bread, Jesus'
body is no less physical, but it is now extendable: it can incorporate
other bodies by being incorporated by them. Transposable now as well
as transfigurable, the body of Christ can cross gender boundaries:
"Jesus' body as bread is no longer Christ as simply and biologically
male" (168).

The breaking of bread now gives way to the breaking of Jesus' body,
resulting in yet more radical displacement. Ward's extended reflection on
the crucifixion narratives—"The male body of Christ is handed over to

---

9 For an independent set of reflections on Ward's arguments, see Thurman in the present volume.

death," is how he epitomizes them (ibid.)—begins by underscoring that body's vulnerability. He ruminates on "the passivity of Jesus before Jewish and Roman authorities," "the two scenes of his nakedness," and "the sexual charge ... evident in the delight taken by the soldiers in abusing his body and in ... the contrast between Pilate's towering authority and Jesus' submissiveness" (ibid.). The narrative "climaxes with the strung-up nakedness of Christ on the cross" (169). The conclusions that Ward draws from these erotic elements are, however, highly debatable. "Throughout the play of these erotic and political power games," he argues, "the actual maleness of the body of Jesus is forgotten.... The body becomes an object acted upon at the point when the dynamic for the narrative is wrenched from Jesus' grasp and put into the hands of the Jewish and Roman authorities.... The body as object is already being treated as mere flesh, a consumable, a dead, unwanted, discardable thing, before Jesus breathes his last" (ibid.). But while these assertions serve Ward's larger arguments about the progressive displacement of the male body of Jesus as we move through the Gospel narratives, they become dubious when set in the context of hegemonic Roman ideologies of gender. Ward would seem to be suggesting that gender is erased during the course of Jesus' trial and execution, but it could more easily be argued, to the contrary, that gender receives intense accentuation precisely at these points in the narratives. Jesus' passivity, his submissiveness, his stripping and whipping, his role as plaything in the rough hands of the soldiers, his "strung-up nakedness" (as Ward himself puts it), penetration, and abject helplessness on the cross would all have conspired, in complicity with the hegemonic gender codes, to throw his masculinity into sharp relief—precisely as a problem. What makes the problem complex, admittedly, is the fact that Jesus' performance throughout his harsh trial and execution by torture might also have invited another reading—a reading no less gendered, however—that would have construed his silence as a bravura exercise in self-mastery, especially in the wake of the Gethsemane episode and the heroic overcoming of the passions there explicitly thematized, all against an encompassing cultural milieu in which self-mastery was construed as the supreme index of masculinity (cf. Neyrey 1998a: 148–51; Moore 2001: 159–64; Moore and Anderson). Of the various scholars surveyed here who have written on masculinity in the Gospels, Ward is the only one who has given any serious consideration to the passion narratives. But here, for once, Ward's formidable erudition seems to fail him; a sizeable body of work on masculinity in the field of classics (crucial to most of the contributors to the present volume) goes unmentioned by him (as by Clines), even though he takes us to the brink of its concerns.

The resurrected body of Jesus, for Ward, "sums up all the modes of displacement ... in evidence before his death" (1999: 173), whether we reflect on the sign of the empty tomb, the seemingly simultaneous tangi-bility and intangibility of the resurrected body, or its resistance to identification or recognition. But it is the ascension that represents "the final displacement of the body of the gendered Jew" (175). After the ascension, "the Church is now the body of Christ, broken like the bread to be food dispersed throughout the world. The final displacement of the gendered body of Jesus Christ, always aporetic, is the multi-gendered body of the Church" (176). And again:

> We have no access to the body of the gendered Jew. So all those attempts to determine the sexuality of Jesus are simply more recent symptoms of the search for the historical Christ—which Schweitzer demonstrated was pointless at the beginning of this century.... It is pointless because the Church is now the body of Christ, so to understand the body of Jesus we can only examine what the Church is.... The body of Christ is a multigendered body. Its relation to the body of the gendered Jew does not have the logic of cause and effect. This is the logic which lies behind such questions as "Can a male saviour save women?" (176–77)

The latter question, originally Rosemary Radford Ruether's (Ruether: 116–38), which Ward also quotes at the outset of his essay, appears to have driven the essay to a significant degree. He explains, however, that he does not intend the essay to be an attack on Ruether herself. "Rather I am attacking the biological essentialism which lies behind many of the recent moves by feminists towards a post-Christian perspective, and attempting to show how a masculinist symbolics can be refigured in a way which opens salvation through Christ to both (if there are only two, which I doubt) sexes" (177 n. 1). Not entirely unexpectedly, perhaps, Ward's handling of Jesus' body, however radical in orientation, is, in the end, highly orthodox. Relatively few theologians would be capable of marshaling the theoretical resources that Ward does in mounting his arguments, yet these arguments are, at base, thoroughly traditional in the way that they decline to take seriously any substantial rift between the Christ of faith and the Jesus of history, together with the way that they erase the specificity of "the body of the gendered Jew" so that it "expands to embrace the whole of creation" (177). The theological legacy to which Ward appeals, however, and for which he assumes the role of apologist, is, to say the least, suspect. Erasing the specificity of the body of the gen-dered *Jew* has had catastrophic consequences for Jews throughout history, enabling Christianity to drive an annihilating wedge between itself and Judaism—an argument that hardly needs belaboring in a post-Holocaust era. Erasing the specificity of the body of the *gendered* Jew is a gesture similarly fraught with risk. Again, this is well-trodden ground. Ruether herself in her "Can a Male Savior...?" chapter essentially anticipates

Ward's position. Notwithstanding the theoretical as well as the theological sophistication of Ward's Christology, it is tempting to see it in the end as merely the latest in the long line of related Christologies critiqued by Reuther in her chapter under the heading "Androgynous Christologies," a line extending from second-century Gnostics through selected medieval and early modern mystics and nineteenth-century romantics. In hindsight, what is especially striking is the seeming inability of these successive androgynous Christologies to yield church structures in which the gender egalitarianism attributed to the spiritual sphere is conscientiously mirrored in the social sphere.

Mikeal Parsons's "Hand in Hand," the last of the four heterogeneous studies in New Testament masculinity that I have selected for discussion, was his contribution to an issue of *Semeia* devoted to autobiographical criticism. Its real topic, however, as gradually becomes clearer the further one reads in it, is masculinity. Unlike the other three studies here surveyed, this one could only have been written by a man: its central theme is the complex relationship of a specific man, Parsons himself, to his own father. Parsons's reflections on the relationship are mediated through the Lukan parable of the Prodigal Son, read in counterpoint with Rembrandt's *Return of the Prodigal* and Clarissa Estes's short story "Sealskin, Soulskin." Alone among the authors here surveyed, too, Parsons has internalized the discourse of the mythopoetic men's movement (although he has not swallowed it whole, as we shall see).[10] It is not that Parsons introduces the movement at the outset and presents his article as a practical illustration of its agenda: the movement is not mentioned by name until the article is almost over. Nevertheless, Parsons's reading throughout both of the parable of the Prodigal and of his relationship with his own father gives vivid expression to themes and concerns characteristic of the mythopoetic men's movement. As Michael Messner has noted, "A major preoccupation with men at mythopoetic gatherings is the poverty of [modern] men's relationships with fathers and with other men in workplaces" (19). Robert Bly, the movement's most influential guru, has insisted repeatedly that "the love unit most damaged by the Industrial Revolution has been the father-son bond" (Bly: 19). Another

---

10 Indeed, I have been unable to discover any other biblical scholar who has written out of this perspective. With its origins in the United States in the 1980s, and its boom period in the 1990s, the mythopoetic men's movement, mainly made up of white, middle-class, middle-aged men, centered on the ritualized rediscovery and reclamation of certain forms of traditional masculinity. For introductions to and critiques of the movement, see Schwalbe; Messner: 16–24; and Hagan. For a series of illuminating exchanges between the movement and its critics, see Kimmel.

characteristic lament of the movement (see Bly: 14–21, for example) is the absence in modern industrial societies of the rituals common in tribal societies whereby adult men initiate adolescent boys into manhood. Parson's reading of the parable of the Prodigal Son proceeds smoothly out of such concerns: "*A man chooses to leave* for the far country before he is fully initiated into manhood" (Parsons: 132, emphasis original). The Prodigal's choice has "a devastating effect on his relationship with his father" (ibid.). This prompts the question, "How many of us men continue to sacrifice one relationship after another for success, security, and status?" (133), and the subsequent suggestion that "the boy is . . . starving for *male* intimacy which only the father can provide. Some of us men, too, are starving for male nurturing, and we are in desperate need of male mentoring" (ibid., emphasis original). But men are also "ensnared by the image of the Great Provider. We can't stop work because so many depend on us. We must learn to go home when we are emotionally dried-up and spiritually spent" (ibid.).[11]

This eventually segues into Parsons's autobiographical narrative: "I was suffering the pain of watching my ailing marriage die a slow and tortuous death, and I knew I needed to go home, spiritually and geographically. So I traveled with my daughters to visit my father with whom I had experienced a very strained relationship at best" (135). This journey is but the prelude to another: "That summer, my father and I took a two-week trip together alone to explore the mythic West" (143). But when they arrive at their reserved cabin on the south rim of the Grand Canyon they discover that it contains only one bed. "A wave of homophobic anxiety silently washed over both of us: we had never slept in the same bed together" (ibid.). The intimate encounter that night, however, with his father's body, missing its right arm as the result of a childhood accident, proves to be a healing experience for Parsons: "Through this sensual encounter with my father's body, I felt a deep spiritual connection with him. New insights into my father and into myself as men came through the very physicality of this experience" (144). Parsons's reflection on this pivotal experience enables him to articulate the "authentic male spirituality" for which he has been searching (125): "that night I felt the mystical presence of God reach out to me through the corporeality of my own father. This image of lying in bed overwhelmed by the very physical presence of my father, combined with others in a powerful way for me to underscore this basic point:

---

11 The homiletic tone of these reflections arises from the fact that, as Parsons explains, this portion of his article is a lightly revised version of a sermon originally delivered at the Baptist Theological Seminary in Richmond, Virginia.

male sensuality is an intimate, but relatively unexplored, connection to male spirituality" (144).

Parsons sees his emphasis on male physicality as a path to male spirituality as a challenge to the mythopoetic men's movement, arguing that the latter has relied on "transcendent, universal, essentializing, absolute language" (144–45). Such language has the effect of severing men yet again "from their physical, sensual selves," while realigning women with physicality and sensuality, in the age-old pattern (145). In addition to being critical of the movement's massive investment in gender essentialism and the antifeminism of many of its members, he is also critical of its failure to develop "a well-articulated sociopolitical agenda" (146). All of this leads to the question of why Parsons "choose[s] still to identify with it, albeit from an explicitly profeminist stance" (147). He offers three reasons. First, the movement is not monolithic and can accommodate nuanced positions such as his. Second, men suffer "spiritual malaise" under patriarchy; dealing with such malaise "is a necessary part of the political struggle against the dominant patriarchal structures"; and the mythopoetic men's movement is singularly well-equipped to heal the malaise. And third, the men's movement can learn effectively from feminism and women's movements (147–48). "For these reasons," he concludes, "I continue to identify with, and seek to reform, both the mythopoetic men's movement and the Christian tradition as sources for male spirituality" (148).

Commendable as Parsons's agenda is, one cannot help wondering whether the profeminist male simply saddles himself with an albatross in taking on the conceptual apparatus of the mythopoetic men's movement. Whatever the movement's effects on men's lives, one has to wonder about its effects on women's lives, even when championed by a feminist-sensitized male such as Parsons. Kimmel and Kaufman, for example, have noted a troubling paradox that characterizes the men's retreats organized by the mythopoetic men's movement. Leaders at these retreats address the participants "not as fathers but as sons searching for their fathers," notwithstanding the fact that the majority of the participants are middle-aged men who themselves happen to be fathers. They seldom speak of their own children, least of all their daughters, preferring instead to speak "of their pain as sons estranged from fathers" (Kimmel and Kaufman: 282). Parsons follows this script to the letter, as a passage quoted earlier from his article indicates: "I was suffering the pain of watching my ailing marriage die a slow and tortuous death, and I knew I needed to go home, spiritually and geographically. So I traveled with my daughters to visit my father with whom I had experienced a very strained relationship at best" (Parsons: 135). His daughters are not mentioned again, nor is his wife; instead, his relationship with his father moves to center stage and dominates the subsequent discussion. One might respond, perhaps, that since the biblical text around which the article circles is the parable of the Prodigal Son, the personal relationship in Parsons's own life most pertinent to productive reflection on this text is precisely his relationship with his father. Parsons is not uncritical of the gender dynamics of the parable; he reports being "struck by how male oriented the prodigal son parable is. There are no women in this parable" (131). But in relegating his wife and daughters to the outermost margins of his reflections and bringing his father into the center, is Parsons not, in the end, uncritically replicating the womanless world of the parable—so like the womanless world of the mythopoetic men's movement?

Similar questions arise with regard to Parson's version of male spirituality. He reports, as we recall: "I felt the mystical presence of God reach out to me through the corporeality of my own father. This image of lying in bed overwhelmed by the very physical presence of my father, combined with others in a powerful way for me to underscore this basic point: male sensuality is an intimate, but relatively unexplored, connection to male spirituality" (144). Yet it takes but a moment's reflection to perceive the hazards in such a formulation. Construing the corporeality of his own father as the privileged medium for mystical communion with the divine only serves to reinforce the privileged connection that traditional theology has insistently established between human fathers and God the Father as well as the consequent evacuation of the feminine from the sphere of the divine and the marginalization of women in ecclesial life and social life in general. Even though Parsons presents his corporeal male spirituality as a challenge to the mythopoetic men's movement, it seems that he cannot avoid playing into the latter's hands in the end.

Wars and Rumors of Wars

And when ye shall hear of wars and rumours of wars, be ye not troubled.

                                                    Mark 13:7

These four attempts to mesh masculinity studies and New Testament studies—those of Glancy and Clines, Ward and Parsons—are as different methodologically as chalk and cheese, apples and oranges. Consideration of further examples of such work generated during the 1990s (Howard Eilberg-Schwartz's analysis of the Gospel infancy narratives in their relationship to masculinity, for instance)[12] would serve only to increase rather

---

12 For a summary of Eilberg-Schwartz's arguments, see Anderson and Moore in the present volume.

than decrease this impression of methodological disparity. The essays contained in the present volume, however, seem in contrast, and for better or worse, to suggest the emergence of a more unified methodological front in the study of early Christian masculinities.[13]

Jerome Neyrey begins his "Jesus, Gender, and the Gospel of Matthew" by rehearsing the gender stereotypes that prevailed in ancient Mediterranean culture. He is especially interested in the stereotype that constructed men as "outdoors" and "public" figures. Matthew rarely locates Jesus "inside," notes Neyrey, and ascribes no household duties to him. Indeed, Jesus' primary relationship in Matthew with the institution of kinship consists in encouraging his disciples to resist its pressures to conform. In other respects, however, Jesus' own actions conform to those that would have been expected of honorable, public males. He excels in the challenge and riposte exchange, in particular. Yet his teaching frequently conflicts with the dominant code of honor. He reforms aspects of the code by declaring certain behaviors conventionally deemed honorable to be shameful in the eyes of God and vice versa.

In "Matthew and Masculinity," Janice Capel Anderson and Stephen Moore offer an independent, although not unrelated, analysis of the cultural assumptions regarding masculinity embodied or expressed in Matthew's Gospel. Although Matthew lacks most of the standard terminology used to discuss or construct masculinity in ancient Greek and Roman texts, it abounds in explicit references to male kinship relationships and social roles, notably Father/fathers, Son/sons, brothers, and householders. Building upon a critical analysis of these interdependent roles, Anderson and Moore argue that Matthew enshrines multiple contradictory assumptions regarding masculinity. Their study begins and ends with reflection upon the intensely ambiguous figure of the eunuch (cf. Matt. 19:12), whom they see as epitomizing the counterhegemonic trajectory in Matthew's construction of masculinity.

Tat-siong Benny Liew's "Re-Mark-able Masculinities" similarly appeals to ancient Mediterranean ideals and ideologies of masculinity in his examination of Mark's representation of Jesus. Jesus' masculinity in Mark is constituted in relation, or in contrast, to several significant groups of "others," contends Liew, notably "foreigners," social superiors and inferiors, and women. Within these defining parameters, however, Mark's Jesus embodies competing, even contradictory, conceptions of masculinity. Jesus attempts to subsume these contradictions under an all-encompassing desire to accomplish the will of his God and

---

[13] The essay summaries that follow are frequently based on abstracts originally provided by the authors themselves.

Father. In the process, however, he becomes both a victim and an agent of patriarchal gender norms. Liew is at pains to stress that his reading of Mark arises out of the conviction that meaningful analysis of masculinity is indissociable from a critical consideration of patriarchy.

Eric Thurman's "Looking for a Few Good Men" argues that Mark's uneasy relationship to Roman colonial authority is productive of gender instability within his text. Mark's Jesus mimics both God's and Rome's imperial and masculinist authority, while Jesus is mimicked by his (male) disciples in turn. Jesus is framed as a "bandit" in the passion narrative, but bandits are frequently "gender outlaws" in other novelistic and historical narratives of the period. Similarly, Mark's concepts of messiahship and discipleship resonate with other contemporary discourses that valorize public figures of vulnerability, such as the gladiator, as objects of identification who embody "feminized" yet triumphant stances. Mark's reconfiguration of the masculine subject neither breaks with nor simply inverts hegemonic manhood. Mark attempts both to resist colonialism and maintain male authority, with important consequences for women, whether "inside" or "outside" his text.

Colleen Conway's "Behold the Man!" argues that the Johannine Jesus (also) models traits that exemplified ideal masculinity in the ancient Mediterranean world. For her, moreover, there is an integral connection between the high Johannine Christology and the superior masculinity of the Johannine Jesus. She argues that Philo's construction of Moses offers an excellent parallel of how superior masculinity could coincide with attributions of divinity. The Johannine Jesus is then examined with respect to the essential characteristics that defined a "manly" male. Finally, Conway nuances the now-common notion that the Fourth Gospel presents us with Jesus Sophia, a feminine dimension of the divine. She appeals once again to Philo. Just as Philo pictures Wisdom as masculine in relation to human beings but feminine in relation to God, so too the Johannine Jesus may be seen as ideally masculine when compared to human beings but necessarily feminine in relation to the ultimate male, God.

David Clines's "Paul, the Invisible Man" presupposes his earlier analyses of the masculinities of a cast of biblical characters: Moses, David, Job, the psalmists, and Jesus. In these earlier studies, he argued for a series of common elements constitutive of the masculinity of these characters: strength, violence, powerful and persuasive speech, male bonding, and womanlessness. His essay on Paul (not Paul the historical personage, he is careful to stress, but Paul the fictional character, a composite construct of the Pauline letters, whether "authentic" or "inauthentic") proceeds deductively to examine whether or not the apostle conforms to the model of masculinity set forth in the earlier studies. His conclusion is that, for the most part, Paul does, and he ends the essay with reflection on the ethical implications of this discovery.

Diana Swancutt's "The Disease of Effemination" argues that Rom 1:18–2:16 is best conceived as a biting censure of Paul's leading rivals in Rome, the imperial city's (male) Roman Stoic rulers. Romans 1:26–27 evokes the dominant Greco-Roman gender ideology that touted the naturalness and "manliness" of penetrative intercourse, while the larger context asserts that the gender-destabilizing sex in which the Gentile masses indulge is the direct consequence of their having dishonored God through idolatry (1:18–32). When conjoined to the Greco-Roman convention of the emasculated Stoic ruler, which, on Swancutt's reading, permeates 1:18–2:16, the charge of effeminacy functions rhetorically to debunk the presumed authority of the hypocritical judges of 2:1.

Jennifer Glancy's "Protocols of Masculinity in the Pastoral Epistles" contends that the instruction in all three letters is consistent with the advice found in other second-century Greco-Roman writings, which emphasize the cultivation of the elite masculine self. The Pastor prescribes behavior for freeborn, property-holding Christian men that is indistinguishable from the behavior prescribed for freeborn, property-holding pagan men by authors as disparate as Plutarch and Athenaeus. The version of Christian masculinity endorsed by the Pastor is, however, at variance with other early images of Christian masculinity. Other early Christian writings represent John the Baptist, Jesus, and Paul as anomalous men in their passions, eschewal of matrimonial and paternal roles, and, in the case of Jesus, shameful death.

Mary Rose D'Angelo's "Knowing How to Preside over His Own Household" argues that not only the Pastorals but the *Shepherd of Hermas* and Luke-Acts envisage governance of a household as a qualification for participation in developing, but still less than clearly defined, structures of church leadership. Whether concerned with manliness or with the distinction of male from female social roles, these texts not only affirm household government as a measure of manly virtue but also reflect and respond to a growing interest in ascetic practice, including sexual abstinence. In response to Roman imperial power, moreover, each of these texts engages in a dialectic of resistance and accommodation whose terms are established in part by the desire of Trajan and Hadrian to reassert the "family values" that played a substantial role in Augustus's consolidation of power.

Chris Frilingos's "Sexing the Lamb," finally, examines the intimately interrelated themes of masculinity and sexualized activity/passivity in Roman culture in general and in the book of Revelation in particular. Frilingos uses the novel *Daphnis and Chloe* as his point of departure in his opening reflections on Roman ideologies of sex and gender. Turning to

Revelation, he contends that its central character, the "Lamb standing as if slain" (Rev 5:6, 12; 13:8), undergoes a telling transformation as the narrative unfolds: at first a "feminized" creature, the Lamb is subsequently "masculinized" through a commanding performance of virility. But the metamorphosis, Frilingos suggests, remains partial. What his reading unveils in Revelation, he argues, is not a linear progression from one gender to another but an unstable complex of gendered meanings that "follow[s] the Lamb wherever it goes" (Rev 14:4).

Unlike the four studies surveyed earlier—and without any editorial prodding—all the contributors to the present collection (with the rule-proving exception of David Clines) tackle the topic of masculinity in the various texts they examine primarily by probing its similarities to and differences from other constructions of masculinity in ancient Mediterranean culture(s). In order to do so, moreover, most of the contributors have, to a greater or lesser degree, made strategic incursions into the neighboring field of classics,[14] a field that, in recent years, has spawned a copious body of work on Greek and Roman masculinities.[15] (It is not by chance, then, that two of the invited respondents to the present collection are prominent classicists who have themselves helped to shape the new gender studies in their own discipline.)

Whether this methodological uniformity in the analysis of early Christian masculinities perdures through future studies or proves merely to have been a momentary alignment preceding a return to methodological fragmentation remains to be seen. The present essay purports neither to speak for the collection it introduces, beyond the level of generality just ventured (for the contributors do not themselves speak with one voice, beyond this same level), nor to remark on the virtues or deficiencies of the collection (that being the proper task of the respondents). Nevertheless, I will conclude with a caveat regarding these recent raids on classics (which is intended, first and foremost, as a memo to myself).[16]

The New Testament critic who strays through the subfield of masculinity studies within the broader field of classics, plucking an argument here, a hypothesis there, is tripping blithely through a battlefield (to put a melodramatic spin on an essentially bookish enterprise). For a series of

---

14 As have D'Angelo (2002) and Moore (2001: 133–72) elsewhere.

15 The best one-volume entrée to this proliferating subfield, perhaps—certainly the most encyclopedic—is that of Craig A. Williams. (That the main title of Williams's book, notwithstanding its focus on masculinity, should be *Roman Homosexuality*, is no accident, as we shall see.) For further examples of work in this area, see §4 in the classified bibliography in the present volume.

16 Border raids on classics have, of course, long been a feature—at times even a constitutive feature—of New Testament scholarship.

"sexuality wars" have recently been raging in classics, as Marilyn Skinner (1996), reporting from the front lines, has warned. The opening salvo was fired by Amy Richlin, it seems (Richlin 1991), and aimed at the influential Foucault-infused studies of ancient Greek sex and gender produced by David Halperin and John Winkler (Halperin 1990a; Winkler 1990a). While appearing to acknowledge their debts to feminism, charges Richlin, these studies manage nonetheless to erase earlier feminist work on Greek (and Roman) sexual ideologies in the very process of replicating them. What makes Richlin's allegations especially disturbing is the fact that Halperin's and Winkler's studies are widely seen as marking the inception of a Foucauldian "school" within classics, impelled by the second and third volumes of Foucault's *History of Sexuality* (Foucault 1985; 1986)—volumes that themselves elide gender and sideline feminism, according to Richlin (1991; 1998) and other critics.

But if Foucault, Halperin, and Winkler lay themselves open to charges of erasing feminism (egregiously so in the case of Foucault, more subtly so in the cases of his successors), to attempt to harness the work of all three—for the study of early Christian masculinities, say—is to run the risk of a another sort of erasure. A signal feature of Halperin's and Winkler's work on ancient sex and gender is that they each "confront the discipline [of classics] from a politicized gay male position," as Skinner pointedly puts it (1996: 4),[17] and the same might be said of Foucault himself (cf. Halperin 1995: 15–125 passim, a chapter titled "The Queer Politics of Michel Foucault"). To appropriate the Foucauldian "legacy" in classics, then, is run the risk of depoliticizing and domesticating it, unless, of course, its queer politics be appropriated along with it—or, alternatively, unless it be appropriated for feminist ends (not that queer studies and feminist studies are mutually exclusive enterprises), as has happened repeatedly in recent classical studies, the feminism originally rendered invisible *by* Foucault now resourcefully reasserting itself *through* Foucault.

The Foucauldian legacy in classics does not, of course, account for all of the work that has been done on Greek and Roman masculinities, but it does account for an extremely influential, if intensely controversial, and widely diffused component of it (cf. Skinner 1996: 1–3). The moral is plain, in any case, for those of us in New Testament and early Christian studies who would make incursions into this subfield of classics the better to excavate the external features and internal operations (not least, the internal contradictions) of early Christian masculinities: to remain

---

17 Page numbers of Skinner's article are taken from the online version.

ignorant of the history of heated debate within this contested subfield is to risk replicating within our own fields the very exclusions and elisions that provoked the debate in the first place.

MASCULINITY STUDIES: A CLASSIFIED BIBLIOGRAPHY

Janice Capel Anderson, University of Idaho,
with the assistance of Stephen D. Moore
and Seong Hee Kim, Drew University

1. GENERAL

Adams, Rachel, and David Savran, eds. 2002. *The Masculinity Studies Reader.* Oxford: Blackwell.

Berger, Maurice, Brian Wallis, and Simon Watson, eds. 1995. *Constructing Masculinity.* New York: Routledge.

Bly, Robert. 1990. *Iron John: A Book about Men.* Reading, Mass.: Addison-Wesley.

Bourdieu, Pierre. 2001. *Masculine Domination.* Translated by Richard Nice. Stanford, Calif.: Stanford University Press.

Bordo, Susan. 1999. *The Male Body: A New Look at Men in Public and in Private.* New York: Farrar, Straus & Giroux.

Brittan, Arthur. 1989. *Masculinity and Power.* Oxford: Basil Blackwell.

Brod, Harry, ed. 1987. *The Making of Masculinities: The New Men's Studies.* Boston: Allen & Unwin.

Brod, Harry, and Michael Kaufman, eds. 1994. *Theorizing Masculinities.* Thousand Oaks, Calif.: Sage.

Butler, Judith. 1995. Melancholy Gender/Refused Identification. Pages 21–36 in *Constructing Masculinity.* Edited by Maurice Berger, Brian Wallis, and Simon Watson. New York: Routledge.

———. 1999. *Gender Trouble: Feminism and the Subversion of Identity.* 2d ed. New York: Routledge.

Chapman, Rowena, and Jonathan Rutherford, eds. 1988. *Male Order: Unwrapping Masculinity.* London: Lawrence & Wishart.

Cheng, Cliff, ed. 1996. *Masculinities in Organizations.* Thousand Oaks, Calif.: Sage.

Clatterbaugh, Kenneth. 2000. Literature of the U.S. Men's Movements. *Signs* 25:883–94.

Connell, R. W. 1985. Masculinity, Violence and War. Pages 4-10 in *War/Masculinity.* Edited by Paul Patton and Ross Poole. Sydney: Intervention.

———. 1995. *Masculinities.* Berkeley and Los Angeles: University of California Press.

Digby, Tom, ed. 1998. *Men Doing Feminism.* New York: Routledge.

Di Stefano, Christine. 1991. *Configurations of Masculinity: A Feminist Perspective on Modern Political Theory.* Ithaca, N.Y.: Cornell University Press.

Downing, Christine. 1993. *Gods in Our Midst. Mythological Images of the Masculine: A Woman's View.* New York: Crossroad.

Dutton, Kenneth R. 1995. *The Perfectible Body: The Western Ideal of Physical Development*. London: Cassell.

Edwards, Tim. 1997. *Men in the Mirror: Men's Fashion, Masculinity and Consumer Society*. London: Cassell.

Faludi, Susan. 1999. *Stiffed: The Betrayal of the American Man*. New York: William Morrow.

Farrell, Warren. 1996. *The Myth of Male Power*. New York: Berkley.

Franklin, Clyde W. 1984. *The Changing Definition of Masculinity*. New York: Plenum.

Friedman, Richard C., and Jennifer I. Downey, eds. 1999. *Masculinity and Sexuality*. Washington, D.C.: American Psychiatric Press.

Gardiner, Judith Kegan, ed. 2002. *Masculinity Studies and Feminist Theory: New Directions*. New York: Columbia University Press.

Goldstein, Laurence, ed. 1994. *The Male Body: Features, Destinies, Exposures*. Ann Arbor: University of Michigan Press.

Guggenbuhl, Allan. 1997. *Men, Power, and Myths: The Quest for Male Identity*. New York: Continuum.

Haddad, Tony, ed. 1993. *Men and Masculinities: A Critical Anthology*. Toronto: Canadian Scholars' Press.

Hadley, D. M., eds. 1999. *Masculinity in Medieval Europe*. New York: Addison Wesley Longman.

Hagan, Kay Leigh, ed. 1992. *Women Respond to the Men's Movement: A Feminist Collection*. San Francisco: Pandora.

Halberstam, Judith. 1998. *Female Masculinity*. Durham, N.C.: Duke University Press.

Harding, Jennifer. 1998. *Sex Acts: Practices of Femininity and Masculinity*. Thousand Oaks, Calif.: Sage.

Hatty, Suzanne. 2000. *Masculinities, Violence and Culture*. Thousand Oaks, Calif.: Sage.

Horowitz, Roger, ed. 2001. *Boys and Their Toys? Masculinity, Class and Technology in America*. New York: Routledge.

Horrocks, Roger. 1994. *Masculinity in Crisis: Myths, Fantasies, and Realities*. New York: St. Martin's.

———. 1995. *Male Myths and Icons: Masculinity in Popular Culture*. New York: St. Martin's.

Jardine, Alice, and Paul Smith, eds. 1987. *Men in Feminism*. New York: Methuen.

Joy, Donald M. 1993. *Men under Construction*. Wheaton, Ill.: Victor.

Justad, Mark J. 1996. A Transvaluation of Phallic Masculinity: Writing with and through the Male Body. *Journal of Men's Studies* 4:355–74.

Keen, Sam. 1991. *Fire in the Belly: On Being a Man*. New York: Bantam.

Kimmel, Michael S. 1996. *Manhood in America: A Cultural History*. New York: Free Press.

Kimmel, Michael S. ed. 1987. *Changing Men: New Directions in Research on Men and Masculinity*. Thousand Oaks, Calif.: Sage.

———. 1995. *The Politics of Manhood: Profeminist Men Respond to the Mythopoetic Men's Movement (and the Mythopoetic Leaders Answer)*. Philadelphia: Temple University Press.

Kimmel, Michael S., and Michael A. Messner, eds. 2000. *Men's Lives.* 5th ed. Boston: Allyn & Bacon.

Lakoff, Robin Tolmach, and Raquel I. Scherr. 1984. Men and Beauty. Pages 209–44 in *Face Value: The Politics of Beauty.* Boston: Routledge & Kegan Paul.

Lees, Clare A., ed. 1994. *Medieval Masculinities: Regarding Men in the Middle Ages.* Minneapolis: University of Minnesota Press.

Leiris, Michel. 1992. *Manhood: A Journey from Childhood into the Fierce Order of Virility.* Translated by Richard Howard. Chicago: University of Chicago Press. [French ed. 1946]

May, Larry. 1998. *Masculinity and Morality.* Ithaca, N.Y.: Cornell University Press.

May, Larry, and Robert Strikwerda, eds. 1992. *Rethinking Masculinity: Philosophical Explorations in Light of Feminism.* Lanham, Md.: Littlefield Adams.

McCloughry, Roy. 1992. *Men and Masculinity: From Power to Love.* London: Hodder & Stoughton.

McKay, Matthew, and Patrick Fanning. 1993. *Being a Man: A Guide to the New Masculinity.* Oakland, Calif.: New Harbinger.

Messner, Michael A. 1997. *Politics of Masculinities: Men in Movements.* Thousand Oaks, Calif.: Sage.

Mosse, George L. 1996. *The Image of Man: The Creation of Modern Masculinity.* Oxford: Oxford University Press.

Pease, Bob. 2000. *Recreating Men: Postmodern Masculinity Politics.* Thousand Oaks, Calif.: Sage.

Perchuk, Andrew, and Helaine Posner, eds. 1995. *The Masculine Masquerade: Masculinity and Representation.* Cambridge, Mass.: MIT Press.

Pleck, Joseph H. 1981. *The Myth of Masculinity.* Cambridge, Mass.: MIT Press.

Pleck, Joseph H., and Jack Sawyer, eds. 1974. *Men and Masculinity.* Englewood Cliffs, N.J.: Prentice-Hall.

Polk, Kenneth. 1994. *When Men Kill: Scenarios of Masculine Violence.* Cambridge: Cambridge University Press.

Porter, David, ed. 1992. *Between Men and Feminism.* New York: Routledge.

Pendergast, Tom. 2000. *Creating the Modern Man: American Magazines and Consumer Culture, 1900–1950.* Columbia: University of Missouri Press.

Rosen, David. 1993. *The Changing Fictions of Masculinity.* Urbana: University of Illinois Press.

Rotundo, E. Anthony. 1997. *American Manhood: Transformations in Masculinity from the Revolution to the Modern Era.* New York: Basic Books.

Schacht, Steven P., and Doris W. Ewing, eds. 1998. *Feminism and Men: Reconstructing Gender Relations.* New York: New York University Press.

Schehr, Lawrence R. 1997. *Parts of an Andrology: On Representations of Men's Bodies.* Stanford, Calif.: Stanford University Press.

Schwalbe, Michael. 1996. *Unlocking the Iron Cage: The Men's Movement, Gender Politics, and American Culture.* Oxford: Oxford University Press.

Sedgwick, Eve Kosofsky. 1985. *Between Men: English Literature and Male Homosocial Desire.* New York: Columbia University Press.

———. 1992. Gender Criticism. Pages 271–302 in *Redrawing the Boundaries: The Transformation of English and American Literary Studies.* Edited by Stephen

Greenblatt and Giles Gunn. New York: Modern Language Association of America.

———. 1995. Gosh, Boy George, You Must Be Awfully Secure in Your Masculinity! Pages 11–20 in *Constructing Masculinity*. Edited by Maurice Berger, Brian Wallis, and Simon Watson. New York: Routledge.

Segal, Lynne. 1990. *Slow Motion: Changing Masculinities, Changing Men.* New Brunswick: Rutgers University Press.

Seidler, Victor J. 1989. *Rediscovering Masculinity: Reason, Language, and Sexuality.* New York: Routledge.

———. 1997. *Man Enough: Embodying Masculinities.* Thousand Oaks, Calif.: Sage.

Silverman, Kaja. 1992. *Male Subjectivity at the Margins.* New York: Routledge.

Simpson, Mark. 1994. *Male Impersonators: Men Performing Masculinity.* New York: Routledge.

Stearns, Peter N. 1990. *Be a Man! Males in Modern Society.* New York: Holmes & Meier.

Stoltenberg, John. 2000. *Refusing to Be a Man: Essays on Sex and Justice.* London: UCL Press.

Taylor, Gary. 2000. *Castration: An Abbreviated History of Western Manhood.* New York: Routledge.

Thomas, Calvin. 1996. *Male Matters: Masculinity, Anxiety, and the Male Body on the Line.* Urbana: University of Illinois Press.

Traister, Bryce. 2000. Academic Viagra: The Rise of American Masculinity Studies. *American Quarterly* 52:274–304.

Tuana, Nancy, et al., eds. 2001. *Revealing Male Bodies.* Bloomington: Indiana University Press.

Wiegman, Robyn. 2001. Object Lessons: Men, Masculinity, and the Sign of "Woman." *Signs* 26:355–88.

2. Race and Ethnicity

Baker-Fletcher, Garth Kasimu. 1996. *Xodus: An African American Male Journey.* Minneapolis: Fortress.

Belton, Don, ed. 1995. *Speak My Name: Black Men on Masculinity and the American Dream.* Boston: Beacon.

Boyarin, Daniel. 1997. *Unheroic Conduct: The Rise of Heterosexuality and the Invention of the Jewish Man.* Berkeley and Los Angeles: University of California Press.

Brakke, David. 2001. Ethiopian Demons: Male Sexuality, the Black-Skinned Other, and the Monastic Self. *Journal of the History of Sexuality* 10:501–35.

Carby, Hazel V. 1998. *Race Men.* Cambridge: Harvard University Press.

Clarke, John R. 1996. Hypersexual Black Men in Augustan Baths: Ideal Somatotypes and Apotropaic Magic. Pages 184–98 in *Sexuality in Ancient Art: Near East, Egypt, Greece, and Italy.* Edited by Natalie Boymel Kampen. Cambridge: Cambridge University Press.

Creese, Gillian. 1999. *Contracting Masculinity: Gender, Class, and Race in a White-Collar Union, 1944–1994.* Oxford: Oxford University Press.

Duneier, Mitchell. *Slim's Table: Race, Responsibility, and Masculinity*. Chicago: University of Chicago Press.

Eng, David L. 2001. *Racial Castration: Managing Masculinity in Asian America*. Durham, N.C.: Duke University Press.

Harper, Phillip Brian. 1996. *Are We Not Men? Masculine Anxiety and the Problem of African-American Identity*. Oxford: Oxford University Press.

Krishnaswamy, Revathi. 1998. *Effeminism: The Economy of Colonial Desire*. Ann Arbor: University of Michigan Press.

Robinson, Sally. 2000. *Marked Men: White Masculinity in Crisis*. New York: Columbia University Press.

Ross, Marlon B. 1998. In Search of Black Men's Masculinities. *Feminist Studies* 24:599–626.

Savran, David. 1998. *Taking It Like a Man: White Masculinity, Masochism, and Contemporary Culture*. Princeton: Princeton University Press.

Sharpe, Sue. 2000. *Uncertain Masculinities: Youth, Ethnicity, and Class in Contemporary Britain*. New York: Routledge.

Sinha, Mrinalini. 1995. *Colonial Masculinity: "The Manly Englishman" and the "Effeminate Bengali" in the Late Nineteenth Century*. Manchester: Manchester University Press.

Staples, Robert. 1982. *Black Masculinity: The Black Male's Role in American Society*. San Francisco: Black Scholars Press.

Stecopoulos, Harry, and Michael Uebel, eds. 1997. *Race and the Subject of Masculinities*. Durham, N.C.: Duke University Press.

3. ANTHROPOLOGY

Almeida, Miguel Vale de. 1996. *The Hegemonic Male: Masculinity in a Portuguese Town*. Providence: Berghahn Books.

Blok, Anton. 1981. Rams and Billy-Goats: A Key to the Mediterranean Code of Honor. *Man* 16:427-40. Reprinted as pages 51–70 in *Religion, Power and Protest in Local Communities: The Northern Shore of the Mediterranean*. Edited by Eric Wolf. New York: Mouton, 1984.

Brandes, Stanley. 1980. *Metaphors of Masculinity: Sex and Status in Andalusian Folklore*. Philadelphia: University of Pennsylvania Press.

Coleman, Eli, Philip Colgan, and Louis Gooren. 1997. Male Cross-Gender Behavior in Myanmar (Burma): A Description of the Acault. Pages 287–93 in *Que(e)rying Religion: A Critical Anthology*. Edited by Gary David Comstock and Susan E. Henking. New York: Continuum.

Collier, Jane, and Sylvia Yanagisako, eds. 1987. *Gender and Kinship: Essays toward a Unified Analysis*. Stanford, Calif.: Stanford University Press.

Cornwall, Andrea, and Nancy Lindisfarne, eds. 1994. *Dislocating Masculinity: Comparative Ethnographies*. New York: Routledge.

Delaney, Carol. 1991. *The Seed and the Soil: Gender and Cosmology in Turkish Village Society*. Berkeley and Los Angeles: University of California Press.

———. 1999. Abraham, Isaac, and Some Hidden Assumptions of Our Culture. *The Humanist* 59:14.

Dubish, Jill. 1986. *Gender and Power in Rural Greece*. Princeton: Princeton University Press.

Gilmore, David D. 1990. *Manhood in the Making: Cultural Conceptions of Masculinity.* New Haven: Yale University Press.

———. 1996. Above and Below: Toward a Social Geometry of Gender. *AA* 98:54–67.

———. 2001. *Misogyny: The Male Malady.* Philadelphia: University of Pennsylvania Press.

Gilmore, David D., ed. 1987. *Honor and Shame and the Unity of the Mediterranean.* Washington, D.C.: American Anthropological. Association.

Gutmann, Matthew C. 1996. *The Meanings of Macho: Being a Man in Mexico City.* Berkeley and Los Angeles: University of California Press.

———. 1997. Trafficking in Men: The Anthropology of Masculinity. *Annual Review of Anthropology* 26:385–410.

Herdt, Gilbert. 1982. *Rituals of Manhood: Male Initiation in Papua New Guinea.* Berkeley and Los Angeles: University of California Press.

———. 1992. *Guardians of the Flutes: Idioms of Masculinity.* Chicago: University of Chicago Press. [Orig. 1981.]

Herdt, Gilbert, ed. 1993. *Ritualized Homosexuality in Melanesia.* Berkeley and Los Angeles: University of California Press.

Herzfeld, Michael. 1985. *The Poetics of Manhood: Contest and Identity in a Cretan Mountain Village.* Princeton, N.J.: Princeton University Press.

———. 1987. "As in Your Own House": Hospitality, Ethnography, and the Stereotype of Mediterranean Society. Pages 75–89 in *Honor and Shame and the Unity of the Mediterranean.* Edited by David D. Gilmore. Washington, D.C.: American Anthropological Association.

Loizos P., and E. Papataxiarchis, eds. 1991. *Contested Identities: Gender and Kinship in Modern Greece.* Princeton: Princeton University Press.

MacCormick, Carol, and Marilyn Strathern, eds. 1980. *Nature, Culture, and Gender.* Cambridge: Cambridge University Press.

Morris, Rosalind C. 1995. All Made Up: Performance Theory and the New Anthropology of Sex and Gender. *Annual Review of Anthropology* 24:567–92.

Ong, Aihwa, and Michael G. Peletz, eds. 1995. *Bewitching Women, Pious Men: Gender and Body Politics in Southeast Asia.* Berkeley and Los Angeles: University of California Press.

Ortner, Sherry B. 1996. *Making Gender: The Politics and Erotics of Culture.* Boston: Beacon.

Ortner, Sherry B., and Harriet Whitehead, eds. 1981. *Sexual Meanings: The Cultural Construction of Gender and Sexuality.* Cambridge: Cambridge University Press.

Peletz, Michael. 1996. *Reason and Passion: Representations of Gender in a Malay Society.* Berkeley and Los Angeles: University of California Press.

Rogers, Susan C. 1975. Female Forms of Power and the Myth of Male Dominance: A Model of Female/Male Interaction in Peasant Society. *American Ethnologist* 2:727–55.

———. 1985. Gender in Southwestern France: The Myth of Male Dominance Revisited. *Anthropology* 9:65–86.

Rubin, Gayle. 1975. The Traffic in Women: Notes on the "Political Economy" of Sex. Pages 157–210 in *Toward an Anthropology of Women.* Edited by Rayna R. Reiter. New York: Monthly Review.

Strathern, Marilyn. 1988. *The Gender of the Gift: Problems with Women and Problems with Society in Melanesia.* Berkeley and Los Angeles: University of California Press.

Tuzin Donald F. 1997. *The Cassowary's Revenge: The Life and Death of Masculinity in New Guinea Society.* Chicago: University of Chicago Press.

Yanagisako, Sylvia, and Carol Delaney, eds. 1995. *Naturalizing Power: Essays in Feminist Cultural Analysis.* New York: Routledge.

4. Classics

Ancona, Ronnie. 1989. The Subterfuge of Reason: Horace, Odes 1.23 and the Construction of Male Desire. *Helios* 16:49–57.

Andouche, I., and P. Simelon. 1995. Stance et la mortalité masculine. *Latomus* 54:319–23.

Balot, Ryan K. 1998. Foucault, Chariton, and the Masculine Self. *Helios* 25:139–62.

Barton, Carlin A. 1992. *The Sorrows of the Ancient Romans: The Gladiator and the Monster.* Princeton: Princeton University Press.

———. 1994a. All Things Beseem the Victor: Paradoxes of Masculinity in Early Imperial Rome. Pages 83–92 in *Gender Rhetorics: Postures of Dominance and Submission in History.* Edited by Richard C. Trexler. Binghamton, N.Y.: Center for Medieval and Early Renaissance Studies.

———. 1994b. Savage Miracles: The Redemption of Lost Honor in Roman Society and the Sacrament of the Gladiator and the Martyr. *Representations* 45:41–71.

———. 1999. The Roman Blush: The Delicate Matter of Self-Control. Pages 212–34 in *Constructions of the Classical Body.* Edited by James I. Porter. Ann Arbor: University of Michigan Press.

———. 2001. *Roman Honor: The Fire in the Bones.* Berkeley and Los Angeles: University of California Press.

Bassi, Karen. 1997. Orality, Masculinity, and the Greek Epic. *Arethusa* 30:315–40.

———. 1998. *Acting Like Men: Gender, Drama, and Nostalgia in Ancient Greece.* Ann Arbor: University of Michigan Press.

Braund, Susanna Morton, and Christopher Gill, eds. 1997. *The Passions in Roman Thought and Literature.* Cambridge: Cambridge University Press.

Brakke, David. 1998. The Passions and the Social Construction of Masculinity. Paper delivered to the Hellenistic Moral Philosophy Section, AAR/SBL Joint Annual Meeting, Orlando, Florida.

Cantarella, Eva. 1992. *Bisexuality in the Ancient World.* Translated by Cormac Ó Cuilleanáin. New Haven: Yale University Press.

Clarke, John R. 1993. The Warren Cup and the Contexts for Representations on Male-to-Male Lovemaking in Augustan and Early Julio-Claudian Art. *Art Bulletin* 75:275-94.

———. 1996. Hypersexual Black Men in Augustan Baths: Ideal Somatotypes and Apotropaic Magic. Pages 184–98 in *Sexuality in Ancient Art: Near East, Egypt, Greece, and Italy.* Edited by Natalie Boymel Kampen. Cambridge: Cambridge University Press.

———. 1998. *Looking at Lovemaking: Construction of Sexuality in Roman Art 100 B.C.–A.D. 250.* Berkeley and Los Angeles: University of California Press.

Dixon, Suzanne. 1992. *The Roman Family*. Baltimore, Md.: Johns Hopkins University Press.

Dover, Kenneth J. 1989. *Greek Homosexuality, Updated and with a New Postscript*. Cambridge: Harvard University Press. [Orig. 1978]

duBois, Page. 1997. The Subject in Antiquity after Foucault. Pages 85–103 in Larmour, Miller, and Platter.

———. 2003. *Slaves and Other Objects*. Chicago: University of Chicago Press.

Dupont, Florence, and Thierry Éloi. 2001. *L'érotisme masculin dans la Rome antique*. L'Antiquité au Présent. Paris: Belin.

Edwards, Catherine. 1993. *The Politics of Immorality in Ancient Rome*. Cambridge: Cambridge University Press.

Fantham, Elaine. 1991. Stuprum: Public Attitudes and Penalties for Sexual Offences in Republican Rome. *Echos du Monde Classique/Classical Views* 35:267–91.

Foucault, Michel. 1985. *The Use of Pleasure: The History of Sexuality 2*. Translated by Robert Hurley. New York: Random House. [Orig. 1984]

———. 1986. *The Care of the Self: The History of Sexuality 3*. Translated by Robert Hurley. New York: Random House. [Orig. 1984]

Foxhall, Lin, and John Salmon, eds. 1998a. *Thinking Men: Masculinity and Its Self-Representation in the Classical Tradition*. New York: Routledge.

———. 1998b. *When Men Were Men: Masculinity, Power and Identity in Classical Antiquity*. New York: Routledge.

Gamel, Mary-Kay. 1998. Reading As a Man: Performance and Gender in Roman Elegy. *Helios* 25:79–85.

Garrison, Daniel H. 2000. *Sexual Culture in Ancient Greece*. Norman: University of Oklahoma Press.

Gleason, Maud W. 1990. The Semiotics of Gender: Physiognomy and Self-Fashioning in the Second Century C.E. Pages 389–416 in Halperin, Winkler, and Zeitlin.

———. 1995. *Making Men: Sophists and Self-Representation in Ancient Rome*. Princeton: Princeton University Press.

———. 1999. Elite Male Identity in the Roman Empire. Pages 67–84 in *Life, Death and Entertainment in the Roman Empire*. Edited by D. S. Potter and D. J. Mattingly. Ann Arbor: University of Michigan Press.

Graver, Margaret. 1998. The Manhandling of Maecenas: Senecan Abstractions of Masculinity. *AJP* 119:607–32.

Goldhill, Simon. 1995. *Foucault's Virginity: Ancient Erotic Fiction and the History of Sexuality*. Cambridge: Cambridge University Press.

Hallett, Judith P., and Marilyn B. Skinner, eds. *Roman Sexualities*. Princeton: Princeton University Press.

Halperin, David M. 1990. *One Hundred Years of Homosexuality: And Other Essays on Greek Love*. New York: Routledge.

———. 1994. Historicizing the Subject of Desire: Sexual Preferences and Erotic Identities in the Pseudo-Lucianic *Erôtes*. Pages 19–34 in *Foucault and the Writing of History*. Edited by Jan Goldstein. Oxford: Basil Blackwell.

Halperin, David M., John J. Winkler, and Froma I. Zeitlin, eds. 1990. *Before Sexuality: The Construction of Erotic Experience in the Ancient Greek World*. Princeton: Princeton University Press.

Hannah, P. A. 1998. The Reality of Greek Male Nudity: Looking to African Parallels. *Scholia* 7:16–40.

Hans, Herter. 1959. Effeminatus. *RAC* 4:620–50.

Hanson, Ann Ellis. 1999. The Roman Family. Pages 19–66 in *Life, Death and Entertainment in the Roman Empire*. Edited by D. S. Potter and D. J. Mattingly. Ann Arbor: University of Michigan Press.

Hobbs, Angela, 2000. *Plato and the Hero: Courage, Manliness and the Personal Good*. Cambridge: Cambridge University Press.

Hooper, Richard W. 1999. *The Priapus Poems*. Urbana and Chicago: University of Illinois Press.

James, Sharon L. 1998. From Boys to Men: Rape and Developing Masculinity in Terence's *Hecyra* and *Eunuches*. *Helios* 25:31-48.

Johns, Catherine. 1982. *Sex or Symbol? Erotic Images of Greece and Rome*. Austin: University of Texas Press.

Kellum, Barbara. 1996. The Phallus As Signifier: The Forum of Augustus and Rituals of Masculinity. Pages 170–83 in *Sexuality in Ancient Art: Near East, Egypt, Greece, and Italy*. Edited by Natalie Boymel Kampen. Cambridge: Cambridge University Press.

Keuls, Eva C. 1985. *The Reign of the Phallus: Sexual Politics in Ancient Athens*. Berkeley and Los Angeles: University of California Press.

Laqueur, Thomas. 1990. *Making Sex: Body and Gender from the Greeks to Freud*. Cambridge: Harvard University Press.

Larmour, David H. J., Paul Allen Miller, and Charles Platter, eds. 1997. *Rethinking Sexuality: Foucault and Classical Antiquity*. Princeton: Princeton University Press.

Leitao, David D. 1995. The Perils of Leukippos: Initiatory Transvestism and Male Gender Ideology in the Ekdusia at Phaistos. *Classical Antiquity* 26:130–63.

Lindheim, Sara H. 1998. Hercules Cross-Dressed, Hercules Undressed: Unmasking the Construction of the Propertian *amator* in Elegy 4.9. *AJP* 119:43–66.

Loraux, Nicole. 1990. Herakles: The Super-Male and the Feminine. Pages 21–52 in Halperin, Winkler, and Zeitlin.

———. 1995. *The Experiences of Tiresias: The Feminine and the Greek Man*. Translated by Paula Wissing. Princeton: Princeton University Press.

Montserrat, Dominic. 1993. The Representation of Young Males in "Fayum Portraits." *JEA* 79:215–25.

———. 1996. *Sex and Society in Graeco-Roman Egypt*. New York: Columbia University Press.

Martin, Dale B. 2000. Contradictions of Masculinity: Ascetic Inseminators and Menstruating Men in Greco-Roman Culture. Pages 81–108 in *Generation and Degeneration: Tropes of Reproduction in Literature and History from Antiquity to Early Modern Europe*. Edited by Valeria Finucci and Kevin Brownlee. Durham, N.C.: Duke University Press.

Mehl, E. 1974. *Gymnastik und Athletik im Denken der Roemer*. Amsterdam: Gruener.

Moxnes, Halvor. 1997. Conventional Values in the Hellenistic World: Masculinity. Pages 263–84 in *Conventional Values of the Hellenistic Greeks*. Edited by Per Bilde, Troels Engberg-Pedersen, Lise Hannestad, and Jan Zahle. Aarhus, Denmark: Aarhus University Press.

Murnaghan, Sheila. 1988. How a Woman Can Be More Like a Man: The Dialogue between Isomachus and His Wife in Xenophon's *Oeconomicus*. *Helios* 15:9–22.

Osborne, Robin. 1997. Men without Clothes: Heroic Nakedness and Greek Art. *Gender and History* 9:504–28.

Pomeroy, Sarah B. 1999. *Plutarch 's Advice to Bride and Groom and A Consolation to His Wife: English Translations, Commentary, Interpretive Essays and Bibliography.* Oxford: Oxford University Press.

Porter, James, ed. 1999. *Constructions of the Classical Body.* Ann Arbor: University of Michigan Press.

Richlin, Amy. 1984. Invective against Women in Roman Satire. *Arethusa* 17: 67–80.

———. 1991. Zeus and Metis: Foucault, Feminism, Classics. *Helios* 18:160–80.

———. 1992. *The Garden of Priapus: Sexuality and Aggression in Roman Humor.* 2d ed. New York: Routledge. [Orig. 1983]

———. 1993. Not before Homosexuality: The Materiality of the Cinaedus and the Roman Law against Love between Men. *Journal of the History of Sexuality* 3:523–73.

———. 1997a. Foucault's *History of Sexuality:* A Useful Theory for Women? Pages 138–70 in Larmour, Miller, and Platter.

———. 1997b. Gender and Rhetoric: Producing Manhood in the Schools. Pages 90–110 in *Roman Eloquence: Rhetoric in Society and Literature.* Edited by William J. Dominik. New York: Routledge.

———. 1997c. Pliny's Brassiere. Pages 197–220 in Hallett and Skinner.

———, ed. 1992. *Pornography and Representation in Greece and Rome.* Oxford: Oxford University Press.

Russell, Brigette Ford. 1998. The Emasculation of Antony: The Construction of Gender in Plutarch's Life of Antony. *Helios* 25:121–37.

Rousselle, Aline. 1988. *Porneia: On Desire and the Body in Antiquity.* Translated by F. Pheasant. Oxford: Basil Blackwell.

Santoro L'Hoir, Francesca. 1992. *The Rhetoric of Gender Terms: "Man," "Woman," and the Portrayal of Character in Latin Prose.* Leiden: Brill.

Sauvage, Andre. 1983. Properce et l'ideolologie masculine. *Latomus* 42:819–43.

Skinner, Marilyn B. 1989. Ut Decuit Cinaediorem: Power, Gender, and Urbanity in Catullus 10. *Helios* 16:7–23.

———. 1993. Ego mulier: The Construction of Male Sexuality in Catullus. *Helios* 20:107–30. Reprinted as pages 129–50 in Hallett and Skinner.

———. 1996. Zeus and Leda: The Sexuality Wars in Contemporary Classical Scholarship. *Thamyris* 3:103–23.

Sorkin Rabinowitz, Nancy, and Amy Richlin, eds. 1993. *Feminist Theory and the Classics.* New York: Routledge.

Sullivan, J. P. 1979. Martial's Sexual Attitudes. *Philologus* 123:288–302.

Taylor, Rabun. 1997. Two Pathic Subcultures in Ancient Rome. *Journal of the History of Sexuality* 7:319–71.

Verstraete, Beert C. 1980. Slavery and the Social Dynamics of Male Homosexual Relations in Ancient Rome. *Journal of Homosexuality* 5:227–36.

———. 1982. *Homosexuality in Ancient Greek and Roman Civilization: A Critical Bibliography with Supplement.* Toronto: University of Toronto Press.

Veyne, Paul. 1985. Homosexuality in Ancient Rome. Pages 26–35 in *Western Sexuality: Practice and Precept in Past and Present Times.* Edited by Philippe Ariès and André Béjin. Translated by Anthony Forster. Oxford: Oxford University Press.

Wallace-Hadrill, Andrew. 1996. Engendering the Roman House. Pages 104–15 in *I, Claudia: Women in Ancient Rome.* Edited by Diana E. E. Kleiner and Susan B. Matheson. New Haven: Yale University Press.

Walters, Jonathan. 1991. "No More Than a Boy": The Shifting Construction of Masculinity from Ancient Greece to the Middle Ages." *Gender and History* 5:20–33.

———. 1997. Invading the Roman Body: Manliness and Impenetrability in Roman Thought. Pages 29–43 in Hallett and Skinner.

———. 1998. Juvenal, *Satire* 2: Putting Male Sexual Deviants on Show. Pages 148–54 in Foxhall and Salmon: 1998a.

Waters, Sarah. 1995. "The Most Famous Fairy in History": Antinous and Homosexual Fantasy. *Journal of the History of Sexuality* 6:194–230.

Williams, Craig A. 1995. Greek Love at Rome. *Classical Quarterly* 45:517–39.

———. 1997. *Pudicitia* and *Pueri:* Roman Concepts of Male Sexual Experience. Pages 25–38 in *Queer Representations: Reading Lives, Reading Cultures.* Edited by Martin Duberman. New York: New York University Press.

———. 1998. *Roman Homosexuality: Ideologies of Masculinity in Classical Antiquity.* Oxford: Oxford University Press.

Winkler, John J. 1990a. *The Constraints of Desire: The Anthropology of Sex and Gender in Ancient Greece.* New York: Routledge.

———. 1990b. Laying Down the Law: The Oversight of Men's Behavior in Classical Athens. Pages 171–209 in Halperin, Winkler, and Zeitlin.

Wyke, Maria. 1998. *Parchments of Gender: Deciphering the Bodies of Antiquity.* Oxford: Oxford University Press.

5. Ancient Near East, Hebrew Bible, and Early Judaism

Aune, David E. 1994. Mastery of the Passions: Philo, 4 Maccabees and Earliest Christianity. Pages 125–58 in *Hellenization Revisited: Shaping a Christian Response within the Greco-Roman World.* Edited by Wendy E. Helleman. Lanham, Md.: University Press of America.

Bal, Mieke. 1987. Delilah Decomposed: Samson's Talking Cure and the Rhetoric of Subjectivity. Pages 37–67 in *Lethal Love: Feminist Literary Readings of Biblical Love Stories.* Bloomington: Indiana University Press.

Boer, Roland. 1999. Queer Heroes. Pages 13–32 in *Knockin' on Heaven's Door: The Bible and Popular Culture.* New York: Routledge.

———. 2001. Yahweh As Top: A Lost Targum. Pages 75–105 in *Queer Commentary and the Hebrew Bible.* Edited by Ken Stone. Cleveland: Pilgrim; Sheffield: Sheffield Academic Press.

Boyarin, Daniel. 1993. *Carnal Israel: Reading Sex in Talmudic Culture.* Berkeley and Los Angeles: University of California Press.

———. 1995. Are There Any Jews in "The History of Sexuality"? *Journal of the History of Sexuality* 5:333–55.

———. 1997. *Unheroic Conduct: The Rise of Heterosexuality and the Invention of the Jewish Man.* Berkeley and Los Angeles: University of California Press.

Brawley, Robert L., ed. 1996. *Biblical Ethics and Homosexuality: Listening to Scripture.* Louisville: Westminster John Knox.

Clines, David J. A. n.d. The Book of Psalms, Where Men Are Men: On the Gender of Hebrew Piety. Cited 31 October 2002. Online: http://www.shef.ac.uk/bibs/DJACcurrres/PlayMan.html.

———. n.d. Dancing and Shining at Sinai: Playing the Man in Exodus 32–34. Cited 31 October 2002. Online: http://www.shef.ac.uk/bibs/DJACcurrres/PlayMan.html.

———. n.d. Loingirding and Other Male Activities in the Book of Job. Cited 31 October 2002. Online: http://www.shef.ac.uk/bibs/DJACcurrres/PlayMan.html.

———. 1995. David the Man: The Construction of Masculinity in the Hebrew Bible. Pages 212–43 in *Interested Parties: The Ideology of Writers and Readers of the Hebrew Bible.* JSOTSup 205. Gender, Culture, Theory 1. Sheffield: Sheffield Academic Press.

———. 2002. He-Prophets: Masculinity As a Problem for the Hebrew Prophets and Their Interpreters. Pages 311–28 in *Sense and Sensitivity: Essays on Reading the Bible in Memory of Robert Carroll.* Edited by Alastair G. Hunter and Philip R. Davies. JSOTSup 348. Sheffield: Sheffield Academic Press.

Eilberg-Schwartz, Howard. 1994. *God's Phallus and Other Problems for Men and Monotheism.* Boston: Beacon.

———. 1995. A Masculine Critique of a Father God. *Tikkun* 10:58–62.

Gagnon, Robert A. J. 2001. *The Bible and Homosexual Practice: Texts and Hermeneutics.* Nashville: Abingdon.

Gerstenberger, Erhard. 1996. *Yahweh the Patriarch: Ancient Images of God and Feminist Theology.* Translated by Frederick J. Gaiser. Minneapolis: Fortress.

Goldingay, John. 1995. Hosea 1–3, Genesis 1–4, and Masculist Interpretation. *HBT* 17:37–44.

Goss, Robert E., and Mona West, eds. 2000. *Take Back the Word: A Queer Reading of the Bible.* Cleveland: Pilgrim.

Hoffner, Harry A. 1996. Symbols for Masculinity and Femininity: Their Use in Ancient Near Eastern Sympathetic Magic Rituals. *JBL* 85:326–34.

Jennings, Theodore W., Jr. 2001. YHWH As Erastes. Pages 36–74 in *Queer Commentary and the Hebrew Bible.* Edited by Ken Stone. Cleveland: Pilgrim; Sheffield: Sheffield Academic Press.

Koch, Timothy R. 2001. Cruising As Methodology: Homoeroticism and the Scriptures. Pages 169–80 in *Queer Commentary and the Hebrew Bible.* Edited by Ken Stone. Cleveland: Pilgrim; Sheffield: Sheffield Academic Press.

Koosed, Jennifer L., and Tod Linafelt. 1996. How the West Was Not One: Delilah Deconstructs the Western. *Semeia* 74:167–81.

MacWilliam, Stuart. 2002. Queering Jeremiah. *BibInt* 10:384–404.

Monroe, Irene. 2000. When and Where I Enter, Then the Whole Race Enters with Me: Que(e)rying Exodus. Pages 82–91 in Goss and West.

Moore, Stephen D. 1996. Gigantic God: Yahweh's Body. *JSOT* 70:87–115.

———. 1996. *God's Gym: Divine Male Bodies of the Bible.* New York: Routledge.

———. 2001. *God's Beauty Parlor: And Other Queer Spaces in and around the Bible.* Stanford, Calif.: Stanford University Press.

Moore, Stephen D, and Janice Capel Anderson. 1998. Taking It Like a Man: Masculinity in 4 Maccabees. *JBL* 117:249–73.

Nissinen, Martti. 1998. *Homoeroticism in the Biblical World: A Historical Perspective.* Minneapolis: Fortress.

Olyan, Saul M. 1997. "And with a Male You Shall Not Lie the Lying Down of a Woman": On the Meaning and Significance of Leviticus 18:22 and 20:13. Pages 398–414 in *Que(e)rying Religion: A Critical Anthology.* Edited by Gary David Comstock and Susan E. Henking. New York: Continuum.

Piazza, Michael S. 2000. Nehemiah As a Queer Model for Servant Leadership. Pages 113–23 in *Taking Back the Word: A Queer Reading of the Bible.* Cleveland: Pilgrim.

Rowlett, Lori. 2001. Violent Femmes and S/M: Queering Samson and Delilah. Pages 106–15 in *Queer Commentary and the Hebrew Bible.* Edited by Ken Stone. Cleveland: Pilgrim; Sheffield: Sheffield Academic Press.

Runions, Erin. 1998. Zion Is Burning: "Gender Fuck" in Micah. *Semeia* 82: 225–46.

Satlow, Michael L. 1994. "They Abused Him Like a Woman": Homoeroticism, Gender Blurring, and the Rabbis in Late Antiquity. *Journal of the History of Sexuality* 5:1–25.

———. 1995. *Tasting the Dish: Rabbinic Rhetorics of Sexuality.* Atlanta: Scholars Press.

———. 1996. "Try to Be a Man": The Rabbinic Construction of Masculinity. *HTR* 89:19–40.

Schneider, Laurel C. 2001. Yahwist Desires: Imagining Divinity Queerly. Pages 210–27 in *Queer Commentary and the Hebrew Bible.* Edited by Ken Stone. Cleveland: Pilgrim; Sheffield: Sheffield Academic Press.

Stone, Ken. 1995. Gender and Homosexuality in Judges 19: Subject-Honor, Object-Shame? *JSOT* 67:87–107.

———. 1996. *Sex, Honor and Power in the Deuteronomistic History.* Sheffield: Sheffield Academic Press.

———. 1997a. Biblical Interpretation As a Technology of the Self: Gay Men and the Ethics of Reading. *Semeia* 77:139-55.

———. 1997b. The Hermeneutics of Abomination: On Gay Men, Canaanites, and Biblical Interpretation. *BTB* 27:36-41.

———. 2001. Lovers and Raisin Cakes: Food, Sex and Divine Insecurity in Hosea. Pages 116–39 in *Queer Commentary and the Hebrew Bible.* Edited by Ken Stone. Cleveland: Pilgrim; Sheffield: Sheffield Academic Press.

Tarlin, Jan William. 1997. Utopia and Pornography in Ezekiel: Violence, Hope, and the Shattered Male Subject. Pages 175–83 in *Reading Bibles, Writing Bodies.* Edited by Timothy K. Beal and David M. Gunn. New York: Routledge.

Washington, Harold C. 1997. Violence and the Construction of Gender in the Hebrew Bible: A New Historicist Approach. *BibInt* 5:324–63.

Wold, Donald J. 1998. *Out of Order: Homosexuality in the Bible and the Ancient Near East.* Grand Rapids: Baker.

6. Philo of Alexandria

Aune, David E. 1994. Mastery of the Passions: Philo, 4 Maccabees and Earliest Christianity. Pages 125–58 in *Hellenization Revisited: Shaping a Christian Response within the Greco-Roman World*. Edited by Wendy E. Helleman. Lanham, Md.: University Press of America.

Baer, R. A. 1970. *Philo's Use of the Categories Male and Female*. Leiden: Brill.

Gaca, K. L. 1996. Philo's Principles of Sexual Conduct and their Influence on Christian Platonist Sexual Principles. *SPhilo* 8:21-39.

Harrison, V. E. F. 1995. The Allegorization of Gender: Plato and Philo on Spiritual Childbearing. Pages 520–34 in *Asceticism*. Edited by Vincent L. Wimbush and Richard Valantasis. Oxford: Oxford University Press.

Mattila, S. L. 1996. Wisdom, Sense Perception, Nature, and Philo's Gender Gradient. *HTR* 89:103–29.

Sly, Dorothy. 1990. *Philo's Perception of Women*. Atlanta: Scholars Press.

Szesnat, Holger. 1998. "Pretty Boys" in Philo's *De Vita Contemplativa*. *SPhilo* 10:87–107.

———. 1999. Philo and Female Homoeroticism: Philo's Use of *Gynandros* and Recent Work on *Tribades*. *JSJ* 30:140–47.

7. New Testament and Early Christianity

Aspegren, Karen. 1990. *The Male Woman: A Feminine Ideal in the Early Church*. Edited by René Kieffer. Stockholm: Almqvist & Wiksell.

Attridge, Harold W. 1991. Masculine Fellowship in the *Acts of Thomas*. Pages 406–13 in *The Future of Early Christianity: Essays in Honor of Helmut Koester*. Edited by Birger A. Pearson, A. Thomas Kraabel, and George W. Nickelsburg. Minneapolis: Fortress.

Blickenstaff, Marianne. 2001. The Bloody Bridegroom: Violence in the Matthean Family. Paper presented in the Matthew Section at the 2001 Society of Biblical Literature Annual Meeting. Cited 10 March 2002. Online: http://www .class .uidaho.edu/jcanders/Matthew/marianne_blickenstaff.htm.

Boyarin, Daniel. 1994. *A Radical Jew: Paul and the Politics of Identity*. Berkeley and Los Angeles: University of California Press.

Brakke, David. 2001. Ethiopian Demons: Male Sexuality, the Black-Skinned Other, and the Monastic Self. *Journal of the History of Sexuality* 10:501–35.

Brawley, Robert L., ed. 1996. *Biblical Ethics and Homosexuality: Listening to Scripture*. Louisville: Westminster John Knox.

Brooten, Bernadette. 1996. *Love between Women: Early Christian Responses to Female Homoeroticism*. Chicago: University of Chicago Press.

Brown, Peter. 1990. *The Body and Society: Men, Women and Sexual Renunciation in Early Christianity*. New York: Columbia University Press.

Buell, Denise Kimber. 1999. *Making Christians: Clement of Alexandria and the Rhetoric of Legitimacy*. Princeton: Princeton University Press.

Burrus, Virginia. 2000. *"Begotten, Not Made": Conceiving Manhood in Late Antiquity*. Stanford, Calif.: Stanford University Press.

———. 2001. Queer Lives of Saints: Jerome's Hagiography. *Journal of the History of Sexuality* 10:442-79.

———. Forthcoming. *The Sex Lives of Saints: An Erotics of Ancient Hagiography.* Philadelphia: University of Pennsylvania Press.

Castelli, Elizabeth A. 1991. "I Will Make Mary Male": Pieties of the Body and Gender Transformation of Christian Women in Late Antiquity. Pages 29–33 in *Body Guards: The Cultural Politics of Gender Ambiguity.* Edited by J. Epstein and K. Straub. New York: Routledge.

Clark, Elizabeth A. 1988. Foucault, the Fathers, and Sex. *JAAR* 56:619–41.

Clines, David A. J. 1998. *Ecce Vir,* or, Gendering the Son of Man. Pages 352–75 in *Biblical Studies/Cultural Studies: The Third Sheffield Colloquium.* Edited by J. Cheryl Exum and Stephen D. Moore. JSOTSup 266; Gender, Culture, Theory 7. Sheffield: Sheffield Academic Press.

Conway, Colleen M. 1999. *Men and Women in the Fourth Gospel: Gender and Johannine Characterization.* SBLDS 167. Atlanta: Society of Biblical Literature.

D'Angelo, Mary Rose. 1992a. Abba and "Father": Imperial Theology and the Jesus Tradition. *JBL* 111:611–30.

———. 1992b. Theology in Mark and Q: Abba and "Father" in Context. *HTR* 85:149–74.

———. 2002. The ANHP Question in Luke-Acts: Imperial Masculinity and the Deployment of Women in the Early Second Century? Pages 44–72 in *A Feminist Companion to Luke.* Edited by Amy-Jill Levine, with Marianne Blickenstaff. FCNTECW 3. Sheffield: Sheffield Academic Press.

———. 2003. Εὐσέβεια: Roman Imperial Family Values and the Sexual Politics of 4 Maccabees and the Pastorals. *BibInt* 11:139–65.

Deming, Will. 1990. Mark 9.42–10.12, Matthew 5.27–32, and *b. Nid.* 13b: A First-Century Discussion of Male Sexuality. *NTS* 36:130–41.

Eilberg-Schwartz, Howard. 1995. *God's Phallus and Other Problems for Men and Monotheism.* Boston: Beacon.

Fatum, Lone. 1997. Brotherhood in Christ: A Gender Hermeneutical Reading of 1 Thessalonians. Pages 183–97 in Moxnes.

Gagnon, Robert A. J. 2001. *The Bible and Homosexual Practice: Texts and Hermeneutics.* Nashville: Abingdon.

Glancy, Jennifer A. 1994. Unveiling Masculinity: The Construction of Gender in Mark 6:17-29. *BibInt* 2:34–50.

———. 1996. The Mistress of the Gaze: Masculinity, Slavery, and Representation. *Semeia* 74:127–45.

Good, Deirdre. 1998. *Jesus the Meek King.* Philadelphia: Trinity Press International.

Jasper, Alison. 1998. *The Shining Garment of the Text: Gendered Readings of John's Prologue.* Sheffield: Sheffield Academic Press.

Kahl, Brigitte. 2000. No Longer Male: Masculinity Struggles behind Galatians 3.28? Translated by Brian McNeil. *JSNT* 79:37–49.

Kuefler, Mathew. 2001. *The Manly Eunuch: Masculinity, Gender Ambiguity, and Christian Ideology in Late Antiquity.* Chicago: University of Chicago Press.

Lagrand, James. 1980. How Was the Virgin Mary "Like a Man": A Note on Mt 1:18b and Related Syriac Christian Texts. *NovT* 22:97–107.

Leyer, Blake. 1993. John Chrysostom on the Gaze. *JECS* 1:159–74.

Maier, Harold O. 1997. Staging the Gaze: Early Christian Apocalypse and Narrative Self Representation. *HTR* 92:131–54.

Martin, Dale B. 1995a. *The Corinthian Body*. New Haven: Yale University Press.

———. 1995b. Heterosexism and the Interpretation of Romans 1:18-32. *BibInt* 3:332–55.

———. 1996. *Arsenokoitês* and *Malakos:* Meanings and Consequences. Pages 117–36 in *Biblical Ethics and Homosexuality: Listening to Scripture*. Edited by Robert L. Brawley. Louisville: Westminster John Knox.

Miller, James E. 1995. The Practices of Romans 1:26: Homosexual or Heterosexual? *NovT* 37:1–11.

Moore, Stephen D. 1995. The Beatific Vision As a Posing Exhibition: Revelation's Hypermasculine Deity. *JSNT* 60:27–55.

———. 1996. *God's Gym: Divine Male Bodies of the Bible*. New York: Routledge.

———. 2000. The Song of Songs in the History of Sexuality. *Church History* 69: 328–49.

———. 2001. *God's Beauty Parlor: And Other Queer Spaces in and around the Bible*. Stanford, Calif.: Stanford University Press.

Moxnes, Halvor, ed. 1997. *Constructing Early Christian Families: Family As Social Reality and Metaphor*. New York: Routledge.

Neyrey, Jerome H. 1994. Despising the Shame of the Cross: Honor and Shame in the Johannine Passion Narrative. *Semeia* 68:113–37.

———. 1998. *Honor and Shame in the Gospel of Matthew*. Louisville: Westminster John Knox.

Nissinen, Martti. 1998. *Homoeroticism in the Biblical World: A Historical Perspective*. Minneapolis: Fortress.

Parsons, Mikeal C. 1995. Hand in Hand: Autobiographical Reflections on Luke 15. *Semeia* 72:125–52.

Pilch, John J. 1995. Death with Honor: The Mediterranean Style Death of Jesus in Mark. *BTB* 25:65–70.

Reinhartz, Adele. 1999. "And the Word Was Begotten": Divine Epigenesis in the Gospel of John. *Semeia* 85:83–103.

Saldarini, Anthony J. 1999. Asceticism and the Gospel of Matthew. Pages 11–27 in *Asceticism and the New Testatment*. Edited by Leif E. Vaage and Vincent L. Wimbush. New York: Routledge.

Scroggs, Robin. 1983. *The New Testament and Homosexuality: Contextual Background for Contemporary Debate*. Philadelphia: Fortress.

Seow, Choon-Leong, ed. 1996. *Homosexuality and Christian Community*. Louisville: Westminster John Knox.

Smith, Abraham. 1999. "Full of Spirit and Wisdom": Luke's Portrait of Stephen (Acts 6:1– 8:1a) As a Man of Self-Mastery. Pages 97–114 in *Asceticism and the New Testament*. Edited by Leif E. Vaage and Vincent L. Wimbush. New York: Routledge.

Smith, Mark D. 1996. Ancient Bisexuality and the Interpretation of Romans 1:26–27. *JAAR* 64:223–56.

Stowers, Stanley K. 1994. *A Rereading of Romans: Justice, Jews, and Gentiles*. New Haven: Yale University Press.

Swancutt, Diana. Forthcoming. Sexy Stoics and the Rereading of Romans 1:18–2:16. In *A Feminist Companion to Paul*. Edited by Amy-Jill Levine. Sheffield: Sheffield Academic Press.

Szesnat, Holger. 1995. In Fear of Androgyny: Theological Reflections on Masculinity and Sexism, Male Homosexuality and Homophobia, Romans 1:24–27 and Hermeneutics (A Response to Alexander Venter). *JTSA* 93:32–50.

Tolbert, Mary Ann. 2000. Gender. Pages 99–105 in *Handbook of Postmodern Biblical Interpretation.* Edited by A. K. M. Adam. St. Louis: Chalice.

Van der Horst, Pieter W. 1996. Sarah's Seminal Emission: Hebrews 11:11 in the Light of Ancient Embryology. Pages 112–34 in *A Feminist Companion to the Hebrew Bible in the New Testament.* Edited by Athalya Brenner. Sheffield: Sheffield Academic Press.

Vogt, Kari. 1991. "Becoming Male": A Gnostic and Early Christian Metaphor. Pages 172–87 in *Image of God and Gender Models in Judaeo-Christian Tradition.* Edited by Kari Elisabeth Børresen. Oslo: Solum Forlag.

Ward, Graham. 1999. The Displaced Body of Jesus Christ. Pages 163–81 in *Radical Orthodoxy: A New Theology.* Edited by John Millbank, Catherine Pickstock, and Graham Ward. New York: Routledge.

Wold, Donald J. 1998. *Out of Order: Homosexuality in the Bible and the Ancient Near East.* Grand Rapids: Baker.

Young, Steve. 1994. Being a Man: The Pursuit of Manliness in *The Shepherd of Hermas. JECS* 2:237–55.

8. The Maleness of Jesus

Doss, Erika. 1996. Making a "Virile, Manly Christ": The Cultural Origins and Meanings of Warner Sallman's Religious Imagery. Pages 61–94 in *Icons of American Protestantism: The Art of Warner Sallman.* Edited by David Morgan. New Haven: Yale University Press.

Gree, Elizabeth E. 1999. More Musings on Maleness: The Maleness of Jesus Revisited. *Feminist Theology* 20:9–27.

Gill, Sean. 1999. Christian Manliness Unmanned: Some Problems and Challenges in the Study of Masculinity and Religion in Nineteenth and Twentieth Century Western Society. Pages 160–72 in *Is There a Future for Feminist Theology?* Edited by Deborah F. Sawyer and Diane Collier. Sheffield: Sheffield Academic Press.

Harrison, Nonna Verna. 1998. The Maleness of Christ. *Saint Vladmir's Theological Quarterly* 42:111–51.

Karras, Valerie A. 1997. The Incarnational and Hypostatic Significance of the Maleness of Jesus Christ according to Theodore of Stoudios. *StPatr* 32:175–83.

Loughlin, Gerard. 1998. Refiguring Masculinity in Christ. Pages 405–14 in *Religion and Sexuality.* Edited by M. A. Hayes, W. Porter, and D. Tombs. Sheffield: Sheffield Academic Press.

Raab, Kelley Ann. 1997. Christology Crossing Boundaries: The Threat of Imaging Christ As Other Than a White Male. *Pastoral Psychology* 45:389–99.

Ruether, Rosemary Radford. 1993. *Sexism and God-Talk: Toward a Feminist Theology.* 2d ed. Boston: Beacon. [Orig. 1983]

Suchocki, Majorie. 1983. The Unmale God: Reconsidering the Trinity. *QR* 3:34–49.

Young, Pamela Dickey. 1986. Christianity's Male Savior–A Problem for Women. *Touchstone* 4.3:13–21.

9. Kinship

Aasgaard, Reidar. 1997. Brotherhood in Plutarch and Paul: Its Role and Character. Pages 166–82 in Moxnes.

Balch, David L., and Carolyn Osiek. 1997. *Families in the New Testament World.* Louisville: Westminster John Knox.

Bannon, Cynthia J. 1997. *The Brothers of Romulus: Fraternal Pietas in Roman Law, Literature, and Society.* Princeton: Princeton University Press.

Bartchy, S. Scott. 1999. Undermining Ancient Patriarchy: The Apostle Paul's Vision of a Society of Siblings. *BTB* 29:68–78.

Barton, Stephen C. 1994. *Discipleship and Family Ties in Mark and Matthew.* Cambridge: Cambridge University Press.

Duling, Dennis C. 1995. The Matthean Brotherhood and Marginal Scribal Leadership. Pages 159–82 in *Modeling Early Christianity: Social Scientific Studies of the New Testament in Its Context.* Edited by Philip F. Esler. New York: Routledge.

———. 1997. Egalitarian Ideology, Leadership, and Factional Conflict within the Matthean Group. *BTB* 27:124–37.

———. 1999. Matthew 18:15–17: Conflict, Confrontation, and Conflict Resolution in a "Fictive Kin" Association. *BTB* 29:4–22.

Esler, Philip F. 1997. Family Imagery and Christian Identity in Gal. 5:13 to 6:10. Pages 121–49 in Moxnes.

———. 2000. "Keeping It in the Family": Culture, Kinship and Identity in I Thessalonians and Galatians. Pages 145–84 in *Families and Family Relations As Represented in Early Judaisms and Early Christianities: Texts and Fictions.* Edited by Jan W. Van Henten and Athalya Brenner. Leiden: Deo.

Fatum, Lone. 1997. Brotherhood in Christ: A Gender Hermeneutical Reading of 1 Thessalonians. Pages 183–97 in Moxnes.

Hallett, Judith P. 1984. *Fathers and Daughters in Roman Society.* Princeton: Princeton University Press.

Hellerman, Joseph H. 2001. *The Ancient Church As Family.* Minneapolis: Fortress.

Horrell, David G. 2001. From ἀδελφοί to οἶκος θεοῦ: Social Transformation in Pauline Christianity. *JBL* 120:293–311.

Klauck, Hans Joachim. 1990. Brotherly Love in Plutarch and in 4 Maccabees. Pages 144–56 in *Greeks, Romans, and Christians: Essays in Honor of Abraham J. Malherbe.* Edited by D. L. Balch, E. Ferguson, and W. A. Meeks. Minneapolis: Fortress.

Meye Thompson, Marianne. 2000. *The Promise of the Father: Jesus and God in the New Testament.* Louisville: Westminster John Knox.

Mowery, Robert L. 1988. God, Lord and Father: The Theology of the Gospel of Matthew. *BR* 23:24–26.

Moxnes, Halvor, ed. 1997. *Constructing Early Christian Families: Family As Social Reality and Metaphor.* New York: Routledge.

Pomata, Gianna. 1996. Blood Ties and Semen Ties: Consanguinity and Agnation in Roman Law. Pages 43–64 in *Gender, Kinship, Power: An Interdisciplinary and Comparative History.* Edited by Mary Jo Maynes et al. New York: Routledge.

Quere, Ralph W. 1985. "Naming" God "Father." *CTM* 12:5–14.

Reinhartz, Adele. 1999a. "And the Word was Begotten": Divine Epigenesis in the Gospel of John. *Semeia* 85:83–103.

———, ed. 1999b. *God the Father in the Gospel of John. Semeia* 85.

Sandnes, Karl Olav. 1997. Equality within Patriarchal Structures: Some New Testament Perspectives on the Christian Fellowship and a Brother or Sisterhood and a Family. Pages 150–65 in Moxnes.

Sheffield, Julian. 2001. The Father in the Gospel of Matthew. Pages 52–69 in *A Feminist Companion to Matthew*. Edited by Amy-Jill Levine with Marianne Blickenstaff. Sheffield: Sheffield Academic Press.

10. EUNUCHS

Allison, Dale. 1984. Eunuchs because of the Kingdom of Heaven (Matt. 19:12). *Theological Students Fellowship Bulletin* 8:2–5.

Blinzler, Josef. 1957. Εἰσὶν εὐνοῦχοι: Zur Auslegung von Mt 19:12. *ZNW* 48: 254–70.

Caner, Daniel F. 1997. The Practice and Prohibition of Self-Castration in Early Christianity. *VC* 51:396–415.

Constantin, Daniel. 1968. Esséniens et Eunuques (Matthieu 19, 10-12). *RevQ* 6:353–90.

Dessen, C. S. 1995. The Figure of the Eunuch in Terence's *Eunuchus*. *Helios* 22:123–39.

Dewey, Arthur J. 1992. The Unkindest Cut of All? Matt 19:11–12. *Foundations and Facets Forum* 8:113–21.

Guyot, Peter. 1980. *Eunuchen als Sklaven und Freigelassene in der griechischrömischen Antike*. Stuttgart: Klett-Cotta.

Hanson, R. 1966. A Note on Origen's Self-Mutilation. *VC* 20:81–82.

Heth, William A. 1987. Unmarried "for the Sake of the Kingdom" (Matthew 19:12) in the Early Church. *Grace Theological Journal* 8:55–88.

Kuefler, Mathew. 2001. *The Manly Eunuch: Masculinity, Gender Ambiguity, and Christian Ideology in Late Antiquity*. Chicago: University of Chicago Press.

Long, Jacqueline. 1996. *Claudian's In Eutropium, or, How, When, and Why to Slander a Eunuch*. Chapel Hill: University of North Carolina Press.

Martin, Clarice J. 1989. A Chamberlain's Journey and the Challenge of Interpretation for Liberation. *Semeia* 47:105–35.

Piazza, Michael S. 2000. Nehemiah As a Queer Model for Servant Leadership. Pages 113–23 in *Taking Back the Word: A Queer Reading of the Bible*. Edited by Robert E. Goss and Mona West. Cleveland: Pilgrim.

Pitre, Brant. 1999. Marginal Elites: Matt 19:12 and the Social and Political Dimensions of Becoming Eunuchs for the Kingdom of God. Paper presented in the Matthew Group at the 1999 Society of Biblical Literature Annual Meeting.

Quesnell, Quentin. 1968. Made Themselves Eunuchs for the Kingdom of Heaven (Mt. 19,12). *CBQ* 30:335–58.

Scholz, Piotr O. 2000. *Eunuchs and Castrati: A Cultural History*. Translated by John A. Broadwin and Shelley L. Frisch. Princeton: Markus Wiener.

Spencer, F. Scott. 1992. The Ethiopian Eunuch and His Bible: A Social Science Analysis. *BTB* 22:135–65.

Stevenson, W. 1995. The Rise of Eunuchs in Greco-Roman Antiquity. *Journal of the History of Sexuality* 5:495–511.

Taylor, Gary. 2000. *Castration: An Abbreviated History of Western Manhood*. New York: Routledge.

Tannehill, Robert C. 1975. Matthew 19:12: Eunuchs for the Kingdom. Pages 134–40 in *The Sword of His Mouth*. Philadelphia: Fortress.

11. FURTHER STUDIES IN MASCULINITY AND RELIGION

Boyd, Stephen. 1992. Trajectories in Men's Studies in Religion: Theories, Methodologies, and Issues. *The Journal of Men's Studies* 7:265–68.

Boyd, Stephen, Merle Longwood, and Mark W. Muesse, eds. 1996. *Redeeming Men: Religion and Masculinities*. Louisville: Westminster John Knox.

Claussen, Dane S., ed. 2000. *The Promise Keepers: Essays on Masculinity and Christianity*. Jefferson, N.C.: McFarland.

Doty, William G. 1993. *Myths of Masculinity*. New York: Crossroad.

Ellison, Marvin M. 1993. Holding Up Our Half of the Sky: Male Gender Privilege As Problem and Resource for Liberation Ethics. *JFSR* 9:95–113.

———. 1994. Refusing to Be "Good Soldiers": An Agenda for Men. Pages 335–44 in *Sexuality and the Sacred: Sources for Theological Reflection*. Edited by James B. Nelson and Sandra P. Longfellow. Louisville: Westminster John Knox.

Hall, Donald, ed. 1994. *Muscular Christianity: Embodying the Victorian Age*. Cambridge: Cambridge University Press.

Jordan, Mark D. 1997. *The Invention of Sodomy in Christian Theology*. Chicago: University of Chicago Press.

Krondorfer, Bjorn, ed. 1996. *Men's Bodies, Men's Gods: Male Identities in a (Post-) Christian Culture*. New York: New York University Press.

Ladd, Tony, and James A. Mathisen. 1999. *Muscular Christianity: Evangelical Protestants and the Development of American Sport*. Grand Rapids: Baker.

Long, Ronald E. 1997. "The Sacrality of Male Beauty and Homosex: A Neglected Factor in the Understanding of Contemporary Gay Reality. Pages 266–81 in *Que(e)rying Religion: A Critical Anthology*. Edited by Gary David Comstock and Susan E. Henking. New York: Continuum.

Myers, William R. 1992. "The Men's Movement and the Church: A Critical Review. *RelEd* 87:479–84.

Nelson, James B. 1991. *The Intimate Connection: Male Sexuality, Masculine Spirituality*. Louisville: Westminster John Knox.

———. 1994. "Embracing Masculinity. Pages 195–215 in *Sexuality and the Sacred: Sources for Theological Reflection*. Edited by James B. Nelson and Sandra P. Longfellow. Louisville: Westminster John Knox.

Rambuss, Richard. 1998. *Closet Devotions*. Durham, N.C.: Duke University Press.

Rohr, Richard. 1992. *The Wild Man's Journey: Reflections on Male Spirituality*. Cincinnati: St. Anthony Messenger.

Rowson, Everett K. 1997. "The Effeminates of Early Medina. Pages 61–88 in *Que(e)rying Religion: A Critical Anthology*. Edited by Gary David Comstock and Susan E. Henking. New York: Continuum.

Vance, Norman. 1985. *The Sinews of the Spirit: The Ideal of Christian Manliness in Victorian Literature and Religious Thought*. Cambridge: Cambridge University Press.

Venter, Alexander. 1993. "A Theological Ethical Perspective on the Current Crisis in Masculinity and the Men's Movement. *JTSA* 83:87–101.

Williams, Rhys-H. 2000. Aspects of Promise Keepers Organization. *Sociology of Religion* 61:1–104.

JESUS, GENDER, AND
THE GOSPEL OF MATTHEW

Jerome H. Neyrey, S.J.
University of Notre Dame

1.0. TOPIC AND FOCUS

It is an axiom of contemporary scholarship that gender is a social construct (Brod; Kramer; Lorber and Farrell; Ortner and Whitehead). Ancient Greece (Cantarella; Dubish), Palestine (Satlow), and Rome (Gleason 1995; Kuefler; Hadley) each articulated what it means to be male or female in relationship to their values and institutions. This study focuses on the figure of the male Jesus in Matthew from the perspective of the common gender stereotype in the Hellenistic world at that time. We argue that the ancient world shared a common gender stereotype, that is, a descriptive and often a proscriptive sketch of gender-specific roles, tasks, tools, and places. There are three major sources of information for this stereotype. We find it in its full form in authors such as Xenophon, Aristotle, and Philo. Second, it is also accessible in epideictic rhetoric, which articulates the criterion for the honor and praise of males (Neyrey 1998a: 70–162), and in other places, such as physiognomics (Malina and Neyrey 1996: 104–6, 111–13, 146–48, 179–81). Third, a large body of data on "public/private" from many ancient documents provides yet one more important source of information on the gender stereotype.

This study has two parts: data and interpretation. First we will rehearse the ancient data for the gender stereotype. The thrust of this part of the study points toward males as "outdoors" and as "public" figures, as well as the roles, tasks, and behaviors expected of such males. Second, with this data we will then interpret the figure of the male Jesus in Matthew. We wish to see how much of this stereotype Matthew knows, how he presents Jesus as an ideal male, and what this means for the interpretation of his Gospel.

2.0. The Gender-Divided World of Antiquity

2.1. Ancient Informants on Gender Stereotypes

The ancients perceived the cosmos as totally gender-divided, and so they describe parallel male and female worlds, in which certain places, roles, tasks, and objects are deemed appropriate to each gender. Their descriptions, of course, are cultural constructions of social reality, that is, integral to their attempts to organize and interpret their worlds. The *topos* on "house" and "household" that was popular both in classical Greece and especially Rome (Pomeroy 1994: 69–73) constitutes our first source of information of the ancient gender stereotype.

In figure 1 below, we have in parallel columns four articulations of the *topos* on "house" and "household." While there are many examples of this *topos*, we will examine only these four in the framework of this essay. What do these texts tell us? (1) They span over five centuries (Xenophon, 428–354 B.C.E.; Aristotle, 384–322 B.C.E.; Philo, 15 B.C.E.–50 C.E.; and Hierocles, 117–138 C.E.), and because of their striking similarities, they witness to a common and persistent gender stereotype in antiquity. (2) All consider gender-divided space an important element, whether that is open/covered or outside/inside. While Hierocles does not use the terminology of binary opposite spaces, his tasks position males and females in different places. (3) Corresponding to gender-specific space are gender-specific tasks and roles. Males are either engaged in agriculture or civic affairs (= "outdoors" or "public"); thus they are farmers, herders, traders, or civic leaders. Females, on the other hand, have three tasks associated with the "indoors" or "private" world: child rearing, food preparation, and clothing production. (4) It follows that objects and tools are likewise gender-specific. Plows and draft animals, sheep, weapons, and harvesting tools belong to the male world; looms, pots and pans, and food-preparation instruments belong to the female. (5) Xenophon and Aristotle continue the stereotype by contrasting body types: male bodies are suited to hardship, labor, and strength, whereas female bodies are weaker (Kuefler: 21); if males display courage, females are timid. It is worth noting that both rural and urban locations are in view.

Figure 1: Gender-Divided Space, Tasks, and Tools

[H]uman beings live not in the open air, like beasts, but obviously need shelter.	For Providence has made man stronger and woman weaker, so that he in	Market-places and council-halls and law-courts and gatherings and meetings	Before anything else I should speak about the occupations by which a

Nevertheless, those who mean to win store to fill the covered place have need of someone to work at the open-air occupations, since plowing, sowing, planting and grazing are all such open-air employments, and these supply the needful food. Then again, as soon as this is stored in the covered place, then there is need for someone to keep it and to work at the things that must be done under cover. Cover is needed for the nursing of the infants; cover is needed for the making of corn into bread, and likewise for the manufacture of clothing from the wool. And since both the indoor and the outdoor tasks demand labor and attention, God from the first adapted the woman's nature, I think, to the indoor and man's to the outdoor tasks and cares. (Xenophon, *Oec.* 7.19–22)

virtue of his manly prowess may be more ready to defend the home, and she, by reason of her timid nature, more ready to keep watch over it; and while he brings in fresh supplies from without, she may keep safe what lies within. In handicrafts again, woman was given a sedentary patience, though denied stamina for endurance of exposure; while man, though inferior to her in quiet employments, is endowed with vigor for every active occupation. In the production of children both share alike; but each makes a different contribution to their upbringing. It is the mother who nurtures, and the father who educates. (Aristotle, *Oec.* 1.3.4 1343b 30–1344a 9)

where a large number of people are assembled, and open-air life with full scope for discussion and action—all these are suitable to men both in war and peace. The women are best suited to the indoor life which never strays from the house, within which the middle door is taken by the maidens as their boundary, and the outer door by those who have reached full womanhood. (Philo, *Spec.* 3.169)

household is maintained. They should be divided in the usual manner, namely, to the husband should be assigned those which have to do with agriculture, commerce, and the affairs of the city; to the wife those which have to do with spinning and the preparation of food, in short, those of a domestic nature (Hierocles, *On Duties* 4.28.21).

2.2. "Public" and "Private" Labels for Male Spaces

My research identifies many linguistic expressions for "public/ private." The raw data are extensive in regard to the terms used and the periods of history in which the examples are found.

FIGURE 2: DIFFERENT EXPRESSIONS OF "PUBLIC" AND "PRIVATE"

1. *koinos / idios:* "The deliberative kind is either hortatory or dissuasive; for both those who give advice in private (*idia*) and those who speak in the assembly (*koinē*) invariably either exhort or dissuade." Aristotle, *Rhet.* 1.3.3 1358b

2. *dēmosios / idios:* "What a widespread corruption of the young in private families (*idiois oikois*) as well as publicly in the State (*dēmosia*)." Plato, *Laws* 10 890B

3. *xynos / idios:* "Now he who said, 'The man who would be tranquil in his mind must not engage in many affairs, either private (*idiē*) or public (*xunē*),' first of all makes our tranquillity very expensive if it is bought at the price of inactivity." Plutarch, *Tranq. an.* 465C

4. *rhētores / idioi:* "First, they laid down laws to protect the morals of our children ... then they legislated for the other age-groups in succession, including in their provision, not only private citizens (*peri tōn idiōtōn*), but also the public men (*peri tōn rhētorōn*)." Aeschines, *Tim.* 7

5. *presbeia / idia:* "When any Athenians come to him [Hyrcanus] either on an embassy or on a private matter (*ē kat' presbeian ē kat' idian prorasin*)..." (Josephus, *Ant.* 14.151)

6. *dēmosios / katoikidios:* [S]ecret political councils (*politymatōn*) were meeting in private houses (*en idiais oikais*)." (Dio Halicarnassus, *Ant. Rom.* 11.57.3)

7. *polis / oikos:* "And you will find united in the same persons an interest at once in private (*oikeōn*) and in public (*politikōn*) affairs." Thucydides 2.40.2

8. *polis / idiōtēs:* "Two speeches have been devised that relate to burial. One is common (*koinos pros polin*) to the whole city and is spoken over the war-dead. The other is private and individual (*idia kath' hekaston*), relating to events that frequently happen in peace, when people die at various ages." (Pseudo-Dionysius, *Procedure for Funeral Speeches* [Russell])

9. *publice / privatim:* "We shall do well to heed that sound doctrine of Democritus in which he shows that tranquility is possible only if we avoid most of the activities of both private (*privatim*) and public (*publice*) life, or at least those that are too great for our strength." (Seneca, *Ira* 3.6.3)

10. *privatus:* "Under fortune one inquires whether the person is a slave or free, rich or poor, a private citizen (*privatus*) or an official with authority (*cum potestate*)." (Cicero, *Inv.* 1.25–35).

11. *foris / domi:* "[A]broad versus at home." (Suetonius, *Gramm.*)

These data indicate that males may be located in *three places:* "public" (politics), "private" (nonkinship associations), and "private" (household).

1. Greeks and Romans distinguished between "public" and "private" in terms of male participation in the *"public" or political life* of the city and the *"private" social relations* of an ordinary citizen (see also Hyperides 4.9; Xenophon, *Ages.* 11.5–6; Demosthenes, *Cor. trier.* 15–16; Lysias, *Defense of Mantitheus* 9–13). Demosthenes makes this distinction in one of his speeches:

> There are two sorts of problems with which the laws of all nations are concerned. First, what are the principles under which we associate with one another, have dealings with one another, define the obligations of *private life (peri tōn idiōn)*, and, in general order our social relations? Secondly, what are the duties that every man among us owes to the commonwealth, if he chooses to take part *in public life (tō koinō)* and professes any concern for the State? Now it is to the advantage of the common people that laws of the former category, laws of private intercourse *(peri tōn idiōn)*, shall be distinguished by clemency and humanity. On the other hand it is to your common advantage that laws of the second class, the laws that govern our relations to the State *(pros to dēmosion)*, shall be trenchant and peremptory, because, if they are so, politicians will not do so much harm to the commonalty. *(Tim.* 192–93)

Elite males, then, may participate in public life *(pros to dēmosion)* or restrict themselves to ordinary private life *(peri tōn idiōn)*. Thus, male association with other males occurs in both "public" and "private." Different behavioral expectations characterize male-public and male-private behavior: laws that govern public activity should be "trenchant and peremptory" versus "clement and humane" in private intercourse.

2. Male *public figures* still had *private household* concerns. For example, criteria for bishops and deacons in 1 Tim 3:4–5, 12 indicate that a male can provide appropriate leadership for the church only if he manages his household well. Thus males, who "naturally" belong in the public world with other males, also have roles and duties in the private world of the household. The duties of a male in the private world of the household include: (1) control of his children; (2) procurement of dowries for daughters and wise marriages for them (Isaeus, *On the Estate of Cleonymus* 39–40); (3) proper use of patrimony (Aeschines, *Tim.* 154); (4) funeral rites for parents (Isaeus, *On the Estate of Menecles* 36–37; see Matt 8:21–22); (5) concern for the virtue and reputation of wives and other females in the household (see Lysias, *On the Murder of Eratosthenes* 15–26); and (6) ruling over slaves and servants (Balch: 21–80). This distinction confirms what anthropologists of the classical world regularly argue, namely, that the ancients had only two institutions, politics (= "public") and kinship (= "private").

3. Occasionally we read of males with decidedly *public roles* but who *rarely* appear *in public*. Plato described some rulers remaining in their fortresses and rarely appearing in public:

> And is not that the sort of prison house in which the tyrant is pent? He only of the citizens may not travel abroad or view any of the sacred festivals that other free men yearn to see, but he must live for the most part cowering in the recesses of his house like a woman, envying among the other citizens anyone who goes abroad and sees any good thing. (Plato, *Rep.* 9.579b–c)

While Plato's tyrant keeps to the "indoor" world to escape violence, we read of other monarchs who lived in splendid isolation within their imperial residences and were elaborately insulated from the common world (see 1 Tim 6:16). Therefore, a few elite males remained "indoors," but within the public world of the institution of politics. But males who otherwise remain "indoors" are considered shameful because their place is in "public" (Pomeroy 1994: 276).

4. Finally we consider an example of this stereotype of male public and private space that clearly articulates the *three social venues* to which the ancients thought males belonged. Lysias argues for the honorable character of the accused by calling attention before his male peers how the defendant fulfilled the expected code of proper male behavior in each of the three spheres where males function (*In Defense of Mantitheus* 16.9–12). First he recounts the honorable behavior in regard to the "private" world of the household:

> Although little property had been bequeathed to me, I bestowed two sisters in marriage, with a dowry of thirty minae apiece; to my brother I allowed such a portion as made him acknowledge that he had got a larger share of patrimony than I had; and towards all else my behaviour has been such that never to this day has a single person shown any grievance against me. So much for the tenor of my private life (*ta idia*). (10–11)

As the eldest male in his family, he assumed responsibility for the honorable marriage of the family's daughters; he acted as patron within the family by distribution of the father's patrimony to his male siblings and to the family' s clients.

The speaker turns to the world outside of the household, which, by contrast with the "private" or household world, he labels the "public" world:

> with regard to public matters (*peri de tōn koinōn*), I hold that the strongest proof I can give of my decorous conduct is the fact that all the younger set who are found to take their diversion in dice or drink

or the like dissipations are, as you will observe, at feud with me, and are most prolific in lying tales about me. It is obvious, surely, that if we were at one in our desires they would not regard me with such feelings. (11)

This is not the "public"-political world of the Assembly nor the "private" household world just seen. Rather, we view the nonhousehold world where males entertain themselves in the company of other males with symposia, games, gambling, and the like.

Finally, he turns to the public-political world where the affairs of the city are in view, in this case, the city's army and its defense of its allies:

As regards campaigns in face of the enemy, observe how I discharged my duty to the State. First, when you made your alliance with the Boeo-tians, and we had to go to the relief of Hilartus, I had been enrolled by Orthobulus for service in the cavalry. (12–13)

Mantitheus goes on to say how he volunteered for the more difficult mil-itary task of an infantryman, attesting to his courage and solidarity with that part of the army. And he claims that he has been a model "public," that is, political, person who has "discharged his duty to the State." By recounting his military exploits, he declares that he acted as an honor-able male who has a visible public role in the affairs of the city. Thus, Mantitheus serves as an excellent emic informer on the triple spheres, spaces, and roles that make up the male world, which was both "public" and "private."

2.3. Males and Females vis-à-vis Gender-Divided Space

While "public" versus "private" were used by the ancients primarily in regard to males, our investigation of the ancient gender stereotype surfaced many examples of the way males and females are gender-divided in regard to space.

1. *politikos/katoikidios:* "It saw how unlike the bodily shapes of man and woman are and that each of the two has a different life assigned to it, to the one the domestic (*katoikidios*) life, to the other a civic life (*politikos*), it judged it well to prescribe rules all of which though not directly made by nature were the outcome of wise reflection and in accordance with nature." (Philo, *Virt.* 19)

2. *exō/endon:* "And since both the indoor (*ta te endon*) and the outdoor (*ta exō*) tasks demand labor and attention, God from the first adapted the woman's nature, I think, to the indoor (*epi ta endon*) and the man's to the out-door (*epi ta exō*) tasks and cares." (Xenophon, *Oec.* 7.19–22)

3. *hypaithros/stegnōn:* "Human beings live not in the open air (*en hypaithrō*),

like beasts, but obviously need shelter (*stegōn*). Those who mean to win store to fill the covered space have need of someone to work at the open-air (*en tō hypaithrō*) occupations; since ploughing, sowing, planting, and grazing are all such open-air (*hypaithria*) employments.... again, as soon as this is stored in the covered place (*eis to stegnon*), there is need of someone to keep it and to work at the things that must be done under cover (*ha tōn stegnōn erga*). Cover (*stegnōn*) is needed for the nursing of the infants; cover (*stegnōn*) is needed for the making of the corn into bread, and likewise for the manufacture of clothes from the wool." (Xenophon, *Oec.* 7:20–21)

4. *politikos/oikourios:* "And of the many forms of baseness none disgraces an aged man more than idleness, cowardice, and slackness, when he retires from public offices (*ek politikōn*) to the domesticity (*eis oikourian*) befitting women." (Plutarch, *Old Men in Public Affairs* 784A)

5. *politeia/oikonomia:* "Organized communities are of two sorts, the greater which we call cities (*poleōn*) and the smaller which we call households (*oikonomia*). Both of these have their governors; the government of the greater is assigned to men, under the name of statesmanship (*politeia*), that of the lesser, known as household management (*oikonomia*), to women." (Philo, *Spec.* 3.171)

6. *dēmosios/oikourios:* "Theano exposed her arm. Somebody exclaimed, 'A lovely arm.' 'But not for the public (*dēmosios*),' said she. Not only the arm of the virtuous woman, but her speech as well, ought to be not for the public (*dēmosion*), and she ought to be modest and guarded about saying anything in the hearing of outsiders (*pros tous ektos*), since it is an exposure of herself; for in her talk can be seen her feelings, character, and disposition. Pheidias made the Aphrodite of the Eleans with one foot on a tortoise, to typify for womankind keeping at home (*oikourias*) and keeping silence." (Plutarch, *Conj. praec.* 142C–D)

We saw that while males enjoy exclusively male public and private worlds, they belong also in a second "private" world, the household, and a code of duties accompanies male participation in each realm. Females, however, do not have formal public space vis-à-vis the *polis*, and while the stereotype indicates that they belong to the "indoor" world, that is not to say that they always remain in their houses. What household does not need to import water and fuel, fulfilment of which tasks must take females "outside" of the house? But females enjoy no civic role and so have no public space. The data about females at meals outside their houses in general indicate their absence (MacMullen 1980); as Pseudo-Demosthenes implies, such females are likely slaves or *hetairai* (59.122). About such females the law was not interested (Fantham: 380). In summary, when concepts such as gender-divided space occur, they invariably indicate redundant sets of gender-specific places, roles, tools, and even virtues.

Matthew, we argue, knows this gender stereotype, as is indicated in the following. For example, in Jesus' final discourse he warns all to watch. Illustrative of the gender stereotype is his reference to "males laboring in the fields," which is juxtaposed to "women grinding corn" (21:25–26). Similar to this is the exhortation to "behold the birds of the sky, who do not sow nor reap nor gather into barns," which is balanced by "behold the lilies of the fields, ... who neither toil nor spin" (6:26–28). Males, who labor in the fields, perform male tasks related to farming. Females, who labor in the household, do female tasks related to food preparation and clothing production. Evidently, the tools of each are gender specific. To this we might add the woman with yeast (13:33) who is juxtaposed to farmers (13:24) and merchants (13:45–46).

2.4. "Public" versus "Private" and Human Sexual Organs

The ancient medical writers Herophilus and Galen testify to the ancient belief that male and female genitals were classified as "public" and "private." Although it was argued that male and female sexual organs are similar, the difference was significant: male genitals are outside the body, whereas female genitals are within the body. Thus Galen writes: "All the parts, then, that men have, women have too, the difference between them lying in only one thing ... namely, that in women the parts are within the body, whereas in men they are outside, in the region called the perineum" (*Usefulness of the Parts of the Body* 14.6). External versus internal classification of the genitals, then, replicates the larger stereotype of a gender-divided world.

One important conclusion to draw from this study of a gender-divided stereotype is that, while we have focused on space, the stereotype is replicated in matters of social roles, tasks and tools, behavior, and even biology. It permeates and structures the entire social lives of males and females: (1) It describes the *roles* ascribed to males as husbands and fathers in the "codes of household duties": they were expected to lead and command, whereas their wives should follow and obey. (2) As regards *tasks*, males acquired the art of farming and herding, including the *tools*, such as mastering animals, carpentry, and tool-making required for this; females became adept at food preparation and clothing production. While both males and females touched corn and sheep, males produced the corn and sheared the sheep, whereas females processed the corn and the sheep's wool—different tasks. (3) Finally, males in public were expected to behave in masculine ways: with boldness, aggressiveness, eager to defend and advance their families' interests. Females, on the other hand, were respected when they were patient, subservient, restrained, passive, and defensive of their virtue (Malina 2001b: 48–50).

2.5. Nuancing the Stereotype: Social Location

Does the same set of gender expectations apply equally to elite and nonelite males and females? Needed here is some model of social stratification suitable to the ancient world that can distinguish for us the various classification of persons in the ancient world. Gerhard Lenski, in his survey of advanced agrarian, preindustrial societies, provides just such a classificatory tool. Lenski describes a hierarchical ranking of persons that seems to fit quite well the ancient world, which model has been used by various New Testament scholars with considerable success (Saldarini 1988: 35–49; Fiensy: 155–76; Duling 1992: 99–116; Rohrbaugh 1993: 114–27; Neyrey 1996: 255–67). Atop the social pyramid sat the true elite of ancient society, namely, rulers and/or aristocratic families, who were served by a series of retainers such as soldiers, priests, scribes, slaves, and the like. Dropping off precipitously in terms of social status, the hierarchical pyramid then consisted of merchants, only a few of whom catered to elite tastes and needs, while the rest belonged to the nonelite masses. Peasants, who constituted the vast majority of the ancient population (80 percent), tilled the land, labored in small villages, fished, and served as day laborers. Landless peasants in search of labor made up the bulk of the artisan group, which sought its fortunes in cities. Below them were the unclean, degraded, and expendibles, such as beggars, thieves, prostitutes, and the like. The ancients themselves expressed the radical difference between elites and nonelites as one between "the best" (*hoi aristoi*) and "the rest" (*hoi polloi*) or between the "more reputable" (*honestiores*) and the "more lowly" (*humiliores*) (Garnsey: 221–76).

Accordingly, all males did not enjoy the same social location and role, and hence "honor." Some were free and others, slaves; a few were elites and the rest, nonelites. In a hierarchical world where every person was vertically classified according to conventional notions of wealth, power, and status, kings ranked above peasants, who ranked above slaves, who in turn were above the untouchables. Few males, then, had the opportunity to fulfill the ideal stereotype of masculinity. Peasant males simply had no "public"-political world; leadership roles so characteristic of the male elite were not available to them, nor did they have voice to speak with boldness in public.

More to our purposes, the ancients themselves advise public speakers to make similar distinctions in regard to the social positions of the persons to be described in speeches or called as witnesses. In regard to how a person may be presented to a court, Cicero instructs the orator to select one of the following social locations: "Under fortune one inquires whether the person is a slave or free, rich or poor, a private citizen (*privatus*) or an official with authority" (*Inv.* 1.25.35). Quintilian's version brings out more of the elite/nonelite: "It makes a great difference whether a man be famous or obscure, a magistrate or a private citizen (*privatus*), a father or a son, a citizen or a foreigner, a free man or a slave" (*Inst. Orat.* 5.10.26). All such witnesses, of course, were males, as males alone had public voice. This material will be of considerable importance when we examine Jesus, the peasant from Nazareth, who nevertheless enjoyed public voice.

What do we know if we know this? We have in view a stereotype about human gender that is both ancient and enduring. We may rightly call it a "commonplace" and expect that it both describes ancient social life and prescribes it. It constitutes a code into which all were socialized and according to which praise or blame was awarded. Although we have tended to view the gender stereotype in terms of space and location, the data indicate how it was replicated throughout the various aspects of life in antiquity: space, roles, tasks, tools, biology, and behavior. It was, then, a formidable construct. The ancients, then, had clear and firm notions of what it meant to be male and female.

3.0. Jesus, the Male Stereotype, and the Code of Honor

With this stereotype of male gender in view, we turn to Matthew's Jesus. We claim that Matthew describes Jesus in terms of the cultural expectations about males just examined. And to argue this, we will track various representative elements of the stereotype: (1) space, (2) role and status, (3) tasks and behavior, (4) public speech, (5) objects, and (6) reputation.

3.1. Jesus, Private and Public

Where does Matthew locate Jesus? What does this communicate? Recall that the spatial options for males are "public" (civic space), "private" (with associates), and "private" (household).

3.1.1. Jesus in "Public"-Political Space

With Jesus' entrance into Jerusalem and its temple (Matt 21–22), he enters into "public"-political space and behaves like a male with elite standing. He will, moreover, stand face to face with Israelite and Roman authorities: males in male civic space, namely, courtrooms. Thus Jesus acts as a "public" male in public-political roles.

3.1.2. Jesus in "Private" (Nonkinship) Space

Matthew often portrays him "outside," as the stereotype on gender-divided space indicated: on a river bank with other males (3:13–17), on the shore of the Lake of Galilee (4:18; 13:1; 15:29) or crossing it (8:18 and 9:1; 14:13, 22–33), in fields (12:1), in "lonely places" (4:1; 14:13), and atop mountains (4:8; 5:1–7:29; 14:23; 15:29; 17:1; 24:3–25:56; 28:16). Jesus, moreover, readily frequents public spaces in villages and towns: synagogues (4:23; 9:35; 12:9; 13:54) and open areas, such as marketplaces and village gates (8:5; 9:9, 27; 11:1; 15:1). Jesus travels extensively, speaking and healing through "all Galilee" (4:23), the surrounds of Gadara (8:28), the villages around Tyre and Sidon (15:21) and Caesarea Philippi (16:13). Thus, as far as Matthew narrates, Jesus lived his life outdoors in the male "private" world outside his own home, as one would expect.

Matthew, moreover, presents Jesus "indoors," namely, in "private" space in the company of disciples and nonkinship-related males. For example, Jesus eats at the home of Levi, where "many tax collectors and sinners"—presumably all males—likewise dined (9:10). Although "indoors," this is not "private" in the sense of household but "private" space where nonrelated males gathered; the same holds true for other meals served Jesus (8:14–15; 10:10; 14:13–21; 15:33–39; 22:2–3).

3.1.3. Jesus in the Private Household Space

Matthew narrates in 12:46 that Jesus' mother and brothers "stood outside" and demanded Jesus come to them, while Jesus spoke to his circle "inside." The story contrasts (1) *two social groups,* the blood relatives of Jesus ("mother and brothers") and the fictive kin of Jesus ("Here are my mother and my brothers," 12:49) and (2) *two social spaces* ("outside" and "inside"). Ideally, his family should be "inside" with him and non-kin "outside." But the kinship relationship and the corresponding space are spatially topsy-turvy. When Jesus calls the group "inside" his "mother and brothers," he labels them his kin, albeit fictive kin. His blood relatives, however, are "outside"; Jesus does not obey their request, nor does he imply that he has any obligation toward them. Matthew, moreover, never describes Jesus in the "private" world of kin and household. He is not found there; he rejects the duties expected of him in regard to it; and he speaks against it. The "private" world of the household, then, is the one space that the male Jesus resists and avoids.

3.1.4. Mobility and Male Behavior

While males are expected to be "outdoors," this means the "open air" male-specific places of cities and villages. How, then, should we assess Jesus' constant mobility and so his absence from home and household duties? It belonged to males to protect and supervise the females under their custody, but if absent for long, they risked being thought cavalier about the reputation of those females (Malina 2001b: 140–42). Matthew says that Jesus' mother is still living, although she is not cared for by Jesus, despite the fact that he is her eldest (or only) son (13:55–56). Jesus' absence from the family home and his lack of care for his mother make him suspect; his mobility creates a problem, for he does not appear to support or supervise his family. Matthew's explanation for Jesus' mobility is tied to his obedience to his Father (e.g., Luke 2:49), and thus his regular appearance in "public" places is sanctioned by other aspects of the gender stereotype, namely, loyalty to one's Father (S. Barton: 125–215).

On this topic, let us recall Jesus' sayings that directly and indirectly attack family loyalty and legitimate a male's absence from the "private" world of the household. Because of him, many disciples will be at odds with their families (10:34–38); some will be ostracized by them (5:11–12; see Neyrey 1998a: 168–80). Others, it would appear, "left houses or brothers or sisters or father or mother or children or lands" for his sake (19:29). Thus Jesus' own mobility would have to be assessed in terms of the kind of antifamily stance that creates loyalty to Jesus and his group. Thus one "private" space (household and blood relatives) is replaced by another (fictive kinship). Whether expelled from the synagogue or seeking to forge strong fictive kinship bonds, the disciples are told to prize the "private" world of fictive kinship over all other spaces, even "private"-household space.

In summary, Matthew narrates Jesus' presence and actions in both the "public"-political forum and the "private"-nonkinship world of disciples. He never portrays Jesus in his "private"-household space. Whereas Jesus assumes male roles commensurate with the first two spaces, he rejects the male roles vis-à-vis the household. While one might expect a typical village male to be found "outside," as indeed Jesus is, it is surprising to find such a person in "public"-political space acting in a political role. If Jesus' mobility, moreover, creates any problem in terms of his honor, that is rationalized by his studied rejection of kinship roles and duties and by the rationale that his public activity is demanded by his Father—thus honor is restored.

3.2. Jesus and Male Roles: The Consummate Public Person

Matthew is mute on Jesus' role as husband and father and never presents him as having any role in the "private"-household world. In contrast, most of the roles that Jesus himself claims or that are ascribed to him belong to the "public"-political world. We consider two factors in the following survey of Jesus' public roles: (1) the proclamation and acknowledgment of them take place in the "public"-political world, and (2) the roles acclaimed are all political ones related to politics, the other major institution in antiquity, indeed, the ideal space for honorable males.

Son of God. The proclamation of Jesus as "Son of God," which occurs strategically at the beginning (3:17), middle (17:5), and end (27:54) of the Gospel, is made by political persons, either God or the Roman centurion, and always in public. Although God calls Jesus "Son" (3:17; 17:5), this is hardly a kinship role for Jesus (D'Angelo 1992a; 1992b), for the background of "Son of God" regularly points in the direction of the political roles of monarchs in the ancient world (Gadd: 45–50). It applies as well to kings of the Davidic line (see 2 Sam 7:14; Ps 2:7). It was applied to wonder workers and occasionally to angels, who act as the "public" agents of God in political matters, such as battle or judgment. "Son of God," then, refers to a political role. We take "Son of God," then, to designate Jesus in terms of a "public"-political, not a kinship role.

Son of David. All other titles and roles locate Jesus outside the "private"-household world and within the "public" world of politics. That is, Jesus is not identified with the institution of kinship but rather with that of politics. Whether people call him by any one of the three interrelated titles of "Son of David," "King of the Jews," or "Christ," they look to him to fulfill those roles and perform the tasks associated with "public"-political figures. It is by far the label most frequently ascribed to Jesus, which occurs first in Jesus' genealogy. There Matthew ascribes royal honor to Jesus by blood descent from the founding fathers of the nation, both Abraham and David (1:1, 17). In R. E. Brown's treatment of the functions of genealogies, he highlights one in particular, namely, to "undergird status, especially for the offices of king and priest where lineage is important (see Ezra 2:62–63; Neh 7:64–65)" (R. E. Brown 1993: 65). The status in question is that of a public, political figure. Various people, both males and females, Judeans and Gentiles, acknowledge this claim of Jesus to a public and political role in diverse situations: (1) when they petition Jesus to act as benefactor toward them with the resources reserved to monarchs to bestow (9:27; 15:22; 20:30– 31) and (2) when they herald Jesus' entrance into the royal city (21:9, 15), an event interpreted by the Evangelist as a political act (e.g., "king" in 21:5). Jesus himself explains Ps 110 in such a way as to indicate that the "Son of David" will be enthroned at God's right hand and so enjoy a public status and role superior even to David himself (22:42–44).

King of Israel/King of the Jews. The magi in search of the new king set the reigning king and his retainers in an uproar (2:2); two kings cannot live in Judea at the same time. Later, during Jesus' trial and execution, the central issue is his role and status as "king of the Jews" (27:11, 29, 37, 42). "King" is by far the most contested role in the Gospel, as it upsets Herod, the Jerusalem elites (2:1–4), the Roman procurator and army (27:11, 29,

37) and becomes a source of mockery from Judean passers-by at the cross (27:42). Yet, along with "Son of David," this most honorable title clearly portrays Jesus in a "public" role in the world of politics.

Christ/Messiah. Irrespective of the diverse popular expectations of a messiah (Charlesworth: 3–35), when Matthew narrates that people call Jesus "Christ," they refer to his "public" role in the world of politics (see Horsley and Hanson 1985: 88–134; Crossan: 168–206). It may be ascribed to Jesus by the heavenly sovereign and acknowledged on earth by his followers (16:16–17), but it is also bitterly contested by those who stand to lose political status and power from the presence of their political rival (26:63, 68; 27:22–23).

Lord (Sovereign). The label "lord," a general acknowledgment or description of honorable extrahousehold status, is equivalent to "sir." Thus people address Jesus as "lord" who seek benefaction from him as a patron under this title (e.g., 8:2, 5, 21, 25; 14:28; 15:27). On two occasions, moreover, the Evangelist uses this title for Jesus in the role of a "public" official, not a private citizen. The "Christ" who is the "Son of David" sits at the right hand of the heavenly Lord, and in that context he is himself called "Lord" (22:44–45). A person at the King's right hand enjoys a "public" role in the world of cosmic politics. Second, although the label "Lord" is not mentioned in the context, when Jesus states that "all authority in heaven and on earth has been given to me" (28:18), he claims the kind of executive role predicted of him in 22:42–45.

Prophet. Jesus is often likened to prophets (12:39–40; 16:14) and on one occasion is found in their company (17:3–4). People in the narrative twice acclaim him a prophet, both times in Jerusalem: "This is the prophet Jesus from Nazareth of Galilee" (21:11; see 21:46). Yet all of Israel's prophets, especially Moses, Elijah, Jeremiah, and Jonah, were public figures whose role frequently involved them within the political institution of either forming a people (Moses), criticizing the behavior of Israel's rulers (Elijah and Jeremiah), or calling a nation to conversion (Jonah). Prophets were sent to "Jerusalem," the national political center, which rejected them and killed them (23:37). In regard to Jesus, "prophet" is likewise a public role in the political institution (see Horsley and Hanson 1985: 135–41; Gray: 114–23). Moreover, it involved Jesus in political conflict, for prophets were sent to criticize those in public-political roles.

In summary, from Jesus' genealogy and birth to his death and vindication, Matthew presents him not simply in terms of ordinary male roles and behaviors appropriate to the "private" world outside of the household. On the contrary, Matthew locates Jesus in the ultimate public arena of politics, where he is ascribed and acknowledged as having elite public-political roles. According to Matthew, Jesus was no mere head of a household, artisan, or peasant. God has ascribed to him the political roles of "Son of David," King of Israel," "Lord," and "Christ. God will make him "sit at my right hand" with power to judge and rule.

3.3. Jesus and Male Tasks: No Ordinary Male

Since Matthew locates Jesus mostly in the "outdoors" world and presents him acting according to political roles there, what tasks and deeds does Jesus perform? Are they appropriate to private or public space? to the institution of kinship or politics? How would Jesus' actions be viewed in terms of the gender stereotype?

3.3.1. Few Actions and a Limited Private Role

Matthew narrates no actions or words by Jesus that relate to management of his own household. Yet males in villages also enjoyed a vigorous "private" life with friends independent of the household. We saw how frequently Jesus eats in the homes of disciples (8:14–15) and followers (9:10–13). The "private" conversations with the disciples on the way to Jerusalem (Matt 16:13–20:28) are a special case and will be discussed shortly. Hence, we find Jesus frequently in "private" nonkinship space, where he does what all ancient males did with great frequency, namely, "hang out" in the company of other males.

3.3.2. Shepherd, Warrior, Lawgiver, and Benefactor

Judging from the importance Matthew gives to it, we focus now on what Jesus does in the "public" world where he acts out certain political roles. The simplest way to treat this is to compare Jesus in his "public"-political roles with what David or other kings of Israel did. (1) *Shepherd*. David was shepherd, not simply of sheep, but of the nation; he was also warrior, lawgiver, judge, and benefactor-patron. Matthew describes Jesus as "shepherd" of a leaderless flock (9:36), who benefits them by his healings and feedings, relieves misery by miraculous acts, and forgives debts and sins. (2) *Warrior*. All of Jesus' conflicts with demons are properly the acts of a warrior-ruler attacking a rival, according to the symbolic world of that ancient culture (J. M. Robinson: 33–42). In defense of his power and authority, Jesus mounts an apology to the political charge that he is the agent of the "Prince of Demons"; he explains that kingdoms or·"houses" in civil war collapse. But Jesus the warrior besieges the fortress of a rival warrior, captures him, and plunders his kingdom (12:25–29). (3) *Lawgiver-Judge*. Jesus proposes a law

(5:21–46; 16:24–26) and acts as enforcer of his law, namely, as a judge (16:27). As king, he will sit on his heavenly throne and separate his subjects like sheep and goats, rewarding some but requiting others (25:31–46). (4) *Benefactor*. As expected of a generous monarch, Jesus provides access to God's great storehouse of food, health, and freedom. Despite the cultural perception of a radically limited supply of all good things, Jesus is able to increase the amount of goods, not by taking from others (i.e., spoils), but by divine benefaction that expands the supply and enriches all. In this, Jesus stands head and shoulders over other benefactors of this world, who must despoil many to benefit a few.

3.3.3. Responder to Public, Even Political Challenges

Virtually every *chreia* about Jesus narrates a challenge to him and his response. All challenges, to be effective, must be "public," that is, face to face with Jesus and before the eyes and ears of others. In that culture, every honorable male must not turn the other cheek but deliver a riposte (Neyrey 1998c: 666–81). And Jesus indubitably does so, despite what he told his disciples (5:38–42). Two questions arise: (1) Are Jesus' claims and the challenges to them those of a private or a public-political nature (e.g., "only God can forgive sins?"), and (2) what is the social location of the players who claim and who challenge? The content of most of the claims and of the challenges to them have to do with "public"-political matters. In regard to the social location of claimants and challengers, if the challengers to Jesus were merely private individuals who, out of envy of him (Mark 15:10), challenged him, then his riposte would be the appropriate behavior of a private person. If, however, his challengers are rulers and elites in the political institution, then challenge and riposte games should be upgraded to reflect the conflict over the public role and status of Jesus in that political institution. We saw earlier that at the beginning and ending of the Gospel the political elite plot Jesus' death. The challenge-riposte game, then, is played among the male elite of the "public"-political world.

Does the picture change when we move from the capital city to Galilee? Who are the people who challenge Jesus (12:38) and test him (16:1)? By far the dominant opposition to Jesus in Galilee comes from the Pharisees (9:11, 34; 12:2, 14, 24, 38; 15:12; 19:3). Saldarini (1988: 168–69) notes that in general the Galilean challenges from scribes and Pharisees touch on two areas: food rules (9:6–13, 14–17; 12:1–8; 15:12) and sources of power (9:32–34; 12:22–24). Yet these should not be classified as "religious" issues. Daniel and 2 and 4 Maccabees witness that what one eats is a matter of political loyalty. The Pharisees belong to the retainer class who serve the governing elite (that is, those with wealth and direct political

power) and who ally themselves with them to promote their own pro-
grams for Judaism. In Galilee, they were not the top level of leadership
but influential figures in local village leadership. They were a middle
level of leadership between the governing class and the people and sometimes acted as brokers for the people with their higher contacts (Saldarini
1988: 171–72). Thus Jesus is confronted by a high-level class of retainers
who serve the elite—no mean opponents. Therefore, challengers to Jesus,
whether in the capital city or in Galilee, belong to the public-political
world. The contents of the challenges, moreover, are political issues,
either Jesus' identity and role or his agenda for the way the nation should
act. Thus, both challengers and the topics of conflict confirm the presentation of Jesus as an honorable "public"-political figure. It is exclusively
male behavior to seek honor, make claims, and defend them. It is
uniquely male behavior to engage in combat.

3.4. Jesus and Male Speech

According to the gender stereotype, males in "private" space outside
the household have voice but females do not, a distinction all the more
true of the "public"-political world. But not every male had public voice,
as Plutarch implies in this maxim: "Nature has given us two ears and one
tongue, because we ought to do less talking than listening" (*Listening to
Lectures* 39B). Who, then, has voice? What have age, social location, and
public/private space to do with voice? First, young males generally do
not enjoy voice, as Lysias indicates: "Some people are annoyed at me
merely for attempting at too early an age to speak before the people"
(*Defense of Mantitheus* 16.20; Luke 2:46–47). Second, perhaps Luke had this
cultural issue in mind when he stated that Jesus was "about thirty years
of age" (3:23) when he went to the Jordan. Some scholars read this not so
much as calendar age than as a claim that Jesus was sufficiently mature to
be an elder (Buchanan). Third, elite male citizens had "public" voice, but
not male peasants. Thus, social location indicates whether in the eyes of
others one has the right to speak. In general, then, elders, who are higher
up the status ladder, enjoy public voice; less so, ordinary males and
youth (Rohrbaugh 1995: 192–95; Neyrey 1996: 276–79). Let us examine
now Jesus' public speaking in terms of his social role and the conventions
of an honorable public male.

3.4.1. Jesus' Right to Public Speech

While Matthew remains silent on whether Jesus was "educated" (see
John 7:15), which might qualify him to speak, he narrates that Jesus was
authorized to speak and to act in the public world by the highest-ranking

person in the cosmos. At the Jordan with the Baptizer, John, not Jesus, has public voice. But Matthew notes that Jesus immediately assumed public voice as he "taught in their synagogues and preached the gospel of the kingdom" (4:23). The theophany at the Jordan (3:16–17) functions as the formal commissioning of Jesus to a public role with public voice. Rohrbaugh argued this case for the Lukan narrative (1995: 186–95), and the same can be said of Matthew. God authorizes Jesus for the public role of "Son of God" (3:17), which, while challenged (4:1–11), is subsequently acknowledged by the audiences who hear Jesus' successful speaking and see his actions (4:23–24; see Malina and Rohrbaugh: 304). Later in the narrative, when Jesus begins to speak a new word about the fate of the Son of Man and the "way" of discipleship (16:21–26), God again appears in a theophany and commands the reluctant disciples to "Listen to him" (17:5). Jesus, then, has public voice because God commissions him, authorizing what he is to say and do.

In addition, Jesus himself claims a unique bestowal of esoteric knowledge given to him by God (11:25–27), which he speaks to a select few (11:27). He claims, moreover, legitimacy to speak by comparing himself with Jonah and Solomon, whose public voices were most honorable; only he is "greater than Jonah" and "greater than Solomon" (12:41–42). Thus, Matthew has studiously attended to the issue of the legitimacy of Jesus' public voice. In virtue of his ascribed honor from God, he has a public role with a public voice, even a valid political voice.

3.4.2. The Content of Jesus' Public Speech

The content of Jesus' public speech includes materials from both male and female worlds. Jesus speaks about the ordinary roles and tasks of females: clothing production (6:28–30; 9:16), food preparation (i.e., leavening flour, 13:33) and child rearing (19:13–15; see 18:1–4). Five maids in a noble house (25:1–13) receive praise for performance of their domestic duties. While he mentions the Queen of the South (12:42), he praises her for listening to the wisdom of King Solomon. Not surprisingly, the bulk of his discourse is about male topics. Jesus, artisan and peasant, knows and speaks of the roles and tasks of ordinary males in the outdoor world of the village: carpenters (13:55), fishermen (4:18–22; 13:47–48), sowers (13:3), farmers buying fields (13:44), merchants (13:45), shepherds (18:12–13; 26:31), day laborers (20:1–16), tenant farmers (21:35–39), and servants abroad doing the master's bidding (22:2–10).

Yet in contrast to these ordinary concerns of village nonelites, Matthew presents Jesus speaking of affairs in the public-political world, namely. God's "kingdom" (Chilton; Malina 2001b: 15–35). In a programmatic summary of his public speech, Jesus declares that it is his role to "preach the gospel of the kingdom" (4:23; see also 9:35). And his parables from 13:19 onward speak about the "kingdom." Modern translations of Jesus' words, however, reduce his discourse on "kingdom of God" to the politically innocuous "God reigning." Moreover, modern political ideology separates "church" from "state," making it difficult to interpret "kingdom" except in terms of "religion" that is not embedded in politics (Malina 2001b: 91–95; 1986: 92–101). But these recent trends are anachronistic Euro-American concerns that skew the perspective of religion-embedded-in-politics commonly found in antiquity. We argue that when Jesus speaks of "kingdom," he generally speaks of the public world and the institution of politics.

At first, Jesus' discourse about this political "kingdom" seems problematic because of the metaphors used to describe it. Some compare items and actions within the ordinary male "outdoors" world and the female world of the household. The kingdom of heaven is like a woman putting leaven into flour (13:33) and a man sowing seed (13:24) or a grain of mustard seed (13:31; see 13:44, 45, 47). Balancing these metaphors, Matthew likens the kingdom of heaven to a king's wedding feast for his son (22:1), a significant political event. It resembles some great landowner hiring many workers (20:1) or a king settling great debts (18:23). Some metaphors accentuate the greatness of the kingdom; others stress its lack of honor and significance or its strangeness. Which metaphor Jesus uses to describe the "kingdom," while important, is ultimately less important here than the fact that he talks about it so frequently and claims to know it intimately. He exercises public voice on a most public topic.

Jesus' discourse on "the kingdom" contains many typical topics, the first of which is membership: Who belongs in this kingdom? Jesus declares that some unlikely people will be accepted in the kingdom (8:11–12; 21:43; 22:8–10; 25:34–40), while others who thought they had a claim to it will be cast out of it (22:2–7, 13; 25:41–46). Second, is there social stratification as one finds in a political kingdom? Evidently, for we are told that there are "greatest" and "least," status sometimes based on observance of the rule of Jesus (5:19), sometimes on benefaction (11: 11), and sometimes on the new code of worth and honor proclaimed by Jesus (19:14; see 18:1, 4; 20:21). Third, in it benefaction is practiced (13:11; 11:25–27), albeit a benefaction quite different from that practiced by rulers in the world (20:25–26). Fourth, the ancestors of the kingdom are well remembered, both patriarchs (8:11) and monarchs such as David and Solomon (6:29; 12:3, 42). Finally, Jesus describes the great triumphal approach (*parousia*) of the vindicated monarch (24:27, 37, 39). Thus, a large part of Jesus' speech concerns the "public"-political world in which Matthew insists that Jesus has a valid right to speak.

3.4.3. The Honor Component in Jesus' Public Speech

Finally, we briefly consider the times when Jesus redefines the pre-vailing male value of honor. I have argued elsewhere that Jesus began his Sermon on the Mount declaring "honorable" those who were dis-honored for his sake (5:3–12; Neyrey 1998a: 164–87; cf. K. C. Hanson). Moreover, he called off the typical games whereby males pursued honor and physical, sexual, and verbal aggression (5:21–48; Neyrey 1998a: 190–211), and he demanded that his disciples on select occasions vacate the playing field where honor is claimed and awarded (6:1–18; Neyrey 1998a: 212–28). While the content of this first public discourse is about the male value of honor, Jesus discredits conventional honor-gaining and honor-maintaining behavior. In this regard he challenges much of the prevailing male gender stereotype.

Jesus' redefinition of honor constitutes the commanding feature of other remarks, namely, his teaching of "the Way" on his way to Jerusalem. Although Jesus spoke often to crowds "outdoors," he gave distinctive teaching to the inner circle of disciples he led to Jerusalem. Matthew brackets this material about Jesus' "way" in terms of the group addressed (i.e., inner circle), the time it was spoken (after Caesarea Philippi and before Jerusalem), and the locale (en route to Jerusalem). Of what does Jesus' new honor code consist? We confess to seeing in Jesus' teaching on the way to Jerusalem (16:21–20:28) a new code of honor and shame.

16:21–28	honor comes from taking up one's cross and imitating Jesus
17:14–20	shame comes from having too little "faith"
17:24–27	honor comes from taking tribute, shame from paying taxes
18:1–6	honor comes from being worthless, like a child
18:7–9	discipleship may require the shame of loss of an honorable limb
18:15–20	the honorable (i.e., private) way of correcting deviants
18:21–35	honor comes from forgiveness of wrongs rather than from vengeance
19:1–9/10–12	honor through sexual aggression is denied to disciples
19:16–30	honor comes from loss of wealth and power
20:1–16	generous patrons impartially share their wealth, showing no favoritism
20:20–28	honor comes from being last and servant of all

Most of this instruction seems concerned with the issues of stratifica-tion and social location, generally a male concern. The "greatest in the kingdom of heaven" is not the ruler or leader but a "worthless" child (18:1– 6). Although kings of the earth take tribute and do not pay taxes (17:25), Jesus and his followers, who now are reckoned among that elite, still pay the shekel tax. Jesus denies session at his right and left hands to James and John (20:20–23). The "great ones" and the "first" should be like Jesus, the servant and last of all (20:25–28). The creation of a new social hierarchy challenges that of the public-political world, in keeping with which Jesus denies all elite titles and power to his disciples (23:8–12). Other examples of Jesus' new social hierarchy include:

1. last is first, first is last (19:30; 20:16)
2. least is greatest, greatest is least (18:1–4)
3. humbled is exalted, exalted is humbled (23:12)
4. servant is "a great one" (20:26) or greatest (23:11); slave is first (20:27)
5. no one is greater than John the Baptist, yet whoever is least in the kingdom of heaven is greater than he (11:1)

A social hierarchy there is, which is now based on values not thought of as male or honorable. This constitutes, then, the most egregious variance of Jesus from the male stereotype.

Other materials, however, touch on the manly virtue of courage. Honorable courage is required to face trials (16:21–26), to lose face and worth (18:7–9), to forego vengeance in favor of pardon (18:20–35), to foreswear sexual aggression (19:4–12), and to lose wealth, a typical mark of honor (19:16-30). But clearly most of the remarks of Jesus "on the way" to Jerusalem serve to redefine "honor" for males in the kingdom of God.

This material is all the more striking in view of the "love of honor" (*philotimia*) that characterized the ancients (Neyrey 1998a: 16–19), and Jesus regularly discourses on it. He knows that it is "love of honor" that drives people to public display of socially commended actions. Some practice their piety in public "in order to be seen by others" (6:1, 2, 5, 16). Similarly, Jesus criticizes the Pharisees for their love of honor: they do all their deeds to be seen by others; they make their phylacteries broad and their fringes long, and they love the places of honor at feasts, the best seats in the synagogues, salutations in the marketplace, and being called rabbi by others (23:5–7). These Pharisees appear to be no different from other males in the ancient world: they dress for success, seek prominent social space, and thrive on public acknowledgment of their worth. Even Jesus laments the loss of his share of it when he is not acknowledged at home (13:57). But Matthew relentlessly portrays Jesus opposing this part of the male stereotype. Therefore, we see that the bulk of Jesus' public speech directly engages the conventions of male honor. All, including

Jesus and God, seek acknowledgment of their worth, role, and status by others. What differs in Matthew is the reform of the honor code. Jesus' discourse on honor is a male-gender phenomenon in the "private" outdoors and "public"-political realms.

4.0. Summary and Conclusions

From this study of gender in antiquity we draw the following conclusions. (1) We have clearly in view a stereotype of a radically gender-divided world. The stereotype, moreover, was replicated in the basic institutions of antiquity (politics and kinship) and structured the whole lives of males and females, their roles, places, tasks, and tools. The corollary to this was a set of the social expectations shared by all according to which both males and females would be evaluated and either praised or blamed.

(2) Our ancient informants describe a simple stereotype of gender-divided space (i.e., males/public and females/private), in that male tasks take them "out of doors," whereas female tasks focus them "indoors." Our data urge us to nuance this, for males belong in three places: "public"-political, "private"-household, and "private"-association. Females belong only to the "private"-household world, even if tasks take them out of the house. Thus males are not simply "public," as the ancient stereotypes suggest, but move in and out of relationship to both the political world and the world of the household. The same is not true for females.

(3) In regard to Jesus, Matthew rarely locates him "inside" and mentions no duties that he has toward his household, either to mother, wife, or children. He appears in the "private" world of nonrelated males and females (e.g., in marketplaces, synagogues, dining rooms or traveling to wilderness, mountains, temple, and the like). Moreover, Matthew credits Jesus with an exalted role and status that belong to persons in the public-political world. In our analysis, Jesus has nothing to do with the institution of kinship, except to encourage disciples to stand against its pressures to conform. Thus, Matthew presents the male Jesus in both public and private space, the public-political and private-association realms.

(4) Jesus' actions are generally those expected of honorable, public males. He performs splendidly in the local game of push-and-shove, that is, the challenge and riposte exchange (Neyrey 1998c; Malina and Neyrey 1988: 71–91). His adversaries are generally socially prominent people whose hostility to Jesus only raises his status.

(5) One of the striking features of Matthew's presentation of Jesus is his public voice. Jesus' audiences regularly credit him with public voice by comparing him with others: "he taught them as one with authority,

and not as their scribes" (7:29). Although the contents of his speech cover a wide range of topics, two aspects stand out. First, he speaks often about the kingdom of God, which we consider a genuinely political topic. His high-status, political roles as "Son of God," "King of Israel," "Son of David," and "Christ" go hand in hand with this discourse. Second, the cultural value of honor was a constant feature in Jesus' discourse. His remarks on honor, however, often conflict with those of the great code of honor to which all males in some fashion were socialized. Jesus reforms aspects of the code by declaring that certain behaviors honorable in the eyes of one's family and peers are not praiseworthy before God, and vice versa.

This essay, then, contributes to the study of gender in antiquity by making salient what the ancients understood by male gender, which as a historical matter should not be left to intuition or political correctness. The gender stereotype of a totally divided world is a historical fact. In light of this, Matthew portrays the male Jesus as most honorable: he acts where honorable males should act ("outside" and in public); he behaves as males should, whether in challenge-riposte exchanges or with socially approved voice to speak boldly and authoritatively. Jesus may seem not to conform to the gender stereotype when he demands of his followers that they (1) eschew male games of physical and sexual aggression to gain honor; (2) vacate the public forum to perform their piety; (3) endure shameful actions, such as ostracization; (4) forsake family wealth; and (5) become lowly and serve others, but these shameful actions actually become the way to honor in the eyes of God and Jesus. Thus, knowing the ancient gender stereotype allows a reader of Matthew to assess the Gospel presentation of Jesus as an ideal, honorable male.

MATTHEW AND MASCULINITY

Janice Capel Anderson, University of Idaho
Stephen D. Moore, Drew University

Eusebius's *Ecclesiastical History*, like so many other ancient histories, is richly studded with anecdotes. One of the more intriguing concerns Origen's painfully literal reading of Matt 19:12:

> At that time, while Origen was performing the work of instruction at Alexandria, he did a thing which gave abundant proof of an immature and youthful mind, yet withal of faith and self-control [*sōphrosynēs*]. For he took the saying, "There are eunuchs which made themselves eunuchs for the kingdom of heaven's sake," in too literal and extreme a sense, and thinking both to fulfil the Saviour's saying, and also that he might prevent all suspicion of shameful slander on the part of unbelievers (for, young as he was, he used to discourse on divine things with women as well as men), he hastened to put into effect the Saviour's saying, taking care to escape the notice of the greater number of his pupils. But, wishful though he might be, it was not possible to hide a deed of this nature. (6.8.1–3)[1]

Though this anecdote is not the focus of the present study, it does prompt an arresting question about the ideologies of masculinity in the Gospel in which the eunuch logion (not attested in any other New Testament source)[2] is embedded: What sort of text would impel an ancient Mediterranean male to "unman" himself? That the Gospel of Matthew might

---

* The authors would like to express their gratitude to the Society of Biblical Literature Group on the Literary Aspects of the Gospels and Acts to whom an earlier version of this article was presented in 1997 and to respondents Fred W. Burnett and Shawn Kelley in particular. We would also like to thank Virginia Burrus for an incisive critique of a later draft of the piece. The cliché holds true, however: all remaining errors *are* ours alone.

1 LCL. Scholars differ as to the credibility of this anecdote. For a range of opinion, see Caner: 401; Chadwick 1959: 68; cf. 9–12; 1966: 67; Cox: 88–90; R. Hanson; Kuefler: 261; and Trigg: 54. Eusebius's "Life of Origen" occupies most of book 6 of the *History*. On Eusebius's treatment of Origen's masculinity in the "Life," see Burrus 2000: 25–28.

2 The issue of whether or not the logion is attributable to the historical Jesus is not our concern. For discussion and bibliography, see Davies and Allison 1988–97: 3:24–25, 28–30.

have had such an effect—or be imagined by Eusebius to have had—is all the more remarkable given that its general "message" regarding masculinity is far from transparent. On the contrary, as we shall see, it is profoundly ambiguous and thoroughly contradictory. This is a self-divided and as such thoroughly ambivalent text that presupposes a hegemonic ideology of masculinity, on the one hand, while simultaneously interrogating and subverting it, on the other, thereby proffering an "alternative" masculinity alongside, and in tension with, a more traditional one. But before turning to trace the contours of this ambivalent design, a more fundamental issue must be addressed: How, for purposes of this study, is "masculinity" to be understood?

MASCULINITIES

To begin with the obvious, anatomy alone does not make the man, and what it means to be a man is subject to variation across cultures, and even within individual cultures. Certain of these variants might be classified as hegemonic and others as subordinate, as Andrea Cornwall and Nancy Lindisfarne (3) have suggested:

> [I]t is useful to think of those ideologies which privilege some men (and women) by associating them with particular forms of power as "hegemonic masculinities." Hegemonic masculinities define successful ways of "being a man"; in so doing, they define other masculine styles as inadequate or inferior. These related masculinities we call "subordinate variants." ... [O]ne reason the rhetoric of hegemonic versions of masculinity is so compelling is that it rests on an apparent certainty: that "a man is a man" everywhere, and everywhere this means the same thing.

If concepts of masculinity are not universal, but culturally determined, neither are they autonomous. They are "always already" imbricated with other culturally constructed categories of difference, such as kinship, age cohort, sexual preference, socioeconomic status, and race or ethnicity.[3]

What of ancient Mediterranean masculinities? The Greco-Roman sex/gender system, it would seem, is best mapped as a gradient (see Mattila) or sliding scale.[4] Clustered at one end of the scale were those

---

3 The social construction of gender involves many variables and domains of discourse. It is constructed relationally. Marilyn Strathern (ix) defines gender as the "categorization of persons, artifacts, events [and] sequences ... which draw upon sexual imagery [and] make concrete people's ideas about the nature of social relationships."

4 There were distinctions between Roman and Greek masculinities, but we are discussing what in large part was shared.

who, notionally at least (for the scale was treacherously slippery and unstable), qualified as the supreme exemplars of hegemonic masculinity: adult male citizens, primarily, although not exclusively, those of high social standing: rulers, heads of elite households, powerful patrons, and so on. Clustered at the other end of the scale were countless others who, in different ways and to different degrees, seemed (in the eyes of the elite, in any case) to fall into a catchall category that might best be labeled *unmen:* females, boys, slaves (of either sex), sexually passive or "effeminate" males, eunuchs, "barbarians," and so on.[5]

That factors other than anatomy were in play in this gendered hierarchy is evident from the fact that free adult females, for example, were generally higher on the scale than adult male slaves. From the hegemonic perspective, the subordinate and unmanly status of the lesser groups derived from their inability to master others or even themselves, unlike those who were more fully men. Mastery of others and/or of oneself emerges as definitive of masculinity in many surviving Greco-Roman texts, the emphasis arguably shifting increasingly to self-mastery during and after the Augustan epoch (Foucault 1986: 84–86, 94–95). Frequently in these texts, such mastery is represented as requiring a fully developed rationality or intellect, troped as masculine, as fitting ruler of the self. The intellect controls the irrational senses, passions, and desires, which in turn are troped as feminine and slavish. Control of self and control of others, therefore, are routinely represented as being intimately related. For Aristotle, for instance, the free male citizen is the fitting ruler over citizen women, children, and slaves because he possesses the rational portion of the soul in full, whereas the female citizen "has it, but without full authority," "the [male] child has it, but in an undeveloped form," and the slave does not have it at all (*Pol.* 1260a, LCL). (Undoubtedly overtidy even for his own time, Aristotle's abstractions would have been especially taxed by selected slaves of the *familia Caesaris* and other wealthy and powerful Roman slaves.)

Philo of Alexandria for his part, subsequently embroidering on these enduring themes, tropes the mind as masculine and the senses as

---

5 We have adopted the term *unmen* from Walters 1991: 31; cf. Walters 1997: 41. We hasten to point out the obvious, however: this (implicit) distinction between "men" and "unmen" rests on texts that were authored, not by those at the "unmen" end of the gender continuum—extant texts from this vast group are all but nonexistent—but by free adult males. Would low-status males (agricultural slaves, for instance) themselves have subscribed to this distinction? Santoro-L'Hoir has suggested that they might have (see esp. 203), yet it is exceedingly difficult to generalize on the basis of the existing evidence (see further C. A. Williams: 153–59).

feminine and construes their relationship symbolically in terms of social and political mastery:

> [I]n us mind corresponds to man [*andros men echei logon ho nous*], the senses [*aisthēsis*] to woman; and pleasure encounters and holds parley with the senses first, and through them cheats with her quackeries the sovereign mind itself: for when each sense has been subjugated to her sorceries, delighting in what she proffers, . . . then all of them receive the gifts and offer them like handmaids to the Reason as to a master. . . . Reason is forthwith ensnared and becomes a subject instead of a ruler, a slave instead of a master, an alien instead of a citizen, and a mortal instead of an immortal. (*Opif.* 165–66, LCL; cf. *QG* 2.49; *Leg.* 1.86–87)

Earlier in the same work, Philo explains why Moses mysteriously lauded the "snake fighter" (Lev 11:22 LXX): the latter is "a symbolic representation of self-control [*enkrateia*], waging a fight that never ends and a truceless war against intemperance [*akrasian*] and pleasure [*hēdonēn*], producing softness and voluptuousness in soul and body" (*Opif.* 164).

Philo stands apart from pagan Hellenistic authors in extolling *enkrateia* through allegorical exegesis of Jewish scripture, needless to say, but in underscoring its importance for manliness he is wholly conventional. In classical Greek literature, and in Stoic and Cynic literature (including some Hellenistic Jewish literature), *enkrateia* is regularly cloaked in martial and athletic metaphors and held up as a supremely masculine virtue (Foucault 1985: 65–70, 72–74; Moore and Anderson: 258–59). *Enkrateia*, together with *sōphrosynē* ("temperance," one of the four cardinal virtues—*andreia*, "[manly] courage," was another), kept a male from setting foot on the slippery slope that would speedily plunge him into the inchoate morass of femininity. Yet even females were not doomed to chronic femininity but could, on occasion, exhibit, even exemplify, "masculine" virtues (Murnaghan: 9–22; Aspegren; Castelli 1991; Moore and Anderson: 265–72). "Abstract" markers of masculinity, nevertheless, such as the possession of certain virtues, could also be associated with concrete physical markers. *Malakos* ("soft"; *mollis* in Latin), in particular, is a loaded adjective regularly deployed to differentiate women, girls, youths, and "effeminate" males from "true" men (Walters 1991: 29; Dover 1989: 79; Gleason 1995: 65, 69; C. A. Williams: 127–32). What is most striking overall, however, about the hegemonic concept of gender in the ancient Mediterranean world is not its reification of anatomy, but rather its relativization of anatomy. We are presented not so much with a simple hierarchical opposition, a masculine/ feminine dichotomy anchored in unambiguous anatomical markers, as with a hierarchical gender gradient or continuum, as noted earlier, in whose middle ranges masculinity begins to shade over almost imperceptibly into femininity, and vice versa, so that swift slippage from a more manly to a less manly status is an ever-present possibility even for the socially advantaged male subject (cf. Gleason 1995: xxii, 159).

MATTHEW

That the Gospel of Matthew is an androcentric text hardly needs belaboring. One need look no further than the patrilineal genealogy (1:1–17); the birth and infancy narratives, in which a passive Mary contrasts with a correspondingly active Joseph (1:18–24; 2:13–15, 19–23); or the Sermon on the Mount in which peacemakers are styled "sons of God" (5:9) and the (male) audience is admonished against lusting after women and instructed about divorcing wives (5:27–28, 31–32). The Gospel is replete with references to householders, brothers, sons, and fathers, including God as heavenly Father. But given its undeniable androcentricity, what cultural assumptions regarding masculinity does the Gospel of Matthew embody? Our own answer, as intimated earlier, is that Matthew embodies multiple, contradictory assumptions regarding masculinity. Arriving at this or any answer, however, is a surprisingly difficult process.

When one scans Matthew for standard terminology associated with masculine virtue—terminology commonly found in other Greco-Roman literature—the pickings are exceedingly slim. The term *andreia* ("[manly] courage") is nowhere to be found in Matthew, for example, nor are any of its cognates: *andreios, andreioō, andrizomai,* and the like.[6] Neither do less explicitly gendered terms, such as *enkrateia* or *sōphrosynē,* crop up, terms frequently expressive of masculine virtue in other Greek literary and philosophical texts of the period, as we earlier observed. Nor does Matthew contain any explicit reflection on reason as master of the passions, of the sort found in Philo or 4 Maccabees (see Aune 1994)—even though the Matthean Jesus does demonstrate consummate mastery of his own passions, particularly from his arrival in Gethsemane on the night of his arrest through to his ordeal on the cross (although it could be argued that his self-control crumbles towards the end of that ordeal, Matt 27:46), and he does demand of his male addressees in the Sermon on the Mount absolute control of anger, lust, desire for revenge, pride, avarice, and anxiety (5:21–6:34).[7] Neither the brief treatment of sexual desire (5:27–30),

---

6 In sharp contrast to 4 Maccabees, say, a roughly contemporary Jewish narrative text (see Moore and Anderson: 253–57).

7 These promising themes deserve further attention. Several recent books have begun addressing issues related to masculinity in Matthew. On the Matthean Jesus' self-mastery, however, see Neyrey 1998a: 148–62.

moreover, nor any other passage in Matthew broaches the issue of active versus passive sex (such activity or passivity being yet another important measure of masculinity in ancient Mediterranean culture). Matthew does contain one occurrence of the phrase "male and female" (*arsen kai thēly*) in the context of a pronouncement on marriage and divorce (19:4)—and an enigmatic statement on eunuchs (19:12), as we have seen.

Although Matthew lacks most of the standard terminology used to represent masculinity in Greco-Roman literature, it does abound in explicit references to male kinship relationships and social roles, and certain of these references contain assumptions not only about masculinity but also about male sexuality. Masculinity in Matthew pivots in part on the male ability to generate heirs and found households—whether literally or spiritually. Much about traditional patriarchal householder masculinity, and the mastery of others it entails (see Torjesen: 59–65), is thoroughly presupposed in this text. Such assumptions underlie a number of the Matthean parables in particular, where male heads of households exercise hegemony over women, children, slaves, and land. But let us turn first to the Matthean genealogy.

Genealogy

The Matthean genealogy is patrilineal, embodying the standard Greco-Roman assumption that the male "begets" or "generates" (*gennaō*) the child, thereby playing the crucial role in reproduction. To be male was to be capable of generation.[8] Important medical works in the Greco-Roman world from Aristotle forward supported and "naturalized" this notion (Dean-Jones 1994a, esp. 197; 1994b: 176–224; Laqueur: 25–62; Pomata: 51–57; Reinhartz 1999a: 87–90; D. B. Martin 2001: 83–96; Yanagisako and Delaney: 7–9). Aristotle, for example, influentially argued that males are "hotter" than females. He held that mature males can turn blood into semen through their heat while females cannot (Pomata: 52–54; Reinhartz 1999a: 87–90; Yanagisako and Delaney: 7–9). Whether holding to a one-seed theory (only men produced seed) or a two-seed theory such as the one held by Galen, "the preeminence of the male over

---

8 D. B. Martin 2001: 83–84 writes: "A male could prove his masculinity by begetting, or at least by demonstrating his capacity to. The ability to impregnate or ejaculate, and in some cases the actual deed, was a signifier of manhood" (83). Martin notes, "The notion that generation is especially the prerogative of the male—that is, that generation is masculine and it is masculine to generate—is reflected in the way semen was seen to function in impregnation" (84). There is also a "conflicting notion that it is particularly masculine to *avoid* sexual intercourse" (86). This relates to the importance of self-control in defining manliness.

the female role in generation" is advocated (Pomata: 56; see also D. B. Martin 2001: 84–85). Male preeminence also informs the following statement of Philo:

> [N]ature has trained men to sow the germs of life and women to receive them, and the mating of these two is the cause of generation and the permanence of the All, while on the other hand is it the nature of the soul which is impotent and barren, or rather has been made so by emasculation, to delight in costly bakemeats and drinks and dishes elaborately prepared? For such a soul is neither able to drop the truly masculine seeds of virtue nor yet to receive and foster what is so dropped, but like a sorry stony field is only capable of blighting the successive growths. (*Ebr.* 210-13, LCL)

We can also see in Philo the agricultural metaphor of the active male sower of seed and the passive female field that was frequent (Buell: 34–49). This is a metaphor that has had an ongoing life, as Delaney points out in *The Seed and the Soil*, her ethnography of a modern Turkish village.

Of course, there is one important difference in the manner in which the Matthean Jesus is generated. While the genealogy traces Jesus' patriline through Joseph back to Abraham, Jesus is actually generated through the intervention of the Holy Spirit rather than by a human father (Matt 1:16, 18). A common interpretation of this aberration is that Jesus becomes Joseph's adoptive son through naming and thereby son of David and son of Abraham (R. E. Brown 1993: 138–43; Davies and Allison 1988–97: 1:185). In obedience to the divine will, Joseph adopts or acknowledges Jesus as his son. While the women preceding Mary who interrupt the otherwise all-male genealogy (1:3, 5–6) may have had irregular sexual unions, thereby anticipating Mary's own (Anderson 1983: 8–9), only Mary has had no human sexual partner.[9] The active male role conventionally inscribed in Greco-Roman representations of generation is strikingly absent.[10]

What is the significance for masculinity of a patrilineal genealogy based not on a physical or literal form of descent but rather on a spiritual or fictive form of descent? Howard Eilberg-Schwartz has reflected incisively on this question and is worth quoting at length:

---

[9] Note that the term *patēr* is never applied to Joseph in Matthew, and Jesus is never explicitly referred to as Joseph's son (see 1:21, 23, 25; 2:13, 14, 20, 21; 13:55–56).

[10] R. E. Brown argues that, in Mary's case, God "overcomes the total absence of the father's begetting" (1993: 74; cf. 71–74). For feminist discussions of the genealogy and birth narrative, see Schaberg's survey.

[T]he point of Matthew's genealogy was to contest the Jewish conception of paternity which until that time had been figured through the male line. Jesus is said to be the son of David in exactly the way that gentiles are said to be Jews. Just as gentiles are the spiritual heirs of Abraham, Jesus is incorporated into a lineage that is not his by birth. Jesus is thus the spiritual descendant of both God and David. His human father is completely irrelevant to his status both as son of God and as Messiah. It is no accident that Matthew recorded the genealogy first and then appended the story of the virgin birth subsequently. In ordering things in this way, the virgin birth story would have shocked Jewish readers into rethinking what the genealogy meant....

The myth of the virgin birth thus signaled a new attitude toward fatherhood and a transformation of the meaning of masculinity. The reproduction of the father's line was no longer centrally important and this change would have effects on men's attitudes toward their own bodies and to sexuality in general. For if the religious role of masculinity was no longer to continue the lineage of the fathers, then the male organ of generation would begin to lose the positive value it once had. Paul's attitude toward circumcision has already indicated how the sexuality of the male body was being demoted. The circumcised penis was no longer a religious symbol of what it meant to be a member of the community, and as this symbolic link was broken, procreation and sexuality began to move to the woman's domain. This is another reason for the importance of the women's names in Matthew's genealogy.... Procreation and sexuality were feminized, leaving men with a divided understanding of themselves. Their own relationship to their sexual bodies was seen as analogous to their relationships with their wives; their relationship to their intellectual and spiritual selves became symbolic of their relationships to God. In short, procreation and sexuality became foreign elements in the territory of manliness. (233–35)[11]

Eilberg-Schwartz's reading of the Matthean genealogy and birth narrative, while speculative (it smacks here and there of Freudian psychohistory), does have the advantage of providing a conceptual framework within which to situate the countercultural inflections that masculinity receives in this Gospel—not least the fact that Jesus himself is apparently unmarried, a highly anomalous state for a first-century adult male Jew. "Since masculinity was no longer defined in terms of procreation, it did not matter that Christ had no consort," Eilberg-Schwartz argues. "Indeed, Christ's masculinity was not only tolerable

---

11 Boyarin similarly notes (e.g., 1994: 27, 80–81) how Paul allegorizes circumcision and emphasizes spiritual genealogy and filiation over literal to champion a universalist position.

but confirmed the configuration of masculinity in the religious community. With Jesus all genealogies came to an end" (236).

We find further support for Eilberg-Schwartz's thesis on Matthean masculinity in the reference to "children [*tekna*] of Abraham" that crops up soon after the genealogy. In 3:7–10 John the Baptist is depicted as cautioning the Jewish religious elite that they cannot count henceforth on physical Abrahamic descent. The hint would seem to be that if God can effortlessly raise children for Abraham out of the very stones (3:9), then he can just as easily effect the same transformation on Gentiles. This subtext comes to explicit expression in 8:5–13, where the Gentile centurion's faith is said to outstrip that of "the sons [*huioi*] of the kingdom" (8:12). But the new possibilities for Gentiles that Matthew proclaims are inextricably bound up with new possibilities for masculinity.

Extrapolating further from Eilberg-Schwartz's analysis, we suggest that Matt 1–2 simultaneously upholds and undercuts traditional valuations of literal fatherhood and patriarchal propagation. In a real sense, this sets the scene for all that follows in the narrative. The downplaying of literal familial relationships, and the corresponding elevation of spiritual or fictive kinship, thereby clearing the way for alternative models of masculinity, is followed through in the remainder of the Gospel— although not without ambivalence, as we shall see.

Here, in summary fashion, is the situation of Matthean masculinity, as we see it. Hierarchical male-to-male relationships, whether of fathers to sons, masters to slaves, or teachers to disciples, are central to this Gospel. God, too, is assigned hegemonic masculine roles, such as father, or master of the house, writ large. Male relational positions more or less on the same level—brothers and fellow disciples, in particular—also define masculinity in Matthew. As in chess, Greco-Roman masculinities, whatever their specific configurations, inevitably entail the assumption of a position on the social board that determines the specific male's relationship at any given moment to every other piece in the game.[12] In Matthew, masculinity is frequently played out in terms of male kinship ties. Literal kinship, however, repeatedly gives way to spiritual or fictive kinship. Literal kinship ties are portrayed as problematic, involving discord and rejection. The spiritual kinship categories of Father, brother, and son, as well as the (largely) homologous categories of master/slave, master/disciple, and king/subject,

---

12 We take the image of the chessboard from Alcoff: 433–34, employing it for related but different purposes.

define each other through their interrelationships—and redefine "masculinity" in the process.[13]

The gender identity narratively constructed for male disciples in Matthew amounts to an *anomalous* masculinity when measured by traditional Greco-Roman standards. They are enjoined not only to be sons of the heavenly Father and brothers but also to be fictive/spiritual slaves and children (see especially 18:1–5; 19:13–15; 20:24–28; 23:11–12), as are the male members of the Matthean audience by extension. At the same time, they are enjoined *not* to be spiritual fathers, masters, or teachers (23:8–10). Even should they marry, therefore, and legitimately be in a position to have literal children and/or slaves of their own (unless, of course, they happen themselves to be slaves), their status as free male householders must be drastically qualified by their status as disciples (see S. C. Barton: 217). Significantly, the term *anēr*, which could mean "husband" as well as "man," is seldom used in Matthew. Instead, fatherhood and brotherhood dominate male kinship categories, fatherhood being the special domain of God and brotherhood the special domain of the disciple.[14] Let us now look more closely at each of these kinship ties in turn.

FATHERS

The term *patēr* appears frequently in Matthew, as is well known. Of particular interest to us, however, is the recurrent replacement of the literal meaning of the term with a metaphorical reference to God. Of the sixty-three instances of *patēr* in Matthew, no less than forty-four refer to God, all such references being found exclusively on the lips of Jesus, as he addressed his disciples, audiences composed of the disciples and "the crowds," or God himself (Mowery: 24–26; Sheffield: 52–53).[15] Few literal

---

13 We are dealing in this essay largely with male categories. The relationship of male categories to female categories would be an important area for future research.

14 We take the notion of certain male relational roles dominating the general category "male" from Peletz, who notes that in Negeri Sembila male relational roles such as husband/father and elder brother "may well dominate the category of 'male' and, in addition color the meanings of all other male relational (and 'positional') roles" (314). With reference to Matthew, Saldarini observes: "Kinship is the dominant metaphor in Matthew for internal group relationships. Father-son and brother-to-brother relationships are most common. Closely related to these kinship metaphors is the master-disciple relationship" (1994: 90). Joseph is described as an *anēr* in Matthew, Peter has a mother-in-law, and there are two teachings about divorce. Nonetheless, father and brother language predominates overall.

15 According to Sheffield, "Thirty-one (70%) of Matthew's 44 uses of πατέρ for God are unique to Matthew" in comparison to the other Synoptics (53). Meye Thompson also discusses the use of father for God in Matthew (105–14.)

fathers appear as characters in the narrative, even if we include Joseph as Jesus' adoptive father. (Whether the centurion of 8:5–13 is to be seen as a father depends on whether one understands *ho pais* [8:6, 8, 13] to mean "child" or "servant.") None of Jesus' disciples is ever portrayed as a father (except implicitly in 19:29). Most of the literal fathers who do appear in the narrative are objects of desertion or rejection (4:21–22; 8:21–22; 10:21, 35, 37; 19:5, 29; 23:9), moreover, precisely because most Matthean references to "earthly" fathers are related to the radical devaluation of literal kinship in favor of fictive or spiritual kinship noted above. This demotion of literal kinship—not only that between fathers and sons but of other familial relations as well—can be traced from the beginning of the Matthean narrative right through to its conclusion.[16]

The devaluation begins in the birth stories, as we have seen, where God is Jesus' real father and Joseph merely his adoptive father. It continues with John the Baptist's claim that God can construct children for Abraham out of stones (3:9) and other early episodes, such as James and John's instant abandonment of their father Zebedee in response to Jesus' peremptory summons (4:21–22). In 8:21 Jesus advises a would-be disciple not to waste valuable time burying his deceased father. In the Missionary Discourse he predicts that because of his name "brother will betray brother to death, and a father a child, and children will rise up against parents and have them put to death" (10:21–22)—but by then the male disciple (note that Jesus' audience here is restricted to the Twelve [10:1, 5]) will have switched his allegiance from his earthly father to his heavenly Father anyway: he is assured that in the moment of trial it is not he himself who will be speaking "but the Spirit of [his] Father speaking through [him]" (10:20).[17] Jesus also declares that he has come "to divide a man against his father, a daughter against her mother, a daughter-in-law against her mother-in-law" and that "a man's enemies will be members of his own household" (10:35–36). He teaches his disciples that "the one who loves father or mother more than me is not worthy of me and the

---

16 English translation of Matthew in this essay is based on the NRSV, except where otherwise indicated. S. C. Barton presents a helpful review of subordination of kinship and household ties in Greco-Roman sources as well as a detailed discussion of relevant passages in Mark and Matthew. Concerning Matthew, Barton concludes that "normally legitimate ties of household and kinship are strongly relativized by the demands of discipleship of Jesus" (217). Riches speaks of "passages which explicitly reject the importance of physical kinship-ties" in his discussion of ethnicity and kinship ties in Matthew (225, see also 208–11). Sheffield writes about the "displacement" of earthly fathers (58–65). She also describes a "reconstitution of the heavenly father's family" (65).

17 Mark 13:11 ("it is not you who speak, but the Holy Spirit") has here been given a paternal inflection (cf. Luke 12:11–12; 21:15).

one who loves son or daughter more than me is not worthy of me" (10:37). Ties to human fathers and children must be subsumed to ties to Jesus. These radical statements prepare for the Matthean Jesus' own exemplary rejection of his biological family in favor of his heavenly, spiritual, or fictive family: "For whoever does the will of my Father in heaven is my brother, and sister and mother" (12:50)—human spiritual fathers are not mentioned (cf. S. C. Barton: 184; Sheffield: 65). In 19:27 Peter reminds Jesus that he and his fellow disciples have forsaken their own families in response to his summons, and he is assured that "anyone who has left houses or brothers or sisters or father or mother or children or fields, for my name's sake, will receive a hundredfold, and will inherit eternal life" (19:29). Also notable is the pronouncement in 23:8–10 that stresses the primacy of the heavenly Father over all earthly fathers, even metaphorical fathers who instruct metaphorical sons: "But you are not to be called rabbi, for you have one teacher, and you are all brothers. And call no one your father on earth, for you have one Father—the one in heaven. Nor are you to be called *kathēgētai* [tutors, teachers], for you have only one *kathēgētēs*, the Christ."

But does this turn to the heavenly Father support or undermine hegemonic masculinity, or provide a glimpse of an alternative masculinity of brothers? Or all of the above? Schüssler Fiorenza argues that Matt 23:8–9 involves a "discipleship of equals": "This new kinship of the discipleship of equals does not admit of 'fathers,' thereby rejecting the patriarchal power and esteem invested in them" (1983: 150). She adds, "The 'father' God is invoked here, however, not to justify patriarchal structures and relationships in the community of disciples but precisely to reject all such claims, powers, and structures" (ibid.).[18] In contrast, D'Angelo writes of Matthew, especially 23:9, "The saying is special to Matthew; it forms part of polemic that rejects honorific titles within the community; Matthew's community is to have one father (in heaven) and one teacher (the Christ). Thus in a sense the Gospel does indeed reject patriarchal organization within the community, but it does so in the name of the absolute patriarchal claim of God" (1992a: 629). D'Angelo does not see the use of Father for God as nonpatriarchal: "Rather, wherever the word is used, even when it is used as a challenge to imperial claims or to the patriarchal family, it evokes the image of God as the *pater* whose *potestas* exceeds and so affirms, limits, or challenges the power of every other *pater*" (ibid.).

With D'Angelo's comments about imperial claims, it seems important to mention that Matthew's use of the metaphor of Father for God is

---

18 Levine offers a similar interpretation of 12:46–50 and 23:9 (1988 254–55), as does Bartchy of 23:9 (71).

not unique. This metaphor was used in the Hebrew Bible and in early Judaism (D'Angelo 1992a: 617–22; Meye Thompson: 35–55). Similarly, Zeus/Jupiter could be called Father (D'Angelo 1992a: 624–25; Meeks 1993: 170; Carter 2001: 26–29, 63), as could emperors who had the blessing of the gods or were seen as manifestations of a god (D'Angelo 1992a: 624; Carter 2001: 26–29). Augustus and other emperors, for example, had the title of *pater patriae* (D'Angelo 1992a: 623–24). The inhabitants of the empire were sometimes likened to a *familia* (D'Angelo 1992a: 624). In itself, then, the use of the metaphor of the heavenly Father for God in Matthew can be seen *both* as a challenge to the dominant hegemonic masculinity of ordinary human fathers as well as to their imperial counterparts whether gods or men *and* as undergirding the same masculinity by using the *familia* model writ large.

HOUSEHOLDERS

In addition to being the heavenly Father, God, and Jesus as well, are frequently depicted as heads of households in Matthew. The Evangelist's term of choice for this role is *oikodespotēs*, one redolent with hegemonic assumptions about masculine destiny.[19] We prefer to translate the term as "master of the house" rather than the more innocuous "householder" (the term favored by most modern English translators, going back at least to the KJV) so as not to lose sight of the role that free male heads of households played in relation to women, children, and slaves in ancient Mediterranean society.[20] Many Matthean references to *oikodespotai* presuppose this patriarchal role. A number of these references occur in parables in which the master of the house is the central character.

In the parable of the wheat and the tares (13:24–30), a man (*anthrōpos*) owns a wheat field that he has sown with good seed (*kalon sperma*) but that his enemy has oversown with weeds. The man is further identified as an *oikodespotēs* with slaves (*douloi*). In Jesus' allegorical interpretation of the parable, the master of the house is identified as the Son of Man, his field as the world, the good seed as the sons of the kingdom, the weeds as the sons of the evil one, and the enemy as the devil. In

---

19 Mark contains only one occurrence of *oikodespotēs* (14:14), while Luke contains four (12:39; 13:25; 14:21; 22:11). Matthew contains seven occurrences in all, suggesting that this Evangelist has a special preference for the term (see Luz 2001: 63). *Oikodespotēs* is used three times in Matthew in direct apposition to *anthrōpos* (13:52; 20:1; 21:33). For helpful discussions of house and household language in Matthew, see Crosby.

20 For an excellent discussion of "Slaves and Slavery in the Matthean Parables," see Glancy 2000. She notes that in Matthew as in much of Greco-Roman literature slaves, including managerial slaves, were subject to discipline/physical abuse.

play here, too, is a metaphoric association between the agricultural sowing of plant seed and the procreative sowing of male seed, leading in this case to the procreation of spiritual rather than literal sons. As in the genealogy and birth narratives, the generation that matters is supernatural.

In 10:24–25, Jesus is again the master of the house, and his disciples are members of his household: "A disciple is not above his teacher, neither is a slave [*doulos*] above his master [*kyrion*]. Enough for the disciple that he be like his teacher and the slave be like his master. If they called the master of the house Beelzebul [see 9:34; 12:22–29], how much more the members of his household [*oikiakous*]." To be noted is the tacit evocation of traditional hegemonic institutions—slavery, the patriarchal household—within which the Matthean remodeling of masculinity is staged, a recurrent phenomenon, as we are about to see.

In the parable of the workers in the vineyard (20:1–16) we encounter a cluster of references to an *oikodespotēs*/*kyrios* who, once again, represents a heavenly master. The kingdom of heaven is compared to "a man, a master of a house [*anthrōpō oikodespotē*], who went out early in the morning to hire workers for his vineyard" (20:1). In response to the protests that his hiring policy eventually elicits, the master of the house indignantly inquires, "Am I not allowed to do what I choose with what belongs to me [*ouk exestin moi ho thelō poiēsai en tois emois*]? Or is your eye evil because I am good?" (20:15). Again, the world is like a landowner's estate, this time a vineyard, and the master of the house is either God or Jesus, "the Lord" (*ho kyrios*, 20:8). The point of the parable, apparently, is bound up with a reversal of ordinary expectations about how an *oikodespotēs* might treat his day laborers—"Thus will the last be first and the first last" (20:16)—but his innate right to his privilege and wealth, including the right to exercise the former and dispose of the latter according to his whim, is everywhere assumed and nowhere called into question.

Another parable in which "a man, a master of a house" (evidently standing in for God) is said to own a vineyard is 21:33–43. This time he rents it out to tenant farmers (*geōrgois*). He sends first his slaves (*doulous*) and finally his son and heir (*klēronomos*) to claim the product of the tenants' labor. Again, the rhetorical efficacy of the parable relies on unquestioned assumptions about patriarchal household arrangements—assumptions curiously at odds with the ostensible celibate and peasant status of the parabler himself.[21]

When we turn to the parable of the thief in the night (24:43–44), however, the master of the house represents neither God nor Jesus but the

---

21 Glancy 2000: 87–88 notes that the difference between slaves and son is essential to the sense of the parable.

disciple: "But understand this: if the master of the house had known in which watch of the night the thief was coming, he would have stayed awake and would not have let his house be broken into" (24:43). The situation is similar in 13:52: "So he said to them, 'Therefore every scribe who has been trained for the kingdom of heaven is like a man [*anthrōpō*], a master of a house [*oikodespotē*], who brings out of his treasure what is new and what is old.'" Here, no less than four terms are set implicitly in apposition: scribe, man, master of a house, and disciple—notwithstanding the fact that discipleship, in the Matthean sense, stands in sharp tension with traditional householder masculinity, as noted earlier.

In several of the parables and sayings considered above, the master of the house encounters opposition from elements outside his household, whether the male rival who oversows his crops, the day laborers he hires, the tenants of his estate, the thief in the night, or those who brand him Beelzebul. Shortly after Jesus' warning about members of his household being tarred with the same brush as the master of the house himself, however, a saying appears in which the enemies of a man (*anthrōpou*) are said to be the members of his own household (10:36). Here the household members are *literal* kin—father and son, mother and daughter, mother-in-law and daughter-in-law—all set at each other's throats by Jesus. As soon as the rhetorical register switches from the metaphorical to the literal, the hierarchical household arrangements that hitherto had prevailed undisturbed are immediately thrown into disarray.

Depending on his stage and station in life, an ancient Mediterranean male might at one time be a subservient household member and a master of a house at another. He might also be judged successful or unsuccessful in discharging the duties associated with the different roles: son, heir, master of a house, slaveowner, husband, father. For Matthew, however, the terms *son, heir, master of a house, household,* and *slave* primarily serve metaphorical functions. "Master of a house" is most frequently metaphoric for the figures of God and Jesus, as we have seen, whereas the disciples are commonly cast in subservient roles—slaves, day laborers—although there are two occasions in which the disciple is himself elevated to the role of master of a house. In the one case where members of a household refer to literal kin, they are cast in the role of enemies. On the one hand, therefore, that consummately masculine type, the Greco-Roman master of a house, looms exceedingly large in this Gospel, and his traditional hegemonic prerogatives are nowhere explicitly called into question. On the other hand, however, the repeated devaluation or disruption of biological kinship ties, and hence of the male generation of heirs, undercuts the traditional power base of the *oikodespotēs* and threatens its eventual erosion—another instance of the profound contradictions in which masculinity in Matthew is enmeshed.

BROTHERS

The household headed by a father who is also the master often contains other male kin related to the father as sons and to one another as brothers. The term *brother* (*adelphos*) appears thirty-nine times in Matthew, nineteen times more than in Mark (Duling 1995: 165, citing Luz 1989: 54). In Matthew, as with other male kinship terms, we find both literal and metaphorical brothers. Literal brothers appear most frequently in the voice of the narrator (1:2, 11; 4:18, 21; 10:2, 21; 12:46–50; 13:55–56; 14:3, 17:1; 19:29; 20:24; 22:24–25). This begins with the genealogy, where Jacob generates Judah and his brothers (1:2), the eponymous ancestors of the tribes of Israel, and Josiah generates Jeconiah and his brothers (1:11). When the first disciples are called, they appear in the form of two pairs of brothers: Simon and Andrew his brother (4:18), and James the son of Zebedee and John his brother (4:21). The literal brotherhood of these disciples is also mentioned in 10:2; 17:1; and 20:20–28. These pairs of literal brothers called as disciples anticipate the metaphorical brotherhood of disciples Jesus establishes as the one teacher of a cohort of spiritual brothers (23:8; see S. C. Barton: 129-30 and Sheffield: 61, who also note the abandonment of their father by James and John).

The literal male kinship category of brother in the Greco-Roman world generally involves a cohort of males in more or less the same subordinate position to a father—at least until the father dies. The positions of brothers may vary with age and the positions of their mothers, if not born of the same mother. Brotherhood as an ideal involves a close male relationship that does not require the same degree of dominance and submission as a father-son relationship or a male sexual relationship. Literal brothers are thought to be in harmony due to being born of the same seed and/or being nurtured by the same womb. Sharing the same father and growing in the same womb binds, for example, the loyal brothers of 4 Macc 13:14–26, part of whose death-torture inheres in the horror of each witnessing his brothers being tortured along with himself (Klauck: 151–52; Hellerman: 42; Good: 29). The word *adelphos* literally means "from the same womb," a *natural* kinship indeed (BAGD). Brothers over a wide sweep of time in the Greco-Roman world are often compared to paired parts of the same body, such as feet, hands, and eyes, which are meant to work together.[22] Brotherly harmony was an ideal. Brotherly love (*philadelphia*) was "widely discussed in popular morality," according to Malherbe (1986: 93). Paul uses the term of fellow Christians (Rom

---

22 Xenophon, *Mem.* 2.3.17; Hierocles, *On Duties:* "On Fraternal Love" 4.27.20, trans. in Malherbe 1986: 95; Plutarch *Mor.* 478 D–E, 481 C and E; cf. Aasgaard: 171 and Good: 27.

12:10; 1 Thess 4:9). Psalm 133:1 (LXX 132:1) extols harmony between brothers: "Behold, how good and pleasant it is when brothers dwell in unity!" (RSV).

However, discord between brothers was also a common topic, sometimes appearing alongside discussions of harmony.[23] One need only think of the storied brothers Cain and Abel (see Matt 23:35; Davies and Allison 1988–97: 1:510), Jacob and Esau, Joseph and his brothers, and Romulus and Remus. Proverbs 6:19 lists "a man who sows discord among brothers" (RSV; LXX: *kai epipempei kriseis ana meson adelphōn*) as one of the six things God hates. Practical advice was given about how to resolve conflict and maintain harmony (Xenophon, *Mem.* 2.3.1–17; Plutarch, *Mor.* 481F–491C; Hierocles, *On Duties*: "On Fraternal Love" 4.27.20 in Malherbe 1986: 94). Brothers were to be tolerant and forgiving of one another due to their close ties. Esau's response to his mother's request to forgive Jacob in *Jub.* 35:22 provides an example of the pull of the brotherly tie:

> Jacob, my brother, I shall love more than all flesh. And I have no brother in all the earth except him alone. And this is not a great (thing) for me if I love him because he is my brother and together we were sown in your belly and together we came forth from your womb. And if I do not love my brother, whom shall I love? (quoted in Hellerman: 42).

Perhaps because the ties of literal brotherhood were seen as a way of positively binding men in relationship, the metaphorical use of the concept of brotherhood was also common and by no means restricted to Christianity. For example, the relationship of Roman soldiers could be understood as that of brothers, as could the relationship of Roman citizens or friends to one another (Bannon: 192) or even male lovers (ibid.: 4, 9, 62–63, 80–90). Members of various voluntary associations in the Greco-Roman world could be seen as metaphorical brothers (Bannon: 192; Duling 1995: 163–64; Horrell: 296; but cf. Saldarini 1994: 93). *Brother* is

---

23 The twofold aspect of unity and conflict of brothers is strongly stressed by a number of the sources we rely upon, including Aasgaard; Betz: 225–26 (focusing on Plutarch); Hellerman; Esler 2000; and Bannon, who writes in her introduction: "The Augustan poet Tibullus, in denying that Remus was to be Romulus' partner, focuses on an essential dynamic in Roman ideas about brothers—the tension between conflict and cooperation. This book charts the variations on this theme, drawing together Roman expressions of brotherly love and rivalry around an idealized notion of fraternity" (3). Esler 2000: 155–57 stresses the possibility of discord and rivalry, as does Hallett: 195–201 especially among the Roman elite. For a discussion of brotherly love in Paul, Plutarch, and 4 Maccabees related to *prautēs*, see Good: 23–38. For discussions of brotherhood language in Paul, see Aasgaard; Bartchy; Esler 1997; 2000; Fatum; Hellerman; Horrell; and Sandnes.

used in the Qumran Scrolls for a member of the community.[24] *Brother, neighbor,* and "sons of your own people" (RSV) are used to refer to the close relationship that God desires for the Israelites in Lev 19:17–18, a passage Matthew references at least three times (5:43; 19:19; 22:39).[25]

One of the key passages in Matthew where literal and metaphorical brothers meet is 12: 46–50. Jesus' literal mother and brothers seek to speak with him, but Jesus asks, "Who is my mother and who are my brothers?" His answer identifies the disciples as his mother and brothers and concludes with the pronouncement: "For whoever does the will of my Father in the heavens is my brother and sister and mother." No literal or metaphorical human father is adduced in this scene, as we mentioned earlier. This passage concretizes in narrative form the relativizing or rejection of literal family ties[26] already seen in the Missionary Discourse at 10:35–37. There human fathers and sons appear among the family ties that disciples must discount, but neither literal nor metaphorical brothers do. This continues the theme of abandonment of the earthly father in favor of the heavenly that we mentioned above. That the disciples serve as metaphorical brothers is reinforced later in the narrative by Jesus' teaching in the Community Discourse about reconciliation of brothers (18:15, 21, 35). Also, when speaking to the crowds and disciples in 23:8, Jesus warns them not to be called rabbi, "for you have one teacher, and all of you are brothers." He continues with the strong statement that they are to call no man father on earth, "for you have one heavenly Father." Thus, the male role of brotherhood is affirmed while literal and metaphorical fatherhood is rejected. That followers are brothers of Jesus is again reiterated in an eschatological context in 25:40. If Jesus is the King and Lord of 25:31–46, as seems likely, then "the least of these my brothers" are Jesus' brothers, whether they are interpreted as disciples, Christians, missionaries, or simply those in need.[27] The final reference to brothers in the Gospel

---

24 According to Davies and Allison 1988–97: 1:513, who cite CD 7.1–2; 1QS 6.10, 22; cf. Josephus, *J.W.* 2.122; and Duling 1995: 181 n. 12, who cites 1QS 6.1; CD 9.2; Josephus, *J.W.* 2.8.3 (= 2.122). See also Gnilka.

25 Duling 1999: 11–13 sees Lev 19:15–18 as the source of a reproof tradition lying behind Matt 18:15, 21–22. He sees Lev 19:14, 16–17 alluded to or referenced in Matt 5:21–26; Lev 19:17–18a in Matt 5:38–42; and Lev 19: 17 in Matt 18:15, as well as the references in Matt 5:43 and 19:19. Davies and Allison 1988–97: 2:787 also refer to a history of reproof based on Lev 19:15–18 as a background for understanding Matt 18:15–17.

26 S. C. Barton: 184, 217 views Matthew as relativizing, whereas Davies and Allison 1988–97: 2:366–67 leave the issue open.

27 For the various options, see Luz 1996 and Davies and Allison 1988–97: 3:428–29. To support an identification of the King and Lord as Jesus, Luz writes, "But everywhere else in the sayings of Jesus God is 'always the father, never the brother of humans'" (Luz 1996: 291, quoting Wilckens: 379).

appears in 28:10: "Do not be afraid; go and tell my brothers to go to Galilee." There the eleven are identified as Jesus' brothers, and they are reunited with him after fleeing. They are also given the commission to make disciples, baptize, and preach and are promised that Jesus, the Son and their brother, will be with them "to the end of the age" (28: 19–20).

The unity of brothers as a masculine ideal in Greco-Roman literature was also accompanied by the theme of conflict, as we noted above, and Matthew is no exception. Matthew focuses on the reconciliation of brothers in the Sermon on the Mount and in the Community Discourse. The Sermon on the Mount is addressed to a double audience of crowds and disciples. In the first antithesis of 5:21–26 anger with the brother and insulting the brother renders the offender liable to judgment. Who exactly the brother might be has been a matter of dispute among interpreters, who often read the brother transparently as a Christian or community member or sometimes as a fellow Israelite—supporting a metaphorical interpretation. Whether the reference is to literal or metaphorical brothers, the passage enjoins eschewing of anger and insults in the relationship between brothers. It stresses the importance of reconciliation even in the face of offering a gift before the altar. Mastery of one's anger and other passions is a mark of masculinity, as well as the proper attitude in regard to a brother.[28] Matthew's Jesus counsels reconciliation among brothers in much the same way that Xenophon, Plutarch, and Heirocles do when offering advice about conflict between literal brothers. Being lenient, which in other circumstances might be considered a mark of unmanliness, is deemed the appropriate behavior for a brother. The next antithesis, which focuses on adultery and lust, is similarly strong in its enjoining of masculine self-mastery. In 5:43–48, love of enemies and perfection are demanded of the sons of the heavenly Father.[29] Loving those who love you is done even by tax collectors, and the salute of one's brothers is expected even of Gentiles. This contrast of tax collectors and Gentiles with the sons of the heavenly Father along with a similar contrast in 18:17, where an excluded brother becomes as a Gentile and tax collector, is somewhat in tension with the focus on spiritual procreation extending kinship to Gentiles that we discussed

---

28 Cf. Neyrey 1998a: 190–95, who sees the situation here as one in which Jesus forbids normal male aggression in the context of challenge and riposte.

29 The unity of the spiritual brothers is established by the relationship to God as Father and Jesus as brother. In 5:45 the audience members are exhorted to become "sons of the heavenly Father." However, Jesus does not call the disciples or crowds "sons of God." The term *Son of God* is reserved for Jesus alone, according to Saldarini 1994: 94. Jesus does, however, call the peacemakers sons of God in 5:9.

previously. There may be a lingering association between brotherhood and ethnic identity, between "us" and "them."[30] Yet, at the end of the Gospel the eleven disciple brothers will be commissioned to make disciples—and hence brothers—of all nations (28:19).[31] Finally, in the Sermon, Matt 7:1–5 returns again to the issue of proper relations with the brother. One should not be critical of the brother, seeing the speck in his eye but not the log in one's own.

As with other elements of the Sermon, relations with the brother are taken up again later in the Gospel. In the Community Discourse, addressed to the disciples, the Matthean Jesus explains what a disciple is to do if a brother sins against him (18:15–22). Private reproof is recommended, the goal being to regain the brother (see Duling 1999: 11–13). If that does not work, reproof with several witnesses and finally bringing the matter before the assembly (*ekklēsia*) is required. The harmony of the brothers is a primary end, but if it cannot be accomplished the brother becomes "as a Gentile and tax collector" (RSV), outside the bounds of brotherhood, and this is ratified by the Father in heaven. However, forgiveness and seeking the lost seem the watchwords, as the parable of the lost sheep precedes the discussion of one who has sinned against a brother. Jesus' response to Peter, which follows in 18:21, also tells Peter to forgive a brother who sins against him seventy times seven (or seventy-seven times), essentially without limit. There is also the injunction to be like children, to avoid becoming a stumbling block to "little ones" who believe in Jesus, and reiteration of the Sermon on the Mount's call for cutting off body parts that may cause one to stumble.[32] The closing of the Community Discourse is the parable of the talents, with the forgiveness of God, the heavenly father, presented as the model that the slave/brother must follow. The last warning in 18:35 is that the brother may be tortured if he fails to forgive: "So also my heavenly Father will do also to every one of you, if you do not forgive your brother from your heart" (RSV).

So we bring our discussion of the male kinship term *brother* to a close. We have seen that there is only one heavenly Father, whose son Jesus has many brothers. This creates a masculinity in which Jesus' followers are

---

30 Were we redaction critics, however, we might posit an incompletely assimilated tradition.

31 Whether or not these "others" will want to become brothers is not discussed.

32 Davies and Allison 1988–97: 2:751 write, "One can make the case that the three paragraphs before vv. 15–20 and the two that follow serve as buffers of a sort; that is, they emphasize the qualities that are required if one is going to be so bold as to carry out the directions of 18:15–20."

spiritual brothers but not spiritual fathers. Their heavenly father will never die, so they are perpetually in the position of brothers whose father is still alive, subordinate to God as Father and to Jesus as eldest brother and heir—slaves and children of the master of the house. This is true even though Jesus' male followers may marry, as the divorce sayings indicate. The spiritual kinship of the brothers, however, has many benefits, not least the care of the heavenly Father and the brotherly masculinity of unity, attachment, and forgiveness that coheres well with other Matthean discipleship teachings, such as the last being first and the first being last. There is also the possibility of brotherly (and sisterly and motherly) ties across ethnic and literal family borders. Domination and subordination are not supposed to be part of the ideal relations of brothers. That there can be disruption of the ideal is evidenced by the passages that explain how to deal with conflict we discussed above, as well as in 20:20–28, where the ten are "indignant at the two brothers" (RSV), the sons of Zebedee, when their mother requests a special place of honor for them. But spiritual brotherhood entails a masculinity that differs from, even if it does not eliminate, the masculinity of fathers (literal sowers of seed) and masters of the house. This is a brotherhood in which one may honorably become a eunuch for the kingdom of heaven.

EUNUCHS

We end where we began with Matt 19:12, the enigmatic pronouncement on eunuchs. The interpretation not only of this verse but of its antecedent context (19:3–11) has always been controversial, the entire passage being concerned with the perennially contested topics of marriage, divorce, and celibacy. Among the disputed issues are the meaning of *porneia* in 19:9 and whether remarriage is permitted after a divorce occasioned by it; the meaning of the disciples' rejoinder in 19:10 (Does it represent a misapprehension?); whether Jesus' clarification in 19:11 that "not everyone is able to comprehend this word" means that only some will be expected to observe his prohibition in 19:9; and whether 19:12, with its reference to those who make themselves eunuchs for the kingdom of heaven, alludes to the choice of a life of celibacy, or, less drastically, to not remarrying after divorce. Of course, there is a still more painful question, exacerbated by the actions of Origen and others: Is Jesus' pronouncement concerning eunuchs to be taken absolutely literally?[33]

---

33 See Justin Martyr, *1 Apol.* 29, for an anecdote of a young man who seeks to be made a literal eunuch but is denied permission. For a discussion of early interpretation of 19:12, see E. A. Clark 1999: 90–92. Not unexpectedly, perhaps, modern commentators show little

How were eunuchs constructed, culturally speaking, in the ancient Jewish and larger Hellenistic contexts? A recurrent perception of eunuchhood—whether eunuchs were viewed as incapable of sex, on the one hand, or as sexual "studs" with either women or men, on the other— concerned the eunuch's lack of generative capacity.[34] The profound ambivalence embodied in the dual construction of eunuchs as both lacking sexual desire and highly sexed was coupled with an equivocation between competing cultural perceptions of eunuchs as hypermasculine males who efficiently conserve their vital essence, on the one hand, and as feminized or childlike "unmen," on the other (see Rousselle: 122; P. Brown 1988: 19, 169). Some ancient authors clearly had problems in categorizing eunuchs altogether, representing them as both male *and* female, yet neither male *nor* female (an important early example is Plato,

---

inclination to take it literally; see, e.g., Gundry 1994: 382; Hagner: 550; Davies and Allison 1988–97: 3:23. An exception is Kuefler: "But if Jesus was familiar with the *galli* and their self-castration as a religious practice, then it is at least possible that his words were intended literally and that he was recommending to his male followers that they physically castrate themselves. Even if these are not the authentic words of Jesus, the same interpretive possibility remains in that the author of the Gospel of Matthew was recommending that male Christians castrate themselves by attributing the sentiment to Jesus" (259). Critical discussions of the eunuch logion also include Allison; S. C. Barton, 191–204; Blinzler; Carter 1994: 56–89; Daniel; A. J. Dewey; Heth; Keener: 462–72; Luz 2001; McNeile; Pitre; Quesnell; and Tannehill 1975. On the Ethiopian eunuch in Acts 8:26–40, see C. J. Martin; Spencer.

34 On which see Malina 2001a: 159–62; Spencer: 157; Pitre; and especially Stevenson, who provides valuable discussion of and bibliography on Greco-Roman attitudes toward eunuchs. See also Dessen, who notes how two characters are needed in Terence's *Eunuchus* to "express the double social construct of the eunuch. Old and young, ugly and attractive, impotent yet oversexed, physically powerless yet mentally powerful—the eunuch holds all these contradictions within himself, but for this very reason he could never be enacted as one character" (128). Pitre stresses the inability to procreate and the lack of kinship ties of eunuchs. He argues that eunuch in Matt 19:12 is "a code word for the voluntarily childless men in his [the Evangelist's] audience who are promised elite status in the imperial household of God" (1). He holds that it does not mean a voluntary celibate, as (at least some) eunuchs could have sex and marry. Pitre contends that the inability to have children led to an elite as well as a marginal status for eunuchs because they could serve emperors and kings without threatening power passed on through heredity (15–16). This also applies to the heavenly kingdom: "Eunuchs for the sake of the kingdom will become eunuchs in the kingdom of heaven" (19). Deirdre Good in notes from a talk she shared with us also speaks of Jesus' "court" in Matthew. We would like to thank Pitre and Good for sharing their unpublished work with us, as well as Marianne Blickenstaff for putting us in touch with Pitre. Blickenstaff first called our attention to Pitre's paper in "The Bloody Bridegroom," where she discusses Jesus' fictive family. There are interesting parallels between imperial language in the culture at large and in Matthew. It seems to us, however, that even though eunuchs may occasionally have acquired a degree of elite status through serving emperors, they still represented a subordinate masculinity, since they could never fulfill the role of father.

Resp. 479b–c). Josephus, apparently improvising on Deut 23:1 and Lev 21:20; 22:24–25, has Moses denounce eunuchs in the harshest terms:

> Let those that have made themselves eunuchs be had in detestation; and do you avoid any conversation with them who have deprived them-selves of their manhood, and of that fruit of generation which God has given to men for the increase of their kind; let such be driven away, as if they had killed their children, since they beforehand have lost what should procure them; for evident it is, that while their soul is become effeminate, they have withal transfused that effeminacy to their body also. In like manner do you treat all that is of a monstrous nature when it is looked on; nor is it lawful to geld man or any other animals. (*Ant.* 4.290–91, Whiston 1987)

Philo gives vent to similar sentiments, having a eunuch lament as follows:

> I ... am a eunuch..., gelded of the soul's generating organs [*ta gennētika*], a vagrant from the men's quarters, an exile from the women's, a thing neither male nor female, unable either to shed or receive seed, twofold yet neuter, base counterfeit of the human coin, cut off from the immor-tality which, through the succession of children and children's children, is kept alight for ever, roped off from the holy assembly and congrega-tion. "For he that hath lost the organs of generation is absolutely forbidden to enter therein" [Deut. xxiii.1]. (*Somn.* 2.184, LCL; cf. *Ebr.* 210–213; *Leg.* 3.8; *Spec.* 1.325)

Josephus and Philo are each embroidering texts in the Hebrew Scriptures that exclude eunuchs from full participation in the covenant community. But not all the texts in or around these scriptures take an unremittingly negative view of eunuchs. Two further texts, several centuries apart, sug-gest that the production of spiritual fruit is ultimately more important than the physical inability to reproduce. Isaiah 56:3–8 (early postexilic) prom-ises that faithful eunuchs will have "a monument and name better than sons and daughters," while Wis 3:13–15 and 4:1–2 (first century C.E.) bless both the barren woman and the eunuch who bear spiritual fruit. Signifi-cantly for our reading of Matthew, moreover, the Isaian passage couples faithful eunuchs and "foreigners" (LXX: *allogenēs*, literally, of another kin or family) as outcasts whom the Lord will accept in due course.[35]

---

35 Isaiah 56:7 is quoted in Matt 21:13. The connection between eunuchs and Gentiles who attach themselves to God is also prominent, of course, in Acts 8:26–39. C. J. Martin sug-gests that Isa 56:3–7 is important background for interpreting the tale of the Ethiopian eunuch (108–10). She further argues that his ethnic identity as a black African Gentile and his geographic origin are consistent with a Lucan emphasis on universalism (114, 119–20).

Returning to Matt 19:12, one is struck anew by the Matthean Jesus' ready appropriation of eunuchhood as an image for exemplary discipleship, given the generally negative perception of eunuchs that prevailed in the ancient Mediterranean world. What makes this statement particularly striking, however, is that it occurs in the context of a debate on marriage and divorce in which Jesus is represented as explaining that God created humans in male and female form so that they might be united "in one flesh" (19:5).[36] Whereas the traditional masculine roles of husband and father are reaffirmed in Jesus' elucidation of God's "original intention" for marriage as a sublime union of male and female, an altogether different possibility for masculinity appears unexpectedly alongside this statement, within the pronouncement on eunuchs— whether the latter be interpreted as male chastity following a first marriage or chastity for the never-married male. Either way, the possibility cuts against the grain of the hegemonic Greco-Roman conception of "full" masculinity that required a man to engage in the generation of heirs and rule over a household consisting of wife, offspring, and, if possible, slaves. In line with the texts from Isaiah and the Wisdom of Solomon cited earlier, Matt 19:12 proffers a countercultural vision of a physically impotent but spiritually potent masculinity that engenders, not literal children, but spiritual children, spiritual fruit. This vision is couched in the threatening yet fascinating figure of the eunuch, who is poised precariously on the sliding scale between man and unman. In terms of gender scripts, the eunuch leads a boundary-blurring, altogether subversive existence.

And it is surely no accident that the succeeding episodes in Matthew exalt childhood (19:13–15) and the renunciation of possessions (19:16–30) in a reversal of traditional hegemonic masculine values—indeed they entice the male reader/hearer with an irresistible reward for abandoning all ambition to head a household (19:27–29).[37] Sons of the heavenly Father

---

36 There is debate over whether the limitation on divorce in the passage was destructive or supportive of patriarchal norms. On the one hand, the husband's freedom to divorce is severely limited, protecting women from casual dismissal. A marital bond in which the wife becomes "one flesh" with her husband might result in a more egalitarian understanding of marriage, a modified conception of the traditional male role within the household, as Carter 1994 argues (see esp. 59–63, 88–89). On the other hand, limitations on divorce and the notion that marriage was intended to be indissoluble might bind women still more tightly within the institution of the patriarchal household and lead to poverty in widowhood if remarriage was not permissible. See further Levine 1992: 255.

37 It may be too much to argue, as Carter 1994 does, that Matt 19 and 20 cohere essentially because they exhibit *topoi* traditionally found in discussions of Hellenistic household management—marriage/divorce, children, slavery, wealth—with which Matthew's audience

can best advance the interests of the kingdom of heaven by embracing social/spiritual roles that typify subordinate masculinities, if not outright "unman" status: eunuchs, children, slaves. This is the gendered aspect of the more general process whereby the first become last and the last first (19:30; 20:16). As noted earlier, this blurring of gender boundaries and adumbration of alternative models for masculinity—models that no longer pivot on literal patrilineage, the male generation of male heirs— allows for a corollary blurring of boundaries between Jew and Gentile, both of whom may now "bear fruit" (3:8–10; cf. 7:15–20) as spiritual heirs of Abraham and as brothers.

That a Gentile such as Origen could have come to read Matt 19:12 as an injunction addressed directly to him thereby increases in plausibility.[38] Accommodating Matthew to an intellectual milieu characterized by obsessive preoccupation with "masculine" mastery of the passions and desires, this consummate master of allegorical exposition may, paradoxically (in a moment that he later regretted?—see his *Commentary on Matthew* 15.1), have taken Matthew's Jesus more literally than even Matthew himself was prepared to take him.

---

would have been familiar. Compelling, however, is Carter's general thesis that these chapters represent an "inverted household code" (216) and hence a liminal existence. It lends support to the idea that Matthew embodies alternative models for masculinity.

[38] The assumption that Origen was a Gentile hinges principally on Eusebius's assertion that Origen was born to Christian parents in Alexandria (*Hist. eccl.* 6.1-2). For biographical discussions of Origen, see Daley; Cross and Livingstone.

RE-MARK-ABLE MASCULINITIES: JESUS, THE SON OF MAN, AND THE (SAD) SUM OF MANHOOD?

Tat-siong Benny Liew
Chicago Theological Seminary

With critical emphasis generally placed on what is considered "different" or "deviant," what is "male/masculine" has for too long been able to avert and avoid any critical inquiry. Working by passive default as well as active deflection of attention onto what is "female/feminine," masculinity experiences what Jean-Joseph Goux calls a "gradual metamorphosis" into "neutrality" (178).[1] As soon as this veil of neutrality is removed, scholars have (following the scrutiny of what is "female/feminine") emphasized masculinity as a social construction that is not the same as biological maleness.[2] David Gilmore, for example, arrives at two anthropological conclusions regarding masculinity as distinct from biology: first, masculinity means different things to different cultures and at different times; and second, masculinity is not a given, but is to be achieved (1990). Intrigued and informed by the recent explosion of men's or masculinity studies, I intend to investigate in this paper whether Mark's Jesus is portrayed in a way that meets or achieves ancient

---

1 Or, in the words of Monique Wittig: "[T]here are not two genders. There is only one: the feminine, the 'masculine' not being a gender. For the masculine is not the masculine but the general" (64). Even in two recent and decent "handbook" essays on "gender" (Boyarin 1998; Tolbert 2000), the focus is arguably on the "female/feminine" almost to the exclusion of the "male/masculine." A similar story can be told regarding the study of race/ethnicity and the more recent study of "whiteness" (see, e.g, Dyer).

2 More recent scholarship has questioned this neat separation of sex as a biological given and gender as a social construction. In addition to Judith Butler's influential work (1990: 6–7), I think Thomas Laqueur's work on sex as a social construction from "the Greeks to Freud" (subtitle) has helped make the relations between sex and gender messier and much more fluid, especially if one reads it *against* the temptation to use Galen's one-sex theory (the view that human genitals are all the same but only placed externally in men and internally in women) to support a clear-cut position that (only) gender was sociocultural in the ancient Mediterranean. As will become clear in this essay, the neat separation of sex as physiological nature and gender as social construction can hardly be warranted.

Mediterranean understandings of masculinity.[3] Rather than aiming for a simple and final yes or no answer, I am more interested in ways in which Mark may help us think about current debates on masculinity. Let me, however, begin with some reasons for linking an ancient text such as Mark with a seemingly contemporary concern such as masculinity.

METHOD OR MADNESS?

Since I am of the opinion that one's interest in the past is always already related to one's concerns of the present (de Certeau), I have no need to deny that my topic has much to do with my personal, twenty-first-century interests in masculinity.[4] This admission does not mean, however, that this essay is just another mad case of so-called "anachronism."[5] There

---

[3] Studies of what is "male/masculine" are not all the same, but I am not going to appeal to the convenient (and too often oversimplified) difference in labels (that is, between "men's studies" and "masculinity studies"). I should also clarify from the start that different social groups were likely to have different understandings of masculinity in the ancient Mediterranean. After reading James C. Scott's anthropological work on "great and little traditions" (1977) and "public and hidden transcripts" (1990), I do not want to presume or present a monolithic view of the ancient Mediterranean. Since literacy was generally a privilege of the elite in the ancient world, and I am dependent on extant (literary) records in my study of the period, what I have to say (I am afraid) will end up reflecting mainly elitist understanding(s) of masculinity. To say that these literary documents were by the elite does not, of course, necessarily dismiss the possibility that they might reflect, or even advocate, alternative or subversive views, since as we will see, elite is also not a monolithic group or category. For a more general but relevant discussion on this issue of "class" or social groupings in the ancient Mediterranean, see Moore 2001: 140–41. For an example of a Markan scholar who uses Scott's work but sees Mark as a (tran)script of the nonelitist "little tradition," see Horsley 2001. For the term *Mediterranean* as "a concept of cultural heuristic convenience" (Gilmore 1990: 30), see Gilmore 1982. For the term *ancient*, I have in mind the period between the fifth century B.C.E. and the fifth century C.E., a relatively narrower span of time than the "ancient" of, say, Michael Grant and Rachel Kitzinger (1988a: xxv).

[4] There are multiple and complex factors leading to current interests in masculinity. Such interests are partly engineered by men of color and gay men who have long been seen by the dominant culture as being "less than a man" (Eng), as well as partly related to a backlash against feminism and the liberation movement by sexual dissidents (Quinby). As Mark J. Justad comments, "The reconstruction of masculinity may be thought of as a manipulation of an identified oppressive social construct that has historical, but not essential, association with men ... or it may be an effort to re-establish some true or archetypal form of being and acting like men that has been obscured by a larger social or political force such as feminism, or industrialization" (355). It is therefore no surprise (and with good reason) that some feminists remain rather suspicious of what may be broadly grouped under masculinity or men's studies. I would venture to suggest that a similar dose of healthy suspicion is needed toward recent "whiteness" studies.

[5] While this essay is not exactly going against "chrono-logic," it is ultimately not concerned with chronological development, since my focus is not to present a clear delineation

are in my mind at least three other reasons justifying my juxtaposition of Mark and masculinity. First, masculinity was a major concern of the ancient Mediterranean world, which explains why, among other things, older men often express jealousy and resentment toward younger men in the Old Comedy (fifth century B.C.E.) with the same complaint: "in my day men and boys were manlier than they are today, when *eromenoi* [younger men or boys who are pursued] are like women and slaves, and *erastai* [older men who do the pursuing] don't know the difference" (Henderson: 1259). Angela Hobbs has also suggested recently that Plato's writings (fourth century B.C.E.) represent the Greek philosopher's gradual but methodical approach to the question of masculinity; at least masculinity provides Hobbs with a logic to read Plato's discussion of virtue and justice from the *Laches* to the *Republic*. Hobbs's point about Plato's stake in the masculinity issue can be seen, I think, clearly in the way Plato himself expresses how philosophers might be perceived as "utterly inexperienced in men's characters" and "ridiculous and unmanly" (*Gorg.* 484d–85c).[6] In Plato's *Republic*, this problem of being "too slack and no kind of a man" is so severe for the philosopher that even his servants will not hesitate to show their contempt for the philosopher to the philosopher's own son:

> [I]f they [the servants] observe a debtor or any other wrongdoer whom the father [the philosopher] does not prosecute, they urge the boy to punish all such when he grows to manhood and prove himself more of a man than his father. (549d, 549e–50a)

Ancient Mediterranean concern with masculinity can further be seen in the connection between masculinity and moral excellence. In Latin, the word "virtue" and the word "man" (*vir*) are even etymologically related. To be morally excellent, then, was often linked with becoming a "real" man. There was also the practice of a popular "science" known as physiognomy to interpret or decode signs of gender deviance by observing people's physical characteristics and style, such as one's glance, movement, or voice.[7] One of the surviving manuals for physiognomic practice states some of the signs of a "detestable womanly male" as follows:

---

of how understanding(s) of masculinity went through notable shifts over time. For studies that do focus on such chronological developments in late antiquity, see Burrus 2000; Kuefler.

6 Unless otherwise indicated, English translations of Greco-Roman texts are taken from the Loeb Classical Library. English translations of Mark are my own.

7 Physiognomy clearly shows that physiology, biology, or anatomy was not completely separable from gender. For example, since the left part of one's body parts was generally considered to be feminine, a man would be viewed to be "unmanly" if his left eye was bigger than his right (Kuefler: 25).

The signs are ... an unsteady eye and knock-knees; he inclines his head to the right; he gestures with his palms up and his wrists loose; and he has two styles of walking—either waggling his hips or keeping them under control. He tends to look around in all directions. (Quoted in Winkler 1990b: 200)

This ancient Mediterranean concern with masculinity shows that masculinity was, as Gilmore suggests, something valuable that needed to be *won* and *kept*. One can further relate Gilmore's emphasis on masculinity as an "achievement" to Butler's concept of "gender (as) performance" (1990). If Butler's "performance" focuses mainly on "writing on the body" in our contemporary world (to borrow the wonderfully nuanced title of a volume on female embodiment [Medina, Conboy, and Stanbury]), more recent books on masculinity have helped show how Butler's concept may be extended to the time of the ancient Mediterranean (Gleason 1995) as well as to bodies of literary writing (Schoene-Harwood).[8] How, then, would Mark's Jesus come across as a man to ancient Mediterranean people who were concerned with masculinity?

If both Plato's philosophy and his physiognomic practice indicate that the ancient Mediterranean world was madly obsessed with, and actually somewhat methodical about, debating and defining masculinity, one has reason to believe that this masculinity issue was even more politically charged when Mark was written. Biblical scholars have generally agreed that Mark was written closely around the first Jewish-Roman war (66–70 C.E.),[9] yet few have come to associate that "consensus" with the way war and masculinity were often mentioned in the same breath within the ancient Mediterranean world.[10] Whether it is Achilles' eagerness to battle (Homer, *Iliad* 19.146–154 [eighth century B.C.E.]), Menelaus's declaration concerning the Trojan War that "fellowship in fight is the great teacher of all things to men" (Euripides, *Andr.* 683–684 [fifth century B.C.E.]), or Protagoras's characterization of "courage" (*andreia*) with "going to war on horseback" (Plato, *Prot.* 349–350), they all concur and confirm Aristotle's definition of "courage," which has its etymological root in "man" (*anēr*), as

---

8 I am aware that Gleason, unlike Schoene-Harwood, does not refer to Butler in her 1990 book. Nevertheless, I personally see a lot of potential interaction between them, especially given the fact that Butler's institutional title bears the word "rhetoric" and Butler's latest book deals with a figure from ancient Greek mythology (2000).

9 A recent dissenting voice is Horsley's, who seems to hint in his latest book that Mark could have been written as early as the 50s C.E., although he never states this definitively (2001: 131–36).

10 This is recognized by Moore, even though his focus is on the book of Revelation rather than Mark (2001: 3, 5, 173–99).

facing "the noblest form of death [in] battle" (*Eth. nic.* 1115a–b).[11] The general discussion of educating young boys in Plato's *Laches* surrounds the particular art of "armor-fighting" and the advice of two Athenian military generals.[12] Equally important is how ancient Greek paintings done on vases tend to depict males in relation to three things: warfare, horses, and athletics (Sutton: 42–43). As it is often stated among ancient Greeks, "Marriage is for the girl what war is for the boy" (quoted in Garland: 199). On the Roman side, Virgil's popular and influential (hi)story of Rome, *Aeneid* (first century B.C.E.), praises Rome's imperial mission pervasively in terms of both its military and its masculinity.[13] Florus (second century C.E.) is even more direct when he begins his abridgement of Livy's *History of Rome* by comparing Rome's busy engagement in military activity and victory in conquest as the "youth" and "mature manhood" of a man's life (*Epitome of Roman History* 1. Introduction). Marcus Aurelius (121–180 C.E.) illustrates virility or masculinity with the words "like a soldier" (quoted in Kuefler: 27). This intertwining relation between militarism and masculinity is my second reason for mixing Mark with masculinity.

Last but not least, Mark's Gospel has, since the time of the early church, been associated with the symbol of a winged lion. Interestingly enough, the lion has also been a Greco-Roman symbol for masculinity.[14] Homer, for example, repeatedly uses the lion in the *Iliad* as an epithet or epitome of his warrior-hero (11.383; 18.316–323; 20.164–175; 24.41–43), and Aristophanes' (fifth century B.C.E.) Aeschylus refers to the threat of Alcibiades as that of a lion (*Frogs* 1431–1432). This common association is also reflected in Plato's writings when Laches lists the lion as one of several animals that everyone calls "courageous" (*Lach.* 196e–97a) and when

---

11 While I have referred to the etymological connection between the Greek words for "courage" and "man," some classics scholars have no hesitation in translating "courage" directly as "manhood," "manliness," or "virility." See, for example, Kuefler: 28, 32, 44; Shaw 1996: 279, 284, 286, 291.

12 Associating masculinity with the military is no doubt a(n over)simplified picture, since ancient Mediterraneans, such as Ptolemy (second century C.E.), did assign different characteristics or idea(l)s to different stages of a man's life. Having said that, it is noteworthy that in his attempt to coordinate his seven-sphere universe with his seven-stage development of a man's life, Ptolemy chose to relate middle young manhood and manhood (what were generally considered to be the best years of a man's life) to the sun, Mars or the god of war, and Jupiter (Burrow: 51–54).

13 It also seems to have much to do with Homer's *Iliad*, which (as my earlier reference to Achilles shows) is itself a fiction or fashioning of masculinity through militarism (and vice versa); see Gransden.

14 No doubt the lion symbol among early followers of Jesus might also be a reference to the "lion of Judah" in Hebrew scripture (Gen 49:9), but as Moore points out, that "lion" is also one related to military violence and masculinity (2001: 176).

Callicles compares strong or hypermasculine men to lions (*Gorg.* 483e–484c). Did the early church understand Mark as the "masculine" Gospel, and hence its symbolization by the winged lion? If so, what is it about Mark that would lead to such an understanding? Is it because in Mark's portrayal, this "king of the Jews" (15:2, 9, 12, 18, 26) is actually a type of a "lion king"?

OUT THERE AND ON TOP

It seems clear from the very beginning of the Gospel that Mark's Jesus is not a "homebody." When we first meet him in the story, we see him being baptized by John in the Jordan (1:9), having already left his family in Nazareth. After a forty-day sojourn in the wilderness, he comes out proclaiming the good news of God's kingdom and issuing a call to repentance (1:12–15). Whether it is out beside the sea (1:16; 2:13; 3:7; 4:1) or in a synagogue (1:21; 3:1), he is busy with a public ministry of teaching and healing. Despite his family's attempt to "restrain" him or keep him home (3:21, 31–35), he only returns to his hometown once in the whole Gospel (6:1–6). Even then, his purpose is not to enjoy the comfort of home but to continue his ministry of healing and teaching. Because of the "faithlessness" of his townsfolk, he stays but a short time. In fact, Mark's Jesus is always in action, moving from one place to another. He journeys through Galilee (1:9–4:34), takes six boat trips about and across the Lake of Galilee (4:35; 5:21; 6:32, 45; 8:10, 13), goes from Galilee to Jerusalem (8:22–11:1), makes three trips into the temple (11:11, 15, 27), and near the end promises another (resurrected) return to Galilee (14:28; 16:7). While scholars have for a long time understood Mark's Gospel in terms of Jesus' journey from Galilee to Jerusalem (Kelber: 9; Tolbert 1989: 113–21), they have not paid enough attention to the way Mark's Jesus is kept (over-) exposed in the public limelight. His every retreat inside a house or a home ends in encroachment, sometimes even by an explosion of crowds. A "whole city" comes to the house of Simon and Andrew because of Jesus (1:29–33). People literally burst open the door as well as tear open the roof of his home in Capernaum (2:1–4). His family's unsuccessful attempt to "restrain" or keep him is itself occasioned by the fact that Jesus cannot even have a meal in his own home (3:19c–21). When Jesus seeks to hide inside another house in Tyre, Mark's preparatory comment that Jesus "cannot be hidden from notice" and the subsequent intrusion of the Syrophoenician woman (7:24–26) bring to mind Jesus' earlier proclamation about hidden lamps and inevitable disclosure (4:21–22). This proclamation, given in the midst of several sowing parables, turns out to be, at least in part, a self-pronouncement on the part of Mark's Jesus. He is not just in the spotlight; he himself is the light that has captured the public's attention. Starting with areas around Galilee (1:28, 45), people flock to Jesus from everywhere (3:7–8), resulting in a personal entourage that he chooses (3:13–19) as well as mass movements of people following him from place to place (3:7; 10:46; 15:40–41). With his fanfare spreading into the Decapolis (5:20), his popularity not only comes to the attention of King Herod (6:14) but also continues to gain momentum as he travels into Judea and beyond the Jordan (10:1), as well as into Jerusalem (11:7–10).

A man outside the home was a masculine stereotype in the Greco-Roman world. Ancient Mediterranean culture features a strong segregation between male and female. While the sphere of a female's duty belonged to the home, that of a male's work was on the outside. A "manly" man would leave matters of the home, such as its care and management, to the female. This kind of sexual or social segregation can be found explicitly stated as an ideal in Xenophon's *Oikonomikos* (fourth century B.C.E.).[15] A "real" man, in the eyes of ancient Mediterranean people, belonged to the outside, the public, and the open. Ancient Greek myth and literature also reflect this kind of segregation by consistently associating males with the sky, the sun, the city, and its institutions and females with the earth, the moon, and the home (Henderson: 1253–54; Arthur: 6, 14–19). For instance, we have this from a writer in the mid-first century C.E.:

> It is right that a woman's nature is made for domestic cares, a man's for exertions out of doors and outside. So god gave man the endurance of heat and cold, journeys and labours of peace and war, that is to say agriculture and military service, to woman, as he [sic] had made her unsuitable for all these things, he [sic] handed over responsibility for domestic business. (Quoted in Wallace-Hadrill: 107)

Again, we see the link between masculinity and the military. What about the link between masculinity and agriculture? Agricultural work

---

15 This kind of sexual or social segregation also led to the development of a different set of virtues for men and women, as the following paragraph shows: "First of all, if you take the virtue of a man, it is easily stated that a man's virtue is this—that he be competent to manage the affairs of his city, and to manage them so as to benefit his friends and harm his enemies, and to take care to avoid suffering harm himself. Or take a woman's virtue: there is no difficulty in describing it as the duty of ordering the house well, looking after the property indoors, and obeying her husband" (Plato, *Meno* 71e). In addition to the public/private "division," one should note the emphasis on a man's ability to cause harm to others but avoid harm to himself. I am putting "division" in quotes because, in the ancient Mediterranean, the state of a man's household was always already a reflection on his honor and masculinity (Cooper 1996: 3, 12–14).

would certainly take a man outside the home, in the sun and in the rain, but there is more. Talking about this same phenomenon of sexual and social segregation, Robert Garland suggests that many mothers in the ancient Mediterranean would find themselves identifying with Deianeira's complaint of her husband that Garland cites from ancient Greek literature: "Indeed we had children but he never saw them other than as a farmer sees an outlying field, at seedtime and when harvesting" (150).

This quote provides a perfect transition to talk about one of the main—and perhaps most masculine—portrayals of Jesus in Mark's Gospel: Jesus as the sower. The importance of the parable of the Sower (4:1–20) within Mark has been increasingly recognized. Tolbert (1989: 121–24) suggests that this parable and the parable of the wicked tenants (12:1–11) function as two plot synopses within Mark. While the latter parable identifies Jesus' status as the heir and refers to God's resort to direct intervention because of the heir's death, the former categorizes characters within the story in accordance with four possible types of ground or responses to Jesus. Van Iersel gives Tolbert's thesis a little twist and argues that the series of parables about seeds and words (4:2–34) and the long speech about the apocalypse (13:1–37), being the only two extensive discourses by Jesus in Mark, embody the "heart" of Jesus' ministry in Galilee and in Jerusalem respectively. What scholars have continued to (dis)miss, however, is the sexual innuendo and thus the incredibly high level of testosterone present in these parables.[16] Sowing seed was a well-known metaphor in the ancient Mediterranean for what a "real" man did in sexual intercourse (Buell: 21–49, 54–68), which was more often than not understood to be for the purpose of procreation (D. B. Martin 2001: 83–86).[17] Plato's Socrates, for example, talks about the need for

---

16 I am indebted to my colleague at Chicago Theological Seminary, Theodore W. Jennings Jr., for first teaching me and teasing me into considering the sexual innuendo of this parable by showing me a copy of (if I remember correctly) Plato's *Laws*, where it states: "I know of a device for making a natural use of reproductive intercourse—on the one hand, by abstaining from the male and not slaying of set purpose the human stock, nor sowing seed on rocks and stones [*mēd' eis petras te kai lithous speiroutas*] where it can never take root and have fruitful increase; and, on the other hand, by abstaining from every female field in which you would not desire the seed to spring up" (8.838e–839a). Similar uses of sowing on rocks or hard and stony land as references to sexual intercourse between men can be found in Philo (first century C.E.), *Spec.* 3.39; and Philo, *Contempl.* 62. In fact, Pseudo-Lucien (fourth century C.E.?) refers to such a metaphor as a "proverb" for intercourse between men (*Affairs of the Heart* 20); note, however, that Philo also uses the same metaphor to refer to intercourse between a man and a sterile woman (*Spec.* 3.34).

17 Buell, however, also never mentions the parable of the Sower in Mark, as Jennings reminded me after I showed him one of Buell's chapters. Likewise, Martin never mentions

matchmakers "to have the knowledge of what soil is best for each plant or seed" (*Theaet.* 149d–e) and how men "sow upon the womb as upon ploughed soil" (*Tim.* 91d). In a way that resonates with the sower parable in Mark 4 even more clearly, Plato links sowing, ejaculating/ inseminating, and teaching together with the statement that a philosopher-teacher "plants and sows in a fitting soul intelligent words which are able to help themselves and him who planted them, which are not fruitless, but yield seed from which there spring up in other minds other words capable of continuing the process for ever" (*Phaedr.* 276e–277a). What I am getting at will become even more explicit in Philo's words:

> We should know, then, that nature's right reasoning has the functions both of a father and a husband, though the perceptions attached to each are different. It acts as a husband because it deposits the seed of virtue in the soul as in a fertile field. It acts as a father because its nature is to beget good intentions and noble and worthy actions, and then to foster its offspring with the water of the truths which education and wisdom abundantly supply. The mind is likened on the one hand to a virgin, on the other to a woman either in widowhood, or still united to a husband. (*Spec.* 2.29–30)

Assuming the role of Philo's "right reasoning," Mark's Jesus clearly presents himself as the farmer-husband, or husband-man. In other words, he takes the manly or active role in his dealings with every human character in the Gospel.[18] After all, does not Mark's Jesus understand and describe himself as a "bridegroom" (2:18–20)? Unlike Philo, however, Mark's Jesus dismisses the fostering, watering, or nurturing aspect that Philo attributes to the sower or inseminator. After he heals a person, Jesus generally sends the person away rather than asking the

---

Mark's sowing parables, even though he does mention the agricultural metaphor specifically in his discussion of insemination as a signifier of ancient Mediterranean manhood (2001: 84). Going back to the separation between sex as a biological given and gender as a social construct, Moore correctly points out that sexuality is a concept that disrupts this neat separation (2001: 12–14). This well-known trope of sowing and receiving "seeds" clearly indicates that sexuality—or perhaps more accurately, sexual practice—was inseparable from the concept and consideration of gender in the ancient Mediterranean. In Plato's *Gorgias*, for instance, the conversation between Socrates and Callicles about masculinity quickly involves a discussion about sex acts, particularly the masculinity and the life of a male who enjoys being penetrated (495a).

18 What that implies about those who come into contact with Jesus is a question that I will address later. I do want to point out regarding seed and procreation that there seems to exist in the ancient Mediterranean, alongside the emphasis on a single and male seed, a double-seed theory that has both male and female contributing a separate seed to the process of procreation (van der Horst; D. B. Martin 2001: 84–85).

person to stay with him (1:42–44; 2:10–12; 5:18–20, 30–34; 7:29–30; 8:25–26). Moreover, Mark's Jesus is so confident of his ability or virility as an impregnator that the outcome of the insemination lies solely on the part of the soil (if it is hard, rocky, thorny, or good). As Mark's Jesus indicates in another sowing parable in Mark 4, the sower "would scatter seed on the ground, and would sleep in the night and rise in the day, and the seed would sprout and grow, he does not know how. The earth [provided it is good soil] produces automatically" (4:26–28a). Jesus' masculinity is therefore nothing less than a mystery, and masculinity gives Mark's Jesus mystique.

Not only do these two sowing parables by Mark's Jesus have implications for his relationship with other human characters and the quality of Jesus' seed or sperm, but they also point to Jesus' sexual appetite as a man. His sowing is a wide or even wild "scattering" (4:26), which also explains why so many different types of ground or soil will end up receiving his seed. Sexual aggression, sexual prowess, and sexual promiscuity were all characteristics of a "manly" man in the ancient Mediterranean world. For sex, in that world, was not perceived as an activity people jointly engaged in but as an action performed by an "active penetrator" upon a "passive penetrated" (Halperin 1990b: 266; see also Moore 2001: 135–46). To be able to sexually penetrate another person (male or female) was a "sign of superior virility and power" (Krenkel: 1296). A "real" man, therefore, will be "sexually aggressive and active" (Winkler 1990b: 180). Euripides' (fifth century B.C.E.) *Hippolytos* even has a character whose sexual continence is presented as part of his "pathology" (Dover 1974: 103).[19] Alongside such emphases as penetration and promiscuity, ancient Mediterranean masculinity also emphasizes another *p* word: procreation, or more specifically, procreation that would result in a male heir. Garland points out, for example, that it is precisely because of the fear of not having a male heir among ancient Greeks that marriage became a necessity for the "manly" man (199–200). Given its focus on gestation and growth, the parable of the Sower shows that Jesus is constantly and actively seeking to enlarge and build up a family. As we have seen, a second sowing parable effectually places all the responsibilities (and potential blames) on the "receiving" end of any relationship with Jesus (4:26–29). There is yet a third, and last sowing parable in Mark 4 that

---

19 Again, there is an alternative or contradictory emphasis in the ancient Mediterranean that features sexual self-restraint as a mark of the "real" man. Henderson (1253, 1257–58) and Winkler (1990b: 181), for example, both talk about the adoration of men who can hold their own against the temptation of strong appetites such as food, drink, sleep, and sex. See also D. B. Martin 2001: 86–97.

further distinguishes Jesus' seed or sperm as one of "mustard" (4:30–32), thus emphasizing yet once more its fertility and Jesus' virility.[20]

This talk of heir and family raises another interesting question regarding Mark's Jesus and masculinity. Mark's Jesus at times takes on, in Greco-Roman perspective, a "lesser" role than that of the husband in the family. For instance, when he first defines for himself a new fictive family on the basis of "doing God's will," he presents himself as either a son or a sibling of his fictive family members (3:33–35). The rest of the story makes it clear, however, that he is not just any other son or sibling. In the parable of the Wicked Tenants, Jesus is clearly identifying himself as the heir (12:6–8). If I may conflate Tolbert's emphasis on parables and van Iersel's emphasis on the apocalyptic discourse, the parable that ends the apocalyptic discourse further presents Jesus as the "master" or the "lord" of the household (13:35) and reduces Jesus' fictive mothers and siblings to the equivalence of "servants," "slaves," or "doorkeepers" (13:34). I have already argued at length elsewhere that nothing less than tyrannical authority is being ascribed to Jesus in Mark's Gospel (Liew: 93–107); I want to suggest now—in the context of masculinity, sexuality, and family—that Mark's Jesus is nothing short of the ancient Mediterranean *paterfamilias* idea(l). After all, Jesus does refer to his disciples as "sons" of his bridal party (2:19b) and addresses them directly as "children" (10:24). He also calls the woman whom he cured of hemorrhage "daughter" (5:34).

This seemingly confusing shifting of roles (husband, son, brother, and father) makes sense once one recognizes that as a household lord or a masculine master in the ancient Mediterranean, a man's legal authority over his family was so close to being absolute that his wife, mother, siblings, and children were basically interchangeable. They were different forms of material resources under his control and at his disposal, almost the same as his property, his money, or his slaves (Kuefler: 70–71). He could sell or abandon his children when they were born, choose whom they would marry, and take over their assets at will. These same legal rights were given to the housemaster over his wife, his siblings in the absence of their father, and his widowed mother.[21] The father figure is absent when Mark's Jesus defines and

---

20 These parables arguably represent a well-veiled phallus in the Bible, given the history of biblical scholarship. A telling sign is the fact that one cannot find a single entry under Mark 4 in a recent commentary that is supposed to provide Hellenistic texts that are parallel to what we have in the New Testament (Boring, Berger, and Colpe: 175).

21 It is therefore hard for me to agree with those who interpret Jesus' stance on divorce in Mark as liberating for women (10:1–12). Since Augustus decreed that all who divorced must be remarried within a short period of time to avoid a penalty, Jesus' stance against

when he reiterates the reality of his new fictive family (3:33–35; 10:29–31), since Mark reserves this father role to God (8:38; 11:25; 13:32; 14:36). Mark's parable of the Wicked Tenants, however, indicates that the presence of this God-Father is distant and his influence indirect (12:1–6); it further identifies Jesus as the heir (12:6–8). Assuming the rightful role as the *paterfamilias* in the absence of his God-Father, Jesus the heir himself becomes a godfather who is on top, flexing his masculine muscles to run and dominate his family.[22]

MASCULINE COMPETITIONS AND COMPETING MASCULINITIES

As Mark's Jesus identifies himself as the household lord in a parable, he also implies that he, like his absentee God-Father, will be absent and away (13:34–35). A "manly" man of the ancient Mediterranean has to be absent and away because it is not enough for him to be out of the home and hearth. He must stay out, way out, to be in the public world of competition. Xenophon (fourth century B.C.E.) writes in *Hiero* 7.3:

> The pursuit of honor is not a natural component of the irrational animals nor of all human beings; those who have a natural desire in them for praise and honor are at the greatest distance from cattle—they are considered to be men, no longer merely human beings. (Quoted in Winkler 1990: 191 n. 63)

---

remarriage basically functions as a prohibition against all divorce—a situation that would be much more difficult for the woman than the man given the power imbalance in a marriage relationship. Note also that by declaring all remarriages after divorce "adulteries" (10:11–12), Mark's Jesus has not really addressed the different definitions of "adultery" that functioned for men and women of the ancient Mediterranean. While a married woman might be guilty of "adultery" for any and all sexual relations outside of marriage, a married man was not guilty of "adultery" as long as his "out-of-marriage" sex partner was not a married woman (Treggiari: 163–64, 262–319). It is also telling that Mark's Jesus, in his response to the Sadducees' question about resurrection, makes not one objection to the earthly practice of the levirate marriage arrangement (12:18–27).

22 Not only does Mark's Jesus refer to himself as the "lord" of the Sabbath (2:28) or simply the "lord" (11:3), but the demoniac also understands Jesus as the "lord" (5:19–20). Interestingly enough, while Pilch and Malina provide no article on "manliness," their table of contents does list "manliness" and refers readers immediately to three actual articles within the volume, namely, "dramatic orientation," "parenting," and "authoritarianism" (vii). I am not sure if these entries are equally valuable for discussing masculinity in other biblical books, but I do find them appropriate headings for Mark's Jesus. Note also that when Henderson describes the concept of masculinity in ancient Greece, he chooses adjectives such as "autonomous, kinetic, centrifugal and direct" (1253–54).

Masculinity, therefore, is measured by one's willingness to compete in the public world. Not for nothing, then, does Mark's Jesus engage himself in various conflicts. Markan scholars have long focused on Jesus' conflicts with the Jerusalem and Roman authorities as well as his conflicts with his own disciples (Kingsbury: 63–117). These conflicts or contests no doubt function to propel the plot (Rhoads, Dewey, and Michie: 77–78), but they also signify Jesus' manhood. His first miracle, for instance, is framed by comments about Jesus' superior authority over that of the scribes (1:21–22, 27–28). Not only is this conflict over authority repeated and reinforced in the first face-to-face confrontation or controversy story between Jesus and the scribes in Galilee (2:1–12) as well as in the first controversy story in Jerusalem (11:27–12:12), but each controversy story is itself followed by a series of four more controversies in which Jesus shows himself to be more than able to hold his own (2:13–3:6; 12:13–37). The location of the second series of controversy stories further proves that Mark's Jesus has no fear of entering his opponents' territory. In fact, he enters the city of Jerusalem in a royal manner (11:7–10). Later, he even barges right into the headquarters of his opponents, denounces them for committing robbery and corrupting God's purpose, and cleanses or closes the temple (11:15–19; Waetjen: 182). In this conflict over authority (or quest for honor, a performative contest over masculinity in the ancient Mediterranean), Jesus and the Jerusalem authorities gradually switch roles. The first cycle of controversies takes place in Galilee. The Jerusalem authorities are on the offensive. They are the ones who go to Galilee to investigate and incriminate Jesus (3:22; 7:1). Jesus is the one being accused of usurping God's authority to forgive sins (2:6–7) and in danger of being destroyed (3:6). The second cycle happens, however, in Jerusalem. Jesus is now invading their turf, intensifying his charges against them for robbery and corruption (11:17) to usurpation and murder. He even threatens them with *their* future destruction (12:9). After Jesus bests the Jerusalem authorities in three consecutive contests (12:13–17, 18–27, 28–34c), Mark comments, "and no one dared to ask him any question any more" (12:34d). In the fourth, and final controversy in this series, not only does Jesus become the one who initiates the inquisition, but his questions also leave his opponents without any answer (12:35–37). Unwilling to ask Jesus any question and unable to answer Jesus' questions, the Jerusalem authorities are left in silent shame. We literally do not hear from them again until 14:1.

Aggression in competition was valuable—to use a term made popular by Bourdieu—"cultural capital" in ancient Mediterranean masculinity. Jesus' aggressive competition is not only performed in contests with the Jerusalem authorities, but is also rhetorically performed in the "plundering" language that he uses to talk about his relationship with Beelzebul, the ruler of the demons (3:22–27). Such rhetoric repeats and reinforces the idea(l) that "manly" men do not just compete, but they also conquer, since ancient Mediterranean masculinity is often associated with success in public competition. Not only does Mark's Jesus successfully defend himself in these controversies; he also defends his disciples, members of his family (2:18–28; 7:1–13), as a "real" man is supposed to do (Plato, *Gorg.* 483b, 486a–d).[23] Aristotle writes, "it is considered servile to put up with an insult to oneself or suffer one's friends to be insulted" (*Eth. nic.* 1126a). Being "slavish" was a synonym of being "womanish" for all practical purposes (Aristotle, *Pol.* 1260a; see also Henderson, 1251, 1253–54). As the twenty-sixth problem in the fourth book of the Aristotelian *Problems* asks, "Why do some men enjoy sexual intercourse when they play an active part and some when they do not?" (879a–b).[24] It is a "problem" precisely because "real" men are not supposed to enjoy passivity, taking orders, or accepting defeat. Instead, they should seek and manage to penetrate and dominate.[25] Like Mark's Jesus, he should be out there and on top in different aspects of his life. The principle is the same whether a man is putting on the persona of a public quester for honor or a *paterfamilias* in charge of a household: he is to "penetrate and appropriate virgin frontiers" (Flannigan-Saint-Aubin: 241).

The irony is that rather than plundering and punishing the Jerusalem authorities all the way through the Gospel, Mark's Jesus is himself punished and his house plundered. He is bound (15:1) like a slave or a woman, suffers a death sentence, and his disciples end up denying, betraying, or deserting him (14:10–11, 26–31, 43–51, 66–72; 15:6–15). In fact, Mark's Jesus has never managed to have an upper hand in his conflict or contest with his disciples. For over a hundred years since William Wrede, Markan scholars have been pointing out the inability of Jesus to penetrate the thick skulls of his disciples.[26] Shortly after a hint about an

---

23 In ancient Athens, every time there was an official gathering of citizens (for which only men were eligible), the gatherers were reminded of their identities as "householders" of their city and their duty to defend the interests of their dependents in combat of external enemies (Winkler 1990b: 178–79).

24 Note that Winkler has a rather different translation for this question: "Why is it that some men enjoy being acted upon sexually, whether or not they also enjoy being active?" (1990b: 200–201).

25 This becomes clear in the immediately following "problem" in Aristotle that links passivity to shame: "Why are those who desire to submit to sexual intercourse greatly ashamed to admit it, whereas they are not ashamed to admit a desire for eating or drinking or any other similar thing?" (Aristotle, *Probl.* 880a).

26 One may even talk about a conflict between Mark's Jesus and some of the people he heals and sends away. Jesus' command to silence (the other major contribution of Wrede's reading of Mark) is flat out disregarded by both the leper and the deaf person in Decapolis (1:43–45; 7:36).

eventual traitor among his disciples (3:19a–b), Jesus calms a storm. His miracle, however, leads to the disciples' fear rather than faith and their confusion rather than comprehension of Jesus' identity (4:35–41). On their way to Jerusalem, Jesus' disciples cannot exorcize a demon as they have been called to do (3:13–15; 9:14–18), not to mention the by-now classic contrast between this traveling section's frames (where Jesus is able to cure the physical blindness of two persons, 8:22–26; 10:46–52) and its body (where Jesus is unable to cure the spiritual blindness of his disciples regarding his death and their discipleship, 8:27–10:45). How is one sup-posed to reconcile the picture of Mark's Jesus as a man who competes and conquers and the one of him as a man who competes but is confined, cornered, and finally crucified? How is one to reconcile Jesus' experiences with Aristotle's claim that "a courageous man ought not to allow himself to be beaten (*Rhet.* 1367a) and that "high-mindedness" or "greatness of soul" (*megalopsychia*) is characterized by "intolerance of dishonor" (*to mē anechesthai hybrisomenoi; An. post.* 97b16–19)?

I want to suggest that the key to understanding these contrary contours is to realize that even among elites of the ancient Mediter-ranean, there were competing ideologies of masculinity. Going back to Hobbs's book on Plato, her thesis is that Plato is advocating a "kinder" and "gentler" idea(l) of masculinity.[27] The notion of masculinity Plato problematizes is one of external and heroic "performative excellence" (to use Michael Herzfeld's term for contemporary Mediterranean man-hood). Personified by Homer's Achilles, a "real" and "ideal" man is a hero who is always on a quest to conquer other people.[28] Alexander the Great, for example, was so enamored of Achilles that not only did he make a special pilgrimage to pay tribute at Achilles' traditional tomb site near Troy (Arrian, *Anabasis of Alexander* 1.12; Plutarch, *Alex.* 15.4),

---

27 "Kinder" and "gentler" are in quotation marks because Plato's alternative masculin-ity has not exactly been kind to women, as we can see in the *Republic*, where Plato writes, "We will not then allow our charges, whom we expect to prove good men, being men, to play the parts of women, and imitate a woman young or old" (395d). For a fascinating femi-nist and deconstructive reading of Plato, see Loraux 1995: 145–77.

28 Hobbs offers a couple of helpful examples to illustrate Achilles' popularity (175, 201). First, Xenophon's (fourth century B.C.E.) *Symposium* (3.5) has a character named Nicer-atus, who talks about how his father made him learn the entire Homeric corpus in order to make him "a good man" and how he can still recite Homer's *Iliad* and *Odyssey* by heart because of those early lessons. Second, Aristotle claims that when it comes to illustrations, Achilles is the most convenient; since "everybody knows what he [Achilles] did," all one has to do is just to name him (*Rhet.* 1416b). For the importance of Homer in ancient Greek education, see D. R. MacDonald 2000: 4–5. Note that I am also indebted to Hobbs (176–78) for my following argument about the relationships among Achilles, Alexander, and certain Roman emperors.

but he also had a copy of Homer's *Iliad* under his pillow and with him on all of his military campaigns (Plutarch, *Alex.* 8.2). When he was shown a "coffer" to keep the "most precious things," Alexander said he would deposit the *Iliad* for "safe keeping" (Plutarch, *Alex.* 26.1). Fictional or not, these stories show the dominance of this ideology of domination in the fashioning of ancient Mediterranean masculinity, particularly when one considers how Alexander's Achillean military (pre)occupation itself allegedly became a model for Roman emperors such as Caesar (Plutarch, *Caes.* 11.3; Suetonius, *Jul.* 7; Dio Cassius, *Roman History* 37.52.2), Augustus (Suetonius, *Aug.* 18, 50), and Caligula (Suetonius, *Cal.* 52; Tacitus, *Ann.* 6.31). The problem that many people have with philosophers, at least as Plato presents it, is precisely their failure to compete and conquer in traditional public arenas where "men get them[selves] note and glory" (*Gorg.* 485d). Seeing this Achillean version of masculinity as reckless, ruthless, out of control, dangerous, and even selfish, Plato seeks to turn the external focus of this heroic masculinity inward and to emphasize the need for a "real" man to master himself with reason, wisdom, and literary/musical studies. Instead of talking about the heroism of invasion and retribution, for example, Plato extols the heroism of discipline, endurance, and self-sacrifice, even the willingness to submit oneself to punishment and death (*Gorg.* 479a–480d, 522e). In *Phaedo*, Plato even presents philosophy as a separation from the body and states that "the true philosophers practice dying" (66a–67e).

Seneca's *Hercules Furens*, written several hundred years after Plato, shows that debates and definitions of ancient Mediterranean masculinity were far from settled by Plato's intervention.[29] In a way similar to if not exactly the same as Plato, Seneca seeks to redirect masculinity away from the rage, madness, and violence of external conquest. Rather than modeling masculinity on Hercules (that mythological founder of war and himself a hero of Achilles [*Il.* 18.117–121]), Seneca suggests an alternative model in Orpheus, whose instruments are arts of peace rather than arsenals of war and whose timings are more deliberate than immediate.[30]

---

29 I am indebted to Headlam Wells for pointing me to the importance of this tragedy by Seneca (25, 90, 177–81), while Headlam Wells himself credits Robert S. Miola for alerting him to *Hercules Furens*. Note that Shaw also deals with Seneca's struggles with masculinity, but he does so by way of Seneca's *Epistles* (292–93).

30 Suffice it to say that Seneca's model for masculinity, Orpheus, also has an ambiguous relationship with women. His desire and grief for one woman cause him to shun all other women as potential corruption; finally, he is killed by a group of women. Note that while Hobbs does not refer to Seneca, she does nevertheless imply that Plato, like Seneca, provides

Not only do these competing masculinities in the ancient Mediter-ranean help make sense of Mark's Jesus, but they also underscore the reality of Raymond Williams's idea concerning dominant, residual, and emergent elements within a culture.[31] While others such as Moore have tended to understand these competing ideologies about masculinity in a causal (self-mastery as a prerequisite to mastery of others) and thus more or less unified fashion (2001: 159, 197; see also Moore and Anderson: 250, 253–54, 257–58, 272), I think the relations between these competing mas-culinities are less straightforward (in terms either of a "before-and-after" or an "either-or"). For most people and most of the time, competing mas-culinities (or Williams's dominant, residual, and emergent elements) simply co-exist or even become mixed together in a messy and make-shift manner that does not reduce or resolve all the tensions and contradictions.[32] Aristotle, for example, does define "high-mindedness" or "greatness of soul" by one's refusal to submit to dishonorable treat-ment, but he also defines it by "being unaffected by good and bad fortune" (*ei dē to adiaphoi einai eutychountes kai atychountes*). In fact, Aristo-tle even gives Achilles as an example for his first definition and Socrates for his second (*An. post.* 97b15–28). Referring to men's tendency to long for a lost past when masculinity used to be "stable and secure," Harry Brod comments that "identifying the historical inaccuracies of this

---

contrasting or alternative models of masculinity. Referring to Plato's *Hippias Minor* or *Lesser Hippias*, Hobbs is of the opinion that Plato pits Odysseus as an alternative ancient Greek heroic model against Achilles, with Socrates serving as a more contemporary alternative (193–98, 239). Note also in this regard Dennis R. MacDonald's recent work on Mark (2000), where he argues that Mark's Jesus is fashioned in accordance with Homer's depiction of Odysseus in the *Odyssey* and Hector (rather than Achilles) in the *Iliad*. I am not interested in arguing for Mark's dependence on specific literary texts or specific literary characters as MacDonald is, but his work does point to an important cultural register for Mark that Mac-Donald himself (dis)misses: that of Homeric masculinities.

31 I personally prefer Williams's terms and concepts to R. W. Connell's "hegemonic" and "subordinated" masculinity (1995: 77–79), because Williams's terms and concepts make room for a complexity and diversity within each one of Connell's masculinities.

32 My argument here does not deny that some people in the ancient Mediterranean might sometimes understand masculinity in terms of a self-mastery that would qualify one to master others, but it does question if all people in the ancient Mediterranean would think in those terms at all times. Let me use a personal example about two issues that are of con-cern to both masculinity and Mark: honor and wealth. My writing of this essay is no doubt partly motivated by the academic capital—that is, prestige or honor—that may result from its publication. At times I may tell myself and others in a somewhat high-sounding manner that what I care about is academic honor, not monetary reward; at other times, I may tell myself and others that what I hope is to build up my academic capital or honor so that I will get a promotion and a pay raise. Most of the time, I simply have both concerns swimming or circling around the back of my mind without any clearly identifiable patterns or relations.

mythologizing of the past can free men's attentions to encounter present realities more directly" (1987b: 268). Abigail Solomon-Godeau is correct to point out that if masculinity is a social construct, it is historical and provisional; as such, it is always already in crisis (71).[33]

Intertwined in Mark is a picture of Jesus who is less of a reckless brute than one possessed of control and strategic wit.[34] Like Plato's "real" man, he has the internal direction and the self-mastery that enable him to endure many less-than-favorable circumstances and consequences. As Robert Tannehill points out, Mark's Jesus certainly knows the direction of his life (1979: 61). He is to fulfill the commission that he received from God, which is signified in Jesus' baptism (1:9–11). Driven by the Spirit (1:12), he does so with single-mindedness. He is willing to go without food (3:19b–20; 6:30–31) and risk being crushed by the pressing crowd (3:9; 4:1). His commitment to do God's will is not swayed by the "advice" of Peter, one of his closest disciples (8:31–33). The repeated usage of the word "immediately" (e.g., 1:12, 20, 29) communicates a sense of decisiveness in Jesus' actions. At the same time, his many commands to silence (1:42–44; 5:43; 7:36a; 9:9) indicate a prudence that both Plato and Seneca would have admired. He knows who he is and what he is about. In response to two different answers to his one and the same question, "What do you want me to do for you?" (10:36, 51a–b), he chooses to turn down the request of Peter and John in 10:37–45 but honors the plea of Bartimaeus in 10:51c–52. The repeated portrayal of Jesus preparing and praying in solitude (1:12–13, 35; 6:45–46; 14:32–42) also confirms Jesus as someone who has great determination and discipline.

Because of this sense of direction and purpose, Mark's Jesus is not afraid to go against tradition, law, public pressure, or threat. Even before the threat of losing his very life, Jesus will not back down. The three passion predictions (8:31; 9:31; 10:33–34) tell us that Jesus is well aware of the suffering and death that await him in Jerusalem, yet he moves "inexorably" toward the city (Rhoads, Dewey, and Michie: 110), and he even assumes the duty to prepare his disciples on the way (10:32).[35] When the

---

33 Solomon-Godeau looks at late eighteenth- and nineteenth-century French art to argue against Kaja Silverman's suggestion that a crisis of masculinity occurred or started at the end of the nineteenth century. What I am hoping to do here is to help support Solomon-Godeau's contention by showing that crisis of masculinity is not just a modern phenomenon.

34 His "cleansing" or "closing" of the temple notwithstanding (11:15–17), his victories in the controversy stories are won through rhetoric and dexterity. See, for example, Tolbert's commentary on the controversy stories in 12:13–27 (1989: 250–53).

35 There is a tension in Mark's description of Jesus' movements. On the one hand, there is this methodical movement that Jesus makes from Caesarea Philippi (8:27) to Jerusalem (11:1) that communicates plan and purpose. On the other hand, Jesus' movement seems to be

issue of death looms larger and closer in his mind, he deals with it by facing it head on at Gethsemane (14:32–42). Once Jesus realizes the inevitability of his death, he accepts it and perhaps even encourages it. Instead of opposing his foes, he intentionally puts himself into their hands and cooperates in their plans to fulfill his "destiny." Other than an indirect verbal warning, he makes no direct attempt to stand in the way of his traitor (14:17–21). He does not put up a fight at his arrest (14:47–49). When the scribes and elders, even with the use of false witnesses, fail to build a valid accusation against him, Jesus is the one who helps them out by volunteering the "crucial testimony" by which he is sentenced to death (14:53–64). When he is taken to the Roman procurator, Pilate, Jesus turns down his last chance to defend himself by keeping his lips sealed (15:1–5).

Such bravery to face rather than escape pain looks even more impressive in light of what he goes through in the passion narrative. He is spat upon, beaten, and mocked (14:65; 15:16–20, 26–32). He endures the full impact of crucifixion in full consciousness rather than accepting an ancient anesthetic (15:23; Schweizer: 345). Moreover, he faces such suffering all alone. His so-called "disciples," the ones on whom he should be able to depend for comfort and help, have either betrayed him, denied him, or fled (14:10–11, 43–52, 66–72). In isolation, he faces his cross, with no comfort of encouragement or a word of support. Even the criminals who are crucified beside him "insulted" him (15:32). Yet Jesus endures it all. In the act of death, he affirms his virtues and his virility.

SHADOW-BASHING OTHER SELVES

Mark's Jesus, however, is not a stoic Seneca or a Socrates who is trapped in a violent world, because, like Achilles and Hercules, he does have a desire for vengeance and violence.[36] This is arguably best seen in his promise of God's coming and God's destruction of Jesus' opponents

---

makeshift because it is often determined by people's response. His entry into various towns is restricted by the leper's publicity against Jesus' will (1:43–45), his stay at both Gerasa and Nazareth is cut short by people's rejection (5:14–17; 6:1–6a), his plan and movement are often unexpectedly interrupted by people's need (5:21–35; 6:30–44; 7:24–26), not to mention his "planned" trip to Bethsaida that ends up taking two chapters and a convoluted detour (6:45–8:22). This tension results, I think, in a Jesus who is not necessarily an overpowering figure but nevertheless one who has strength to face and endure limitations and opposition.

36 Hobbs suggests that the majority of Achilles' actions in the *Iliad*, from fighting the Trojans and the Greeks to killing Hector, are "motivated by revenge" (183). Believing in a lie that Lycus has cuckolded him, Hercules seeks revenge by murdering his own children and wife in a mad attempt to regain his sullied manhood.

in the parable of the Wicked Tenants (12:9). Similar promises, or threats, can be found in a negative and exaggerated version of the "golden rule" (which I paraphrase as "wrong unto others *more* than what others have wronged unto you," 4:24–25), a subtle "woe" against his betrayer that Judas would one day regret his entire existence rather than just his one act of betrayal (14:21), and a graphic description of an eschatological punishment that is worse than drowning and mutilation (9:42–48). What is most interesting for my present purpose, however, is Jesus' destruction of a fig tree, an action that frames his displeasure or disgust with the temple (11:12–21). Destroying the earth, particularly rocks and woods, out of anger is something that Seneca specifically criticizes Hercules for doing (*Herc. fur.* 939–986). If Mark's Jesus is like a Socratic "great soul" with his disregard for misfortune, he is at the same time also like Achilles or Hercules, a "real" man or even a demigod who is so committed to his version of the ideal (his "God's will," 3:35) that when that ideal is threatened, he will not hesitate to take action to punish the wrongdoers. If his cursing of the fig tree and his "cleansing" or "closing" of the temple are any indications, his threats of vengeance and violence will not be empty.

Jesus' masculinity, whether in terms of Achilles/Hercules and/or Socrates/Orpheus, is even more compelling when one returns to Gilmore's point about masculinity being a social achievement. A social achievement requires interaction with other people, whether in terms of contest (competing with others for masculinity), contrast (defining one's own masculinity in light of others' femininity), and/or consent (acknowledgment from others that one is indeed a "real" man). The importance of social contest, contrast, and consent to one's own identity is clearly shown by Jesus' successive questions to his disciples: "Who do people say that I am?" (8:27), and "But who do you say that I am?" (8:29).

Derrida's and Lacan's relational understanding of language meaning and self-identity respectively are thus important for the meaning and identity of gender (Belsey). Male/masculine and female/feminine make sense only in terms of or, more accurately, in contrast to each other (Segal: 114).[37] Colleen M. Conway is correct in this regard to suggest that gender analysis within Gospel studies should involve a cross-examination or comparative inspection of both male and female characters. Yet a "real" man in the ancient Mediterranean has various opposites or contrasting "Others." In addition to women, these "opposite Others" include at least

---

[37] I take that to be at least part of the reason for Eve Kosofsky Sedgwick's complaint that masculinity "is not always 'about men'" (1995: 12) and that women are also "producers" as well as "consumers" and "performers" of masculinity (13).

"foreigners" and social inferiors (Segal: x).[38] Romans, for example, had a long tradition of equating effeminacy with men of the eastern Mediterranean, whose wealth and luxurious clothing had supposedly made them "most delicate" and "degenerate" and compromised their manhood (Kuefler: 47).[39] "True" men in the ancient Mediterranean were usually of high social standing, while men below were implicitly categorized as "unmen" (Moore 2001: 136, 139, 142–46).[40]

Foreigners

The most obvious "foreign" characters in both Mark's text and context are the Romans. The lone named Roman character in Mark, Pilate, turns out to be a caricature and a foil to heighten Jesus' masculinity. Pilate, despite being impressed by Jesus' stoic silence and convinced of Jesus' innocence (15:5, 10, 14a–b), lacks the courage to stand up to the crowd asking for Jesus' crucifixion (15:14–15).[41] Jesus' masculinity vis-à-vis "foreigners" is perhaps best illustrated in the episode concerning the Gerasene demoniac (5:1–20). Not only does Jesus exorcize and cast the demon, Legion (a Latin word that refers to the Roman armies), into the

---

38 Social inferiors may include many subgroups, such as slaves and children (Moore and Anderson: 262), with the subgroup of "slaves" divisible into more subgroups, such as eunuchs (Kuefler). Rather than addressing different subgroups, I will focus on the disciples as representative of Jesus' social inferiors. Note also that this emphasis on masculinity's connections with race/ethnicity and class is very much in keeping with current developments within masculinity studies. For example, see Creese; Horowitz; Sharpe; Stecopoulous and Uebel.

39 That changed, of course, gradually as the Roman Empire became weaker and weaker. What is interesting for our purpose is that as the empire lost control Romans also began to acknowledge the military strength, and hence the masculinity of, the "foreigners," thus underscoring yet once more the ancient Mediterranean connection between the military and masculinity (Kuefler: 49).

40 These choice "Others" (women, "foreigners," and social inferiors) indicate an intricate relation among patriarchy, xenophobia, and classism. I am borrowing Schoene-Harwood's term (xii) and calling this section "shadow-bashing" because the term conveys a sense of masculinity's own anxiety and thus its need for a relentless self-monitoring process through monitoring others so that they not be(come) part of one's self (Hopkins: 123). These "Others" or "other selves" present a classic "double-bind" for the masculine ideal, since they are simultaneously needed to establish masculinity and avoided for their potential to erode masculinity. These "Others" then may well represent what Kristeva calls the "abject," or "what disturbs identity, system, order … [and] does not respect borders, positions, rules" (4). As we will see, these abjects in Mark turn out to be the Romans, the disciples, and the women characters; all of them have an ambiguous and ambivalent relationship with Jesus.

41 Thus there is here also a contrast between the Roman governor and the Jewish authorities who are working the crowd behind the scene, and outmaneuvering Pilate in his attempt to grant Jesus amnesty (15:6–11).

sea despite Legion's repeated begging (5:9–13), but the Gerasenes themselves are so frightened and worried by Jesus' action that they too "beg" him to leave (5:17). In addition to being able to stand up to a cowardly Pilate and stand out in domination of the Romans and the Gerasenes, Mark's Jesus further establishes his masculinity by being able to supply "foreigners" with food. Since Jesus' second miraculous feeding (8:1–10) follows a healing miracle in Decapolis (7:31–37) without any specific geographical reference, this feeding effactually has Jesus assume the masculine role of provider for the Gentiles. As Mark's story comes to a close, Mark has a Roman centurion articulate and acknowledge what we have been finding out all along: Jesus is truly a man; he is the son or the anointed of God (15:39).

Social Superiors and Inferiors

Despite Jesus' critique—as a response to James and John's quest for honor—of the hierarchical structure of "foreign" politics (10:35–45), his own masculinity is defined by playing off the hierarchical structure of social ranks. When Northrop Frye (33–67) uses solely "scope" or "power of action" as a lens to interpret Aristotle's explication in the *Poetics* of how fictional heroes may be "better" or "worse" than the audience, Frye has prematurely (dis)missed the importance of social ranks, since scope or power of action may well correlate with social status (B. R. Smith: 119–20). Fictional heroes who have greater power than the audience are often also from a higher social rank. Mark tells us that it is partly because of social rank that the Nazarenes find it hard to accept Jesus' greater scope or power of action, since Jesus is only a carpenter's son (6:1–3). The same reason may also explain the difficulty that the Jerusalem authorities have with Jesus. Yet, as we have already discussed earlier in the essay, Jesus consistently shows himself to be more of a man than the Jerusalem authorities by dominating them in every debate and each controversy. A good contrast is the way Jesus is able to handle the Jerusalem authorities' "catch-22" question regarding taxation (12:13–17), almost immediately after the Jerusalem authorities are unable to deal with Jesus' "catch-22" question about John's authority (11:27–33). Worst of all, the people recognize Jesus' domination over the Jerusalem authorities (1:21–22; 7:37; 11:7–10; 12:37c); that is, people acknowledge Jesus' masculinity.[42] The

---

42 This acknowledgment actually also comes from some of Jesus' social superiors, including Jairus, who is a leader of a synagogue (5:22–23), the rich man who sincerely asks about inheriting "eternal life" (10:17–22), a curious scribe who is so impressed by Jesus that he agrees with Jesus' statement about the "first commandment" (12:28–34), and Joseph of Arimathea, a council member who provides a burial for Jesus (15:42–46).

way the Jerusalem authorities are fearful of Jesus and the people (11:18, 32; 12:12; 14:1–2) only causes the Jerusalem authorities, like Pilate, to embody the opposite of Jesus' manhood. Since they are most concerned with the possibility of riot that may cost them their jobs, they show themselves to be cynical politicians who live by expediency rather than "men" who live by higher principle. As they become frustrated and fearful, they lose more of their "cultural capital" as men by losing control of their emotions, as well as losing their honor. They, Mark tells us, resort to "deceit" to murder Jesus (14:1) and do so out of "jealousy" (15:10).

Jesus' masculinity is defined by his defiance of those above him as well as by his domination of those below him.[43] Since my earlier comments on Jesus as the *paterfamilias* are related to this issue, I will now limit myself to explicit examples that concern the comparative masculinity of Jesus and his disciples. If "courage" is etymologically rooted in or even equal to ancient Mediterranean masculinity, the disciples clearly fail to achieve manhood in Mark. Like many others in the Gospel, Jesus' disciples are constantly associated with fear (4:39–41; 6:49–50; 9:6, 32; 10:32).[44] Like the Gerasenes, they are afraid of the miracles they see (4:39–41; 6:49–52; 9:2–6). Like the Jerusalem authorities, they gradually become afraid to ask Jesus questions (9:32). They do not have the discipline to stay awake in Gethsemane, a weakness that becomes doubly problematic because of the immediately preceding emphasis that Jesus gives to watchfulness (13:3–37; 14:32–42). When Jesus is arrested by people armed with "swords and clubs" (14:43), they flee as if they are deserters in a war (14:50). Given the ancient Mediterranean association of masculinity with war, what the male disciples are doing here constitutes a great social stigma. As if that is not enough to underscore their unmanliness, Mark has one disciple even deserting in nakedness (14:51–52). Rather than being in the nude to engage in a "manly" contest like those who do so in gymnasia, this nameless nude dude runs away from a fight.[45] Unlike a robber in Apuleius's *Metamorphoses* (second century C.E.) who resorts to cross-dressing to escape capture, the naked deserter in Mark will find it hard to make the s(h)ame claim that he does

---

[43] This, along with the way Mark's Jesus consistently resists and ridicules the Jerusalem authorities in the name of an even higher-ranking authority, God, should, in my view, warn against any temptations to idealize or idolize Jesus as a revolutionary.

[44] Understanding or knowledge (or lack thereof) is also relevant here. Given the way Mark consistently presents the disciples as "dimwits" who fail to understand or know (4:10–13; 6:49–52; 7:17–19; 8:14–21; 9:9–13), is he also categorizing them as "women," since the latter were, in broad cultural terms, generally excluded from understanding and knowledge?

[45] For an interesting "handbook" entry on "nakedness" or "nudity" in "biblical times," see Neyrey 1998b.

not "fall short of my father's reputation or my own manliness" (7.8; quoted in Kuefler: 57–58).

After the disciples have betrayed (14:42–46), deserted (14:50–52), and denied Jesus (14:54, 66–72), Mark begins to "replace" them with some female followers of Jesus (15:40–41). These female or women disciples, however, also turn out to be full of fear and leave the Gospel with an abrupt and disappointing ending by short-circuiting the communication of Jesus' resurrection message (16:8). To use women to symbolize fear is, of course, a "cultural shorthand." Polemo (second century C.E.) writes:

> The male is physically stronger and braver, less prone to defects and more likely to be sincere and loyal. He is more keen to win honor and he is worthier of respect. The female has the contrary properties: she has but little courage and abounds in deception. (Quoted in Gleason 1995: 60)[46]

This quotation functions to question the disciples' masculinity even more cogently, since their sincerity, loyalty, bravery, and thus masculinity are all suspect.[47] To pick the easiest example, Peter denies Jesus when he is confronted by one who occupies the double negative position of being a woman and a social inferior, a "servant-girl" (14:66–72). Before that, Peter has also made a suggestion in response to Jesus' transfiguration (9:2–8), but Mark tells us that Peter "did not know what to say, for they [Peter, James, and John] were terrified" (9:6). In other words, his suggestion is one made out of fear, and he does not mean what he says. Mark's "cultural shorthand" in the end may then turn out to be a literary undressing. One may read this as Mark's literal or literary rendition of Plato, who writes that "all those creatures generated as men who proved themselves cowardly and spent their lives in wrong-doing were transformed, at their second incarnation, into women" (*Tim.* 90e). Is Mark's "introduction" of the women disciples a pronouncement that the disciples are not men, but women? If so, then the women disciples who

---

46 The inseparable link between sex and gender comes into play yet once more, since the understanding of women as binary opposites of men in moral terms may be related to Galen's "one-sex theory." As Kuefler proposes, if women are but inverts or men turned inside out physiologically, it would be more accurate to call men and women "opposite sexes" than a single sex (20). In other words, men and women as moral opposites is but an extension of them as physiological inverts.

47 One may also want to remember in light of this quote that Mark, as I have already mentioned, specifies that the Jerusalem authorities seek to murder Jesus "by deceit" (14:1). Mark follows up on that statement by describing their bribery of Judas (14:10–11), their arrest of Jesus with arms and in the dark (14:43, 49), as well as their false and made-up testimonies against Jesus (14:56–59). Once again, the Jerusalem authorities come across as feminine vis-à-vis a masculine Jesus.

remain near the end of Mark and maintain their silence at the end of Mark are not "replacement disciples" but disciples relieved of their male drag and revealed for the "women" that they are. As they just did in Jesus' arrest (14:50–52), the (fe/male) disciples once again flee in fear (16:8).[48]

This is, however, still just part of Mark's masterful story about masculinity. Mark's "introduction" (or revelation) of the fearful and failing women disciples at the end is another attempt to bring out faith as the opposite of fear, or bring faith out of fear.[49] What we have here in Mark may be nothing less than the goal of transgendering the women disciples into men. At the same time, as I intimated earlier, the parable of the Sower presents Jesus as the potent male who takes the active role in every relation and interaction, thus effectually marking his disciples as feminine or transgendering his male disciples into women (particularly in light of the highly praised experience of gestation or birthing within the metaphor of this parable). In addition to the sowing parable(s), one can think of Jesus' emphasis on the need for the male disciples to care for children (9:33–37; 10:13–16), which is traditionally a woman's work. Of significance here also

---

48 Mark also uses the same phrase "from a distance" (*apo makrothen*) to describe the way Peter follows Jesus after Jesus' arrest (14:54) and the way the women disciples witness Jesus' crucifixion (15:40). Horsley has recently argued that the number twelve that is used to describe the age of Jairus's daughter and the number of years the hemorrhaging woman has suffered signifies that both are representatives of a restored Israel who, as female, is now ready to give new birth (2001: 206, 212). Let me add that alongside these somewhat complementary representations of women and the disciples are other, more contrasting representations. An example will be the way Mark has the unnamed woman anoint Jesus with a jar of expensive nard (14:3–9) right before his account of Judas's decision to betray Jesus for money (14:10–11). Not only does this scene underscore Judas' desire for wealth; it further underlines the hopelessly feminine position of Judas. He cannot even measure up with a woman.

49 While Tolbert has argued for this in terms of ancient rhetoric (1989: 224, 264), Butler's recent article (1995) on melancholy and masculinity can also help to interpret in psychoanalytic terms the dynamics Tolbert has articulated. Following Butler, one would say the melancholy or unfinished grieving of both Jesus' death and the women's fearful silence leads to an identification with the masculinity that is demonstrated and demanded by Jesus. In light of Mark's rhetorical or emotionally moving ending, one may also understand Mark's "cultural shorthand" more generally in terms of the long association between women and (excessive) emotions that hinder both reason and action. If Mark is using women (who are supposedly emotional) to stir up emotions at the end, what would this injection and infusion of emotions make of the readers in terms of the male/masculine and female/feminine scale? Or, is the women's fearful silence yet another case to justify the position that women's excessive emotions must be controlled to prevent disastrous results? Regarding the Markan opposites of fear and faith (4:40; 5:36), it is clear, for example, from the way Mark's Jesus stresses persecution and suffering (8:34–38; 10:35–39; 13:9–23) that following Jesus in faith is not something for the fearful or the "unmanly." Given the "cultural capital" of masculinity in the ancient Mediterranean, this (apocalyptic) message of persecution, suffering, and death may ironically serve to entice people to as well as repel people from Mark's Jesus.

is Jesus' comparison of resurrected persons, in response to the Sadducees, to "angels in heaven" (12:25), since angelic existence, as far as we can tell from Mark, is limited to serving Jesus (1:13) and to being on call to do his bidding (13:26–27, 32). Given Jesus' pronouncement that people will no longer marry after the resurrection, as well as his self-description as "the bridegroom" (2:19–20), is Jesus implying that everyone in heaven will be his bride, serving him the husband-man like Simon's mother-in-law does in the house the night she is healed (1:29–30)? What should one then make of the sex and gender of the disciples? Given the ambiguities above, Mark's negative description of the disciples as "rocky ground" may yet end up rather apt, since we do know of a hermaphroditic figure, Agdistis, in Greek mythology who is born of a rock that has been "inseminated" by Zeus's seed (Vermaseren: 3–5).[50]

Whether transvestites, transgendered, or hermaphrodites, the disciples are clearly not comparable to their master Jesus in the sliding scale of masculinity. According to the parable of the Sower, Jesus' seed or sperm is aborted by human desire and fear, while Satan moves around to act as a kind of birth control and patrol (4:14–19). Plato has also talked about the problem of fear and desire and proceeds to prescribe courage and/or self-control—both characteristics of ancient Mediterranean manhood—as remedies (*Resp.* 442b–c). In Plato's diagnosis, fear and desire are both problems of "unmanliness." We have already talked much about the problem of fear among many who encounter Jesus. What about that of desire? Pilate's and the Jerusalem leaders' policy of expediency is connected to their desire to hold on to their positions of power, as we have discussed. Mark's Jesus also relates James and John's desire for honor to Gentile leadership style (10:35–45) and ridicules the Jerusalem authorities for lusting after honor and wealth (12:38–44). For Mark, these two "unmanly" problems are intertwined rather than neatly separable, and they plague "foreigners" as well as Jesus' social inferiors and superiors.

---

50 In this light, Moore's recent argument that Romans presents sin and woman as synonyms and thus faith as a gradual "soteriological sex change" to make believers into men has left me much to ponder (2001: 146–69). The same is true of his overall argument about the queer spaces associated with Jesus and Jesus' followers (2001). However, if the gradual soteriological sex change in Mark is more accurately described as hermaphroditic (despite the rhetoric of and reverence for masculinity), then salvation would become almost like a return to the hermaphroditic first humans who conspired against the gods and, as a punishment, were "sliced" into be(com)ing two separates sexes (Plato, *Symp.* 189c–191d). According to the *Gospel of Thomas*, "Jesus said to [his disciples], 'When you make the two into one, and when you make the inner like the outer, and the upper like the lower, and when you make male and female into a single one, so that the male will not be male nor the female be female … then you will enter the Father's domain'" (22:4–7; quoted in Powell: 44).

Women

If Mark uses women disciples as a "cultural shorthand" to emphasize and criticize the disciples' "unmanliness," Mark is likely to use other women characters to bolster Jesus' masculinity. First of all, it is clear that Mark devotes a lot more ink to Jesus' interaction with men than with women, thus implying that Jesus is living out the ancient Mediterranean idea(l) of sexual or social segregation. This idea(l) is, of course, rooted in the fear that spending too much time with women may corrupt a man's masculinity and the correlating assumption that men are both more desirable competitors in one's quest for manhood and more considerable consenters to one's masculinity. This idea(l) also puts Jesus' rejection of his mother and family to do his God-Father's will in a different light (3:31–35).[51] It signifies Jesus' attempt to separate himself from the socialization of his biological mother to enter the public world of men.[52] Not only does Mark repeat the "outsider" status of Jesus' mother and family (3:31–32), but Mark's Jesus also reiterates their action as an opposition to his single-minded zeal to do the will of God, or obey the law of his (absentee) Father (3:20–21, 31–35). In Lacan's psychoanalytic terms, what Jesus does that day can be read as his physical separation from the mother and his entry into the symbolic order. If so, then not only is this "early experience" ("early" at least in terms of Mark's literary or narrative sequence) followed by the cultivation of a social identity through language; it also becomes foundational for Jesus' death drive to escape language and return to his originary wholeness.[53]

---

51 It does make sense in the hierarchical structure of the ancient Mediterranean for Mark's Jesus to relate to God as a masculine Father (8:38; 11:25; 13:32; 14:36), since within that hierarchical logic, the ruling or active part is always masculine.

52 Notice how the people of Nazareth, in talking about Jesus' biological family, mention Jesus' brothers by name but simply refer to his nameless sisters as still being "here with us" (6:3). I take that as a clear indication that Jesus and his siblings are all living out the idea(l) of sexual and social segregation. The presence of his brothers in 3:31–32 is readily explicable by the need for Jesus' mother to be accompanied by adult males when she travels outside her home.

53 It is also on the basis of such sexual and social segregation that Philip E. Slater suggests a "repressed mother syndrome" among Athenian wives, which leads to difficult and ambiguous mother-son relations in the ancient Greek world. Then Slater goes on to argue that the extremely masculine and overbearing heroes in Greek tragedy are merely reflections of the dramatists' own psychic battle with their childhood and adolescent experiences. See Gilmore 1987b for a related discussion in the context of the contemporary Mediterranean world. Although Schoene-Harwood is interested in "literary masculinities" of a different period and time, her treatment of what she calls "domophobia" is nevertheless relevant here (14–15). Note that Jennifer A. Glancy, relating this episode concerning Jesus' family (3:31–35)

When Jesus does interact with women in the Gospel, he constantly does so within a home or house (1:29–31; 5:35–43; 7:24–25; 14:3),[54] and he consistently assumes the dominant role, if not always the (grammatically speaking) active part. He heals Simon's mother-in-law in the house of Simon and Andrew, whose immediate response to her healing is service to and for Jesus (which involves also serving other men who are with Jesus; 1:29–31). Likewise, Jesus defends the woman who anoints him in the house of another Simon (the leper) at Bethany when others criticize her for being wasteful (14:3–9). What is Jesus' defense? He praises the woman for performing "a good service" for him (14:6) and in the process interprets her "service" as a whole-hearted endorsement of his masculine-cum-martyr project(ion) (14:7–9). I will say more about this project(ion) later; let me simply pinpoint now how these contrasting or defining "Others" can function as foils as well as fans to bolster Jesus' masculinity.

Jesus' encounters with women in Mark demonstrate "the contentiousness of men and women as a sport or game" (B. R. Smith: 109). This contentious or gaming aspect is particularly evident in the episodes concerning the woman who has been hemorrhaging for twelve years (5:25–34) and the Syrophoenician woman (7:24–30). Many commentators have pointed out how both women seem to approach Jesus independently without any mediation of a man, yet in both cases Mark develops the episodes in such a way that Jesus appears at the end as their male or "manly" benefactor. The end of the episode undercuts whatever independence and initiative the hemorrhaging woman may have displayed in the beginning.[55] The closing picture reinscribes her inferiority and

---

to the episode of Herodias (6:14–29), hints at a very important question regarding how the relationships between mothers and sons and those between mothers and daughters might be different in this context of sexual and social segregation (42 n. 25)

54 I have argued elsewhere that women in Mark who seem to have traveled and acted somewhat "independently" are women without any male association and/or operating in the absence of men. Examples include the hemorrhaging woman (5:25–34), the Syrophoenician woman (7:24–30), the poor widow at the temple (12:41–44), the woman who anoints Jesus at Bethany (14:3–9), and the women disciples who come to the tomb to anoint Jesus' body (16:1–8). See Liew: 137–38, 142.

55 This particular Markan episode is extremely important for any discussion of masculinity, since we find in it, to use a phrase that Dale B. Martin uses to talk about menstruation in the ancient Mediterranean, "a site where two separate highly overdetermined signs—the female and blood—came together in one place" (2001: 98). What interests me is that this woman's femininity vis-à-vis Jesus' masculinity may actually have been one-sided from the start. In terms of Galenic medicine, blood is an important source of life and virility. Men are, "by nature," better endowed with blood. Paradoxically, too much blood may block some men's capacity for reason and result in Galen's remedy known as "blood-letting" to purge the excessive blood and rebalance the body (Brain: 1–14, 25–27).

indebtedness to Jesus by having her kneel down, reporting the "whole truth" to Jesus, who, in turn, calls her "daughter" and incorporates her into his family and "manly" protection before he dismisses her (5:33–34). Similarly, Jesus sets the terms for his verbal game with the Syrophoenician woman, who also ends up acquiescing that she and her daughter are "dogs" who should not come to Jesus' table as full and equal children (7:24–28).[56] If Jesus seems distant to the Syrophoenician woman from the beginning, he continues to keep his distance from her and her daughter by performing a "long-distance" healing at the end (7:29–30). Given his very immediate response to a similar request from Jairus (both in terms of how willing and where Jesus is in performing the healing, 5:21–24a, 35–43), I personally can think of only two reasons for Jesus' distant response to the Syrophoenician woman: (1) she is a woman without a man; and (2) she is a "foreigner." I have already noted that "foreigners" and women were separately considered to be defining and defiling "others" of masculinity; what the "foreign," Syrophoenician woman represents is then a double otherness, or a doubly dangerous source of feminine corruption of Jesus. Is this the reason for Jesus' distant response to her request?[57]

Even in these "blood-letting" cases, it is important to keep in mind Martin's point that bleeding inevitably points to a problem with one's body (101). What I want to emphasize here is the desperation for a woman who is already less endowed with blood to keep losing blood and how this desperate or disastrous condition further implies the woman's weak, and feminine, position. If Jesus' loss of power is a transfer of blood so the woman can be well by regaining her blood balance, I will admit that I am tempted to interpret this as a veiled reference to Jesus' "sowing" or inseminating specialty (which has just been specified in the previous chapter), particularly since semen is for Galen the highest or most refined form of blood (D. B. Martin 2001: 91–92). If so, may one interpret Mark's parallel reference to people being healed by touching the fringe of Jesus' cloak in the next chapter (6:56) as another indication of Jesus' wide and wild "sowing"? Let me also point out that I personally do not agree with Rita Nakashima Brock's reading that Jesus' loss of power here is a loss of patriarchal power, particularly since Brock herself wants to read this woman's bleeding as an indirect reference to women's menstruation (83–84). How can this episode be a protest against patriarchal power if Jesus heals the woman by causing her bleeding or menstruation to "cease" (5:29)? Since menstruation is, in Brock's own definition, the sign of femaleness (83), Jesus' healing will amount to removing the woman's femaleness. It is also interesting that Mark makes no specific mention of Jesus losing blood during his suffering or crucifixion, although blood is mentioned in the context of the covenant during the Last Supper (14:24). Is this because of Martin's observation that loss of blood implicitly but inevitably implies a loss of manhood in the ancient Mediterranean (104)?

56 Some feminist scholars have argued for a positive reading of the Syrophoenician woman's role in Mark by seeing her as a catalyst who inspires Jesus to understand the inclusive nature of his mission (J. Dewey 1994: 485). Yet women, especially "foreign women," have long been given the role of "inspirer" in texts that are clearly patriarchal and colonial. For examples of such a trope in literary history, see Dube: 70–83, 92–95.

57 Note also the gender implication communicated by the contrast within this episode between a Jesus who travels all over the place and enters a house to seek momentary respite

Despite their apparent differences (in terms of age, ethnicity, nature of the problem, or presence/absence of male mediation), women characters who actually interact with Mark's Jesus all find in him help and protection. To put it in another way, these women are helpless and defenseless without Jesus. Both helplessness and defenselessness are "projections of a narcissistic male desire that constructs the myth of its own monumental potency in diametric opposition to the deficiencies of an equally man-made femininity" (Schoene-Harwood: 6). Mark's Jesus thus ends up looking a lot like what Paul Smith says about Clint Eastwood in many Eastwood movies: he appears as an ally of women, but that alliance also serves to rein women in (92–94).

The most important woman in Mark is, in my view, actually a woman character who has no direct interaction with Jesus. I am thinking of Herodias, who at least partly engineers the beheading of John the Baptizer (6:14–29).[58] A comparison of how Mark depicts Herodias and the women above shows, however, that for Mark women should be helped and protected but never allowed to become decision makers. Bringing in Herodias highlights also a comparison between Herod's femininity and Jesus' masculinity.[59] In contrast to Herod, who displays his capriciousness (and thus his femininity) in his relationship with John the Baptizer (from being perplexed to being joyful and from protector to murderer, 6:20–28), Jesus stays his course in following God as well as in his commitment to his wayward disciples (14:26–28; 16:7). While Herod is outwitted by Herodias, Jesus will not be outdone by the tricks of the hemorrhaging woman.

(which turns out to be unsuccessful) and a woman who meets Jesus inside a house only to return home (7:24–25, 29–30).

58 Without dismissing Glancy's (1994) concern and observation that Herod himself assumes responsibility for John's death (6:16), I do nevertheless think that Glancy's thesis about male masquerade (as anxiety about being a victim of a woman) is not just a projection of modern readers of Mark on Mark but part of Mark's textual and contextual dynamics, since masculinity was very much an object(ive) of Mark's agonistic world, and that agonistic world operated with a "zero-sum" presupposition (D. B. Martin 2001: 93–94). That is to say, whenever a woman turns masculine (as Herodias does), a man has to be made feminine. Glancy's masculine masquerade is so male-centered that she ends up (dis)missing the masculine masquerade (as drag performance) of a woman, Herodias. This kind of male monopoly is, I believe, precisely the "problem" that Sedgwick (1995) points to in her critique of masculinity studies.

59 To relate this back to the other two "shadow groups" of masculinity, Herod, being king, is clearly another social superior who ends up catering to people and thus being less "manly" than Jesus (6:26). Many New Testament scholars have pointed out the parallels Mark makes between Herod and the "foreign" governor, Pilate (Tolbert 1989: 273). Both are authority figures who face an insidious manipulation behind the scene, succumb to people pressure, and execute a God-sent that they actually find intriguing. More importantly for our present purpose, both are deemed cowardly and feminine vis-à-vis Jesus.

Unlike Herod, who becomes a "manipulable" if not powerless cipher in a woman's hands, Jesus will always decide how he will respond to the needs of the Syrophoenician woman. Yet Herod's femininity further shows that Herodias is responsible in this brief episode not only for cutting off John the Baptizer's head but also for castrating John and/or Herod (Anderson 1992: 126–29). As we have discussed earlier, revenge is related to the heroic masculinity of Achilles and Hercules. To seek revenge for honor is a masculine thing to do, and Mark is clear that Herodias (rather than Philip or Herod) "had a grudge" against John the Baptizer because John disapproved of Herod's marriage to his brother Philip's wife (6:18–19).[60] Mark implies, then, that a woman becomes most destructive if she is allowed to become masculine; part of that destruction certainly has something to do with the understanding that a woman who raises herself to masculine status is inevitably lowering men to feminine status.[61] Under such circumstances, men's only choice is to destroy this threatening force or risk being cut up or having body parts "cut off" like John the Baptizer and Herod. One should not forget, of course, that Herodias is also responsible for repeatedly breaking the brotherly bond between men. In addition to presumably coming between Herod and his brother Philip, she also causes Herod to behead the prophet whom he used to protect and listen to with joy (6:20). In Mark, "not-all-men-are-masculine" does not translate into the idea(l) that some women, or any woman, should become masculine. Defining some men as feminine only serves to transmit the message of other men's—in this case, Jesus'—masculinity.

MASCULINITY'S DE(CON)STRUCTIVE MACHINERY

When I was growing up among "born again" Christians, I was taught that Jesus was fully God and fully *man*. When I was in graduate school, I

---

60 Glancy, in too binary a manner, argues that Herodias's act should not be read as a revenge but as a political maneuver to secure her position with Herod (1994: 49). I personally do not see those two views as mutually exclusive.

61 Since men and women are not to be good in the same way, they have different sets of virtues. It is therefore difficult for Greco-Roman men to deal with a woman who exhibits masculine virtues. Some plainly discouraged such a move. In Sophocles' (fifth century B.C.E.) *Electra*, for example, one finds Chrysothemis telling Electra that she, born a woman, should not take up arms (992–998). Likewise, Aristotle, speaking to poets, teaches that "it is inappropriate for a woman to be courageous and clever" (*Poet.* 1454a 23–24). Others would acknowledge such a display by women, with the caveat that this was something unusual. For a good discussion of these various stances and examples, see Hobbs: 70–72. One should also keep in mind Kuefler's reminder that describing certain women as "manly" is a strategy to keep intact the equation of masculinity and moral excellence (30–31); see also Moore and Anderson: 269.

learned that some mainline scholars chose to translate the phrase "Son of Man" in Mark (2:10, 28; 8:31, 38; 9:9, 12, 31; 10:33, 45; 14:21, 41, 62) as "the Human One" or "the Human Being" (Waetjen: 27–61). Now I realize that both of those views are, each in its own ironic and partial way, actually appropriate ways to talk about the masculinity of Mark's Jesus. In the ancient Mediterranean, where being masculine is the norm for being human, Mark's portrayal of Jesus seems to be that of an all-Mediterranean male. He is a master of mastery, sometimes over others and sometimes over himself. Yet it is precisely Mark's juxtaposition of these two non-fully congruent versions of mastery or masculinity, I would like to argue, that betrays masculinity's own de(con)structive dynamics.

According to Headlam Wells, "Heroes do not exist in a vacuum. They depend for their existence on an admiring public; and they tell us as much about ourselves and our own will-to-myth as they do about themselves" (83). Moore, in this light, is correct to suggest that a masculine historical Jesus reflects the self-projection of certain contemporary questers (2001: 107). What, however, can we say about Mark's portrayal or projection of his masculine Jesus? What would Mark's project(ion) tell us about Mark's context and about "ourselves"?

Mark is clearly uncomfortable with a Jesus who is completely and fully on top. Like Plato, who seeks to reconfigure masculinity because of the discrepancies between an Achillean masculinity and his life of philosophy, or Seneca, who seeks to do the same because of a Stoicism that is inseparable from the imperial experiment and Seneca's own imperial experience,[62] Mark's juxtaposition of masculinity as mastery over others and as self-mastery may have much to do with his context of fighting a losing battle—assuming, of course, that the conventional dating of Mark around the first Jewish-Roman war is correct.[63] Ironically, in Mark's tragic

---

62 Paul Veyne (discussed in Cooper 1996: 1–4), and more recently, Kuefler (49–55) have both suggested that the shift from republic to empire had a relatively devastating effect on the power of the Roman aristocracy, of which Seneca was clearly a part. The ups and downs of Seneca's career in imperial service have been well documented and should be well known.

63 Note that Moore has made a similar suggestion regarding a later New Testament book (in terms of both canonical and chronological order): the book of Revelation (2001: 186–87). Beyond the New Testament, Shaw makes a similar argument about how the Greeks in the second century B.C.E. (from Polybius to Posidonios and the [Middle?] Stoics) finally developed the idea that endurance or self-mastery could be victorious and masculine because of their own experiences of victimization (1996: 286–87), while Kuefler's book on late antiquity argues that a similar change in context, or weakening of power on the part of the Romans, led to a rethinking, redefinition, or spiritualizing of masculinity. Keeping in mind that redefinition and reinforcement of "traditional" masculinity are not necessarily mutually exclusive, one may want to "balance" the picture by looking at how Britain's vanishing imperial influence after the world wars resulted in an attempt to reassert masculinity

(con)text,[64] the masculinity Mark ends up emphasizing is no less destructive or even deadly. If Plato and Seneca criticize the masculinity of Achilles and Hercules as reckless, ruthless, or even a kind of madness, it is because dominating others may easily turn into an excuse to kill or destroy without control or to be out of control. Note that Mark's masculinity also demands death as a proof, although it is now the death of oneself rather than that of others.[65] The masculinity that is demonstrated and demanded by Mark's Jesus before the parousia is partly determined by whether one is willing to endure persecution, suffering, and death. Not only does Mark's Jesus compare his own fate to that of John the Baptizer with the summary statement that people would do to either of them whatever they please (9:12–13);[66] he also warns his disciples of inevitable suffering and death (8:34–38; 10:35–39; 13:9–23), along with a particular mention of wars (13:7–8). If the parable of the Wicked Tenants ties those whom God sent in the past with Jesus by means of a common, tragic fate (12:1–11), the apocalyptic discourse in Mark 13 immediately does the same for Jesus and his disciples. In short, Jesus' masculinity in Mark focuses on martyrdom, with Jesus and his followers performing the roles

---

as mastery over others in the figure of the "angry young man" rather than redefine it (Segal: 1–25; Schoene-Harwood: 77–98).

64 Since the context of being at the losing end of a disastrous war should be relatively clear, let me give just a couple of examples for Mark's tragic text. Not only does Mark's Jesus refer to his generation as "adulterous and sinful" (8:38) and "faithless" (9:19), but his ability to do miracles also decreases as the Gospel progresses. In contrast to at least eighteen accounts of or references to miracles in the first eight chapters of Mark, there are only three such accounts/references after Jesus' first passion prediction at 8:31. In that pivotal chapter, Mark's Jesus needs more food to feed fewer people (8:1–10; compare with 6:30–44); he even needs a second try to bring about perfect vision for the blind person at Bethsaida (8:22–26). For a more detailed argument on this point, see Liew: 109–32.

65 Admittedly, the line between killing others and being killed is a fine and fuzzy line within masculinity that emphasizes mastery over others, since its most obvious models, Achilles and Hercules, both end up being killed. Rather than destroying my argument, I think this actually deconstructs the apparent binarism between alternative masculinities (which is precisely my argument). There is a common glorification of death that runs through the masculinities of Achilles, Heracles, Plato, and Mark. For example, Plato himself compares Socrates' willingness to die for philosophy to Achilles' willingness to die to avenge his companion Patroclus (*Apology* 28b–d), despite all the arguments and disagreements he expresses against an Achillean masculinity (see also *Symp*, 179e–180a; *Hipp. maj.* 291d–293b).

66 In Mark, several parallels exist between Jesus and John the Baptizer. Both are initially very popular (1:5, 33, 37–38), and both of their identities have been subjects of an "opinion survey" (6:14–16; 8:27–28). Not only do they both suffer death partly because of a cowardly or feminine authority figure (Herod and Pilate respectively); Mark also describes their tragic experiences with a parallel vocabulary ("being handed over," 1:14; 14:41; 15:1).

of tragic heroes.[67] Masculinity, militarism, and mortality remain linked as another (un)holy trinity. The power differential between Mark and the Romans might well have caused Mark to redefine masculinity. That redefinition, however, turns out to be a mimicry of the deadly or deathly masculinity of his oppressors, and I am not yet referring to the vengeance that will accompany Jesus' parousia (6:11; 8:38–9:1; 12:9).

With this emphasis on masculinity and martyrdom, is it any surprise that Mark shows no passage in Jesus' life as a man, despite the popularity of thinking about a man's life as a sequence of ages or stages among ancient Mediterraneans such as Aristotle, Ptolemy, and Galen (Burrow)?[68] Mark's Jesus shows up as an adult, and the story seems to cover maybe (at most) a year of his life. If there is a sense of passage in Mark's story of Jesus, it is more like the passage of objectifying, torturing, and finally transcending the masculine figure or body that P. Smith talks about in relationship to Hollywood movies starring Clint Eastwood.[69] P. Smith's mention of "transcendence" may also be a helpful way to think about how Mark's tragic message can come across as enticing as well as repelling. One way to forego passage into old age or not consider an early death as lamentable is to downplay the significance of this life. Seneca, in his attempt to redefine masculinity, for example, has "anguished ... self-debates" on this issue precisely because of his resistance to "a literal, renewed life-after-death and a bodily resurrection" (Shaw 1996: 292–94). Note, in that regard, the pervasive references within Mark to the reality of resurrection. Jesus seemingly or supposedly raises Jairus's daughter from death (5:35–43). Herod believes Jesus was John the Baptizer resurrected (6:14). Jesus' three passion predictions are always linked with the promise of resurrection (8:31; 9:31; 10:32–34), and he further bests the Sadducees in their question(ing) of resurrection (12:18–27). Even though Mark does not contain a resurrection appearance on the part of Jesus, Jesus' resurrection is clearly stated and affirmed by the figure in the tomb (16:6–7). Masculine martyrs are promised "eternal

---

67 Mark, read in this light, becomes relevant to Boyarin's recent thesis about masculinity, martyrdom, and the intertwining birth and growth of Judaism and Christianity in late antiquity (1999).

68 We have also seen this in Florus's flaunting of Roman militarism and masculinity, where he initially represents Roman history in terms of a man's life passages (*Epitome of Roman History* 1. Introduction). I am indebted to Janice Anderson for pointing out another pertinent reference in an e-mail: Philo, in his attempt to explain the perfection of the number seven in the creation account, proceeds to link the number to the stages of human growth (*Opif.* 103–105).

69 Moore has similarly hinted at Jesus' body being perfected after death (1996: xi, 102; 2001: 64, 127).

life" (8:34–38; 9:42–48; 10:28–31), in which they will become, in the words of Mark's Jesus, like "angels in heaven" (12:25). Is this why the early church has Mark symbolized by a lion with wings? In Mark, a "real" man will roar, fight, die, but he will also fly away from this life with a better body fitted with wings.[70]

If resurrection eases to a degree the tension of death, it does not fully resolve the tension of either death or masculinity in Mark. As soon as Mark's Jesus accepts his God-given identity as the "beloved son" (1:9–11), he is immediately "sent out" to encounter Satan in the desert (1:12) and travels all over Galilee under divine piloting (1:38–39). Again, as soon as he realizes that God has approved and arranged a new course for him, he moves resolutely toward Jerusalem and toward his own death (8:31; 9:31; 10:33–34, 14:32–42). Mark's Jesus follows something he sees as "God-given" all the way to die on the cross, but this is something that he does not fully understand. The imperative "must" (*dei*) that he uses to describe the suffering and death of himself (8:31) and his faithful followers (13:7, 10) is never fully explained.[71] It is true that the parable of the Tenants seems to explain Jesus' death as a miscalculation of God and the result of human evil (12:6–8), and the parable of the Sower seems to attribute the lack of generation to the degeneration of Satan as well as human fear and desire (4:15–19). Yet Mark's Jesus is adamant that "all things are possible with God" (10:27; see also 9:23). In fact, his prayer at Gethsemane not only restates this point about God's "all-possible" ability, it further links his

---

70 Mark is so concerned to be a "real" man (which is, of course, inseparable from doing or obeying his God-Father's will) that he literally, like his women who show up at the tomb, does not see the dead body or bodies. In contrast to Seneca, who seeks to redefine masculinity without resurrection but with "vivid descriptions of the afflictions vented on the body" (Shaw 1996: 293), Mark, as Moore has insightfully pointed out, is rather restrained in his description of what happens to Jesus' body (1996: 4–6). In Jesus' suffering, for example, there are arguably more depictions of the way people ridicule Jesus (14:65; 15:17–20, 26–32); everything else is just succinctly stated. One can say the same regarding the apocalyptic discourse in Mark 13, where the focus is placed on that of being saved (13:13, 20); warnings of suffering are given without actually descriptions of what may happen to the physical body. Yet, I cannot forget for a moment the cruel reality of war and the potential pileup of dead or maimed bodies behind Mark's rash and rushed rhetoric. In Mark's own words, my "problem" may have to do with the fact that my mind is on the things of human beings rather than those of Mark's God (8:33).

71 Arguably, one may also talk about Jesus using "must" to describe the suffering and death of John the Baptizer (9:11–13). Rigidly speaking, the disciples are the ones who use the word (9:11). Jesus' answer, however, does not dispute that use; he only proceeds immediately to relate the coming of the new Elijah or the Baptizer with the inevitable experience of suffering, contempt, and presumably death (9:12–13). In light of the parable of the Wicked Tenants (12:1–1), one may further extend this imperative of suffering and death from the Baptizer to all the predecessors who have been sent by God before Jesus.

suffering and death somehow not to Satan and human evil but ultimately to God's own will (14:36). That Jesus knows but does not understand why God (partly) wills his suffering and death is evidenced in the question that Jesus utters on the cross to God: "My God, my God, why have you forsaken me?" (15:34).[72] God may have responded to Jesus' question by quickening his death (Tolbert 1989: 293), but God never gives Jesus an explanation that answers Jesus' "why" question.

Is this not the saddest thing about Mark's Jesus and his masculinity? Given the way Mark places an extended episode to highlight Jesus as God's Son in the beginning (Jesus' baptism, 1:9–11), the middle (Jesus' transfiguration, 9:2–8), and the end (Jesus' crucifixion, 15:33–40) of the Gospel, as well as the way Mark's Jesus refers to God as "Father" (8:38; 11:25; 13:32; 14:36), we may well relate Jesus' story in Mark to bell hooks's memorable phrase regarding masculinity: "doing it for daddy." Jesus' masculinity is concerned with "doing it for daddy," although he does not always and necessarily understand what "daddy" himself is doing. As one of his sowing parables puts it, the sower sows and goes to sleep (in the grave?), yet harvest comes even if the sower does not know how (4:26–27). In addition, Mark's Jesus readily admits that he does not know, but only the Father knows, the time of the end (13:32). What you have in Mark, then, is a man who commits himself to do the will or the law of the God-Father all the way to the point of death. He, however, does not know much about the why, the how, or the when of that will or law. Jesus may have told the disciples "everything" he knows (13:23), but everything has not been told him by his God-Father. Yet, despite all these unknowns, he does not hesitate to state that "no one is good but God[-Father] alone" (10:18). Is Jesus' God-Father such a case of ideal(ized) masculinity that Jesus is incapable of doubting its and/or Jesus' own validity?

This invisible God-Father's mastery over Jesus is akin to the omnipotent and omnipresent onus to be a "man" in the ancient Mediterranean, although, given the context of the first Jewish-Roman war, the link that Bhabha seeks to make between love of "Father" and love of nation should also not be ignored here (1995: 59, 63).[73] What Jesus' biological family sees

---

72 Moore points out the importance of Jesus' "cry of abandonment" to Jesus' masculinity in Mark, but he simply interprets it as a weakening of Jesus' self-mastery (2001: 264).

73 It is well known that the Roman emphasis on masculinity as mastery (over others) is inseparable from Rome's imperial and colonial activities. I cannot help but wonder if Mark's version of masculinity as martyrdom does not also have the potential to end up approving, or even advocating, war as a condition to actualize manhood. Recent feminist and postcolonial inquiries have certainly been problematizing nationalism as both a resisting and reinscribing response to colonialism/imperialism. See, for example, Chatterjee 1986; 1993; Kaplan, Alarcón, and Moallem; and Mayer.

as "out of his mind" (3:19b–21) or what the Jerusalem authorities read as demon-possession (3:22) are all really parts of the ancient Mediterranean script(s) for masculine performance (Schoene-Harwood: 51). These invisible but influential script(s) call(s) Jesus to leave mother and home to compete with other men. The will of God that Jesus does, the law of the Father, or, we would say, patriarchal conditioning, motivates masculinity and finally detonates both men and women, but it can be something that escapes one's ability to see (in the double sense of vision and reason).[74] Of relevance here is, of course, Moore's questioning of Jesus' death as a sadistic act of the God-Father (1996: 12),[75] as well as Moore and Anderson's observations on the masculinity presented in 4 Maccabees (257 n. 22). As in 4 Maccabees, masculinity in Mark is assumed, articulated, and asked for but not argued for.

Moreover, Mark's masculinity juxtaposes contradictions and is itself eventually self-contradictory. If the way to affirm Jesus' masculinity despite his lack of mastery over others is that of his *self*-mastery, how are we to understand Jesus' *self*-mastery when he himself is completely and consistently under the control of his God-Father's will? If self-mastery or control of one's emotions is the masculine ideal, then what should we do with the way Mark's Jesus expresses his compassion (1:41; 6:34; 8:2–3; 10:21) and/or anger (3:5; 10:21; 11:12–17)? Why does Mark's Jesus denounce honor and wealth on the one hand (10:21–25; 12:38–40) but talk incessantly about an honor that God grants as well as God's own concern for (material) inheritance on the other (8:38; 9:33–35; 10:29–21,

---

74 Since the part about not seeing God or God's will in terms of "reason" is readily explained by Jesus' unanswered question on the cross to God, I will elaborate only on the part about not seeing in terms of "vision." Not only is the character of God only heard but never shown or seen within Mark (1:11; 9:7); readers of Mark have also seldom seen or paid adequate attention to this character. God(-Father) is not even listed as a character in the chapters on Markan characters by Rhoads, Dewey, and Michie (98–136), and is mentioned without comment in a footnote in Malbon's recent book on characters in Mark's Gospel (192 n. 10) Despite John R. Donahue's call twenty years ago, God therefore remains "a neglected factor" in many readings of Mark. If and when the Gospel of Mark is performed as a drama (a move that is most appropriate in the context of this paper, given the performance language made popular and influential by Butler), God(-Father) will most likely not be a visible character on stage.

75 Moore lists a number of New Testament texts in raising this question, although Mark is not on his list. As Moore himself immediately indicates, this view is related to Anselm's theological understanding of the atonement (1996: 12–17). In addition, one can also link the crucifixion scene to what Kristeva understands as an abject horror that "draws attention to the fragility of the law" (4). Kristeva is, of course, interested in the law of the (God-)Father as well as its contradictions. Referring to Jesus as an abject would for our purposes here destabilize Jesus as a "manly" man.

41–44)?[76] What separates the "vineyard owner" and the "wicked ten-ants" in their common resort to killing or destroying over "inheritance" (12:1–9)? Why is fear an opposite to faith at times (4:40; 5:36) but fear of judgment itself an ingredient of faith at others (8:38–9:1; 9:42–48; 12:9; 14:21)? If women's speech is dangerous (6:24–25; 14:66–72), then why is the silence of the women disciples portrayed negatively (16:8)? How is one to reconcile the severing of John the Baptizer's head by Herod and/or Herodias (6:21–29), the destruction of Jesus' body through flog-ging and crucifixion by the Jerusalem and/or Roman authorities (14:65; 15:15–24), and the future annihilation of the authorities themselves by God and/or Jesus (12:9)? Why is the Baptizer's severed head/penis a symbol of masculine violence gone awry, while Jesus' crucified body and promise of future payback are symbols of masculine vigor? Is the difference defined by the fact that the former is the will and work of Herodias, a woman in drag, and therefore not "genuine" masculinity?

I would like to argue that Herodias in drag does provide for me a way to make sense of the many paradoxes or contradictions within Mark's masculinity. What makes sense is finally not sense, but what has been sanctioned by patriarchy, Mark's God-Father. Masculinity in Mark (as demonstrated and demanded by Jesus) is nothing but a hierarchical setup of patriarchy. "Real" men are allowed, in fact, encouraged to com-pete with and conquer others, but they are also paradoxically required to submit unconditionally to the will and law of the patriarch, even to the point of self-destruction.[77] Both the destination and direction of this quest for manhood may change according to the whims and needs of the Patri-arch. After all, as Mark's Jesus declares, his God-Father has the last say on honor and shame (8:38), on forgiveness (11:25), on the time of the apoca-lypse (13:32), and on what happens and does not happen to whom (10:39–40; 14:36). Masculinity as mastery over others and masculinity as

---

76 There is actually nothing new in what Jesus is teaching here. Plato's struggle with Achillean masculinity also involves his criticism against honor and wealth (*Resp.* 548a), a criticism that is shared by Cicero (*Off.* 1.68) and Aristotle. Aristotle, though, may be most helpful for us here. Like Mark's Jesus, Aristotle criticizes the honor-loving man but also praises him at times as "manly and a lover of what is noble" without giving any specific explanations (*Eth. nic.* 1125b). Jesus' concern with a God-given honor may have to do with Aristotle's teaching that honor has more to do with those who confer it than with those who receive it (*Eth. nic.* 1095b).

77 Self-destruction here clearly refers to the destruction of Jesus' self on the cross, but it may also imply his crucifixion as something that he brings on himself, since he does not seem ultimately to understand the reason for his crucifixion. This self-inflicted implication becomes even more cogent or potent if one understands his God-Father as a product of Jesus' or Mark's own projection or imagination of the ideal(ized) masculine.

self-mastery do not necessarily stand in causal relationship to each other (despite different expressions to explain or rationalize away this paradox); what really needs to be seen and said is that both have a compliant relationship to an incredibly flexible but durable patriarchy (D. B. Martin 2001: 82–83). This is analogous to the way Aristotle concludes his contradictory definitions of "high-mindedness," or "greatness of soul":

> Now I take these two [definitions] and consider what there is in common between indifference to fortune and intolerance of dishonor; and if there is nothing, there must be two kinds of high-mindedness. But every definition is always universal. A doctor prescribes what is salutary not for some one eye but for all eyes, or for the eye in a specific condition. (*An. post.* 97b23–28)

Aristotle's insistence on the "universal" applicability of these contradictory definitions is interwoven with an emphasis on faith or trust in the doctor's medical expertise to make the proper call in a particular situation. This illustrates, I think, Martin's argument that contradictions within masculinity ideology help certify and fortify control, particularly (patriarchal) class-control (106–7).[78] The importance of contradictions or paradoxes for the machinery of patriarchal gender norms becomes even more evident in Cooper's work on "idealized womanhood in late antiquity" (subtitle). When Cooper claims that early Christians "broke the paradox" of Roman masculinity as both sexual restraint and sexual prowess (1996: ix), what she ends up offering is only a new paradox of Christian femininity as virginity and marriage. The contradictory and paradoxical machinery of patriarchy has yet to be broken.

Jesus' (unanswered) question on the cross to his God-Father betrays how patriarchy or a patriarchal masculinity norm often destroys without being seen or known (as opposed to blaming Jesus' death solely on the Jewish and/or Roman authorities); it further shows the sad irony that patriarchy, or a patriarchal gender norm, does not hesitate to destroy even an obedient son such as Mark's Jesus. The way(s) patriarchy and masculinity destroy with an alibi may become more obvious if we return to the case of Herodias. Rather than blaming the Baptizer's death solely on either the menace of Herodias or the whims of a wimpy Herod, one should not lose sight of the fact that both are acting within a structural machinery of masculinity that produces and/or addresses various concerns such as: Whom may one marry? Who may participate in a public

---

78 Contradictions within an ideology are then themselves contradictory sites, providing potentials or spaces for control as well as for change.

meal? Who may entertain men, and how? How may one increase one's honor? Without doubt, more visible within this plot are characters such as Herod, Herod's female adversaries (both Herodias and the daughter), or Herod's guests, but far more vicious is their own systemic subjection to the self-destructive machinery of a patriarchal gender norm. Rather than gazing at either femininity or masculinity, as Glancy puts it (1994: 47), one should be gazing at patriarchy, which "not only ... oppress[es] women, it deforms men" (Cockburn: 222).[79]

While Butler is well known for her argument about the subversive potential of gender parody, Herodias is far less well known or less well read as a performer of drag. Her masculine performance in seeking revenge *and* eliminating John the Baptizer to bolster her political position does, however, illustrate the consequences of patriarchal marriage arrangements as well as the destructiveness of another self-contradictory masculine idea(l): the inherent contradiction of male bonding and battling that was being required of "real" men in the ancient Mediterranean. This contradiction between bonding and battling among men is particularly acute because, as I have already mentioned, masculinity is something that men contest each other for, but also acknowledge in and give to each other. What results, then, is an alternative competition and confirmation among men, as seen in the relationship between Herod and the Baptizer, as well as between Herod and his guests. Both Herod and the Baptizer are participants in this delicate and volatile social dance. In the midst of its push-and-pull, back-and-forth dynamics among men, John the Baptizer loses his head while Herod loses sleep because of guilt. This is really the dance that destroys both Herod and the Baptizer, not the dance of Herod's daughter, and not the drag performance of Herodias.[80]

Jesus and John the Baptizer are, of course, not the only victims of a destructive or even monstrous masculinity. As we have seen, Mark's Jesus continues to pass on the destructive demands of patriarchy and

---

79 Glancy does try to conclude her paper in a less binary way by referring to the "humanity" of both Herod and Herodias. As "humans," Glancy contends, Herod "is weak and compromises himself," and Herodias "attempts to eliminate the man who would remove her from a position of power in her husband's home" (1994: 50). Paraphrasing Mark's Jesus, this "human" focus (yet once more) loses sight of the God-Father (8:33). The Patriarch(y) is culpable, but he/it is often as elusive (or even invisible) as the well-known contemporary godfather Don Gotti or the "Teflon Don."

80 Not only does Herodias's drag performance reveal the destructive dynamics of male bonding and battling, but the fact that she has to be in drag to get her revenge clearly testifies to the unequal relations between men and women. Does Herodias's masculine performance, in this regard, have anything to do with her need to (become a man to) compete with John for Herod's favor? Thus, the episode may further expose the contradictory impulse that an ancient Mediterranean man faces between love of men and love of women.

masculinity to his disciples and, by extension, potentially to Mark's readers. Notice that Mark's Jesus himself actually demonstrates some of the
"unmanly" fears and weaknesses that we see in the disciples. His fear, for
example, is on clear display at Gethsemane (14:32–36). I have suggested
elsewhere that Jesus' praise of the woman who anoints him at Bethany
for doing what she can (14:8)—that is, preparing Jesus' body for burial
because she has accepted her own incapacity to avert Jesus' upcoming
violent death—serves to disclose Jesus' own "futile" or "fatalistic faithfulness" in accepting his own suffering and death as a "necessity" (Liew:
124). What I want to suggest here is that Jesus' praise also discloses Jesus'
occupation of a feminine position similar to that of the woman. He is
completely passive and feminine vis-à-vis his God-Father and his God-
Father's will. Is Jesus' "toughness" with his disciples then partly his own
projection of what he does not like but inescapably sees in himself? Do
the disciples represent Jesus' own (hermaphroditic) position vis-à-vis his
God-Father?[81] Having received the Patriarch's spirit "into" (*eis*) himself
(1:10), and having internalized the insidious imperatives of the masculine
idea(l) to mastering others and/or self under the mastery of the Divine
Masculine Master, Mark's Jesus proceeds to (re)produce the system that
engenders and endangers him. For example, he even demonstrates the
same patriarchal flexibility in exercising exemptions for himself from the
very instructions that he gives others to follow. He scolds the scribes for
exploiting poor widows (12:40–44) and asks a rich man to sell all he owns
to give to the poor (10:17–22), but he allows an undistinguished woman
to anoint him with a jar of expensive nard that could have been sold to
help the poor (14:3–9). Mark's Jesus, as a part of his own man-making in
doing the God-Father's will all the way to the cross, attempts (though he
is finally not able) to make "men" out of the disciples. By replacing or
revealing Jesus' male disciples with (or as) female disciples, Mark and/or
Mark's Jesus (re)produce(s) a "sense of inadequacy [that] engenders ... a
special susceptibility to patriarchal pressure, a susceptibility that will
eventually manifest itself in acts of reckless, overcompensatory heroism"
(Schoene-Harwood: 15). Rather than causing one to question the ideal of
masculinity, the inevitable gap between ideal and reality ironically serves
to spur everyone (Mark, Mark's Jesus, Jesus' disciples, and many of
Mark's readers) on to a senseless chase.[82] Rather than bringing an end to

---

81 For an opposite but overlapping understanding of Jesus that features gender instability, see Schüssler Fiorenza 1994, who suggests that Jesus, though biologically male, is an
incarnation of Sophia, or the female principle of God.

82 Given the language of a chase, one can relate this to the chase or hunt of the lost boys
in William Golding's *Lord of the Flies*. For an excellent reading of this novel's depiction of

a shadowy ideal that is unreal and unachievable, energy is spent in boxing or bashing a shadow self. Or, in Derridean terms, the poison of masculinity is (mis)taken as the medicine or cure. Does this (mis)taking have anything to do with the mystery and hence the mystique of a masculinity (divine and/or human) that is always absent, away, and abstract? If U.S. black women performing domestic services within white families occupy a social location of "outsider-within" (Hill Collins: 10–11), may one understand Mark's Jesus (and other men like him), who seeks to serve an absentee God-Father (and this God-Father's contradictory but pervasive patriarchal gender norm), to be occupying a location of "insider-without"? Does this curious location function to lock Mark's Jesus (and other men like him) into a poisonous prison of masculinity?

Conclusion

Like Plato and Seneca, Mark suggests a different route or direction for masculinity, but in the process he also presents a more direct revelation of masculinity. As demonstrated by Jesus, a "real" man in Mark is one who masters others as well as himself solely under the mastery of the God-Father. This, I suggest, amounts to a male living under various or even contradictory masculine norms under patriarchy. Such a man, however, can never be(come) "real," because his commitment to the Patriarch(y) places him immediately in a passive and feminine position. Unable to understand how the Patriarch(y) operates but voluntarily and perennially placing himself under His/its power, Jesus ends up self-destructing as well as becoming a conduit for passing on this path of self-destruction. If I may adapt Stephen H. Smith's concern to read Mark as a drama of "divine tragedy," I personally find it more apt to view Mark as a melodramatic tragedy of men.

I started this essay talking about the neutrality or invisibility of what is male and masculine. This study shows that behind masculinity there is yet another often invisible and insidious force: patriarchy. Patriarchy may in different times and circumstances allow different definitions of masculinity, but it chews up both men and women in its machinery just

---

masculinity, see Schoene-Harwood: 50–65. Her thoughts on the *Lord of the Flies* there have actually inspired many of my thoughts on the Lord Jesus and the Lord of Jesus as depicted in Mark. D. B. Martin also suggests a similar (psychic) dynamics at work within the masculinity machinery, although he does so by referring to the gaps created by the contradictory idea(l)(s) of masculinity rather than those between ideal and reality (2001: 108). Either way, a sense of vulnerability is created. The stronghold of masculinity becomes more vigorous as masculinity becomes more precarious and precious.

the same. In fact, these different or even contradictory definitions give patriarchy the flexibility to search and destroy. Attempts to redefine masculinity with different arenas (war, philosophy, wealth, or rhetoric) or different rules (mastery of others or of self) may well amount to nothing if the social order between men and women remains unchanged and unchallenged; that is, as long as women are feared, hated, and oppressed or as long as patriarchy is not literally met head on.[83] If partriarchy is elusive and kept out of sight, it is partly because of men's reluctance to talk about it, as both feminist and gay scholars have pointed out (Modleski: 61–111; Bersani). My foray into the views and uses of masculinity in the Gospel of Mark has convinced me that no complete or meaningful analysis of masculinity can be made in separation from a thorough examination and critique of patriarchy.

---

[83] See, in this regard, Solomon-Godeau's warning against being too optimistic about the subversiveness of so-called "nonphallic" masculinities (73, 76). Solomon-Godeau's target, as we have seen, is Silverman. Another critic who is more optimistic or hopeful about the subversive potential of these alternative masculinities is Segal. In reference to Markan studies, Brian K. Blount may also turn out to be a little bit too optimistic when he reads Mark as solely "sowing pockets of resistance." When it comes to issues of masculinity and patriarchy, Mark demonstrates far more cultural replication than resistance.

LOOKING FOR A FEW GOOD MEN:
MARK AND MASCULINITY

Eric Thurman
Drew University

> *The question... "Who then is this...?" is the crisis at the heart of the Christology in Mark. It is a crisis without resolution—the Christology cannot be neatly summed up, it can only be engaged with, as the representation provides for that engagement. ... In other words, Jesus Christ is the crisis of representation itself.*
>
> G. Ward 1994: 14

> *To speak of masculinity in general, sui generis, must be avoided at all costs. It is as a discourse of self-generation, reproduced over the generations in patrilineal perpetuity, that masculinity seeks to make a name for itself. "He," that ubiquitous male member, is the masculinist signature writ large—the pronoun of the invisible man; the subject of the surveillant, sexual order; the object of humanity personified. It must be our aim not to deny or disavow masculinity, but to disturb its manifest destiny—to draw attention to it as a prosthetic reality—a "prefixing" of the rules of gender and sexuality; an appendix or addition, that willy-nilly, supplements and suspends a "lack-in-being."*
>
> Bhabha 1995: 57

Taking the measure of masculinity in the New Testament has typically not been on the agenda of academic biblical studies.[1] Recently, however, a handful of essays and an occasional book have begun to put the spotlight on men *as men* and on the social construction of masculinity in bibical texts and in ancient cultures. Several efforts were sparked in particular by recent developments in classical studies that revisit Greek and Roman ideologies of gender and sexuality in the wake of

---

1 Thanks to Stephen Moore, Virginia Burrus, and Janice Capel Anderson for helpful comments on earlier drafts of this essay. While their suggestions strengthened my arguments and my prose, any limitations or shortcomings remain, of course, my own.

feminism and of Michel Foucault's *History of Sexuality* (see now Moore 2001: 135–45 for bibliography and overview). While drawing on the work of classicists myself in this essay, my reading of Mark is also framed by a consideration of Graham Ward's theological reflections on masculinity. As a theologian, Ward's writing ranges broadly over the intersection of contemporary critical theory and theological discourse. Several of his works are engaged in rethinking the relationships between transcendence, desire, and sexual difference (Ward 1995; 1996; 1998), including the theological reconfiguration of masculinity in light of contemporary feminist theory. Ward's sophisticated insights merit careful consideration by religious scholars interested in the complexities of gender, sexuality, and religious discourse. Since Ward occasionally performs close readings of biblical texts as well, biblical scholars interested in the construction of gender also ought to consider carefully his interpretations and their implications (1994; 1995; 1999).

For example, on Ward's reading, Jesus' "constitutional representation" in Mark, his role as the "official substitute ... for what is absent and unrepresentable," generates an epistemological crisis with respect to his identity (1994: 12). Ward maintains that Mark participates in and self-consciously fosters this crisis of understanding, in part by highlighting the unpredictable behavior of Jesus, epitomized by his parabolic speech. The parables convert everyday items and experiences into signifiers imbued with the potential for new significance as well as the risk of having none at all, just as Jesus himself evokes responses of faith and charges of madness (1994: 9, 13). Jesus' identity remains ungraspable, but traceable, throughout the Gospel. Mark invites readers to link up with the "chain of substitutions—from God to Christ, from Christ to the Twelve, from the Twelve to the Church" and join the mimetic process that aims to make present that which is absent (1994: 4–5, 18). "Jesus' life is the performance within which the salvation promised by God is made effective for all; just as the narration of Jesus' life is the performance (re-enacted by each reader/listener) by which the salvation effected by God in Christ is made available for all" (1994: 12).

If Jesus in Mark's Gospel "is the crisis of representation itself," might we also find his masculinity to be "in crisis"? One might draw such a conclusion from a more recent essay by Ward, "The Displaced Body of Jesus Christ." There Ward argues that the body of "Jesus the gendered Jew" undergoes a series of "displacements" in the Gospel narratives (read theologically in light of early church traditions) that destabilize the singularity of masculine identity. Pivotal events in Jesus' carnal life—such as his incarnation, circumcision, transfiguration, Eucharist pronouncement, crucifixion, resurrection, and especially the ascension—work to transform his male body, so that "the particularities of one sex give way to particular bodies which are male and female," ultimately achieving, on Ward's view, a "multigendered" church (1999: 163). Stressing that "none of us has access to bodies as such, only to bodies that are mediated through the giving and receiving of signs," Ward underlines the "textuality of these bodies" (1999: 163, 174).

> The body of Christ crucified and risen, giving birth to the ecclesial corpus, the history and transformations of that ecclesial body—each of these bodies can materialize only in, through and with language. The continual displacement of their bodies, the continual displacement of their identities, is not only produced through economies of signification, it is a reflection (a mimesis or repetition) of an aporetics intrinsic to textuality itself. (1999: 174)

Here the semiotic undecidability manifested in Mark's representation of Jesus' authority and identity is intrinsically bound up with a somatic instability that seems to deconstruct his gender as well (1999: 178 n. 4).

Masculinity, authority, and representation in Mark's Gospel comprise the central preoccupation of this essay, as I take up Ward's insights in order to resituate some and resist others. Ultimately, I suggest that the ambiguity surrounding Jesus' gender in Mark belongs, not simply to an "aporetics intrinsic to textuality itself," but to the specific problematics of colonial representation, especially the ambivalence inherent in colonial gestures of mimicry.[2] Postcolonial theorist Homi Bhabha understands "colonial mimicry" as the process of (imperfect) imitation of the colonizer by the colonized. Commanded to be both like and unlike the colonizer, the colonial subject stands as "a reformed, recognizable Other, *as a subject of difference that is almost the same, but not quite*" (Bhabha 1994: 86, emphasis original). Bhabha highlights the ambivalence of this "partial presence" by noting how the "incomplete" and "virtual" replication of the colonizer's culture inevitably eludes the colonizer's control and may subtly work to undermine his authority (1994: 85–92; 102–22). Colonial subjects may reproduce the signs of the colonizer's authority, while simultaneously deploying those signs for subversive purposes, such as the native's deferential greeting that draws attention away from the hand that picks

---

2 Mark is hardly the first (and certainly not the only) example of mimicry discernible in pre-Constantinian Christianity, the Apocalypse of John arguably providing the New Testament's most stunning performance of this colonial script. See Moore forthcoming. Postcolonial studies is beginning to make inroads in biblical scholarship; see Dube; Horsley 2001; Liew; Moore 2000; and Sugirtharajah. Burrus's "Sexing Jesus in Late Antiquity" (2001) gives a Bhabhaian reading of the Chalcedonian Christ's hybridity that enabled many of my observations in this essay.

the master's pocket, to cite one of Bhabha's examples (1994: 119). Such gestures of silent insubordination render the signs of colonial authority "less than one and double" by insinuating a slippage of power and signification into the very act of duplicating the colonizer's culture (1994: 119).[3] Foregrounding the gender instability generated by Mark's ambivalent attachment to colonial authority is the main task of my essay. To oversimplify somewhat here at the beginning, I will argue that Mark both reinscribes and resists Roman imperial ideology, especially the assumption that the ability to dominate others implies the right to do so (see Liew: 93–108). That power is, of course, unmistakably masculine, indeed standing as one pole on the continuum of hegemonic masculinity in the Greco-Roman world (see Moore and Anderson: 250). Hegemonic masculinity and imperial conquest seemingly then go together like the proverbial hand in glove. Yet the rise of Roman autocracy, as I will note further, also produced a "crisis" of sorts in the hegemonic construction of masculinity for elite men who were denuded of much of their traditional authority. Mark's response to empire, I hope to show, betrays a similar destabilizing of hegemonic masculinity, marked by neither an (impossible) outright rejection nor a simple inversion but by an ambivalent imitation of masculine ideals.

Before reading Mark's mimicry of masculinity, I want to situate Jesus' gender ambiguity in a colonial frame by (re)locating Mark's text within the proliferation of fictional narratives and philosophical discourses written under the political conditions of imperial rule.[4] Ancient novelistic literature, several of whose literary traits Mark shares,[5] offered

---

3 Bhabha marks a distinction between mimesis and mimicry: "What emerges between mimesis and mimicry is a writing, a mode of representation, that marginalizes the monumentality of history, quite simply mocks its power to be a model [for the colonized], that power which supposedly makes it imitable. Mimicry *repeats* rather that *re-presents*" (1994: 87–88, emphasis original). Bhabha's poststructuralist take on mimicry aims to undermine the distinction between original/copy characteristic of modern notions of mimesis and representation. Graham Ward's interpertation of mimesis, also informed by poststructuralism, comes close in some respects to Bhabha's view of mimcry: both highlight the indeterminacy of representation. By reading Ward with Bhabha, my aim is to implicate Mark's mimetic process within the economy of colonial knowledge and power articulated by Bhabha.

4 On the novel and empire, see Hägg: 81–86, 104–8; Doody: 15–32, 60–81, 160–72; Bowersock: 29–55; Perkins 1995: 41–76; Konstan 1998: 121–38; 1994: 218–33; Tolbert 1989: 35–79.

5 Wills says that "[t]the relation of the gospel to the novel is mainly in the area of technique, in the description of the individual, character, and psychology, as Erich Auerbach saw fifty years ago" (1997: 12). Tolbert 1989: 55–79, esp. 70–79, provides a more detailed discussion of literary traits shared by Mark and the ancient novels. Additional work on Mark and the novels includes Hedrick 1995; 1998; Hock 1996; 1998: 126–28; Shiner; D. R. MacDonald 1998. Also relevant is D. R. MacDonald 2000.

an "open form for an open society" (Hägg: 89), a mode of representation in which newly destabilized identities accompanied both the blurring and heightening of distinctions between "Greek" and "barbarian," male and female, slave and free, past and present, and truth and fiction. Greco-Roman erotic novels such as Chariton's *Chaeras and Callirhoe*, Xenophon of Ephesus's *An Ephesian Tale*, Achilles Tatius's *Leucippe and Clitophon*, and Longus's *Daphnis and Chloe* in particular registered the cultural shifts brought by empire through the complex gendering of the protagonists, often upsetting conventional expectations in the process (see Konstan 1994: 8; Perkins 1995: 91; Boyarin 1997: 8-12).

Surprisingly, perhaps, it is not the romantic hero but the figure of the bandit (*lēstēs; latron*), as profiled in fictional and historical narratives, who clues us into the "prosthetic reality" of Jesus' masculinity. Menacing the Roman state's authority by replicating its use of organized violence (Shaw 1984: 5–52, esp. 24-28; see Horsley 1979; 1981; 2001), bandits provide a striking instance of Bhabhaian "colonial mimicry." Camouflaged in the trappings of Roman militarism, yet removing the use of violence from a legal base, bandits split the discourse of Roman authority into "less than one and double" (Bhabha 1994: 119; cf. Shaw 1984: 44–49). Bandits sneak through the "interstitial passage between fixed identifications" (Bhabha 1994: 4) and occupy an indeterminate conceptual space in Roman legal discourse, being somewhere "between persons within the scope of the law ... and enemies of the state" (Shaw 1984: 22), a borderline status that itself mirrors the geographical borderlands in which they often operated (Shaw 1984: 49).

If, as classicist Brent Shaw says, bandits "were, quite literally, 'outlaw'" (22), they were no less "gender outlaws" as well in the eyes of the elite. Symptomatic of the intimate relationship between imperialism and masculinity, the bandit appears in both fictional and historical narratives as public enemy number one, a threatening, parasitic double of the true *vir*. A rap sheet on bandits in the ancient novels would include the following charges: inclined to undisciplined and luxurious "soft" (and thus "feminine") living and unkempt appearance; prone to excessive drinking, insatiable lust, and despair from unrequited same-sex love; practioners of human sacrifice and cannibalism; and likely to meet an ignoble death (Hopwood; cf. Shaw 1984: 44–48). Both excessive and deficient, these fictional bandits stand as parodic imitations of Roman, especially martial, masculinity, for "despite their superficial resemblance to soldiers in their carrying of arms, they were everything a soldier was not" (Hopwood: 195)—or, at least not meant to be. Livy records an instance of the anxiety aroused by the bandit's "partial presence," his resemblance to the solider that is "almost the same, but not quite" (Bhabha 1994: 86). Here an officer who failed to follow orders

earns the reprobation of the consul Papirius, despite winning an important victory:

> When military discipline has been defiled even once, the soldier will not
> obey his centurion, nor the centurion his tribune, nor the tribune his
> legate, nor the legate his consul, nor the master of the horse his dictator.
> No-one would have respect for men or for Gods; neither commands of
> generals nor the auspices would be heeded; soldiers would wander
> about without leave in peace and war; careless of their military status
> they would go wherever they wished, by their own whim; the scattered
> standards would be abandoned, and soldiers would not muster to com-
> mands, nor would they distinguish day from night, favourable or
> unfavourable terrain, but they would fight whether ordered or not
> ordered by their general and they would not respect standards or posi-
> tions; it would be blind and by chance like banditry, not like the solemn
> and sacred rites of war. (8.34.7–11; cited in Hopwood: 195–96)

The consul's histrionic warnings uncover, only to disavow, the unsettling
similarities between the bandit's and the soldier's occupations. On closer
inspection, the model soldier's discipline appears as "an appendix or
addition, that willy-nilly, supplements and suspends a 'lack-in-being'"
(Bhabha 1995: 57) detectable in the distorted mirror image of the bandit.

Under feminist and postcolonial cross-examination, I will argue, the
otherwise silent figure of the bandit in Mark's passion narrative, who
shadows Jesus from his arrest (14:48) to his crucifixion (15:27; cf. 15:7),
eventually "rats" Jesus out and testifies to the colonial mimicry animating
Jesus' gendered performance as the Messiah and the Son of God. Both
roles are heavily implicated in hegemonic masculinity: the Messiah as a
Davidic military and political (8:29; 13:21–22; cf. 11:1–10; 12:35–37; 15:2, 9,
12, 18, 26, 32; see also Moore 2001: 173–99) and divinized authority figure
(1:1; 12:35–37; 14:61–62; Boring 1999: 454–55); the Son of God as a similarly divinized heir of patriarchal (1:1, 11; 9:7; 14:61–62) and imperial
authority (15:39; cf. A. Y. Collins 2000: 93–100) who must also respect the
Father's wishes (12:6; 14:32–36; Boring 1999: 452–53). As I hope to show,
Mark's representation of Jesus' crucifixion, where Jesus' identity as the
Messiah and the Son of God obtains its ironic fulfillment in his death,
unveils even as it covers up the lack between Jesus' divine, imperial dominance and his human submission. It is across this divide, I argue, that we
can measure Jesus' masculinity as the imperfect imitation of divinity (cf.
Burrus 2001: 9–11).

Jesus' (male) disciples can also be picked out of this lineup of
"mimic men" as accomplices who share his authority (3:13–19; 6:7–13;
13:10) and who are expected to share his fate (8:34–38; 10:28–31, 35–39,
42–45; 13:9–13; cf. 14:31). Here, too, a postcolonial reading historicizes

Graham Ward's movement from "Christ to the Twelve to the Church" (1994: 4–5, 18). The Twelve, along with all of Jesus' would-be followers, participate in a counter-cultural formation with an anticolonial bent (cf. Liew; Horsley 2001; Tolbert 1995: 334–36; Myers: 5–8, 39–90; Blount: 5–10; 55–65). All disciples are enjoined to "take up their cross" (8:34)[6] and to "lose their life for [Jesus'] sake and for the sake of the gospel" (8:35). They should expect to be "hated by all" (13:13), "persecuted" (10:30; 13:9–13), "betrayed" (13:12), and "handed over" to religious and political authorities (13:9–13) during a time of great suffering (13:14–20). Jesus also instructs his fame-seeking (male) followers to become "last of all and servant of all" (9:35), indeed a "slave of all" (10:43–44), just as he himself dies a slave's death in order "to serve and to give his life a ransom for many" (10:45). "The decisive point is that [Jesus] sees in [service] the thing which makes a man His disciple" (Beyer: 93). Or, that would make a man out of his disciple, as we will see.

Mark's preoccupation with (male) suffering and servility, I suggest, resonates with Greco-Roman philosophical discourses that reveal shifting trends in male self-fashioning. Under Roman political autocracy, elite men throughout the Mediterranean found themselves stripped of much of their traditional civic authority, and occasionally found themselves directly at the mercy of the emperor himself (Burrus forthcoming: 1–13; cf. C. A. Barton 1993; 1994a; Gleason 1995; Perkins 1995; Boyarin 1997; Shaw 1996). In certain quarters, men responded by invoking and contesting traditional masculine conventions, making calculated identifications with "feminized" positionalities and turning those stances to strategic advantage. While bandits largely remained figures of social unrest, other marginal men of ambiguous gendering—paradigmatically the gladiator, the slave, and later the martyr—became objects of identification for elite males dealing with a "crisis" in their manhood. Gladiators, in an even more acute manner than the bandit, split hegemonic masculinity into "less than one and double": slavish, ignoble, and hence unmanly but also models of courage and martial skill. Ambivalent attraction to public figures of vulnerability such as the gladiator funded the anxious male imaginary with new role models and promoted a self-consciously performative embodiment of gender itself, as several historians of antiquity point out (Burrus forthcoming; C. A. Barton 1993; Gleason 1995; Shaw 1996). Listen briefly to Seneca the Younger compare the Stoic life with that of the gladiator:

> You have promised to be a good man; you have enlisted under oath; that is the strongest chain which will hold you to a sound understanding.

6Unless otherwise noted, all biblical translations are from the NRSV.

Any man will be but mocking you, if he declares that this is an effeminate and easy kind of soldiering. I will not have you deceived. The
words of this most honourable compact are the same as the words of
that most disgraceful one, to wit: "Through burning, imprisonment, or
death by sword." From the men who hire out their strength for the
arena, who eat and drink what they must pay for with their blood, security is taken that they will endure such trials even though they be
unwilling; from you, that you will endure them willingly and with
alacrity. The gladiator may lower his weapon and test the pity of the
people; but you will neither lower your weapon nor beg for life. You
must die erect and unyielding. Moreover, what profit is it to gain a few
days or a few years? There is no discharge for us from the moment we
are born. "Then how can I free myself?" you ask. You cannot escape
necessities, but you can overcome them. "By force a way is made." And
this way will be afforded you by philosophy. (*Ep.* 37.1–4)

Seneca's "good man" (*virum bonum*), like the enslaved warrior he emu-
lates, locates in his subjection to a world without discharge a stage for a
paradoxical display of masculine virtue. Both the philosopher and the
gladiator produce a hybridized (and hyperbolic) imitation of "lost" mastery and virtue "in an almost parodic enactment of the position in which
every subject of empire found him-(or her-) self" (Burrus forthcoming: 4;
cf. C. A. Barton 1993: 14). I will argue that on Mark's understanding male
disciples, like Jesus himself, similarly hybridize hegemonic masculinity
by strategically taking up a "feminized" positionality of servile suffering in explicit resistance to Roman colonial models of domination. The
"displaced" and unstable gendering of Jesus and his male disciples in
Mark points up the necessity for readings that "disrupt the manifest
destiny" of masculinity. And it is to a critical interrogation of Mark that
I now turn.

OF MESSIAHS AND MEN

*He took the twelve aside again and began to tell them what was to
happen to him, saying, "See, we are going up to Jerusalem, and the
Son of Man will be handed over to the chief priests and the scribes,
and they will condemn him to death; then they will hand him over
to the Gentiles; they will mock him, and spit upon him, and flog
him, and kill him; and after three days he will rise again." (Mark
10:33–34)*

*[The phrase "taking it like a man"] seems tacitly to acknowledge that
masculinity is a function not of social or cultural mastery but of the
act of being subjected, abused, even tortured. It implies that masculinity is not an achieved state but a process, a trial through which
one passes. But at the same time, this phrase ironically suggests the*

precariousness and fragility—even, perhaps, the femininity—of a
gender identity that must be fought for again and again and again.
For finally, when one takes it like a man, what is "it" that one
takes? And why does the act of taking "it" seem to make it impos-
sible for the one doing the taking, whoever that might be, to be a
man? Why does this little word, "like," with the annoyingly imi-
tative relationship that it denotes, always get in the way? Why can
the one doing the taking only take it like a man? (Savran: 38)

Let us catch up with Jesus and his disciples as they head toward
Caesarea Philippi. Jesus questions them "on the way" (8:30) concerning
his identity. Peter, speaking for the Twelve, answers: "You are the Messiah" (8:30). But what kind of Messiah? Jesus speaks of the "great
suffering" shortly in store for the Son of Man (8:31), a qualification, if not
outright rejection, of unspoken assumptions about a messiah's role.
Peter counters Jesus' reinterpretation, perhaps imagining instead a
unvanquished military leader, Peter's mind being "not on divine things,
but on human things," according to Jesus (8:32–33; Myers: 241–45; Nineham: 226; Taylor: 380). In this passage and other more explicit ones,
Mark, like Josephus, seems to have little patience for the messianic hopes
harbored by some of the Judean revolutionaries of 66–74 C.E. Placing
Mark's community in a "temporal and spatial proximity" to the events
of that struggle, Joel Marcus takes the reference to "false christs" at 13:6,
21–22 as Mark's warning against messianic pretenders involved with the
revolt, such as Simon bar Giora and Menahem (1992: 446–48; 1998: 33–
37). Marcus also nominates the revolutionary instigator Eleazar ben
Simon as a likely candidate for the "abomination of desolation" of 13:14
(cf. Dan 9:27; 11:31; 12:11). Mark, he suggests, appropriates Daniel's
vision of the temple's desecration in the eschatological "time of trouble"
and applies it to the rebels' use of the temple during the revolt. Eleazar's
occupation of the temple, ultimately precipitating the carnage created by
the various rebel factions fighting within its precincts, also prompted
Josephus to describe the revolutionaries' actions as "defiling" God's holy
place (J.W. 4.3.10, 12 §163; 4.6.3 §388; 6.2.1 §95; Marcus 1992: 454–55). By
reading Mark from this perspective, the rebels begin to resemble the
bandits Josephus often takes them to be.

For the rebel's polluting ways were not confined to the temple or to
bloodying its floors, claims Josephus. Throughout his history of the war,
Josephus explicitly tars many of the revolutionary groups with the label
"bandit" (J.W. 2.13.3 §254; 2.13.6 §264–265; 2.21.1 §585–589; 4.3.3–9
§135–161; 4.9.9 §555; Marcus 1992: 449; see also Horsley 1981; M. Smith
1999). Several accounts of the rebels' behavior echo the depiction of *lēstai*
in the ancient novels. Here is Josephus's description of rebels fighting and
pillaging in the streets of Jerusalem:

> With an insatiable lust for loot, they ransacked the houses of the wealthy; the murder of men and the violation of women were their sport; they caroused on their spoils, with blood to wash them down and from mere satiety unscrupulously indulged in effeminate practices, plaiting and painting their eyelids to enhance their beauty. And not only did they imitate the dress, but also the passions of women, devising in their excess of lasciviousness unlawful pleasures and wallowing as in a brothel in the city, which they polluted from end to end with their foul deeds. Yet, while they wore women's faces, their hands were murderous, and approaching with mincing steps they would suddenly become warriors and whipping out their swords from under their dyed mantles transfix whomsoever they met. (*J.W.* 4.8.10 §560–564)

Though speaking here specifically of Galilean troops loyal to John of Gischala, Josephus says that Simon offered an even "bloodier reception" to any who attempted to escape the chaos (*J.W.* 4.8.10 §565). During the famine, rebels horrendously tortured people in their search for food (*J.W.* 5.10.3 §434–437). After Titus entered the city, they fought among themselves for scraps and, Josephus suspects, "had not capture forestalled them, they would in their excess savagery have tasted the very corpses" (*J.W.* 6.7.3 §373; cf. 4.9.8 §538–544).

According to Marcus (1992: 448–56), Jesus' decrying of the temple as a "cave of bandits" (11:17: *spēlaion lēstōn*; my translation) likewise registers Mark's (indirect) denunciation of the revolutionaries. Mark uses *lēstēn* in two other instances to which I will turn shortly. Both of these imply seditious activity, supporting a similar meaning at 11:17. Mark opposes the rebels' occupation of the temple as the embodiment of a "nationalist," anti-Gentile ideology, as the contrast between a "cave of bandits" and a "house of prayer for all the nations" implies. Jeremiah, from whom Mark takes the phrase "cave of bandits" (Jer 7:11 LXX), preaches against those who "steal, murder, commit adultery, swear falsely, make offerings to Baal, and go after other gods" and then enter the temple for worship, saying "We are safe!" On Marcus's reading, Mark similarly critiques rebels who enter the temple with the intent of murderously advancing their political aims, which perhaps included the "ethnic cleansing" of the temple itself (Marcus 1992: 451, 454–55; Blount: 151–56). To this constricted view of Israel Mark juxtaposes Isaiah's vision of international worship (56:7 LXX), a statement reflecting Mark's own "inclusive" (and arguably expansionist, cf. 13:10, 27) politics (Marcus 1992: 450–55). The destruction of the temple by Titus, ironically prefigured by Jesus' prophetic cursing of the fig tree (11:12–14, 20–24; Graham and Moore: 450–53) and his own "cleansing" of the temple (11:15–17), signaled for Mark, and Josephus, divine judgment on the rebels' cause (cf. 12:9; 13:1–2; Marcus 1992: 455–56; Blount: 156–60).

Like Josephus, Mark (implicitly) casts the revolutionaries as unlawful, usurping bandits in order to underwrite the legitimacy of his own divinely chosen hero (Mark 1:2–3, 11; 8:29; 9:7; 14:62; 15:39; *J.W.* 5.8.3 §367; 5.8.4 §378; 6.5.4 §312–314). Yet Jesus, too, comes on the scene as an "outlaw" of sorts, breaking and entering into "the strong man's house," tying him up, plundering his property, and so bringing Satan's dominion to an end (Mark 3:22–27; cf. Matt 24:43 = Luke 12:39; Luke 16:1–18, 18:1– 8; *Gos. Naz.* 8; *Gos. Thom.* 98). Jesus styles himself in terms of symbolic banditry in response to scribal charges that "he has Beelzebul and by the ruler of demons he cast out demons" (3:22). The scribes attempt to exploit the moral uncertainty surrounding Jesus' exorcisms, accusing him of conspiring with Satan in an ambiguous doubling of divine power, and introducing slippage into the masculine identification of Jesus as the "Son of God" (cf. 1:11; 3:11; 5:7). Jesus counters with a parable: "How can Satan cast out Satan?" For "if Satan has risen up against himself," his "empire" (3:24: *basileia;* my translation) and "house" are "divided," and "he cannot stand, but his end has come" (3:25–26). Implied in Jesus' parable is the belief that Satan is the present ruling spiritual power, a belief echoed in other literature of the period (*1 En.* 6:1–8; 85–90; *T. Dan* 6:1–14; *Jub.* 5:6; 10:7–8; 4Q286 10 ii.1–13; cf. Marcus 1998: 273, 283; Witherington: 157). Satan in effect administers a colonial regime, his "empire" made manifest through demonic possession, the violent annexation of human "territory." Jesus, spearheading God's own in-breaking "empire" (cf. 1:15; my translation), menaces Satan's authority through his exorcisms, displays of (spiritual) strength that outdo the demonic "strong man" on his own terms and reclaim God's stolen property (cf. 1:7; 5:4; Horsley 2001: 139–40; Marcus 1998: 274, 282–83). Like a bandit or an insurrectionist, Jesus resists Satan's colonial control on behalf of an alternative imperial male power.

Richard Horsley observes a parallel between insurrectionists such as Judas the Galilean and Simon bar Giora and Jesus in this regard:

> Just as these popular kings [by sacking Herod's storehouses were] taking back from the royal fortresses what the oppressive king Herod's soldiers had taken from the people, so Jesus is taking from Satan's house what his demons had seized from the people's houses. (2001: 273 n. 30; *Ant.* 17.271, 274)

Yet the parallel may actually go further, for strength and a capacity for violence are as constitutive of Jesus' masculinist authority as that of militant revolutionaries such as Simon (Aichele 1998; Clines 1998: 355–58; cf. Moore 1996: 105–17; on Simon's strength, see *J.W.* 4.9.3 §503). As God's "Holy One" and beloved Son, Jesus is equipped to conduct guerilla-style (spiritual) warfare in which his exorcisms play a strategic role. Jesus' public campaign begins in Capernaum, where he commences to "destroy"

(1:24: *apolesai*) the demonic ranks by "rebuking" (1:25: *epetimēsen*) an unclean spirit in the manner of a divine warrior (Horsley 2001: 137; cf. Pss 9:6; 68:31; 78:6; 80:16; Zech 3:2). Tellingly, the Qumran *War Scroll* speaks of God conquering Belial (Satan) and his forces, using the Hebrew cognate (*ga'ar*, usually translated "rebuke" but carrying the sense of "subject" in some instances) of Mark's language for Jesus' inaugural and final exorcisms, as Horsley notes (2001: 137–38; Mark 1:25; 9:25; cf. 4:35–41; 1QM 14:9–11, with 4Q491). In his encounter with the Gerasene demoniac, Jesus stages a reenactment of the defeat of Pharaoh's armies by drowning "in the sea" a "legion" of unclean spirits, who perhaps duplicate and stand in for Roman occupational forces (5:13; Horsley 2001: 140–41). Though Jesus parades in messianic form on the way to Jerusalem (11:1–11), his demonstration in the temple the next day (sometimes also read as a messianic performance) culminates his banditlike activity (Aichele 1996: 183–84; Horsley 2001: 148; Myers: 166, 302–4). "Breaking" into the "house of the Lord," he casts out buyers and sellers in a way that recalls his earlier exorcisms (11:15; cf. 1:34, 39; 3:15) and in effect declares that this house cannot stand (11:15–17; cf. 11:12–14, 20–24).

Jesus here sets in motion the events that ultimately lead to his arrest, trial, and execution as an outlaw in the eyes of Rome, a drama that adds another layer to his roguish identity. For "when the chief priests and the scribes heard [his teaching in the temple] they kept looking for a way to kill him" (11:18; cf. 12:12; 14:1–2). Often lacking an adequate police force, Roman governors relied heavily upon betrayal to facilitate the capture of bandits (Shaw 1984: 16). Though he is wanted by Judean officials rather than Roman, Jesus' arrest appears to be no exception. The chief priests and scribes find their man in Judas, who leads "a crowd with swords and clubs" at night to Gethsemane and the waiting Jesus (14:10–11, 43). Seeing that they expect armed resistance (cf. 14:47), Jesus recognizes himself as an accused brigand: "Have you come out with swords and clubs to arrest me as though I were a bandit [*hōs epi lēstēn*]? Day after day I was with you in the temple teaching, and you did not arrest me. But let the scriptures be fulfilled" (14:48–49). The positioning of Jesus as a political troublemaker continues when the crowd asks Pilate to release a prisoner in light of the impending Passover festival (15:6–15). Jesus the son of the Father (cf. 14:36) is paired with his nonidentical twin, Barabbas, another "son of the father" according to the Aramaic etymology of his name. Barabbas, Mark informs us, was "in prison with the rebels who had committed murder during the insurrection" (15:7). Beginning the destabilizing play of masculine identity that runs throughout the spectacle of Jesus' crucifixion, the appearance of Barabbas, the revolutionary, mockingly duplicates Jesus' criminal status. The crowd decides to have Barabbas, a would-be "king of the Jews," released and to have

Jesus crucified. This opens the narrative space for the ironic interpella-tion of Jesus as the "king of the Jews" (15:9–15, 25; Aichele 1996: 13–17; cf. R. E. Brown 1994: 1:787–820). It is on the cross that Jesus is associated with outlaws for the final time. Two bandits (*duo lēstas*) are crucified with him, "one on his right and one on his left" (15:27; cf. 10:37, 40). "The inscription of the charge against him read, "The King of the Jews" (15:26), marking Jesus, like the two bandits, who may be co-conspirators with Barabbas, as a threat to Roman elite, male hegemony (cf. R. E. Brown 1994: 2:968-71; Myers: 387). Having denounced the "bandits" operating in the temple, Jesus now finds himself condemned as a bandit, raising questions about his difference from them (Mack: 292). Bandits, as noted above, presented a specific menace to Roman state control and to hegemonic masculinity through their parodic doubling of the emperor and the soldier. Executed as a rival king and insurrectionist, Jesus, too, emerges as a "mimic man." Within a postcolonial frame, I suggest, Jesus' hold on masculinist and imperial authority is troubled by the trauma of the cross, pointing up his ambivalent imitation not only of the Roman princeps and his soldiers but of divinity. For Mark's main concern throughout the passion narrative is how the details of Jesus' suffering ironically confirm his identification as the Messiah and as God's Son (Matera: 61–66). As it turns out, Mark's deity is himself an imperial pre-tender, being a partial projection of the colonial ideology internalized by Mark (cf. Liew: 123 n. 22).

Let us begin to unpack the "colonial mimicry" suffusing Mark's text with the help of Tat-siong Benny Liew. Liew argues that Mark both resists *and* reproduces an unmistakably imperial (and, I would add, male) ideol-ogy of "authority as power." Jesus exercises this authority in a number of ways, from the appropriation of prophetic texts and the performance of miracles to his relationship with disciples (93–108). No display is more dramatic, however, than Jesus' role at the parousia (13:26–27; 14:61–62), the apocalyptic endgame in which he will decisively beat the Romans at their own game of "tyranny, boundary, and might" (Liew: 108; 103–7). Ultimately, Liew says, "Mark's politics of parousia remains a politics of power, because Mark still understands authority as the ability to have one's commands obeyed and followed, or the power to wipe out those who do not" (108). Like the Roman emperors and governors whose parou-sia ritually marked the arrival of imperial authority, Jesus returns with the full complement of the "empire of God" (cf. 8:38; 13:27).

Mark, in other words, essentially endows Jesus with a sizable "impe-rial phallus" (to borrow Daniel Boyarin's phrase [1997: 82]). That is, Jesus' hegemonic authority, and the means at his disposal to enforce it, not only intensifies the "might-is-right" ideology that supports imperialism (Liew: 107) but is of a piece with hegemonic masculinity. As Liew reminds us,

Jesus' authority derives chiefly from his representative status as God's sole son and heir (Liew: 97; cf. Mark 12:6). Jesus also occupies the privileged position of an aristocratic householder in the discourse on the parousia: there he returns as the "lord of the house" (13:35), whereas his followers are characterized in subordinate terms as "slaves" (13:34a), and elsewhere as "children" (Liew: 99–102; Mark 2:29b; 10:13–16, 24).

Mark, on Liew's reading, perpetuates imperial dominion as an all too familiar father-and-son business. Homi Bhabha comments on the relationship between masculine and nationalist identifications in his essay, "Are You a Man or a Mouse?": "The instinct for respect—central to the civic responsibility for the *service* of nation-building—comes from the Father's sternness, which is an effect of his 'peripheral' position in the family" (1995: 59, emphasis original). That is, in nationalist discourse, the father mirrors self-worth and identity and the mother physical well-being within the familial metaphor, of which Mark makes much use (cf. Liew: 99–102). Bhabha also says that it is the father's absence, or better, absent presence, "that constitutes the principle of national self-identification and the *service* of the nation" (Bhabha 1995: 59, emphasis original). From the beginning of the narrative, God's "phallic peripherality" (ibid.) shadows Jesus. Lacking legitimate representation on earth (in light of Mark's condemnation of Judean leaders and institutions), God's spirit interpellates Jesus at this baptism (1:10–11) and drives him into the wilderness (1:12–13) and into the service of the "imperial rule" of God (1:14–15; my translation). Jesus not only "enacts the role properly ascribed to God" (G. Ward 1994: 12); he mimics God's masculine and imperial authority as well. "What is this? a new teaching—with authority!" (1:27; cf. 1:24; 2:7, 10; 3:11; 5:7, 19–20; 9:7; 12:1–11; 13:26–36; 14:62). Yet the son is almost, but not quite, the Father (cf. 10:18; 13:32), and this slippage introduces an ambivalence in Mark's mimetic discourse. Jesus' opponents give voice to this indeterminacy as they point up the lack in his performance and raise questions about his identity. "By what authority are you doing these things? Who gave you this authority to do them?" ask the chief priests, the scribes, and the elders (11:28; cf. 8:11–13). Is Jesus of God (1:24; 2:7, 29; 5:7; 12:1–11; 14:62) or of Satan (3:22)? Is he the son of Mary (6:3) or John the Baptist *redivivus*, Elijah, or one of the prophets (6:14–15; 8:28)?

This ambivalence becomes more pronounced in Jesus' prayer in Gethsemane. On the way to Jerusalem, Jesus tells his disciples "quite openly" of the (divine) necessity (*dei*) of his coming suffering, death, and resurrection (8:31; cf. 9:31; 10:33). He even acknowledges being cast for this script(ure)ed role long ago (9:12; 14:49). Here at Gethsemane, however, Jesus' sure-footed stride to Golgotha stutter-steps onto the path of a different desire. The beloved son's love for the Father grows anxious as his service requires suffering for the sake of the empire (cf.

10:45; Bhabha 1995: 58–60). Jesus begins his prayer: "Abba, Father, for you all things are possible; remove this cup from me" (14:36). Luke's Jesus focuses on God's will rather than on God's power, only to discover that God in fact intends his death. "Father, if you are willing..." (Luke 22:42). "For Luke, God's will is otherwise, and Jesus' will disappears" (Ruprecht: 11). Matthew has Jesus qualify his plea: "My Father, if it is possible...." As Matthew's Jesus speaks again, he moves closer to accepting a prophetic necessity God apparently cannot change: "My Father, if this cannot pass unless I drink it...." (Matt 26:42, 54). By declaring that God can alter his fate, Mark's Jesus opens the real possibility that his request will be heard and granted. Earlier, Jesus taught his disciples that "whatever you ask for in prayer, believe that you have received it, and it will be yours" (11:22–24). Mark has also led the reader to expect compassion from God, given his earlier declarations of love (1:11; 9:7; Ruprecht: 12). Now, however, God remains deaf to his son's plaintive longing, and Jesus is forced to wrestle with his submission. Jesus' prayer echoes that of another novelistic hero. Habrocomes, the male lead in Xenophon's *An Ephesian Tale*, similarly prays to a considerably different god, Eros, to be released from his fate (Xenophon of Ephesus 1989: 130–31). Habrocomes' prayer, like Jesus', exhibits an anguishing, resistant will, acknowledges the divine orchestration of his fate, and wishes for an alternative outcome. Habrocomes paints himself as a prisoner and a slave ultimately forced to submit. Jesus, too, substitutes his will for another: "yet not what I want, but what you want" (14:36b). His own desire remains suspended, neither fulfilled nor surrendered (Ruprecht: 12; Tolbert 1989: 214–16).

Jesus withholds his full consent—yet he goes. One can trace the increasing passivity and hence "feminizing" of Jesus as he is continually "handed over" (*paradidōmi*): from Judas (14:44) to the chief priests to Pilate (15:1) and finally to the Roman soldiers, who abuse and crucify him (15:15; cf. G. Ward 1999: 168–73). Demonstrating Mark's interest in theatricality, the soldiers perform a mime, dressing and saluting Jesus as caricatured royalty while spitting upon and beating him (cf. R. E. Brown 1994: 1:862–77; A. Y. Collins 1994: 494–95). Jesus remains silent, almost invisible like Habrocomes, who after being falsely accused of adultery silently and passively endures torture, only later to break down in tears (Hansen: 21). During Jesus' trial Pilate is "amazed" at Jesus' failure to respond to the strenuous accusations of the chief priests. Some interpreters see Jesus stoically bearing physical abuse and defiantly refusing to confess his guilt (Gundry 1993: 925; Myers: 378–79). But Jesus' silence, like Habrocomes', may indicate his submission and acquiescence (cf. Konstan 1994: 15–26; Perkins 1995: 91). Pilate may be simply amazed at Jesus' refusal to defend himself.

Throughout the scene of his crucifixion, Jesus' tormentors mockingly (15:20, 31: *enepaixan autō; empaizontes*) address him as a royal pretender and a son of god. The Roman soldiers abuse and salute him: "Hail, King of the Jews!" (15:18). The chief priests and scribes, along with other passers-by, deride him: "Let the Messiah, the King of Israel, come down from the cross now, so that we may see and believe" (15:32). A centurion responds to Jesus' death: "Truly this man was a son of a god" (15:39, my translation). Jesus' masculine identity is at once called into question and paradoxically affirmed through the ironic performance of these characters (cf. Tolbert 1989: 98–103; 277–78; Rhoads, Dewey, and Michie: 60–61, 114). Jesus' suffering produces a fault line in his subjectivity, now displayed in split-screen fashion: crucified criminal and God's promised messiah—a crucified Christ.

Jesus' hybridity comes to the foreground here as his masculine identity is revealed in the "interstitial passage" (Bhabha 1994: 4) briefly glimpsed between the two perspectives offered on his death, the human and the divine. The narratological aperture widens, affording an omniscient view on the events that matches Jesus' own divine power to predict them (G. Ward 1994: 20). Jesus himself, though, no longer upstages other characters; he blends into the background of action, allowing the reader to see, along with the narrator, the whole stage. The reader is thus positioned as an "insider," one "to whom the mystery of the kingdom of God has been given" (4:11) and thus able to understand the ironic truth of the characters' statements about Jesus. Knowing Jesus' origin and identity, the reader's eye is on "divine things" (8:33; cf. Tolbert 1989: 103; Rhoads, Dewey, and Michie: 141; G. Ward 1994: 6). The soldiers, chief priests, and bystanders, however, gaze upon Jesus with literal, human perception. "Let the Messiah, the King of Israel, come down from the cross now, so that we may see and believe," they demand (15:32). They indeed "look, but do not perceive" (4:12) the meaning of the cross. Mark's discourse here exhibits a double-consciousness as the irony admits of more than one dimension to Jesus' identity. What Graham Ward takes as the multiplication of meaning in the passion narrative, a "madness born of mimesis," becomes, when placed against Mark's colonial background, the heightened instability of imperfect mimicry. Jesus' suffering on the cross exposes his ultimate lack of divinity, and hence masculinity, expressed in his cry of abandonment (15:34). Yet, paradoxically, the cross is also the crowning moment of his kingship and his obedience as a son, and Jesus' broken male body is taken up (especially through resurrection) into the divine emplotment of history. Jesus approximates the masculine identity of Messiah and Son of God precisely and paradoxically by enduring the feminizing shame and humiliation of the cross. His masculinity—fractured and unstable—emerges from a "third space" between his humanity and his divinity (Bhabha 1994: 36–39; cf. Burrus 2001: 9–11). On the cross the difference between these two dimensions of Jesus' hybrid identity becomes not only visible but recognizable, from a postcolonial perspective, as a human imitation of divinity. The Son of Man, it seems, can only take it *like* a man.

A Few Good Men

Let us now bring in Mark's (male) disciples for questioning. As it turns out, they have questions of their own for Jesus, raising their hands several times in the stretch of text from 8:22 to 10:52 and once more at 13:4. Scholars typically review these Q&A sessions with an eye for how Mark understands "discipleship" (see Horsley 2001: 79–98) Several teachings directed pointedly to Jesus' twelve male disciples hint that Mark is not simply defining faithful following; he is looking for a few good men. What the reader finds, I suggest, is a desire not for just any men but for subversive "mimic men" whose gendering is anything but stable.

On the road to Jerusalem, after Jesus relates to the twelve for the third and final time his impending date with death, the brothers Zebedee make a request of him: "Grant us to sit, one at your right hand and one at your left, in your glory" (10:36). James and John, notes Ben Witherington, "expect Jesus, once he enters Jerusalem, to restore its former glory and reestablish David's throne. They understand Jesus' messiahship as royal and political" (437). Seats at Jesus' right and left may signify privileged positions at the messianic banquet or, more likely, in light of the reference to Jesus' "glory," thrones at the eschatological judgment (Gundry 1993: 583; Myers: 278; cf. 8:38; 13:26). Matthew's Jesus, responding to Peter's charge that the disciples have left everything to follow him, explicitly promises his followers "twelve thrones" for "judging the twelve tribes of Israel" (19:28; cf. Luke 22:30). When pressed, James and John affirm their ability to swim in the overwhelming tide of suffering that is Jesus' baptism, a tempest poured out of the cup from which they too will drink (10:38–39; cf. Gundry 1993: 584; Witherington: 287). Jesus agrees. They will share his fate, but the seats belong not to them, he says, but to "those for whom it has been prepared," perhaps ironically alluding to the bandits who will be crucified on either side of him (Gundry 1993: 578). Apparently upset that the Zebedees have jumped the gun on them, the other ten male disciples grow angry at their presumption (10:41; Witherington: 288). Earlier, in Galilee, all twelve had argued about who among them was "the greatest" (9:34; cf. 9:38–41; 10:13–16; cf. Myers: 260–62). In both scenes, the twelve betray their investment in hegemonic masculinity as they vie for the limited resources of male honor they expect to be available in Jesus' messianic new world order (on the notion of "limited good," see Malina 2001a: 81–107).

As before, Jesus begins to teach. Now, however, it is an explicit lesson in (anti)colonial politics (10:42; cf. 9:35). "You know that among the Gentiles those whom they recognize as their rulers have dominion over them, and their great ones exercise authority over them," he says (10:42; my translation; cf. K. W. Clark: 207–12; Carter 1994: 170). By addressing the pretensions of Roman domination in the context of the Zebedees' ambitions, Jesus implies that his disciples' understanding of messianism amounts to a replication of colonialism (Horsley 2001: 228) and elite male hegemony. He critiques his male disciples' interest in being "first" or "great" as a desire to hold power over others, acknowledging a "partial presence" of the imperial rule that will shortly kill him (cf. 10:33–34). Once again describing his own take on authority, Jesus now intends to mark a difference between the community formed in his name and that of the dominant colonial power: "But it is not so among you; but whoever wishes to become great among you must be your servant, and whoever wishes to be first among you must be slave of all. For the Son of Man came not to be served, but to serve, and to give his life a ransom for many" (10:43–45; cf. 9:35). Yet the Son of Man, no less than the Sons of Thunder, still finds himself bound to the logic of "tops" and "bottoms." Mark's Messiah reconfigures the hegemony of being "first" and "great" through an inversion that fails to undo fully the structure of hierarchy. Mark's (male) disciples may become "first" and "great" precisely by assuming the position of servant and slave, a script of self-fashioning that pivots on and thus reinscribes the very distinction between "top" and "bottom" it intends to resist (Myers: 278; Witherington: 290; Seeley 1993: 234, 239; cf. Carter 1994: 170). "Servant" and "slave" retain something of their stigmatized "otherness" in Mark's discourse on discipleship. Though Jesus' followers will preach and perform exorcisms as he did (3:13–19; 6:7–13) and so appear similarly as bandit-like rebels in Satan's realm, the disciples are here invited to imitate the slave's "feminized" social postition, while paradoxically defining their status as "first" and "great" in contrast to the slave's inferiority. Like other philosophical appropriations of the slave and the slave solider, the gladiator, Mark's discipleship discourse complicates the disciples' masculinity, as we will see.

With what shall we compare Mark's version of "servant leadership"? When Paul says that though a free man, he makes himself "a slave to all" (1 Cor 9:19) so that he might win more people for Christ, he presents himself as a populist leader, according to Dale Martin (1990: 86–116; 124–26; 132–35). A debated and at times despised figure in antique political philosophy, the "enslaved leader" aims to benefit his constituency most effectively by identifying (in appearance at least) with their status, inviting charges of hypocrisy, opportunism, and ignoble *levitas* from his opponents and other conservative *politicos* (D. B. Martin 1990: 91–114). Neither Paul, the populist, nor Mark's I would add, completely surrender their authority, as Martin notes:

> The populist who lowers himself does not really give up power or cease to be a leader. The enslaved leader actually gains power by a step down in status. The populist does not completely give up the patronal form of social structure but steps outside the normal patronal structures of status and authority to appeal directly to the masses. ... The power is shifted, not lost. ... It is an exercise of authority, but a more subtle, ambiguous authority that is not based on normal social position and normal status hierarchy. (1990: 134–35)

Like the "enslaved leader" of populist rhetoric, the Cynic philosopher undergoes a kind of subjection in the exercise of his (divine) office; indentured to the deity, rather than the masses, he affects an indifference to social convention that frees him to move down the ladder of status without fear of shame (cf. Epictetus, *Diss.* 3.24.67–77; 3.26.32–36; 4.1.114–116; D. B. Martin 1990: 85–88). David Seeley hints that for both Epictetus and Mark (though not the populist politician) such voluntary and metaphorical submission expands to incorporate the actual slave's exposure to physical abuse (Seeley 1993: 240–45; Fitzgerald: 91–92; Epictetus, *Diss.* 4.1.76–79; cf. Seneca, *Ben.* 3.20). Epictetus's discourse, "On the Calling of a Cynic," like several of Mark's discipleship passages (cf. 8:34–9:1; 10:17– 22), invites an inquisitive interlocutor to consider his interest in philosophy carefully. For not unlike the disciples who will be "beaten in synagogues" (13:9), the Cynic, too, "must needs be beaten like an ass," though "while he is being beaten he must love those who beat him, as though he were the father or brother of them all" (3.22.54; my translation; cf. 4.1.76–79), if, that is, he is to wield the "staff of Diogenes" (3.22.58). Who, then, can befriend a Cynic? Only one with a herculean capacity for pain, a fellow Cynic who also shares "with him his scepter and kingdom" and proves himself a "worthy servant" (3.22.63; 55–67; my translation).

Epictetus's wandering wise man performs as a solo *sophos*, since marriage (in the present social order) distracts from "the service of God" (3.22.69). As "one who shares in the government of Zeus," (3.22.95; cf. 3.22.48–49; 63; 72; 76; 79), the Cynic engages in a politics far nobler than any other (3.22.83–85). Unlike the "kings and tyrants of the world" who rule by force, the Cynic's "power" to govern comes from his "conscience"; his every thought "is that of a friend and servant of the gods" (3.22.95; 94–96). Service here, as in Mark's discourse, encompasses suffering for others. Epictetus remarks of Diogenes:

> Come, was there anybody that Diogenes did not love, a man who was so gentle and kind-hearted that he gladly took upon himself all those troubles and physical hardships for the sake of the commonweal? But what was the manner of his loving? As became a servant of Zeus, caring for people indeed, but at the same time subject unto God. (3.24.64–65)

Of his pain—whether in the form of poverty, loss of status, exile, or even the tyrant's sword—the philosopher takes no notice. Listen as Epictetus literally loses his voice extolling the freedom from fear made possible by being subject to the will of God alone:

> Who is there, then, that I *can* any longer be afraid of? ... For I regard God's will as better than my will. I shall attach myself to Him as a servant and follower, my choice is one with His, my desire one with His, in a word, my will is one with His will. (4.7.19–20)

As "servants" of the community (cf. Gundry 1993: 586) Jesus' (male) "followers" model their servile suffering supremely on his own (Gundry 1993: 589; Myers: 279; Witherington: 288; Tolbert 1989: 317–18; cf. Seeley 1993: 246). The Son of Man "serves," too, giving his very life "as a ransom for many" (10:45). John N. Collins points out that here "to serve" is not "expressing directly the idea of servanthood but the activity of the servant in respect of his commission" (251). Though "the commission itself can be to any kind of activity," Jesus' charge "to give his life" specifies his divine appointment (ibid.). In effect, he slides from service into outright servitude, dying a slave's death that (paradoxically) manumits "many" and (con)fuses submission and subversion (cf. Myers: 279). Jesus' fate is prefigured by the persecuted prophets, who appear as slaves in the parable of the Wicked Tenants (12:2, 4; cf. Matt 23:29–35; Jer 7:25; 25:4; Josh 14:7; Amos 3:7; Zech 1:4–6; Ps 94 [95]; Myers: 279; Witherington: 320). Similarly, according to Ronald Hock, John the Baptist appears in the wilderness as God's slave-messenger (1:2–3), respecting the aristocratic protocols of the returning landlord by preceding Jesus, the heir of God's estate (1996: 315–19). Speaking of the return of the glorified Son of Man, Jesus is represented in the parable of the Doorkeeper both as the sojourning "master of the house" and, like the disciples, as a slave (13:32–37). Not simply one slave among many, according to Timothy Geddert, Jesus is himself the doorkeeper who faithfully keeps watch throughout the hours of his passion and who exhibits the unwavering vigilance and unconditional obedience expected of all God's "slaves" (Geddert: 105–6).

If both Mark and Epictetus appropriate for themselves the slave's obedience and vulnerability, adopting this strategically "feminized" stance affords both disciple and philosopher an alternative stage for the performance of masculine virtue. Recall the comments, quoted earlier, of Mark's contemporary, Seneca the Younger, comparing the Stoic life with that of an enslaved warrior, the gladiator (*Ep.* 37.1–4; cf. Epictetus, *Diss.* 1.29.37). At once despised and praised, desired and derided, the gladiator stood as a magnetic figure of honor lost and (impossibly) regained, simultaneously repulsive and attractive to a cultural elite humiliated under imperial rule. By his oath, his *sacramentum*, the gladiator both announced his slave status and expressed his volition, "and so, at the very moment that he [became] a slave condemned to death, he [also became] a free agent and a man with honor to uphold," as classicist Carlin Barton notes (1993: 15). For Seneca, the athlete's and the gladiator's victorious suffering mirrors the philosopher's moral triumph, a "reward [that] is not a garland or palm or a trumpeter ... but rather virtue, steadfastness of soul, and a peace that is won for all time" (*Ep.* 78:17).

For later Christian writers, such as Tertullian and Cyprian, the martyr took up, with surpassing severity, the gladiator's *sacramentum* (C. A. Barton 1994: 56). Mark lacks the oath, but not, I suggest, its logic. Let us briefly return to two points on the way laid out for Jesus' disciples. In Caesarea Philippi, after upbraiding Peter for misunderstanding his vocation, Jesus addresses the men and women of the crowd along with his disciples and spells out for the first time his expectations of his followers:

> If any want to become my followers, let them deny themselves and take up their cross and follow me. For those who want to save their life will lose it, and those who lose their life for my sake, and for the sake of the gospel, will save it. For what will it profit them to gain the whole world and forfeit their life? Indeed, what can they give in return for their life? Those who are ashamed of me and of my words in this adulterous and sinful generation, of them the Son of Man will also be ashamed when he comes in the glory of his Father with the holy angels. (8:34–38)

Enlisting with Jesus requires a willingness to die for his sake and for the sake of the message of his counter-empire (cf. 1:14–15). Talk of denying oneself and taking up a cross registers the legal and even imperial contexts in which a disciple may expect to make the ultimate sacrifice (Myers: 246). Addressing Peter, James, John, and Andrew on the Mount of Olives, Jesus makes this explicit:

> As for yourselves, beware; for they will hand you over to councils; and you will be beaten in synagogues; and you will stand before governors and kings because of me, as a testimony to them. And the good news must first be proclaimed to all nations. When they bring you to trial and hand you over, do not worry beforehand about what you are to say; but say whatever is given to you at that time, for it is not you who speak, but the Holy Spirit. Brother will betray brother to death, and a father his

child, and children will rise against parents and have them put to death; and you will be hated by all because of my name. But the one who endures to the end will be saved. (13:9–13)

Playing the slave to Jesus, the master (13:33–37), the ideal disciple publishes his good news to "all the nations" (13:10) and stands as a witness to hostile governors and kings (13:9; 8:35). Like the gladiator, this disciple exhibits his or her voluntarism ("if any wish") through an act of self-renunciation (indeed, self-destruction; *apolesei*, 8:35), one that commits one to endure hatred, persecution, betrayal, beatings, and death. And the "name" by which the disciple worked miracles (9:37–41; cf. 13:6; Witherington: 739–41) now signifies the performance of a "savage miracle," a transformation that exceeds in reach the gladiator's own paradoxically exalted status. For where the gladiator's fearlessness in the face of death might win him the philosopher's applause as a moral *exemplum*, the honor of a *vir fortis*, the disciple regains that which neither the philosopher nor the gladiator could (or would) imagine—his very life—as well as honor in the eyes of the returning Son of Man (cf. 8:38; 13:26–27).

Neither the gladiator nor (especially) the martyr won unequivocal admiration, as is well known (C. A. Barton 1994b). Tertullian testifies to the public's contradictory love for the condemned swordsman: "Men give them their souls, women their bodies too.... On one and the same account, they glorify them and degrade and diminish them.... Yet, they love whom they punish; they belittle whom they esteem; the art they glorify, the artist they debase" (*Spect.* 22; C. A. Barton 1993: 12). I suggest that it is from this "interstitial" space between art and artist, a space marked by an ambivalent *artifice*, that the gladiator's gender comes into view, neither "feminized" nor fully masculine, as with the bandit. Like the rituals of sadomasochism, the rituals of the arena involve the play of mimesis and mimicry. Lynda Hart's theorizing of sadomasochism as a kind of (Bhabhaian and Irigarayan) mimicry contrasts the two modes of representation: "Mimicry repeats rather than re-presents; it is a repetition that is nonreproductive. Mimesis operates in the order of the model/copy. Mimicry performs its operations in the realm of the simulacrum" (86). In the erotically charged complicity between actor and audience, the gladiator's compulsion is elided by a mutual desire for what Hart calls the "impossible-real, not the real of the illusion that passes for reality, but the Real that eludes symbolization," an unpremeditated and unscripted encounter (91). As a spectacle of the "impossible reality" of restored honor, the gladiator aims to please his masters by reproducing the free man's courage in the face of death (C. A. Barton 1993: 25–36). Yet should the gladiator fail to be sufficiently brave and fierce, the mask slips and his performance is revealed *as* a performance; he stands exposed as a scripted simulacrum of masculinity, bearing a resemblance to the valiant soldier that is "almost the same, but not quite" and unveiling the whole production to be both a sham and a shame (C. A. Barton 1993: 22–24).

Such constitutive gender instability inheres in the performance of Mark's male disciples as well. Returning to the conversation between Jesus and the Zebedees with which we began this section, we may now read Jesus' reinscription of "first" and "great" as an ambiguous mimicry of the masculinist and colonialist authority those accolades represent. As I mentioned earlier, Jesus reiterates the (implicitly colonialist) distinction between "tops" and "bottoms." Like all acts of imitation, however, Jesus' gesture is "almost the same, but not quite," troubling the stability of this hierarchal difference. Mimicry is closely aligned with hybridity in Bhabha's thought. He writes:

> Hybridity is the revaluation of the assumption of colonial identity through the repetition of discriminatory identity effects. It displays the necessary deformation and displacement of all sites of discrimination and domination. It unsettles the mimetic or narcissistic demands of colonial power but reimplicates its identifications in strategies of subversion that turn the gaze of the discriminated back upon the eye of power. (1994: 112)

Mark, as I have been suggesting, repeats the devalued identity of the slave, reimplicating the slave's obedience and suffering in a "strategy of subversion" (cf. ibid.). Mark's replication of the visible signs of authority—"first" and "great"—thus splits their conventional meanings into "less than one and double" by introducing this slippage into the discourses of hegemonic masculinity and colonialism. Valorization of service and suffering as the path to authority produces an ambivalent masculine identification for the male disciple, as registered by the ambiguity surrounding the virtue of "endurance." Seneca may draw no distinction with respect to manliness between patiently enduring a siege and attacking the enemy (*Ep.* 66:12; Shaw 1996: 293), yet he does so only by transposing the "feminine," passive virtue into an active, public feat of strength (*Ep.* 78:15–19). Enduring persecution to the "end" (13:13), Mark's male disciple "takes it like a man" in a performance that always risks leaving him one step away from simply "being" a man (cf. Savran: 38).

Concluding Remarks

By way of conclusion I want to return briefly to Graham Ward's observations on Jesus' "displaced" masculinity. As noted at the beginning of the essay, Ward suggests that Jesus' masculinity is reconfigured as it is caught up in the indeterminacy of mimesis and representation. Placing Mark in a postcolonial frame, I have attempted to read Jesus' unstable masculinity instead as a performative mimicking of hegemonic authority. Adopting momentarily the perspective of the dominant colonial orders (Rome and Satan), I read Jesus as an "outlaw," like the bandits of ancient Hellenistic novels, who challenges colonial hegemony by duplicating the signs of its authority. Jesus' execution as a bandit provided an interpretive key for viewing his performance as a strategically failed mimicry of divinity and hence masculinity. While Jesus' humiliating death signaled his lack of divinity to his enemies, it also ironically inscribed his divine status through the confirmation of prophecy and scripture. The scene of Jesus' crucifixion retains the trace of Jesus' human difference, which appears as faithful and "feminized" submission from the perspective of Mark's prior confession of his divinity (cf. 1:1). Holding open the space between Jesus' humanity and divinity in the passion narrative, I highlighted the fractured masculinity that appears as the imitation of divinity. Like Jesus, his male disciples too mimic hegemonic masculinity. To the extent that Jesus' male disciples continue Jesus' struggle against the present colonial order(s), they, too, play the role of bandits and take on an ambiguous gendering. Yet it is Mark's valorization of the unmanly slave that provides a key to the male disciples' destabilized masculinity. Just as Greco-Roman writers expressed an ambivalent attachment to the gladiator as a model for rethinking male identity, so too Mark appropriates the slave's subservience and capacity for suffering as models for his male disciples. Here I noted the seeming contradictions of a masculine identity reconstructed to incorporate "feminized" stances. From a postcolonial perspective, masculinity in Mark is destabilized by the play of power across a number of thresholds: between slave/master, last/first, suffering/glory, dying/saving, colonizer/colonized, and human/divine.

How, then, might a postcolonial reading of masculinity in Mark differ from Graham Ward's interpretation of masculinity in the Gospels? Where Ward implies that Jesus' masculinity is self-subverting as it is able to become "the body of Christ ... a multigendered body" (1999: 177), a postcolonial reading attends more closely to the imbalances of power remaining in the text. Mark's reconfiguration of masculinity hardly achieves the results Ward's theological reading points toward. To give just one example, though the women disciples who follow Jesus to the cross (15:40–41) alone exemplify the "service" (*diakonia*) that is the cardinal trait of leadership and basis of authority for Mark (cf. 10:42–45), twelve male disciples alone are addressed as would-be authorities in the community. Despite his reconstructing of and at moments resistance to hegemonic masculinity, Mark fails to question male privilege at a fundamental level. So *contra* Ward's reading of the Gospel texts, it is not the reconfiguration of masculinity by Mark (or by the theological tradition alone) that holds out hope for the "multigendered body" (1999: 176). Rather, it is feminist and postcolonial critique that disrupts what Bhabha describes as masculinity's "manifest destiny" (1995: 57). As feminist scholars have pointed out, Mark's uneven narrative attitude toward women reveals faithful female followers whose actions already interrupt hegemonic masculinity's ambitions (cf. 5:25–34; 7:24–30; 12:41–44; 14:3–9; 15:40–41). Since Mark's desire for a few good men disavows the contradictions of the masculinity he constructs, tracing the effects of mimicry and hybridity unveil masculinity's ultimately "prosthetic reality" (Bhabha 1995: 57).

"BEHOLD THE MAN!"
MASCULINE CHRISTOLOGY AND THE FOURTH GOSPEL

Colleen M. Conway
Seton Hall University

INTRODUCTION

Since the Council of Chalcedon in 451 C.E., Jesus has been confessed as "perfect in Godhead and ... perfect in manhood, truly God and truly man" (Kelly: 339). The Fourth Gospel played a central role in the development of this confession, with its unabashed display of the divinity of Jesus. Not coincidentally, I suggest that Jesus' manliness is also fully displayed in this Gospel. In other words, the desire to show the true divinity of Jesus, a desire that shapes the "high" Christology of this Gospel, results in a particularly masculine Christology. My primary aim in this essay is to show how the Johannine Jesus models the traits that defined ideal masculinity in the first-century Mediterranean world. In this sense, I want to make explicit the masculine Christology of the Fourth Gospel.

Such a project is likely to raise protests from those who argue that the Gospel presents Jesus Sophia, a feminine dimension of the divine (e.g., Englesman; A. Y. Collins 1982; M. Scott). Indeed, this Gospel has been an important resource for feminist scholars seeking a ray of light in the dark world of patriarchy. And it is certainly clear that the Gospel evokes wisdom traditions. From the prologue to the passion, Jesus speaks in ways that sound much like the personified Wisdom figure of the Jewish tradition (R. E. Brown 1966: cxxii–cxxv; Dunn 1983; Willett; M. Scott). The question is what the evocation of this Wisdom figure implies about the gender identity of the Johannine Jesus.

Thus, this essay will explore two aspects of the Johannine Jesus: evidence of his ideal masculinity on the one hand, and the implications of Wisdom imagery on the other. It may well be that one can find both masculinity and femininity in the Johannine Jesus. However, if one considers the connotations of these categories in the first-century context, a different picture of Johannine Christology may emerge. For this reason, I turn first to a discussion of the meaning of masculinity (and necessarily femininity) in the ancient Mediterranean.

But first, a few words about terminology, which tends to be a tricky issue in discussions of sex and gender. Typically, scholars have made a distinction between the social construction of gender and the biological fact of sex. To speak of gender one might use terms such as *masculine/ feminine,* while references to biological sex might use *male/female.* However, this essay draws on theories of ancient sex/gender construction that render problematic the modern sex/gender distinction. Soon it will become clear that what moderns consider biological bedrock in terms of sex difference was a rather fluid and shifting category in the ancient Mediterranean world. Thus, when dealing with texts from this period, the typical sex/gender distinction cannot be maintained so easily either in concept or in language. Nevertheless, insofar as possible, I will use the terms *man, manly,* and *masculinity* to indicate constructions of identity. *Male/female* will be reserved for instances in which biological indications of difference are at issue.

Masculinity in the Ancient Mediterranean World

To some readers, the masculinity of Jesus seems self-evident, especially in a Gospel that emphasizes the enfleshing of the Word. Certainly this would need to be sexed flesh, and clearly Jesus was male. Yet, as we will see, the biological fact of a male sexed body would not go far in providing evidence for Jesus' masculinity. (This is aside from the fact that the Fourth Gospel provides no incontrovertible hint of biological maleness, such as Luke's mention of circumcision in 2:21.) If the Johannine Jesus were to be viewed as a true man, he would need to demonstrate certain key traits.

As is now well recognized, in the ancient world "manhood was not a state simply to be definitely achieved, but something always under construction and constantly open to scrutiny" (Gleason 1995: xxii).[1] Rather than biological difference, what mattered was one's position on the vertical continuum that structured the cosmos. The perfect man was featured at the top with other less complete or perfect versions of masculine identity falling at various lower points on the axis. In this view, woman was understood not as the biologically opposite sex of man but

---

1 Along with Gleason, there is a growing collection of studies on the construction of gender and sexuality in the ancient Mediterranean world. See Laqueur; Winkler 1990a; 1990b; Halperin 1990a; Cadden; Montserrat 1996; 1998; Walters 1993; Thornton; Foxhall and Salmon 1998a; 1998b; Garrison. For succinct overviews, see Stowers; Satlow.

as an imperfect, incomplete version of man. As Thomas Laqueur has aptly demonstrated, this view was rooted in the "natural truths" espoused by physicians and philosophers and readily linked to constructions of the body (25–62). Thus, the second-century physician Galen echoes Aristotle in his treatise, *On the Usefulness of Parts of the Body*, stating:

> Now just as mankind is the most perfect of all animals, so within mankind the man is more perfect than the woman, and the reason for his perfection is his excess of heat, for heat is Nature's primary instrument. (2.630; Aristotle, *Gen. an.* 775a)

Galen's anatomical theory construes the human reproductive system in ways that fit the so-called natural order of male dominance. He leads his reader through imaginary exercises to turn a man's reproductive organs outside in and the woman's reproductive organs inside out. The female body quite literally becomes the unfinished, underheated, inversion of the abundantly heated male body. The result is that "instead of being divided by their reproductive anatomies, the sexes are linked by a common one" (Laqueur: 26).

As mentioned, in all of this Galen is heavily influenced by Aristotle. Indeed, not only does Aristotle speak of men as perfected by heat; he understands women to be "natural deformities" (*Gen. an.* 4.3 737a25–30). They represent reproduction gone wrong. Some glitch in the process has produced a female rather than a male. Nevertheless, even as a deformity, women are a necessary and natural deformity since further reproduction requires their participation.

What this one-sex model of humanity (to borrow Laqueur's phrase) meant for daily life is difficult to say. On the one hand, people were certainly aware of bodily differences between men and women. On the other hand, stories of corporeal instability—female bodies sprouting penises or male bodies becoming effeminate—reveal a genuine trepidation about the possible slippage from one gender to another (Laqueur: 122–34).[2] In short, this one-sex model of humanity made for a precarious situation especially for men. If woman were not different in kind, but simply a lesser, incomplete version of man, and if one's anatomy was not determinative in assigning gender, what was there to keep men from sliding down the axis into the female realm?

----

2 Though Laqueur cites stories from Renaissance authors, these authors all ground themselves in ancient tradition. They cite Pliny the Elder, who asserts that the "transformation of females into males is not an idle story." Pliny then provides several examples, including an eye-witness account of a woman changing into a man on the day of her marriage (*Nat.* 7.4.36–38).

The fear generated by this question created a situation in which the cultural polarity between the male and female was made internal to the masculine gender (Winkler 1990b: 182). As a man, one needs to be ever vigilant as to the state of one's manliness. And in the end, what mattered most was where one was located on the sliding gender scale. Whether one had a penis was not as essential as whether one proved to be a manly male or womanly male. Moreover, since gender identity was always a relative thing, it was also the case that one could have multiple masculinities. That is, in certain contexts one would be positioned as more masculine in relation to those lower on the gender hierarchy but not so masculine when compared to other more masculine men.

Given all this, what was the measure of masculinity? How did one gain position on the gender axis? While there were certain corporeal indications of masculinity (Gleason 1990), it was particularly critical to demonstrate manliness through the practice of particular virtues and characteristics. Among the most significant of these virtues with respect to one's manly status was mastery of self and others. Self-mastery was discussed in terms of mastery of the passions, especially lust. Giving in to lustful desire was an indication of sliding down the scale from male to female, since unbridled sexual passion was viewed as a feminine characteristic. In addition, virtues such as courage, honor, justice, and scorn of luxury were also important indicators of masculinity. Lack of these qualities suggested softness and effeminacy.

Displays of anger were also considered to be unmanly, since an angry man is one who has lost control (Brakke). For instance, Plutarch points to how the "countenance, color, gait, and voice" change (*Mor.* 455f) so they appear in a state "contrary to nature" (456b), making the angry man's behavior undignified and unmanly. The point seems to be that if one cannot exercise proper domination over oneself, how can one properly rule over another?

Still, Plutarch also admits to a competing perspective. Apparently there are "many" for whom the drive and ferocity produced by anger indicate "activity," "boldness," "force of character," "firmness of resolution," even "hatred of evil" (*Mor.* 456f). In this view, rather than threatening one's masculinity, anger actually displays it. As Brakke puts it:

> Because anger motivated a man to action in righting wrongs to himself and others, because its opposite appeared to be passivity in the face of challenges from other males, because—to put it simply—it raised the body's temperature, anger appeared to be a characteristic of masculinity, a sign that a man was indeed a manly man. (26)

On the possibility of "proper anger," Brakke cites Basil, the fourth-century bishop who speaks of the use of anger that is linked to "hatred of sin." That such anger aids the cause of masculinity is clear in Basil's description of its effects. "If the soul should become enervated from pleasure," he argues, "anger hardens it as with a tincture of iron and restores it from a most weak and flaccid state to strictness and vigor" (456).

Brakke suggests that the differing views of anger in philosophical literature from this period reflect an instance in which the Greco-Roman ideology of masculinity is at odds with itself. As we will see, the alternative view of anger will prove significant in the examination of the Johannine Jesus as the ideal man.

Apart from considering masculinity as the mastery of particular passions, we need to attend to the ways in which masculinity was woven into a whole range of status categories. Again, Brakke's work is useful, as he points to literature from this period that presents "a manliness that is not merely masculine rather than feminine, but also free rather than servile, governing rather than governed, Greek or Roman rather than barbarian" (3). In short, the higher societal status that one achieved, the more masculine one became and vice versa.

> Those who lack sufficient manliness are not only women, but also slaves, penetrated men, and persons not ethnically Greek. When, therefore, the elite male slipped in manly self-control, he could do so along several axes and so become not only more feminine, but also more servile, more passive, more barbarian, or any combination thereof. That is, he looked more fit to be ruled, than to rule. (Brakke: 6)[3]

As we examine the Fourth Gospel, attending to this matrix of masculinity will be important. The Gospel does not set out to discuss the manliness of Jesus. However, it is directly concerned with questions of Jesus' power and authority. It also contains rhetoric of slavery and freedom. In other words, the masculinity of Jesus can be read through a whole web of social relationships rather than simply through a contrast with femininity.

Here one brief example of how the relationship between status and masculinity is implicit in the Fourth Gospel may be helpful. The example can be found early in the presentation of John the Baptist. He is, of course, never "the Baptist" in this Gospel but rather the witness to Jesus. What is striking is that John witnesses to Jesus with what amounts to emascula-

---

3 Brakke cites evidence from Pseudo-Aristotle's *Physiognomonica*, which associates traits such as complexions that are too light (like women) or too dark (like Egyptians or Ethiopians) with cowardice. High-pitched voices (like women and cowardly animals) are problematic, especially since they indicate sexually passive men; hair growing down on the forehead instead of receding from it appears servile (6).

tion of himself. His first testimony identifies the respective rank of both of them. Jesus "ranks ahead" of John because he was before him (1:15, 30). John also places himself in a position of humility and submission—he is not worthy to untie Jesus' sandal, a task typically reserved for women and slaves (1:30). Later John will tell his disciples, "He must increase, but I must decrease" (3:25). John must move down the hierarchy, becoming less masculine compared to Jesus. As a result, Jesus' status is elevated. He emerges as the more masculine leader.

Returning to the exploration of masculinity in the ancient Mediterranean, we find that the equation of masculinity with status extended into the higher regions of the cosmos as well. Masculinity was understood to be more divine than femininity. Aristotle, for example, explains the existence of males and females by noting that whenever possible the two should be separate entities, since the male is better and more godlike (*theioteron*) than the female. This is the case because the male is associated with the generative process of creation, whereas the female merely provides the necessary material (*Gen. an.* 732a7–9).

Philo shares similar philosophical ideas, associating an increase in piety with a movement toward maleness. As he puts it, progress is indeed nothing else than giving up of the female genus by changing into the male, since the female class is maternal, passive, corporeal, and sense-perceptible, while the male is active, rational, incorporeal, and more akin to mind and thought (*QE* 1.7).[4]

This logic is peppered throughout his writings as Philo points to the inferiority of the female (e.g., *Spec.* 1.200–201, 3.178; *Fug.* 51; *QG* 1.25, 27, 37, 43, 45, 3.3; 4.15, 38). Even more telling, however, is Philo's depiction of Moses. Here we have a ready example of a "perfect man" who reaches the heights of divinity. A brief look at Philo's rather explicit construction of Moses' masculinity will prepare the way to examine the more implicit construction of the Johannine Jesus as the ideal man in the Fourth Gospel.

PHILO'S MOSES AS A MANLY MAN

As Philo begins his *Vita Mosis* he sets out to relate the story of Moses, "the greatest and most perfect among men" (*Mos.* 1.1). He then proceeds to paint a picture of Moses as a strong, handsome, intelligent, man who

---

4 Note the similar formulation of Jesus in the *Gospel of Thomas:* "I myself will lead [Mary] in order to make her male, so that she too may become a living spirit resembling you males. For every woman who will make herself male will enter the kingdom of heaven" (logion 114; J. M. Robinson 1988: 138).

early on demonstrated extraordinary control of his passions. From the time of his adolescence, Moses "tamed and assuaged and reduced [his passions] to mildness; and if they did but gently stir or flutter he provided from them heavier chastisement than any rebuke of words could give" (*Mos.* 1.26).

Philo does not detail what form this chastisement takes—we are left to our imaginations. He does indicate that Moses not only tames his passions but also manages to forget all about the pleasures of sex. It only enters Moses' mind in the context of the "lawful begetting of children" (*Mos.* 1.28). But most telling is the reaction of his associates. Philo reports that on account of such behavior, those who knew Moses speculated as to "whether [his mind] was human or divine or a mixture of both so utterly unlike was it to the majority, soaring above them and exalted to a greater height" (*Mos.* 1.27). Here we find one of the key determinants for masculinity, control over the passions, leading to speculation about divinity.

Philo also depicts Moses as having the knowledge of what makes a man and encouraging others on this course. Thus he tells the enslaved Israelites to "bear their condition bravely" and to "display a manly spirit" (*Mos.* 1.40). In contrast, Moses chastises ill-mannered shepherds who try to steal water from young girls as "masses of long hair and lumps of flesh, not men … who go daintily like girls." As Moses continues to berate the bully shepherds, they become submissive and do his bidding (*Mos.* 1.51–57).

Finally, as a reward for Moses' consistently high performance, Philo states that God gave Moses "the greatest and most perfect wealth" (*Mos.* 1.155). This Philo describes as "the wealth of the whole earth and sea and rivers, and of all the other elements and the combinations which they form" (*Mos.* 1.154–155). Moses was made a "partner" in God's possessions and even more "was named god and king of the whole nation, and entered we are told, into the darkness where God was" (*Mos.* 1.158). According to Philo, Moses has set before the reader, "in himself and in his life displayed for all to see … a piece of work beautiful and godlike, a model for those who are willing to copy it" (*Mos.* 1.158). Still, Philo also implies that while copying such a godlike life is ideal, it is far from possible for most human beings. That is, he quickly adds the caveat that one should at least strive to imprint the image on one's soul or have an unflinching desire to attain such a level of virtue (*Mos.* 1.158).

Thus, with the example of Philo's Moses, we move from a depiction of ideal masculinity to the "reward" of divinity. With the Johannine Jesus, the situation is different. The assumption from the beginning is that Jesus is divine. Indeed, as is often noted, the Johannine Jesus is among the most godlike presentations of Jesus in the New Testament. But if divinity goes hand in hand with masculinity, as Philo and his contemporaries indicate, then one would expect that Jesus is also depicted as the ideal man. This, I will argue, is what we find with the Johannine Jesus. In what follows, I examine elements in the narrative that point to Jesus' exemplary masculinity. Of course, in many instances, the case could be made that my illustrations point to Jesus' divinity. This is just the point. I mean to suggest that the very qualities that make Jesus appear to be "true god" are closely related to those qualities that matched the ancient world's definition of the ideal man.

WHAT MAKES THE JOHANNINE JESUS A MAN?

Jesus As Son of God

We can begin with the most straightforward foregrounding of Jesus' masculinity. As is frequently observed, no other Gospel is so permeated with references to the Father-Son relationship of Jesus with God. This Gospel uses "Father" as a referent to God some 118 times, compared to four times in Mark, forty-four in Matthew, and twenty in Luke. Similarly, the Fourth Gospel uses "the Son" as a reference to Jesus nineteen times, compared to one instance in Mark (13:32) and its parallel in Matthew (24:36). Matthew 11:27 and Luke 10:22 also refer to Jesus as "the Son" in language much like the Fourth Gospel, hence this Q saying's identification as a "Johannine logion."[5] The frequent occurrences of this father and son language (not to mention the masculine leader titles such as King of Israel, Messiah, or rabbi) provide a continual reminder of the masculinity of both God and Jesus.

Contemporary perspectives on the Gospel typically treat this language as metaphorical: the relationship between Jesus and God is *like* that of father and son. However, drawing on parallels between the prologue and Aristotle's account of human reproduction (*epigenesis*), Adele Reinhartz raises the possibility that the Gospel's father-son terminology could well bear a more literal meaning (1999). The opening words of the Gospel, *en archē*, echo Aristotle's notion of "first principle" of generation. The term accompanies the *logos*, which refers to both the rational purpose for the thing created and the source of movement that sets the creative process in motion. Thus, the role of the *logos* in the Fourth Gospel may recall "the role of the motive cause in Aristotelian embryology, that is, the

---

5 My count is only of occurrences of "the Son." I omit references to Son of Man, Son of God, or Son of David that run through the Synoptic tradition, since here I am interested in the father-son relationship.

principal mover in the process of generation" (Reinhartz 1999: 92). If so, the prologue may be closer to a birth narrative than has been recognized.

Added to this are the various uses of *ginomai* that link with Aristotelian thought, in particular *sarx egeneto* (1:14). Reinhartz suggests the phrase would better be translated "the Word was born flesh," so as not to miss the generative sense of the verb. Pointing also to the term *monogenēs*, She argues that, against the background of Aristotle's *epigenesis*, the prologue would communicate that "Jesus' uniqueness rests in the fact that he is the only one in the human or indeed divine realms who has come forth from, or been generated directly by, the divine seed" (1999: 94). Since, in Aristotle's view, ideal generation results in the perfectly formed male, understanding the prologue through this lens would accentuate the maleness of both God and Jesus (99).

Masculinity in Textual Absences

Once Jesus is begotten from the Father, there are further indications of Jesus' gender and social status, although some are suggested only implicitly through what is *not* stated. For example, aside from the mention of "flesh" and "glory," the Gospel provides no description whatsoever of Jesus' body. Unlike Moses, we do not know if he is handsome or not.[6] The text provides no clues as to the appearance of his eyebrows, eyelids, neck, complexion, hair, and the like that might support the presentation of a manly man. Still, this lack of description itself may be an indicator of gender and social status.

Montserrat's study of the male body in Roman Egypt notes such an absence of description for free men in papyri of the first three centuries C.E. (Montserrat 1996; 1998). Whereas the bodies of runaway slaves were typically described in specific detail (e.g., height, weight, hair color, complexion, facial hair, nature of walk), descriptions of free men were much more circumspect. Even when the papyri contain an order to arrest a free man (thereby removing his privileged status), only names and occupations are stated. While Monserrat acknowledges the practical aspect of detailed bodily descriptions of runaway slaves, he suggests that there may be a subtext to their inclusion. Much of the language used to describe the slaves is couched in passivity, subjection, and infantilization. A slave cannot be a "real man," and "the adjectives applied to his body serve both to set him physically apart and render him ridiculous" (Montserrat 1998: 158–59).

---

6 Though influenced by christological readings of Isaiah, early tradition suggests otherwise (Moore 1998b).

In contrast, the bodies of free men are rarely described, the two exceptions being when free men were victims of violence and when men served as witnesses to documents. In the latter case, the descriptions remain quite general compared to the detailed descriptions of slaves. In the first case, the emphasis is on the nature of the wounds that "rendered [the man] passive and vulnerable" (Montserrat 1998: 160). In light of this material evidence, the lack of description of Jesus' appearance and especially the lack of emphasis on his wounds is suggestive. If descriptions of a wounded body potentially meant a glimpse at a vulnerable or feminized Jesus, the Gospel provides the reader little opportunity for such a glimpse. Jesus' status as a free man is reinforced by the reticence of the passion narrative. Notably, where the narrative does attend to wounds, Jesus' *unbroken* legs are contrasted to the broken legs of the thieves beside him (19:32–33), and the wound that the already dead body of Jesus receives, a pierced side, pointedly does not indicate vulnerability but rather the saving power of Jesus even after his death (19:34–35; see R. E. Brown 1970: 950).

The Passions of Jesus

There are other ways that Jesus' masculinity is made apparent in the absences in the narrative. As mentioned above, a true man was one who could master his passions, especially lust and anger. In terms of lustful passion, there is no indication in any of the Gospel traditions of Jesus being tempted by sexual passion, so there seems little room to comment on his accomplishments in this area (Kazantzakis's *The Last Temptation of Christ* notwithstanding). Still, this complete silence on the subject of sexual desire may itself be a confirmation of Jesus' superior manliness, especially in the case of certain passages. Two scenes in particular seem designed to evoke expectation in the reader with respect to male/female intimacy, but in both instances the expectations remain unfulfilled.

The first such scene occurs between Jesus and the Samaritan woman (4:1–42). As is commonly recognized, this story appears to follow the pattern of a biblical betrothal scene. A man and a woman meet at a well, they talk, they draw water, they feast with the woman's family, and they become engaged. Isaac, Jacob, and Moses all meet their future wives in such a fashion (Gen 24:10–61; 29:1–20; Exod 2:15b–21). Thus, the scene in John 4—Jesus meeting a woman at a well—would naturally raise the expectation of an emerging relationship between this man and woman.[7]

---

7 For discussion of the betrothal type-scene, see Alter: 52. For the presence of this type-scene in John, see Duke; Eslinger; Reinhartz 1994.

However, even while Jesus skirts close to the matter of the woman's sexuality, in the end he speaks only of spiritual matters. No yielding to temptations of the flesh here. Similarly evocative allusions occur in John 20:1–2, 11–18, where Mary Magdalene's actions parallel the longing of the woman searching for her lover in Song of Songs (Cambre; Winsor). Still, Jesus sounds nothing like the male lover from the poem as he warns Mary not to touch him (20:17). In short, even when the narrative suggests passionate associations between Jesus and a woman, apparently Jesus is so far beyond such desires that they need not be addressed. There is no need to tell the reader of Jesus' self control, as in the case of Philo's Moses—the Johannine Jesus makes such control evident.

When it comes to anger, there are several places in the Gospel that indicate a Jesus who loses his temper. Filled with protective jealousy for his "Father's house" in 2:13–17, the Johannine Jesus wields a whip of cords on unsuspecting cows and sheep. He makes a big mess of coins and tables. Plutarch would likely flinch at this undignified display and loss of control, yet, as we have seen, Plutarch's view of the relationship between anger and masculinity was not the only view in the ancient world. Recalling the earlier discussion of anger in ancient Mediterranean culture, one could well imagine support for Jesus' angry displays as a sure sign of his masculinity. Here is Jesus—bold, active, hater of evil, exhibiting the appropriately righteous anger of a virtuous man.

The Johannine Jesus also gets angry or at least emotional at the death of his friend Lazarus (11:33–38), but this hardly comes close to the undignified loss of control that worried the philosophers. Notably, the place where one might expect at least a momentary loss of control, the place where the Synoptic Jesus agonizes over his impending death (Mark 14 and parallels), the Johannine Jesus instead notes almost matter-of-factly that his "soul is troubled" (12:27). Far from expressing anguish, this Jesus faces death with the strength and courage of a superhero. Indeed, in this equivalent to the Synoptic Gethsemane scene, Johannine Jesus nearly scoffs at the weakness of the Synoptic Jesus. "What shall I say—'Father, save me from this hour?' No, it is for this reason that I have come to this hour" (12:27). Instead of praying for deliverance, this Jesus states, "Father, glorify your name" (12:28).

Jesus in Control

The Johannine Jesus' strong self-assurance shades into control over others in the arrest scene (18:1–11). There he approaches the large cohort bent on arresting him, asking whom they seek. At their response, "Jesus of Nazareth," Jesus overpowers the soldiers and police with words alone. At his revelatory *egō eimi* they retreat and fall to the ground (18:5). Jesus then allows the arrest to proceed, scolding Peter for his attempt at armed resistance (18:10–12). Jesus has controlled his own arrest from beginning to end. In doing so, he shows himself to be the ruler rather than the ruled.

This is the case throughout the passion narrative. Jesus makes clear that he lays down his life of his own accord; no one takes his life from him (10:17–18). Later, he argues that there is no greater love than giving one's life for friends (15:16). In this way, the Johannine Jesus indicates that his will be a noble, voluntary death for the benefit of others. By Greco-Roman philosophical standards, such a death is the sign of a good and strong man (Seeley 1990). After orchestrating the final moments with a symbolic exchange with his mother and disciple, he announces, "It is finished," and gives up his spirit (19:26–30). Thus, Jesus has control even over his own death. Is it coincidental that the Johannine Jesus has proceeded in a manly fashion throughout his passion, demonstrating impeccable control over his passions?

Woven through the presentation of this Jesus-in-control is a discourse on power. From the very beginning of the Gospel, in a proleptic view of the benefits that come to Jesus' believers, Jesus is depicted as the dispenser of power. To those who believed in his name, "he gave power to become children of God" (1:12). The rest of the Gospel represents Jesus as one with the power to bestow such a gift. Unlike the synoptics, "power" in this Gospel is never expressed in terms of *dynamis*, that is, ability or demonstration of power. Instead, it is always *exousia*, indicating absolute, ruling, authoritative power—the kind of power reserved for men who have proved themselves as men.

Along this line, the Johannine Jesus claims an astounding range of authority, from that of executing judgement (5:27) to power over his own life and death (10:18) to power over the lives and deaths of others (5:21; 6:40, 11:1–44). Indeed, only in this Gospel does Jesus claim the power to raise himself from death.[8] If this were not impressive enough, added assurance of the totality of Jesus' power comes in the midst of the farewell discourse. There the Johannine Jesus assures his disciples that "the ruler of this world" has no power over him (14:30). In prayer, Jesus claims that the Father has given the Son "power over all flesh" (17:2). Later, when Pilate threatens Jesus with his authority over him, Jesus points out that Pilate has no authority over him on his own accord (19:11).

Considering the Gospel through the matrix of masculinity with its multiple oppositions also provides a different perspective on the rhetoric

---

8 For examples of the standard confession, "God raised him," see Matt 20:19; Acts 3:15; 4:10; 5:30; 1 Cor 6:14; Rom 4:24–25; 8:11; 10:9; 1 Pet 1:21.

of slavery and freedom. Notably, along with a promise of power to become children of God (1:12) comes the promise of knowledge of truth and attainment of freedom (8:31–32). As a free man in a ruling status, Jesus has the ability to make slaves free (8:34–36). This is, in fact, what happens to his disciples. Those who do Jesus' command are no longer slaves but beloved (*philoi*) of God (15:15). The implication is a rise in status for Jesus' followers. Not only are they no longer slaves, but the language of friendship evokes the philosophical rhetoric of intimacy between free men. In this way, the salvific benefits offered by the Johannine Jesus are in certain respects an offer for his followers to become more manly, that is, to enjoy the benefits that a truly free man would enjoy.

To be sure, even after the indication of this new status, there is still an assumption that the disciples remain slaves with respect to their master Jesus (15:20, cf. 13:16). However, this does not negate a rise in social status. If one is the slave of a person with high social status, one's own standing is also improved (D. B. Martin 1990: esp. xxii, 47–48, 56–57, 76–77, 132–33).

In sum, the Fourth Gospel presents Jesus as a quintessential man. He reveals no weakening to the passions that might undercut his manly deportment. Instead, Jesus proves himself through disciplined self-control throughout his ministry and in the face of suffering and death. He presents himself as a free man who offers the possibility of freedom to others. At the same time, he insists on his fundamental authority over others and has followers who readily submit themselves to him.

Still, this discussion has not yet attended to the places in the Gospel that evoke the figure of Sophia. As mentioned in the introduction, consideration of a masculine Christology in the Fourth Gospel demands attention to claims that the Johannine Jesus, as Wisdom incarnate, evokes a feminine dimension of the divine. With this in mind, we turn now to a discussion of the implications of this Wisdom imagery for the gender construction of Jesus.

A FEMININE DIMENSION OF JOHANNINE CHRISTOLOGY?

Today it is clear that the portrayal of the Johannine Jesus is heavily influenced by the Jewish wisdom traditions (R. E. Brown 1966: cxxii–cxxv; Dunn 1983; Willett; M. Scott). As one who saw this connection early on, Raymond Brown argues that the Fourth Evangelist sees in Jesus the "supreme example of divine Wisdom active in history, and indeed divine Wisdom itself" (1966: cxxiv). At the time this comment was made, the gender implications of the association between Wisdom and Jesus were a nonissue. The only attention Brown gives to gender identity is in a comment that Sophia is personified as a woman because of the feminine gender of *ḥokmâ* (1966: cxxii).

Others, however, have attached a great deal of importance to the feminine aspect of Wisdom and its implications for Johannine Christology. For example, Englesman argues the Fourth Gospel's presentation of Jesus produces "the most feminine of the Gospels" (199). Feminist theologian Elizabeth Johnson relies heavily on Wisdom imagery from the Fourth Gospel and elsewhere in the New Testament to find an alternative vision to the male God. Taking a step further, Martin Scott sees the Gospel as intentionally attending to the divine feminine. He argues:

> The point of John's Wisdom Christology is precisely that Jesus Sophia is not mere man, but rather the incarnation of both the male and the female expressions of the divine, albeit within the limitations of human flesh. (172)

In Scott's reading, one needs to imagine a gender-blending in the Johannine Jesus. "Jesus is a *man* who exhibits all the characteristic traits of the *woman* Sophia" (174).[9]

While also celebrating "divine Woman Wisdom," Schüssler Fiorenza makes quite a different case for the use of wisdom traditions in the Fourth Gospel. In her view, any feminine aspect of God in the Gospel has been marginalized and silenced by the male rhetoric of the Gospel. The Johannine Jesus has displaced Sophia.[10] As she puts it,

> By introducing the "father-son" language in the very beginning and using it throughout the Gospel, the whole book reinscribes the metaphorical grammatical masculinity of the expressions "logos" and "son" as congruent with the biological masculine sex of the historic person of Jesus of Nazareth. The Fourth Gospel thereby not only dissolves the tension between the grammatical feminine gender of Sophia and the "naturalized" gender of Jesus but also marginalizes and "silences" the traditions of G*d as represented by Divine Woman Wisdom. (1994: 153)

The point was made even earlier by Wayne Meeks, who notes that "in the Fourth Gospel there is no trace of the usual feminine Sophia; she has

---

9 Scott's own imagination appears reluctant to drift too far in this direction. In the end, it seems that he envisions not a gender blend but a gender split—Jesus' inherent maleness is preserved and his feminine side is reflected in (or projected on to?) the Gospel's female characters (250).

10 Schüssler Fiorenza draws here on Petersen, who, although not concerned with gender categories, nevertheless focuses on the way the Gospel's use of wisdom traditions displaces Sophia (which has already displaced Moses in Second Temple Jewish literature) in favor of Jesus (Petersen: 114–19).

become entirely the masculine Logos, the Son of Man" (1972: 72). Judith McKinlay takes a more nuanced approach but arrives at essentially the same place. She points out that the Gospel draws on multiple images to portray Jesus, so that the feminine Wisdom stands as one among many other masculine images. In her view, "Certainly the Wisdom parallels allow the feminine dimension to remain as part of the expression of the divine, but with that divinity expressed through a male Jesus, the feminine has now receded even further than before" (206; see also Schottroff: 85).

Completing the range of interpretations are Judith Lieu and Michael Willett (Newheart). Lieu argues that just because Wisdom is personified as woman in some instances does not mean that every reference to Wisdom has gender implications (228–29). At the far end from Englesman, Willett reads the Gospel's portrayal of Jesus as Wisdom as an affirmation of maleness, at least within the Johannine community. Although women in the community might have been attracted to leadership roles, ultimately, "Wisdom becoming flesh in the male Jesus, to whom a male disciple bore witness, would have reinforced the primary leadership positions in the community held by males" (147–48).

Such wide-ranging interpretations reflect the difficulty of the question. What are we to understand about the gender construction of the Johannine Jesus if, on the one hand, he is presented in full masculine glory and, on the other, he speaks the language of Sophia? One way of gaining clarity on the issue is to examine the ways that Wisdom is gendered in literature roughly contemporary to the Gospel (see Webster). Doing so reveals that the adoption of Wisdom imagery does not necessarily lead to a choice of either displacement or revelation of the feminine dimension of the divine. Instead, the literature reveals a certain fluidity of gender connotations around the figure of Wisdom. In other words, Wisdom is not consistently personified as feminine (though there are certainly instances of this) but can also be viewed in gender neutral and masculine ways as well.

In examining these various personifications, it may be best to begin with texts in which Sophia appears at her most erotically feminine. Ben Sira presents a Wisdom figure designed to arouse desire and pursuit from her followers. For example, Webster provocatively notes the progression of the seeker in 14:22–27 as he "penetrates [Sophia's] locative, visual, auditory space to climax in the midst of her" (67). The image then shifts to Sophia as mother and young bride, feeding her follower with bread and giving him water to drink (15:2–3). The theme of sustenance is repeated later in the book as Sophia urges those who desire to come and eat their fill of her fruits: "For the memory of me is sweeter than honey, and the possession of me sweeter than the honeycomb" (24:19–21).

Not only are these images erotically suggestive, but one can easily find similar themes associated with the Johannine Jesus. He is also sought and pursued (1:37; 6:2, 24); he also offers sustenance to his followers (4:14; 6:51–58). Yet even as these Wisdom themes are evoked, there are consistent indications that the Johannine Jesus is superior to this tradition. Whereas those who eat of Sophia will hunger and thirst for more (Sir 24:21–24), those who eat and drink of Jesus will be eternally satisfied (John 4:14; 6:58).

In fact, in each of the cases in which Jesus is designated as the true version of something—*true* bread, *true* light, and *true* vine (1:9; 6:32; 15:1)—one hears Sophia traditions in the background (bread, Sir 15:3; light, Wis 7:27, 29; vine, Sir 24:17). This seems to imply that the Sophia traditions as expressed apart from Jesus are false, perhaps because they are linked to Torah and/or Moses and not to Jesus (Petersen: 110-32). Indeed, it is also clearly the case that Jesus surpasses Moses in the Gospel as one who provides something greater than the manna from Moses (e.g., 6:31–34, 58). Given the first-century depiction of Moses presented in Philo, it is tempting also to understand Jesus as surpassing the ideal masculinity of Moses. In any case, it seems clear that the masculine figure of Jesus as *true* bread, light, and vine does imply superiority and does effect a displacement of the feminine personification of Wisdom, especially with respect to the sustaining functions of Wisdom.

However, it is also apparent that Wisdom is not personified as a woman in every instance, and we should attend to that as well. For instance, when we look to the Wisdom of Solomon we find mixed gender imagery. To be sure, Sophia is here also sought after and desired as a bride (6:12–14; 8:2). On the other hand, masculine imagery is also used in these personifications. Wisdom "penetrates all spirits" and "pervades and penetrates all things" (Wis 7:23–24). She "passes into holy souls" (7:27; Webster: 76). Moreover, Wisdom teaches self-control, prudence, justice, and courage—just those traits that make a man a man (8:7).

At the same time, this text has Wisdom imagery that seems to have no gender connotations. Wisdom is spoken of as a spirit (1:6-7; 9:17), a fashioner of all things (7:22), a breath of the power of God (7:25). Throughout these texts, Wisdom is still referred to with feminine pronouns, but there is no emphasis on erotic connotations, as in Ben Sira. This diversity of language suggests that Wisdom did not in all cases suggest a feminine image.

Perhaps most informative, however, is yet another example from Philo. In the case of his writings, the gender of Wisdom is relative. Indeed, his discussions of Wisdom provide a marvelous example of how fluid and functional gender categories could be in the ancient world. First, Philo has no qualms in arguing that Sophia is in principle masculine, since she has the generative power of masculinity. Still, Philo needs to explain why she has a feminine name. The answer, he argues, concerns her relative position to God. Philo explains,

All the virtues have women's titles, but powers and activities of perfect men. For that which comes after God, even if it were chiefest of all other things, occupies a second place, and therefore was termed feminine to express its contrast with the Maker of the universe, who is masculine, and its affinity to everything else. (*Fug.* 51–52)

This gender fluidity extends to discussions of Wisdom in relation to humanity. Wisdom can be woman or man, impregnator or impregnated, depending on her partner in procreation. While the texts are too numerous to examine here, the point is conveyed well by this summary:

Wisdom is made pregnant by God, and impregnates man while herself remaining a virgin. Feminine in regard to God, Wisdom becomes masculine with regard to man, who is made masculine by her, and begets, but who should not affirm his fatherhood of this offspring which is the work of God in him. The defilement of virtue in a soul is remedied by intercourse with wisdom, which restores the pristine condition of virginity to deflowered virtue. (Laporte: 118–19)

If we take this gender fluidity seriously, it provides a new way of understanding the gender construction of the Johannine Jesus. Perhaps what we find in the Fourth Gospel is a narrative expression of what Philo relates philosophically. With respect to the people who populate the Gospel, Jesus is certainly an exemplar of masculinity. Yet when it comes to his relationship with God the Father, he assumes a less masculine status. He is obedient, submissive, can do nothing on his own (John 5:19, 30; 6:38; 7:16; 12:49; 15:10). In other words, when compared to God, Jesus takes a less-masculine position in much the same way that John the Baptist did in relation to Jesus.

Thus, in the same way that Philo pictures Wisdom as relatively masculine and feminine, so is Jesus relatively masculine and feminine. For Philo, the feminine aspect of Wisdom is only that (s)he is second to God. The same could be said of the Johannine Jesus. In every way he fulfills the expectations of masculinity. Indeed, he is such a supreme example of masculinity that he takes on divine status. As *logos*, Jesus is masculinity at its active, generative, and spiritual best, at least in terms of the gender ideology of the ancient world. When compared to the ultimate male, God, the Johannine Jesus assumes a second, less-masculine position on the gender hierarchy.

CONCLUDING REFLECTIONS

Research on the construction of masculinity in the ancient Mediterranean world has made possible a more nuanced analysis of gender and

Christology in the Fourth Gospel. Much of the evidence suggests that Jesus is presented as the manliest of men. This presentation would be fully commensurate with his characterization as divine Word made flesh. Like Philo's Moses, whose ideal masculinity approaches the heights of divinity, so the deified Jesus is incarnate as the ideal man.

To be sure, this masculine Christology may be complicated by the links between Jesus and Sophia in the Gospel. One might read such links as indicators of a feminine dimension to the divine, but in the context of the first century, a feminine aspect in the presentation of Jesus would speak more to his position vis-à-vis God than to a positive expression of feminine qualities. In other words, highlighting Jesus' "feminine" side through the presence of Wisdom motifs would be to highlight the ways in which he is second to the ultimate male, God.

The same principle applies to the Gospel's depiction of female characters in general. Many have looked to the Gospel's positive portrayal of women as a resource for feminist reflection on leadership in the church (R. E. Brown 1975; Schneiders; M. Scott). Characters such as the Samaritan woman, Martha, and Mary Magdalene have been read as exemplars of faithful discipleship and leaders in the Johannine community, but this analysis suggests that in the end these characters take shape only in the broader framework of the Gospel's masculine Christology. Yes, there are strong women characters in the narrative. However, their consistently positive portrayal may be because as women they are already in the proper position with respect to the dominant male characters in the Gospel, Jesus and God. In other words, women characters pose no threat to the divine/human gender hierarchy. They are very clearly "women" with respect to Jesus and God in a way that is not so readily apparent with the male characters. Ironically, then, the prominence of women in the Gospel functions to preserve and accentuate the masculine images of Jesus and God.[11]

In the end, focusing on the construction of masculinity seems a bleak road to take for feminist interpretation of the Fourth Gospel. It becomes one more way of saying that the Bible, in this case the Fourth Gospel, is inherently infected by patriarchy. Yet communities, including women, have always found ways to read against the text in their reflections of the Christ or to read in ways that highlight the ultimate instability of the text. Indeed, just as in the ancient world sex/gender was a fluid and unstable category, feminist scholars can assume that it is so in the Gospel as well. The very fact that the Fourth Gospel works so hard to present a masculine Christology betrays the difficulty of sustaining such a project.

---

11 I develop this idea in Conway 2003.

Paul, the Invisible Man

David J. A. Clines
University of Sheffield

I know that most of the books about Paul are about his thought and that Paul as a human being is on the fringes, but you would have thought that someone somewhere would have found it interesting—I mean, *really* interesting for the understanding of his thought—that Paul is not just a Jew, a Pharisee, a scholar, a thinker, a traveller, an author—but also a *man*.

Being a man has never been the same as being a human being. It has always imposed certain obligations and scripts upon those brought up as men as well as offering them special male roles and privileges—without, of course, their being aware necessarily of their specificity as men or thinking there is anything unnatural, which is to say, constructed, about being men. Not surprisingly, those who have written about Paul, almost all of them men, have not usually given a moment's thought to the masculinity of Paul; presumably they have all been too busy writing books about Paul to think very much about their own masculinity either.

Paul therefore may be dubbed the invisible man. Time, then, for the outing of the bachelor from Tarsus, that Jewish, Mediterranean male who has imprinted himself and his values so deeply on Western culture and, probably, upon you—if you are anything like me. All the same, the full apostolic monty will offer us nothing more dramatic or titillating than what we all know but never speak about—Paul's male equipment, both for being and for thinking.

I have been studying over the last few years the ways masculinity is inscribed in the biblical texts and have looked in turn at David, Job, the psalmists, Moses, and Jesus.[1] What I have found to be characteristic of

---

1 See my "David the Man: The Construction of Masculinity in the Hebrew Bible" (Clines 1995a); "*Ecce Vir;* or, Gendering the Son of Man" (Clines 1998); "He-Prophets: Masculinity As a Problem for the Hebrew Prophets and their Interpreters" (Clines 2002). Other papers on the theme may be found in prepublication form at http://www.shef.ac.uk/uni/academic/A-C/biblst/DJACcurrres/Articles.html. They are "Dancing and Shining at Sinai:

masculinity in the relevant texts are these elements: strength, violence, powerful and persuasive speech, male bonding, and womanlessness. So that is what I am looking for in the depiction of Paul. There are, of course, other male characteristics, not least the honor/shame outlook so typical of Mediterranean cultures ancient and modern. But the elements I am focusing on are remarkably cross-cultural.

I need to say that I am not considering the historical personage Paul but the fictional character Paul whom I meet with in the letters written by him and ascribed to him and in the Acts narrative about him. I say "fictional," not to deny the historical existence of a Paul, but to underline the fact that everything we read about him, even in his authentic letters, is constructed, fictive. The harmonized Paul is the Paul that most Bible readers know of, in contradistinction from the "historical Paul" engineered by that tiny circle of Bible readers known as biblical scholars. In a paper such as this, I see no call to distinguish between *authentic* and *inauthentic* in the figuration of Paul, for that is the language of historical criticism, and I am engaged in another project: uncovering the masculinity of the fictional character Paul, whether the fiction is his own creating or someone else's.

1. Strength

It is fundamental for the traditional male to be strong. Weakness is not a desirable male trait in traditional societies; even in modern society lack of physical strength in a boy or a man is still deplored to a degree it is not in a girl or a woman.

For Paul, too, to be a man is to be strong. Says he, "Watch ye, stand fast in the faith, quit you like men, be strong" (*andrizesthe krataiousthe*; 1 Cor 16:13 KJV). For him, then, *andrizō* is *krateomai*; strength is definitional for males.[2] It is, to be sure, not Paul but Peter who speaks of women as "the weaker vessel" (*asthenesteron skeuos*; 1 Pet 3:7), but he would no doubt be in accord. He certainly knows about strong men entering houses by force and making slaves of "weak women, silly women, womenettes" (*gynaikaria*; *ek toutōn gar eisin hoi endynontes eis tas oikias kai aichmalōtizontes gynaikaria sesōreumena hamartiais, agomena epithymiais poikilais*; 2 Tim 3:6). For him, males are plainly stronger than females, and strength is a fundamentally important attribute.

Playing the Man in Exodus 32–34"; "Loingirding and Other Male Activities in the Book of Job"; "The Book of Psalms, Where Men Are Men: On the Gender of Hebrew Piety."

2 C. K. Barrett (1968: 393) remarks that *andrizō* "inculcates a virtue recognized in antiquity," as if he himself recognizes masculinity as a virtue.

Paul evidently sees himself as the ultimate Can Do male. To use his own language, he has "the strength for everything—through him who empowers me" (*panta ischyō en tō endynamounti me*; Phil 4:13 NAB).[3] It is not of much consequence whether he thinks he is innately strong or is empowered from without; anyone who says *panta ischyō* fancies himself as Superman, even if his physical appearance is unimpressive as Clark Kent (*hē de parousia tou sōmatos asthenēs*; 2 Cor 10:10).

In his work as an apostle, he pictures himself as a man of strength. He strives "with all the energy that [Christ] inspires within me in strength" (*kopiō, agōnizomenos kata tēn energeian autou tēn energoumenēn en emoi en dynamei*; Col 1:29). His preaching is accompanied with power: "by the power of signs and wonders, by the power of the Spirit" (*en dynamei sēmeiōn kai teratōn, en dynamei pneumatos hagiou*; Rom 15:19). His speech and message have been accompanied by demonstration of the Spirit (which is a token of force) and of power (*to kērygma mou ... en apodeixei pneumatos kai dynameōs*; 1 Cor 2:4).

When it comes to opposition from other preachers, it is a test of strength with them that Paul looks forward to, for it is by strength (however that is defined) that validity in apostleship is attested: "But I will come to you soon, if the Lord wills, and I will find out not the talk of these arrogant people but their power" (*eleusomai de tacheōs pros hymas, ean ho kyrios thelēsē, kai gnōsomai ou ton logon tōn pephysiōmenōn alla tēn dynamin*; 1 Cor 4:19).

As for his "brothers," as he calls his fellow-males in his churches, Paul prays, for example, that the Colossian brothers[4] may like himself have an access of power and that they may "be strengthened with all power, according to [Christ's] glorious might" (*en pasē dynamei dynamoumenoi kata to kratos tēs doxēs autou*; Col 1:11). Likewise the Ephesians will fulfill their mission if they are "strong in the Lord and in the strength of his might" (*endynamousthe en kyriō kai en tō kratei tēs ischyos autou*; Eph 6:10).

To be in the sphere of strength, according to Paul, whether it is divine strength infused internally or simply divine strength exercised

---

3 "The 'self-sufficiency' of the apostle is not after all the same as the *autarkeia* of the Stoic, even though he has used the Stoic word a moment before. The Stoic knew no power outside himself from which he might derive strength to bear the hardships of life.... He did not think of himself as a strong soul, who needs no outside support" (Beare: 153). Gordon D. Fee comments: "'Everything' in this case, of course, refers first of all to his living in 'want or plenty.' Paul finds Christ sufficient in times of bounty as well as in times of need.... Paul's point is that he has learned to live in either want or plenty through the enabling of Christ" (1995: 434–35), but we might well wonder what help Paul might require in times of plenty.

4 He is addressing "brothers" specifically in 1:2.

on one's behalf, is itself to be strong. Paul wants his Ephesians to recognize how they are on the receiving end of divine strength: he prays
that they will be enlightened so as to know "what is the immeasurable
greatness of his power for us who believe, according to the working of
his great power" (*ti to hyperballon megethos tēs dynameōs autou eis hēmas
tous pisteuontas kata tēn energeian tou kratous tēs ischyos autou;* Eph 1:19
NRSV).

There may seem to be something a little strange with all this talk of
strength in Paul, for he makes great play as well with "weakness," even
to the point of paradox, saying, for example: "Whenever [*hotan*] I am
weak, then am I strong" (*hotan gar asthenō, tote dynatos eimi;* 2 Cor 12:10).
Christiaan Beker says that this means that for Paul power "manifests
itself as weakness" (197–98),[5] but it seems rather that Paul is more interested in power, which he likes, than in weakness, which he does not
like—and he has thought of a way in which weakness can be seen as
power. Thus he does not say, "When I am strong, then am I *weak*," as if
weakness were the state he really wants to experience. The bottom line
is that whether weakness is only apparent, or weakness is a path to
strength, or weakness really *is* strength, what matters is *strength*.[6] If the
weakness of God is stronger than humans (*to asthenes tou theou ischy-
roteron tōn anthrōpōn;* 1 Cor 1:25), that is a paean of praise to strength,
not to weakness.

2. Violence

Being strong is not an end in itself. The purpose of being strong as a
man, and especially of being stronger than other men, is to be able to
overcome them and if need be kill them. The name for strength in action,
in traditional male terms, is violence. And the name for the violent action
of men in groups is war.

Paul is no warrior, but he is a traditional male, and he participates in
violence in the ways open to him, given the historical and social setting
supplied for him in texts by him and about him.

We notice first how Paul constructs his acolyte Timothy as a soldier.
This is not a female role, we hasten to add. Timothy must see himself as
"a good soldier of Christ Jesus," "wag[ing] the good warfare," not

---

5 Barrett glosses the sentence thus: "when I am weak (by human standards), then am I
strong (not in myself but in that *Christ's power rests on me*)" (1973: 317). Philo also uses a similar phrase (*Mos.* 1.69), *to asthenes hymōn dynamis estin,* but the sense is different.

6 I am a little surprised to find that the *mega*- root occurs only seventeen times in Paul,
and then without any distinctive usages, so far as I can see.

"entangled in civilian pursuits" and living with the sole aim of pleasing "the one who enlisted him" (*tautēn tēn parangelian paratithemai soi, teknon Timothee ... hina strateuē ... tēn kalēn strateian;* 1 Tim 1:18; *synkakopathēson hōs kalos stratiōtēs Christou Iēsou;* 2 Tim 2:3; *oudeis strateuomenos empleketai tais tou biou pragmateiais, hina tō stratologēsanti aresē;* 2 Tim 2:4). Quite what kind of violence Paul has in mind for Timothy to be engaged in we cannot tell. If it is the same image as in 2 Cor 10, the opponents of the Christian soldier are supernatural powers ("Though we live in the world we are not carrying on a worldly war, for the weapons of our warfare are not worldly but have divine power to destroy strongholds" (*en sarki gar peripatountes ou kata sarka strateuometha, ta gar hopla tēs strateias hēmōn ou sarkika alla dynata tō theō pros kathairesin ochyrōmatōn, logismous kathairountes;* 2 Cor 10:3-4).

Christian soldiers (all male, since female soldiers are hardly in view) appear elsewhere also: "Let us then cast off the works of darkness and put on the armor of light" (*apothōmetha oun ta erga tou skotous, endysōmetha de ta hopla tou phōtos;* Rom 13:12). Christian soldiers are armed "with the weapons of righteousness for the right hand and for the left" (*dia tōn hoplōn tēs dikaiosynēs tōn dexiōn kai aristerōn;* 2 Cor 6:7). They gird their loins, as only men do,[7] in preparation for battle and arm themselves with breastplate and helmet (*stēte oun perizōsamenoi tēn osphyn hymōn en alētheia, kai endysamenoi ton thōraka tēs dikaiosynēs;* Eph 6:14; *endysamenoi thōraka pisteōs kai agapēs kai perikephalaian eipidos sōtērias;* 1 Thess 5:8).

Curiously enough, though, fighting itself (*machomai, machē*) is a bad word for Paul; *machai* in 2 Tim 2:23 are quarrels, which Timothy must avoid, and likewise *machai nomikai,* quarrels over the law (Titus 3:9). Fighting (*machē*) is what Paul's opponents do, not an activity in which he engages (2 Cor 7:5). What takes the place of the *machē* in Paul is the *agōn,* the contest rather than the fight. Whether this is the athletic contest or the struggle of the martyr against wild beasts in the theater is not always easy to determine. In the one case, the opponents of the agonist are his competitors; in the other, they are envisaged as wild animals threatening his life. Either way, this is an important image of Paul's self-understanding as a male, since he sees himself as competing either for honor or for his life.

Sometimes the *agōn* is the athletic contest. In 1 Tim 6:12 ("Compete well for the faith. Lay hold of eternal life, to which you were called when you made the noble confession in the presence of many witnesses";

---

7 I have studied this language, of girding the loins, in an as yet unpublished paper, "Loingirding and Other Male Activities in the Book of Job" (available in prepublication form at http://www.shef.ac.uk/uni/academic/A-C/biblst/DJACcurrres/Articles.html).

agōnizou ton kalon agōna tēs pisteōs, epilabou tēs aiōniou zōēs, eis hēn eklēthēs, kai hōmologēsas tēn kalēn homologian enōpion pollōn martyrōn) and in 2 Tim 4:7 too ("I have competed well; I have finished the race; I have kept the faith"; *ton agōna ton kalon ēgōnismai, ton dromon teteleka, tēn pistin tetērēka*), it is evidently an athletic contest, as of course it is in 1 Cor 9:25, in which the athlete in the games is explicitly a role model for Paul ("Every athlete exercises discipline in every way. They do it to win a perishable crown, but we an imperishable one"; *pas de ho agōnizomenos panta enkrateuetai, ekeinoi men oun hina phtharton stephanon labōsin, hēmeis de aphtharton*).

Elsewhere, on the other hand, it is as if life itself is an *agōn*, a struggle against largely unnamed forces, which seem more animalistic or gladiatorial than merely competitive. So in Rom 15:30 ("I urge you, [brothers,] by our Lord Jesus Christ and by the love of the Spirit, to join me in the struggle by your prayers to God on my behalf" [NAB]; *Parakalō de hymas, adelphoi, dia tou kyriou hēmōn Iēsou Christou, kai dia tēs agapēs tou pneumatos, synagōnisasthai moi en tais proseuchais hyper emou pros ton theon*), Phil 1:30 ("Yours is the same struggle as you saw in me and now hear about me" [NAB]; *ton auton agōna echontes hoion eidete en emoi; kai nyn akouete en emoi*), Col 2:1 ("For I want you to know how great a struggle I am having for you and for those in Laodicea and all who have not seen me face to face" [NAB]; *thelō gar hymas eidenai hēlikon agōna echō hyper hymōn kai tōn en Laodikia, kai hosoi ouch heōrakasi to prosōpon mou en sarki*), and 1 Tim 4:10 ("For this we toil and struggle, because we have set our hope on the living God, who is the savior of all, especially of those who believe" [NAB]; *eis touto gar kopiōmen kai agōnizometha, hoti ēlpikamen epi theō zōnti, hos estin sōtēr pantōn anthrōpōn, malista pistōn*).

3. POWERFUL AND PERSUASIVE SPEECH

When I was studying masculinity in the David story, I came to realize that persuasive speech was in ancient Israel a typical mark of male behavior. I found it also in the depictions of Job and Jesus, and I shall not be surprised if it crops up again in Paul. What I will expect is that it will be a form of strength and thus an especially male characteristic.

You know already what key text I am tending toward. In 2 Corinthians Paul quotes his opponents as saying, "His letters are violent and strong, but his bodily presence is weak, and his speech of no account" (*hai epistolai men, phēsi, bareiai kai ischyrai, hē men parousia tou sōmatos asthenēs kai ho logos exouthenēmenos*; 2 Cor 10:10). We only have Paul's word for it, of course, but since in this sentence he plainly gives himself two other bad marks, perhaps he is representing his opponents correctly in describing his written words as "violent and strong."[8] The point is not that Paul is not a good public speaker—which is the matter that interests the commentators, C. K. Barrett even suggesting that Paul's weakness was his proneness, when speaking excitedly, to tie himself in grammatical knots (1973: 261). The point rather is that being persuasive and effective in speech is one of Paul's key values. He would like to be the opposite of a nothing (*exouthenēmenos*) in speaking.[9] It must be some consolation to him that in writing at least he is acknowledged as "strong" (*ischyros*) and "forceful" or "violent" (*barys*), not "weighty," as most English versions (NAB: "severe");[10] the term is used of wolves in Acts 20:29 and of wind, thunder, hail, the baying of dogs, and violent anger or hostility in other Greek literature (Schrenk: 1:556–57). If that is his letters, just imagine his e-mails.

Persuasion is a rather ambivalent project for Paul. While he is quite happy to acknowledge that he himself is persuaded of various things (Rom 8:38; 14:14; 15:14; 2 Cor 2:3; Phil 1:6; 2 Thess 3:4; 2 Tim 1:5, 12), he is very unhappy to accept that he might be in the persuasion business himself. "Who am I supposed to be trying to convince now? Men? God?," he asks in Gal 1:10 (*Arti gar anthrōpous peithō; ē ton theon...*). When he admits in 2 Cor 5:11 (*Eidotes oun ton phobon tou kyriou anthrōpous peithomen, theō de pephanerōmetha*), "Yes, of course I try to persuade people," we surely hear an overtone of some charge against him,[11] which he must weaken with the rider, "but only in such a way as I can answer for it to God." In Acts 26:28 Paul has a testimonial from Agrippa that he is persuading him to become a Christian (or whatever *en oligō me peitheis Christianon poiēsai* means), so perhaps the apostle doth protest too much that he is no persuader. He wants, nonetheless, to affirm that his speech has not been "meant to convince by persuasive words, but to demonstrate the convincing power of the Spirit" (*kai ho logos mou kai to kērygma mou ouk en*

---

8 "Whether Paul would have shared this estimation of his letters is problematical..., but he did expect the letters to be read, heeded and acted upon (1 Cor 14:37, 38; cf. Col 4:16; 1 Thess 5:27), though not to be blindly obeyed as an imperious *diktat* (Phil 3:15, 16)" (R. P. Martin: 312). One should certainly hope not! I too would never regard any letter I wrote expecting it to be "read, heeded and acted upon" as an "imperious *diktat*," but I would not be surprised if those receiving such a letter would think of it as just that. Just whose point of view is being represented here?

9 "Above all, Paul lacked *aretē* 'divine power' ... and *pneuma*, thought of as a dynamic and impressive force to convey powerfully the triumph and effectiveness of his message" (R. P. Martin: 312).

10 So too, for example, R. P. Martin: "weighty (i.e., impressive) and forceful" (311).

11 Bultmann (13) acutely observed that this *peithō* must be the word of Paul's opponents, for he himself would have used *parakaleō*, "exhort," as he does in 6:1.

peithois sophias logois, all' en apodeixei pneumatos kai dynameōs; 1 Cor 2:4).
Persuasive words seem to have something underhand about them in his
book, but what, we may ask, are words of power, which he approves of,
if they are not persuasive words? He is slippery-tongued, you are persuasive, I speak words of power. He does not mean that he hits people over
the head, but if he gets results, he has been persuasive.

"Proclaim the message," is his charge to Timothy, "press it home on
all occasions, convenient or inconvenient; use argument, appeal and
reproof" (2 Tim 4:2, Michael Grant's [21] translation of *kēryxon ton logon,
epistēthi eukairōs akairōs, elenxon, epitimēson, parakaleson*). That sounds
authentically Paul (even though, by the canons of historical criticism, it is
in an inauthentic epistle). *Eukairōs akairōs*—it is the motto of telesales personnel and apostles alike.

4. Male Bonding

Male bonding is a feature of male behavior that has been attested
throughout history but that has only recently been given a name.[12] Typical of such male friendship are a strong sense of loyalty, a dyadic
relationship with an exclusive tendency, a commitment to a common
cause, and a valuing of the friendship above all other relationships. In
such a male friendship there is not necessarily a strong emotional element; the bond may be more instrumental and functional than affective.

Paul has bonds with a lot of men. On a quick count, I find fifty-six
men mentioned by name in the letters[13] and just eleven women.[14] Paul is

---

12 The term seems to have been first used by Lionel Tiger, in his *Men in Groups*. See also
Cohen; Wolf, 1966, distinguishing emotional from instrumental friendship (10).

13 Achaicus (1 Cor 16:17), Alexander (2 Tim 4:14), Amplias (Rom 16:8), Andronicus
(Rom 16:7), Apelles (Rom 16:10), Apollos (1 Cor 16:12), Aquila (Rom 16:3), Archippus (Col
4:17), Aristarchus (Col 4:10), Aristobulus (Rom 16:10), Artemas (Titus 3:12), Asyncritus (Rom
16:14), Barnabas (Col 4:10), Carpus (2 Tim 4:13), Crescens (2 Tim 4:10), Demas (Col 4:14),
Demas (2 Tim 4:10), Epaenetus (Rom 16:5), Epaphras (Col 4:12), Epaphroditus (Phil 4:18),
Erastus (Rom 16:23), Erastus (2 Tim 4:20), Eubulus (2 Tim 4:21), Fortunatus (1 Cor 16:17),
Gaius (Rom 16:23), Hermas (Rom 16:14), Hermes (Rom 16:14), Herodion (Rom 16:11), Jason
(Rom 16:21), Jesus Justus (Col 4:11), Linus (2 Tim 4:21), Lucius (Rom 16:21), Luke (Col 4:14),
Mark (Col 4:10), Narcissus (Rom 16:11), Nereus (Rom 16:15), Olympas (Rom 16:15), Ones-
imus (Col 4:9), Onesiphorus (2 Tim 4:19), Patrobas (Rom 16:14), Peter (Gal 2:7), Philologus
(Rom 16:15), Phlegon (Rom 16:14), Pudens (2 Tim 4:21), Quartus (Rom 16:23), Rufus (Rom
16:13), Sosipater (Rom 16:21), Sosthenes (1 Cor 1:1), Stachys (Rom 16:9), Stephanas (1 Cor
1:16), Tertius (Rom 16:22), Titus (2 Tim 4:10), Trophimus (2 Tim 4:20), Tychicus (Col 4:7),
Urbane (Rom 16:9), Zenas (Titus 3:13).

14 Claudia (2 Tim 4:21), Euodia (Phil 4:2), Julia (Rom 16:15), Junia (Rom 16:7), Mary
(Rom 16:6), Nympha (Col 4:15), Phoebe (Rom 16:1), Priscilla (Rom 16:3), Syntyche (Phil 4:2),
Tryphena (Rom 16:12), Tryphosa (Rom 16:12).

obviously bonded with, in turn, Barnabas and Silas. But he is most strongly bonded with Timothy, whom he has "taken" and circumcised (by hand, it sounds like, *labōn perietemen auton*; Acts 16:3).[15] You have a special bond with a man who has personally circumcised you (when you are already an adult). Paul has a variety of affectionate terms for this young man with whom he is bonded; he calls him my fellow-worker (*ho synergos mou*; Rom 16:21), my beloved and faithful child (*Timotheon, hos estin mou teknon agapēton kai piston en kyriō*; 1 Cor 4:17), the brother (*ho adelphos*; 2 Cor 1:1; Col 1:1), my true child in the faith (*Timotheō gnēsiō teknō en pistei*; 1 Tim 1:2), son (*teknon Timothee*; 1 Tim 1:18), my beloved child (*Timotheō agapētō teknō*; 2 Tim 1:2).[16] It is as a son with a father that Timothy has served with Paul in the gospel (Phil 2:22).

Paul is homosocially related to these men, and there is, at least with Timothy, a marked emotional element in the relationship, at least from Paul's direction. He is full of advice and encouragement for the younger man, even to the extent of suggesting that he "drink no longer water" (*mēketi hydropotei, all' oinō oligō chrō dia ton stomachon kai tas pyknas sou astheneias*; 1 Tim 5:23 KJV) but take a little wine for his digestion's sake— and for his frequent "weaknesses," for we cannot have a fine young man of the masculine Pauline circle "weak," now, can we? At another moment Paul urges him, for example, to "let no one underrate you because you are young" (*Mēdeis sou tēs neotētos kataphroneitō*; 1 Tim 4:12 REB)—how will Timothy arrange that, we wonder? No problem, though, in knowing who he has in mind when he says, "Never be harsh with an older man; appeal to him as if he were your father" (*Presbyterō mē epiplēxēs, alla parakalei hōs patera*; 1 Tim 5:1 REB). All the same, there is remarkably little that is personal in 1 Timothy, since, as is frequent enough with male bonding, it is the common enterprise that almost completely absorbs Paul; and while he ends by urging Timothy to "keep safe what has been entrusted to you" (*tēn parathēkēn phylaxon*; 1 Tim 6:20 REB), he so far forgets himself as to sign off with "Grace to you all" (*Hē charis meth' hymōn*; 1 Tim 6:21), as if he were concluding an encyclical rather than a personal letter (cf. 1:2).

On the other hand, 2 Timothy is a lot more personal; here Paul tells Timothy he is missing him terribly (mentioning him in his prayers constantly day and night, to use the Pauline language, 2 Tim 1:3; *adialeipton*

---

15 I can find no comment on the significance of the apparently otiose participle *labōn* "having taken."

16 Here is an appreciation of the relationship between the two: "[I]n Lystra he renewed acquaintance with a young man whose career was henceforth to be interwoven with his own.... Timothy was plainly so attracted by Paul that he counted the world well lost for the sake of accompanying such as man as his aide-de-camp" (Bruce: 213).

echō tēn peri sou mneian en tais deēsesi mou, nyktos kai hēmeras) and longing
to see him again so as to make his happiness complete (*epipothōn se idein
... hina charas plērōthō*; 1:4). Naturally, he wants Tim to be "strong" (*Sy
oun, teknon mou, endynamou*; 2:1), like a soldier, an athlete, a farmer
(2:3–6), or any other muscular male occupation you can think of. Do your
best to join me soon, he presses him; I am all alone, and everyone has
deserted me (4:9–10), and I am thinking of you all the time. Paul is calling
in his investment in his young man, who, he is reassured to recall, has
"observed closely [his] teaching and manner of life, [his] resolution, [his]
faithfulness, patience, and spirit of love, and [his] fortitude under persecution and suffering" (*Sy de parēkolouthēsas mou tē didaskalia, tē agōgē, tē
prothesei, tē pistei, tē makrothymia, tē agapē, tē hypomonē, tois diōgmois, tois
pathēmasin*; 3:10–11)—and who is not a real man if he does not know how
to be loyal to his old buddy.

Paul's orientation to male bonding is not quite the same thing as
being against sex. That is a possibility that is contemplated by Michael
Grant, among others; he opines that "Paul's hostility to sex cannot be
entirely attributed to [his] belief in the imminence of the Second
Coming"(24). Quite so; we can be sure that if he had been interested in
sex, he would have found an excellent theological justification for it. It is
not so much that he is against it; rather, he finds it unnecessary, for he has
all he needs from his male friends.

5. THE WOMANLESS MAN

It is widely recognized that one of the concomitants of strong male
bonding is a relative minimizing of cross-sex relationships. The male
Paul, true to type, is everywhere surrounded by male friends; it is therefore not surprising that Paul gets on well without women. He has his
female friends, usually wealthy and high-ranking women, as far as we
can tell, since he is a bit of a snob, but he does not treat them as women.
Interestingly enough, in his vision of the ideal community there is neither male nor female: "There is neither Jew nor Greek, there is neither
slave nor free, there is neither male nor female; for you are all one (male
person)[17] in Christ Jesus" (*ouk eni Ioudaios oude Hellēn, ouk eni doulos oude
eleutheros, ouk eni arsen kai thēly: pantes gar hymeis heis este en Christō Iēsou*;
Gal 3:28). This is not such good news for women as is often thought, for
a doctrine of the equality of women can be a way of not recognizing

---

17 Donald Guthrie saw the point: "The full force of the masculine gender of *heis* (one)
should be retained, for the idea is not of a unified organization but of a unified personality"
[which is, inevitably, male] (1969: 116).

them as women (just as we are more than a little suspicious if someone says, I don't notice if a person is black).[18] "[A]n anti-sex attitude," says Hyam Maccoby, "can often lead to a doctrine of the equality of women, since the obliteration of sex also brings about the obliteration of sex differences, so that all human beings are regarded as belonging to a neuter sex" (200).

In Paul's construction of masculinity, a man is better off womanless. Marriage with a woman is a fetter, in which a man is bound: "Are you bound to a wife? Do not seek to be free" (*dedesai gynaiki? mē zētei lysin;* 1 Cor 7:27). Being unmarried is "looseness," "freedom" (*lysis*). He thinks it would be better if every man were like him on this very score, that is, womanless ("I wish that all were as I myself am"; *thelō de pantas anthrōpous einai hōs kai emauton;* 1 Cor 7:7). His advice to men is: "Are you free from a wife? Do not seek a wife" (*lelysai apo gynaikos; mē zētei gynaika;* 1 Cor 7:27). And those who are already with a woman would be better off living a womanless existence ("let those who have wives live as though they had none"; *Touto de phēmi, adelphoi, ho kairos synestalmenos estin: to loipon hina kai hoi echontes gynaikas hōs mē echontes ōsin;* 1 Cor 7:29). That is the slogan of a real man—of the most unreconstructed kind, I mean, of course: while using women, live as if they did not exist.

Paul will not however deny himself the right to a wife, the right to lead around (*periagō*) a sister-wife[19] ("Do we not have the right to be accompanied by a wife, as the other apostles and the brothers of the Lord and Cephas?"; *mē ouk echomen exousian adelphēn gynaika periagein, hōs kai hoi loipoi apostoloi kai hoi adelphoi tou kyriou kai Kēphas;* 1 Cor 9:5). For the freedom to deny himself a woman is a freedom he cherishes. It is not simply that he *happens* to be unmarried, never found Ms. Right. He wants to make a *principle* of it, to make such a decision out of his own free choice, for this being unmarried coheres closely with his construction of his own masculinity.

It is not, I should add, that Paul does not want children. In Timothy he has actually found a way of having a son without the burden (or

---

18 "He does not say that the Church should try to alter the civil status of women or slaves or other less privileged persons. Hoping, as he most probably did, that the Parousia would occur within a generation, he did not think it important to attempt a revision of social institutions" (Bligh: 328). Bligh quotes an interesting sentence from the well-known leader of the "social gospel" movement, W. Rauschenbusch, "Paul was a radical in theology, but a social conservative" (102).

19 Not many have followed Clement of Alexandria (*Strom.* 3.6. §53) in taking the term *adelphē gynē* as signifying he would have treated any wife as a sister, that is, would not have had a sexual relationship; but it is an interesting thought. See also Bauer: 94–102, noting that a rabbi would not have been able to travel around with a woman who was not his wife.

"fetter," as he would say) of having a wife. Forget parthenogenesis; pain-less male reproduction is the goal of a real man.

Conclusion

What all this adds up to is a claim that the Paul we meet in the New Testament is more of a man than we have been inclined to notice. His masculinity is pretty normal and, at least in the aspects I have been con-sidering, not particularly culturally conditioned. But it is quite palpable, and it permeates the characterization of him.

Perhaps I should make my own position clear. Just because Paul is male, indefeasibly and unmistakably male, it does not mean that there is something wrong with him. There are those of us in the world who are male, even if not entirely indefeasibly and unmistakably, and we do not intend to be wrongfooted on that account alone. So I would not like it to be thought I have said that because Paul is male he is somehow bad. What is bad is if people think Paul is human rather than male, that he speaks as a human being *simpliciter* and not in the name of masculinity.

But I need to say also that, for my part, just because something is male I do not necessarily approve of it. My response to the maleness of Paul ranges right across a spectrum: for example, the violence and domi-neering aspect of his behavior and speech I find distasteful, whereas his penchant for powerful and persuasive speech hardly troubles my con-science at all.

If Paul had been less of a man, and more of a human being, his writ-ings would have been very different—but also, I admit, they would probably not have sold as well. But he was a man, and we had better not forget it.

"The Disease of Effemination": The Charge of Effeminacy and the Verdict of God (Romans 1:18–2:16)

Diana M. Swancutt
Yale Divinity School

What shall we say of this insanity? ... not only are you [men] made into a woman, but you also cease to be a man; yet you are neither changed [fully] into that nature, nor do you retain the one you had. Rather, you become a betrayer of both.
John Chrysostom, *Homilies on Romans* 4.2.3

Romans scholars usually argue that a condemnation of homosexual intercourse as unnatural (1:26–27) clinches Paul's censure of all humanity for dishonoring God as the Creator of nature (1:18–2:16). But as this comment by Chrysostom shows, most ancients thought 1:26–27 condemned gender transgression, particularly effeminating intercourse that threatened to effect a sex-change in men, turning them, contrary to nature, into *androgynes* or, worse, *women*. This essay follows their lead, arguing that 1:26–27 censures gender-transgressive, gender-shifting sex. Further, it argues that in 1:18–2:16 the charge of gender-transgressive sex predominates in a political and philosophical censure of specific rivals to Paul's gospel in Rome, Stoicized Roman judges (2:1). Evidence for this reading derives from two sources: the ancient gender ideology elicited in 1:26–27, which touted the naturalness of masculine (i.e., penetrative) intercourse; and the Greco-Roman convention of the emasculated Stoic ruler, which permeates 1:18–2:16. Read against that double backdrop, 1:18–2:16 reads as an indictment of hypocritical Roman Stoics who touted natural living, proclaimed themselves perfect ruler-judges, and judged the behavior of others, all the while engaging in "unnatural," effeminizing sex. This stereotyped censure of the Stoic judges' poor judgment functions rhetorically to impugn their credibility as teachers and political leaders and, when compared with the just judgment of God, to eliminate them as Paul's rivals in Rome. At the time (ca. 54–58 C.E.), Stoicism was the most popular philosophy among the Roman elite, many Stoics served as

Roman magistrates, and Seneca guided Nero Caesar's governance of the empire. Thus, Paul's censure of Stoic judges for effeminacy was a powerful proof of the superiority of Paul's gospel even to the power of Rome. According to Paul, that judgment was in fact the verdict of God.

THE ARCHITECTURE OF A CENSURE, PART ONE:
GENDERING THE GRECO-ROMAN BODY/POLITIC

The Immateriality of Homosexuality to an Ancient Reading of Romans 1:26–27

Modern interpreters often assume that Rom 1 treats homosexual activity as the seminal *semeion* of a condemned humanity. As Joseph Fitzmyer states, "Homosexual behavior is the sign of human rebellion against God, an outward manifestation of the inward and spiritual rebellion. It illustrates human degradation and provides a vivid image of humanity's rejection of the sovereignty of God the creator" (276). Unfortunately, scholars' characterization of 1:26–27 as reproving "homosexual behavior" presumes the modern concept of homosexuality, and the influence of that concept on their reading of Rom 1 is so thoroughgoing that the inaugural censure of Paul's letter to the Romans (1:18–2:16) is rendered incomprehensible as a piece of ancient rhetoric. For Rom 1 to be read in its ancient context, homosexuality must be treated as immaterial and the language of homosexuality abandoned.

As scholars who study ancient constructions of gender know well, the reason is that neither heterosexuality nor homosexuality existed in the Greco-Roman world. Ancients lacked the concept of "sexuality," the modern, Western notion that humans possess a constitutional drive distinct from biological sex that orients them sexually, in binarized fashion, toward a person of the same or other sex (Halperin 1990a: 24–26). Ancients also lacked the scientific conceptual apparatus upon which the definition of sexuality depends: the ideas that two biological sexes exist; that biological sex is fixed and genetically based; and that sex is distinct from gender, which is socially based and changeable (Laqueur: 29–30, 61–62). Greeks and Romans, on the other hand, conceived of sex acts as merely one type of *gendered* sociopolitical activity. Hence, *gender expression* (for men, masculinity), not sexuality, was the central feature of identity called into question by, and maintained through, sexual activity. As David Halperin described over a decade ago:

> Before the scientific construction of "sexuality" . . . sex was a manifestation of personal status, a declaration of social identity.... sexual partners came in two significantly different kinds—not male and female but "active" and "passive," dominant and submissive. That is

why the currently fashionable distinction between homosexuality and heterosexuality ... had no meaning.... there were not, so far as they knew, two different kinds of "sexuality," two differently structured psychosexual states or modes of affective orientation corresponding to the sameness or difference of the anatomical sexes of the persons engaged in the sexual act. (1990a: 21, 32–33)

Sexuality, therefore, is not a universal characteristic of human life.[1] It is rather a modern, Western "cultural production ... represent[ing] the *appropriation* of the human body and of its erogenous zones by an ideological discourse" (Halperin 1990a: 25).

If the concept of sexuality did not exist in the ancient world, then Romans, as a first-century letter, could not have condemned homosexuality. Even New Testament scholars who deem Rom 1 directly relevant to modern debates about homosexuality generally acknowledge this point. As Richard Hays (200) put it, "the whole conception of 'sexual orientation' is an anachronism when applied to this text" (cf. Furnish: 52–83, esp. 66). Interpreters have consequently shifted away from portraying 1:26–27 as a description of "homosexuality" to that of "homosexual" or "same-sex *behavior*." This terminological shift has not solved the conceptual problem, however. Because scholarly interpretations usually retain two crucial features of the modern definition of "sexuality"—a central emphasis on the sex of one's object choice and the assumed existence of only two sexes—their treatments of 1:26–27 still presume the concept of sexual orientation. As a result, their comments about same-sex intercourse often slip into condemnations of homosexuality (D. B. Martin 1995b: 340). Note, for example, the linguistic shift from "homosexual behavior" to "homosexuality" in Hays's interpretation of Rom 1:18–32:

Modern commentators ... universally agree that the purpose of the passage as a whole is to proclaim that the "wrath of God" is now being revealed against all who do not acknowledge and honor God.... in Romans 1 Paul portrays homosexual behavior as a "sacrament" (so to speak) of the anti-religion of human beings who refuse to honor God as creator.... Thus Paul's choice of homosexuality as an illustration of human depravity is not merely random: it serves his rhetorical purposes by providing a vivid *image* of humanity's primal rejection of the

---

1 See Nussbaum (1990: 49; cited by D. B. Martin 1995b: 49): "[T]here was for the ancient Greeks no salient distinction corresponding to our own distinction between heterosexuality and homosexuality; no distinction, that is, of persons into two profoundly different kinds on the basis of the gender of the object they most deeply or most characteristically desire. Nor is there, indeed, anything precisely corresponding to our modern concept of 'sexuality.'" For additional bibliography, see D. B. Martin, 1995b: 340 n. 21.

sovereignty of God the creator.... [Paul] speaks out of a Hellenistic-Jewish cultural context in which homosexuality is regarded as an abomination. (187, 189, 191, 194)

Hays repeatedly describes Paul as censuring homosexuality despite asserting that Paul had no concept of it (cf. 200, 202–4, 210). As Dale Martin has said, such interpreters of 1:26–27 assume the constitutive, orientational character of homosexuality: they "believe that Paul is *referring* to homosexual desire, even if he is not actually *condemning* it" (1995b: 340).

This kind of conceptual slippage is problematic for an ancient reading of Romans not simply because scholars wrongly presume that we share with ancients a common conceptual category of activity called "homosexual behavior" (cf. Hays: 205, 210). Rather, the primary problem is that scholars' imposition of sexual orientation on the text leads them to read 1:26–27 backwards, interpreting 1:26 in light of 1:27, so that 1:26 becomes a reference to female homosexual intercourse and Rom 1:26–27 becomes a judgment of all human homosexual behavior. This modernization of 1:26–27 has, in turn, prevented scholars from seeing the ancient gender assumptions that governed Paul's larger argument in 1:18–2:16. As I will show, the women of 1:26 are censured because the "unnatural masculinity" of female sexual *activity* (rather than passivity; cf. Brooten: 216, 246) foregrounds the more important charge of male sexual and sociopolitical *effemination* that follows in 1:27.

In short, imposing the conceptual framework of homosexuality on 1:26–27 blinds moderns to a demonstrably more ancient reading of 1:18–2:16: that the charge of unnatural gender transgression *among men* is the rhetorical key to Paul's censure of both the idolatrous Gentiles of 1:18–32 and the hypocritical Gentile judges of 2:1–16.[2] Pelagius said of 2:1–16: "Judges and princes are being put on trial. By a natural process everyone pronounces a sentence that fits the crime and knows that justice deserves reward while injustice should be punished" (*PCR* 69). John Chrysostom interpreted the text likewise: "Paul says this with the rulers of the city in mind, because at that time they ruled the entire world. He was telling [the Romans] ... that when they pass sentence on someone they are passing sentence on themselves as well" (*NPNF*[1] 11:360). As the

---

2 For the argument that the judge of 2:1 is a boastful Gentile, see Stowers (31, 83–138). For the argument that the judge is a hypocritical Stoic and for the importance of that characterization to Paul's larger protreptic censure in 1:18–2:16, see Swancutt ("Sexy Stoics and the Rereading of Romans 1:18–2:16," forthcoming). This article builds on the philosophical rhetoric and stereotyping described in "Sexy Stoics" in order to offer a more developed, political interpretation of 1:18–2:16. For the argument that Romans addresses Gentiles, see also Nanos (14); Engberg-Pedersen (185); Swancutt (2001: 1–102).

patristic authors saw, the charge of unnatural sex in 1:26–27 functions to undercut the authority of the male political leadership in Rome, the "judges" of 2:1–3.

Passivity and Passion: Gendered Sex (Un)Made the Man

> *The greatest government is the ruling of the passions and the con-*
> *trol of the womb and things yet within it. For if reason does not*
> *permit a wise man to move even his finger randomly, as the Stoics*
> *assert, how much more ought the sexual part to be controlled by*
> *those in pursuit of wisdom?*
>   Clement of Alexandria, *Pedagogue* 2.10

To make this political reading of 1:18–2:16 plausible, we must first discover how the activities described in 1:26–27, especially the "same-sex intercourse" of 1:27, could have been conceived fundamentally as a gender error. Greek and Roman medical and philosophical writers provide an answer, for they defined "males" sociopolitically as naturally superior, sexually penetrative citizens. They also deemed a wide range of behaviors (e.g., pederasty, depilation, transvestitism, sexual receptivity) to be intimately related acts of weakness that could emasculate both men and society because they flowed from the same source, femininity. According to these writers, two interactive gender matrices characterized and controlled femininity: the hierarchical ordering of the cosmos and the regulation of desire.

The first of these ideological matrices, the Greco-Roman cosmic hierarchy, ranked humans within a vertically ordered spectrum of "natural" bodily and political assignments that embodied contemporary sociopolitical standards for "masculinity" and "femininity."[3] As examinations of medical texts have shown, ancients did not conceive of the people assigned to the ends of the spectrum as referring to two genetically differentiated sexes, male and female. Rather, ancients constructed the human physique on a one-body, multigendered model with the perfect body deemed "male/man."[4] Greek and Roman males/men were consequently described with cultural superlatives that reflected their

---

3 Laqueur: "What we take to be ideologically charged social constructions of gender ... were for Aristotle indubitable facts, 'natural' truths.... Social categories are themselves natural" (28–29).

4 Aristotle, *Gen. an.* 728a18–20; 737a25–35; 775a15. Laqueur (29) discusses medical texts from Aristotle to Soranus (second c. C.E.) and demonstrates their conception of the one "sex" body.

perfect "natural" state: physical and political strength, rationality, spirituality, superiority, activity, dryness, and penetration. Females/women, on the other hand, were said to embody humanity's negative qualities (physical and political weakness, irrationality, fleshliness, inferiority, passivity, wetness, and being penetrated), but not because they were the "opposite" biological sex.[5] Rather, because all bodies were thought to contain more- (masculine) and less-perfect (feminine) elements that required constant maintenance to produce the perfect male/masculine body, females/women and the other gendered beings (e.g., androgynes, *kinaidoi* [effeminates], and *tribades* [dominatrices][6]) were deemed differently imperfect versions of the male body, versions whose imperfections (e.g., breasts, fat, menstruation, weak sperm, inverted internal penises) were manifestations of their impaired physiological health (Laqueur: 25–62).[7] Thus, the Greco-Roman cosmic hierarchy conjoined biological sex with gender expression, and defined sex/gender sociopolitically as the natural, hierarchically-inscribed interrelation of masculinity or femininity (superior/inferior), societal status (more/less powerful), and sex role (penetrator/penetrated).[8]

The fundamentally sociopolitical character of sex/gender meant that its bearers both embodied and faced cultural risks. On the one hand, females' anomalous state as imperfect males meant that they were not only weak but also inherently dangerous to family and state. "Intimate with formlessness and unbounded in their alliance with the wet, the wild, and raw nature," they were "pollutable, polluted, and polluting in several ways at once" (A. Carson: 158–59). In other words, because females/women embodied the worst qualities of the cosmic gender hierarchy, they represented both the weaknesses of, and the dangers to, the good government of society. The cosmic hierarchy was dangerous for citizen-males, on the other hand, because they could lose their high status as its governors

---

5 Hellenistic Jews attributed this inferiority to their divine laws (e.g., Josephus, *C. Ap.* 2 §199).

6 See below for a discussion of these genders. Philo of Alexandria imagined a sixth gender, the "unnatural monsters" produced when women or men mated with animals, "whence possibly the Hippocentaurs and Chimeras and the like, forms of life hitherto unknown and with no existence outside mythology, will come into being" (*Spec.* 3.43–45).

7 Ancient physiognomists known to have conceived of women anatomically as men with imperfect, internal genitalia include Herophilus, Hippocrates, and Galen (see A. E. Hanson 1990: 309–38, esp. 390–91). For Hippocrates and Galen, who thought male and female seed commingled after sex, the constructed character of sex/gender meant that a baby's gender was not absolute at conception but depended on "which type of seed predominated or the temperature of the uterine quadrant in which it lodged" (A. E. Hanson 1990: 391).

8 On the Roman sex/class system, see Richlin (1993: 532, 533 n. 24).

(Winkler 1990a: 50; see also A. Hanson: 391; Stowers: 42–82). Since ancients did not conceive of gender as a stable personality characteristic independent of sexuality but as a spectrum of culturally assigned, mutable, and binarized acts, *maleness was an achieved state synonymous with rule.* The natural stability of maleness and society was therefore vulnerable at three points. By penetrating an unacceptable partner (a freeborn youth or another *vir* [*similes*]), a citizen-male could cause his sex-partner's effemination, thereby aiding the subversion of his superior male nature and the divine order it represented. Alternatively, by taking up feminine practices (feminine dress, hairstyles, hair length, cosmetics, receptive intercourse), a man could actually become more female, mutating physically into a *cinaedus* or androgyne. Finally, a woman could become androgynous by assuming masculine habits and/or acting as a *tribas*, a dominatrix who sought to penetrate boys, girls, men, or other women.[9]

The implication of this logic is that boundary-blurring sexual acts were deemed socially dangerous gender violations. The *tribas*, for example, was despised because the increased maleness wrought by her sexual domination of others threatened the stability of the societal-cosmic hierarchy (Laqueur: 53). Martial's *Epigr.* 7.67, 70 presumes this "common knowledge" when it presents Philaenis as the ultimate *tribas* ("a *tribas* of the very *tribades*") who, "quite fierce with the erection of a husband," buggered boys and battered eleven girls a day. As in other ancient portraits of *tribades*, Philaenis appears as a sexually aggressive pederast who penetrated multiple, and differently gendered, targets (cf. Ovid, *Trist.* 2.365; Plutarch, *Lyc.* 18.9; Shenute, *Vit. mon.* 21, 26). As other writers did of *tribades*, Martial also depicts Philaenis as a third-gendered being whose sexual exploits are linked to other masculine qualities, ranging from a penchant for wrestling (Brooten: 46), to penile growth (Laqueur: 53; Dover 1989: 60–68; Halperin 1990a: 166 n. 83), balding (Seneca, *Ep.* 95.20), the sexual pursuit of both women and men (ibid.), and the occasional need for cliterodectomies (to prevent penetration; Brooten: 25). Ancients such as Martial castigated *tribades* because their mannish sexual aggressiveness caused them to shift genders away from their natural, passive-female state, thereby destabilizing the cosmic hierarchy and the masculinist society it symbolized and sustained.[10]

---

9 Cf. Szesnat. In our post-Cartesian world, it is worth underscoring that ancients treated the mind as the highest aspect of the physical body, not as an element or entity distinct from the physical body (contra Brooten: 45). Hence, the masculinization or effemination of the body could include or be evidenced by the unnatural alteration of its highest aspect, the mind. Men could become foolish (weak, effeminate) and women, wiser (stronger, masculine).

10 Highlighting the puzzle tribadic intercourse presents to an ideology that assumed a penetrating penis, Brooten posits that *tribades* were women-loving women whose intercourse

Importantly, ancient moralists criticized male pederasty for the same reasons. Although they usually described pederasty as appropriately asymmetrical, marked by accepted sexual and sociopolitical power differentials between citizen-males and boys, critics sometimes denounced both the penetrated boys and their penetrators.[11] When they derogated the boy (*puer*) as a *mollis* ("soft" or "unmasculine"), their criticisms were not based on his having had sex with another male (in point of fact, the boy was not yet a "male/citizen," a *vir*). Rather, moralists worried that by assuming the feminine, receptive sex role habitually, a freeborn *puer* would grow to like passivity too much and would therefore fail to mature into a *vir*.[12] Philo of Alexandria assumes this ancient bit of common sense when he asserts, in *Spec.* 3.37–41, that by taking up gender-bending behaviors such as receptive sex, cosmetics, and hair-coiffing, the boy abandoned his male sex-nature and shifted genders, *becoming* an androgyne deserving death for the disgrace it brought on its person, home, country, and fellow humanity:

threatened society because it rendered "irrelevant the [normal ancient sociosexual] distinction between active and passive" (6; cf. 8–10, 17, 185). Brooten further posits that ancients responded to this threat by caricaturing one of the two women as becoming like a man, "that is, as having a [natural or crafted] physical organ wherewith to penetrate her female partner," or by classifying both partners equally as *tribades* "worthy of death" (6). Unfortunately, there is no evidence that female homoerotic intercourse rendered irrelevant the seminal ancient distinction between penetrator and penetrated, that women who had sex with other women called themselves *tribades* or *frictrices* (7), or that the title was applied only to such women. Rather, as Brooten rightly sees, ancient men uniformly described women who pursued sex with other women, *boys, girls, and men* in active/passive, masculine/feminine terms and called the problematic partner a "penetrator" (*fututor*) or "rubber" (*frictrix*). In short, all we know about *tribades* is that they were characterized as physically mannish and sexually aggressive toward a variety of sexual objects, and the reasons for their denunciation are similar to the womanish *cinaedi*, gender transgression (mannish sexual domination) and indulgence of desire. For a full critique of the view that the *tribas* was a "woman-loving woman" and an alternative explanation of the social history and functions of the term, see my essay-in-progress, "*Still* before Sexuality: The Personae of the Tribas and the Imperial Politics of Roman Masculinity."

11 Authors did display a general disgust for boy-prostitutes and for those who enslaved them. See 1 Tim 1:10.

12 See the texts cited by Richlin 1993: 537. Cf. also Plutarch, *Mor.* 10.751C, E, which refers to Plato's condemnation of the sex-role of the penetrated male as "contrary to nature" ("they allow themselves to be covered and mounted like cattle"). He was disparaged because his "gender-bending" behavior was evidence that he had abandoned his male superiority. As D. B. Martin puts it, "[Same-sex] penetration affronts nature due to its disruption of the male-female cosmic hierarchy.... What is unspoken but clearly presupposed is that it is perfectly 'natural' for women to be 'covered and mounted like cattle'" (1995b: 193).

Pederasty is now a matter of boasting not only to penetrators but also to the passives, who habituate themselves to endure the disease of effemination ... and leave no ember of their male sex-nature to smolder. Mark how conspicuously they braid and adorn the hair of their heads, and how they scrub and paint their faces with cosmetics and pigments and the like, and smother themselves with fragrant unguents (for of all such embellishments, used by all who deck themselves out to wear a comely appearance, fragrance is the most seductive); in fact their contrivance to transform, by scrupulous refinement, the male nature to the female does not raise a blush. These persons are rightly judged worthy of death by those who obey the law, which ordains that the androgyne who debased the currency of nature should perish unavenged, suffering not to live for a day or even an hour, as a disgrace to himself, his household, his homeland, and the whole of humanity (see also *Contempl.* 60–61; *Abr.* 135–136).

The pederast's major vice was his effemination of this future citizen-male: "He sees no harm in becoming a tutor and instructor in the grievous vices of unmanliness and effeminacy by prolonging the bloom of youth and emasculating the flower of their prime, which should rightly be trained to strength and robustness" (*Spec.* 3.37).[13] The condemnation of *puer* and pederast was spurred by male-citizens' fear of the "disease of effemination" and the loss of social status engendered when one "transform[ed] the male nature into the female."[14]

Writers cast similar aspersions on adult-passives, whom they called *kinaidoi* (Latin, *cinaedi*) or *androgynoi*. According to the lexicographer Pollux, the term *cinaedus* had a range of meanings similar to *malakos*, covering territory from generalized moral reproach to softness, sexual passivity, and prostitution. Generally treated as sexual deviants, *cinaedi* were overwhelmingly characterized by their effeminacy, the same characteristics they attributed to androgynes. Indeed, Pollux equated them (6.126–127), the second-century physiognomist Polemo described them identically,[15] and Quintilian told his pupils to avoid their mannerisms (mincing walk; shifty eyes; provocative glance; limp, upturned hands; thin voice; *Inst.* 11.3.76, 78–79, 69, 83, 126, 128–129; cf. also Seneca, *Ep.*

---

13 Pliny discusses natural substances (hyacinth root, ant eggs, lamb testicles) used to halt boy-prostitutes' maturation (21.170; 30.41; 30.132). Seneca also bemoans the state of the *puer* (*Ep.* 47.7).

14 Cf. Athenaeus, *Deipn.* 12.540F, 528D; Aristophanes, *Eccl.* 1058, and other texts cited by D. B. Martin (1995a: 117–36). See also Richlin (1993: 531) and A. E. Hanson (1990: 396–97). A slave, who was not a *vir* (his citizenship was not at issue), could be called a *puer* all his life because of his sexual vulnerability.

15 Gleason 1990: 389–415, esp. 395. According to Polemo, *cinaedi* were fleshy of hip, fluid of gate, fainthearted, weak kneed, and dry eyed.

52.12). Among the Roman Stoics, the *cinaedus* was even portrayed as depilating his beard—*the* sign of adulthood—and otherwise crafting his body to remove his *vir*ility (Gleason 1990: 399–402). As Maud Gleason notes, "Stoics liked to moralize about hair because it was a term in the symbolic language of masculinity that could be construed as not merely a conventional sign, but as a symbol established by Nature itself" (1990: 401). Thus, Musonius Rufus, Seneca, and Epictetus railed against coiffing and depilating since the presence and roughness of hair announced from afar, "I am a man. Approach me as such."[16] Influenced by Stoic thought, Dio Chrysostom and Clement of Alexandria also aligned this behavior with debauchees who "violated nature's laws" and engaged in "unnatural acts."[17] Attempting to approximate womankind so successfully that he was sometimes indistinguishable from an androgyne, the *cinaedus*, like the *puer* and the *tribas*, was defined socially by the destabilizing effects of his own gender deviance on the cosmic hierarchy.[18]

This sociopolitical definition of gender is further illuminated by the second ideological matrix that governed conceptions of intercourse, the regulation of desire. Greeks and Romans considered desire a common reservoir of pleasure and danger that, while morally neutral, could be indulged too much. Since the danger of pleasure was the weakness and lack of self-control inherent in women (Aristotle, *Eth. nic.* 7.1150b), overindulgence in sex made a man weak and womanish. Overly passionate behavior was therefore gender trouble that led easily to gender deviance. As philosophers knew, that gender deviance could extend even to the mind, the highest or ruling aspect of the body (D. B. Martin 1995a: 3–37). Seeking to live wisely, philosophers in particular gendered foolishness, or the lack of mental self-control, feminine. They consequently counseled students to moderate the passions by cultivating the

---

16 Musonius Rufus, frag. 21; *Diss.* 1.16.11; 3.1.26–27, 31; Seneca, *Ep.* 52.12; 95.21. Cf. also Athaeneus's report about Diogenes, who censures a man with a plucked chin by saying, "It cannot be, can it, that you fault nature because she made you a man instead of a woman?" (*Deipn.* 13.565B–C).

17 Dio Chrysostom, *Or.* 33.52, 60; Clement, *Paed.* 3.15.1–2, 19.1. See *Paed.* 3.3.19.1, in which Clement describes the beard as the "symbol of the stronger nature."

18 See Gleason 1990: 411. Cf. especially *Chaereas and Callirhoe* 1.4.9, the Pseudo-Aristotelian *Physiog.* 808a34, and Laertius, *Vit. Phil.* 6.54. These texts denounce effeminates who dainty themselves up in preparation for their pursuit of women (D. B. Martin 1995a: 126). Gleason (1990: 398) describes astrological alignments that explain how *cinaedi* might be born effeminate, but this hypothesis is exceptional and does not negate the general ancient assumption that boys and men remade themselves into *cinaedi* by means of their actions.

masculinity of mind (toughness, asceticism, and rationality) critical to the good government of the body (cf. also Epictetus, *Diss.* 3.24.31–37). As Stanley Stowers has said, "Life [was] war, and masculinity [had] to be achieved and constantly fought for" (45). The winning strategy in this battle with passion was an ethic of self-management called self-mastery (*enkrateia*),[19] and the goal was *sōphrosynē*, "moderation" or "self-restraint" in the use of sex.[20]

In the imperial period, Roman Stoics intent on governing both their bodies and the body politic *kata physin* ("according to nature") were perhaps best known of all the philosophers for seeking to stem emasculation through the self-mastery of the passions. To that end, Roman Stoics strove to extirpate desire (and its consequence, foolishness) by circumscribing natural sex to dispassionate procreativity (see Nussbaum 1987; 1994). Hence, although Stoic founder Zeno approved the communal sharing of wives and bade "men and women to wear the same dress,"[21] Musonius Rufus proclaimed procreative, married sex the only natural form of intercourse (R. B. Ward 1990: 281–89), and several Stoics characterized adultery as "contrary to nature."[22]

Interestingly, Roman Stoics' success at stemming desire through "natural" sex seems to have encouraged them to charge others, not only pederasts and *cinaedi* but also opponents, with effeminacy (Halperin 1990: 68). Believing themselves alone capable of self-rule, Stoics dismissed as "girlish fools" the masses who preferred hotter pursuits, such as pederasty, group trysts, and bestiality, to more mundane, procreative sex with their wives. As Dio Chrysostom said, the uncontrolled man abandoned as "utterly feminine" the natural sexual use of women for reproduction and, inflamed, turned to adultery, prostitution, and assaults on boys.[23] Seneca professionalized this complaint, condemning

---

19 For the link between manliness and philosophy, cf. Lucian, *The Eunuch* 12, where practicing philosophy is compared to penetration of a woman. To be a sage, you had to have the right parts and use them correctly.

20 Ancient writers did not treat the Aristotelian distinction between *sōphrosynē* and *enkrateia* as absolute. See 4 Macc 1:31, where the terms overlap in meaning. (For this reference I thank Brent Nongbri, a Yale graduate student currently working on a fascinating essay entitled, " 'There Is No Male and Female,' Only Male: Paul's Masculinization of Gentiles in Galatians.")

21 On chasing boys, cf. Diogenes Laertius, *Vit. Phil.* 7.17, 21. On Zeno's advocacy of communal marriages and transvestitism, 7.33, 131. Zeno was esteemed as most temperate, 7.27.

22 *Diss.* 2.4.10–11; Origen *Cels.* 7.63; *SVF* 1.58.11–15; Fr. 244. Panaetius also banned all references to genitals or sexual intercourse (Cicero, *On Duties* 1.104, 127).

23 *Oration* 7.133–136, 149, 151–152. Dio's emphasis on reproduction within marriage as the "normal [*kata physin*] intercourse and union between male and female" (133–136) sets the tone for the denunciation of lustful pursuits that follows.

the *voluptas* of Epicureans and repeatedly coupling it with the traits of an effeminate (e.g., *Vit. beat.* 7.3; 13.2–3; *Clem.* 4.2, 13; *Ben.* 4.2.1). Epictetus also castigated Epicureans, saying that according to nature the sage's duties were "citizenship, marriage, begetting children, reverence to God … to hold office, judge uprightly … [thus] no woman but your wife ought to look handsome to you, [and] no boy" (*Diss.* 3.7.26, 21). In other words, Stoics decried passionate sex as unnatural, proclaimed themselves the manliest citizen-judges, and judged the behavior of all others girlish by comparison. The sociopolitical fear of effemination had led Roman Stoics to hypermasculinize their ethics and to portray non-Stoics as foolish and immoderate effeminates.

Since Stoicism and Roman ideology were coupled under the Republic and early Empire (Swancutt 2001: 193–253), Stoic teaching on this matter influenced Roman politics, strengthening already-tough Roman standards for manliness and giving Roman politicians means to criticize others for effeminacy. The Stoic politician Scipio Africanus, for instance, won a reputation for great self-control, condemning the pederasty that reportedly increased among young Romans after the introduction of Greek culture to the city (Polybius, *Histories* 31.25.2). In 141 B.C.E., he even attacked the soldier P. Sulpicius Galus by charging that if he made himself up in front of a mirror, wore a woman's tunic, and plucked his eyebrows, he was most certainly a *cinaedus* (Gellius, *Noct. Att.* 6.12.5; see also Macrobius, *Sat.* 3.14.7). Lucilius repeated Scipio's hatred for *cinaedi*, charging Scipio's political opponent Appius Claudius Pulcher with being *pulcher* ("fine") and an *exoletus* (a pathic; Rudd: 216). Importantly, however, Velleius also decried the perceived degeneracy of Rome by decrying the luxury and effeminacy that Scipio's son Aemilianus had introduced there. Both the elder and younger Senecas agreed, roundly condemning freeborn Romans who welcomed the advances of their elders and charging a loss of imperial virility as the source of Rome's problems (Rudd: 219, 221; Seneca the Elder, *Contr.* 1, *praef.* 8; Seneca the Yonger, *Ep.* 114.22; *Nat.* 7.31.2–3). The Stoic satirist Persius did likewise, repeatedly accusing corrupt Romans of a loss of virility (*Sat.* 1.87–89, 103–104; 1.15–20, 32–35; 4.1–10). The implication is clear: effeminacy was a threat to empire that had to be eradicated lest the Romans be left as *cinaedi* servicing another man's imperial house.

Not without reason, then, did Clement of Alexandria, echoing the Stoics, teach Christians pursuing wisdom that "the greatest government [was] the ruling of the passions and the control of the womb" (*Paed.* 2.10). Through the ideological interaction of the cosmic hierarchy and the regulation of desire, elite Greeks and Romans constructed both intercourse and good government socially as the pursuit or abandonment of masculinity. Intercourse thereby unmade citizen-men who indulged in passion or passivity. "The actions of the mollis and the tribade were thus unnatural not because they violated natural heterosexuality but because they played out—literally embodied—radically, culturally unacceptable [gendered] reversals of power and prestige" (Laqueur: 53).[24] As Philo's comments about the "disease of effemination" demonstrate, Jews reacted as strongly as Gentiles to the cultural dangers of effemination (however much they insisted that Gentiles alone felt its effects).[25] In the imperial period, however, Roman Stoics were perhaps best known for their rigor in eradicating effeminacy by extirpating the passions, circumscribing natural sex to procreative intercourse, and by censuring others as *cinaedi*. They, and the Romans they influenced, knew and used to their political advantage the "natural truth" that pederasty, coiffing, depilating, and sexual passivity were gender transgressions that threatened societal stability with emasculation, and they battled hard the unnatural disease of effemination at work in the bodies of its bearers and the Roman society in which they lived.

It's a (Real) Man's World: God the Creator and the Impiety That Effeminates through Sex Contrary to Nature (Romans 1:26–27)

So, I argue, did Paul. Bent on entrapping the hypocritical Roman judges of Rom 2:1–16 in their self-righteous judgment of others, Paul first

---

24 Amy Richlin has offered the only substantive argument against this position. She insists, contra David Halperin and John Winkler, that homosexuals did exist in ancient Rome (1993: 525–28). According to Richlin, "it would really be fair to say that Suetonius describes Claudius as a 'heterosexual,' Galba as a 'homosexual,' Caesar and Augustus as having had 'homosexual' phases or episodes in their youth, and Nero as a no-holds-barred omnisexual Sadeian libertine" (532; cf. *Jul.* 52.3; *Aug.* 71.1; *Claud.* 33.2; *Ner.* 28–29; and *Gal.* 22). She also emphasizes the materiality of the *cinaedus* in ancient Rome and argues that *cinaedi* were passive homosexuals. Unfortunately, her detailed and interesting argument is riddled with conceptual difficulties. First, she equates passive homosexuality with homosexuality, using the terms interchangeably. (It is significant that moderns do not have a constitutional, psychologically, and physiologically demarcated sexuality called "passivity." Male-penetrator/female-penetrated is an ancient, not a modern, framework for sex.) Richlin's account also assumes the stability of biological sex and a two-sex dimorphic body, two decidedly modern concepts. At the same time, she ignores or downplays evidence that the *cinaedus* was not conceived of as a "homosexual," such as depictions of *cinaedi* who penetrate women (532–33 and n. 24), who are recognized as such by their nonsexual feminine activities, and whose overindulgence of desire is the source of their effemination. Finally, in her system, a *cinaedus* should not be equated with an androgyne; thus, she avoids evidence that he was. Richlin does not adequately recognize the overriding importance of gender and desire in the social definition of the *cinaedus*.

25 Boyarin (1995) and Olyan provide detailed evidence and arguments that Jews of the biblical, Second Temple, and early rabbinic periods interpreted Lev 18:22 and 20:13 on the gender model described above, rather than on "a system of sexual orientations defined by object choice" (Boyarin 1995: 335). On the Jewish charge that effeminacy and same-sex intercourse were uniquely Gentile gender transgressions, see Swancutt (forthcoming).

censures the Gentile masses for impiety (1:18–32),[26] and he presents the unnatural intercourse of 1:26–27 as the prime somatic evidence of their failure to recognize and worship God as the creator of nature. He seeks to prove that "those who forsook the author of nature could not keep the order of nature" (Pelagius *PCR* 67). To that end, Paul invokes regnant assumptions about the cosmic hierarchy and desire to accuse Gentile men of abandoning their natural gender—including their God-given sex role as dominators of women—by taking up a lusty and effeminating form of intercourse with men. Like the deformity said to result from this act (1:27c–d), the effect of this rhetoric is to signal somatically what Gentiles should have known naturally: the "order of nature" (the masculinist cosmic hierarchy) was in fact the creation of God, and any people fool enough to ignore *His* supremacy over it would be emasculated by their own actions.

Paul's rhetorical play on masculinity comes to the fore in 1:24–27 with the correlation of unnatural intercourse and impiety. There the false reasoning about nature that led Gentiles to foolishness and idolatry (1:23–25) facilitates women and men's free exercise of the passions in unnatural sex (1:26–27):

> Although they knew God they did not honor him as God.... they became futile in their reasonings and their senseless minds were darkened. Claiming to be wise they became fools and changed the glory of the imperishable God into an image resembling perishable man, birds, animals, and reptiles. Therefore God handed them over to the lusts of their hearts, into impurity that dishonors their bodies amongst themselves.... God handed them over to passions of dishonor.[27] Their women exchanged the natural use [of sex] for what is contrary to nature, and the men likewise gave up the natural use of the woman. Burning in their yearning for each other, men cultivated deformity [*aschēmosynē*] in men and received in their own persons the due penalty for their error.

According to patristic commentators, Paul linked impiety and unnatural sex through the repeated correlation between dishonor and deformity in 1:23–27. That is, God allowed Gentile fools to dishonor and degrade their

---

26 Patristic interpreters uniformly understood the men of 1:18–32 to be Gentiles. Cf. Irenaeus, *Haer.* 33.1; John Chrysostom, *Hom. Rom.* 3; Pelagius, *PCR* 66; Augustine, *Exp. prop. Rom.* 3; Ambrosiaster, *Com. Ep. Paul.* 81:47, 49; Gennadius of Constantinople, *Ep. Rom.* (*NTA* 15) 358.

27 The genitive is a genitive of apposition. Paul does not admit of passions that are honorable.

bodies through unnatural sex[28] because by refusing to honor him as the Creator of nature, they had first *changed* the majesty of God (*ēllaxan tēn doxan*, 1:23), degrading it to the status of mere idols in physical form.[29]

Modern commentators, on the other hand, suggest that Paul links unnatural sex to impiety by displaying the way homosexual intercourse *per se* contravened the Creator's plan for heterosexual complementarity (Hays: 191) or, in the case of "lesbians," the way same-sex intercourse challenged power differentials ancients thought naturally existed between women and men (Brooten).[30] To argue thus, scholars must first characterize 1:26 as a depiction of female same-sex intercourse. Significantly, however, Paul never names the women's sex-partners (a glaring omission in this highly structured piece of rhetoric).[31] Indeed, linguistic

---

28 The NEB captures the sense of "dishonor" here well by translating the phrase in 1:24, "the degradation of their bodies."

29 The importance of actually altering God's glory through their actions must not be overlooked in translation. The text does not say "they exchanged [*metēllaxan*] the glory of God ... for an image" but "they changed [*ēllaxan*] the glory of God into an image." For the role of this verse in the larger censure, see the discussion of 1:23 below in the section entitled, "Censuring the Roman Judge in 1:18–2:16: The Judgment of Living Contrary to Nature."

30 While the creation is inarguably a pivotal basis for the proofs lodged against the idolaters in Rom 1, and the actions in 1:26–27 functioned as the prime example of mindless idolatry, the narrative does not function as Hays claims. Ancients did not interpret Rom 1:18–32 as an exegesis of Gen 1–3 representing the "natural complementarity between women and men" as moderns understand it. Complementarity as Hays construes it, a "natural" compatibility between men and women that extends beyond procreation (the ancient view) into other realms such as work and social intercourse, is a modern concept born in nineteenth- and twentieth-century American discussions of women working outside the home. See Kessler-Harris; Rosenberg.

31 To argue that that 1:26 depicts female same-sex intercourse, scholars must read the adverb *homoiōs* ("likewise," "in the same way," 1:27a) as supplying the sex objects of 1:26 (e.g., Brooten: 249). In other words, they must read the text backwards, inferring from men's forsaking of "the natural use of women" that women likewise exchanged sex with men for sex with other women:

Rhetorical Focus of Modern Reading
(bold = supplied by us)

Subject		Object		Action
females	+	**females**	=	unnatural sex

"in the same way"

| males | + | males | = | unnatural sex |

clues in 1:26–27a suggest that Paul was far less interested in their identity than he was in depicting the inversion of natural sex roles in 1:26–27, sex roles in which men were active penetrators of passive women. Present but presented in inverted order is the gender pairing (woman-man) common to the cosmic hierarchy.[32] More importantly, Paul portrays the women of 1:26 as actively "exchanging" (*metēllaxan*) the natural use of intercourse for the unnatural (thereby embodying idolatry in their intercourse; cf. *hēllaxan*, 1:23), whereas the men of 1:27 passively "gave up [*aphentes*] the natural use of women."[33]

Linguistic evidence that the "unnatural" refers to sex-role inversion is supported by patristic readings of 1:26. To my knowledge, of the early interpreters of Romans, only Ambrosiaster explicitly identifies the sex partners of the women as other women.[34] Clement of Alexandria's *Paed.*

However, the gender of women's sex partners cannot be gleaned from *homoiōs*. Elsewhere in the Pauline letters, *homoiōs* occurs only three times, in 1 Cor 7:3–4, 22. In 1 Cor 7:3–4, it suggests that conjugal "rights" due the husband are also due the wife. But this use of *homoiōs* does not mean that *homoiōs* connotes same-sex intercourse in Rom 1:26–27. The most cursory concordance search of New Testament texts indicates that *homoiōs links actions without necessarily implying or determining the direct or indirect object of the verb.* In Mark 4:16, for example, *homoiōs* refers to two acts of sowing, but they occur in different places. In Luke 3:11, it refers to sharing, once of a coat, but then of food. In John 6:11 and 21:13, it connects distribution of loaves with that of fish. In 1 Cor 7:22 it links two exchanges of status position but does not thereby equate them. Finally, in 1 Pet 3:1, *homoiōs* connects a call to submission but demands different types of submission from slaves and wives. Moreover, in 3:7 *homoiōs* links entirely different actions; husbands should be considerate just as wives are submissive. These functions of *homoiōs* indicate that the important connection between Rom 1:26 and 27 is the action, the "exchange/forsaking of the natural use for what is contrary to nature." In other words, the Romans would have heard a parallel drawn between women and men who had "exchanged/given up the natural use of sex," but what women exchanged "the natural use" *for* is not clarified by *homoiōs*. Thus, 1:26 *lacks the critical data at the foundation of the modern reading of 1:26–27.*

32 Paul previously alluded to the Hellenistic cosmic hierarchy in 1 Cor 11, where he described the relationship of the cosmic gender hierarchy to God (see Corley and Torjesen).

33 See Brooten: "The active verb (*metēllaxan*) with a feminine subject is striking. The specific verbs for sexual intercourse are usually active when they refer to men and passive when they refer to women ... in the context of the widespread cultural view of women as sexually passive, for women actively to 'exchange natural intercourse for unnatural' stands out" (245–46). For a poignant example of the unnatural results of women's gender-bending sexual activity, cf. Plutarch, *Mor.* 12.997 2B: "just as with women who are insatiable in seeking pleasure, their lust tries everything, goes astray, and explores the gamut of profligacy until at last it ends in unspeakable practices [Empirius renders it, 'into manly practices,' *eis ta arrena*]; so too intemperance in eating passes beyond the necessary ends of nature and resorts to cruelty and lawlessness to give variety to appetite."

34 "Paul tells us that ... a woman lusts after another woman because God was angry at people for their idolatry.... For what is it to change the use of nature into a use which is contrary to nature if not to take away the former and adopt the latter, so that the same part of

2.10 is far more typical of patristic responses to 1:26. Displaying a total disinterest in the identity of the women's sex objects, Clement highlights the gender-transgressiveness and lustiness of women's sexual activity. He also lists several possible sex acts as "contrary to nature":

> It is surely impious for the natural [*kata physin*] designs to be irrationally perverted into customs that are not natural [*para physin*].... desire can alter the character of somebody already formed.... the point of this parable [concerning the excessive desire and sexual activity of the female hare] is to advise abstinence from excessive desire, mutual intercourse [*epallēlōn synousiōn*], relations with pregnant women, reversal of roles in intercourse [*allēlobasias*], corruption of boys, adultery, and lewdness.

Clement assumes that women who indulged desire in excess would act *para physin* in various types of intercourse ranging from adultery and sex while pregnant to "mutual intercourse" and a "reversal of sexual roles."[35] As John Boswell saw, Clement's emphasis on "mutual intercourse" and the "reversal of sex roles" reflects his discomfort with women who unnaturally assumed the masculine, penetrative role in sex, whether that penetration was of women or of men (Boswell: 358; contra Brooten: 331). The desire that caused gender-transgression could, as Clement notes, alter the character of women. Hence, Clement sought to emphasize that women like those in Rom 1:26 who engaged in unnatural sex both "harm[ed] themselves" and upset the "design of nature."[36] As Pelagius

---

the body should be used by each of the genders in a way for which it was not intended? Therefore if this is the part of the body which they think it is, how could they have changed the natural use of it if they had not had this use given them by nature?" (CSEL 81:51). The dearth of explicit references to women as the sex objects in Rom 1:26 indicates that a careful rereading of the patristic evidence presented by Brooten (303–62) is in order. The fathers most certainly discussed woman-woman sex (among a number of other gender-transgressive sexual activities, e.g., adultery, prostitution, exchange of sexual position), but they did not argue that woman-woman sex was the unique referent of 1:26. Brooten's account obscures this fact.

35 See also Augustine (*Nupt.* 20.35), who interprets 1:26 as referring to nonprocreative intercourse between women and men (Brooten: 353).

36 It is the treatment of *para physin* in passages such as *Paed.* 2.10 that finally convinces me that Brooten is incorrect in identifying Rom 1:26 as a reference to female homosexual sex. Her main argument, that "ancient sources depict sexual relations between women as unnatural" (250), works only if ancient sources *only* depicted sexual relations between women as unnatural. But the bottom line is that they do not (and when they do discuss same-sex intercourse, it is the psychic and/or physical manliness of one of the women that is deemed unnatural). Brooten does not discuss Clement's list at any length. She dismisses the relevance of Philo, who clearly says that sex with menstruants and nonprocreative sex are unnatural (248–52). She also fails to discuss Roman Stoic depictions of sex *para physin* (251 nn. 101, 103), which, like Clement, circumscribe natural sex to desire-free procreativity. If, as Clement did, we account for the standards of Stoics such as Musonius Rufus, Epictetus, and

and Chrysostom said, their gender transgression "turned everything on its head" (*PCR* 67; *NPNF*[1] 11:355–56).

In 1:24–27, the indulgence of the passions in women and men's inversion of "nature" only underscores this point. Verses 24–27 literally scream the language of their passion-in-excess, from "the lusts (*epithymia*, 1:24) of their hearts" to "passions of dishonor" (*pathē atimias*, 1:26) and men's "consumption in their burning" (*orexei*, 1:27) for each other. Given the convergence of the cosmic hierarchy and the governance of desire in ancients' maintenance of natural gender boundaries, we should expect that in 1:24–27 immoderately indulged passion would turn natural gender relations on their head.

This is exactly what happens in 1:27, the rhetorical center of the censure. After introducing the subject of gender reversal in 1:26b–27a with allusions to the gender hierarchy (woman-man) and inverted sex roles (women's active "exchange" and men's passive "giving up" of natural sex), the narrative moves quickly to highlight what was most important rhetorically, the actions of men "who gave up the natural use of women" for unnatural intercourse (1:27):

Initial Focus of Attention

Subject	Action	Object
females/women →	**exchange of natural use of sex for unnatural**	[unknown]
	likewise	
males/men →	**gave up the natural sexual use**	of women

↓ ↓

Main Focus of Attention

males/men	**consumed with burning working/producing unseemliness receiving in themselves**	for each other in men penalty for their error

---

Seneca, the *Romans* could have treated as unnatural *any* unmarried, nonprocreative sex—including women pursuing another woman's husband, women penetrating boys, men, girls or women, and the forms of "unnatural sex" Brooten lists and dismisses. Given that *homoiōs* does not specify the identity of the sex objects in 1:26, that ancients describe a variety of forms of sex involving women as unnatural, and that only one early patristic interpreter of Romans explicitly identified female same-sex intercourse as the subject of 1:26, naming the sex objects of the women in Rom 1:26 is probably a fruitless (and for Paul, at least, an unnecessary) exercise.

Since the phrase "the natural use of the woman" connoted the appropriately hierarchical penetration of a woman by a man (Brooten: 245, 250), the clause "giving up the natural use of the woman, the men were inflamed in their burning for each other" (1:27a–b) frames 1:27c–d as the inversion of the cosmic penetrator-penetrated gender paradigm by means of inordinately indulged passion (D. B. Martin 1995b: 339–49). The participial phrases of 1:27c–d confirm this framing, using the language of gender transgression to allude to the result of their behavior, effeminacy: "by working unseemliness [*tēn aschēmosynēn katergazomenoi*] in men, men [who gave up the natural use of women] received in themselves the penalty fitting for their error." Gender transgression inheres in the participial phrase *tēn aschēmosynēn katergazomenoi*, but typical translations of it obscure this effect. The RSV and NRSV render the Greek, "men committing shameless acts with men and receiving in their own persons the due penalty for their error," translating the singular *tēn aschēmosynēn* with the plural "shameless acts" to emphasize repetition. But if Paul had wished this effect, he could have used the plural *aschēmosynai* rather than the singular *aschēmosynē*.[37]

The functions of *aschēmosynē* in other ancient texts suggests an interestingly different reading of 1:27c–d. In addition to connoting the shame that controlled this honor-shame culture, *aschēmosynē* meant "deformity," "unseemliness," and "disgrace," and writers employed it to describe the unmanly weakness that accompanied passionate behavior and prohibited the pursuit of virtue. In the Old Greek scriptures, its connection to sex is clear in its normal function as a euphemism for genital nakedness and intercourse (cf. Exod 20:26; Lev 18:6–20; Rev 16:15). Philo, for example, interpreted Deut 23:14, where *aschēmosynē* referred to excrement, as applying to the "unruly desires" associated with food, drink, and sex that tested a man's self-control: "Let a shovel, that is, reason [*logos*], follow passion, preventing it from spreading abroad ... and bringing the shovel to bear you will cover your *tēn aschēmosynēn*" (Philo, *Leg.* 3.156–157). Philo assumed that God could only use the scriptures (*logos*) to educate men to do his will if they buried the *aschēmosynē* of passion. Plutarch likewise used the synonymous adjective *aischros* to describe the effeminizing results of unnatural indulgence in food:

> Intemperance in eating passes beyond the necessary ends of nature and results in cruelty and lawlessness to give variety to appetite [*orexis*]. For it is in their company that organs of sense are infected and won over and

---

37 For the singular as "shameful act," see Josephus, *Ant.* 16 §223. For the plural as shameless acts, see Philo, *Leg.* 2.66.

become licentious when they do not keep to natural standards.... From this our luxury and debauchery conceive a desire for shameful [*aischros*] caresses and effeminate titillations.... Just so intemperate intercourse follows a lawless meal, inharmonious music follows unseemly debauches, barbarous spectacles follow shameless songs and sounds. (*Mor.* 997 2B–C; cf. also Dio Chrysostom, *Or.* 71.6)

In short, the "unseemliness" of *aschēmosynē* alluded to the threat of effemination that rendered a man impotent to act virtuously and shamed him in others' eyes. When *aschēmosynē* as the "unseemliness/disgrace" of passion is paired in 1:27c with *katergazomenoi*, which emphasizes the effect wrought by work,[38] the phrase "men working unseemliness in men" connotes the cultivation of gender transgression that both shamed participants and effeminated their bodies.

Significantly, early interpreters of Rom 1 read verse 27 in precisely this way. First, they uniformly treated the sexual activity of *men* (1:27) as the rhetorical climax of Paul's censure. John Chrysostom, for example, frames his *Homily 4* commentary on 1:26–27 with the statement, "The passions in fact are all dishonorable ... but the worst of all is a mania for males." Chrysostom seems to assume that Paul's teaching on 1:26–27 is encapsulated in a denunciation of lustful sex between men. Origen similarly assumes the centrality of the men's actions in a comment on Paul's use of *paredōken* ("he handed over"): "This [1:26] is the third time that the apostle uses the phrase 'God gave them up' ... it is therefore better to take all three instances [of *paredōken*] together and regard them as a single cause for the abandonment *of men to their lusts*" (*CER* 1:156). Ambrosiaster offers the most complete picture of the rhetorical importance of the men:

Because the Gentiles had deified images and relics of things, dishonoring the Creator God, they were given over to illusions. They were handed over ["to their desires and the degradation of their bodies," 1:24] ... that they might willingly damage each other's bodies with abuse. For

---

38 *Katergazomai* meant to produce, cultivate, or do something. Of twenty-two occurrences of the verb in the New Testament, nineteen are Pauline. The majority of these occur in Romans: the first is 1:27, the last 15:16, and most of the remainder are in chapter 7. Paul used *katergazomai* with each of the three connotations: to produce, to cultivate, or to do. Hence, 1:27c could be interpreted as emphasizing the act itself, "men did/committed a shameless act." However, the presence of the article, the use of *aschēmosynē* as a euphemism for the weakness associated with indulgence in passion, the linkage of it with *katergazomai*, and the explicit language of result in the following participial phrase indicate that *katergazomai* is better understood as connoting the effect wrought by work—what is produced or cultivated through an act. Cf. esp. Rom 2:9 and 5:3–5, where *katergazomai* also meant "produce," emphasizing actions with negative and positive results, respectively.

even now there are men of this type who are said to dishonor each other's bodies.... It is clear that because they "changed the truth of God into a lie" they changed the natural use [of intercourse] into that use by which they were dishonored.... It must be said that they changed into another order. (CSEL 81:47, 49, 51, 53)

Despite recognizing the presence of women in 1:26, patristic interpreters treated the physical decay wrought by sex between *men* as the signal proof of Gentiles' punishment for damaging God's honor.

Ambrosiaster's allusion to the "changing of orders" points to early interpreters' second main point of agreement, that bodily effemination and a consequent loss of status as real men was God's penalty for Gentiles' prior assault on his honor. Patristic scholars from Clement of Alexandria (*Paed.* 2.10) and Chrysostom to Novatian and the authors of the *Physiologus* and *Epistle of Barnabas* agree: 1:27 applied to pederasts and sexual passives whose overly passionate intercourse made them "less than men" physically. According to the author of the *Physiologus*, "You must not therefore become like the hyena [who 'is a male-female'] taking first the male and then the female nature; these, he says, the holy Apostle reproached when he spoke of 'men with men doing what is degrading.'"[39] *The Epistle of Barnabas*, on which he may depend, argues similarly: "You should not eat the hyena so that you may not become an adulterer or seducer or like them. Why? Because this animal changes its gender annually and is one year a male and the next a female" (Boswell: 137–38). Of the "hare-type," which represents the pederast, Novatian goes even further, saying that such judgments refer to "men who made themselves women."[40] In an attempt to protect nature from a charge of inconsistency, Clement argues against these common positions while simultaneously revealing their popularity (*Paed.* 2.10):

Nature is never constrained to change, and that which is once formed cannot simply will to reverse itself wrongly, since desire is not natural. Desire can alter the character of something already formed, but it cannot remake its nature.... (Hence) it cannot be believed that the hyena ever changes its nature or that the same animal has at the same time both types of genitalia, those of the male and the female, as some have thought, telling of marvelous hermaphrodites and creating a whole new type—a third gender, the androgyne, in between a male and female.

---

[39] Boswell: 142. In the *Physiologus*, *allassein* refers to a change of sex (138–39 n. 5).

[40] Boswell: 141. The text of *De cibis Judaicis* (PL 3:957–58) reads, "Accusat deformatos in feminam viros."

They are certainly wrong not to take into account how devoted nature is to children, being mother and begetter of all things.[41]

Clement knows that his contemporaries treat gender-shifting to an androgynous state as a consequence of overly passionate sex. Confirming the reading of *Barnabas* and the *Physiologus,* he also defines androgyny as the physical condition of gender liminality (being male-female) or gender flux (shifting between male and female forms). The relevance of these assumptions about androgyny to Rom 1:27, particularly that of shape-shifting, is confirmed by the Naassenes. Reading the *aschēmosynē* of 1:27 as a reference to "formlessness," they argue that the intercourse of 1:27 shifted men's gender to an androgynous state.[42]

For early readers of Rom 1:26–27, therefore, it was the danger of lust-induced somatic change in men and the consequent destabilization of the cosmic gender hierarchy that explains the importance of "unnatural sex" in Paul's argument. Chrysostom states the matter clearly in *Homily* 4.1, 3:

> This [1:27a] is clear proof of the ultimate degree of corruption, when the genders are abandoned. Both he who was called to be a leader of the woman and she who was called to become a helpmate to the man now behave as enemies to one another.... what shall we say of this insanity [1:27], which is inexpressibly worse than fornication? ... Not only are you made [by it] into a woman, but you also cease to be a man. Yet neither are you changed [fully] into that nature nor do you retain the one you had. You become a betrayer of both.... Just to demonstrate my point, suppose someone came up to you and offered to change you from a man to a dog. Would you not try to get away from such a degenerate? Yet you have changed yourselves from men not into dogs but into a much more loathsome animal than this. A dog at least is useful, but a male prostitute is good for nothing ... for it is not the same thing to be changed into the nature of a woman as it is to become a woman while yet remaining a man or, rather, to be neither one nor the other.

Women and men who indulged the passions were thought to contravene the Creator's plan for the sex roles, to unnaturally embrace the sexual role

---

41 See Boswell (140, 356–57). The tension in Clement's protest against the possibility of sex-change becomes clear when he later decries "incomplete androgynous unions" as among the sexual acts that result from men's indulgence of passion and are prohibited by Rom 1.

42 Brooten: 338–43. According to Hippolytus, the Naassenes treated this as a good change. They thought androgyny presented the primal human condition, and they deemed the rejection of procreative sexual relations implied by Rom 1:27 as yielding them the reward of returning to this blessed "formless" state. On the masculinity of primitive androgyny, see D. B. Martin (1995a: 230–33) and D. R. MacDonald (1987: 98–101).

of the other (women became "leaders," men "helpmates"), and through their gender transgression to invert, or at the least badly trouble, the naturally hierarchical character of male-female gender relations. The women's sexual activity or "leadership" symbolized the abandonment of their natural passive sex role, thereby foregrounding the sexual and sociopolitical effemination wrought in the male antagonists of 1:27. Moreover, the men who gave up their high gender-status as cosmic governors and their God-given sex role as dominators of women found themselves in a physical "no man's land," their bodies morphing and their status falling until they were left with androgynous, shape-shifting bodies of less worth than a dog. The effemination wrought through their exchange of natural for unnatural sex roles is therefore the signal *semeion* or sign of their total lack of judgment. And this, of course, is the main point of 1:18–32. Paul's rhetorical play on unnatural sex-role inversion (1:26–27) vividly displays the physical consequences of the mindlessness that led Gentiles to degrade God's honor by refusing to worship him as the Creator of nature (1:21–23). The ultimate consequences of their effeminized judgment are of course as dire as their emasculation of God's *doxa*: according to God's just decree, they are "more and more reduced to idiocy," unmanning not only themselves but their relations with others (1:28–31) in the process (Ambrosiaster, CSEL 81:53).

The Architecture of a Censure, Part Two:
The *Topos* of the Hypocritical Stoic Ruler and the Critique of the Roman Body/Politic

For the reading of Rom 1:18–2:16, the question then becomes why and how Paul turns this censure of Gentile effeminacy on the hypocritical judges of 2:1–3. The reason, at least, is simple. As I have argued elsewhere, Paul's letter to the Romans is a protreptic speech that seeks, among other things, to demonstrate to his Roman audience the superiority of his gospel to all rivals (Stowers: 162; Swancutt 2001: 4 n. 4). Sent to the Romans in the height of the quinquennium of Nero (54–58 C.E.), which was widely lauded as the return of the golden age, Paul's letter logically begins with a censure of his chief cultural rival, a representative of *Romanitas* or the Roman way of life (Swancutt 2001: 4–7). Paul's judgment of the masses for impiety and unmanliness (1:18–32) is therefore rhetorically valuable because it can easily be turned on elite Romans who, concerned with the health of the empire, derided effeminacy in others while being vulnerable to the charge themselves.[43]

---

43 For the argument that the judge *cannot* be a Jew, but must be an elite, philosophic Gentile, see Swancutt (forthcoming). Several patristic authors—Origen, John Chrysostom,

The means by which Paul effects this censure is more complex, how-ever. Employing a rhetorical technique typical of protreptic, diatribal censure of and argument with stereotypically personified rivals, Paul criticizes Stoicized Roman judges stereotypically for hypocritically con-travening the Stoic *summum bonum*, life in accord with nature. The social logic behind this rhetorical move is that Stoicism had become the most popular philosophy among the Roman elite of the imperial period. As a result, many Stoics were Roman leaders, and Stoic ideals were inter-woven with Roman imperial ideology thoroughly enough to become a main thread in the fabric of Roman culture. During the quinquennium of Nero, the Stoic Seneca even served as tutor and chief counselor to Nero. In other words, Paul's Roman audience, some of whom actually served in the imperial household (Rom 16:10–11), could not help but be reminded daily of the political associations between Stoicism and *Romanitas* (Swan-cutt 2001: 204–30).

This sociopolitical situation explains why in 1:26–27 Paul charges the Gentile masses with unnatural, effeminate sex and why, as I will now show, Paul delivers a political and philosophical censure of Stoicized Roman judges in 1:18–2:16 by evoking a well-known Greco-Roman con-vention of the effeminated Stoic ruler. By indicting hypocritical Roman Stoics who touted natural living and judged others weak while them-selves engaging in unnatural sex, Paul undermines the credibility of the Romans as political leaders and of *Romanitas* as a rival to Paul's gospel.

The popularity of the stereotype of the hypocritical Stoic ruler, which was explicitly applied by and to Roman rulers, provides strong support for the argument that the judges of 2:1 refer to Stoicized Roman magis-trates. The primary element of the *topos* as expressed by non-Stoic satirists and moralists was that Stoics possessed a preposterous but unshakable belief in their own perfection. According to both Greek and Latin sources, Stoics asserted that, unlike the foolish masses, they were models of strength, consistency, and virtuosity. This consistent virtuosity meant that they alone were a living law and, thus, that they alone were perfect rulers or judges.[44] Satirists and enemies scoffed at these perceptions,

---

Ambrosiaster, Augustine, Pseudo-Constantius, and Prosper of Aquitaine—interpreted Rom 1 as addressing philosophers as fools and traitors to nature. Origen, *CER* 1:142, 156, 158; Chrysostom, *Ep. Rom.* 3 (*NPNF*¹ 11:354), 5 (11:360); Ambrosiaster, *Com. Ep. Paul.* (CSEL 81:43); Augustine, *Exp. Ep. Rom.* 3, *Civ.* 8.10; Pseudo-Constantius, *Frag. Paul* 25; Prosper of Aquitaine, *Grace and Free Will* 12.4 (FC 7:380). Origen even underscored the fact that the judgment of 2:1–8 addressed Gentile philosophers and others promoting heresies (*CER* 1:174, 182, 184, 186).

44 See Chryssipus (Plutarch, *Mor.* 9.1035C), Cicero (*Leg.* 1.6.18), Musonius Rufus, and Diogenes of Babylon, who said a Stoic should govern and judge since he alone was a living

reveling in Stoics' imperfections while repeating the conventions. For example, the Greek moralist Plutarch (45–120 C.E.) and the biographer Diogenes Laertius (early third century C.E.) said that the Stoic alone considered himself wise, manly, just, and self-controlled (Plutarch, *Mor.* 13.2 1034.7D; Diogenes Laertius, *Vit. Phil.* 7.92). Addressing the Stoic self-identification as rulers, the early Latin satirist Horace (65–8 B.C.E.) quipped: "the wise man is only surpassed by Jove, He is well off, respected, handsome, the free king above all kings. And above all being RIGHT in the head, He's always quite well … lest a cold keeps him in bed" (*Ep.* 1.1.106–108). In *Lives at Auction*, Lucian likewise sniped, "[In the Stoic] I see virtue itself, the most perfect of philosophies…. he is the only wise man, the only beautiful, just, manly man—a king, rhetor, wealthy man, lawgiver, and everything else there is" (*Vit. auct.* 20, 23). Quoting Menander acidly, Plutarch added, "If one has gotten virtue from the Stoa, one can ask, 'if there's anything you wish: all will be yours.'"[45]

Cicero, Laertius, and Dio Chrysostom likewise attributed to Stoics such as Chrysippus the notions of perfection and unique ability to rule, judge, or execute other public duties (*kathēkonta*).[46] Plutarch, on the other hand, cared less about which Stoic authored the notion than about its usefulness for charging Stoics with inconsistency:

> Zeno, his conciseness considered, wrote quite a bit, Cleanthes much, and Chrysippus a very great deal about government, ruling, being ruled, judging, and pleading cases; and yet in the career of none of them can there be found any military command or legislation or attendance in council or advocacy at the bar or military service. (*Mor.* 13.2 1033.2C)

---

law. Cf. also Plutarch, *Alex.* 329 A–B (*SVF* 1:262); Laertius, *Vit. Phil.* 2.7.87–89, 128; Pindar frag. 69 *On Law* (*SVF* 3:314, 1:537, lines 2, 24); Epictetus, *Diss.* 1.24.13; 3.24.42; Klassen; and Martens (55–67, esp. 64–66). On the necessity of being a good judge, see also Epictetus, *Diss.* 3.7.21, esp. 30–33. On kingship, see *Diss.* 3.22.34.

45 *Mor.* 13.2 1058. Of course, Plutarch thought this made Stoics into leeches, and he retorted that the only sources of income acceptable to them were gifts from kings and friends and, as a last resort, lecturing (1043).

46 On Stoic duties, see Laertius, *Vit. Phil.* 7.108–110. On judging and rule, see Cicero, *Fin.* 4.74; cf. also *SVF* 1, frag. 222. The assumption is also present in the discourses of Dio Chrysostom (40–120 C.E.) on kingship, particularly in *Or.* 1.9; 3.4–11 to Trajan. Formerly against Stoicism, particularly that of Musonius Rufus, Dio later embraced Stoic and other schools of thought, including the Stoic *topos* of the ideal king. Laertius, *Vit. Phil.* 7.122: "Moreover according to them not only are wise men [*sophoi*] free, they are also kings; kingship being irresponsible rule, which none but the wise can maintain. So Chrysippus in his treatise vindicates Zeno's use of terminology. For he holds that knowledge of good and evil is a necessary attribute of the ruler, and that no bad man is acquainted with this art. Similarly the wise and good alone are fit to be magistrates, judges, or orators, whereas among the bad there is not one so qualified. Furthermore the wise are infallible, not being liable to error."

As many as do enter government, however, are contradicting their own doctrines still more sharply, for in holding administrative and judicial offices, in acting as councilors and legislators, in meting out punishments and rewards they imply that they are taking part in the government of genuine states and that those really are councilors and judges who are at any time so designated by lot ... so when they take part in government they are inconsistent too. (*Mor.* 13.2 1033.3)

Well then, should the first object of our proceedings be the common and notorious notions which even they (Stoics) in easy-going admission of the absurdity themselves entitle paradoxes, their notions as to who alone are kings, and who alone are opulent and fair, and alone are citizens and judges...? (*Mor.* 13.2 1060B)

In short, Greek and Latin authors from the first century B.C.E. to the third century C.E. roundly charged Stoics with hypocrisy for asserting that they were perfect and uniquely qualified to rule, judge, and guide affairs of state.

They also criticized the basis of the commonplace, the Stoic tenet that the universe, or nature (*physis*), was the source of their ethics. Much as Stoics themselves had, Plutarch, Cicero, and Laertius said Stoics portrayed nature as permeated with *logos* or *pneuma* and described their own minds (*nous*) as singularly capable of apprehending its rationality. Thus Stoics alone truly lived "according to nature" (*kata physin*). As Laertius said, Stoic teachers taught that "virtue is the goal toward which nature guides us" and "living virtuously is equivalent to living in accordance with [nature]" (*Vit. Phil.* 7.87). Because the idea that the strong ruled over the weak was fundamental to the Greek concept of nature, Stoics' ability to be a "living law" and to think and live *kata physin* was the reason they thought they should rule over the masses.[47] According to critics, two other results followed from Stoic claims that their minds were attuned to nature: first, Stoics could rely on their mental reasonings (*syneidēsis, dialogismoi*) to give them the self-control (*autarcheia,*

---

[47] This notion crystallized only later in Cicero as a *nomos physeōs* (*lex natura* in *Rep.* 3.33), although early Stoics discussed a common law that existed by nature, was equivalent to *logos*, attributed to Zeus, and comprehended only by the sage. Although unlike early Stoics Cicero argued that proximate goods enabled men to become virtuous gradually, the function of "nature" and "natural law" in Cicero and the early Stoics were compatible, enabling later Stoics to assert that those who acted according to nature, right reason/*nous*, and their *syneidēsis* could live well and free themselves from troubling passions (*pathē*). Cf., e.g., Marcus Aurelius 7.31. Thus, attendance to nature made the Stoic a living law. On the strong ruling the weak as a guiding principle of nature, cf. Plato, *Gorg.* 483A7–484C3; Cicero, *Rep.* 3.23–33; Lactantius, *Inst.* 6.8.6–9.

sōphrosynē) they needed to avoid passions (*pathē, epithymia*).[48] Second, the passionate behavior Stoics used their natural reasoning to avoid was self-deception, an involuntary error (*planē*) of judgment.[49] Athenaeus assumed both *apatheia* and the importance of mind for right action when he applauded Celts for "stoical endurance" and cited the Stoic Posidonius as saying "other people cannot control themselves because of the weakness of their minds" (Athenaeus, *Deipn.* 4.160E, 6.263). As for *kata physin*, it is true that many philosophers talked about living naturally; Aristotle's *Protrepticus*, written in the fourth century (384–332) B.C.E., may be the earliest famous exhortation for humans to live in harmony with nature. However, Seneca did say, "our motto, as you know, is 'Live According to Nature'" (*Ep.* 5.4: "Nempe propositum nostrum est secundum naturam vivere."). His statement assumed that people associated this phrase with Stoics. His contemporaries Persius (34–62 C.E.) and Plutarch confirm the assertion (cf. also Laertius, *Vit. Phil.* 7.86–110; Athenaeus, *Deipn.* 7.233C; Clement of Alexandria, *Strom.* 2–3). Speaking about non-Stoics, the satirist Persius said that "the self-evident law of nature limits/the actions of incompetents and half-wits" (*Sat.* 5.98–99). Likewise, Plutarch remarked testily that "the common nature and the common reason of nature [must be] destiny and providence and Zeus, of this not even the Antipodes are unaware, for the Stoics keep harping on them everywhere."[50] Hence, criticisms of Stoics' proprietary claims to live and to rule others *kata physin* evidence a general awareness of the commonplace.

This criticism leads to the seminal component of the *topos*. Although satirists and moralists did not usually level this charge at other specific philosophical groups, they frequently denounced Stoics who espoused "natural" living but effeminized their boyfriends by means of shaving or sexual penetration or effeminized themselves by means of sexual passivity or transvestitism.[51] In the third and second centuries before the

---

48 On *nous* in Stoic thought and Rom 7, see Stowers (260–84); Epictetus, *Diss.* 1.20; 3.22.30–22. On Stoics as passionless wise men, cf. Laertius, *Vit. Phil.* 7.117.

49 On both error and passion, cf. Laertius *Vit. Phil.* 7.110–115.

50 *Mor.* 13.2 1050. Plutarch's repeated denunciations of Stoics for not thinking consistently about nature or not living *kata physin* consistently assume that Stoics were well known for the tenet. Cf. *Mor.* 13.2 1060.4C–6E on nature, 1069.A–E on benefit, 1071.B and 1072.B–E on the goal (*telos*) of philosophy, and 1073.A–D on love. I discuss *eros* (desire) below. Cf. also Laertius, *Vit. Phil.* 7.86–87, who says Zeno of Kition was the first to designate "life in agreement with nature" as the *telos* of the philosophical life.

51 Greek and Roman authors of the imperial period charged various individuals and groups (e.g., soldiers, statesmen, philosophers), but not particular schools of philosophy other than the Stoa, with effeminacy and/or sexual passivity. These barbs were generally

Common Era, the poets Cercidas and Hermeias and the biographer Antigonus of Carystus called Stoics "merchants of twaddle" and "verbiage-fakers" for having sex with boys (Cercidas, *Meliamb.* 5.5–15; 6.14–15; Athenaeus, *Deipn.* 13.563D–E [citing Hermeias] and 565D–F [citing Antigonus]). Athenaeus followed suit, charging Stoics with controverting nature through transvestitism and with requiring their boyfriends to shave their bodies in order to extend pederastic liaisons until their "boys" reached the extraordinarily advanced age of twenty-eight. "Your wise Zeno," he said, "[saw] the lives you would lead and your hypocritical profession … that you give the name of effeminate [*kinaidos*] to those who put on perfume or wore slightly dainty garments. You shouldn't then, when rigged up in that fashion … take in your train lover-lads with shaven chins and posteriors" (Athenaeus, *Deipn.* 13.564F, 605D [*para physin*]; see Halperin 1990a: 88, 181 n. 6).

Lucian and Plutarch repeat this commonplace in order to imply that Stoics inverted the appropriate (hierarchical) relationship between themselves and their students, making themselves passive recipients of their students' sexual advances and thereby corrupting their common pursuit of virtue. In *Vit. auct.* 24, Lucian assumed the convention of the sexually passive sage in his attack on Stoics who charged their students fees for their "educational" services:

> Buyer: Then we are to say the same of the fees that you get for your wisdom from young men, and obviously none but the scholar will get paid for his virtue?
>
> Stoic: Your understanding of the matter is correct. You see, I do not take pay on my own account, but for the sake of the giver himself: for since there are two classes of men, the *disbursive* and the *receptive*, I train myself to be receptive and my pupil to be disbursive.
>
> Buyer: On the contrary, the young man ought to be receptive and you, who alone are rich, disbursive!
>
> Stoic: You are joking, man. Look out that I don't shoot you with my indemonstrable syllogism.

---

used to poke fun at, embarrass, or humiliate the accused, thereby reducing their status in the eyes of others. "Philosophers" as a generic group also received such insults. On this subject, see Rudd (215–25). However, among first- and second-century philosophers, Stoics were uniquely repudiated as hypocrites for their effeminacy and sexual passivity (Martial, *Epigr.* 9.47, which targets individual philosophers of different schools [Democritus, Zeno, Plato, Pythagorus], is the exception that proves the rule). Stoics seemed to have inherited this dubious honor from Socrates and his ilk, who were regularly the butt of jokes in classical Athens. See Richlin (1993: 523–73, esp. 544).

Buyer: What have I to fear from that shaft?

Stoic: Perplexity and aphasia and a sprained intellect...

The inversion of power and sexual position between sage and student occurred even earlier in Plutarch's *Moralia*, which argued that sex between Stoic teachers and their students undercut Stoic claims to live "according to nature." The first passage alludes to the ugliness of the neophyte and contends that even though he tries to pass as a just king, the Stoic is really a foolish, effeminate youth:

> the sage of the Stoics, though yesterday he was most ugly and vicious, today all of a sudden has been transformed into virtue.... the Stoic love consorts with the ugliest and most unshapely and turns away when by wisdom these are transformed into shapeliness and beauty.... Among the Stoics the one who is most vicious in the morning, if so it chance to be, is in the afternoon most virtuous. Having fallen asleep demented and stupid and unjust and licentious, and even, by heaven, a slave and a drudge and a pauper, he gets up the very same day changed into a blessed and opulent king, sober and just and steadfast and undeluded by fancies. He has not sprouted a beard or the tokens of puberty in a body young and soft. But in a soul that is feeble and soft and unmanly and unstable has got perfect disposition, knowledge, free from fancy, and an unalterable habitude and this not by any previous abatement of his depravity but by having changed instantaneously into what may almost be called a kind of hero or spirit or god. (Plutarch, *Mor.* 13.2 1057.2E–1058.B)

In the second passage, Plutarch used the same language to claim that by extending sexual liaisons with students into adulthood, Stoic sages obliterated their claim to live naturally:

> Diadumenus: ... All members of the school are involved in the absurdity of the philosophical tenets of the Stoa, which are at odds with the common conceptions on the subject of love. For [the Stoic] position is that while the young are ugly, since they are base and stupid, and the sages are fair, none of these who are fair is either loved or worth loving. And this is not yet the awful part. They say further that, when the ugly have become fair, those who have been in love with them stop. Now, who recognizes love like this, which at the sight of [depravity] of soul together with depravity of body is kindled and sustained and at the birth in them of beauty together with prudence accompanied by justice and sobriety wastes away and is extinguished? Lovers like that, I think, do not differ at all from gnats, for they delight in scum and vinegar but palatable and fine wine they fly from and avoid....
>
> Comrade: Yes, for love, they say, is a kind of chase after a stripling who is undeveloped but naturally apt for virtue.

Diadumenus: Why then, my dear sir, are we now trying to do anything else but convict their system...? For if passion is not at issue, no one is trying to keep the zeal of sages about youths from being called a "chase" or a "friend-making"; but one ought to call "love" what all men and women understand and call by the name: "All of them hotly desired to be couched by her side in the bride bed." ... Yet, while casting their theory of morals off upon troubles like [*eros* (desire)], "twisted, unsound, and all circuitous," they belittle and disparage the rest of us as if they alone uphold nature and common experience. (*Mor.* 13.2 1073.A–D)

The subject of the passage is the inconsistency of the Stoic doctrine of *eros*, which most people assumed was desire for sex, but according to Plutarch and Diogenes Laertius (2.7.130), Stoics defined as "an impulse to make friends." However, of greatest interest to us is Plutarch's allusion to "ugly, stupid" youths who matured into "beautiful, wise" men while retaining their sex appeal to pederastic sages. Since the description is common to both passages, and since Athenaeus repeated the criticism of Stoics for effeminacy and unnatural sexual relations with maturing youths, these passages of the *Moralia* probably criticize Stoics by alluding to the confusion of appropriate sex roles between sages and their students. Like Lucian and Athenaeus, therefore, Plutarch assumed that the Stoic *desideratum* was a ruse. The Stoic could not live or rule *kata physin* if, through sexual penetration or the depilation of their body hair, he effeminated maturing students he instructed in natural living or if he allowed them to effeminate him by penetrating him.[52]

Significantly, the Roman satirists Martial (40–103 C.E.) and Juvenal (60–130 C.E.) also scourged Stoics for portraying themselves as manly Roman leaders when they were really *cinaedi*. In *Epigr.* 1.24, for example, Martial needles a lawyer named Decianus for appearing the stern-faced, patriotic Stoic while acting the sexual passive (cf. 1.8, 2.5; cf. Martial, *Epigr.* 2.36; 6.56; 7.58; 12.42). In *Epigr.* 1.96, a jurist named Maternus gets much the same treatment. As in 1.24, Maternus is never explicitly named a Stoic but is rather identified as one by his hypocritical "manly" behavior: walking about somberly attired and critical of others' gay apparel, he nevertheless loves effeminate colors and gazes longingly at stiff and strapping athletes. Juvenal brings these elements of the *topos* together even more fully in *Sat.* 2 (100–112 C.E.),[53] when he describes Rome as lying in ruins because of the unnatural behavior of Roman Stoic judges. Initially unidentified by Juvenal, these fools appear masculine—with hirsute

---

52 The same complex occurs in Athenaeus, *Deipn.* 13.605D, with the phrase *para physin.*

53 Juvenal's first five satires, which were "published" as one book, contain a reference to the trial of Marius Priscus (1.49–50) and were therefore written before 112 C.E.

limbs (2.11), taciturn speech (2.14), and crew cuts (2.15)—and as such go about their normal civic roles, defending Rome from license (2.39) as judges and lawmakers (2.51, 76).[54] Using the voice of the female character Laronia, Juvenal only later unveils the culprits as "our Stoic brethren" (2.64) who swish about like women soliciting advances from manly men. Taunting them with hypocrisy, Laronia sneers, "Do any of *us* plead at the bar, or set up to be experts in civil law? ... *You* card wool, and when you've finished, you carry the fleeces back in baskets, twirl the big-bellied spindle, and finger the fine-spun thread" (2.51–57). After the woman's work is done, Juvenal chimes in, satirizing a particularly debauched judge named Creticus, who wore a transparent toga to court (2.64–81) and visited people who dressed in drag (2.84–116), donned chartreuse outfits (2.97), and held mirrors, props always associated with women (2.99).[55] Juvenal even thanks Nature for rendering these "androgynous monsters" sterile (2.138–139). As he puts it, their houses might be "crammed with plaster casts of Chrysippus," but in these Stoics a "third Cato" has hardly fallen from the skies (2.5, 40). Juvenal's point is clear: the judgment of cinaedic Stoics is too impaired to cleanse Rome of the effeminacy killing the imperial body.

In sum, the charge of Stoic hypocrisy based on effeminacy and unnatural sex had an august history. Flowering fully in the first and second centuries C.E., the convention of the cinaedic Stoic enabled various authors to undercut the school's claims to sagacity and Romans' claim to right rule. In Martial's *Epigrams* and Juvenal's *Sat.* 2, even unnamed Stoics had their political clout as perfect Roman judges and legislators erased through allusions to hypocritical effeminacy. Likewise, Plutarch, Lucian, and Athenaeus deployed the convention to subvert Stoics' authority both as natural rulers and as manly instructors of maturing youths. In the first century of the Common Era, therefore, denouncing even unnamed Stoic judges as transvestites, sexual passives, or pederasts who effeminated their students was a typical way to strip authority from Stoic claims to live naturally and lead Rome well. In a first-century Roman environment in which Seneca *tutored* the young Nero and their government of the empire was publicly *conjoined*, to censure a Roman judge using the *topos* of the unnatural, sexy Stoic was therefore a thoroughgoing emasculation of *Romanitas*. It was equivalent to saying that the Roman Empire was run by women.

---

54 Richlin 1993: 544. On the very old connection between manliness and lawmaking, cf. Plato, *Resp.* 429c.

55 I am paraphrasing Richlin's colorful description (1993: 545).

CENSURING THE ROMAN JUDGE IN 1:18–2:16:
THE JUDGMENT OF LIVING CONTRARY TO NATURE

Paul says this with the rulers of the city in mind, because at that
time they ruled the entire world. He was telling [the Romans] ...
that when they pass sentence on someone they are passing sen-
tence on themselves as well.

John Chrysostom (*NPNF*[1] 11:360)

This is exactly the charge Paul levels at the judges of 2:1. Read in light
of the *topos* of the hypocritical Stoic, 1:18–2:16 resounds with Stoic com-
monplaces turned rhetorically in 2:1–16 to censure Roman leaders who
"ruled the whole world" according to nature and yet judged others for
unnatural acts in which they themselves indulged (Pelagius, *PCR* 69). Present in Romans are common understandings of the Stoic concept of the
cosmos, attention to nature through a mind attuned to reason, manly sex,
public duties, and perfect wisdom and judgment. Within the censure of
impiety in 1:18–32, these aspects of the convention constitute a critique of
the masses and of rival philosophies with which Paul's Stoic opponents can
concur. They function to remind Paul's Roman audience that Roman Stoic
elites deemed their lessers foolish effeminates. Within 2:1–16, Paul then
turns this Stoic rhetoric of judgment back upon them, the effect of which is
to eliminate the now-emasculated *Romanitas* as a rival to Paul's way of life.

Paul's deployment of the *topos* of the hypocritical Stoic follows immediately on the heels of his declaration of God's verdict of death against
the impiety and injustice of Gentile idolaters (1:18; cf. 1:32). The first
proof, which is strong enough to leave the adjudged without a defense
(1:20; 2:1), is that the created world teaches them what can be known of
God (1:19–20). This statement coheres nicely with the Stoic *topos*, which
depicts the universe, or nature, as revealing divinity because the divine
rationality permeates it. Although Stoics were known for identifying the
universe *as* God, even the language of God as "Creator" of nature (1:20)
and of the impiety (*asebeia*) of those who did not worship God (1:18, 21) is
consistent with Stoic thought. According to Laertius, "The deity, [Stoics]
say, is a living being, immortal, rational, perfect, intelligent in happiness,
allowing entry to nothing evil, taking providential care of the world and
everything in it, but he is not of human shape. He is, however, the artificer of the universe and the father of all, both in general and in the
particular part of him that is all-pervading."[56] As James Dunn notes while

---

56 Laertius *Vit. Phil.* 7.147; cf. also 7.134–136. Chrysippus identified the Universe
with God (Cicero, *Nat. d.* 2.38), but this did not prevent Epictetus from talking about God

highlighting Stoic terminology in 1:20, the language in Romans coheres with this portrait:

> The language here is scarcely characteristic of earliest Christian thought (*kathorao*, "perceive" and *theiotes*, "divinity, divine nature," occur only here in the NT; *aidios*, "eternal" elsewhere only in Jude 6; and *poiema*, "what is made," only here and Eph 2:10). It also for the most part plays an insignificant role in the OT. But it is familiar in Stoic thought: the closest parallel to the *aorata/kathoratai* wordplay comes in Pseudo-Aristotle, *de Mundo* 399b.14ff. ... and for *theiotes* cf. particularly Plutarch, *Mor.* 398A; 665A.... Paul is trading upon, without necessarily committing himself to, the Greek (particularly Stoic) understanding of ... [reality known] through the rational power of the mind. (Dunn 1988: 57–58)

The role of mind (*nous*) in recognizing the relationship of nature to the divine introduces the second allusion to the *topos*. Inaugurated by the *aorata/kathoratai* (invisible things/perceive) wordplay in 1:20, the language of (false) reasoning skyrockets in Rom 1:21–23: knowing (*gnontes*) God is juxtaposed to the befuddling (*emataiōthēsan, emōranthēsan, eskotisthē*) of those who are senseless (*asynetos*) in their reasonings (*dialogismois, kardia*; Stowers: 253). As in the Stoic convention, the involuntary false thinking of senseless minds leads fools into other forms of falsehood (1:23, 25), which are also involuntary errors of judgment (see *planē*, 1:27).

According to patristic commentators such as Origen and Ambrosiaster, their leading error is "changing" or damaging God's glory by mindlessly mistaking "the image of the likeness of perishable man" for its maker, the invisible, immortal Creator (1:23).[57] Significantly, the charge that God's *doxa* could actually be damaged by the mindlessness of men coheres nicely with charges Stoics leveled against Epicureans. According

---

as creating its constituent parts. *Diss.* 1.14.10: "Is God not able to oversee all things and to be present with all and to have a certain communication from them all? ... Is He who has created the sun, which is but a small portion of Himself in comparison with the whole, and causes it to revolve, is He not able to perceive all things?" Likewise, Laertius emphasizes that Stoics saw themselves as both godlike and pious worshipers of the gods or God (7.119). Paul distinguished God from the universe in a way Stoics did not, but this distinction is not important for 1:18–32 to function as a censure of Stoics; Paul's opponent at 2:1, and thus, a Stoic interlocutor, only had to believe that people were judged for not recognizing God-in-nature and that God was worthy of worship.

57 Ambrosiaster (CSEL 81:45, 47): "So blinded were their hearts that they altered the majesty of the invisible God ... not into men, but what is worse and is an inexcusable offense, into the image of man." Origen (*On Prayer* 29.15): "These people have lowered to a body without soul or sense the identity of the One who gives to all sentient and rational creatures not only the power of sentience but also of sensing rationally, and to some even the power of sensing and thinking perfectly and virtuously."

to Epicureans, the gods appeared as human in form and were apprehended as "images" nature imprinted on the mind (Cicero, *Nat. d.*
1.43–49). For that reason, unless the mind was devoid of unworthy
beliefs, "the holy divinity of the gods" could be "damaged by you" and
they will "do you harm.... You will be unable to visit the shrines of the
gods with a calm heart and incapable of receiving ... the images of their
holy bodies which travel into men's minds to reveal the gods' appearance. The direct effect on your life is obvious" (Lucretius, *Rer. nat.*
6.68–79). Stoics typically denounced this conception of the gods as foolish, otherwise "it must be denied that the gods exist, as Democritus in
effect does by introducing his 'likenesses' and Epicurus does with his
'images'" (Cicero, *Nat. d.* 2.75–76). Seneca (*Ben.* 4.19.1–4; 4.4.1–3) even
parrots Epicurus's own arguments back to him in order to demonstrate
that his theology strips the divine of his power and majesty and makes it
madness to address "deaf divinities and ineffectual gods." In Rom 1:23,
Paul evokes this Stoic censure of Epicureanism, using the very theology
of Epicureans against them in order to maintain the Stoic principle that
the mind of the true sage could not have been so damaged (*Vit. beat.* 7.4).
Paul's reversal of the categories of the wise man and fool in 1:22 (cf. 1:14)
underscores the rhetorical consequences of this mistake: those, like Epicureans, who claimed to be philosophic (*sophoi*) while maintaining false
conceptions of God demonstrated the weakened state of their minds.[58]

This point leads to the third allusion to the convention, which occurs
in 1:24–27: the false reasoning about nature that led both masses and
pseudosages to dishonor God now precipitates their involuntary exercise
of dishonorable passions (1:26–27).[59] In 1:24–27, as in the convention, the
vice of unnatural sex is a "form of ignorance of those things whereof the
corresponding virtues are the knowledge."[60] The virtue or "good" (cf. 2:8,
10) is, of course, intercourse in which male and female partners enacted
"natural" sex roles in accord with the will of the Creator. As I argued
above, the language of 1:26–27a indicates that the idolaters were guilty of
reversing this hierarchically gendered norm. Hence, the depiction of
thēleiai (women/females) and *arsenes* (men/males) engaging in unnatural
sex undoubtedly functioned as the critical proof of their mindlessness, of

---

58 Pseudo-Constantius lists Democritus and Epicurus among the philosophers accused
of foolishness in Rom 1:22 (*The Letter of St. Paul to the Romans*, ENPK: 25).

59 The involuntary character of the actions is underscored by Paul's repeated use of
paredōken. God is portrayed as the actor who "hands over" the idolaters to their lusts (1:24,
26). The idolaters then act on their lusts, but the point of the narrative is that false thinking
inevitably leads to these consequences, and God causes these results.

60 *Vit. Phil.* 7.94. Laertius was discussing Stoics' understanding of vices in general.

the ignorance that caused their failure to honor God as the Creator of nature. Significantly, the thrust of 1:24–27a parallels that of Epictetus's discourse on providence (*pronoia*): "Assuredly from the very structure of all made objects we are accustomed to prove that the work is the product of a technician.... do not visible objects and vision and light reveal him? And the male and female, and the zeal they have for sex, and the faculty which makes use of the organs that have been constructed for this purpose, do not these things reveal their artificer?" (*Diss.* 1.6.8–9). In 1:24–27, as in Roman Stoicism, women and men's exchange of natural for unnatural sex represented a mindless inversion of the cosmic hierarchy, arguably the most important work of the Artificer.

This point is further illuminated by the second allusion to the convention in 1:24–27, the role of passion and desire in the inversion of the cosmic hierarchy. Like the *topos*, passion is portrayed as the result of false thinking; it is the inevitable consequence of mindlessness. As Laertius put it, according to the Stoics, "falsehood results in distortion, which extends to the mind ... from this distortion arise many passions, which are causes of instability. Passion is, according to Zeno, an irrational and unnatural movement in the soul or an impulse in excess." Desire (*epithymia*), one type of passion (*pathē*), is an "irrational appetitive burning" (*orexis*) that exhibits itself, among other things, as love (*Vit. Phil.* 7.110, 113). Since, as I showed, 1:24–27 screams precisely this language of passion (*pathē, epithymia, orexis*), it points inexorably forward to the effeminacy of mind and body realized through men's "error" (*planē*), their "consumption in their burning" (*orexei*, 1:27) for each other. Immoderately indulged passion turned natural gender relations on their head and cultivated effemination in the bodies of its bearers. As Epictetus described the consequences of indulging the passions, "the wages of fighting against God and disobedience [*apeitheias*] will not be paid by 'children's children,' but by me myself in my own person" (*Diss.* 3.24.24; for the extended argument, see 3.24.22–39). In short, from its emphasis on nature to its inversion of the cosmic hierarchy through indulged passion, Rom 1:24–27 coheres with Stoic denunciations of non-Stoic philosophers (particularly Epicureans) and others as "the foolish masses" (1:22) who ignored the reason of nature and who practiced immoderate, unnatural sex.

Romans 1:18–32 ends with one more allusion to the convention of the hypocritical Stoic ruler, the idea that idolaters' effeminated minds prohibited them from doing their natural duties as citizens (*kathēkonta*). The Stoic founder "Zeno was the first to use the term *kathēkon* of conduct," which is "an action in itself adapted to nature's arrangements." By extrapolation:

> Befitting acts [*kathēkonta*] are all those which [natural] reason prevails upon us to do; and this is the case with honoring one's parents, brothers,

and country, and intercourse with friends. Unfitting or contrary to duty [*para to kathēkon*] are all acts that reason deprecates, which are these very things [*ta toiauta*]: to neglect one's parents, to be indifferent to one's brothers, not to agree with friends, to disregard the interests of one's country, and so forth. (*Vit. Phil.* 7.107–109; see also 7.25)

In Rom 1:28–32, Paul evokes the Stoic notion of natural duties left undone (*ta mē kathēkonta* 1:28) to extend the theme of the unnatural results of ignorance from their effeminizing effects on idolaters' bodies (1:24–27) to their enervating effects on the body politic (1:29–31). This rhetorical effect is wrought in 1:28 by: charging the idolaters with ignorance for a fifth time ("failing to keep God in mind," 1:18–19, 21, 23, 25, 28); juxtaposing their effeminated minds and poor judgment about God in a wordplay on mental fitness (*edokimasan/adokimon*); describing them for a third time as "handed over by God" (1:24, 26, 28) to an unfit mind (*adokimon noun*) that disabled acts of justice toward others (*adokia*, 1:29); and listing vices (1:29–31) that emphasized the passions with interpersonal consequences.[61] Precisely the kind of errors listed above by Laertius, these passions also underscore the contrast between idolaters' mindless injustice and the justice of the God who now judged them (1:17–18, 32).

Hence, the reference to Gentile idolaters' knowledge of God (*epignontes*) in 1:32 is an ironic *inclusio* of both 1:28–32 and 1:18–32 as a whole: the irony is that idolaters' effeminacy of mind is so complete, and their distance from the Creator of the nature by which they supposedly determine right action so total, that they think highly (*syneudokousin*) of those guilty of the unnatural acts that God deemed worthy of death.[62] In other words,

---

61 Cf. Laertius, *Vit. Phil.* 7.110–115. According to Stoics, examples of other passions included contentiousness, envy, rivalry, jealousy, anger, resentment, grief, pity, anguish, and distress.

62 Commentators widely agree that God's *dikaiōma* ("just verdict," 1:32), that "those who practice such things are worthy of death," does not refer to a specific judgment of the Jewish law but appeals to a current, culturally accepted "truth," placed in God's mouth, that people who are so wholly out of tune with acceptable conduct are refuse worthy of the worst punishments. Verse 32 reflects the widespread idea that God or the gods punish these people, who are unjust, for the passions that ruin their minds (see esp. 13:3–4, where rulers are empowered by God to inflict capital punishment for wrongdoing [Dunn 1988: 764]). Even though Stoics actively taught that death was inconsequential and not to be feared *by sages*, the idea of punishment *of fools* is present in Stoic thought (Stobaeus, 1.3.50, attributed to Epictetus the sentiment that God punished the unjust). Epictetus also said that punishment, including "destruction" of the faithful man, followed from disobeying God (*Diss.* 3.7.36); an unpleasant death awaited those who lived passionately (3.2.15); the greatest offenses reaped the greatest punishments (3.24.41–43); and a shameful death was especially dreadful (2.1.13).

their unnatural indulgence of the passions both evidenced and facilitated their total loss of judgment. In *Ep.* 39.3–6, Seneca makes the same point by describing the man who had wholly succumbed to passion and, thus, wholly lost his mind:

> No man of exalted gifts is pleased with that which is low and mean.... The only excuse that we can allow for the incontinence [*inpotentiae*] and mad lust [*insanae libidini*] of [certain men prone to excess] is the fact that they suffer the evils which they have inflicted upon others. And they are rightly harassed by this madness, because desire must have unbounded space for its excursions, if it transgresses nature's mean.... for this reason they are most wretched, because they have reached such a pass that what was once superfluous to them has become indispensable. And so they are the slaves of their pleasures.... *Then the height of unhappiness is reached, when men are not only attracted, but even pleased, by shameful things,* and when there is no longer any room for a cure, now that those things which once were vices have become habits.[63]

In Rom 1:18–32, the impious fools who dishonored God were precisely these insanely passionate men. Thus, from its emphasis on the importance of knowledge and judgment, unnatural sex, and failure to do one's natural public duties, to the idea that the universe revealed its Creator through a mind attuned to nature, Rom 1:18–32 coheres with criticisms ancients thought Stoics used to censure the "uncivilized" and to prove themselves more sagacious than rival philosophers.

Exit ROMANITAS: THE ROMAN JUDGE AND THE JUDGMENT OF GOD (2:1–16)

> *Therefore you are without defense, you Sir, each one of you who judges. For in that which you judge the other, you condemn yourself, for you, the judge, do the very same things. We know that the judgment of God rightly falls upon those who do these very things. Do you suppose, Sir, you who pass judgment on those who practice such things and yet do them yourself, you will escape the judgment of God?*
>
> Romans 2:1–3

The very coherence of the convention of the Stoic wise ruler within 1:18–32 is what makes it so devastating as a critique of Stoicized Roman judges' hypocrisy in 2:1–16. The convention shows that even

---

63 On foolishness as insanity, see also Epictetus, *Diss.* 2.15.13–15. For another parallel to 1:32, see *T. Ash.* 6:2.

when criticized anonymously, as he is in Rom 2:1–3, the Stoicized Roman ruler was widely recognized for thinking himself the perfect judge of the empire and the perfect instructor of young men in virtue. Epictetus's censure of an Epicurean indicates that Stoics did as well (*Diss.* 3.7.21):

> Drop these doctrines [of yours], Sir (*anthrōpe*). You live in an imperial state! It is your duty to hold office; to judge uprightly; to keep your hands off the property of others; [therefore] no woman but your wife ought to look handsome to you, no boy, and no silver or gold plate. Look for [Stoic] doctrines consistent with these principles of conduct, doctrines which will enable you to refrain gladly from matters so persuasive to attract and overpower a man.

However, as the convention also shows, the problem with Epictetus's censure of Epicureans was that both Stoic sages and the Roman leaders who followed Stoic principles were as vulnerable as Epicureans to Stoic charges of acting "contrary to nature." Stoic founder Zeno was known to chase his students and encourage androgynous dress. Likewise, Roman leaders acted effeminately in whatever ways they wished even as Roman Stoics touted strict gender differentiation, circumscribed natural intercourse to procreative sex, and called for the renewed virilization of the empire. Thus, of all the possible targets of Rom 2:1, the Stoicized Roman leader was the most vulnerable to censure for being the opposite of the "perfect judge" he claimed to be.

Like Martial's *Epigrams* and Juvenal's *Sat.* 2, which excoriate unidentified, or initially unidentified, Roman Stoic leaders who judge others while behaving effeminately, Rom 2:1–16 accuses an unnamed judge, in the vocative ("you Sir"), of just this kind of hypocrisy. Hear again the parallel with Juvenal:

> Why every street is full of you stern-faced pederasts. How can you lash corruption when you are the most notorious furrow among our Socratic fairies? ... It's a happy age [in Rome] that has you, Sir, to reform its morals.... what a garb for presenting new laws and enactments before a community.... think of what *you* would say if *you* saw such clothes being worn by a judge. I question if even a witness would appear in chiffon! (*Sat.* 2.9–10, 38–39, 72, 75–76)

The patristic commentators had good reason indeed for thinking that Paul had "the rulers of the city in mind." The judge of Rom 2:1 did the same unnatural things as Juvenal's Roman Stoic judge and exactly the same unnatural things (1:32; 2:1–2) as the fools upon whom he passed judgment in Rom 1:18–32. He lived in complete contradiction to his *summum bonum,* a life in accord with nature. He effeminated maturing youths and was effeminated by them (1:27), made a mockery of his dedication to his public duties (1:28–31), and demonstrated his total mindlessness. In fact, he was (to echo Seneca) so insane, his mind so thoroughly effeminated, that he "approved of" people who acted unnaturally (1:28–32, esp. 32). Obviously, he lacked the masculinity of mind necessary to effect his natural Stoic duty (*kathēkon*) of judging people justly (1:28; 2:1).

Depicting himself rhetorically as the instructor of the Roman judge, Paul then highlights the political consequences of these judgments in a careful comparison (*synkrisis*) between the emasculated reasoning of the Roman judge and the superior judgment of God (2:3–16). Paul argues fundamentally that the representative Roman's effeminacy of mind and body proves that neither life "in accord with nature" nor, by extension, the Stoicized *Romanitas* it sustained could, by itself, be rewarding. He does so in diatribal style. Paul instructs the Stoic judge, first, that his unnatural actions and inability to honor God as the Author of nature proved his mental weakness and lack of judgment (2:3). Deploying an assumption fundamental to the Greco-Roman concept of nature, the idea that the strong (masculine) should rule over the weak (feminine), Paul then argues that God's superior power (*dynamis* 1:16, 20) and benevolence (2:4) gave him the right to rule over and judge the Roman. By extrapolation, only God could choose the standard by which men would be evaluated, accounted just (*dikaioi*), and granted the benefits of "glory, honor, and immortality" (2:7; 1:17). Luckily for the Roman judge, Paul argued, God's justice was defined by liberality, patient endurance of misdeeds (2:4), and the impartial extension of his mercy to *everyone*, not first or only to high-status Greeks (1:14) but, first and foremost, to the Jews (2:9–10). The Roman's only chance at life was therefore to recognize the superior justice of Paul's God in refusing to act toward him as he had toward others (i.e., in refusing to condemn the hypocritical judge to death immediately as he would have done to the masses; 1:32; 2:4, 12). The Roman judge must accept the opportunity to "change his mind" (*metanoia*, 2:4)[64] and take up Paul's way of life as his own. After all, Paul argued, the gospel promised "wise" Gentiles like him, who said they could do the good naturally, the chance to do so and, thus, to have their

---

[64] On *metanoia* as a "change of mind" in protrepsis, see Swancutt (2001: 36, 62). Cf. Rom 12:2, where God is the metamorphosizer of believers' minds. On *metanoia* as "repentance," see, e.g., Ezek 33:11; Pseudo-Aristeas 188. Unlike the Stoics, Jews such as Philo considered *metanoia* a virtue, the mark of a man of wisdom (*Virt.* 177; *Abr.* 26; *Somn.* 1.91; *Spec.* 1.103; *QG* 2.13; for a positive portrait of "change of mind/heart," in non-Jewish texts, cf. esp. Lucian, *Nigr.* 38). Paul clearly did as well, arguing in 2:4 that "change of mind" was the moment at which, and the means by which, an unjust man began to "seek after glory and honor and imperishability" (2:7).

deeds evaluated in the future according to the lawful judgment of God (2:12–16).[65]

Apropos of the Stoic *topos,* however, the Roman judge is portrayed as silently impenitent of mind. Because of his supposed natural superiority (2:5, 8), Paul's threat of death seems not to concern him (2:7).[66] In the rhetorical space left after Paul's rapid-fire questions of 2:3–4, the following judgment therefore seems to echo: the judge's effeminacy of mind rendered him impotent to recognize not only his own "unnatural acts" but even his need for the mercy of a superior Judge. This unstated rhetorical logic may explain why Paul ends his censure of the Roman judge with a warning: all those like himself who continued their self-interested (*ex eritheias*) and unjust behavior (2:8–10) were "storing up wrath for themselves" in God's final judgment of deeds (2:5–7). They would, he promised, reap death as their reward (2:8–10, 12, 15–16; cf. 5:12–21)—not at all a good portent for the Roman judge.

Thus, into a city in which many Stoics served as magistrates and Seneca and Nero crafted the ideology of the quinquennium as the golden age of a Stoic ruler, Paul sent a letter inaugurated by a censure of a Stoicized Roman judge for governing himself and the masses "like a girl." Romans 1:18–2:16 is therefore a biting denunciation of *Romanitas.* It undercuts the cultural power of Rome and the rule of the Stoic *summum bonum* over Paul's audience by weaving a censure on Gentiles' mindless assault on the Creator of nature, a vivid allusion to gender transgression and its unnatural somatic consequences, and several allusions to the *topos* of the hypocritical Stoic ruler, into a comparison between the injustice of

---

65 I read 2:12–15a as placing Gentiles as well as Jews under the evaluation of God's law (2:6–8). The Jewish assumption underlying 2:12–16 specifically and 1:18–2:16 in general is that nature always points beyond itself to God and his law. I translate 2:12–15a as follows: "Whoever has sinned lawlessly [as in 1:18–32] will perish lawlessly, and whoever sins under the aegis of the law will be evaluated through the law. It is not hearers [students] of the law who are just men before God, but doers of the law who will be justified: when Gentiles who do not have the law do naturally the things of the law, those not having the law are a law to themselves. They demonstrate the work of the law is written on their hearts." A detailed explanation of this exegesis of 2:12–16 can be found in Swancutt (forthcoming).

66 See *Diss.* 3.7.7–11; 3.10.13–14. Stoics treated death as inconsequential to the sage (cf. 3.3.15; 3.18.2). According to Epictetus, death (is merely) "the time for the 'stuff' of which you are constituted to be restored to those elements from which it came.... thus I have been set free by God, I know his commands, no one has power any longer to make a slave of me, I have the right kind of emancipator and the right kind of judges [the natural elements]" (4.7.15–18). Stoics such as Posidonius, Seneca, and Marcus Aurelius interpreted the myth of Hercules to mean that after passing through the fire that liberated their spirits/souls at death, sages who lived according to nature were raised to the level of gods and enjoyed immortality as their reward.

an effeminated Roman judge and the justice of Paul's powerful Jewish God. Paul's rhetoric of masculinity forces his Roman audience to ask the following question about *Romanitas:* If elite Roman Stoics who touted living naturally acted effeminately "contrary to nature," how could their "wisdom" rival that of Paul's God? The answer is that it could not. Romans 1:18–2:16 deploys gender stereotypes about unnatural intercourse and effeminacy to shatter the credibility of *Romanitas* as a cultured way of life and to eliminate the independent authority of the Stoic philosophy of "natural living." As Paul had argued from the beginning, nature had always pointed beyond itself to the sovereign justice of Paul's God (1:18–23; 2:13–15). Hence, the justice of God must rule the cosmos so that all peoples, both Jew and Greek, had an equal chance at "glory and honor and immortality" (cf. 1:16–17; 11:32; 12:1; 15:12). Compared to *that* kind of justice, the mindless "insanity" of Roman rule was no rival.

PROTOCOLS OF MASCULINITY
IN THE PASTORAL EPISTLES

Jennifer A. Glancy
Le Moyne College

> *I am tired of cursing the Bishop,*
> *(Said Crazy Jane)*
> *Nine books or nine hats*
> *Would not make him a man.*
>
> W. B. Yeats

In three epistles written in Paul's name, the early second-century author whom I will call the Pastor claims the biography of the apostle Paul as his own.[1] In selective allusions to Paul's story, the Pastor supplies a thumbnail sketch of himself as the young Paul, "enslaved to various passions and pleasures [*douleuontes epithymiais kai ēdonais poikilais*]" (Titus 3:3). The Pastor implies, however, that in his maturity he has mastered the passions and pleasures that once controlled him. He can even suggest that others should regard him as a model to emulate. "Now you have observed my teaching, my conduct, my aim in life, my faith, my patience, my love, my steadfastness" (2 Tim 3:10). In his youthful hotheadedness, the Pastor suggests, Paul had failed to exhibit the self-mastery that was a hallmark of respectable Greco-Roman manhood. The Pastor insists on a different persona for Paul as a mature man: patient, steadfast, and purposeful.

The Pastoral Epistles articulate a protocol of masculinity informed by contemporary codes of masculinity. In discerning the contours of these codes, the writings of Stoic philosophers and other moralists are

---

1 I regard the Pastoral Epistles as products of the second century. For a synopsis of the arguments on provenance, see Bassler 1996: 17–20. Although I treat the pastoral epistles as the work of a single author, I recognize that the Pastor, as I present him here, is a construct dependent on my reading of the text. I am primarily concerned with the ideology and rhetoric of masculinity in these epistles; I am not concerned with the individual psychology of the author. An argument for multiple authorship would not be inconsistent with my arguments regarding the structures of masculinity on display in the epistles.

of particular, though not exclusive, relevance. Others have established that the Pastoral Epistles are close to Stoic sources in their values, their preferred virtues, and even their use of medical terminology and metaphors (e.g., Davies 1996a: 11; Malherbe 1980, 1994; Villiers). James Francis argues that during the first and second centuries, Stoics adopted the "customs of the upper class ... the Romans made duties of their own conventions" (4). Moralists such as Plutarch embraced both the cultivation of the self through the control of the passions and the cultivation of household harmony through the assertion of the householder's will as the rule for other members of the household, with full acknowledgement that, among other costs, the householder's wife would have to subordinate and even negate her own will. In the Pastoral Epistles as well, cultivation of a self-controlled masculine self is coupled with the cultivation of a harmonious household, subject to the will of the male householder.

Michel Foucault's writings on sexuality in the Greek and Roman worlds are widely cited as the catalyst for a generation of scholarly work on sexuality, particularly male sexualities, in the ancient world. Foucault argued that, during the first centuries C.E., pagan ethical codes focused increasingly on "the manner in which the individual needed to form himself as an ethical subject" (1986: 67). What emerged was not a more intense ascetic code but "an intensification of the relation to oneself by which one constituted oneself as the subject of one's acts" (41). Foucault's male subject is freeborn, property-owning, cognizant of his duties toward older men and his responsibilities toward younger men, and in control not only of his wife, offspring, and slaves but, perhaps more importantly, of his own desires, liberated from any enslavement to passions and pleasures (cf. Titus 3:3). In the decades since the publication of Foucault's work, classicists have both qualified and challenged various tenets of his model, thus offering more complex visions of masculine self-definition at the height of the empire. Maud Gleason (1995), for example, argues that the second century witnessed competing paradigms and postures of masculinity. Amy Richlin, who identifies herself as a feminist critic of Foucault, claims that Foucault "meets his sources dressed in their Sunday best; it is hard to recognize in Foucault's contemplative, self-disciplined, married pederasts the men who made so many jokes about rape and ugly women" (1992: xiv). Even the ancient authors whose writings inform Foucault's story of the cultivation of the masculine self acknowledge that some contemporaries perceived masculinity in terms less rarefied than their own. Plutarch laments that, while those who are sick in body acknowledge their illnesses, those who are sick in soul are typically unable to identify their maladies, which they may even misdiagnose as virtues. He writes, "For although no one has ever called a fever 'health,' nor consumption 'excellent condition,' nor gout 'swiftness of foot,' ... yet many call hot temper 'manliness' [*thymon de polloi kalousin andreian*]" (*Mor.* 501.B.3).

What is a real man? How do young males learn to embody codes of masculinity? In arguing that the Pastoral Epistles codify a protocol of proper Christian masculinity consistent with coeval pagan articulations of masculinity, I do not assume that a single norm of masculinity prevailed throughout the empire. One can easily imagine a second-century father as crudely proud of his son's sexual organs as Augustine's father, observing his son's budding masculinity in the baths and boasting about such developments (*Conf.* 2.3). Cultivated men defined masculinity as a moral achievement, but on the streets and in the baths many would have based their own estimations of who qualified as a man on anatomical configuration and physical prowess.[2] Precisely the existence of competing modes of manhood (some self-reflective, others forged in bravado and a culture of communal nudity, drinking, and sexual aggressiveness) invites the kind of articulation of norms we find in the Pastoral Epistles. Gleason suggests that, in the second century, "efforts to articulate and formalize an empire-wide code of elite deportment might be welcomed by provincial aristocrats who suddenly found themselves faced with a wider world" (1995: xxv). She finds a confirmation of this desire for the formalization of codes of masculinity in the second-century proliferation of "physiognomical treatises, moral essays, medical advice manuals, and rhetorical handbooks" (ibid.). In the Pastoral Epistles, we find such a specification of what constitutes legitimate masculinity, ranging from a valorization of self-control as the epitome of virtue to an insistence that Christian men should exert a controlling influence over their wives and offspring.[3] The Pastoral Epistles serve as a Christian hornbook of masculine propriety.[4]

---

2 For evidence concerning the extent of nudity in the baths, see Fagan: 24–26.

3 In this article I will not consider the vexed translation of *arsenokoitēs* (1 Tim 1:10). Exploring possible translations of the term, Dale Martin concludes, "I am not claiming to know what *arsenokoites* meant, I am claiming that *no one* knows what it meant" (1996: 123). He argues that an association of *arsenokoitēs* with sexual exploitation for financial gain is at least as likely as a more general association of *arsenokoitēs* with male homosexual sex. Perhaps the use of the term is part of the Pastor's discourse of masculinity; however, it seems less central than the topics I treat here, including control of the passions, control of household members, and control of language, among the concerns to which the Pastor repeatedly returns.

4 Noted, although not developed, by Pervo: "In this light the PE [= Pastoral Epistles] are quite easily read as edification for boys or young men, dealing with both their own moral development and with the nature of the church.... By telling young men how to rule their own lives and how the church should be managed, they could serve as works seeking to inspire young men to pursue leadership in the church" (38).

Real Men

Both in 1 Timothy and in Titus, the Pastor sets forth qualifications for various church offices, including deacons, bishops, and elders. Although women seem to number among the deacons (1 Tim 3:11), the Pastor passes quickly over their presence in the ranks of deacons, emphasizing rather what is expected of men who seek to hold church office. Scholarly discussion over the requirements for church office tends to revolve around questions of the degree of development of church hierarchy and the precise functions of the various offices, which are poorly defined. These questions need not detain us here. I am interested instead in what the qualifications for church office establish, more broadly, regarding the Pastor's paradigm for legitimate masculinity. The Pastor presents bishops, deacons, and elders as exemplars for the community, setting standards of behavior for other men to emulate (Davies 1996a: 81). Officeholders should be above reproach; married one time and able to control their children and their households; temperate, sensible, respectable, not arrogant, not quick-tempered, not prone to brawling, not quarrelsome; not addicted to wine; not avaricious; and able to teach sound doctrine in a straightforward manner. In setting forth these requirements, the Pastor implicitly specifies norms for the behavior of mature Christian men. Many of these qualities are associated with properly self-controlled masculinity in pagan writings of the era, as well (Davies 1996a: 81). For example, as we will see, displays of temper and avariciousness were interpreted as symptoms of effeminacy.

According to Gordon Fee, the Pastoral Epistles require that, "Above all, they [elders and other officeholders] must be exemplary family men." He then backpedals by defining an exemplary family man minimally, as a "husband of one wife" (1985: 148). (Nonetheless, Fee's invocation of the phrase "family man," with its cultural location in modern discourses of family values, remains problematic.) The Pastor seems to value first of all the mere fact of marriage and procreation of legitimate children, a value in keeping with Augustan legislation encouraging men to marry and to beget legitimate children. By the time the Pastor wrote, this imperial value had already infiltrated the writings of Stoic philosophers such as Epictetus, who was "adamant regarding marriage and raising children as a social duty" (Francis: 18).

Beyond the brute requirement of marriage and child-rearing, the Pastor advocates a display of masculinity in the householder's control of members of the household. A bishop "must manage his own household well, keeping his children submissive and respectful in every way—for if someone does not know how to manage his own household, how can he take care of God's church?" (1 Tim 3:4–5). The Pastor's recitation of the qualities necessary for a bishop immediately follows his prescription for women's behavior in assemblies of worship. Women must learn in silence with full submission, they must not teach or have authority over men, and they must remain silent (1 Tim 2:11–12). Surely implicit in the Pastor's instruction to men to control their households is an imperative to control wives as well as children. An emphasis on managing children and other members of the household recurs in the Pastor's other lists of qualifications for church office, including the qualifications for deacon in 1 Tim 3:12. In Titus, the Pastor specifies the nature of the control desired over one's offspring. An elder should be a man "whose children are believers, not accused of debauchery and not rebellious" (3:6).

Writing in roughly the same period as the Pastor, Plutarch delivers advice on conjugal happiness to a bride and groom. "Whenever two notes are sounded in accord the tune is carried by the bass; and in like manner every activity in a virtuous household is carried on by both parties in agreement, but discloses the husband's leadership and preferences" (*Mor.* 139.D.11). The Pastor regards it as the duty of older women to encourage younger women to love and moreover to submit to their husbands, since a Christian woman's failure to submit to her husband might discredit the word of God (Titus 2:3–5). Sensitive to feminist concerns, readers in the twenty-first century are likely to find the burden for family harmony that both Plutarch and the Pastor impose on wives, who are enjoined to subordinate their own voices and wills to the dominant note sounded by their husbands, to be alienating. Plutarch even states that "the wife ought to have no feeling of her own [*houtō tēn gynaika mēden idion pathos exein*], but she should join with her husband in seriousness and sportiveness and in soberness and laughter" (*Mor.* 140.A.14). (Plutarch thus promotes a gendered distortion of the Stoic virtue of *apatheia*, in which a wife transcends enslavement to her own desires and emotions only to surrender to her husband's.) Acknowledgement of the restrictions on women's autonomy that these writings impose, however, should not preempt our simultaneous recognition of the obligations of masculinity that both Plutarch and the Pastor prescribe. The male householder has the duty to ensure submission and compliance from all members of the household: as a husband, from his wife; as a father, from his children; as a slaveholder (in those households that include slaves), from his slaves.

Thus, for the Pastor, Christian performance of masculinity encompasses control of the behavior of other members of his household. Equally central to the conduct of the Christian male, however, is *self-*control. Officeholders, themselves exemplars for other Christian men, are expected to be temperate, sensible, respectable, not arrogant, not quick-tempered, not prone to brawling, and not quarrelsome. The Pastoral Epistles are peppered with additional reminders to adopt such behavior.

When men pray, they should lift up their "holy hands without anger or argument" (1 Tim 2:8). Community members should avoid harsh speech, speaking with the respect due each generation (1 Tim 5:1–2). Dissension and wrangling are symptoms of depravity (1 Tim 6:4–5; cf. 2 Tim 2:14, 23–25). God has given members of the church a spirit of power, of love, and of self-discipline (*pneuma sōphronismou*, 2 Tim 1:7). One should particularly guard against youthful passions (*neōterikas epithymias*, 2 Tim 2:22). Older men should be prudent (*sōphronas*) and younger men self-controlled (*sōphronein*, Titus 2:2, 6). The appearance of God's grace should train community members to reject worldly passions (*kosmikas epithymias*) and to live lives of self-control (*sōphronōs*, Titus 2:12). In this pursuit of the self-controlled life, Paul himself stands as a model of a man who moved from enslavement to youthful passions to a maturity characterized by sobriety and self-control (Titus 3:3; 2 Tim 3:10). Abraham Malherbe notes that the Pastoral Epistles represent Paul as "the apostle of moderation" (1994: 204). Margaret Davies likewise points out that the Pastor's ideal officeholder is "a moderate man, free from destructive passions, a picture which would appeal to contemporary Greeks and Hellenistic Jews" (1996a: 76).

The location of the Pastoral Epistles within moral and philosophical discourses at the height of the empire is thus well-established (F. Young: 84–91).[5] Specifically, the Pastoral Epistles valorize self-control as a pivotal virtue for Christian life, an evaluation consistent with the privileged place accorded to self-control in the varieties of Stoicism that flourished in the first and second centuries C.E. Foucault argued that self-control was the defining characteristic of elite masculinity in that era.[6] While subsequent writers on classical masculinity have modified various dimensions of Foucault's portrait of Roman sexualities, they generally endorse his identification of control, including self-control, as the key masculine trait. According to Craig Williams's definition, for example, "[Roman] Masculinity meant being in control, both of oneself and of others, and femininity meant ceding control" (137). Despite Williams's (seemingly exhaustive) taxonomy of Roman men's sexual practices, he insists that

---

5 Contrast Villiers, who comments on "how close these letters are to the Graeco-Roman world in terms of its ethics" (38). These letters are not *close* to the Greco-Roman world; they *belong* to the Greco-Roman world.

6 Along with his repeated admonitions to men to exercise self-control, the Pastor also encourages young women to exhibit self-control. However, self-control in Hellenistic thought is a gendered virtue. Whereas *sōphronsynē* evokes a spectrum of behaviors that a man must moderate to achieve the masculine norm of self-mastery, for women, *sōphronsynē* refers more narrowly to sexual self-control, to chastity. Lucinda Brown has noted the relevance of this distinction for the Pastoral Epistles (84).

"masculinity was not fundamentally a matter of sexual practice; it was a matter of control" (141). Williams lists a number of oppositional pairs that, in Roman thought, correlate with the columns masculine/feminine. Masculinity/femininity correspond not only with courage/timidity, strength/weakness, and activity/passivity but also with hardness/softness and moderation/excess (142); excess is associated with a softening and therefore a feminization of the body and soul. The Pastor's mistrust of passions and pleasures is thus a crucial component of his code of masculinity.[7]

A man enslaved to passions and pleasures is feminized not only by indulgence of his desires for luxury items that would soften the body and weaken the character, but also by indulgence of his anger and desire for retaliation. Seneca is clear about the feminizing qualities of anger. "Thus, anger is a most womanish and childish weakness [*Ita ira muliebre maxime ac puerile vitium est*]. 'But,' you will say, 'it is found in men also.' True, for even men may have womanish and childish natures [*Nam viris quoque puerilia ac muliebria ingenia sunt*]" (*Ira* 1.20.3). As Gleason observes in another context, what appear to be markers separating men from women often "divide the male sex into legitimate and illegitimate players" (1995: xxviii). Just as Plutarch notes that many misprise hot temper for manliness (*Mor.* 501.B.3), Seneca also recognizes that his perception of anger as a feminizing trait is not universally held. He writes, "Let him who thinks that anger reveals the great soul, think that luxury does the same; it [luxury] desires to rest on ivory, to be arrayed in purple, to be roofed in gold.... Let him think that avarice also betokens the great soul; it travels over heaps of gold and silver.... Let him also think that lust betokens the great soul; it swims across straits, it unsexes lads by the score [*puerorum greges castrat*]" (*Ira* 1.21.1). Seneca thus concedes that his elevation of self-control and moderation as cardinal masculine virtues bucks against some popular characterizations of masculinity. Nonetheless, he insists that the blustering, lusty male does not reveal himself as the epitome of manhood but instead unmans himself by his lack of self-control, a womanish deficiency. Through his emphasis on self-control and moderation, not only of pleasures but also of anger and other passions, the Pastor contributes to the same discourse of masculinity.[8]

Although one might suppose that the Pastor's advocacy of control of the passions would be incompatible with the exercise of violence against the bodies of recalcitrant members of the household, contemporary

---

7 The phrase "mistrust of the pleasures" is Foucault's (1986: 39).

8 On the ancient association between women and anger, see Harris: ch. 11. Harris writes, "The angry emotions were feminine" (264). Nonetheless, he contends that women, unlike men, lacked legitimate outlets for their anger.

writings represent self-control as consistent with the authorization of such violence. In the *Attic Nights*, Aulus Gellius recounts a story about Plutarch and a slave characterized as worthless and insolent. Plutarch commanded that the slave be stripped and flogged, presumably by another slave. The "worthless" slave had listened to his owner's orations on the subject of anger and absorbed their content. As he was being beaten, the slave castigated Plutarch for shaming himself through a display of anger. Plutarch calmly replied, "'What makes you think, scoundrel, that I am now angry with you. Is it from my expression, my voice, my colour, or even my words, that you believe me to be in the grasp of anger? In my opinion, my eyes are not fierce, my expression is not disturbed, I am neither shouting madly nor foaming at the mouth and getting red in the face." The anecdote concludes with the observation that Plutarch instructed the man wielding the whip to continue his work while the debate continued (*Noct. Att.* 1.26). We know that the Pastor held the male householder responsible for control of household members, explicitly for the behavior and attitudes of his offspring, by extension for the behavior and attitudes of his wife and slaves. Although slaves were certainly more likely than wives or legitimate offspring to feel the sting of the whip (Saller), all subordinate members of the householder were ultimately subject to the disciplinary strategies of the householder. The philosophical and cultural tradition in which the Pastor participated did not stress the danger posed by anger to the one(s) victimized by an angry person; the tradition stressed that anger represented a danger to the person in whom its heat surged. Although a man should restrain the anger he might feel, the heating of his body and soul, he still had an obligation to maintain discipline and order in his household. Masculine exercise of control over self and others thus had latent costs for those excluded from the category of masculinity, that is, women, children, and slaves.

According to Seneca, containing one's behavior and demeanor when in the grip of anger was imperative, but ultimately less desirable than avoiding the passion of anger altogether. He advocated training oneself to avert the experience of anger. Such training should be a perennial part of a man's life. Nonetheless, training during formative years would yield greater results than training after a man's character had been largely established: "Just as in caring for the body certain rules are to be observed for guarding the health, others for restoring it, so we must use one means to repel anger, another to restrain it.... The period of education calls for the greatest, and what will also prove to be the most profitable, attention; for it is easy to train the mind while it is still tender, but it is a difficult matter to curb the vices that have grown up in us" (*Ira* 2.18.1–2). For Seneca and others of the era, the explanation for the greater efficacy of early training lay in physiology. Youth was associated with heat and heat with anger; thus, one was considered most susceptible to the fiery effects of anger early in life. At the opposite extreme, old age was associated with dryness: "In the dry periods of life anger is powerful and strong, but without increase, showing little gain because cold succeeds heat which is now on the decline. Old men are simply testy and querulous, as also are invalids and convalescents and all whose heat has been drained either by exhaustion or loss of blood" (Seneca, *Ira* 2.19.4–5). The Pastor depicts Paul as a slave to the passions in his youth, when his blood would have been most fiery and he would have been most susceptible to anger and other strong emotions. Paul moved not to a querulous old age, according to the Pastor, but to a serene and composed maturity. To effect such a transition required careful training and cultivation of the self.

What kind of training would promote the transcendence of anger and other passions? Although extreme physical privations of asceticism were not an end in themselves, writers of the era argued that some forms of physical privation could promote *apatheia*. The time for such training was youth. At twelve, for example, Marcus Aurelius wore rough clothing and spent his nights on the hard ground. Seneca also advocated that elite young men spend time living in conditions of poverty. Francis writes: "The object is *apatheia*, teaching that physical want, should it befall him, is nothing to be feared since deprivation cannot harm the soul" (24). In a parallel fashion, the Pastoral Epistles emphasize spiritual askesis over physical askesis: "Train yourself in godliness [*gymnaze de seauton pros eusebeian*], for, while physical training [*sōmatikē gymnasia*] is of some value, godliness is valuable in every way, holding promise for both the present life and the life to come" (1 Tim 4:7b–8). The Pastor relies elsewhere on images of athletic and military training as metaphors for the proper comportment of men pursuing the Christian life: "The soldier's aim is to please the enlisting officer. And in the case of an athlete, no one is crowned without competing according to the rules" (2 Tim 2:4b–5). The Christian male is able, moreover, to rely on the grace of God to support the project of self-cultivation he shares with his pagan peers: "The grace of God has appeared … educating us [*paideuousa hēmas*] to renounce impiety and worldly passions to live lives that are self-controlled [*sōphronōs*], upright, and godly" (Titus 2:11–12). Coached by the grace of God, the Christian has a distinct advantage over his pagan counterpart in the cultivation of a proper masculine self.

Because the Pastor emphasizes the youth of the recipients of these letters, his invocation of training metaphors is particularly apt. In addressing Timothy and Titus as beloved and loyal children, the Pastor constructs an impression of generational difference between writer and recipients (1 Tim 1:2; 2 Tim 1:2; Titus 1:4). Timothy's youthfulness is a factor in the advice the Pastor extends. Timothy is to set a model for the other Christians in Ephesus: "Let them not despise your youth" (1 Tim 4:12). More immediately relevant to the Pastor's prescriptive masculinity is his instruction to Timothy to "shun youthful passions" (*tas de neōterikas epithymias pheuge*, 2 Tim 2:22a). As we have seen, the notion of the hot-blooded youth was not a metaphor but a diagnosis; the property of heat was understood to dominate the temperaments of young men, making them susceptible to passions at the very time their characters were being refined. Thus, in a variety of ways, the Pastor encourages Timothy and Titus, pictured as men still young, to submit themselves to physical and spiritual disciplines that would help them evolve from hot-blooded youths to properly self-controlled men, a transition the Pastor implies that Paul had successfully made.

Timothy's presumptive age and stage of training underlie an otherwise peculiar directive the Pastor delivers: "No longer drink only water, but take a little wine for the sake of your stomach and frequent ailments" (1 Tim 5:23). This instruction is disconnected from the surrounding context, disrupting a discussion of the impact of sin on the community and its leaders. Perhaps, as some commentators have suggested, the Pastor introduces this injunction here lest the reader construe the preceding call to purity as an invitation to the kind of dietary asceticism the Pastor finds offensive (1 Tim 4:3–5; Dibelius and Conzelmann: 80–81; Bassler 1996: 102). However, the instruction remains surprising in light of the Pastor's reiterated censure of men and women who indulge excessively in alcohol (1 Tim 3:3, 8; Titus 1:7; 2:3). The verse ultimately leaves many readers at a loss: "The relevance of verse 23 is a mystery" (Bassler 1996: 102). The Pastor's encouragement to imbibe, however, is consistent with his project of mentoring Timothy and, by extension, the intended recipients of the text toward a mature and proper performance of masculinity. As others have noted, moderate consumption of wine was a component of ancient medical and self-care regimes (Davies 1996b: 44; Bassler 1996: 102). Nonetheless, because younger men were perceived to be more fiery, they were understood to be physiologically susceptible to the negative effects of alcohol. Some training regimens therefore recommended that younger men avoid or severely minimize drinking wine.

"No longer drink water only," writes the Pastor, creating an impression that Timothy, though young, is entering his maturity. Timothy, the Pastor implies, had pursued a course of physical training, not as an end in itself, but as a path toward godliness. Now a leader in the congregation, he has crossed the threshold into manhood and is no longer as vulnerable to deleterious effects of alcohol. Moderate consumption of wine, ostensibly for medical purposes, would also permit him to participate more fully in a social life that in a Greco-Roman city such as Ephesus, where the Pastor locates Timothy, inevitably revolved around alcohol. Through this instruction, the Pastor also allows those readers who have followed an ascetic lifestyle to recast their rejection of drink (and food? and marriage?) not as a permanent choice, but as youthful training toward godliness.

A healthy body, reasoned the Pastor's contemporaries, should be able to resist unhealthy passions, "desires that are vehement, intractable, unwanted, and hard to dispossess" (Plutarch, *Mor.* 127.A.9). Therefore, a man cultivating himself through the discourse of philosophy had a concomitant obligation to develop his knowledge of medicine (*Mor.* 122.E.1). Rather than having constant recourse to physicians or pharmacological concoctions, a man should know his own body and treat minor ailments with the simplest of available treatments: moderation of diet, occasional fasting or enemas, or temporary substitution of water for wine (*Mor.* 134D).[9] Moderate consumption of wine appears as a routine component in such regimes of physical self-maintenance. Athenaeus, for example, connects the consumption of wine to the beneficial irrigation of the digestive tract. He reports that wines treated with salt water, which he claims do not cause headaches, "loosen the bowels ... and assist digestion" (*Deipn.* 1.32.3). The state of medical knowledge suggested that wine increased the body's heat. Moreover, some minimum level of heat was considered essential to the maintenance of masculine identity. The medical writer Galen even averred that a decline in a man's heat could result in a "womanish" character (Corbeill: 109). While wine caused susceptible temperaments to overheat, by the same logic, sipping a little wine contributed to the maintenance of a balanced man's persona. The Pastor's recommendation to "take a little wine for the sake of your stomach and frequent ailments" is consistent with a prophylactic regimen of physical and spiritual hygiene.

Such wine bibbing, however, should remain moderate. The Pastor's concern that the men who lead the church should avoid drunkenness reflects his aversion to behavior that, because unrestrained, exhibits a lack of masculine self-mastery. Therefore, Seneca suggested, those with fiery temperaments should stay away from wine altogether, lest they boil over (*Ira* 2.20.1). The very potion that produces health in some persons and some circumstances produces, in other instances, a shameful lack of

---

9 In an extraordinary analogy, Plutarch compares the effect of medications on the digestive tract to swarming masses of immigrants in a Greek city: "The violent disturbances lower down in the bowels resulting from medication, by decomposing and liquefying the existing contents, increase rather than relieve the overcrowding. Just imagine that anybody, feeling much troubled at the crowd of Greeks living in his city, should fill up the city with Arab and Scythian immigrants" (Plutarch, *Mor.* 134.D.22).

propriety. Athenaeus includes a compendium of quotations from authors who weigh the positive and negative effects of wine. Eubulus, for example, writes that the temperate drink only three kraters of (mixed) wine: one for health, one for pleasure, and one for sleep. After that, "the fourth bowl is ours no longer, but belongs to violence"; continued downing of kraters of wine leads successively to uproar, revels, barroom brawls, and even madness (*Deipn.* 2.36.C). Moderate drinking, which has a role in maintaining (directly) a man's physical well-being and (indirectly) his mental balance, could easily deteriorate into drunkenness, associated with emotional displays and outbursts that would unman the drinker. Moreover, in the context of the banquet hall, drunkenness would be associated not only with greed but also with indiscriminate sexual behavior unbefitting a man (Corbeill).[10]

The risks were most serious for fiery youth still disciplining their bodies and minds toward the goal of self-control. Athenaeus ascribes to Timaeus of Tauromenium a drinking yarn that emphasizes the vulnerability of youthful drinkers to the fire of alcohol. At a house in Agrigentum, a party of young men drank until they were entirely overheated. They became convinced, in their alcohol-induced delirium, that the house was in fact a ship. They deduced from their unsteady gait that the ship was rocking because of a ferocious storm. To stabilize the putative ship, they threw furniture through the windows. When they were called before the magistrates the next day, the leader of the group mounted a seaworthy defense: his crew had thrown the excess cargo overboard in order to save their own lives as their ship weathered the storm. The magistrates concluded that their behavior was not so much criminal as inebriated and sentenced the young men to restrain their future consumption of alcohol.[11] In narrating the story, Athenaeus emphasizes the youth of the offenders, the heating effects of alcohol, as well as the excesses and disorderliness of their behavior (*Deipn.* 2.37.C–E). Counsel that the young should abstain from wine boasted a distinguished pedigree. Athenaeus argued that Homer, recognizing *sōphrosynē* as the most desirable virtue for young men, advocated that they live abstemiously because their "passions and pleasures," especially their desires for food and drink, were so strong. Learning to curb these strong desires would establish a pattern of self-control that would be maintained through the vagaries of life (*Deipn.* 1.8.F). Seneca told his readers that, because heat dominated the temperaments of youth, Plato

---

10 Note that Corbeill draws the majority of his examples not from writers contemporaneous with the Pastoral Epistles but from writers of the late Republic.

11 Directors of undergraduate residence halls continue to tell such tales today.

did not think young people should even drink wine, "protesting against adding fire to fire" (*Ira* 2.20.1). "No longer drink water only," writes the Pastor to his Timothy. The reader infers that Timothy's rejection of alcohol had been the praiseworthy choice of a youth in training to control his passions and pleasures. Presenting his invitation to pour some wine as sagacious medical self-help advice, the Pastor pictures Timothy stepping into the circle of mature male company, sufficiently in control of himself and his world that indulgence in alcohol (not truly an indulgence but a gesture toward health) would not jeopardize his self-possession and thereby his status as a man.

A final kind of appetite against which the Pastor repeatedly warns is avarice, although this counsel must be distinguished from a condemnation of wealth. Desire for wealth rather than possession of wealth is the quality that the Pastor identifies as inappropriate for church leaders (1 Tim 3:3, 8; Titus 1:7). The Pastor does deliver particular instructions to the rich: those with abundant resources should rely not on their storehouses but on God. They should share generously (1 Tim 6:17–19). However, the Pastor does not condemn the wealthy for their treatment of the poor (contrast, for example, Jas 2:6; 5:1–5). If neglect or abuse of the poor is not the source of the Pastor's warning against avarice, what is? The Pastor opens the discussion with advocacy of self-sufficiency, which, rather than invoking Jesus' encouragement of simple living, echoes the formulations of Hellenistic philosophy (Davies 1996b: 49). He continues, "Those who want to be rich fall into temptation and are trapped by many senseless and harmful desires [*epithymias pollas anoētous kai blaberas*] that plunge people into ruin and destruction. For the love of money is a root of all kinds of evil, and in their eagerness to be rich some have wandered away from the faith and pierced themselves with many pains" (1 Tim 6:9–10). The sentiment is hardly original. A variety of writers preserve versions of a saying that identifies the love of money as the root, mother, or mother-city of evils (Dibelius and Conzelmann: 85–86). The Pastor's very lack of originality underscores his participation in a wider ethical discourse and protocol of masculinity. Once again, what disturbs the Pastor is behavior that would incline a man to surrender to desire, a feminizing inclination.

A craving for money had a particular reputation as a womanish longing. In the *War with Catiline*, Sallust writes:

> But at first men's souls [*animos hominum*] were actuated less by avarice than ambition—a fault, it is true, but not so far removed from virtue; for the noble and the base alike long for glory, honour, and power, but the former mount by the true path, whereas the latter, being destitute of noble qualities, rely upon craft and deception. Avarice implies a desire for money, which no wise man covets; steeped as it were with noxious

poisons, it renders the most manly body and soul effeminate [*ea quasi vene-nis malis imbuta corpus animumque virilem effeminat*]; it is ever unbounded and insatiable, nor can either plenty nor want make it less. (11.3)

Although Sallust wrote in the late Republic, Gellius's account of an informal debate orchestrated by the eunuch sophist Favorinus suggests the currency in the Pastor's day of Sallust's diagnosis of the feminizing tendencies of avarice (*Noct. Att.* 3.1).[12] Gellius and Favorinus were walking in the baths as Sallust's *War with Catiline* was read to them. After listening to Sallust's discussion of avarice, Favorinus, who might claim expertise in the characteristics of the feminized body, asked, "How does avarice make a man's body effeminate? [*Quo pacto corpus hominis avaritia effeminate?*] For I seem to grasp in general the meaning of his statement that it has that effect on a manly soul [*animum virilem*], but how it also makes his body effeminate I do not yet comprehend." Gellius comments that he had wondered that very thing for a long time. A disciple of Favorinus offers an opinion he had gleaned from Valerius Probus (a scholar of the late first century C.E.). On this view, Sallust used a poetic circumlocution in this passage, "for a man is made up of body and soul." Favorinus rejects this interpretation.

The discussion continues. Favorinus consults a learned man sharing the promenade. The man speculates that those possessed by avarice are so consumed that they neglect "manly toil and physical exercise." Thus, their bodies languish. Favorinus challenges the learned man. If this is the case, how do we account for avaricious men who have muscular (hard, masculine) bodies? For such exist. His conversation partner suggests that Sallust's verdict would apply only to a man whose avarice is so fierce that pursuit of wealth excludes all other activities, "so that because of that one passion he has regard neither for virtue nor physical strength, nor body, nor soul." Only in such an extreme case could one conclude that avarice causes effeminacy not only of soul but also of body. Favorinus's response is equivocal, noting that either the learned man's analysis must be correct or that Sallust's contempt for avarice led him to speak in indefensibly strong terms.

I rehearse this exchange at length to establish that the identification of avarice as a womanish desire was not simply an idiosyncratic position held only by Sallust but had far wider currency. Even before entering into discussion of Sallust on this occasion, participants in the dialogue seem familiar with the proposition that avarice has feminizing effects, at least

---

12 Gleason discusses the passage from Gellius in the context of Favorinus's bravura performance of masculinity (1995: 143).

on the soul. Favorinus concedes from the outset that avarice feminizes a man's soul; the debate centers on the question of whether avarice additionally feminizes a man's body. How does avarice feminize a man's soul? As the Pastor says, the love of money traps avaricious persons in senseless and harmful desires and is thus the source of all manner of evils. What kinds of evils? Avarice is particularly vicious because, in Sallust's words, "it renders the most manly body and soul effeminate." The Pastor's prohibition on admitting avaricious men to leadership positions thus reinforces other components of his protocol of masculinity.

As we read the Pastoral Epistles through our twenty-first-century gender codes, it is easy to interpret the Pastor's advice, apart from a few passages explicitly addressing the roles of men and women within the church, in gender-neutral terms. However, the eponymous recipients of the letters are men. As we examine the Pastor's instructions to his readers in the context of second-century protocols of masculinity, we recognize the extent to which a prescriptive code of manhood conditions his counsel. So far, I have presented the Pastor's directions as straightforward coaching for proper masculinity, not so far removed from, say, the intergenerational advice of Polonius to Laertes ("And these few precepts in thy memory/See thou character"). The delivery of such advice would not necessarily imply that the Pastor was familiar with churches that tolerated or promoted deviant masculine postures. However, one strand of advice in the Pastor's writing suggests strongly that he is writing defensively, that is, that persons with opposing outlooks have become influential in the very circles over which he seeks (or seeks to maintain) influence. In his admonitions against these opponents, the Pastor focuses repeatedly on the character of their speech. He expresses a particular concern with those who insinuate themselves into other men's households and, through their words, enthrall the women of those households. In the next section, I consider the Pastor's warnings against his opponents, arguing that the Pastor delivers his straitlaced advice in order to undermine the authority of men whose seductive speech he views as symptomatic of their deviance from gender norms. The specter of men who violated conservative imperial gender norms threatened the Pastor's sense of order and excited his desire not only to control his own masculine self but also to define, more generally, a proper self for Christian men.

IMAGINARY MEN

I have located the Pastor's protocol of masculinity in the context of a discourse of masculinity favored among educated men in the first and second centuries. In this section, I complicate the story by insisting on the contested character of manhood in this same milieu. The Pastor delimits the boundaries of proper masculine behavior not simply to help young men trying to negotiate the transition to a mature and tempered manhood. Rather, the Pastor writes to counterbalance other modes of masculinity, modes that have captured the imagination of Christians he hopes will endue this letter with the same authority accorded Paul's own letters. The Christian masculinity prescribed by the Pastor is at odds with images of other possible Christian masculinities. Early Christian writings represent John the Baptist, Jesus, and Paul as anomalous men in their passions, in their eschewal of matrimonial and paternal roles, and, in the case of Jesus, in shameful death. Writings by both Christians and non-Christians from the second century suggest that a number of men attracted by the gospel enacted such alternative masculinities. The Pastor attempts to overwrite their script of masculinity with his own.

As Jouette Bassler writes, "Cultural norms control the ethical perspective throughout these letters [i.e., the Pastoral Epistles], making it sometimes difficult to determine which admonitions were given because they were an ethical commonplace, and which reflect concrete problems with the community" (1996: 63). Because of the Pastor's vehement attacks against those whose words disrupt families and seduce women away from the roles he approves, I agree with scholars of widely varying hermeneutical perspectives who argue that the Pastor addresses what he perceives to be a serious threat within the communities he attempts to guide. Fee, for example, accepts that the false teachers in the epistles to Timothy are "insiders, teachers, elders with influence over women" (1985: 144). He writes that 1 Timothy is intended to "to respond in a very *ad hoc* way to the Ephesian situation with its straying elders. To put that another way: What we learn about church order in 1 Timothy is not so much organizational as reformational" (146). With a very different evaluation of the significance of the situation, Linda Maloney proposes that the Pastor presents himself as a "frightened would-be authority on the defensive against powerful and intelligent opponents who are *not* attackers from the outside" (362, her emphasis). Although Fee and Maloney disagree on the identities of the Pastor's opponents and the merits of the opponents' presumed agenda, both agree that the Pastor addresses an actual rather than a hypothetical challenge and that the opponents are insiders rather than outsiders to the community in question. I argue that the Pastor and his opponents embody conflicting postures of masculinity and that the Pastor seeks to undermine the authority of his opponents by employing invective that would have been widely understood as derisive of his opponents' identities as men.

What clues do the Pastoral Epistles provide concerning the identity of those the Pastor views as agitators? Idle or frivolous talkers (*mataiologoi*), they disrupt entire households (Titus 1:10–11). At the same time, they do not understand what they are talking about (1 Tim 1:6–7). Their speech is empty sound (*kenophōnia*), their word a contagious disease (2 Tim 2:16–17). They spread "profane myths and old wives' tales," against which the Pastor urges Timothy to inoculate himself by a manly regimen of training himself for godliness (*gymnaze de seauton pros euse-beian*, 1 Tim 4:7–8). The Pastor sounds the same note repeatedly, warning Timothy to turn aside from "profane chatter [*bebēlous kenophōnias*] and the contradictions of what is falsely called knowledge" (1 Tim 6:20).

It was widely believed that a person's speech, delivery as much as content, conveyed his or her character. Quintilian asserted, "As a man lives, so he speaks" (Connolly: 132). The supposed babbling of women and slaves, for example, was at once a foil and a trap for free men, whose rhetorical self-presentation often came dangerously close to employing the manipulative strategies associated with females and servile males. Arguing that speech plays a "role ... in the maintenance of gender boundaries," Gleason attributes to Dio Chrysostom the position that "the voice that blurs the boundaries of gender is more hideous than the voice that crosses the boundaries of species" (1995: 82). She writes further:

> The very word that Plutarch selects to characterize a woman speaking is not the basic Greek word for talking (*legein*), but what linguists would call a marked form that connotes babble or idle chatter (*lalein*). Plutarch's use of the marked form in this context points to the possibility that women's speech and men's speech, in some vital but largely irrevocable sense, were felt to be qualitatively *different*. If speech itself is gendered, then the possibility of confusion of gender boundaries is inherent in any spoken encounter. (98, emphasis original)

Gleason examines at length the rivalry between two second-century Sophists whose modes of self-presentation derived from competing postures of masculinity. Through his mastery of the art of oratorical performance, the eunuch Favorinus (whom we first encountered walking in the baths) managed to enact a masculine identity, although Polemo, his more conventionally equipped rival, never stopped drawing attention to Favorinus's deficiencies. Polemo did not focus exclusively on Favorinus's physiology but instead challenged the virility of Favorinus's discourse. Gleason recounts, "When Polemo's old teacher, the Cynic Timocrates, remarked, 'What a talkative creature that Favorinus has become!' Polemo was quick to jibe, 'Just like every other old crone'" (1995: 27–28). With such mockery men policed the boundaries of masculinity in a climate of competing approaches to manly self-presentation (76). "It is important to remember," writes Gleason, "that the strictures of hirsute moralists [such as Polemo or the Pastor] did not command universal assent" (74). The seductive appeal of Favorinus's accomplished and inviting voice cast an irresistible spell, which established, for some, his manliness, and for others, the ultimate proof of his degenerate gender-identity.

Gleason's work helps us glimpse the tension between rival postures of masculinity among educated men early in the second century in the Greek-speaking eastern empire. Favorinus was particularly associated with Ephesus, Polemo with Smyrna (Gleason 1995: xxvii). The Pastoral Epistles, addressed to Timothy in Ephesus and Titus in Crete, share this cultural context. The Pastor's invective against his enemies focuses precisely on their patterns of speech, insinuating that they use hollow, foolish, and ultimately effeminate modes of discourse to seduce women away from their proper roles and to corrupt young men such as Timothy. The setting of the Pastoral Epistles in a cultural milieu of contested masculinity inclines me to hear the Pastor's warnings as expressions of anxiety about the posture of masculinity proper for Christian men.

The Pastor explicitly warns Timothy to guard against those who, by forbidding marriage and demanding abstinence from various foods, will disrupt the normal functioning of households. (As we have seen, through the Pastor's counsel to begin drinking wine for medicinal purposes, readers who had in the past abstained from wine would be invited to represent that self-denial, and by analogy other abstemious behavior, as a component of a youthful training regimen [1 Tim 5:23].) The Pastor asks Timothy to share his instructions on these matters with "the brothers." As a prophylaxis against the opponents' teachings, the Pastor urges Timothy to cultivate himself: "Have nothing to do with profane myths and old wives' tales. Train [*gymnaze*] yourself in godliness" (1 Tim 4:3–7). We can attach names to the characters whose speech the Pastor derides as weak and, by extension, womanish: "Avoid profane chatter, for it will lead people into more and more impiety, and their talk will spread like gangrene. Among them are Hymenaeus and Philetus, who have swerved from the truth by claiming that the resurrection has already taken place. They are upsetting the faith of some" (2 Tim 2:16–18). The Pastor relies on vocabulary of disease to characterize his opponents' speech and thereby to dismiss their authority. While the Pastor expresses repugnance for what they represent, others in the community, notably certain women, find this rival message more compelling than that articulated by the Pastor. (Given the fictive setting of the letter, I do not assume that Christians named Hymenaeus [also named in 1 Tim 1:20] and Philetus were actual persons known to the author of the Pastoral Epistles, nor that the Pastor transmitted a historical memory of men with these names, although either of these scenarios is possible. Rather, within the implicit narrative of the epistles, these names anchor the Pastor's concern about men whose speech threatens his sense of proper Christian masculinity.)

The false teachers, according to the Pastor, have penetrated Christian households, presumably without the sanction of male householders: "There are also many rebellious people, idle talkers and deceivers, especially those of the circumcision; they must be silenced, since they are upsetting entire households by teaching for sordid gain what is not right to teach" (Titus 1:10–11). Joy Connolly observes that ancient gender ideology held that "wives, daughters, mothers, slaves, and freedmen [and freedwomen, we should add] are the primary sources of corruption, the weak spots in the household's defenses, or at least, the sites at which vice enters the *familia*" (146). This observation is borne out by the Pastor's description of what he presents as the teachers' infiltration of Christian households:

> For among them are those who make their way into households and captivate silly women [*gynaikaria*], overwhelmed by their sins and swayed by all kinds of desires, who are always being instructed and can never arrive at a knowledge of the truth. As Jannes and Jambres opposed Moses, so these people, of corrupt mind and counterfeit faith, also oppose the truth. But they will not make much progress, because, as in the case of those [Jannes and Jambres], their folly will become plain to everyone. (2 Tim 3:6–10)

The Pastor presents female nature as inherently lacking in *sōphrosynē*. According to the rules by which he lived, a proper woman would not welcome an unrelated, unauthorized male caller. Once she agreed to do so, her weak female nature could mount few defenses against his mesmerizing words. The Pastor sketches the scene with erotic overtones: the false teachers captivate, or take prisoner, women who are overcome by all kinds of longings, desires over which women were understood to have little if any sway. Since the teachers reject marriage, presumably their encounters with female Christians are not overtly sexual. (Unless, of course, their rejection of marriage is based on libertine rather than ascetic precepts; of this, however, I sense no suggestion.[13]) Nonetheless, by coaxing women away from their proper roles, the teachers just as surely violate the strictures of patriarchal control within marriage.

Or at least, this is how the Pastor casts the situation. Here, as elsewhere, we should avoid the trap of simply reinscribing the Pastor's constrained and constraining assumptions about the dynamics of gender and control, both inside and outside the legitimating structure

---

13 "If one assumes a libertine tendency among the heretics, one could point to the 'desires' which the author mentions here. But if he had wished to accuse his opponenets of unchastity, he would probably have said it much more clearly" (Dibelius and Conzelmann: 116).

of marriage. The imagery of captivating or capturing women belongs to the Pastor, not to the rival teachers nor to the women with whom they associate. The Pastor is indifferent to women's subjectivity and their active role in shaping scenes in which they may well see themselves as participants and not as pawns.

Although I concentrate on the prescriptive masculinity that laces the Pastoral Epistles, I rely on the work of other feminist scholars who argue that the participation and leadership of independent women in Christian congregations disturbed the Pastor's sense of order. So, for example, the Pastor may be thinking of a specific woman or women when he forbids women/wives to teach or to have authority over men/husbands (1 Tim 2:12). This is still clearer in the Pastor's discussion of the role of widows in the church, where he expresses agitation over the activities of some women in the community. He stipulates that younger women should be barred from receiving the benefits enjoyed by widows: younger widows "learn to be idle, gadding about from house to house; and they are not merely idle, but also gossips and busybodies, saying what they should not say" (*lalousai ta mē deonta*, 1 Tim 5:13). The author recommends that younger women, instead of participating in the autonomous work of the widows, should assume what he sees as their proper roles as wives and mothers, safely contained within households, "faithful representatives of the community's virtue" (M. Y. MacDonald 1999: 248). Feminist scholars have argued convincingly that these women who moved freely from house to house would not have recognized themselves in the Pastor's caricature of their work with one another.

Joanna Dewey argues that in 1 Timothy, "the author seems particularly concerned to control the behavior of women" (1992: 353). Yes, but what apparatus of control does the Pastor employ? In seeking to rein in these autonomous women, the Pastor directs Timothy, a surrogate for other male leaders, to oversee and to regulate the activities of Christian women. The existence of autonomous females in the household of God signals that the householders, the male leaders of the church, have not mastered the congregation as the Pastor demands. Someone in the congregation should restrain the widows, and that someone, I think, must be a man, so that when the Pastor directs, "Give these commands as well, so that they [the widows] may be above reproach" (1 Tim 5:7), the chain of command goes from man to man. For the Pastor has written, "Let a woman [*gynē*] learn in silence with full submission" (1 Tim 2:11). To enroll a woman as a widow or to refuse to enroll her would not be a decision best left to women (the would-be widow herself or a community of widows) but should be in the capable hands of male leadership. In the first section of this essay, I analyzed the Pastor's prescription for masculinity, but the tonic prescribed has toxic side-effects; in order for men to be men, women must be silent.

The Pastor uses the verb *lalein* to characterize the speech of the young widows. As Gleason notes, *lalein* is a marked linguistic form connoting babble; its use here underscores negative stereotypes of women's speech current in the early second century. The stereotypic association of women's speech with senseless discourse creates the possibility of impugning a male speaker's manhood by describing his voice as weak and his rhetoric as foolish. As Gleason writes regarding Polemo's policing of gender, "notions of gender identity depend on polarized distinctions (smooth/hirsute, high voice/low voice, pantherlike/leonine, etc.) that purport to characterize the gulf between men and women but actually serve to divide the male sex into legitimate and illegitimate players" (1995: xxvii). Even so, we noted earlier, Polemo derided his rival Favorinus by labeling him a talkative old crone. Philosophical polemic deployed comparisons with old women's communications to dismiss rival claims (Dibelius and Conzelmann: 68). Celsus weighed both the teachings of Christianity and the ramblings of an old woman, and the balance tipped against Christian doctrine: "Would not an old woman who sings a story to lull a little child to sleep have been ashamed to whisper tales such as these?" (Origen, *Cels.* 6.34). This context shapes my reading of the Pastor's warning, extended specifically to Timothy, to avoid "profane myths and old wives' tales" (1 Tim 4:7) by persevering in his (manly) course of training toward piety. Some feminist scholars have argued that, with his warning against old wives' tales, the author of the Pastoral Epistles cautions against women engaged in a preaching ministry (e.g., Dewey 1992: 356). Given the conventional use of gendered barbs to dismiss the authority of male speakers, I find it more likely that the author uses such language to stain the image of his male opponents by associating their teaching with (what is characterized as) the prattling of old women. Moreover, in instructing Timothy (a surrogate, I have suggested, for male readers) to guard himself against such old wives' tales by training himself for godliness, the Pastor exhibits anxiety about the effects of what he considers effeminate speech on upright Christian men. In this all-male exchange, the use of gender invective has particular valence as a tool for social regulation.

But there seem to be some Christian men who, preferring mixed company, do not apply to the men's club the Pastor convenes. What kind of a man would seek to make his way into respectable households to capture women's hearts and minds? Lucian's *Runaways* narrates a similar account of teachers, in this case aspiring philosophers, who infiltrate and undermine the patriarchal household.[14] "Some even carry off the wives of their hosts...," Lucian writes, "pretending that the women are going to become philosophers; then they tender them, as common property, to their associates and think they are carrying out a tenet of Platonism" (*Fug.* 18). At the same time, Lucian claims, these would-be Cynics hypocritically condemn adultery and lewdness. They lack even the virtues of dogs: "guarding property, keeping at home, loving their master, or remembering kindnesses." They are doglike instead in their "barking, gluttony, thievishness, excessive interest in females ... and hanging about tables" (16). Lucian thus characterizes them as deficient in the rhetorical skills and self-mastery essential to his protocol of masculinity. That is, they bark, they overeat, and they chase women.

Both Lucian and the Pastor describe faux teachers who make illicit overtures to women who are, in the Pastor's words, "overwhelmed by their sins and swayed by all kinds of desires" (2 Tim 3:6). According to second-century standards for proper masculine behavior, such descriptions would be no more flattering to the teachers than to the women they instructed. Although men might take female or male sexual partners outside their own marriages, they were expected to defer to the household boundaries of other men. Improper contact with another man's wife (or legitimate daughter or son) would indicate that a man was so deficient in self-control as to violate a central understanding of social harmony.[15] According to Roman law and custom, a man apprehended in adultery was subject to physical and sexual abuse, including beatings and penetration, both oral and anal; the symbolic degradation of such corporal violation was intended to unman the adulterer, both socially and sexually (Walters 1997: 39; Dupont and Éloi: 165–68).[16] An adulterous man was thus understood to be so softened by desire that he was willing to risk compromising his bodily integrity and, with that, his claim to manhood. A man exposed a deficiency in masculinity by actively pursuing women as well as by being sexually penetrated (C. A. Williams: 143). Once a man lost control of himself, ancient sources imply, anything was possible. When the Pastor describes Christian missionaries who insinuate themselves into

---

14 Francis (162–78) points out parallels between Lucian's satiric treatment of ascetics, Celsus's depiction of Christians, and the forms of Christianity reflected in the apocryphal Acts.

15 In his treatment of *stuprum*, C. A. Williams discusses the social compact that censured men for engaging in sexual activities with the wives and the legitimate sons of respectable men (ch. 3).

16 The vulnerability of the adulterer to humiliation at the hands of the aggrieved husband is also consistent with Greek practice. Davidson argues, moreover, that in classical Athenian thought, "the woman-lover and especially the adulterer was considered to have been himself somehow womanized by his womanizing and was pictured as an effeminate" (165).

other men's households for the purpose of enthralling their women, he does not flatter them with cryptic references to their virility but derides their manhood by playing up their illegitimate, if celibate, relations with women.

As Dennis MacDonald argues, the Pastor's condemnation of those who seduce women away from their proper household roles, not toward sexual profligacy but toward sexual renunciation, resonates with tales from the apocryphal Acts of men's missionary activities among women from respectable households. Most immediately, since the Pastoral Epistles rely on Paul's name as the foundation for their own authority, the Pastor's denunciation of teachers who disrupt households appears to be an attempt to construct an image of Paul as a defender of marital boundaries, an image calculated to counter the apocryphal representation of Paul. In the *Acts of Paul*, Paul's voice coaxes women from their sanctioned roles within proper households. Before Thecla even sees Paul, she sits by her window night and day in order to hear him speak. Theocleia, Thecla's mother, reports to Thamyris, her daughter's fiancé, that Thecla has been listening day and night to Paul as he speaks "deceptive and subtle words": "And my daughter also, like a spider bound at the window by his words, is controlled by a new desire and a terrible passion. For the virgin concentrates on the things he says and is captivated" (3). Thecla's conversion is described precisely as a disturbance to the household: Thamyris mourns his intended wife, Theocleia her daughter, and the female slaves (improbably enough) their mistress.[17] Within the world of the apocryphal Acts, however, such disruption of patriarchy is sanctioned rather than censured; the apocryphal Paul exhibits no interest in joining the other men at the Pastor's club.[18]

Francis suggests that, in the late second century, Celsus formed his low opinion of Christianity on the basis of acquaintance with a form of Christianity familiar to us via the apocryphal Acts (166). Celsus's account of Christian missionary activity focuses on the influence of unlettered men over ill-educated members of households, including women and children: "In private houses also we see wool-workers, cobblers, laundry workers, and the most illiterate and bucolic yokels, who would not dare to say anything at all in front of their elders and more intelligent masters.

---

17 Perkins situates the negative attitude of the apocryphal Acts toward marriage in the context of a second/third-century shift *away* from "the Classical/Hellenistic concept of a human 'self' who pursued self-mastery as a moral goal while finding personal meaning in civic life and institutions" (1996: 258).

18 A full discussion of the complex representation of masculinity in the apocryphal Acts is, unfortunately, beyond the scope of this essay.

But whenever they get hold of children in private and some stupid women with them, they let out with some astounding statements as, for example, that they must not pay any attention to their father and school-teachers" (Origen, *Cels.* 3.55). While the speech of these teachers is persuasive to gullible persons, Celsus clearly differentiates their untutored discourse from that of elite males, before whom they instinctively fall silent. Francis notes, "This infiltration of family life is framed in terms of a challenge to the traditional authority of the *paterfamilias*" (157). Both Celsus and the *Acts of Paul* depict male Christians who win converts by transgressing the boundaries of respectable households; their attitudes toward the sanctity of those boundaries, however, differ. The Pastor shares both Celsus's veneration of the patriarchal household and his perception that (at least some) Christians lack respect for that institution. Both the Pastor and Celsus represent the discourse of the intrusive teachers as weak, hollow, and senseless: in short, as unmasculine.

Celsus's account clearly reflects prejudice based on social status. Similar prejudice is also evident in Lucian's account of faux Cynics who, among other nominal outrages, corrupt women from respectable households. The character of Philosophy describes these fraudulent philosophers: "There is an abominable class of men, for the most part slaves and hirelings, who had nothing to do with me in childhood for lack of leisure, since they were performing the works of slaves or hirelings or learning such trades as you would expect their like to learn.... Well, while they were following such occupations in youth, they did not even know my name" (*Fug.* 12; see Francis: 64). Lacking the cultivation of true philosophers, Philosophy claims, the self-styled Cynics coin themselves as counterfeit philosophers by donning the outward garb of her true disciples. Does the Pastor's derisive representation of his opponents as babbling intruders encrypt a status/class prejudice akin to that so evident in Celsus and Lucian? Although the Pastoral Epistles do not supply sufficient evidence to offer a definitive answer, the possibility is worth considering.

According to the Pastor, his opponents do not even understand their own senseless discourse (1 Tim 1:6–7). Although the Pastor does not develop the point as Celsus and Lucian do, he may expect his readers to recognize that the ignorance of the would-be teachers, so great an ignorance that they do not recognize their own limitations, signals a lack of cultivation, of the *paideia* by which elite males learned to fashion themselves into men. The achievement of masculinity through *paideia* was a prerogative of elite males; others were excluded from even attempting such self-fashioning through their want of "time, money, effort, and social position" (Gleason 1995: xxi). Status differences would have surfaced in the quality of voice that men exhibited: the eloquence of elite men versus the so-called barking (Lucian's term) of the less privileged. These disparities would have been evident to those who had enjoyed oratorical training; whether such disparities would have been equally evident to those who lacked such opportunities for self-cultivation is an open question. Normative conceptions of masculinity and femininity were informed by consideration of social status; thus, an effective bias toward *elite* males would be consistent with the Pastor's project of regulating performance of masculinity within the Christian community. This scenario, however, in which the Pastor derides the manliness of those whose low status disbars them from the category of masculinity as defined among elite males, is importantly different from Gleason's sketch of a contest of manhood between two men, each of whom predicated his achievement of masculinity on the qualities he had cultivated through *paideia*.

For Celsus, the corruption of masculinity among Christians is even more blatant than the Pastor insinuates: Celsus assimilates Christian men to the *galli*, the self-castrated priests of Cybele. Origen writes that Celsus "compares those who believe … to the begging priests of Cybele" (*Cels.* 1.9). According to Origen, Celsus claims that Christians overwhelm worshipers "by playing flutes and music like the priests of Cybele who with their clamor stupefy the people whom they wish to excite into a frenzy" (*Cels.* 3.16). Celsus's mocking words probably reflect standard tropes of gender polemic rather than the practices of actual Christians (although there is some irony that Origen, remembered as an autocastrate, repeats and attempts to refute this charge). Williams argues that, within Roman polemic, the figure of the *gallus* functions to establish the limits of proper masculinity: "We might say, in other words, that the *cinaedus* and above all the *gallus* were ideological scare-figures for Roman men: a man who flaunted his breaking of the rules of masculinity could be said to have taken the first step on the dangerous road toward becoming a castrated priest of the Mother Goddess" (C. A. Williams: 177). By associating Christian practices and practitioners with the tactics of the *galli*, Celsus stigmatizes Christian males as irredeemably effeminate. Such ridicule was a regular part of the invective that played a significant role in social regulation. Marilyn Skinner observes that, in Roman discourse, "accusations of effeminacy may have been intended to tap audience prejudice against nonconformist lifestyles" (1997: 5).

We find further characterizations of Christian males in terms derisive of their masculinity in other pagan writings of the second century. In telling the story of the erstwhile Christian Peregrinus, Lucian plays up details of his biography that would have been understood as evidence of defective manliness. Some of these details precede and others are subsequent to Peregrinus's career as a Christian. Lucian writes ironically that, as soon as Peregrinus entered manhood, he was caught in an act of adultery. The aggrieved husband beat Peregrinus, who, stuffed with the conventional radish, ignobly and shamefully escaped by jumping from a roof. Peregrinus further demonstrated his lack of self-control by seducing a beautiful and respectable youth; he got out of that scrape by paying off the young man's equally respectable but impoverished parents (Lucian, *The Passing of Peregrinus* 9). For a time after Peregrinus converted to Christianity, Lucian claims, he was almost as revered as the one "who was crucified in Palestine because he introduced this new cult into the world" (11). Lucian thus implies that a man such as Peregrinus, enslaved to passions and pleasures, is the type of unman situated at the heart of the Christian cult. In recounting the further history of Peregrinus, Lucian delights in describing him in the midst of a storm at sea, so little in control of his fear that he is "wailing along with the women" (43). Peregrinus ends his life in a public act of self-immolation. Lucian describes the scene. While some by-standers urged him to save his own life, "the more virile [*hoi de andrōdesteroi*]," including, apparently, Lucian himself, encouraged him to complete the deed (33).

Something about the behavior of some Christian men made the Pastor uncomfortable, sufficiently uncomfortable that he also employed the rhetoric of gender derision in attempting to establish his own authority. By such language, he separated himself, and, by extension, Paul, from the suspiciously soft teachers who chose to spend unaccountable time with women in the community. His concern was not only the regulation of his own masculinity, however. He also attempted to police the boundaries of proper masculinity for other Christian men. Writing from outside the church, Lucian and (especially) Celsus make extreme claims about a degenerate masculinity that they picture dominating the Christian cult. Writing from inside the church, the Pastor disassociates himself from fellow Christian men he perceives as insufficiently virile. He prescribes for his fellow Christian males a style of self-presentation conforming to his own interpretation of imperial gender norms. Both the career of Peregrinus and Celsus's composition of his anti-Christian treatise (almost certainly) postdate the writing of the Pastoral Epistles. The Pastor could not have been familiar with the perilous public life of Peregrinus, Lucian's sketch of Perigrinus's mishaps, or Celsus's writings. However, I find it interesting that these pagan observers of Christianity employed the rhetoric of gender derision to question the reputation of the Christian cult and its adherents, especially in light of the Pastor's concern that officeholders should enjoy good reputations with those outside the church (1 Tim 3:7); perhaps the Pastor codified his protocol of masculinity not only out of visceral anxiety arising from the affect and behaviors of other Christian men and women, but also as a response to what was to become a long-standing pattern of pagan gender-baiting.

But how did those other Christian men, the ones who made the Pastor squirm, imagine themselves? Did they refuse to define themselves as men? Or did they see themselves as embodying, perhaps in response to the gospel, alternative postures of masculinity? In resisting the Pastor's straitlaced protocol of masculinity, these second-century Christians could easily have imagined themselves as imitators of those seminal figures of the first century, John the Baptist, Jesus, and Paul. Whether the Pastor would have been at ease living in close quarters with his spiritual fore-bears is another matter. If we look over the Pastor's shoulder, the shadow of the Galilean falls uncomfortably close to the shadow of the *gallus*.

The reputation of Christianity was inevitably linked to the character of Jesus. Celsus knew this; on his telling, Jesus had been born of an adul-terous union and therefore marked with shame from birth. Jesus traveled to Egypt with his mother when her husband expelled them from his home. There, Jesus apprenticed himself to magicians (Origen, *Cels.* 1.28), practitioners of an art widely associated with the deceptions of women (Janowitz: ch. 6). The seedy persona of Jesus bears fruit, Celsus implies, in the overtly scandalous actions of his followers, who comport themselves like *galli*. Origen attempts to convert the tale of Jesus' lowly and shameful origins to a triumphant narrative of masculine self-fashioning, turning on Jesus' successful achievement of a masterful speaking style. Origen emphasizes that, by Celsus's own description, Jesus "had no general edu-cation and had learnt no arguments and doctrines by which he could have become a persuasive speaker" (*Cels.* 1.29). That is, Jesus lacked the resources necessary to gain access to *paideia*, through which elite males of his era cultivated themselves as men. Nonetheless, Jesus controlled the manly art of oratory. He addressed large crowds and attracted followers. Origen asks, "How could such a man, brought up in this way, who had received no serious instruction from men (as even those who speak evil of him admit), say such noble utterances ... that not only rustic and illit-erate people were converted by his words, but also a considerable number of the more intelligent...?" (*Cels.* 1.29).

John the Baptist, Paul (especially as represented in the legends pre-served in the apocryphal Acts), and Jesus embraced behaviors and attitudes alien to the Pastor's gender code. Here, I am not concerned with the question of whether these three would have appeared as securely or defectively masculine in their first-century contexts. I am concerned instead with the question of how gender policemen like the Pastor and Polemo would have responded to the memories of these passionate men. The reactions of Polemo, Celsus, and other pagans who shared their gender-prejudices are important because of the likely impact of their ridicule on the willingness of Christians such as the Pastor to tolerate variation of gender-expression among fellow believers; derision is a powerful tool for enforcing social conformity. I imagine Plutarch dismissing Jesus, John the Baptist, and Paul by sniffing that they represent the sort of persons who confuse hot temper with manliness. None of the three married or procreated, minimal requirements in the Pastor's articulation of a protocol of manhood. Each, in other words, rejected the position of head of household, a position in which one enacted masculine identity at least in part through control of other persons: a wife, legitimate offspring, and, frequently, male and female slaves. Furthermore, they prescribed an alternative gender protocol for their followers; Jesus encouraged men to disdain family ties, the historical Paul recommended that unmarried persons who were able to maintain their self-control should not marry, and the apocryphal Paul campaigned systematically against marriage and procreation.

In what ways did the Pastor's second-century church remember that these founding figures had rejected for themselves and discouraged others from the roles of husband and father? Was walking in their footsteps attractive to some men who did not want to perform a script of masculinity that relied on women, children, and slaves as props for selfhood? The Pastor's repetition of the expectation that men should play the roles of husband and father, and play them exactly, ensuring the compliance of children and the submission of wives, hints at a desire to distinguish his own image, not only from fellow believers derelict in their adherence to a stabilizing protocol of masculinity, but also from his unmarried, childless forerunners.

A curious feature of the Pastor's Christology is his omission of any reference to Jesus' crucifixion, although the Pastor does point in several places to the significance of Jesus' death (Davies 1996b: 52). Failure to mention the crucifixion sharply differentiates the Pastoral Letters from the authentic Pauline letters. Paul never ceases to invoke not only the cross but also the scandal of the cross. For the Pastor, the crux of the scandal could have been Jesus' death in a manner unbefitting a man.[19] Jesus' imprisonment and trial are represented as clearly emasculating in, for example, the Gospel of Mark: "Some began to spit on him, to blindfold him, and to strike him.... The guards also took him over and beat him" (Mark 14:65–66). The ability to protect one's body from violation was an essential dimension of the Roman code of masculinity (Walters 1997). Jesus' vulnerability to corporal abuse stigmatized him as less than a man, since he was unable to sustain an honorably masculine self-presentation.

---

19 For a different approach to the gendering of Jesus' death, see Moore, who argues that, even as Jesus' submissive death marks him as feminine, the self-mastery he exhibits marks him as masculine (2001: 163–64).

Influenced by Roman codes of masculinity, the Pastor would have understood the blindfolding of Jesus as yet another element in his unmanning; to be looked upon, to be the object of the gaze without the ability to return the gaze, was a mark of dishonor: "Toxic shaming occurred when one felt that there was no inhibition in the eyes of others, when the eyes of others would 'desoul' you" (C. A. Barton 2001: 248). The abuse continued throughout his imprisonment, as soldiers undressed him, mocked him, crowned him with thorns, and even struck his head. Mark's description of the crucifixion itself is less explicit, but an ancient audience would not have required a detailed description, since they would have been familiar with the ritualized stripping of masculinity in crucifixion: the exposure of the body, the lack of control over even breathing, and the contempt of onlookers. Finally, Mark's rendition of Jesus' desperate cry of abandonment from the cross marks Jesus as a man who has utterly lost control of himself as he passes from life to death.

Although Christians redeemed the ignominy of the crucifixion through their own interpretations, to an outside observer such as Celsus, the mode of Jesus' death yielded one more token of his defective masculinity. Celsus's discussion of Jesus' arrest, imprisonment, and crucifixion itemizes a number of details that the Pastor omits. Of these episodes in Jesus' life, the Pastor writes only that Jesus Christ "in his testimony before Pontius Pilate made the good confession" (1 Tim 6:13). Celsus, on the other hand, labels Jesus' arrest disgraceful and calls attention to some of the more shameful aspects of Jesus' ordeal, including his mock investiture in a purple robe and crown of thorns (Origen, *Cels.* 1.31, 34; Origen offers a counter-interpretation of these incidents as evidence of heroic self-control, since Jesus refrains from responding in anger [*Cels.* 7.55]). Finally, Celsus contrasts Jesus' muteness under torture with Epictetus's self-controlled eloquence. "When his [Epictetus's] master was twisting his leg he smiled gently and calmly said, 'You are breaking it. . . .' What comparable saying did your God utter while he was being punished?" (Origen, *Cels.* 7.53; not surprisingly, Origen claims that Jesus' very lack of speech testifies to his self-control: "We would reply to him that by his silence under the scourge and many other outrages he manifested a courage and patience superior to that of any of the Greeks who spoke while enduring torture" [*Cels.* 7.55]). Thus, according to one second-century pagan observer of Christianity, Jesus demonstrated in his dying, as in his living, a deficiency of the dignity and virtue requisite for manliness.

While the Pastor does not allude to the mode of Jesus' death, he invokes in several places the unusual metaphor of Christ's *epiphaneia*, his appearing or manifestation, phrasing that can refer both to Christ's eschatological return as well as to his fleshly presence among humans as part of human history (1 Tim 6:14; 2 Tim 1:10; 4:1, 8; Titus 2:13; Davies 1996b: 53). *Epiphaneia* is cultic terminology, part of the vocabulary of the ruler-cult: Caesar's title included the declaration, for example, that he was "God manifest" (Dibelius and Conzelmann: 104). In developing his Christology, the Pastor thus emphasizes imagery that magnifies the dignity and even majesty of Jesus while obscuring elements of his story understood (for example, by the pagan Celsus) as symptoms of a shameful want of masculinity. The communities for which the Pastor wrote knew the manner of Jesus' death. They knew, that is, that he had been beaten, mocked, exposed, and pierced. Nonetheless, the Pastor does not encourage the letters' recipients to meditate on the image of the crucified and thereby emasculated Jesus but on the glorious image of his imperial manifestation.

Through his self-presentation in the Pastoral Epistles, the Pastor separated himself from predecessors who adhered to other practices of masculinity. He did this in part by encoding Paul's story as a narrative of exemplary masculine development. He did this in part by omitting ignominious elements of Jesus' biography. The historical Paul had written, "I bear in my body the marks of Jesus " (Gal 6:17), identifying his own scars with the violations Jesus incurred in the ordeals of imprisonment and crucifixion. Unconcerned that he would be emasculated by his corporal hosting of a crucified man, Paul had announced, "It is Christ who lives in me" (Gal 2:20). In contrast, with his silence on the crucifixion, the Pastor separated himself from the unmanly image of the crucified Christ. Such distance was a necessary prerequisite for the Pastor's prescription of a socially conservative protocol of masculinity for male followers of Jesus.

"Knowing How to Preside over His Own Household": Imperial Masculinity and Christian Asceticism in the Pastorals, Hermas, and Luke-Acts

Mary Rose D'Angelo
University of Notre Dame

In the late first and early second century, early Christian texts begin to express explicit interest in and anxiety about the confirmation of a masculine role. In many of them, the early Christian masculinity they construct is specifically tied to the conduct of a household and is manifested in responsiblity for its inferior members. This concern is articulated by the query of 1 Tim 3:5: "If some one does not know how to preside over [*prostēnai*] his own household, how will he attend to [*epimelēsetai*] the church?"[1] "Presiding over a household" required the display of women, children, and slaves who manifested appropriate submission, as well as the other virtues that promised individual and social good order. The governance of a household is a marker of masculinity that is of particular interest to me as feminist, for it demonstrates the ways that male status functions by making its mark upon its "others." Both the significance of household governance for masculinity and its impact on "others" in the household emerge in a *dictum* from the *Sentences of Sextus*, a gnomic text that probably originated in the (later) second century and was popular in Christian circles for many centuries: "Dismissing his wife, a man confesses not to be able to rule a woman" (246). In what follows, I am concerned not only with how the Pastorals, the *Shepherd of Hermas*, and Luke-Acts construct masculinity but even more with the question of how the masculinities they construct structure power relations in their audiences. The Pastorals (1 and 2 Timothy; Titus) articulate the principle, while the

---

* Much of the research for this essay was done on a research leave supported by a Henry Luce III Fellowship in Theology 2000 and by the University of Notre Dame.
1 Translations in this essay are my own unless otherwise noted.

Shepherd of Hermas voices its author's anxiety about his own failures in paternal authority. Elsewhere I have drawn a broad picture of concerns with masculinity in Luke-Acts, a work in which gender plays a central and widely remarked role (D'Angelo 2002; cf., e.g., Parvey; Schüssler Fiorenza 1986; D'Angelo 1990a; 1990b; 1999; Seim, 1994a; 1994b; Reimer; Reid). Together these texts manifest creative variations on the motif of the imperial *paterfamilias* whose virtue is guaranteed by the good conduct of his dependents and guarantees the good order of the community.

The Pastorals, the *Shepherd of Hermas,* and Luke-Acts share a constellation of concerns with gender whose individual elements appear in a number of early second-century texts. Each of these works constructs a conversation between (an inscribed, perhaps fictive) author and a specified reader or readers. All three of these "authors" are men of some status, and their readers, and, in case of the *Shepherd*, readers and hearers, are also evoked in ways that construct gendered relations among the audiences. Whether concerned with manliness or with the distinction of male from female social roles, these texts envisage governance of a household as a qualification for participation in the developing but still less than clearly defined structures of leadership. While all these texts affirm household government as a measure of manly virtue, all three reflect and respond to a growing interest in ascetic practice, including sexual abstinence. In response to Roman imperial power, the Pastorals, *Hermas,* and Luke-Acts engage in a dialectic of resistance and accommodation whose terms are set in part by the desire of Trajan (98–117) and Hadrian (117–138) to reassert the "family values" that played a substantial role in Augustus's consolidation of power.

Imperial Family Values in the Second Century and Early Christian Sexual Politics

Trajan acceded to an imperial throne that was still shaky from the effort of dislodging Domitian; the propaganda that sought to solidify his hold upon it rearticulated the claim to restoring the republic that had become a leitmotif of imperial succession. Both he and Hadrian touted their military campaigns and victories, evoked reminiscences of the Augustan era through visual cues, and recalled other aspects of the Augustan ideological program. Prominent among the latter was the "family values" campaign in which Augustus celebrated his use of legal means and personal example to restore the *mos maiorum* (ancestral mores) with regard to marriage, family, consumption, social distinctions, sexual morality, and devotion to the gods (D'Angelo 2003a). Among these measures, the marriage laws (*lex iulia de adulteriis, lex iulia de maritandis ordinibus*) were particularly central, providing, as Catherine Edwards remarks, "the last word in rhetorical invective" (1993: 62). The activities and virtues of Livia were likewise deployed in this effort (Fischler). The increase in the prestige and public function of marriage in the early second century discerned by Peter Brown (1987: 246–48) reflects not so much a new prestige as new ways of propounding a supposedly traditional morality.

One window into the early second-century discourse of family values is to be found in Pliny's speech of thanks to Trajan on his assumption of the consulship (100 C.E.); his expanded and published version is now known as the *Panegyric*. Pliny's effusions tactfully insinuate his own hopes for the relatively new regime, but, as Julian Bennett concludes, they also reflect Trajan's own publicity (63–64). Both Nerva and Trajan are characterized as *parens*, much is made of the title *pater patriae* (21; 56.3) and the relations of the empire and the emperor are characterized as *pietas* (the virtue that comprises familial duty and devotion and duty and devotion to the gods; 3.2). Capitoline Jupiter is said to have chosen Trajan (94.1–4), and an analogy is drawn between the emperor and the divine father of all (88.8). Trajan's distributions of largesse (25–28) and grain (29) are characterized as the product of the emperor's parental care. His virtues remove the need for coercion in childbearing and rearing; both women (20.3) and men (27) are eager to have children (cf. *Letters* 10.2). These public virtues are reflected in his personal moderation and the conduct of his "house and bedroom" (82–83). The emperor's wife, Pompeia Plotina, and his sister, Ulpia Marciana, are lauded for their civic and modest personae (83.7; 84.1) and the harmony with which they collaborate in the imperial household (84.5). Pliny is careful to make clear that their virtues are the product of Trajan's molding and example (cf. 83.7, 8; 84.4: *te enim imitant, te subsequi student*). He draws upon the conviction that the husband is to be the moral and intellectual instructor of his wife. This conviction appears also in the gift of Plutarch, Pliny's contemporary, to Pollianus and Eurydice, a couple who were both Roman citizens as well as members of the nobility of Delphi (*Conj. praec.* 47–48 [*Mor.* 145A–146A]; Pomeroy 1999: 42–44), in Pliny's own description of his young wife's attentiveness to his writing (*Letters* 4.19), and, less pleasantly, in Juvenal's loathing for learned women (*Sat.* 6.434–456, cf. 185–199).

Coinage and inscriptions from the reign of Trajan enlist the virtues of Plotina and Marciana and of his niece Matidia and her daughter Sabina in imperial propaganda (R. A. G. Carson: 39 plate 10; Temporini: 100–107, 190; Bennett: 183). Despite (or perhaps because of) Hadrian's supposed incompatibility with Sabina his wife and his highly public devotion to Antinous, he took care to continue the celebration of familial virtue. During his reign, coins were struck in honor of Plotina, Marciana, Matidia, and Sabina; these and other images identified the imperial women with Vesta, guardian of the hearth and of Rome itself, and with the personifications of virtues that had both marital and imperial significance, such as *Pietas*, *Fides*, and *Concordia* (R. A. G. Carson: 43 plate 12; Temporini: 100–115, 255–61 plates 1–5). "What makes the second century significant," in the view of Peter Brown, "is the frequency with which domestic concord associated with the nuclear family was played up symbolically, as part of a public desire to emphasize the effortless harmony of the Roman order" (1988: 16). This is not to deny the real influence of these women or the importance of marriages in the creation of a sort of dynastic succession for the adoptive emperors. But their role in the imperial discourse from this period affirms Kate Cooper's suggestion "that wherever a woman is mentioned a man's character is being judged—and along with it what he stands for" (1996: 19). Chadwick's commentary on *Sentences of Sextus* describes saying 236 as "striking for its purely Hellenic quality, unqualified by any Christian appeal to divine and dominical sanction, basing its disapprobation of divorce on the ground that it is a slight to male pride" (1959: 173). Probably Chadwick's claim of "pure Hellenism" suggests that the saying did not originate from Christian reflection. But in the second century, its context is not pure Hellenism, but Roman political moralism. A man "not able to rule a woman," like a man unable to rule himself, was un-Roman, devoid of the virtues that justified universal rule to Rome (see, e.g., Dionysius of Halicarnassus, *Antiquities* 1.3.5).

For Christians of the early second century, one catalyst in the need to develop and display "family values" of recognizable excellence was the Roman policy on Christians attested in the exchange between Pliny and Trajan (Pliny the Younger, *Ep.* 10.96–97). This policy prescribed the "ultimate punishment" for those who clung to the name Christian but chose not to pursue Christians unless they were arrested for other crimes or formally denounced as Christians. Thus Christians could practice their faith and even proselytize quite aggressively—until they incurred the wrath of an outsider. The reactive character of this policy fostered Christian hopes of taking a place in imperial society. The distinction between an externally imposed and a perceived crisis is sometimes used to explain an early Christian sense of tribulation in the absence of sustained and widespread persecution (A. Y. Collins 1984: 84–110; Osiek: 12). But throughout the first half of the second century, the threat of persecution was by no means merely perceived. Rather, as a threat that was both suspended and capricious, it generated a permanent state of crisis. And the imperial reactions, if intermittent, were savage once aroused. Christians were given the strongest possible motivation for arguing for the blamelessness, indeed the exemplary character, of their mores, whether to avoid denunciation or to validate the deaths of those who had been denounced.

In the later second and third centuries, the Christian writers who produced the apologetic genre responded by arguing explicitly that the moral superiority of the Christians made them the emperor's best allies in achieving order in the empire (Justin, *1 Apol.* 12–17; Tertullian, *Apol.* 2–3). The complexities of the early Christian situation and the importance of marriage, family, and sexual mores in it are well illustrated in Justin's narrative of an incident from the city of Rome in the mid-second century: martyrs were made when a woman converted to Christianity and then divorced her husband (*2 Apol.* 2). Her conversion and even her attempts to get her husband to change his sexual practices seem not to have caused problems (2.4), but in response to the divorce, her husband denounced her and her Christian teacher, one Ptolemeus. The teacher and at least two others died (2.11–20), and Justin expected to follow them (3.1). Justin recounts this story in part to show that the Christians were persecuted for the very superiority of their sexual mores. This was a view apparently not shared by either the husband or the magistrate. On the contrary, what Justin sees as evidence of superior chastity they identify as a breach of marital fidelity. This disjuncture illuminates the difficulties facing Christian attempts to argue for moral superiority and may shed light on Ignatius's stipulation that ascetics should not only refrain from boasting but even be known only to the bishop (*Pol.* 5.2).

The Pastorals, *Hermas,* and Luke-Acts make similar, less formal apologies that respond both to the Roman policy on Christians and to the imperial ideology described above. This combination of pressures is most easily demonstrated for the early second century, and all these texts have been attributed to this period by at least some interpreters on other grounds. But the dates of each continue to be disputed; arguments have been made that place both the Pastorals and Luke-Acts in the later first century.[2] To my mind, the strongest argument for a date in the early second century is the way these texts appear to respond to Trajan's policy on Christians. But it is not certain that the policy on Christians was Trajan's innovation; it may have been inherited from earlier practice.

---

2 Luke Timothy Johnson continues to attribute the Pastorals to Paul (26–31), while Dennis MacDonald (1983) wishes to locate them in the same milieu as *Acts of [Paul and] Thecla;* Quinn and Wacker give a overview of arguments, choosing a date in the late first century (18–22), while Margaret MacDonald prefers the second (1996: 154–71). *Hermas* has been attributed to dates between the very late first century and 155; Osiek (18–19) and Jeffers (106–12) review the evidence. Luke-Acts has been located at a wide range of dates, from before the death of Paul to about 135; Conzelmann delineates the debate until 1966, opting for a date shortly after 70; in the same volume, John Knox prefers a date around 125. For a more recent argument suggesting a date as late as 135, see Wills 1991.

Nor does emphasizing the imperial context of the sexual politics in the Christian texts establish that all or any of them dates from this period. Neither the imperial discourse nor the Christian appropriation is so new that the details can be precisely dated. I do not expect this essay to resolve the questions about the dates of these texts. Unlike some interpreters of ancient social history (Dixon 1997b), I do believe in social change, even over relatively short periods of time and even in the ancient world, which was so firmly committed to an ideology of moral nostalgia. But I am less convinced of scholarship's ability to delineate change with certainty. The second century emperors were reasserting and revising aspects of Augustus's propaganda; further, it is difficult to distinguish motifs of the reigns of Trajan and Hadrian from that of Domitian.[3] The complaints of an elite in service to his successors make a poor basis for reconstructing Domitian's social policies (cf. D'Ambra: 7–10). Suetonius accuses him of personal sexual depravity (*Dom.* 22) but also recounts his revival of Augustan social measures and assiduous (not to say terrifying) correction of morals (3–4). The material remains that survived the attempt to erase him from Roman memory are slender (Flower), but enough remains to confirm the literary evidence for his revival of Augustan moral themes; in particular, a frieze from the forum he built as a monument to the Flavian dynasty provides a striking display of female domestic virtue (D'Ambra: see esp. 59–60, 78–108). Thus, if the moral dicta favored in the reigns of Trajan and Hadrian cannot be used to date the Christian texts, it is equally important to be clear that attributing one or all of them to an earlier date does not exclude the observations I make below.

Imperial masculinities of the second century were by no means monolithic. Maud Gleason's study of second-century masculinity juxtaposes the postures of two famous rhetors. Polemo's construction of a masculine self by rigorously eliminating all that might suggest the feminine stands in striking contrast to the high-risk, paradoxical masculinity of Favorinus, who celebrated his own status as a "eunuch who was yet accused of adultery" (Philostratus, *Lives of the Sophists* 489; Gleason 1995). In David Konstan's reading of the romances of the second century, their dependent, distraught, and complaining lovers provide a contrast to the virtues of the epic hero (1994: 15–26) and, one might add, to the self-control and authority expected of a *paterfamilias* (A. E. Hanson 1999: 29; Gleason 1999a: 69–73). But the novels resolve this opposition by their teleological drive toward a marriage that affirms the authority of

---

3 But see Kleiner, who argues for a distinct difference in the use of imperial women in official art of the Flavian dynasty, on one hand, and that of Trajan and Hadrian, on the other (53).

family, city, and empire (Perkins 1995: 72–76; see also Egger). The early Christian texts are likewise involved in complex negotiations over the meanings of masculinity, negotiations that are more complex in that the households they rule and provide for often lie at or outside the horizon of imperial family values. Early Christian patterns of masculinity, then, should be expected to offer not uniformity but variations on themes. In the Pastorals, *Hermas*, and Luke-Acts, governance of the household offered one strategy for defining masculinity while negotiating a stance toward the empire: leadership that was credible to insiders and outsiders alike and ascetic practice, particularly sexual asceticism.

The Pastorals

Gendering the Conversation: Man-to-Man Counsel

The three letters known as 1 and 2 Timothy and Titus present themselves as man-to-man talks, a set of dispatches[4] from the aging and threatened (i.e., matryred) Paul to his younger apprentices Timothy and Titus. The "suffering self" of this Paul, that is, the memory of Paul's fame and his martyrdom, plays a special role in undergirding the message. Second Timothy is set in the midst of the trial that will end in his death (4:16), but the voice of this "Paul" speaks from beyond the grave, awaiting only final vindication: "I have fought the good fight, I have finished the race, I have kept the faith" (4:6–8). Lesser suffering also plays a role in characterizing him; he complains of being betrayed and abandoned (2 Tim 1:15; 4:14–15, 9–13, 16), emphasizing that his only support in his "first defense" was the Lord (4:16–17). As an example for the audience, he is the foremost object of divine pity, rescued from his former status as "greatest of sinners" (1 Tim 1:13–17).

Both recipients are addressed as Paul's "true (legitimate) child" (1 Tim 1:2, Titus 1:4). Titus receives very little further characterization, except in so far as his authority is established by the counsels he receives to pass on. "Timothy" emerges much more clearly; youthful and therefore insecure in his authority (4:12), he is yet well qualified for it. Called "beloved" by "Paul" (2 Tim 1:2) and the child of a believing

---

4 The question of whether these letters are the product of a single author has been disputed; indeed, the unity of *Hermas* and Luke-Acts has also been questioned. I assume that *Hermas* and Luke-Acts have undergone a complex development. I shall treat the Pastorals as a body of work, assuming that if they are not the work of a single author, one provides the models for the others—that is, the Pastorals as I discuss them are the creation of the author who supplied the latest of the three.

mother and grandmother (2 Tim 1:5), Timothy was raised in the scriptures (3:15) and singled out by prophetic designation and the laying on of Paul's hands (1:6; cf. 1 Tim 1:18; 4:14). As disburser of Paul's instruction, he is to act like a banker or, more likely, a man of means, who has been given a deposit and is responsible for it. And he is responsible; he is not merely sober but overly abstemious and frequently ailing (1 Tim 5:23), so that "Paul" must urge him to take a little wine. He is exhorted under the images of soldier (1 Tim 1:18; 2 Tim 2: 3–5) and athlete (1 Tim 4:7–8), images of manliness drawn from the undisputed letters (1 Cor 9:7, 24–26; 2 Cor 10:3, 4; Phil 3:12–14) and from common parenetic stock (Dibelius and Conzelmann: 32–33, 68–69) but redirected in 2 Tim 4:6–8 to focus upon Paul's martyrdom. It is likely that the first readers also knew Timothy as a martyr, for he is urged to "co-suffer" with the gospel (2 Tim 2:3, 11; cf. 4:5).

Throughout the second century Paul's authority, though significant, was by no means uncontested. Like the evocation of his martyrdom, the prophecies of false teaching, defections, and general wickedness (1 Tim 4:1–5; 2 Tim 3:1–9) impose an authoritative interpretation on events known to the first audience and so prove Paul's prophetic gift, shoring up his authority and that of his disciples, including the writer. The parenetic counsels likewise not only seek to change or influence the communal relations of the second-century Christians but also to enhance Paul's prestige. The intent, however it may have been received, was probably to impress at least some readers with the moral excellence of these dispositions of good conduct in the household of God. The codes establish this "Paul" as one who is well able to guide/preside over the conduct of the church at large. This does not mean that the dispositions the letters make reflect the real arrangements of the Christian communities to which they are supposedly addressed; as has frequently been observed, they should be taken as prescriptive rather than descriptive.

This observation, of course, raises the question of the earliest "real" readers of the letters. Lucinda Brown's analysis of 1 Timothy led her to conclude that the letter might be addressed only to those already ensconced in positions of leadership (83), whereas Linda Maloney has suggested that "the whole rhetoric of the Pastorals is addressed as much to women as to men" (369). If Maloney is right, then that rhetoric has been calculated to perform what it also prescribes: a kind of chain of command. While the leaders, perhaps even all the men of the congregation (1 Tim 2:8), might have placed themselves in the role of either Paul or Timothy, women, children, and slaves are kept very much to the side of, or below, the conversation: they are not so much hearers as overhearers of this instruction.

Judith Perkins's study of the "suffering self" in the second century emphasizes the deployment of suffering as resistance, as enacting a "subversion of deference and hierarchy" in the martyr acts of the later second and third centuries (1995: 104–23). But, despite the celebration of Paul and Timothy as martyrs and of Jesus as the one "who attested the good confession before Pontius Pilate" (1 Tim 6:13), the complaining masculinity presented in these letters enforces rather than subverts "deference and hierarchy," seeking a place in the Roman imperial order. The Pastorals have a widely noted concern with the views of outsiders (1 Tim 3:7; 5:14; Bassler 1996: 31–33; M. Y. MacDonald 1996: 154–78), and the largest pressure from the outside world comes from the imperial interest. "Paul" instructs Timothy to cause prayers to be offered "for emperors and all those who are in authority, that we may lead a quiet and peaceful life" (1 Tim 2:1–2). Titus also is told that the Cretan churches must be reminded "to be subject to rules and authorities, to obey, to be prepared for every good deed, to offend no one, to be pacific, clement, demonstrating meekness to all human beings" (3:1). More than prayer is required in this effort; most of 1 Timothy and Titus are devoted to encouraging the community to adopt behavior that the author expects will obtain or protect "a quiet life" in which they can live out their piety.

Household Governance and Conducting the Household of God

Although the Pastorals celebrate martyrdom and inculcate the other virtues, they include no exhortation to the display of courage or manliness (*andreia*) as does, for instance, 4 Maccabees. Instead, they construct masculinity by a careful distinction of male from female roles: men from women, elder men from elder women, younger men from younger women. Central to these distinctions is the order of the household. The phrase "preside over one's own household" especially describes the task of the *episkopos*: "an *episkopos*[5] must be blameless, husband of one wife ...

---

5 The three terms *episkopos*, *diakonos*, and *presbytēr* are difficult to translate because of their prominence in later church office. The traditional choice for translation has been between "bishop, deacon, presbyter" and "overseer, minister, elder." Other options could be more helpful. The terms *episkopos* and *diakonos* designate roles in civic and ritual contexts in Greek and Roman cities, as well as having some place in household terminology. BAGD leans heavily toward "guardian" for *episkopos* and "agent, intermediary" (1) and "assistant" (2) for *diakonos*, while LSJ prefers "inspector" and "servant , messenger" (I.1) and "attendant or official" (I.2) respectively. Using "guardian" for *episkopos* and "attendant" for *diakonos* might help to evoke the ancient civic and religious contexts while avoiding overspecification. But for this essay, I prefer to transliterate the first two terms and use "elder" for the third.

presiding well over his own household, and holding children in submission [*en hypotagē*], with all holiness. For if someone does not know how to preside over his own household, how will he attend to the household of God?" (3:1, 4, 5). These verses illuminate the dual aspects of "presiding": it involves both providing for (cf. Titus 3:8, 14) and controlling those under one's charge (cf. 1 Thess 5:12). The term is used to describe the functioning of *episkopoi, diakonoi,* and elders (1 Tim 3: 4, 5, 12; 5:17). The *diakonoi,* like the *episkopoi,* are expected to be "husbands of one wife, presiding well over their children and their own households" (3:12). Does this imply that they also are to preside over the church, or is there a distinction between those who preside and "those who have ministered/acted the *diakonos* well" (3:13)? Elders, who receive much less attention in 1 Timothy, may include both *episkopoi* and *diakonoi* and are said to preside, apparently in the community (5:17). Titus seems to use the terms *elder* and *episkopos* interchangeably and prescribes that elder/*episkopos* be "husband of one wife, having children who are faithful, not guilty of uncleanness or rebellious [*anypotakta*]" (1:5–6).[6]

The importance of "regulating the household" extends beyond the use of the word "preside." Titus 1:7 explains the *episkopos* as *theou oikonomoi,* God's household manager, who stands in and speaks for the divine *paterfamilias.* In contrast to the disputes and speculation arising from "the teaching of oddities, or clinging to myths and genealogies" (1 Tim 1:3–4; 2 Tim 2:14; Titus 3: 9–10), Timothy is to instruct the communities in *oikonomian theou* (1 Tim 1:4, "the household management of God" or "godly education"; Dibelius and Conzelmann: 15). Paul sees himself as trusted with an *oikonomian* (1 Cor 9:17; cf. 4:1–3), apparently meaning stewardship, and Ephesians uses the word to refer to the divine plan (Eph 1:10; 3:2, 9; Col 1:25). But here the word seems almost to function as a title for the codes that are so central to both 1 Timothy and Titus. As Paul's testament, 2 Timothy establishes this instruction as a "last word" of Paul, repudiating the controversies so likely to arise from the undisputed letters, "in which are many things hard to understand" (2 Pet 3:16). Their nuanced and dialectical theologizing is replaced in the Pastorals by instruction in "how one must behave in the household of God" (*pōs dei en oikō theou anastrephesthai,* 1 Tim 3:15).

Although 1 Tim 3:4–5 identifies "presiding over one's house" with controlling children and prescribes submission for slaves (1 Tim 6:1–2;

---

6 The Pastorals may have been conceived on the model of Ignatius's *To Polycarp,* which is also from a (potential) martyr to an individual, accompanies letters to communities, charges the recipient with the task of passing on the martyr's message, and offers counsel for the regulation of communal life.

Titus 2:9–10), "Paul" seems most exercised over threats to household order and therefore male status from women, who must be in "all submission" (*en pasē hypotagē*, 1 Tim 2:11; cf. Titus 2:5). This is particularly noteworthy in 1 Tim 2:8–15. At first reading, this passage seems to consist of a single verse concerned with men (*andres*, 2:8), followed by six about women. But women are defined in relation to men throughout; 2:8–10 prescribes attitudes at prayer for both men and women. Men are to avoid wrath and dispute, women ostentatious and seductive dress (cf. *Pan.* 83.7, where Pliny praises Plotina as "modest in dress" [*modica cultu*]; Plutarch, *Conj. praec.* 26 [*Mor.* 141E]). The next four verses establish the primacy of men over women in the community through an exegesis of Gen 2–3 that justifies "Paul's" insistence that a woman not assume authority or teach but rather learn from her husband.

With the strictures on widows (1 Tim 5:3–16), the prediction of heretical seducers (2 Tim 3:5–6), and the stipulations on elder and younger women (Titus 2:3–8), 1 Tim 2:8–15 offers not only bursts of perfervid misogyny but also noteworthy reflections of the Augustan marriage laws. The suspicion of female susceptibility to seduction and to "lusts of every kind" (1 Tim 2:14; 5:6, 11–12; 2 Tim 3:5–6) is reminiscent of the fears enshrined in the *lex iulia de adulteriis*. The command that younger widows keep marrying until they are sixty (well past the age to bear children [1 Tim 5:9, 14]) and the claim that childbearing will bring women salvation (1 Tim 2:15; cf. 5:14) seem particularly close to the stipulations of the *lex iulia de maritandis ordinibus*, which required that women remarry until a fixed age and offered rewards for the bearing of children (D'Angelo 2003b: 158–62). The Roman laws bore also (although less than equally) upon men (see Pliny's request for the right of three children in *Ep.* 10.2), but the Pastorals show a certain realism in the assumption that control of women is central to the ideology of familial piety.

The contradictory character of the instructions to widows has frequently been noted (Bassler 1996: 33–34). The conflict between "Paul's" command that women marry and continue to remarry until the age of sixty and his requirement that only women who were wives of one husband should be enrolled as widows mirrors a similar conflict in Roman practice: the legal stipulation and long-established social preference that widows (and the divorced) remarry conflicted with the idealization of the *univira* (Tregiarri: 233–35). As Jouette Bassler points out, the author appears to wish to curtail the number of widows (1996: 34–35); indeed, combined with ancient life expectancies, this pair of stipulations would have reduced them to virtual nonexistence. The women the author appears to have found most objectionable were the young widows who might change their minds and wish to marry (5:11–12); these women may have been, or included, "virgins called widows" (Ignatius, *Smyrn.* 13.1), celibate women in the service of the community (M. Y. MacDonald 1996: 157–64; Maloney: 371).

The treatment of widows comes between a brief instruction to "Timothy" on how to treat elder men and women (5:1–2) and the counsel that "elders who have presided well" deserve a double honorarium (5:18–19). While some scholars and translations treat the male and female elders of 5:1–2 as older men and women and the (lexically masculine) elders of 5:18–19 as presbyters, this distinction is far from certain. The category of widows served a dual purpose: leadership and support. As Bassler points out, the widows received social benefits as well as financial ones (1996: 34–35). She focuses upon celibacy as freedom, but the recognition of widows as a group is likely to have involved prestige and authority as well. Thus the community seems to have recognized women elders, among them widows, and women *diakonoi* (1 Tim 3:11). The general strictures on women in 2:8–15 and the prescriptions for widows seek to limit their status and ministry to the one attributed to the women elders in Titus 2:3–5: teaching younger women to be good (submissive) wives and mothers. The author's goal in attempting to restrict the widows to as few as possible of the literally elderly, poor, and bereft seems to be to reduce these women from the status of leaders to that of dependents. Financial issues also are likely to have played a role in the attempt to reduce their numbers. First Timothy accuses the teachers of oddities of considering "piety" as a livelihood, so it would seem that a similar question could arise about male teachers (6:5–6; cf. Titus 1:11). But in contrast to the tight social regulation of widows, the qualifications for male leaders focus on moral excellence (including lack of the love of money). Except for the stipulation that the *episkopos* must not be a neophyte (1 Tim 3:6) and that both *episkopos* and *diakonos* be "husband of one wife" (3:2, 12), there is no attempt to curtail access to leadership for men.

Sexual Asceticism: Anxieties and Ambitions

That celibacy allowed women a greater degree of communal leadership may have had a role in the author's expressed hostility to the practice of sexual asceticism or rather to the false teachers who are said to "forbid marriage" (1 Tim 4:3). As Gail Corrington Streete points out, the Pastorals manifest their own form of ascetic practice, of the integrative type. It appears as the practice of the cardinal virtue moderation or temperance (*sōphrosynē* and related forms: 1 Tim 2:9, 15; 3:2; 2 Tim 1:7; Titus 1:8; 2:2, 4, 5, 6, 12; L. A. Brown, esp. 93; cf. *temperantia* attributed to Trajan's personal habits in *Pan.* 82.9). In contrast, *enkrateia* (continence), the word that became associated with more disruptive forms of Christian asceticism, appears only once (*enkratē,* Titus 1:7; see 1 Cor 7:9; 9:25; Gal

5:23; Acts 24:25; 2 Pet 1:6; see also Hunter: 106–7) and "to abstain" is used only negatively (*apechesthai*, 1 Tim 4:3).

While "Paul" castigates those who forbid marriage, he does not go so far as to proscribe celibacy—except for young widows who might disgrace it.[7] Some forms of sexual abstinence do seem to be affirmed, such as that of widowed male leaders. The stipulation that an *episkopos* or *diakonos* be "husband of one wife" does not appear to proceed from Roman ideology. That a husband had had only one wife was an indication of good fortune for Roman writers, but it is not a staple in Roman-period epitaphs, as are *univira* and its equivalents in the epitaphs of women (Treggiari: 235). If "husband of one wife" does not imply that the *episkopoi* and *diakonoi* are required to be married, but only forbidden to remarry if widowed, sexual abstinence is also demanded of some of them—and permitted, perhaps even esteemed, in others—like the models the letters provide. Unless Paul is understood by the author of the Pastorals to have married between 1 Cor 7 and Philippians, where he addresses an unnamed interlocutor as *syzyge* (yokefellow, partner, 4:3), these stipulations are offered by a counselor whose gift (*charisma*) is his ability to practice continence (*enkrateuontai*, 1 Cor 7:7–9). As for Timothy (unless he is supposed to be too young to have married), he appears to have chosen to "remain like" Paul. His grandmother Lois and mother Eunice seem to provide the household that guarantees his respectability (2 Tim 1:5). More importantly, the household that Paul and Timothy know "how to preside over" is the church; sexual abstinence is dangerous when and because it plays a role in the preaching of the unsubmissive (*anypotaktoi*, Titus 1:10), who lead whole households astray (1:11).

Thus in the man-to-man conversation in the Pastorals, the voice of the elder, celibate "Paul" exhorts the young, apparently unmarried "Timothy" to be sure that communal leaders are "husbands of one wife" and in control of their own households, while women are required to stay married and bear children to the absolute end of the period in which they might be fertile. For men, submissive, believing children are a commendation for leadership; for women, the grounds of salvation (1 Tim 2:15). While many of the same virtues are required of men and women, women in general are suspect. In 1 and 2 Timothy, as for Juvenal, fear and loathing are inspired by the spectacle of women trying to learn (*manthanein* = be disciples?) and

---

7 The accusation that some "forbid marriage" may misrepresent the ascetics. In the *Acts of Thekla,* the insidious Demas and Hermogenes accuse Paul of making celibacy a requirement for resurrection (12), but his own words never do this—in the beatitudes of his sermon purity is a pledge but not a requirement of the resurrection (5–6).

to teach. For this Paul, household governance is a strategy for defining a masculinity that affirms Roman family values, protecting the Christian community against the charge that women, children, and slaves run around loose and absolving male Christian sexual ascetics who imitate Paul and Timothy from the charge that they are hostile to marriage.

HERMAS

Gendering the Conversation: Prophecy among the Men and Women Elders

The *Shepherd of Hermas* also ties masculine status to presiding over a household, despite very notable contrasts with the Pastoral Epistles. This author appears to speak in his own voice, though it is difficult to distinguish autobiographical details from the symbolic elements of the dream visions, the revisions of memory, and literary restructuring (Osiek: 8–10). The conversation set up in the *Shepherd* is heavily populated in comparison with the Pastorals' fictive exchange between two authoritative men. The "elder woman" of the visions commands Hermas to write her revelations in a book that he will read to "this city" among the elders, while two copies are entrusted to Grapte, who will exhort the widows and orphans, and Clement, who will send the book to communities beyond Rome (*Vis.* 2.4.3).[8]

Like the human mediators of *Hermas*'s message, its heavenly intermediaries are both male and female. Rhoda, Hermas's former and apparently deceased owner, and the elder woman who is progressively made younger (*Vis.* 1–3) are the first heavenly visitors. The elder woman represents not only the church and (ultimately) the Holy Spirit but also Hermas's own spirit—her age reflects his energy. At least three male mediators also appear: a "youth" (*Vis.* 3.10.7), the shepherd (*Vis.* 5.1), and the angel of repentance (*Man.* 12.6.1). The angel and the shepherd seem to be differing manifestations of one spirit and indeed are not easy to distinguish from the Son of God and the Lord of the tower. While not every image of a shepherd in early Christianity is to be identified as Christ, all

---

8 The readings and the circulation of the books help to validate the prophecy. According to *Man.* 11.9, prophets are to be tested by their lives, by their repudiation of consulting roles, and by communal performance: by speaking after prayer in an assembly of "righteous men"(*andres*), where they show that they are filled with the Holy Spirit and not privately or by consultation (11.13–14). Hermas's visions are private in a sense: located on the road (*Vis.* 1.1.3; 2.1.1; 4.1.2; *Sim.* 2.1.1; 10.1.1), in his house (*Vis.* 3.1.2; 5.1.1; *Sim.* 6.1.1), off in a field, country, or plain (*Vis.* 3.1.4; *Sim.* 7.1.1), so the communal readings and circulation beyond Rome substitute for the prescribed communal inspiration.

the revealers in this text, including the elder woman, the church, are manifestations of the Holy Spirit (*Sim.* 9.1.1), and the Spirit is not clearly
distinguished from the risen Christ (Osiek: 16, 34–36).

"Manliness" (*andreia*) is not included in the *Shepherd's* virtue lists, but
it does carry moral significance. The heroic manliness of the angels who
build the tower is stressed by calling them "six lofty and glorious men"
(*hex andres hypsēlous kai endoxous*); the shepherd, the Son of God, and the
Lord of the tower are all described as "a glorious man" (*anēr tis endoxos,*
Vis. 5.25.1; cf. *Sim.* 9.84.1; 9.89.7; 9.89.8). Manly behaviors can be attributed to female as well as to male figures in the visions: the virgins who
support and carry the stones for the tower are described as acting coura-
geously/in a manly fashion (*andreiōs, Vis.* 3.7.2; *Sim.* 9.2.6). Twelve
women dressed in black serve as their counterparts, as the foolish woman
does to wisdom in Prov 7–9; it is desire for these women that causes some
to be excluded from the tower. Although they also carry stones, they are
not described as manly (*Sim.* 9.9.5–6; 13.8). Hermas may be aware of the
distinction of virgins from women and is willing to attribute manliness
only to virgins (Castelli 1986: 74–78; D'Angelo 1995: 145, 149, 157 n. 61,
158 nn. 83–85).[9] The moral connection of manliness and purity enter the
Christology: the flesh (*sarx*) God chose for the Holy Spirit to dwell in no
way soiled the Spirit but always collaborated with it, behaving in strong
and manly fashion (*ischyrōs kai andreiōs anastrapheisan*) so that God made
"the flesh" partner (*koinōnon*) and heir with the Holy Spirit (*Sim.* 5.5.5–6).
While it is not clear that this "manly behavior" is to be understood as
sexual abstinence, the language is certainly resonant of it.

Gender appears not to form the rigid social boundaries for *Hermas*
that it does for the author of the Pastorals; the author does not experience
communal roles as assigned by gender. Grapte's responsibility for the
"widows and orphans" can be interpreted as a socially female role, allowing her authority only over other women and underage children who
have no *paterfamilias* (Osiek: 59). But "widows and orphans" seems to be
synonymous with "widows and the destitute" in the *Shepherd*; it may
well be an echo of the biblical phrase, referring more generally to those in
need or dependent for their living upon the community. To shelter (*skepa-*
zō) widows and the destitute seems to be particularly central to the
ministry of the *episkopoi* (*Sim.* 9.27.2).[10] By the mid-second century, Justin

---

9 But at their first appearance in *Vis.* 3.7.2 the virtues are called women.

10 See, e.g., *Sim.* 9.26.2 and 9.27.2, where the Shepherd contrasts the *diakonoi* who ministered badly, plundering the life of widows and orphans, to those *episkopoi* who "always
sheltered [*eskepasan*] the poor and the widows by their ministry [*diakonia*] continually." The
difference between the two is not different offices but the way the ministry is exercised, and

attributes to the "one who has presided" (at the weekly Eucharist) the task of caring for "the orphans and the widows, and those in necessity because of sickness or some other reason, and the prisoners and the aliens in residence and simply anyone in need" (*1 Apol.* 67.7). Grapte may well have been counted among the *episkopoi* or elders of the Roman communities; Osiek suggests that the elders among whom *Hermas* is to be read may refer to heads of house churches, both men and women (59 n. 12; she is, however, inclined to see Grapte as a deacon).

Manliness, Ministry, and Enkrateia

Stephen Young identifies the emergence of Hermas's manliness as a plot device in the *Shepherd.* He locates Hermas's manhood in his role in the house-church, a threefold role: prophet, *paterfamilias*-patron, and pastor (247). For Young, the "perceived crisis" to which the visions respond is Hermas's failure in the role of *paterfamilias* and leader, because he lacks authority (or courage) to keep the church he leads and hosts from the temptations arising from commerce. He suggests that Hermas's transfer of allegiance from the female "role-model," Rhoda, and the female mediator, the church, to the male models and mediators, the shepherd and the angel of redemption, is essential to his attainment of manly status. In part this analysis is based on the command/encouragement the elder woman gives at the end of the first vision: "play the man/be courageous, Hermas" (*andrizou, Herma, Vis.* 1.4.2). In the final *Similitude,* the shepherd gives a similar command: "behave manfully in this ministry" (*viriliter in ministerio hoc conversare,* 10.4.1).[11] But there are problems with interpreting the femaleness of the first intermediaries as reflecting or constituting a defect in Hermas's manliness. Already in the second *Vision* the elder woman's youth is partially restored. The youth who explains this to Hermas compares him to an old, discouraged man who receives an unexpected inheritance and "is renewed in spirit and made manly [*andrizetai*] again" (*Vis.* 3.12.2). What revives Hermas's virility and enables him to take off his "softness" (lack of manliness, *malakia*) is the revelation given through the woman church (3.12.2–3).

---

the resonance between the noun and verb drives it home; the true *episkopoi* are those who have sheltered (*eskepasan*) the poor. See also *Mand.* 8.10: "to take charge of the widows, to care [*episkeptesthai*] for the orphan and the needy" are the commands that follow from faith; *Sim.* 1.1.8: "care for [*episkeptesthe*] widows and orphans"; 5.3.7 "give [the money saved by fasting] to the widow or orphan or needy."

11 Young suggests that the Greek had another use of *andrizomai,* but the phrase can be translated into Greek word by word: *andreiōs en tautē tē diakonia anastraphēs.* This version is based on *Sim.* 5.5.6.

For Pliny and the Pastorals the conduct of a household reflects the moral character of its *paterfamilias*. Hermas also exhibits this conviction, and it inspires in him deep anxiety. The elder woman reveals to him that his failure to control his household is the source of divine displeasure (*Vis.* 1.31.1; 2.2.–4); the shepherd tells him that he is being punished for the sins of his household because he is its head (*kephalē*, *Sim.* 7.3). Stephen Young takes all the references to Hermas's household as references to a house church, which, like the prophecy as a whole, extends to the larger circle of the house churches of Rome and Christian communities beyond the city. But, as Osiek points out, some of these references seem to envisage the members of Hermas's immediate and literal household, that is, a wife and children whose sins undermine his role as *paterfamilias* (22–24). The most prominent charge against the children is double: they have "blasphemed [*eblasphēnēsan*] the Lord" and become known as "betrayers of parents" (*prodotai, Vis.* 2.2.2; cf. 1.3.1: "acted lawlessly against God and against you, their parents"). Betrayal and blasphemy suggest that their misdeeds relate in some way to the context or threat of persecution, a threat that emerges throughout the elder woman's instruction (2.7–3.3; see also Osiek: 54) and is made explicit in *Vis.* 4. Their betrayal has involved Hermas so that he is corrupted in financial matters (*Vis.* 1.3.1). In addition, the children have committed sins that the elder woman describes as excesses (*aselgeias,* a word with sexual overtones) and piled up wickednesses (2.2.2). Hermas's wife, on the other hand, is accused of doing evil by not restraining her tongue (2.2.3). In contrast, the instructions the elder woman gives to the "children" who are the community concern the relation of rich and poor (3.9; but see also 2.2.6).

Along with concerns for his household's integrity and the obedience and good order of its members, Hermas is deeply concerned with ascetic practice, especially the practice of sexual asceticism. In the *Shepherd*, *enkrateia* (continence) is a virtue, or, in Hermas's words, a power (*dynamis*) of the Son of God, second only to faith (*Vis.* 3.8.3; *Sim.* 9.13.2), and is essentially manly, as it is in 4 Maccabees (Moore and Anderson: 257–62). Personifed by the second among the virgins who build the tower, *enkrateia* is described as *hē perizōsamenē kai andrizomenē*. In Kirsopp Lake's translation (LCL), she "is girded and looks like a man" (47); in Osiek's, she "is girded and acts like a man" (76). Osiek rightly interprets the participles together, suggesting that she wears "a heavy belt such as a man might wear for a journey or for battle, and has other stereotypically masculine characteristics, such as strength and assertiveness" (77–78). The image can be further elaborated; the belt's effect is to shorten her tunic to or above the knee, to facilitate war, travel, or work. Thus she both looks mannish and acts manfully; the shepherd figures of the second and third centuries wear such short, belted tunics, as does Artemis, the virgin huntress. In other early Christian texts the gesture of girding is associated with the passover flight (1 Pet 1:13; cf. Exod 12:11) and with armor (Eph 6:14) but especially with labor, most often serving at table (John 13:4; 21:7, 18; Luke 12:35, 37; 17:8). In keeping with the nonelite character of Hermas (Osiek: 20–21) and perhaps with his past experience as a slave, manliness is not imaged by athletic or military prowess, as in 4 Maccabees and the Pastorals, but by the ability to stand up to and excel in hard labor.

The practice of *enkrateia* is not limited to sexual abstinence or restraint in this work, but takes in a wide variety of abstentions and engagements (*Mand.* 8). Sexual violations are, even so, first in the list of acts from which one must refrain (8.3). The elder woman calls Hermas "the continent" (*ho enkratēs*) to underline her denial that the desire for Rhoda was the sin that caused divine displeasure with him (*Vis.* 1.2.4). The *Mandates* also pay special attention to chastity. *Mandate* 4 on purity (*hagneia*) deals with the questions of how a husband may cohabit with a wife whom he discovers in some sort of adultery (4.1.4) and whether a widowed husband or wife may remarry (4.4.1). The solutions given by the shepherd bear a tense relationship to the stipulations of the Julian laws. He opines that it is better for the widowed to remain unmarried, though they do not sin if they remarry (4.4); the Julian law penalized, but did not criminalize, widows who did not remarry.

The case of adultery differs. The shepherd rules that a husband must divorce a wife if he knows her to be adulterous; if he does not, he shares her sin (cf. Matt 19:9; 5:32). In this he concurs with the Julian law's prescription that a husband who discovers his wife *in flagrante* must divorce and prosecute her; to do otherwise would leave the husband liable to a legal charge of pandering (*lenocinium*; Tregiarri: 288–90). Pandering was equated with adultery, and both were crimes. In contradistinction to the legal prescription, the shepherd then requires that the husband remain alone and take back his wife should she repent. Both aspects of this decision seem legally problematic: remaining single evades the requirement to stay married until the fixed age, while taking back a wife accused of adultery was also seen as immoral (Osiek: 110–11). How far the latter was enforced is unclear. Suetonius credits Domitian with having eliminated from the equestrian order a man who had divorced a wife for adultery and then remarried her (*Dom.* 7.3), but also accuses Domitian of having divorced Domitia for the same cause and then remarried her (3.1; see on this D'Ambra: 9–10). In the *Shepherd*, the provision for repentance is central to the message communicated by the shepherd, who is also the angel of repentance. He feels obligated to defend the stipulation of forgiveness for the repentant against the charge of providing a pretext for sin (4.1.11); thus the message of repentance is elaborated in *Mand.* 4.2–3.

The ruling that the husband remain single in order to leave room for his wife to repent is not wholly motivated by the message of repentance; purity is also of concern. Whether or not repentance takes place, the spouse, whether husband or wife, who remarries after divorcing a partner for adultery is made adulterous by remarriage (4.1.6, 8, 10; cf. Mark 10:10–12; Matt 19:9; 5:32; Luke 16:18). Even more stringent is the prescription that one may not live with another who "does according to the likeness [*homoiōmata*] of the Gentiles" (4.1.9). Decoding this euphemism is quite difficult. If "live together" refers to being a sexual partner, it may envisage a situation such as Justin's woman; she refused to live with her husband because of his sexual practices (2 *Apol.* 2.3–5). But all the pronouns in *Man.* 4.1.9 are masculine; the commandment may envisage refusing to share a house with anyone, relative or friend, whose sexual practices or other morals do not meet Hermas's standards.

Hermas is required to adopt the practice of sexual abstinence for himself—and for his wife. Sexual abstinence may be seen by Hermas as a condition of prophecy (Osiek: 54); this decision appears to be celebrated and reinforced in his night of fraternal revelry with the twelve virgins (*Sim.* 9.11). But the stipulation is made by the elder woman when she instructs him on how to correct his family: "Make these words known to all your children, and to your wife, who shall be to you as a sister. For she also does not abstain [*apechetai*] her tongue." Perhaps this sexual abstinence is to protect Hermas from sharing the taint of her lack of restraint. Although Hermas occasionally remembers to note that the stipulations apply to women as well as men, *Man.* 4 is articulated in terms of the responsibility of the husband. This reflects Hermas's deep internalization of the social mores that make the *paterfamilias* responsible for his family's actions, as well as the legal stipulations that enforce it (Osiek: 110–11).

The masculinity constructed in the *Shepherd* admits of women as mediators of prophetic knowledge. Hermas assumes and relies upon the authority of Grapte, both to lend authority to his book and to instruct (*nouthetein*) those under her supervision. He shows no explicit interest in excluding women from leadership, though it is possible that the "unrestrained tongue" of his wife is actually her participation in prophetic speech or communal leadership (Osiek: 54). His visionary experience includes female mediators, though it also reflects misogynist stereotypes (such as the twelve women in black). These "wild" women seem to inspire in Hermas some fear, but not the loathing so prominent in the Pastorals. They are dangerous because they are desirable. Hermas's successive visions of the once-desired Rhoda, the elder woman/the Sybil/the church, then the virgins and the women in black seem to bear out Emma Stafford's observation that female forms or idealized women personify abstract ideas because in ancient discourse these feminine forms convey the ability of the abstraction to arouse desire—whether for good or ill.

Hermas and the Imperial Order

Unlike the Pastorals, Hermas foresees no potential truce with the imperial order. The shepherd requires Hermas to avoid committing himself to the possession of lands and buildings in the city from which the lord of this city (the emperor) can and will expel him when he chooses. Instead of buying into Rome, he is to consider himself an alien, while waiting for the day when he will be expelled from the city for rejecting the laws of its lord for the law of his own city (*Sim.* 1.1–6). While this image recalls the emperors' periodic expulsions of various undesirable elements from the city of Rome, it may be an allusion to the threat of martyrdom, the ultimate expulsion from the empire. In *Sim.* 1.7, the pronoun shifts from singular to plural: not only Hermas but all the community are to purchase the lives of the downtrodden instead of lands and to care for widows and orphans (*Sim.* 1.1.7–11). Perhaps because of his own experience of enslavement, Hermas appears to promote the practice of expending charitable and perhaps communal funds for buying slaves and captives (cf. *Man.* 8.10).

Undoubtedly, Hermas has as little desire to attract hostile attention from outsiders, including the emperor, as does the author of the Pastorals. But the imperial order bears upon multiple aspects of his life. Male slaves in antiquity never attained manhood but were always liable to the appellation "boy" (*puer, pais*). Nor could they acknowledge a family of origin or found a new one. In so far as he shares Roman family values, Hermas may be resisting the powerlessness of his own past. The fragility of the slave family unprotected by formal marriage and subject to dissolution by sales and the construction of slaves as moral inferiors made freedpersons the more eager to display the moral excellence of their newly acquired families (D'Angelo 1990b: 68–69, 82–83). By exerting control over his wife and children as their father and head, Hermas establishes his worthiness to speak in the spirit to and among the leaders of a larger household, the church (*Vis.* 3.9.7–9).

LUKE-ACTS

Gendering the Conversation: Men Fit to Appear before Emperors and Assemblies

Like the Pastorals, Luke-Acts is set into the frame of an exchange between two men of status, a frame created by the much-studied prologues

(Luke 1:1–4; Acts 1:1). The addresses to Theophilus, whether they are seen as a literary device or a debt owed by the author, place these works within a familiar ancient practice: the two books represent service rendered to a patron (Moxnes 1991: 267; more tentatively, Alexander: 190–91). This service is of a professional character: Loveday Alexander links the prologues by content and diction with the scientific literature of antiquity (passim, esp. 172–76). The author they present is conscious of and well able to negotiate the difficulties of sifting evidence, estimating witnesses, and creating an orderly narrative. Although some interpreters have suggested that this author was a woman, the masculine participle in 1:3 (parēkolouthēkoti, Luke 1:3) establishes a masculine persona for the narrator (D'Angelo 1990a: 443).

Theophilus's elite status is intimated by the epithet kratiste, a Greek equivalent of "Optimus," the epithet awarded to Trajan by the senate and connected by Pliny to Jupiter Optimus Maximus ("best and greatest"; Pliny, Pan. 2.7; 88.4–8; Letters 10.1.2; see Bennett 105–6).[12] In Acts, kratiste is used by Paul to address the Roman procurators Felix (23:26; 24:3) and Festus (26:25). Thus the masculinity inscribed in the prologues is elite not only by the more general criterion of literacy, but even by the standards of Roman social stratification: governors of minor provinces (such as Felix and Festus) were drawn from the equestrian rank (Edwards 1993: 13–15). In turn, the author acquires status from his relationship with his elite patron.[13] He undertakes to guide his benefactor on an expedition in search of the very thing that the Roman officials of Acts seek but cannot attain: surety (tēn asphaleian, 1:4; cf. Acts 21:34; 22:30; 25:26) about the things accomplished in their midst. The success of the author and readers is itself sure: the narrator offers assiduous research upon the accounts of "many others," and his information derives from eyewitnesses and the guardians of the message who succeeded them (Luke 1:1–2), while his reader has been instructed in these events (1:4) and so is well able to discern the superiority of his account.

Theophilus, as representative of the reader, provides a sort of dramatic, personified captatio. The early Christian readers and hearers take up a position at his side, among the elevated ranks from which imperial

---

12 Vernon K. Robbins compares the "inscribed author" to Josephus, who also presents the events of his narrative to an "inscribed reader with a Roman name" (314). It should be noted, however, that neither Theophilos nor Epaphroditos is, strictly speaking, a Roman name; both names are actually Greek, though either could be used as a cognomen with a real Roman name, a gentilicium, as is the case with Flavius Josephus (304–32, 321).

13 Robbins notes that the "inscribed author" places himself in a subordinate position to the "inscribed reader" (322), but this observation does not exclude the narrator's acquisition of status from their relationship.

governors are drawn. Like Theophilus, they investigate with the privileged knowledge of Christian instruction. That Theophilus is the readers'
exemplar does not, of course, imply that the author expects an audience
exclusively composed of male Christians of the equestrian rank. Paul's
speech to Agrippa addresses him exclusively, but the author stresses
Berenike's presence (Acts 26:2, 19; cf. 25:23; 26:30). The Gospel includes
more stories about women than its two (generally acknowledged)
sources combined; this increase probably reflects a concern with the
instruction of women (Parvey: 138–41; D'Angelo 1990a: 447–48). Nor is it
the case that Luke-Acts would have been intelligible only to instructed
Christians. Of all the early Christian texts, Luke-Acts seems most accessible to exoteric readers. Even though as an example he is both exotic and
elite, the portrait of the Ethiopian eunuch in Acts 8 gives evidence that
the author is quite conscious of the potential interest of uninitiated readers. Rather, readers and hearers are deemed to share the privilege of the
elite male Christian—elite within Roman imperial society and informed
as Christian.

The prologues' construction of an elite Christian masculinity serves a
central concern of Luke-Acts, that of enabling the early Christian message
to be heard on the world stage of imperial Rome: "Public speaking, even
more than literary writing, was the hallmark of the socially privileged
male" (Gleason 1999a: 67). The author's diction also serves this end. The
other Gospels rarely use the term *anēr* (man as male, hero, or husband)
except to mean husband. In Luke-Acts it appears frequently. In some
cases, it is used interchangeably with *anthrōpos* (human being, person), as
long as the referents are male. If this change of usage is a conscious move
on the part of the author, it probably reflects no more than the desire to
elevate the language of the Gospel's sources toward literary Greek and
that of the Septuagint. A more deliberate dramatic choice appears in Acts,
where speakers address crowds as "men" (*andres*) usually with a modi-
fier that suggests a civic context. In Athens, for instance, Paul uses the
address "men, Athenians" (*andres, Athenaioi*, Acts 17:22), so reminiscent
of Socrates in the *Apology* (17A, B; 18A, E; 21E; 22A; 24A, C; 26A, etc.).
Peter addresses the Jewish crowds as "men, brothers" (*andres, adelphoi*,
e.g., Acts 2:14). The ambassadors of Christianity must be fit to appear
before "Gentiles and emperors" (9:15; 27:24), like Paul the Roman citizen,
who is not only bilingual but eloquent enough to tempt a Jewish king and
imperial administrator like Agrippa to "play the Christian" and fit in
every way to make known to the world that "it is not in a corner that
these things were done" (26:26).

In keeping with the author's desire to address the imperial public, a
clear succession of masculine leaders is presented. Jesus carefully selects
a council of twelve named men who will undertake his mission

(6:13–16); when a further seventy missionaries are named, they are not said to be men, but it is easy to assume so (10:1). When a successor to Judas must be found (by the scripture and the Holy Spirit), it is from among the men (*andrōn*) who were with the movement "from the baptism of John until the day when he was taken up from our midst" (Acts 1:21–22). The twelve settle disputes about the widows by the appointment of seven named "Hellenists" to minister to the widows; all are men, in contrast to Grapte, who seems to be in charge of a similar ministry in Hermas's Rome. Luke-Acts does not use the term *diakonos* at all but speaks of ministry and ministering as generic terms. Although women are disciples in Luke-Acts (Luke 10:40; Acts 9:36, *mathētria*) and mentioned as ministering (Luke 4:39; 8:3), the widows of Acts are those who are in need and ministered to (6:1–6; 9:39). Acts speaks of the authorities in Jerusalem as the apostles and elders (11:30; 15:2, 4, 6, 22, 23; 16:4; 21:18); among this group, only men are mentioned. Paul and Barnabas appoint elders in every city (14:23); in his testamentary farewell to the elders of Ephesus, Paul refers to them as *episkopoi* (20:17, 28). If there are women elders, the text gives no indications of them.

As Paul is proved a citizen of Rome with more impeccable claims than his Roman jailer, so also the envoys of Christianity are shown to excel in the practice of those Roman family values that legitimate the Romans' claim to imperium and the emperors' claim to the throne. First and foremost is the representation of men behaving well, with women, children, and slaves following suit. Unlike the Pastorals and the *Shepherd*, Luke-Acts does not directly address prescriptions to the situation of its Christian audience but communicates them through its narrative. Even the teaching sermons of Jesus are directed first to the narratives' internal audiences: the crowds, disciples, and Jewish leaders; their prescriptions must be reapplied or even revised by Luke's audience. Virtues are for the most part not listed or praised but performed in the narrative and communicated through example. Masculine virtue is constructed by the display of men who "know how to preside over (the) household" and of well-regulated households, in which the women, children, and slaves follow the direction and example of the male head of the household—or of those who take their place.

Imperial Family Values in the Narrative of Luke-Acts

Reflections of Roman family values and examples of the household virtuously ruled by its head appear even in the infancy narratives, which belong to the distant and foreign world of the "law and the prophets" and in which women are allowed prophetic speeches. The miraculous birth of John not only echoes biblical narratives, but also appeals to the imperial ideology in which childbearing is a sign not only of good fortune but also of pious duty. Elizabeth names her newborn child against the choice of those who are conducting the circumcision, who seek to name him after his father. She might appear to be following the pattern of the biblical matriarchs, but the narrative makes clear that she acts on her husband's behalf, carrying out Gabriel's command, which she may know only through prophetic inspiration (1:57–65).

A more explicit appeal to the picture of a well-regulated and submissive household is made in the aftermath of Jesus' appearance among the teachers at the age of twelve. Questioned by his mother, he declares his allegiance to his (true, heavenly) father's concerns. But the narrative concludes with the declaration that he returned to Nazareth and was subject to his parents (*hypotassomenos*, 2:51; cf. 1 Tim 2:11; 3:4; Titus 1:6). Having demonstrated his authority and its source, he conforms to the demands of Roman family values for a son in *patria potestas*, appearing again only at the age of "about thirty" (3:23), the right age for a Roman man to enter into public office.[14]

Throughout the body of the Gospel, the Spirit is identified with Jesus, who emerges as *anēr prophētēs* (man/hero and prophet; 24:19). Women and men characters alike serve this portrait, but women's appearances especially help to construct and enhance this heroic masculinity. The representations of women in the Gospel set Jesus up to step in and rescue or correct. The desperation of the widow of Nain gives way to the acclamation of Jesus as prophet (7:11–17); the sinful woman is defended and forgiven for her love and repentance, as Jesus demonstrates his prophetic knowledge of her heart and his censorious host's (7:36–50); the "daughter of Abraham" bent over for eighteen years Jesus liberates as he bests his accusers in argument (13:10–17). As in Mark, the cures of Peter's mother-in-law (4:38–39), the daughter of Jairus, and the woman with the flow of blood (8:40–56) are all narrated to demonstrate the spiritual power and compassion of Jesus. The same is true in the case of stories about men, of course. But in Luke, miracle stories about women are put in a different light. Mary Magdalene and the other women who accompanied and supported the twelve are explained not as disciples and ministers (as they are in Mark 15:41) but as benefactors, because they have been beneficiaries, in a sense clients of Jesus—they "follow along," become fellow travelers, not because they were called, like the twelve, but because they were cured,

---

14 The usual age for entry into the quaestorship, the first-level magistracy of the *cursus honorum* was between twenty-seven and thirty years; it was set by Sulla at thirty, but the age was advanced to twenty-five during the Principate. The traditional ages for the magistracies were frequently flouted during the empire, especially for the imperial family.

and the most famous of them was also the most demon-infested (8:1–3). In Acts, Peter raises the disciple (*mathētria*, 9:36) Tabitha-Dorcas; the narrative presents her good works and alms in highly gendered terms—she made tunics and cloaks for the widows (see D'Ambra: 101–8)—and at the same time stresses the helplessness of the widows who depended upon her (9:39). Thus Peter becomes the provider of her ministry to the widows. Thus where women minister to others, their work is attributed to or brought under the authority of a male figure.

The story of Martha and Mary (Luke 10:38–42) has been among the most fraught of Lukan narratives for feminist interpreters, in part because of its long and problematic history of application to the roles of women (Reid: 144–58). At the revival of arguments for the ordination and ministry of women, interpreters suggested that the text endorsed discipleship for women by Jesus' approval of Mary who takes up the position of a disciple "at his feet" (Parvey: 141). Developing feminist critical thought began to raise questions about the text's denigration of the work of sustaining life so long allotted to women. Recognizing the communal function of Martha's *diakonia* further suggested that Jesus' reproof of Martha, if it approved the discipleship of women, actually sought to limit, subordinate, or discourage the participation of women in ministry (Tetlow: 104; Schüssler Fiorenza 1986: 30–31; D'Angelo 1990a: 455; 1990b: 77–79). Although the story reflects aspects of gender and leadership in Luke's context, the focus of the narrative is actually not on the women but on the characterization of Jesus. The women are placed in the "competition that is born of proximity and equal status and inflamed by envy" (Pliny, *Pan.* 84.2) that Pliny sees as a particular weakness of women in the same household. Trajan's superior instruction and example, he claims, enable Plotina and Marciana to avoid it. Similarly, Jesus' instruction of Martha manifests the wisdom with which he acts to replace such competition with harmony. Only one other woman is allowed a speech in the body of the Gospel, the woman who blesses Jesus' mother. She too is corrected, in a fashion that demonstrates the appropriate *pudor* of Jesus, who refuses any special honor for his mother, and therefore for himself (11:27–28). Jesus' prediction of the destruction of Jerusalem to the women on the way to the cross not only demonstrates his prophetic knowledge, but also exhibits the same self-deprecating *pudor:* "weep not for me, but for yourselves and your children" (23:27–32; C. A. Barton 2001: 223–30; 1999).

Luke also pays more attention to the image of God as father than does either Mark or Q. The use of "father" for God plays a role in the Christology, particularly in establishing the status of the church as heir to Jesus. Jesus has received a reign from his father, which he can with confidence bequeath to his "little flock" (12:32; 22:29). The characterization of Jesus in the passion as exemplary martyr deploys use of this designation for the deity in prayer both for release from the trial of martyrdom (22:42) and for divine acceptance of it (23:46). A third prayer using this address asks for forgiveness of Roman soldiers who crucify him and divide his garments (23:42). The textual attestation for this verse is divided, but its content fits well with the apologetic concerns in the acquittal of Jesus reiterated three times by Pilate (23:4, 14, 22) and once by the centurion who crucified him (23:48).

The Gospel produces images of divine fatherhood that undergird conventional social structures. Among the most influential of the Lukan parables is the narrative called the Prodigal Son (15:11–32). This story manifests significant likenesses to and differences from a case presented for debate in the elder Seneca's *Controversiae* 3.3, thus circulating well before the composition of Luke-Acts:

> A father had two sons, one moderate [*frugi*] and one profligate [*luxurio-sum*]. He disowned the profligate one. The moderate son set off abroad; he was captured by pirates and wrote to his father to be redeemed. Since his father delayed, the profligate went ahead and redeemed him. The moderate one returned, and adopted his brother. Now he is being disowned.

The cast is notably similar to that of Luke, but they appear in a plot that pitches grudging paternity against fraternal solidarity, reversing a far more common narrative pattern in which the *paterfamilias* is the hero and the younger son the villain (Dixon 1997a: 152). Like other *Controversiae*, it is meant to be provocative, even outré. By contrast, Luke's parable affirms the more socially conservative pattern; the heroic *paterfamilias* rescues the younger, profligate son in response to the son's recognition of his own iniquity and the beneficence of his father's household regime. This pattern structures the response of the audience: they are to identify with the profligate younger son, the representative of the tax collectors and sinners. The parable thus offers a reassuring antidote to the harsh antifamilial tradition reiterated in 14:46: "if someone comes to me and does not hate his father..." (cf. 12:53).

Ascetics within the Good Order of the Household

Luke-Acts evinces concern with sexual asceticism, but one that is discreet enough to have garnered attention only as interest in gender and ascetic practice has increased. The prohibition of divorce from Mark 10:2–10 never appears in Luke, but the prohibition of remarriage does (16:18; cf. Mark 10:11–12; D'Angelo 1990a: 456–57). The wording of the saying assumes that only the behavior of the man is at issue. Indeed, a wife is among those that one may/must leave for the sake of the kingdom

(Luke 14:26; 18:29). For Peter alone among the apostles, the text implies that he at least once had a wife (4:38–39); interestingly, his call occurs in Luke only after the cure of his mother-in-law (5:1–11), when he left behind "his own," which included his wife (18:28–29). In the parable of the Banquet, a marriage is represented as one of the pretexts on which the invitation to God's reign may be refused (14:20). Jesus' debate with the Sadducees (Mark 12:18–27) is revised by this author in ways that suggest that the problem of the woman married successively to seven brothers is resolved not by disclaiming the relevance of marriages in the eschatological future but by endorsing the assumption of angelic celibacy in the present as "sons of the resurrection" (20:34–36; Seim 1994a: 208–9; 1999: 119). The critique of marriage and endorsement of celibacy in the Gospel is both eschatologically oriented (Seim 1999) and a facet of the cultivation of discipline and self-mastery (Garrett; A. Smith).

Like the rest of the parenetic material (as in the other Gospels), the ascetic sayings are articulated in androcentric terms, and endorsements of celibacy for women are less explicit. A husband may have to leave a wife for God's reign, as one may have to leave parents or children, sisters or brothers. But no such eventuality is foreseen for a wife. Whereas in *Gos. Thom.* 79 Jesus' correction of the woman who blesses his mother and the woe pronounced upon the pregnant and nursing provide an endorsement of women's celibacy, in Luke these two sayings appear separately (11:27–28; 23:27–28) and do not speak with as clear a voice. In the context of the other sayings they suggest, if not an exhortation to abstinence, at least a rejection of the stigma on childlessness that is reflected both in biblical narratives and in Roman law.

The narrative does supply two cases in which women are presented as ascetic practitioners; both are also identified as prophets (though they are given no prophetic speeches). Acts 21:18 briefly identifies the four daughters of Philip as both virgins and prophets. More detail is given about the prophet Anna (Luke 2:36–38). Caution must be used in treating her as an exemplar for women readers of the Gospel; she belongs to the distant and foreign era of "the law and the prophets." But she is clearly seen by the author as some sort of ideal. Like the widows the author of the Pastorals desires, she is at prayer day and night (2:37; cf. 1 Tim 5:5), and she has been married only once (Luke 2:36; 1 Tim 5:9). Otherwise she conforms poorly to that author's prescriptions, for since she was married for only seven years, she must have been a young widow, and there is no suggestion that she bore children (1 Tim 5:10). She forms a notable contrast with the widowed mother of seven sons from 4 Maccabees, who stresses not only her carefully guarded premarital virginity and marital chastity, but also the fact that she remained with her husband as long as she was fertile (18:9; D'Angelo 2003b: 152–57).

For Luke-Acts, then, sexual abstinence is an important, if risky, business: it is presented with discretion, indeed, nearly with a disguise. In 1990, I referred to the author's presentation of pairs of women and men as "marital pairs" (1990a: 450). But this term appears increasingly inadequate. Some pairs, such as Anna and Simeon, Agrippa and Berenike, are very clearly not married; others, such as Dionysius and Damaris, occur with no suggestion of marriage. The ascetic counsels raise other questions about the interpretation of pairs who appear to be identified as man and wife, such as Prisca and Aquila (Acts 18:2–4). Are they also "sons of the resurrection" (20:36), living in chastity? The pairs of male and female figures in Luke-Acts help to present or perhaps veil Christian ascetic practice in the context of familial mores in which men conduct households, even if at a remove. Luke-Acts allows for women heads of household, but in the narrative they appear only to yield the stage to men: Martha submits to the direction of Jesus; the mother of John Mark is mentioned only to identify the house Peter seeks when liberated from prison; and Lydia's household becomes Paul's base of operations in Philippi. Despite their preference for sexual abstinence and critique of marriage, the Christians are not enemies to the moral order of the household. Rather, they outdo the Roman conviction that their claim to empire is based upon their own moral superiority (Edwards 1993: 20–29). Trajan and Hadrian both displayed the imperial women as an attestation to their own moral worth and to the beneficence and harmony of their relation to the empire. As Peter Brown notes, marital harmony had become a sign for imperial concord (1988: 16, cited above). But it is not only the harmony of a marital pair that these emperors advertised. Pliny treats Marciana as the equal of Plotina, and for Hadrian, Plotina and Matidia (his mother-in-law) were as important as Sabina. These emperors deal in images of household *concordia, pietas,* and *fides.* Luke-Acts also can deploy images of women brought into appropriately ordered virtue by men who practice continence as they bring whole households to the truth.

In the apologetic of Luke-Acts, the Christians are personified by Paul: more Roman than his jailers (16:37–40), he shows himself morally and socially fit to rule those who imprison him (Lentz: 43–50, 95–100). Himself continent, he is able to bring order to the wildness of a possessed mantic servant girl and the female-headed household of Lydia (16:12–15). Knowing that he is bound to see Rome (19:21), Paul gives an account of his own stewardship, making clear that he has presided well, having both fulfilled his responsibility for the lives of persons and dealt with the communal finances with utter probity (20:17–38). Called before Felix and Drusilla, he discourses upon justice, continence, and the coming judgment (*peri dikaiosnēs kai enkrateias kai tou krimatos tou mellontos,*

Acts 24:25), themes that Felix ought to be versed in, as a judge for many years (24:10). But these themes inspire only fear in Felix, for he is prey to the vice so common to governors and so detrimental to to the imperial order: he hopes for a bribe from Paul (24:26). This man (*anēr*) in whom the Roman authorities can find nothing out of place (*atopon*, 25:5, 25) offers the magistrates of the imperial order the hope of becoming their best selves.

The ways that Luke-Acts' construction of masculinity marks its "others" differs notably from the misogyny of the Pastorals and Juvenal. Overt hostility to women and any depiction of "bad women" is avoided, even erased: Mark's lurid anecdote of the death of the Baptist (6:17–29) does not appear in Luke, and Berenike's dubious reputation does not follow her into Acts. Like Plutarch (*Virtues of Women*, Preface [*Mor.* 242A]), Luke-Acts prefers not to be silent about women but to praise good women, albeit in their proper relation to men (Foxhall; Stadter). The use of pairs of men and women throughout the Gospel and Acts harmonizes well with Plutarch's comparison:

> We see the moon, when she is away from the sun, manifest and shining, but it disappears and is hidden when she comes near him, but the virtuous [*sōphrona*] woman must, on the contrary, be seen most when she is with her husband, but stay at home and be hidden when he is not there. (*Conj. praec.* 9 [*Mor.* 139C])

In Luke-Acts, women can, indeed should, be disciples and learners, ministers at least as benefactors, and in the case of Priscilla, even teach, if in the company of a male partner (Acts 18:26, although the word *didaskein* is not used here).

What of the woman reader or hearer in the conversation of Luke-Acts? As I suggested above, the prologues set up the two-volume work as an exchange between elite males, and unlike *Hermas,* the author directs no explicit attention to other readers. But the effect is very different from the man-to-man exchange of the Pastorals. The broad narrative panorama of Christian beginnings also offers a broad range of actors, including the slavewoman (*paidiskē*) Rhoda, who answers the knock of Peter after his miraculous release from prison (Acts 12:13–17). A slavewoman such as Rhoda hearing or reading Luke-Acts would find herself included in the narrative. Her social subjugation would be confirmed, but she would not miss the realization that though Rhoda (like the women at the tomb) is dismissed by the assembly, she is right; she knows what she knows. Similarly, her privileged knowledge offers the slavewoman a place alongside the noble Theophilos: instructed in the events of the fulfillment of God's promises and in the know about their surety—at least as long as she accepts Luke's narrative.

Conclusions

For the Pastorals, the *Shepherd of Hermas*, and Luke-Acts, "knowing how to preside over his own household" is a marker of masculine worth and one that equally marks the members of the community over whom it is exercised. All three to some degree draw upon household governance to protect Christian continence from the appearance of undermining marriage and family values: sexual asceticism is or is presented as a strategy of holy behavior within marriage. In all three texts, the structures of communal leadership have begun to emerge, and the terms used for them have at least some resonance of household offices and functions: elders, *diakonoi* (or those who perform *diakonia*), *episkopoi*, and widows. All experience to some degree the ambivalence produced by Trajan's policy on Christians: their communities flourish in a sort of suspended animation, knowing that incurring the hostility of neighbors may invite denunciation and bring them to the trial. But these three texts modulate their appeals very differently, and the masculinity they present differs also.

The "Paul" of the Pastorals is a severe and continent household manager of God. Full of tenderness in his directions of his "true child" Timothy or Titus, he requires the *episkopoi* especially, but also the *diakonoi* and elders, to show similar severity and gravitas in their conduct in the household of God. Toward women he evinces suspicion that modulates into misogyny; he is particularly concerned to exclude women from teaching and learning and to reduce widows in numbers and status—only those who have no other recourse are to be enrolled; they are not benefactors, but dependents of the church. He enjoins behavior that will preserve for the communities "a quiet life" even under the dangerous regard of those outside, particularly of "emperors and governors." Masculine worth is imaged in the standard moral metaphors of service in the army and competition in the games, metaphors that make a claim on the civic life of the empire.

Luke-Acts pitches its conversation at a more elevated level: author and addressee are of the intellectual and social elite, and the men who are the focus of the two-volume history are heroic figures, fit to be spokesmen for the divine word and will on the world stage—even before Caesar. In this work, the primary marker of masculinity is fitness to speak in public and for the community; household governance is evidence for this capacity. Although Luke's Christian orators have foregone wives and households of their own (Luke 18:28–29), they bring social and moral order where they enter. Men teach, although women appear to learn well from them—and, in the single case of Priscilla, share in the instructing (Acts 18:26). For Luke-Acts the prospect of martyrdom is the opportunity to instruct the empire in its true task of justice and continence; deference and hierarchy assert the moral ascendency of the

Christian leaders and promise a future harmony under the fatherly reign of the true but unknown God. Women follow along, minister, and learn/are disciples but are not apostles, the ambassadors of God. Widows represent the poor—as the author of Pastorals wishes them to do.

To some extent, the *Shepherd of Hermas* stands over against the Pastorals and Luke-Acts. Unlike the "inscribed authors" of these two texts, Hermas seems to have no hope of converting the empire and its rulers and no secure expectation of obtaining from them a "quiet life." In contrast to the man-to-man exchanges constructed in the other works, the *Shepherd* constructs a conversation that is both complex and diverse. Hermas locates himself as both author and audience: he hears from the female and male intermediaries and speaks to and alongside the men and women who lead the church. Hermas assumes and relies upon the authority of Grapte, both to lend authority to his book and to instruct (*nouthetein*) those under her supervision; he shows no interest in excluding women from leadership. His visionary experience includes female mediators, though it also reflects misogynist stereotypes (such as the twelve women in black). But for Hermas also, manly status includes the moral oversight of his household: he is liable to divine displeasure for the sins of his wife and children and responsible for their guidance and correction.

Two final points emerge from this study. First, to recognize that these early Christian assertions of manliness and moral worth respond to Roman imperial family values does not suggest that the authors adopt these values without either sharing in them or submitting them to critique. Examining the three texts has shown both connections and corrections of Roman legal stipulations and the moral ideals that the emperors adopted and fostered. The writers and communities behind them display in the men who preside and the families they preside over an excellence that surpasses what is best in Rome.

Second, Kate Cooper's observation "that wherever a woman is mentioned a man's character is being judged—and along with it what he stands for" has proven itself in a sort of reverse. In an attempt to look directly at masculinity in the male worlds of these texts, it has been easiest to see and understand its workings on the persons of those who are other-than-men: women, children, and slaves.

SEXING THE LAMB

Chris Frilingos
Michigan State University

The critical and commercial success of the recent film *Gladiator* suggests that the ancient Roman combatants fascinate modern Americans. The hope of appealing to this interest would seem to be what inspired a recent United States Marine Corps television advertisement, which features a kind of gladiatorial contest. Fast and furious, the ad tells its tale in less than thirty seconds. At first a gigantic arena filled with cheering spectators looms on the horizon. Then we see a young man in a T-shirt and jeans against a dark, animated background of thunderclouds and whirring machinery, a scene from some science-fiction, postapocalyptic wasteland. As we watch him negotiate treacherous obstacles to enter the stadium, the scene shifts: suddenly, he's joined in battle with an immense but amorphous gray-black beast with yellow eyes. In an instant, the contest is over. Our gladiator in blue jeans grabs a glistening sword, slices the beast wide open, and metamorphoses into a Marine in a shiny, new uniform.

The visual effects are stunning, but the ad's narration also deserves comment. As the hero swings for his opponent, a baritone voice intones: "If you can master your fear, outsmart your enemy, and never yield, even to yourself—then you will be changed forever. The few, the proud, the Marines." This message assigns the monster a double identity. On one level, the beast represents an external threat to the hero: the ideal Marine will "outsmart" and defeat this villain. On another, the shadowy behemoth symbolizes the internal fear that must be mastered, the inner chaos to which the soldier must not yield. This is a story about the (trans)formation and mastery of the self, a story that reflects an axiom formulated by Stephen Greenblatt in his now classic study of Renaissance subjectivity: "Self-fashioning is achieved in relation to something perceived as alien, strange, or hostile" (9). The spectators in this gloomy arena view two contests: one between the hero and the monster and another between the hero and himself. Triumph over these opponents turns a civilian into a Marine and a boy in blue jeans into a man.

These themes bear a striking resemblance to the moral prescriptions outlined by Roman writers during the early Roman Empire. Imbued with a "Stoicizing ethics," the writings of ancient moralists uniformly testify that happiness and well-being result from the mastery of the self (Swain: 120). Philosophers such as Musonius Rufus, Seneca, Plutarch, and Epictetus agree that the struggle to maintain "control" (*enkrateia*) over the emotions characterized the moral man. For Michel Foucault, the relation between morality and self-mastery intensified during this period and coalesced into a technology of the subject, which he labels the "cultivation of the self" (1986: 39–68). Extending the work of Paul Veyne, Foucault maintains that this increased attention to the "relations of oneself to oneself" ran parallel to a shift in the organization of imperial Roman society. The change of orientation occurred in the realm of pleasure, specifically with respect to the rules governing how desires were satisfied: domination and subjugation were no longer enjoined, but reciprocity and harmony instead. The household served as the proving grounds for this new ethics of the self, and moralists such as Musonius observe that the violent subduing of household members—slaves, wives, and children—has no part in the virtuous life. Rather, as Plutarch advises a pair of newlyweds, "marriage and the household shall be well attuned through reason, concord, and philosophy" (*Conj. praec.* 138C).[1] No one benefitted from this irenic atmosphere more than the head of the *domus* himself, who thus fulfilled the moral imperative: "care for oneself."

But Foucault's judgment of Roman "self-mastery" is incomplete. As much scholarship since *The History of Sexuality* has pointed out, he fails to consider the significance of gender. Despite the ostensible goal of uncovering the power relations masked by the rubric "sexuality," Foucault's (and Veyne's) analysis neglects masculinity and femininity, categories inextricably linked to the very discourse—sexuality—that Foucault attempts to historicize (Richlin 1991; cf. Skinner 1996; E. A. Clark 1988). Kate Cooper, for example, contends:

> The rhetoric of conjugal unity in antiquity served primarily as a means by which aristocratic families could broadcast the moral character of their menfolk, a point of much significance which has been missed by the much-discussed attempts of Paul Veyne and Michel Foucault to explicate the Roman rhetoric of affection between the spouses. (1992: 151)

---

1 Texts and translations of ancient sources are generally from the Loeb Classical Library. Other translations consulted include Reardon; Apuleius; Artemidorus. Translation of *Acts of Paul and Thecla* is from Elliott. Text and translation of *Martyrdom of Perpetua and Felicitas* are from Musurillo. Biblical citations (including 4 *Ezra*) are from the NRSV.

"Self-mastery," then, had less to do with a political or social shift than with the "shoring up" of Roman masculinity. Similarly, gender enables a different understanding of the USMC television commercial. The narration remains to a certain extent "gender neutral," but the images portray a "masculine" hero who conquers the other with a thrusting sword. Further, the imagery of spectacle frames the hero's pursuit of victory: the boy becomes a man inside a colosseum filled with cheering fans. And by watching the battle, the arena spectators (as well as the television viewers) participate vicariously in this realization of masculinity, calling to mind the notion of the "male gaze" elaborated in recent feminist film criticism (Mulvey; de Lauretis: 127–48). Not only the hero's sword but also the gaze of onlookers vanquishes the beast.

So, too, penetration and the gaze were components in the economy of power sustained by Roman sexuality. This essay explores an intersection between these themes of Roman society and the book of Revelation. I begin with a discussion of gender and Roman sexuality: the Greek novel *Daphnis and Chloe* serves as the point of departure. Then, turning to the Apocalypse, I argue that the book's central character, the "Lamb standing as if slain" (Rev 5:6, 12; 13:8), undergoes a kind of transformation: at first a "feminized" creature, a commanding performance of virility "masculinizes" the Lamb. But this transformation, a process I label "sexing the Lamb," remains partial. As we shall see, the Lamb does not simply "progress" from one gender to another; rather, Revelation assigns to the figure a complex of gendered meanings. Indeed, the gender of the Lamb is not essential but perspectival: as the creature slides between subject positions—between object and subject of the textual gaze—so the Lamb is feminized and masculinized.

EDUCATING DAPHNIS

We begin our investigation of ancient sexuality with one of the five extant Greek erotic novels. *Daphnis and Chloe*, a second-century C.E. romance written by Longus, tells a tale of love deferred. The plot is typical of the genre: boy meets girl, boy and girl fall madly in love, boy and girl's every attempt to consummate their relationship meets with frustration. Despite the "simple" structure and conventional subject matter of these stories, however, they were not mere pulp fiction for the masses. Rather, as Simon Goldhill (1995) argues cogently, the Greek romance provides ironic versions of classical and Hellenistic philosophical discussions about nature, knowledge, and desire. By engaging and parodying lofty discussions of epistemology, the genre contributes to the formation of an ancient discursive field of gender and sexuality. The ancient romance, like the philosophical and medical texts of Foucault's investigations, simultaneously reflected and inscribed "normativity" vis-à-vis sexual relations and gender construction in Roman culture. There are serious dimensions to the romance's erotic play.

Serious dimensions, however, are difficult to detect at first blush. Central to the plot of Longus's novel is a running joke about the sexual naivete of children: Daphnis, the young goatherd, and Chloe, a shepherd and Daphnis's beloved, simply do not know how to "do it." The pair's ardent quest to consummate their relationship—dressed, undressed, lying down, standing up—makes for slapstick humor, furnishing the fictional account with a "country bumpkin" atmosphere. From first to last, the novel presents itself as a tale untouched by metropolitan sophistication: the setting is rural, the names of the characters are pastoral, and the action—from goatherding to bungled lovemaking, which always occurs "in the woods," on the outskirts of society—remains unhurried and innocent.

While the story might have brought a smile to the faces of its ancient audience, the romance also taught the gentle reader a lesson in the "big city" sexual values and gender roles of Mediterranean society, a society over which Rome cast a long shadow. Indeed, the novel emphasizes instruction in a memorable scene that pairs sex and violence. Here Daphnis catches the eye of the urban and urbane Lycaenion, a seductress whose motives for bedding the boy are at once altruistic and self-centered. Lycaenion knows that the couple's intimate moments have left both Chloe and Daphnis dissatisfied, and, according to the narrator, "she sympathized with their trials and saw a twofold opportunity: for rescuing them and satisfying her desire" (*Daphnis and Chloe* 3.15). Daphnis, who had earlier pledged his unflagging devotion to Chloe, quickly assents to the elder woman's plan to teach him how to make love. So the lesson commences: Lycaenion has intercourse with Daphnis in a forest, away from prying eyes. After their lovemaking, Lycaenion explains to Daphnis what just happened between them. The goatherd, for his part, is eager to find Chloe in order to show her what he has learned. But Lycaenion stops him short with a speech, drawing a sharp distinction between herself and Chloe as a sexual partner/object:

> You've still got this to learn, Daphnis. Because I happen to be an experienced woman, I didn't suffer any harm just now (long ago another man gave me this lesson, and took my virginity as his reward). But if Chloe has this sort of wrestling match with you, she will cry out and weep and will lie there, bleeding heavily as if slain [*kathaper pephoneumenē*]....
> remember — I made you a man [*egō andra ... pepoiēka*] before Chloe did. (*Daphnis and Chloe* 3.19)

"As if slain": Lycaenion's chilling admonition puts Chloe *on display*. Like the Lamb of Revelation, she appears wounded, penetrated, murdered.

This is not the image of sexual reciprocity, of household harmony and conjugal unity, that one expects to encounter in the society imagined by Foucault's philosophers, but a set of relations forged under the violent sign of patriarchy.

At first Daphnis fears that he might hurt Chloe: "Daphnis thought about what she [Lycaenion] had said, lost his previous impulse, and shrank from pestering Chloe for more than kisses and embraces" (*Daphnis and Chloe* 3.20). The initial hesitation of Daphnis to fulfill a "manly" role, his reluctance to "educate Chloe," leads John J. Winkler to wonder whether the romance confirms patriarchal force or "problematizes" it (1990a: 101–26). But the reservations of the goatherd dissipate in the novel's conclusion, which describes the lavish marriage of the pair, a ceremony that the entire city attends: Daphnis, it seems, forgets his prior misgivings and "deflowers" the virgin Chloe. The chamber door closes behind the newlyweds, but the wedding guests stand immediately on the other side, singing "with harsh, rough voices, as though they were breaking up the earth with forks, not singing a wedding hymn" (*Daphnis and Chloe* 4.40). Then, relates the narrator with a wink and a nod,

> Daphnis and Chloe lay down naked together, embraced and kissed, and had even less sleep that night than the owls. Daphnis did some of the things Lycaenion taught him; and then, for the first time, Chloe found out that what they had done in the woods had been nothing but "children's games" [*paidiōn paignia*]. (*Daphnis and Chloe* 4.40)

The moral of the romance now emerges: sex is not a private act "in the woods" but a public performance authorized by the civic gaze. Further, the novel's conclusion confirms what has been evident in the story all along, that not just Chloe but also Daphnis receives an "education"—first from Lycaenion, then from the community. The nuptial sanctuary, a symbol of societal approbation, mitigates the apprehension of Daphnis about "inflicting" intercourse upon his beloved. The robust voices of those gathered to bear witness to Daphnis's manly achievement create a mimetic dynamic, driving him onward, urging the goatherd "to break up the earth with forks." Daphnis has become a man, and this is what men do.

The Penetration Grid

Daphnis and Chloe points up assumptions about sex, gender, and the social order under the Roman Empire that require elaboration. "Roman sexuality was a structuralist's dream"; so says one scholar of ancient gender and sexuality (Parker: 48). As is well known by now, informing ancient society was a traditional grid that divided sexual roles according to "active" and "passive" positions (Richlin 1992: 131–39; Halperin 1990a: 15–40). Gender—the behaviors and appearances constitutive of both "masculinity" and "femininity"—was linked inextricably to this system, ordering for Romans the details of their culture. As Bernadette J. Brooten remarks: "Active and passive constitute foundational categories for Roman-period culture; they are gender coded as masculine and feminine respectively.... for this reason they [Romans] described passive men as effeminate and active women as masculine" (116; cf. Gleason 1990). According to the grid, "masculinity" corresponded to "activity" and could be demonstrated by penetrating the orifices of the body (Walters 1991: 26). The genitalia of this object-body had little if any bearing on the gender coding of the "active" partner: a male penetrator was "manly" no matter the physiology of his mate. Indeed, as Amy Richlin discusses, ancient poetry based on invective sometimes defends the fortress of Roman masculinity with the threat of male on male sexual assault (Richlin 1992: 105–33). Likewise, a woman who sexually penetrated another (but this is rarely reported) was also "manly" (Brooten: 29–72). And—as one might expect in a structuralist's dream—the reverse held true: the breached body, male or female, was "feminine" or "effeminate." The basic question of Roman masculinity is thus "who's penetrating whom?" (Parker: 53).

As we have seen, providing a socially acceptable response to this question forms at least part of the impetus for "educating Daphnis." The goatherd learns to penetrate—how to be manly—while Chloe learns to distinguish between playful embraces and being penetrated, an important difference marked at the linguistic level for Greeks. As Dale B. Martin describes succinctly:

> Greek language seems almost always to have constructed sexual inter-course as a one-way street; the pleasure was assumed to belong naturally to the penetrator, and the penetrated was expected to submit without enjoyment. Whoever enjoyed being penetrated was considered weak, unnatural, or at least suspect—or (to sum up all three terms into one body) a woman. (1995a: 177)

The warning of Lycaenion makes the difference between penetrator and penetrated palpable, fleshly: Chloe's body, like the bodies of classical Greek tragedy examined by Nicole Loraux (1987: 14–15), is painted in bloody hues. In the Greek theater the female body is a spectacle of death; the heroines of Euripides are brought into focus at the moment they embrace the sword. In the literature of the Roman Empire sex, sword, and death compose an erotic triangle of metaphors, a geometry illustrated by the erotic banter of Photis and Lucius in *The Golden Ass*. Before he turns into an ass, Lucius is eager to take part in "Venus' gladiatorial games [*gladiatoriae Veneris*]" with the comely Photis (*Metam.* 2.15). After noticing his aroused state, Photis exhorts Lucius to

> Engage ... and do so bravely. I shall not yield before you, nor turn my back on you. Direct your aim frontally, if you are a man [*si vir es*], and at close quarters. Let your onslaught be fierce; kill before you die [*et occide moriturus*]. Our battle this day allows no respite. (*Metam.* 2.17)

Later in the story, during a different night of debauchery, Lucius recounts: "When I was finished with her feminine generosity, Photis offered me a boy's pleasure as a gift" (*Metam.* 3.20). The sexualized Photis, the object of Lucius's desire, is a collection of orifices made available for the pleasure of penetration.

This is not to suggest that Lucius becomes a model of "hypermasculinity," for, as Winkler observes, the hapless hero is "at once armed yet vulnerable" in these encounters with Photis and presents himself as a "victim" to Cupid's arrow (Winkler 1985: 175). Lacking self-mastery, both Photis and Lucius repeatedly succumb to their mutual passion. Yet, if the *Golden Ass* hints at a praxis of sexual reciprocity in its account, the "truth" of the sex between Photis and Lucius takes shape according to the rules of penetration. Photis serves the wants of Lucius, changing from "woman" to "boy" to provide pleasure for him. And this same "truth" reveals itself in the romance, in which the "sexual symmetry" of Daphnis and Chloe's nonpenetrative foreplay—their "children's games" in the countryside—is finally displaced and erased by the wedding chamber and "adult" society (cf. Konstan 1994: 89).

Scenes such as the one in which Photis plays both a "woman" and a "boy" are not only, or even primarily, about sexual positions or differentiation. Rather, the effect of such language and "gender-bending" is to "masculinize" a subject position and to (re)inscribe a relation of power. There exist two prongs to the process that I shall explore briefly: the social meanings assigned to the body and the mechanism of the gaze. The body of the mature Roman male was to be inviolable. Mastery of the self includes the power to protect one's body from intrusion. Further, this body represented the Roman ideal, standing at the top of a social pyramid. As Jonathan Walters observes, "the impenetrable boundaries of the social body are being drawn around those of the [adult male] physical body" (1997: 37). In this system, the right to protect the body against physical assault corresponds directly to social standing. Penetration, for Romans, equals domination: in such a system, sexuality and gender remain expressions of mastery (Moore and Anderson: 272). Aristocratic women and free youths were thus afforded some legal protection; slaves, on the other hand, were treated in terms of property: the rape of a slave represented the invasion of the master's *domus* not of the slave's body.

The second-century C.E. "Interpretation of Dreams" of Artemidorus vividly reproduces this social pattern, placing status on an axis of penetration (Foucault 1986: 4–36; Winkler 1990a: 17–49). A dream depicting the dreamer (assumed here, it would seem, to be a free adult male) being penetrated by his slave, for example, is "inauspicious," but

> having sexual intercourse with one's servant, whether male or female is good; for slaves are possessions of the dreamer, so that they signify, quite naturally, that the dreamer will derive pleasure from his possessions, which will grow greater and more valuable. (*Oneir.* 78)

Sex is only "active" or "passive" in Artemidorus's guide: one either penetrates or is penetrated. And the status shading of this opposition illustrates the close alignment of the body with the body politic, making the *Oneirocritica* a "dream" text indeed for both Claude Lévi-Strauss and Mary Douglas. In this text, *dreaming* of passivity is not always "inauspicious," not if the penetrator ranks higher on the social scale than the dreamer: "For a man to be penetrated by a richer, older man is good," writes Artemidorus, "for the custom is to receive things from such men" (*Oneir.* 78). The penetration grid, superimposed over both fantasies and reality, confirmed a basic principle of Roman hierarchy: at the top of the social ladder stood the impenetrable penetrator.

But the structuralist connection between grid and society should not erase the gender fashioning at work in the discourse of penetration, an operation intimately related to visual representation. The narrative descriptions of Chloe and of Photis as penetrated not only reinforce social hierarchy; they also frame these characters as sexual objects. Chloe and Photis connote, in the words of Laura Mulvey, "to-be-looked-at-ness" (11). Their physicality emerges in the eyes of the penetrator: Lucius becomes a "phallus with eyes," describing the "supple movements" of Photis's back and her adroit sexual positioning (see Frontisi-Ducroux: 81–100). Compounded with a "fetishized" attention to parts of the female body is the language of war and battle, a "divide and conquer" approach, as it were, to the objectified, feminized body. In these episodes images of death—Chloe's torn flesh parallels Photis's sacrificial "kill me"—and aperture are brought close together, engendering a desire that seeks to dominate the other. In such scenes the "gaze carries with it the power of action and of possession," so that the subject position of the gazer is not "male" but "masculine" (Kaplan: 31). That is to say, the "feminized" body and the "masculine" gaze are not "essential" expressions of anatomy; rather, viewing animates a relation of power, a structure of domination and submission. In short, the bearer or subject of the gaze occupies a position superior to the one inhabited by the object of the gaze (Glancy 1998).

Ancient texts draw close connections between viewing, penetration, and desire. Tracing the "tactile gaze" back to Platonic theories of vision, in which "a fire within the eye flows outward to create a visual ray of such force that it 'collides' with its object," Georgia Frank shows the close association of sight and touch in antiquity (124). Not all philosophers simply adopted this "extramission" theory of the gaze; some, like Aristotle, spoke of images being stamped upon the eye, and others, like the Epicureans, devised an "intramission" system of "images flowing off objects" and striking the eye. Still, all of these theories "retained the idea of vision occurring through contacts" (Frank: 124). When we turn to accounts of the "desiring eye" in ancient literature, examples of tactile "sexual" viewing are not difficult to find. For some, sight triggered arousal: as Aline Rousselle notes, there exists a widespread assumption in ancient medical texts that "the presence of women or young boys generally aroused male desire and that erotic pictures or stories aroused desire in the normal woman" (65). But the erotic look is not simply the prelude to intercourse; in some texts, it is intercourse (see, e.g., Matt 5:27–29). In *Leucippe and Cleitophon*, the penetrative stare is "enfleshed" in advice given to Cleitophon by Cleinias, who urges his friend to gaze at Leucippe:

> This pleasure is greater than that of consummation, for the eyes receive each others' reflections, and they form there from small images as in mirrors. Such outpouring of beauty flowing down through them into the soul is a kind of copulation at a distance. This is not far removed from the intercourse of bodies. (*Leucippe and Cleitophon* 1.9)

Again, such a text, which emphasizes reciprocity, would seem to point to the "sexual symmetry" of partners, but when the desirous Cleitophon acts on Cleinias's advice a few passages later, masculine desire exposes itself through the gaze. Rather than reciprocal viewing, an exchange of glances, Cleitophon narrates how he arranges to look at Leucippe while she, distracted, looks elsewhere. Taking the plumes of a peacock as his starting point, Cleitophon tells a slave standing nearby about mating practices in nature, a lecture that engrosses the eavesdropping Leucippe. The "erotic lesson" allows Cleitophon to stare with impunity on the object of his affection, while Leucippe gazes at the peacock. Mission accomplished, Cleitophon paints a vivid picture of his beloved:

> I was looking at the young lady to see how she reacted to my erotic lesson. She discreetly indicated that she had not been displeased by my discourse. The radiant beauty of the peacock struck me less forcefully than that glance from Leucippe. The beauty of her body challenged the flowers of the field: her face was the essence of pale jonquil; roses arose

on her cheeks; her glance was a revelation of violet; her hair had more
natural curls than spiral ivy. Such was the meadow of Leucippe's face.
(*Leucippe and Cleitophon* 1.19)

Cleitophon's seemingly innocent ruse, part of a plot to bring him near
to Leucippe, makes Cleitophon the bearer of the gaze and Leucippe the
object. He, like Lucius, presents himself first as a victim, struck by the
"glance of Leucippe," but the flesh that lingers is Leucippe's, a body
revealed by the eye of the impassioned Cleitophon. Here, in a "grove of
very pleasant aspect," surrounded on all sides by erotically charged
flowers, fruits, and birds, mutuality gives way to masculinity (*Leucippe
and Cleitophon* 1.15).

The preceding discussion has meant to suggest the pervasive nature
and recalcitrance of the penetration grid in the Roman society of John the
Seer's day. Even when this grid of gender and sexuality seems to weaken
under the pressure from notions of reciprocity, domination and control
are ultimately reasserted. *Leucippe and Cleitophon* expresses the erotic gaze
through the portrayal of the female body, framed by a fecund, sexualized
landscape. Treated to scene after ecphrastic scene of objectified, feminized flesh, the reader exercises an "unabashed voyeurism" (Goldhill
1995: 72). The effects of this textualized relation are well described by
Blake Leyerle: "The gendered gaze ensures a hierarchical positioning of
male and female encoded in terms such as active/passive and subjective/
objective," for both fictional characters and audience (159). The following
analysis will suggest that the same "positioning" is carried out in the
book of Revelation. The Apocalypse, we shall see, employs images of
penetration and the passive body to conceptualize power and desire.

The Feminized Lamb

In view of the vehemently anti-Roman stance taken by the book of
Revelation, it is surprising to discover that the Apocalypse holds significant points of contact with Augustan morality (see now Royalty: 82–96;
but cf. Bauckham: 45). After all, this same text repeatedly attacks the
city—"the great city that rules over the kings of the earth"—and its
empire (Rev 17:18), veiling Rome as the prostitute Babylon, a "haunt of
demons" fated to drown in a lake of fire. Yet the book's stirring, final
vision of the "promised land," the utopian New Jerusalem that descends
from the heavens, holds much in common with the moral themes
espoused by Foucault's philosophers and promoted by Augustus.
Granted, evidence in the Apocalypse for such a parallel is cast in negative
terms: the persons barred entrance to the New Jerusalem, those who
remain outside its walls, include "cowards, the faithless, the polluted, the
murderers, promiscuous persons, sorcerers, idolaters, and all liars" (Rev

21:8). To add to the list of vices, we should note that the book blocks the entrance to paradise for at least one courtesan, Babylon, and her serpentine consort. Likewise, Augustan Rome sought to proscribe immoral behavior within the sacred boundaries of the city. Augustus, like emperors after him, was deeply interested in establishing a pattern of morality and piety for imperial subjects to emulate. Augustus further reinforced his moral example with legislation aimed at forcing members of aristocratic families to marry (Jacobs: 109–13). In Augustan Rome, adulterers were subject to legal action and capital punishment under the *lex Iulia de adulteriis* of 18 B.C.E., while the activities of the "infamous"—including actors, performers who "lied for a living," and prostitutes—were repeatedly restricted (Edwards 1993: 124). Magicians, as Ramsay MacMullen discusses, were perennially numbered among the "enemies of the Roman order" (MacMullen 1966: 95–127).

But to eyes and ears informed by Roman sensibilities, *deiloi* ("cowards") are the most detestable moral failures on Revelation's list. Such persons are hopeless degenerates, unable to control their fears; they lack *virtus*, the Roman term for "manliness," whose connotations include "courage" and "moral excellence." And Romans, as every Roman knew, led the world in this quality: "The Roman nation is unquestionably the most outstanding in *virtus*," writes the elder Pliny (*Nat.* 7.130). Cowardice thus stands for the "unRoman"; it smacks of softness, passivity, and effeminacy, all obstacles for the Roman man to hurdle in his tireless pursuit of masculine self-mastery. An opposition commonly invoked during this period pitted Roman manliness against Greek *mollitia* ("softness") in everything from warfare to literary style. (Greeks, of course, had their own views, and *andreia* ["manliness"] remains a cardinal virtue for them, despite Roman defamation to the contrary [Moore and Anderson: 253].) Martial mocks a Corinthian's "effeminate" appearance (*Epigr.* 2.86), while Cicero highlights the Roman moral superiority over Greeks (*Tusc.* 1.1.2). To distinguish between "morality" and "manliness" in this context is unhelpful. The society of imperial Rome ranked values according to patriarchal principles, and morality consisted, to a large degree, in being manly, evoking the martial ethic and military traditions of imperial Rome. Revelation, too, glorifies the art of war and uses the vocabulary of masculine achievement: it counts among the blessed a potent army of 144,000, "a few good men" who have not "slept with women" (Rev 14:5), and "to everyone who conquers" (*tō nikōnti*), the book promises entrance into "the paradise of God" (Rev 2:7). Revelation, like Rome, is enamored of virility (Moore 1998a: 183–98).

But this is only part of the apocalyptic story. Indeed, the "Lamb standing as if slain" (*arnion hestēkos hōs esphagmenon*, Rev 5:6) seems to contradict openly the preceding assertion about Revelation's close association with the "manly," dominating ideal of Rome. Further, the conflict is not only external to the text, not only between "Christianity" and the "Roman Hellenistic world." Rather, as the destruction of Babylon in Rev 18 indicates, themes of aggression and a struggle for dominance permeate Revelation. Against this textual backdrop, the Lamb seems out of place. The Lamb is weak and compromised when it appears in the heavenly throne room (Rev 5), its posture bearing witness to the death and defeat of the crucified Christ. Parts of the animal's anatomy struggle to overcome its apparent impotence: the horns of the slaughtered Lamb represent authority and might, the kind of power symbolized by another member of the animal kingdom, the lion (Laws: 27–31). And this association is made by the text itself, in which a heavenly elder identifies the creature as the conquering "Lion of the tribe of Judah" (Rev 5:5). The Lamb's physical bearing stands at odds with the honor and authority it is assigned. This tension, we shall see, is absent from the book's other messianic characters, making the Lamb's "weakness" even more apparent.

If we locate this figure inside the Roman penetration grid, the pressure applied to the manly narrative by the wounded Lamb becomes palpable. Following the elder's introduction, the chapter accents the passivity of the Lamb (cf. T. B. Slater: 169). The Lamb's open wounds inspire song in the diverse members of the heavenly court: "You were slaughtered [*esphagēs*], and by your blood you ransomed God's saints," they sing, "worthy is the lamb that was slaughtered" (Rev 5:9, 12; cf. 7:14; 12:11). The participles are different—*pephoneumenē* in the romance, *esphagmenon* in Revelation—but Lycaenion's speech to Daphnis includes the same imagery. Just as Lycaenion's violated Chloe lies in a pool of blood, so the violence inflicted upon the Lamb leaves broken skin. To be sure, indications of fleshly fissures precede (and follow) the appearance of the Lamb in Rev 5. The book's first chapter, for example, follows a reference to "Jesus Christ, the faithful witness ... [who] freed us from our sins by his blood" with an allusion to Dan 7:13: "Look! He is coming with the clouds; every eye will see him; even those who pierced [*exekentēsan*] him" (Rev 1:6–7). But Rev 5 provides the fullest description of the creature: its seven horns, seven eyes, and bleeding body come into focus most clearly at this moment. The Lamb is both penetrated and "visually" dominated. The repeated attention the text calls to the Lamb's open wounds and profuse bleeding—in short, the attention called to the Lamb's feminized body—reproduces the "divide and conquer" scheme we have already encountered in the depiction of Chloe and Photis, a mode of representation that reveals far more about masculine desire than about "women." Does a similar desire take shape in the book of Revelation?

Answering this question in full would take us beyond the scope of this essay. For now, I note briefly that some salient evidence exists in the book's wicked characters, Babylon and the beast. Not only is the figure of Babylon monstrous, but this figure is also penetrated (Pippin: 64). The prostitute's body is on display; outfitted at first in purple and scarlet, she lies "drunk with the blood of the saints and the blood of witnesses to Jesus" (Rev 17:6). Quickly, however she is disrobed, and kings tear at her body in what is perhaps the most gruesome moment in the book: "they will devour her flesh and burn her up with fire" (Rev 17:16). The "amazing" beast with seven heads, like the Lamb, is wounded, and one of the beast's heads appears "as if slain" (*hōs esphagmenēn*), a life-threatening injury that is miraculously healed (Rev 13:3). Revelation, it seems, like Roman culture, constructs a patriarchal worldview, subduing the Other by masculine aggression. Does the "feminized" other include the pierced Lamb? Perhaps, but only for a moment, for an important distinction exists between the Lamb and its opponents. While both Babylon and the beast remain under the threat of penetration throughout the narrative, the Lamb, by contrast, overcomes the problem of penetration—momentarily, at least—through a demonstration of masculinity. To this episode we now turn.

Momentary Masculinity

At first glance the dead but alive, "slain" but "standing," Lamb alters and indicts the values of Roman society. When Longus put words about the "slain" Chloe into Lycaenion's mouth, he was simply adding skin, blood, and bone to conventional notions of gender and sexuality under the Roman principate. Revelation's Lamb, on the other hand, "breaks the rules" and manifests the narrative's socially dissident character (Kerner: 286–302). In this strange figure, some scholars argue, a new value system takes shape: the apocalyptic animal exercises authority *because* of its passivity; it receives praise and honor *because* of its sufferings. It is, in short, difficult to imagine a more *un*-Roman character than the Lamb (Schüssler Fiorenza 1991: 61; A. Y. Collins 1977: 247). Small wonder that the vulnerability evinced by the figure has given rise to much elegant hyperbole on the part of commentators: one scholar writes, for example, that the Lamb remains "one of the most mind-wrenching and theologically pregnant transformations of imagery in literature" (Boring 1992: 708).

A recent treatment, mindful of gender and sexuality in the Roman world, argues that Revelation modifies or, more precisely, reformulates the Roman concept of masculinity. Stephen Moore contends that the book is a "proto-martyrology" that defends "passive resistance as a legitimate masculine stance," an idea that disrupts the penetration grid of imperial Rome (Moore 1998a: 197 n. 8). His discussion of the Apocalypse, while controversial, stands in a long line of scholarship that separates the book from Greco-Roman society. If the book at all "mimics" aspects of Roman culture, this is only "window-dressing"; Revelation's ambitions and objectives ought to be viewed as culturally subversive and, some would say, politically revolutionary. Such evaluations naturally alight on the Lamb as a symbolic rejection of societal values: in a world that idealizes domination, the broken Lamb portends a reversal of the status quo.

But the Lamb does not remain broken in Revelation. An infamous passage describes the Lamb presiding over the eternal agonies of the doomed: "Those who worship the beast and its image, and receive a mark on their foreheads or on their hands ... will be tormented with fire and sulfur in the presence of the holy angels and in the presence of the Lamb [*enōpion tou arniou*]" (Rev 14:9–10). This episode has caused commentators no little consternation: Is it possible that this book, like other contemporary apocalypses, shows the righteous reveling in the woes of the wicked (cf. Aune 1998: 835)? The account of judgment day in 4 *Ezra*, for example, includes this chilling passage:

> Then the pit of torment shall appear, and opposite it shall be the place of rest; and the furnace of Hell shall be disclosed and opposite it the Paradise of delight. Then the Most High will say to the nations that have been raised from the dead, "Look now, and understand whom you have denied, whom you have not served, whose commandments you have despised! Look on this side and on that; here are delight and rest, and there are fire and torments!" (7:36)

Later Christian writers, too, indulge in the apocalyptic gaze: Tertullian writes of the rapturous joy that fills his heart when he imagines the suffering of Roman governors on judgment day (*Spect.* 30). In Moore's words, these texts picture "a spectacle calculated to fill [the onlookers] with grim satisfaction, or outright delight, since it manifests the Divine Sovereign's impartial justice and implacable hatred of sin" (1996: 20). The remainder of the chapter continues in this vein: "And the smoke of their torment goes up forever and ever. There is no rest day or night for those beast-worshipers and for anyone who receives the mark of its name" (Rev 14:11). A punishment of Foucauldian proportions awaits the beast's followers: the condemned announce their guilt in the number pressed into their flesh, and their bodies, tossed about in the flames, testify to the truth of the divine judgment found against them (cf. Maier: 143). The book labels the scene "a call for the endurance of the saints, those who keep the commandments of God and hold fast to the faith of Jesus" (Rev 14:12). The followers of God and the Lamb are expected to find comfort in the graphic description of their enemies' demise.

As a form of discipline, the Lamb's "torture chamber" resembles spectacles of the Roman arena. Here, too, masculinity emerges as a salient theme. Ancient texts suggest the close association of *virtus* with gladiator combats, beast hunts, and the public execution of criminals (Wistrand: 15–39). For a few, the valor and skill of the gladiator made him an exemplar. Martial, for example, writes of an evenly matched contest that ended in a draw: "to both men Caesar sent palms; thus *virtus* and skill had their reward" (*Spect.* 31). The vast majority of Roman writers, however, regarded gladiators—often slaves or criminals—with disdain or, at best, ambivalence. As performers, gladiators, along with actors and prostitutes, suffered *infamia*, "the loss of their identity as respectable citizens" (Wiedemann: 28; C. A. Barton 1994a). Only the rare gladiator proved a model of "Roman-ness." The locus of arena masculinity lay not in the nobility or courage of the combatant but in the gruesome exhibition itself or, more precisely, in the viewing of the spectacle. As Thomas Wiedemann observes, "it was meant to be part of the Roman character to be able to watch the bloodshed of the arena" (138). What seems to modern commentators to be a perverse thirst for blood among Romans befits a society built on domination. The younger Pliny, in an encomium to Trajan, praises the shows of the imperial *editor:*

> Then there was seen a spectacle neither feeble nor dissolute nor likely to soften and break the manly spirit [*nec quod animos virorum molliret et frangeret*], but one to rouse them to beautiful wounds and scorn for death [*ad pulchra vulnera contempumque mortis accenderet*], when even in the bodies of slaves and criminals [*cum in servorum etiam noxiorumque corporibus*] the love of praise and the desire for victory was visible. (*Pan.* 33.1)

It is important to note the sharp distinction Pliny makes between the audience and the "entertainment." The observers might find inspiration in "beautiful wounds," the trophies collected by the Roman soldier in the field of battle, by watching slaves and criminals die. These "infamous" groups, however, do not thereby become models of *virtus*. Rather their performance—"neither feeble nor dissolute"—provides an opportunity for the audience to refine its own masculinity. So Pliny lauds the "desire for victory" (*cupido victoriae*) in the performers, but they remain useful only to the degree that they inspire manliness in the spectators.

The penetration of bodies was a central theme of the Roman arena. Seneca, who readily expresses contempt for the hordes that eagerly gather at the amphitheater, describes the cries of outraged spectators: "Kill him! Lash him! Burn him! Why does he meet the sword in so cowardly a way?" (*Ep.* 7.4). To be sure, this is not the *virtus* that Seneca himself espouses, but the shouting crowds embody a kind of Roman manliness, a masculinity that calls out for broken, burned, and torn flesh. The same masculinity takes shape in the "fatal charades" of Roman capital punishment, dramatic executions in which animals sometimes raped female prisoners (Coleman: 50–52). Outside of the arena, community-sanctioned violence often included various forms of sexual assault, against men as well as women. In Lucian's satire *The Passing of Peregrinus* an anonymous witness testifies against Peregrinus: "as soon as he came of age, [he] was taken in adultery in Armenia and got a sound thrashing [*pollas plēgas ellaben*] ... with a radish stopping up his vent [*rhaphanidi tēn pygēn bebusmenos*]" (*Peregr.* 9). For the indiscretion Peregrinus is systematically emasculated: his accusers twice penetrate his body, first with rods, then with a vegetable (Dover 1989: 106).

Against this cultural backdrop the episode of divine punishment in Rev 14 expresses more than a vengeful streak in the Lamb. To state the obvious: the "tables have turned." The Lamb presides over the punishment of these prisoners, a scene that thus transforms the creature from *passive* to *active*. In the Roman world such a development would have been viewed as a gendered mutation from effeminacy to masculinity. The penetrated Lamb is now an agent of discipline, issuing divine retribution to its former persecutors, "even those who pierced him" (Rev 1:7). The structure of power remains stable, the hierarchy of domination and submission remains intact, but the actors have changed positions. Elsewhere authority is ascribed to the Lamb through symbol or acclamation (Rev 5–8), but here the Lamb *performs* power, controlling and tormenting the enemies of God. The meanings assigned earlier to the passive flesh of the "slain" Lamb are thus transferred to the unfortunate bodies that writhe "in the presence of angels and of the Lamb." Most important, the Lamb harnesses the "power of the gaze" in this scene: the Lamb is not the viewed but the viewer. It is not insignificant that the Lamb is described as "standing as if slain" before and not after Rev 14:9–10: this performance of masculinity closes the creature's gaping wounds, and the formerly "slouching" Lamb now towers over its opponents. The Lamb's passive, bleeding body—the "to-be- looked-at-ness" of the creature—receives no narrative attention in Rev 14. The Lamb sees but is not seen, while the bodies of the condemned suffer in its presence.

Further light may be shed on this episode by placing Rev 14:9–10 in the context of biblical literature that describes the ocular dimension of divine judgment (Maier: 140–43). The book of Psalms, for example, states simply, "His eyes behold, his gaze examines humankind" (Ps 11:4b). The letter to the Hebrews suggests further the force of the divine stare:

> The word of God is living and active, sharper than any two-edged sword, piercing [*diiknoumenos*] until it divides soul from spirit, joints from marrow; it is able to judge the thoughts and intentions of the heart. And before him no creature is hidden, but all are naked and laid bare to the eyes of the one to whom we must render an account. (Heb 4:12–13)

So too Revelation explicitly acknowledges the sharp gaze of divine and semidivine figures: in an allusion to Jer 17:10a, the "one like a son of man" announces: "I am the one who searches minds and hearts [*egō eimi ho eraunōn nephrous kai kardias*], and I will give to each of you as your works deserve" (Rev 2:23). Biblical literature attests to the invasive force of the divine gaze of judgment, but we will have to look elsewhere to comprehend the gender and sexual valences of the Lamb's spectacular conquest in Rev 14:9–10.

Two examples, drawn from the world of early Christian female martyrs (Miles: 53–80), illumine the play of gender in Rev 14:9–10 and bring into clear focus the manly potency of the Lamb's gaze. The first comes from the *Acts of Paul and Thecla*. Paul's young disciple finds herself in deep trouble for rejecting both a marriage proposition and a rape attempt. To punish this nonconformity, the governor sentences Thecla to expire in the arena. While the account never diminishes the threat posed by the wild beasts, a different danger rivals the mere prospect of death. After Thecla throws herself into a pool containing fierce seals, the narrator notes, "there was round her a cloud of fire so that the beasts could neither touch her nor could she be seen naked" (*Acts of Paul and Thecla* 34). The fiery cloud turns back the beasts that seek to devour Thecla; it also keeps her safe from exposure to the eyes of her captors (Burrus 1994: 29). In the arena, the beasts are menacing; equally so is the lecherous gaze of the spectator, and both forms of assault must be blocked for Thecla to survive the ordeal.

The second example comes from the *Martyrdom of Perpetua and Felicitas* (Castelli 1995: 13–16). This episode, by contrast, shows little or no interest in protecting the female body from either spectators or death, while making explicit the same associations implied by the fiery cloud that surrounds Thecla. Like Thecla, Perpetua and Felicitas are thrown into an arena and stripped of clothing. The nakedness is momentary, however, for the sight of Felicitas, "fresh from childbirth with the milk still dripping from her breasts" (*Martyrdom of Perpetua and Felicitas* 20), horrifies the crowd. So as not to spoil the entertainment, both women are dressed again in tunics. Then the restless spectators, having already watched bears and other beasts maul the women's male companions, demand that the execution of the Christians proceed in front of them. "But the mob asked for their [the martyrs'] bodies to be brought out into the open," says the narrator, "so that their eyes could share [*comites*] the killing as the sword entered [*penetranti*] their flesh" (*Martyrdom of Perpetua and Felicitas* 21). Perpetua is finally executed, and though she dies a noble death, it is the corporeality, not the courage, of the martyr that surfaces in the description: "she screamed as she was struck on the bone" (*Martyrdom of Perpetua and Felicitas* 21). If Trajan's games inspired "a manly spirit" in the spectators, the account of Perpetua's death presents the gaze of the crowd as a "manly" weapon that could effortlessly pierce the flesh on display.

Body, punishment, and the spectator: the combination of these three elements in Rev 14:9–10 make it a crucible of masculinity. By exacting divine vengeance upon the bodies of the condemned, I submit, the Lamb realizes *manliness*. Revelation 14:9–10 not only shows the difference between viewed and viewer; it makes apparent the hierarchical structure of domination and submission that informs this difference. And while the Lamb does not slice open the suffering bodies with a sword or prod them with a pitchfork, the creature's seven eyes invade the condemned even as the sulfur melts their skin. Most important, the Lamb, in this moment, gains mastery of other and of *self*. The flesh of the unrighteous remains exposed—"you are wretched, pitiable, poor, blind, and naked" (*gymnos*), the "one like a son of man" warns the "lukewarm" Laodiceans (Rev 2:17–18; cf. 16:5)—but the body of the Lamb disappears from the text. Hidden from view, the Lamb is now in control: it is active, not passive, and the bearer, not the subject, of the gaze. More Daphnis than Chloe now, the Lamb becomes manly.

The imagery that follows in the wake of this transformation remains coextensive with the Lamb's newly achieved masculinity. A pastiche of blood, death, and farm implements, the chapter continues to articulate the theme of divine wrath—"poured unmixed into the cup of his anger" (Rev 14:10)—that the Lamb's "torture chamber" introduces. First, "one like a son of man," he of the fiery, intrusive gaze, appears "with a golden crown on his head, and a sharp sickle [*drepanon oxy*] in his hand!" (Rev 14:14). On his heels follows a different character, an angel, "and he too had a sharp sickle" (Rev 14:17). Both figures "reap the earth" with their sickles, and the grapes that they toss into "the great winepress of the wrath of God" unleash a great flow of blood, "high as a horse's bridle, for a distance of about two hundred miles" (Rev 14:20). In a narrative that seems to valorize manliness—the book rails against cowards, urges conquest, idealizes war—it is difficult not to view these sickles and the deeds they accomplish in phallic terms (Moore 1998a: 186–87). The agents of God conquer the world with sharp instruments, tools meant for breaching the skin and for "feminizing" opponents. The Lamb's participation in heaven's victory is at first a matter of words: it receives glory and honor and is "worthy" to open the seven seals of a scroll filled with plagues, but the Lamb remains wounded, "standing as if slain." Revelation 14, in contrast, fulfills the promise of this earlier acclaim, changing words of praise into action, into discourse: the Lamb, the "Lion of the tribe of Judah" (Rev 5:5), and its allies conquer the foes of heaven.

But no sooner have the brandishing sickles of Rev 14 seemingly confirmed the Lamb's masculinity than they call into question the gender coding of the figure. There is no doubt that the Lamb occupies a position of authority in the Apocalypse, but the creature seems to exercise this authority for only a fleeting moment. Other righteous figures that execute the will of God are constantly engaged in waging war, in domination, in conquest. Two prominent envoys of God in Revelation—"one like the son of man" and the rider on the white horse—both "lead the charge," while the Lamb fades into the background, preserved from conflict. The "one like a son of man" has already been mentioned in this discussion. He appears immediately following John's salutation, a conflation of two figures in the book of Daniel: the "Ancient of Days" (Dan 7:9) and "the one like a son of man" (Dan 7:13–14; 10). Revelation describes the physical attributes of the "one like a son of man" in lavish detail:

> and in the midst of the lampstands I saw one like a Son of Man, clothed with a long robe and with a golden sash across his chest. His head and his hair were white as white wool, white as snow; his eyes were like a flame of fire, his feet were like burnished bronze, refined as in a furnace, and his voice was like the sound of many waters. (Rev 1:13–15)

Is this yet another "divide and conquer" representation? Initially, perhaps, but then the figure's manliness is unveiled: "and from his mouth came a sharp, two-edged sword" (*rhomphaia distomos oxeia*, Rev 1:16). The body of the "one like the son of man" indicates domination not submission. Further, the figure "walks like a man" in the remainder of the narrative: he possesses a penetrating gaze, he reaps the earth with a sickle, and, in a disturbing scene of sexual violence, he throws "that woman Jezebel" onto a bed (Rev 2:22).

The "rider on the white horse," likewise, performs masculine deeds. The audience encounters this figure in Rev 19: he wears "a robe dipped in blood" and his body is marked—"he has a name inscribed that no one knows but himself" (Rev 19:12)—and his "thigh" is revealed (Rev 19:16). In this scene, which most scholars agree describes the messianic "parousia," the enemies of God fall before the sealed armies gathered earlier in the narrative (Rev 7:3–8; 14:1–3). The war is over before it begins: the rider and his army utterly destroy their opponents. The two beasts of Rev 13 are captured and cast into "the lake of fire that burns with sulfur," while the beastly infantry, "those who had received the mark of the beast," are killed by the "white horseman," by "the sword that came from his mouth" (Rev 19:20–21). Two aspects of this passage deserve immediate comment. First, this story "plays out" the saying of Rev 13:10: "If anyone is for captivity, to captivity he will go; if anyone with the sword is to be slain, he with the sword will be slain." While this passage is sometimes taken both as an indictment of warfare in the book and as a warning to the faithful about the suffering they must endure, the events of Rev 19 suggest that a proleptic purpose, too, lurks within this saying: the beasts become prisoners, and their followers are massacred by the sword. Second, and more important for the present discussion, the masculinity of "the rider on the white horse" is palpably evident here. The armies that follow the rider stand far behind their leader, watching as he engages the hosts of hell with his "sharp sword" (*rhomphaia oxeia*). This rider "will shepherd them [i.e., the nations] with an iron rod" (*poimanei autous en rhabdō sidēra*, Rev 19:15). Commenting on this passage, Moore makes a playful but salutary allusion to Freud: "sometimes a rod of iron is just a rod of iron" (Moore 1998a: 188). In the Roman world, however, a sword is never "just" a sword: penetration invokes the opposition between conqueror and conquered, domination and submission, masculine and feminine. When the audience peers at the rider's "thigh," they see not the naked thigh of Perpetua nor the open wound of the Lamb but a sharp, "double-edged" device that belongs to the "King of kings and Lord of lords" (Rev 19:16).

Revelation's trio of messianic figures—the "one like a son of man," the "rider on the white horse," and the Lamb "standing as if slain"— share in the victory over the enemies of God and, to varying degrees, share in the violent subjugation of heaven's opponents. Compared to the first two characters, however, the Lamb is a "shrinking violet." Revelation grants the Lamb a moment of manliness in Rev 14, only to *replace* the Lamb in successive chapters with its more aggressive colleagues. Even before Rev 14 reaches a conclusion, the "son of man," not the Lamb, wields a sharp sickle, reaps the earth, and sheds blood. Further, the interpreting angel (*angelus interpres*) tells John that the allies of the beast will make war on the Lamb, "and the Lamb will conquer them, for he is Lord of lords and King of kings" (Rev 17:13); and earlier, in the heavenly throne room, the Lamb, an elder tells John, will be a "shepherd" (Rev 7:17). Yet when the battle is joined, the Lamb is nowhere to be found. Rather, the rider, not the Lamb, destroys the allies of the beast; the rider, not the Lamb, becomes a shepherd (Rev 19:15). The "demasculinization" of the Lamb, we shall see, continues in the New Jerusalem, where the figure is once again made subject to the gaze.

Following in the Lamb's Footsteps

The most telling evidence of the Lamb's "momentary masculinity" shows itself in a lack, an absence. As the world comes to an end in the Apocalypse, the Lamb, in an unlikely parallel to Daphnis, prepares for a signal performance of masculinity: "for the marriage of the Lamb has come, and his bride has made herself ready" (Rev 19:7). And like the testosterone-filled conclusion to *Daphnis and Chloe*, Revelation makes the wedding a public occasion. The witnesses are gathered, and the heavenly congregation shouts songs about the torment of Babylon, about the destruction of the great city, about the judgment of God upon her (Rev 18–19). It is tempting to suggest that these hymns are sung "with harsh, rough voices, as though they were breaking up the earth with forks, not singing a wedding hymn" (*Daphnis and Chloe* 4.40). But this is where the parallels end: for unlike the conclusion to the novel, the consummation of the Lamb's wedding remains deferred. A wedding feast is held (Rev 19:9), and the bride, "the holy city, the new Jerusalem, coming down out of heaven from God, prepared as a bride adorned for her husband" arrives (Rev 21:2). But there is no "wedding night" for the bridegroom and bride. The Lamb is preserved for a different, *objectified* role: the Lamb sits on the throne of God in the New Jerusalem, and the citizens of the city "see his face" (Rev 22:1, 3). The Apocalypse thus returns the Lamb to a position of "to-be-looked-at ness."

Not only the citizens of the New Jerusalem but also the *extratextual* audience, the "readers" of Revelation, gaze on the Lamb. This audience, too, "follows the Lamb wherever it goes" (Rev 14:4). To measure the effects of the Lamb's "gender-bending" on this audience, I return briefly to the USMC television advertisement that inspired the introductory meditation on penetration and spectacle. A striking and instructive difference in presentation emerges if we compare the televised scene to the scenes of torment and destruction narrated by the Apocalypse. While the commercial invites the television audience to participate in self-mastery and masculinity, its astounding special effects permit, at most, only a vicarious experience for the viewer. One simply does not encounter such monsters in the streets of modern America.

The Lamb of the Apocalypse, however, models a performance— spectatorship—to which readers of this text have direct and immediate access. Surrounded by public displays of punishment and death, Revelation's "colosseum" of horrors tethers the book to Roman culture. And just as this culture made the arena a training ground for masculinity, the book of Revelation allows its audience to exercise a spectator form of manliness. In Rev 14 the reader *watches* the Lamb *watch* the fiery torments and the smoke that "goes up forever and ever." After studying the Lamb's viewing example, the audience encounters the suffering for themselves: they witness the rape of Babylon (Rev 17–18); they watch as the armies of the beast are killed and their flesh fed to the birds (Rev 19:20–21). They are the spectators when the beast is "tormented day and night" (Rev 20:10) and when the smoke of the burning Rome "goes up forever and ever" (Rev 19:3). Like the shows of Trajan, Revelation inspired a "manly spirit" in the early Christian audience that gathered to witness the spectacles of the apocalypse.

ANCIENT MASCULINITIES

Page duBois
University of California at San Diego

For a classicist, the very existence of Christianity sometimes appears as a shock and a scandal. I am still in the thrall of Eric Auerbach's *Mimesis* of 1946, which posits a dramatic, almost violent break between the texts of classical antiquity and the Gospel of Mark. Commenting on a scene from the Christian text, Auerbach insists on the radical rupture into a new world: "the nature and the scene of the conflict ... fall entirely outside the domain of classical antiquity" (42). "What we see here is a world which on the one hand is entirely real, average, identifiable as to place, time, and circumstances, but which on the other hand is shaken in its very foundations, is transforming and renewing itself before our eyes." (43); "the stylistic convention of antiquity fails " (44); "the deep subsurface layers, which were static for the observers of classical antiquity, began to move" (45). "[T[here is no room for ethical and rhetorical standards in the sense of the ancients" (ibid.). "A scene like Peter's denial fits into no antique genre" (ibid.). Auerbach cites what he calls a "symptom," "the use of direct discourse in living dialogue," unheard of in the ancient historians, to mark the radical difference between these two bodies of work. And he attributes the stylistic discontinuity he notes to a difference in audience between the classical and the early Christian texts: Petronius and Tacitus looked down from above, while the New Testament text is written "directly for everyman" (47). "The story speaks to everybody; everybody is urged and indeed required to take sides for or against it. Even ignoring it implies taking sides" (48). He argues that there is a dramatic separation, an antagonism between sensory appearance and meaning, that "permeates" "the whole Christian view of reality" and that such an antagonism was absent from the Greco-Roman representations of reality, "perfectly integrated in their sensory substance" (49).

---

* The essays by D'Angelo and Swancutt were not available when this response was composed.

His is, of course, a problematic move for us as contemporary readers. We now assume that history does not change with such abruptness; we recognize that there were other important traditions present in the Europe that provides the landscape for Auerbach's narrative, Jewish and Islamic textual traditions, for example, that must qualify our sense of Europe and the West as homogeneous and contained.

One of the great virtues of this collection of essays on New Testament masculinities is the authors' frequent concern to bridge the great intellectual, spiritual, and disciplinary divide between classical studies, its study of ancient societies, and the discipline of the study of early Christianity. My thinking on the question of ancient gender has been much enriched by these essays. Tat-siong Benny Liew's essay, "Re-Mark-able Masculinities," usefully draws the reader's attention to the crucial issue of patriarchy and reminds us that masculinity is performed in the shadow of an overarching patriarchal domination. Janice Capel Anderson and Stephen Moore's rich and subtle essay, "Matthew and Masculinity," refuses a reductive reading and remains faithful to the complex contradictoriness of their object of study. Jennifer Glancy, in "Protocols of Masculinity," makes the crucial methodological move of considering the rhetorical status of the Pastoral Epistles. "Paul, the Invisible Man," by David Clines, violating certain codes by using the first-person singular, calls attention to the rhetoric of writing by insisting on the subjective nature of readings of these crucial texts. The reader finds in Colleen Conway's "Behold the Man!" a careful and historically rigorous definition of terminology that clarifies much appearing in other essays even as it supports Liew's conclusions considering the masculinity of Jesus subordinated to the patriarchy of the greater god. Jerome Neyrey's authoritative article, "Jesus, Gender, and the Gospel of Matthew," while insisting on a positivist approach, demonstrates a crucial recoding of honor that marks a difference between ancient and Christian ideology, and that for me cast light on the scandal of the crucified god of Christianity. Chris Frilingos's "Sexing the Lamb," risking anachronism in the deployment of film theory, offers a strikingly dynamic reading of the Apocalypse, showing the instability of the ideologies of masculinity and femininity in this text, and again conscientiously considering the rhetorical effects on contemporary readers, ancient and postmodern, of the revelations. Eric Thurman's essay, "Looking for a Few Good Men," has changed my mind completely about the value of postcolonial theory for thinking about ancient societies. Again, pedantically, I had condemned it as anachronism, forcing the categories of modernity and postmodernity on an inappropriate object. I still think that a sloppy use of Judith Butler and Homi Bhabha can tell us very little about ancient cultures. Yet Thurman's nuanced, careful, historically attuned discussion of bandits and mimic men goes far toward turning a disciplinary wound, the split between classicists and historians of early Christianity, into a scar, weaving the genres of romance and Gospel together, making it seem possible that they existed in the same world.

One point that is touched on by some of these papers, but that could be emphasized more, is the historical difference between modern notions of "masculinity" and those of antiquity. It is possible to project ahistorical heterosexist assumptions about a natural pairing of male and female onto the concept of masculinity, when, as several of the authors make clear, virility was in antiquity associated not with the heterosexual dyad but rather with mastery. One strain of ancient thinking would regard as most masculine a man who dominated sexually boys, or other men, rather than one who consorted with women, who could have a debilitating, even effeminizing effect. The *Secret Gospel of Mark*, edited by Morton Smith, suggests that there may have been aspects of the cult of Jesus that more fully resembled initiation rites, mysteries, and homoerotic bonding than have been registered in the canonical Gospels. Certainly the symposium of antiquity was a site of homoerotic desire and even fulfilment of desire; Dionysiac symposia were participated in by men, often lovers, as we see in a scene such as that portrayed on the Tomb of the Diver in Paestum. The depiction of the symposiaic scene, with two male lovers kissing, on a tomb, may also hint further at the associations between Dionysos, death, and the underworld. The *Secret Gospel of Mark* is accessible only through a letter of Clement of Alexandria, apparently denouncing the unspeakable (*arrhētous*) teachings of the Carpocratians, who in their libertine understanding of Jesus' message may have advocated homoerotic love. The term *arrhētous*, "unspeakable," is used of the sexual symbolism of the Eleusinian mysteries. The passage of the *Secret Gospel of Mark* cited by Clement, to clarify something he sees as exaggerated and illegitimate in the practice of the Carpocratians, does allow for the possibility of some kind of initiation rite and homoeroticism, although such an interpretation has been strenuously objected to by a homophobic tradition. Jesus is said to have raised a young man from the dead:

> straightaway, going in where the youth was, he stretched forth his hand and raised him, seized his hand. But the youth, looking upon him, loved [*ēgapēsen*] him and began to beseech him that he might be with him. And going out of the tomb they came into the house of the youth, for he was rich. And after six days Jesus told him what to do and in the evening the youth comes to him, wearing a linen cloth over his naked body [*peribeblēmenos sindona epi gymnou*]. And he remained with him that night [*nykta*, accusative of duration of time], for Jesus taught him the mystery of the kingdom of God. (M. Smith 1973: 447)

Concerning this passage Smith argues:

> Since the Carpocratians had a reputation for sexual license, ... it is easy
> to suppose that the Carpocratians took the opportunity to insert in the
> text some material which would authorize the homosexual relationship
> Clement suggested by picking out *gumnos gymnô*. Similar developments
> might be thought to lie behind the celebration of baptism in Acta
> Thomae 27 as *hê koinonia tou arrenos* ... and sayings like Gospel of
> Thomas (Leipoldt) 108, "Jesus said: 'He who will drink of my mouth will
> become like me, and I shall be he, and the hidden things shall be
> revealed to him.'" (1973: 185)

Smith further points out that the word *neaniskos*, used of the resurrected
youth, connects him with others (e.g., Mark 14:51, a youth wearing a
sheet over his naked body was [almost] caught with Jesus late at night;
M. Smith 1973: 109). In any case, Clement cites the *Secret Gospel of Mark*,
going on to deny that the words "naked man with naked man" (*to de
gymnos gymnō*) and "the other things about which you wrote" are found
in the text. Later in Clement's letter, the youth is referred to as "the
youth whom Jesus loved [*ēgapa*]." Certainly, in the context of early
Roman imperial civilization, sexual acts between men were commonplace and unremarkable. Yet Paul refers to such homosexuality,
condemning it, in his letter to the Romans, who of course like the whole
of the Greco-Roman world had been practicing pederasty and homosexual acts for centuries:

> God gave them [those who by their wickedness suppress the truth
> (1:18)] up to degrading passions. Their women exchanged natural inter-
> course for unnatural, and in the same way also the men, giving up
> natural intercourse with women, were consumed with passion for one
> another. Men committed shameless acts with men and received in their
> own persons the due penalty for their error. (1:26)

Such condemnation of the commonplace homoeroticism of antiquity
comes to justify subsequent homophobias and to distort our reading of
ancient and early Christian masculinities.

To a classicist, studies of Christianity can often seem "contaminated"
by belief and by traditions of cult. Many scholars of early Christianity
come from backgrounds of belief and piety, and these circumstances
affect their relationship to the ancient objects. I say this not to find fault.
Classicists, having the convenience of studying gods in whom (almost)
no one still believes, are drawn to their objects for various reasons, sometimes having to do with a sense of elite privilege, the mysteries of
languages unknown to the masses, or to what are imagined to be the joys
of paganism, perhaps as a reaction against a hegemonic monotheism in

Western societies, until recently dominated absolutely by Christianity and Judaism. Psychoanalytic categories can illuminate the practices of historical scholarship. Disavowal, like the themes of the unconscious, projection, transference, and countertransference, adduced to account for the operations of the human mind, acknowledges the difficulties, even impossibility, of a pure, immediate access to our objects of inquiry. Psychoanalysis tries to recognize and name, but never fully to master, all that inevitably interferes with a perfect, true, and objective knowledge of one's self, of others, of texts, of all that one encounters in life. Psychoanalysis, with its rich vocabulary for describing the troubling, noisy, interfering investments we bring to any object, opens up new kinds of reading. To the confidence of the positivist working toward a clear, unblemished account of the ancient past, I prefer the self-conscious, self-critical, self-reflexive mode of knowing recorded in Freud's accounts. As Freud and Nietzsche insist, every perspective is particular, internally troubled, marked by conscious or unconscious investments. One can never know or understand all the determinants of one's inquiry, never fully represent the object. There is no single, true, whole picture of the past. It is impossible to get it right, to see clearly a distant past, to bracket successfully our own desires and needs vis-à-vis the objects of scholarly work. It seems to me better to acknowledge and meditate upon them rather than to pretend they can be overcome, or mastered. In Latin, *contamino* can mean "to render (a sacred object, etc.) ritually unclean, profane, pollute, desecrate." Who we are "contaminates" what we write. I mean contamination in this etymological sense, that contact produces mingling, impurity, hybridity, not necessarily a negative infection or pollution; better to acknowledge this fusion of temporalities than to claim a pure, unmediated access to the past.

There are two ways in which these matters affect my reactions to these pieces. The writers' desire affects the object. And what is written is rhetoric produced in the present, that is to say, an intervention in debates of the twenty-first century. In the case of masculinity, these are political interventions marked by desires and investments, in debates about gender, about religion, belief, and practices, and about the conduct of politics. The texts of the New Testament considered here exist as rhetorical interventions themselves, as writing meant to communicate with an audience, contemporary and subsequent, as do the essays assembled in this valuable collection. The debate about masculinities engaged here will have its effects not only on our view of the Hellenistic world but also on the living of masculinities, by men and women, in present and future.

BY WHOSE GENDER STANDARDS (IF ANYBODY'S) WAS JESUS A REAL MAN?

Maud W. Gleason
Stanford University

What would Polemo have made of Jesus? An elite rhetorician as well as a self-proclaimed physiognomist, this pagan "gender policeman" (to use Glancy's felicitous phrase) liked nothing better than to expose the pretensions of males who were not, by his exacting criteria, real men. "Soft dark hair, flabby hips, sinews on the skinny side? Effeminate, my dear Watson." Alas, Polemo lived a century too late to meet Jesus in the flesh, and early Christian written traditions preserved for posterity no physical particulars of the founder's appearance.[1] But in the context of Greco-Roman gender protocols, even without any physiognomical evidence, Jesus' masculinity was a problem.

For one thing, Jesus had no *paideia*. He did control "the manly art of oratory" (so Glancy, also Clines), in the sense that he could control the attention of a large crowd, but most of his crowds were composed of rustics. Greco-Roman gentlemen had no use for such persons: they cut their gender-teeth discoursing with other of their own social kind, in a literary dialect that was probably over the heads of even those rustics whose native language was some kind of Greek. Indeed, while the ability to dominate a crowd verbally may well have been part of a pan-Mediterranean koine of masculinity, educated elites who excelled in *paideia* were actually suspicious of speakers who were excessively popular with audiences of low degree, stigmatizing them as illegitimate players at the game of words. Some of these suspect speakers were, like Jesus, entrepreneurs in the religious sphere: people such as the quasi-Christian Peregrinus and the snake-oracle-monger Alexander of Abonuteichos. So, though Jesus could control an ignorant crowd, in

---

1 Pagans, by contrast, were showing a heightened interest around this time in the physical appearance of the Homeric heroes, as we can see from Philostratus's *Heroikos*, now translated by Maclean and Aitken.

the eyes of the educated Jesus' public-speaking ability would have been at best an ambiguous component of his masculinity.

What Jesus clearly did not control was the boundaries of his own body. This inability, in the eyes of educated men and those who accepted their value system, was related to his educational limitations: one of the chief benefits of *paideia* was its power to protect the body-boundaries of the educated person from violation, particularly from violations by the agents of the imperial criminal justice system.[2] The *only* thing that the Gospel narratives tell us about Jesus' body is that it was thus violated. This issue is explored by both Glancy and Frilingos, who writes: "The breached body, male or female, was 'feminine' or 'effeminate'" (Frilingos: 302). As Frilingos notes, the Lamb of Revelation's flesh, like that of Jesus, is penetrated and visually dominated by the scopophilic gaze of onlookers trained (we might suppose) to this domination-practice by grisly Roman entertainment forms. But then, in a particularly fascinating passage, Frilingos shows us how the Lamb shifts position, from the gazed-on to the dominant one who gazes upon others. The Lamb redeems his compromised masculinity by presiding over the spectacle of the tortured bodies of the damned. This shift brings up the crucial question, touched upon in several papers, of the extent to which the Roman Empire's equation of masculinity with domination influenced the way Jesus' life and message were interpreted by his early followers. "The last shall be first" can be read as a model of triumphalist reversal (as in Tertullian's *De Spectaculis* and *Revelation*) in which the underdog takes over the position of the erstwhile top dog in the same old status game. But Jesus can also be seen as proposing a new game altogether, one that entails not just a reversal but an actual transformation of masculinist ideology. Thurman's contribution shows how Mark struggles with a destabilized masculinity, and Anderson and Moore explore how Matthew presents a "countercultural vision of a physically impotent but spiritually potent masculinity" (90).

Some Christians apparently did take Jesus' destabilized masculinity as a paradigm authorizing experimentation with traditional gender protocols, as we can infer from the faint traces of anxiety about proper masculine deportment in the Pastoral Epistles and other early Christian texts. D'Angelo captures well a fateful historical moment when Christians' need to appear socially respectable in the eyes of skeptical and occasionally murderous "Others" promoted the development of an ethic of masculinity that resembles the moral program of the Roman emperors

---

2 I have written a little more on this in Gleason 1999b.

in emphasizing hegemonic control over self and underlings in the household and in the Christian community. This ethic was not fully formed (if present at all) in Jesus' ragtag band of household-less followers. Even though the author of *Hermas* appears to have more complex, if not fully egalitarian, relations with real and visionary females, he still feels the male householder's sting of shame for his failure to control the behavior of his wife and offspring. Another window on the early Christians' anxiety about inadequate male control over the household opens up for us when we read between the lines of Origen's *Contra Celsum*. Celsus appears to have ridiculed Christian households in which women and children ignored the prescriptions of their *paterfamilias* in favor of the so-called "wisdom" they drank in from low-status Christian teachers in the wool-dresser's shop. As Glancy observes, there may have been "a long-standing pattern of pagan gender-baiting" (260). This would not surprise me, since pagan rhetoricians, both Greek and Roman, made hay with any chinks in their opponents' gender-armor that they could find.[3]

Though I cannot do justice to the full range of topics and texts covered in this volume, I would like to raise for a moment the question of cultural specificity. Though many contributors discuss classicists' work on Greek and Roman gender ideology, I think we need more discussion of the extent to which the social construction of gender in Aramaic-speaking Palestine followed the same lines. Jesus' original auditors had read no Aeschylus or Seneca. How much more Hellenized were the next few Christian generations? To the extent that readers of early Christian texts, whatever their ethnicity, were not members of the educated elite, we must ask of each text's probable audience: What were its specific gender-norms? Jewish views on male nudity and male-male sexual contact, to mention just two examples, were clearly at odds with the views of the Greco-Roman elite (which were probably themselves much more varied and complex than we classicists have made them out to be!). With all humility I must say that we do not know to what extent nonelite residents of a Greek city shared the gender-values of their betters.

---

3 On this unedifying spectacle, see, among many others, Gleason 1995.

MANHOOD AND NEW TESTAMENT STUDIES AFTER SEPTEMBER 11

Jeffrey L. Staley
Seattle University

It is a good time to be a man—a manly man—in America. My son turned seventeen this past summer, and he loves to show me how powerful he is. He says to me, "Come here, Dad, I've got something to show you in the living room." And I fall for him every time. He grabs me, tries to trip me, and wrestle me to the floor. As he pins my arms behind my back, I protest and complain that I am much too old for this sort of roughhousing. I'm over fifty. My bones are getting brittle. But that doesn't seem to dissuade him. He forces me to the floor anyway. He has a need to flex his muscles, to test his strength "mano a mano."

I should wear a steel cup for all the times he walks past me in the kitchen or dining room and sucker-punches me in the balls. The behavior must be symbolic of *something*, it happens so regularly. Maybe his actions somehow represent the passing of the male baton to the next generation. I am old and slow. He is young, strong, and agile. He is old enough to drive. I wear bifocals but still hit curbs occasionally just so I know where I am on the street. It is true that I would die for my son, but he is nearly old enough to die for his country—in Iraq or Afghanistan—or some other place where American interests seem to need protection. Are United States military personnel issued steel cups? I hope so.

Two years ago, terrorists invaded our sacred American space. They penetrated our most holy and private places: our centers of male power, with sleek, pen-shaped jets. The twin towers, those "legs of alabaster columns set upon bases of gold" (Song 5:15), exploded in pain and agony, and we were powerless to stop the iron rods of Allah's anger. Not once, but twice, jets hit the towers. Then the Pentagon. And only the spontaneous act

---

* The essays by D'Angelo, Liew, and Swancutt were not available when this response was composed.

of a few good men on United Airlines Flight 93 averted further disaster at the United States capitol. So buckle on your steel cups, ye men of valor. Sharpen your pens, ye hooded professors of New Testament. Flex your muscles as my son does, and forge your pens into bayonets. Pass the baton. The New Testament and this volume have something to say to US about manhood. A couple of years after 9/11.

Jerome Neyrey tells us that in the ancient Mediterranean world, "All challenges, to be effective, must be 'public,' ... every honorable male must not turn the other cheek but deliver a riposte" (59). Likewise, we biblical scholars fight with words on the public battlefields of Semeia Studies and *JBL* in order to prove our "manhood." So how, in good agonistic fashion, shall we New Testament critics divide and conquer the textual geography our editors have now set before us? Every good war—paper or otherwise—starts with deployment. Perhaps this paper war should also begin with organizing the troops. Men and women in leadership positions—the managers, supervisors, editors—make sure that everything is properly ordered. So let's choose the terrain and set out our troops.

Thrust into the forefront of the battle, I have decided to meet the manly crisis with the following strategy: social-scientific/social-description essays will be my first line of attack. Since the essays of Jerome Neyrey, David Clines, Jennifer Glancy, and Colleen Conway primarily focus on how masculinity operated in the ancient Mediterranean Basin, what masculinity was like in the eastern Roman Empire during the late Augustan era, their essays function as shock troops. They tell us (again and again) that the contours of masculinity were much different then than in the twenty-first-century Western world. Yet, how the General Reader is to apply that newly acquired knowledge (if it can be applied at all) is the general's own problem, and not the primary interest of these authors. It's like firing salvos at a distance. Analyze the evidence embedded in the ancient social map of the Bible and elsewhere, but don't worry about the text as a living canon aimed at US. It is too far away, pointed in the opposite direction, and we are out of range anyway. It won't hurt us.

So Neyrey, Clines, Glancy, and Conway just map the contours of masculinity in the ancient Mediterranean world. And they do it well. For example, Neyrey's statement of purpose works fairly well for all four writers: "This study has two parts: data and interpretation. First we will rehearse the ancient data for the gender stereotype" (43). Since his focus is on Matthew, "with this data we will then interpret the figure of the male Jesus in Matthew. We wish to see how much of this stereotype Matthew knows, how he presents Jesus as an ideal male, and what this means for the interpretation of his Gospel" (ibid.). This first group of essays push beyond the first skirmishes of "social-scientific biblical criticism" in the 1980s and early 1990s, where there was virtually no attempt to nuance the elite ideal models for more narrowly defined subgroups—especially for those who were outside the culture's spheres of status and honor.

Neyrey, a point man in the battlefield of applying cultural anthropological models to New Testament studies, has learned to ask a slightly different question than he was asking ten years ago. His current inquiry focuses on the issue "Does the same set of [ancient Mediterranean] gender expectations apply equally to elite and nonelite males and females?" (52). And Neyrey is led to conclude that "Few males ... had the opportunity to fulfill the ideal stereotype of masculinity" (52). In his analysis, Jesus is at "egregious variance ... from the male stereotype" (64), but while "Jesus may seem not to conform to the gender stereotype when he [makes certain] demands of this followers.... [Nevertheless,] these shameful actions actually become the way to honor in the eyes of God and Jesus" (66). Neyrey's point is well taken: the author of Matthew does not step unarmed into no man's land. He still lives in an androcentric, patriarchal honor-shame world, for despite Jesus' apparently dishonorable death, Jesus ultimately is pronounced honorable in the sight of God and exalted to a status superior to any human (Matt 21:42; 26:64; 28:17). However, in view of the Jewish revolt of 70 C.E., I wonder whether the "honor" of enduring shameful actions (42) may have lost some of its luster for Matthew's community. In light of the events of 70 C.E., is the author of Matthew trying to restore martyrdom to a place of male honor in his community? If Q had no passion narrative, as is often argued (and so must have represented a different construal of Jesus' masculine honor), does Matthew's coupling of Q and Mark represent a reconfiguring of that tradition's masculinity? It would be interesting to see how Neyrey might assess the historical trajectory of masculinity in Matthew's community in light of Matthew's use of Q traditions.

In my estimation, the essays of David Clines, Jennifer Glancy, and Colleen Conway do not stray far from Neyrey as point man. Like his essay, these also center largely on the collection of male stereotyped data. One finds only minor forays into such issues as how their interpretations might relate to contemporary communities of faith who read these texts as part of a religious canon.

David Clines's essay on Paul emphasizes Paul as a "pretty normal" male (192). But perhaps because Clines eschews the sort of taxonomies of which Neyrey is so fond, he can go on to say that Paul is "not particularly culturally conditioned" (ibid.). Surely Neyrey would find Clines's last statement problematic—while solidly affirming the former. But I would want to push the question further: Is there a hermeneutical strategy that one can develop from this "pretty normal but not particularly culturally conditioned" Paul? One that can address or challenge United States manhood after 9/11?

Jennifer Glancy's essay on masculinity in the Pastorals suggests that New Testament constructions of the ideal male may not be quite the impregnable fortress that Neyrey presumes. Like Neyrey, she sets out a wealth of extrabiblical material to prove that the "pastor's" construction of masculinity in the Pastoral Epistles is no different from what one finds in other first-century Mediterranean texts. But where she differs from Neyrey and Clines is in her qualification that other characters in early Christian texts (Paul, Jesus, John the Baptist) reflect "alternative masculinities" (250) that the "Pastor" seeks to "overwrite" (ibid). For her, the Pastor's "silence on the crucifixion" makes it possible for him to separate "himself from the unmanly image of the crucified Christ" (264). This observation, usually stated only in the context of the Pastoral Epistles' non-Pauline Christology, becomes a significant masculinist insight in her analysis. To put her observation in the context of Matthew and Q: If Q existed as a Gospel without a passion narrative, it would seem to fit the Pastor's masculine sensibilities quite well. Furthermore, Matthew's decision to combine Q with Mark could, perhaps, be seen as a Glancian challenge to Neyrey's argument that when all is said and done Matthew still "fits" the model of the ideal ancient Mediterranean male. To stir up a hornets' nest: Q and the "Pastor" represent the ideal ancient Mediterranean masculinity. Matthew is a challenge to it.

These first three essays share a common approach to the ancient biblical text. None of them spend any time theorizing or excavating sources behind the Gospels or epistles in an attempt to delineate a trajectory of "masculinity" in the early church the way Elizabeth Schüssler-Fiorenza did so masterfully for feminist biblical studies twenty years ago. But Colleen Conway's essay is a bit different from the first three. In her exploration of masculine Christology in John she does address the roots of the book's supposed feminized wisdom theology and Christology. However, she problematizes the wisdom language in such a way that Jesus is both "an exemplar of masculinity" in relation to the people in the story (179) and a feminized character in his relationship to God. Thus her reading of Jesus in the Fourth Gospel reveals a person who is more fluid (like water?), one who sometimes has masculine characteristics and sometimes has feminine attributes. Conway's essay ends on a note that is more pointedly hermeneutical and moves in the direction of the final three essays under consideration. Her conclusion speaks of those communities that "have always found ways to read against the text in their reflections of the Christ or to read in ways that highlight the ultimate instability of the text" (180). For me, this is the point at which we move into a no man's land that can be life giving; where the canon as weapon turns in upon itself and becomes a fecund opening to a world of restructured masculinities.

In company with the first four scholars, Thurman, Frilingos, and Anderson and Moore also mine ancient Mediterranean texts (e.g., Philo, Greco-Roman erotic novels, patrisitic theologians) for constructions of masculinity. Here again we are on a familiar battleground (the Gospel of Mark, the book of Revelation, and Matthew), and we half expect to find ourselves taking body counts and checking dog tags rather than engaging in live action. But surprise! Thurman uses postcolonial discourses to challenge and complicate the ideal of Mediterranean masculinity; Frilingos explores the images of penetration in Revelation, showing how those are linked to "gender-bending" (317) and domination through the metaphor of the slain Lamb that the reader "watches" (ibid.). And Anderson and Moore hear contrapuntal voices in Matthew that challenge its stereotyped Mediterranean male values. These essays thus share a slightly different orientation, one that I find more constructive when considering the ongoing ethical dimensions of the Christian canon. To my way of thinking, these latter authors all seem to be consciously looking for an intratextual and intertextual hermeneutic for biblical texts that can challenge the dominant, hegemonic, binary framework of ancient Mediterranean masculinity. Thinking about rhetorical constructions of United States masculinity after 9/11, I believe these scholars' probings offer a more fruitful ethical orientation for contemporary communities of faith. Their intertextual tapestries highlight the blurred borders and edges of male identity rather than its bright center. For example, Thurman takes the reader on a provocative analysis of the term *lēstēs* in Greco-Roman novels and, with Homi Bhabha's postcolonial concept of mimicry, leads the reader into the gladiatorial arena to reveal a Jesus who "emerges as a 'mimic man'" and an "imperial pretender" (149). For Thurman, this means "Mark fails to question male privilege at a fundamental level" (160). But rather than end on this dispirited note, Thurman adds that "feminist and postcolonial critique ... disrupts ... masculinity's 'manifest destiny'" (161).

Anderson and Moore likewise challenge a Neyreyan reading of Matthew by reading on the edges of its masculine discourses. Especially helpful are the ways in which they show how the Mediterranean language of kinship is rescripted by Jesus in such a way that the image of the ideal male is disrupted (86–87). This disruption is seen most clearly in their discussion of eunuchs (87–91), who are boundary-blurring people of "'unman' status" (91). Finally, Chris Frilingos's observation that "Penetration, for Romans, equals domination: in such a system, sexuality and gender remain expressions of mastery" (303) eerily evokes the rhetoric of our post-9/11 world. I must confess that I read Chris's essay first, before any of the others, because I was also working on an essay on the book of Revelation. Because of his essay, the politics of penetration is still with me. I wonder how much of Frilingos's choice of metaphor was influenced by the events of 9/11.

Penetration and power, shame and honor. The phallus twins of New York turned inside out, vaginal. Ground Zero. The great hole of Babylon. Some go to gape—and others come, but avert their eyes. Is it the apocalypse? A postcolonial Mark of devastating mimicry? Matthew rescripted? A Pall hovering, invisible still? We cannot afford simply to discuss New Testament masculinities as though they have no connection to contemporary Christian communities or United States global policies. Ethically responsible biblical interpretation—whether it is historical-critical, literary, social-scientific, postcolonial, or postmodern—must find ways to translate its New Testament visions (versions) of manhood into socially responsible critiques and action. Whether that means finding new ways of reading ancient texts, as in the case of Thurman, Frilingos, and Anderson and Moore, or whether it means rejecting these texts outright, as the first set of essays might seem to imply, we ignore them at our own peril. All too quickly the gamesmanship of challenge and riposte gets transformed into "martyrdom," violence, and annihilation. These texts as canon should mean more to us than that. Somehow the canon must be redirected, retrained, reconfig*uerred.*

It seems to me that what is largely lacking in this series of essays on New Testament masculinities is a sense of what is at stake for living, present-day communities of men and women who claim these texts as authoritative, who claim that these texts, in some way, hold sway over their lives, who claim these texts as "canon." To say that Matthew's Gospel reflects ancient Mediterranean constructions of masculinity is not surprising; to argue that Paul fits within first-century social-world constructions of the male is barely interesting. We, as biblical interpreters and scholars, need to be thinking hermeneutically, asking whether there is a hermeneutical framework or interpretive angle to these canonical texts that can lead to fresh visions of manhood.

Analyses of New Testament masculinity must somehow address the question: What effect does "canon" have upon our strategies of reading masculinity in New Testament texts? Surely there is value, post-9/11, in recognizing that challenges and ripostes continue today in international politics, that saving face is of deadly importance. But are there ways to restructure rhetorical situations (canonical or otherwise) so that challenge and riposte are seen for the tropes they are and not as incendiary preludes to violence?

Finally, how might issues of postcolonialism—especially as a strategic exercise in broadening our intertextual repertoire—relate to reading masculinity in the New Testament? For example, how might reading New Testament masculinities with matriarchal or matrilinear honor/shame texts and cultures affect those constructions of masculinity? I'm thinking here particularly of the Bible's reception in different Native American tribal cultures. But African American texts might come into play here as well.

So what do I tell my son at seventeen, strong, virile, flexing his muscles. The one who wrestles me to the floor to prove his manhood (and I let him); the one who is ready to graduate from high school and take on the world? So much a man he is, but there is a nation lurking in the shadows, hungry to pounce on him and devour his body as a brave witness, a martyr for ... for what new snake oil?

I want to say to that bush burning (and still not consumed), the Bush fiery with an unquenchable, fierce anger directed at Saddam's sandcastles in the desert, "You can't have my son; this dusky-shaped jewel of masculinity." So much of him is his own, so much of him is mine—and this *homoousios* that is us seems only vaguely formed and molded by the canon. But still I want to speak back to the bush burning. I want to say: "We will not fold under the warped rhetoric of your evangelistic, apocalyptic, hot-through-the-whole-with-hyped-up-male-dominated language." And I am hoping that some of US New Testament scholars will have the balls to use our canon in such a way that it turns inside out, quenches those flame-fed masculinities, and gives birth to a new generation of word-wrestling readers.

WORKS CONSULTED

Aasgaard, Reidar. 1997. Brotherhood in Plutarch and Paul: Its Role and Character. Pages 166–82 in Moxnes 1997.

Adkins, Arthur W. H. 1960. *Merit and Responsibility: A Study in Greek Values.* Chicago: University of Chicago Press.

Aichele, George. 1996. *Jesus Framed.* Biblical Limits. New York: Routledge.

———. 1998. Jesus' Violence. Pages 72–91 in *Violence, Utopia, and the Kingdom of God.* Edited by Tina Pippin and George Aichele. New York: Routledge.

Alcoff, Linda. 1988. Cultural Feminism versus Post-Structuralism: The Identity Crisis in Feminist Theory. *Signs* 13:433–34.

Alexander, Loveday. 1993. *The Preface to Luke's Gospel: Literary Convention and Social Context in Luke 1.1–4 and Acts 1.1.* Cambridge: Cambridge University Press.

Allison, Dale. 1984. Eunuchs Because of the Kingdom of Heaven (Matt. 19:12). *Theological Students Fellowship Bulletin* 8:2–5.

Alter, Robert. 1981. *The Art of Biblical Narrative.* New York: Basic.

Ambrosiaster. 1966. *Ambrosiastri Qui Dicitur Commentarius in Epistulus Paulinas.* Edited by H. J. Vogels. CSEL vol. 81.1. Vienna: Hoelder-Pichler-Tempsky.

Anderson, Janice Capel. 1983. Matthew: Gender and Reading. *Semeia* 28:3–27. Reprinted as pages 25–51 in *A Feminist Companion to Matthew.* FCNTECW 1. Edited by Amy-Jill Levine, with Marianne Blickenstaff. Sheffield: Sheffield Academic Press, 2001.

———. 1992. Feminist Criticism: The Dancing Daughter. Pages 103–34 in *Mark and Method: New Approaches in Biblical Studies.* Edited by Janice Capel Anderson and Stephen D. Moore. Minneapolis: Fortress.

Apuleius. 1994. *The Golden Ass.* Translated by P. Walsh. Oxford: Oxford University Press.

Aristotle. 1942. *Generation of Animals.* Translated by A. L. Peck. LCL. Cambridge: Harvard University Press.

———. 1944. *Aristotle in Twenty Three Volumes.* Vol. 21. Translation by H. Rackham, Cambridge: Harvard University Press. Cited 27 December 1997.Online: www.perseus.tufts.edu/cgi-bin/text?lookup=aristot.+pol.

Arnal, William E. 1977. Gendered Couplets in Q and Legal Formulations: From Rhetoric to Social History. *JBL* 116: 75–94.

Artemidorus. 1975. *The Interpretation of Dreams.* Translated by R. White. Park Ridge, N.Y.: Noyes.

Arthur, Marilyn B. 1973. Early Greece: The Origins of the Western Attitudes toward Woman. *Arethusa* 6: 7–58.

Aspegren, Karen. 1990. *The Male Woman: A Feminine Ideal in the Early Church.* Edited by René Kieffer. Stockholm: Almqvist & Wiksell.

Athenaeus. *The Deipnosophists.* Translated by Charles Burton Gulick. 7 vols. LCL. New York: Putnam's Sons.

Auerbach, Erich. 1953. *Mimesis: The Representation of Reality in Western Literature.* Translated by W. Trask. Garden City, N.Y.: Doubleday Anchor.

Aune, David E. 1994. Mastery of the Passions: Philo, 4 Maccabees and Earliest Christianity. Pages 125–58 in *Hellenization Revisited: Shaping a Christian Response within the Greco-Roman World.* Edited by Wendy E. Helleman. Lanham, Md.: University Press of America.

———. 1998. *Revelation 6–16.* WBC 52B. Dallas: Word.

Balch, David L. 1981. *Let Wives Be Submissive: The Domestic Code in 1 Peter.* Atlanta: Scholars Press

Bannon, Cynthia J. 1997. *The Brothers of Romulus: Fraternal Pietas in Roman Law, Literature, and Society.* Princeton: Princeton University Press.

Barrett, C. K. 1968. *A Commentary on the First Epistle to the Corinthians.* London: Black.

———. 1973. *Commentary on the Second Epistle to the Corinthians.* London: Black.

Bartchy, S. Scott. 1999. Undermining Ancient Patriarchy: The Apostle Paul's Vision of a Society of Siblings. *BTB* 29:68–78.

Barton, Carlin A. 1993. *The Sorrows of the Ancient Romans: The Gladiator and the Monster.* Princeton: Princeton University Press.

———. 1994a. All Things Beseem the Victor. Pages 83–92 in *Gender Rhetorics: Postures of Domination and Submission in History.* Edited by Richard Trexler. Binghamton, N.Y.: Center for Medieval and Early Christian Renaissance Studies.

———. 1994b. Savage Miracles: The Redemption of Lost Honor in Roman Society and the Sacrament of the Gladiator and the Martyr. *Representations* 45: 41–71.

———. 1999. The Roman Blush: The Delicate Matter of Self-Control. Pages 212–34 in *Constructions of the Classical Body.* Edited by James I. Porter, Ann Arbor: University of Michigan Press.

———. 2001. *Roman Honor: The Fire in the Bones.* Berkeley and Los Angeles: University of California Press.

Barton, Stephen C. 1994. *Discipleship and Family Ties in Mark and Matthew.* Cambridge: Cambridge University Press.

Basil. 1950. Against Those Prone to Anger. Pages 457–61 in *Ascetical Works.* Translated by M. Monica Wagner. FC 9. Washington: Catholic University of America Press.

Bassler, Jouette M. 1984. The Widow's Tale: A Fresh Look at 1 Tim 5:3–16. *JBL* 103:232–41.

———. 1996. *1 Timothy, 2 Timothy, Titus.* ANTC. Nashville: Abingdon.

Bauckham, Richard. 1993. *The Theology of the Book of Revelation.* New Testament Theology. New York: Cambridge University Press.

Bauer, Johannes B. 1959. "Uxores circumducere" (1 Kor 9,5). *BZ* 3:94–102.

Beare, F. W. 1959. *Commentary on the Epistle to the Philippians.* BNTC. London: Black.

Beker, J. Christiaan. 1980. *Paul the Apostle: The Triumph of God in Life and Thought.* Edinburgh: T&T Clark.

Belsey, Catherine. 1980. *Critical Practice.* New York: Routledge.

Bennett, Julian. 2001. *Trajan, Optimus Princeps: A Life and Times.* 2d ed. Bloomington: Indiana University Press.

Berger, Maurice, Brian Wallis, and Simon Watson, eds. 1995. *Constructing Masculinity.* New York: Routledge.

Bersani, Leo. 1995. Loving Men. Pages 115–23 in Berger, Wallis, and Watson.

Betz, Hans Dieter. 1995. *The Sermon on the Mount.* Hermeneia. Minneapolis: Fortress.

Beyer, Herman. 1964. διακονέω, διακονία, διάκονος. *TDNT* 2:81–93.

Bhabha, Homi. 1994. *The Location of Culture.* New York: Routledge.

———. 1995. Are You a Man or a Mouse? Pages 57–68 in Berger, Wallis, and Watson.

Blickenstaff, Marianne. 2001. The Bloody Bridegroom: Violence in the Matthean Family. Paper presented in the Matthew Section at the 2001 Society of Biblical Literature Annual Meeting. Cited 10 March 2002. Online: www.class .uidaho.edu/jcanders/Matthew/marianne_blickenstaff.htm.

Bligh, John. 1970. *Galatians: A Discussion of St Paul's Epistle.* London: St. Paul Publications.

Blinzler, Josef. 1957. Εἰσὶν εὐνοῦχοι: Zur Auslegung von Mt 19:12. *ZNW* 48: 254–70.

Blok, Anton. 1981. Rams and Billy-Goats: A Key to the Mediterranean Code of Honor. *Man* 16: 427–40. Reprinted as pages 51–70 in Wolf 1984.

Blount, Brian. 1998. *Go Preach! Mark's Kingdom Message and the Black Church Today.* Maryknoll, N.Y.: Orbis.

Bly, Robert. 1990. *Iron John: A Book about Men.* Reading, Mass.: Addison-Wesley.

Bordo, Susan. 1999. *The Male Body: A New Look at Men in Public and Private.* New York: Farrer, Straus & Giroux.

Boring, Eugene M. 1992. Narrative Christology in the Apocalypse. *CBQ* 54:702–23.

———. 1999. Markan Christology: God-Language for Jesus? *NTS* 45:451–71.

Boring, Eugene M., Klaus Berger, and Carsten Colpe, eds. 1995. *Hellenistic Commentary to the New Testament.* Nashville: Abingdon.

Boswell, J. 1980. *Christianity, Social Tolerance, and Homosexuality.* Chicago: University of Chicago Press.

Bourdieu, Pierre. 1984. *Distinction: A Social Critique of the Judgement of Taste.* Translated by Richard Nice. Cambridge: Harvard University Press.

Bowersock, G. W. 1997. *Fiction As History: Nero to Julian.* Sather Classical Lectures 58. Berkeley and Los Angeles: University of California Press.

Boyarin, Daniel. 1994. *A Radical Jew: Paul and the Politics of Identity.* Berkeley and Los Angeles: University of California Press.

———. 1995. Are There Any Jews in "The History of Sexuality"? *Journal of the History of Sexuality* 5:333–355.

———. 1997. *Unheroic Conduct: The Rise of Heterosexuality and the Invention of the Jewish Man.* Contraversions: Critical Studies in Jewish Literature, Culture, and Society 8. Berkeley and Los Angeles: University of California Press.

———. 1998. Gender. Pages 117–33 in *Critical Terms for Religious Studies.* Edited by Mark C. Taylor. Chicago: University of Chicago Press.

———. 1999. *Dying for God: Martyrdom and the Making of Christianity and Judaism.* Stanford, Calif.: Stanford University Press.

Boyd, Stephen. 1992. Trajectories in Men's Studies in Religion: Theories, Methodologies, and Issues. *The Journal of Men's Studies* 7:265–68.

Brain, Peter. 1986. *Galen on Bloodletting: A Study of the Origins, Development and Validity of His Opinions, with a Translation of the Three Works.* Cambridge: Cambridge University Press.

Brakke, David. 1998. The Passions and the Social Construction of Masculinity. Paper delivered to the Hellenistic Moral Philosophy Section, 1998 Society of Biblical Literature Annual Meeting, Orlando.

Brandes, Stanley. 1980. *Metaphors of Masculinity: Sex and Status in Andalusian Folklore.* Philadelphia: University of Pennsylvania Press

Brock, Rita Nakashima. 1988. *Journeys by Heart: A Christology of Erotic Power.* New York: Crossroad.

Brod, Harry. 1987a. A Case for Men's Studies. Pages 263–77 in *Changing Men: New Directions in Research on Men and Masculinity.* Edited by Michael Kimmel. Beverly Hills: Sage.

———, ed. 1987b. *The Making of Masculinities.* Boston: Allen & Unwin.

Brod, Harry, and Michael Kaufman, eds. 1994. *Theorizing Masculinities.* Thousand Oaks, Calif.: Sage.

Brooten, B. 1996. *Love between Women: Early Christian Responses to Female Homoeroticism.* Chicago: University of Chicago Press.

Brown, Lucinda A. 1992. Asceticism and Ideology: The Language of Power in the Pastorals. *Semeia* 57:77–94.

Brown, Peter. 1987. Late Antiquity. Pages 235–311 in *From Pagan Rome to Byzantium.* Vol. 1 of *A History of Private Life.* Edited by Paul Veyne. Cambridge: Harvard University Press.

———. 1988. *The Body and Society: Men, Women and Sexual Renunciation in Early Christianity.* New York: Columbia University Press.

Brown, Raymond E. 1966. *The Gospel according to John I–XII.* AB 29. New York: Doubleday.

———. 1970. *The Gospel according to John XIII–XXI.* AB 29A. New York: Doubleday.

———. 1975. Roles of Women in the Fourth Gospel. *TS* 36:688–99.

———. 1993. *The Birth of the Messiah.* 2d ed. ABRL. New York: Doubleday.

———. 1994. *The Death of the Messiah: From Gethsemane to the Grave: A Commentary on the Passion Narratives in the Four Gospels.* 2 vols. New York: Doubleday.

Bruce, F. F. 1980. *Paul: Apostle of the Free Spirit.* Rev. ed. Exeter: Paternoster.

Buchanan, George W. 1995. The Age of Jesus. *NTS* 41:297.

Buell, Denise Kimber. 1999. *Making Christians: Clement of Alexandria and the Rhetoric of Legitimacy.* Princeton: Princeton University Press.

Bultmann, Rudolph. 1947. *Exegetische Probleme des zweiten Korintherbriefes: Zu 2. Kor. 5,1–5; 5,11—6,10; 10–13; 12,21.* SymBU 9. Uppsala: Wretmans.

Burrow, J. A. 1986. *The Ages of Man: A Study in Medieval Writing and Thought.* Oxford: Clarendon.

Burrus, Virginia. 1994. Word and Flesh: The Bodies and Sexuality of Ascetic Women in Christian Antiquity. *JFSR* 10:27–51.

———. 2000. *"Begotten, Not Made": Conceiving Manhood in Late Antiquity.* Stanford, Calif.: Stanford University Press.

———. 2001. Sexing Jesus in Late Antiquity. Unpublished paper.

———. Forthcoming. Torture and Travail: Producing the Christian Martyr. In *A Feminist Companion to the Patristic Period*. Edited by Amy-Jill Levine. FCNTECW. Sheffield: Sheffield Academic Press.

Butler, Judith. 1990. *Gender Trouble: Feminism and the Subversion of Identity*. New York: Routledge.

———. 1995. Melancholy Gender/Refused Identification. Pages 21–36 in Berger, Wallis, and Watson.

———. 2000. *Antigone's Claim: Kinship between Life and Death*. New York: Columbia University Press.

Buttrick, George Arthur, ed. 1954–76. *The Interpreter's Dictionary of the Bible: An Illustrated Encyclopedia*. 4 vols. (1954) and a supplementary vol. (1976). Nashville: Abingdon.

Cadden, Joan. 1993. *Meaning of Sex Difference in the Middle Ages*. New York: Cambridge University Press.

Cambre, M. 1962. L'Influence due Cantique des Cantique sur le Nouveau Testament. *Revue Thomiste* 62:5–26.

Caner, Daniel F. 1997. The Practice and Prohibition of Self-Castration in Early Christianity. *VC* 51:396–415.

Cantarella, Eva. 1987. *Pandora's Daughters*. Baltimore: Johns Hopkins University Press.

Carson, A. 1990. Putting Her in Her Place: Women, Dirt, and Desire. Pages 135–69 in Halperin, Winkler, and Zeitlin.

Carson, Robert Andrew Glindinning. 1990. *Coins of the Roman Empire*. New York: Routledge.

Carter, Warren. 1994. *Households and Discipleship: A Study of Matthew 19–20*. JSNTSup 103. Sheffield: Sheffield Academic Press.

———. 2001. *Matthew and Empire: Initial Explorations*. Philadelphia: Trinity Press International.

Castelli, Elizabeth A. 1986. Virginity and Its Meaning for Women's Sexuality in Early Christianity. *JFSR* 61–88.

———. 1991. "I Will Make Mary Male": Pieties of the Body and Gender Transformation of Christian Women in Late Antiquity. Pages 29–33 in *Body Guards: The Cultural Politics of Gender Ambiguity*. Edited by J. Epstein and K. Straub. New York: Routledge.

———. 1995. *Visions and Voyeurism: Holy Women and the Politics of Sight in Early Christianity*. Edited by Christopher Ocker. Protocol of the Colloquy of the Center for Hermeneutical Studies NS 2. Berkeley: Center for Hermeneutical Studies.

Chadwick, Henry. 1959. *The Sentence of Sextus: A Contribution to the History of Early Christian Ethics*. Texts and Studies: Contributions to Biblical and Patristic Literature NS 5. Cambridge: Cambridge University Press.

———. 1965. *Origen: Contra Celsum*. Cambridge: Cambridge University Press.

———. 1966. *Early Christian Thought and the Classical Tradition*. Oxford: Oxford University Press.

Charlesworth, James H. 1992. *The Messiah: Developments in Earliest Judaism and Christianity*. Minneapolis: Fortress.

Chatterjee, Partha. 1986. *Nationalist Thought and the Colonial World.* Minneapolis: University of Minnesota Press.

———. 1993. *The Nation and Its Fragments: Colonial and Postcolonial Histories.* Princeton: Princeton University Press.

Chilton, Bruce. 1994. The Kingdom of God in Recent Discussion. Pages 354–80 in *Studying the Historical Jesus.* Edited by Bruce Chilton and Craig Evans. Leiden: Brill

Clark, Elizabeth A. 1988. Foucault, the Fathers, and Sex. *JAAR* 56:619–41.

———. 1999. *Reading Renunciation: Asceticism and Scripture in Early Christianity.* Princeton: Princeton University Press.

Clark, Kenneth Willis. 1980. *The Gentile Bias and Other Essays.* Brill: Leiden.

Clines, David J. A. 1995a. David the Man: The Construction of Masculinity in the Hebrew Bible. Pages 212–43 in *Interested Parties: The Ideology of Writers and Readers of the Hebrew Bible.* JSOTSup 205. Gender, Culture, Theory 1. Sheffield: Sheffield Academic Press.

———. 1995b. *Interested Parties: The Ideology of Writers and Readers of the Hebrew Bible.* JSOTSup 205. Gender, Culture, Theory 1; Sheffield: Sheffield Academic Press.

———. 1998. *Ecce Vir;* or, Gendering the Son of Man. Pages 352–75 in Exum and Moore.

———. 2002. He-Prophets: Masculinity As a Problem for the Hebrew Prophets and Their Interpreters. Pages 311–28 in *Sense and Sensitivity: Essays on Reading the Bible in Memory of Robert Carroll.* Edited by Alastair G. Hunter and Philip R. Davies. JSOTSup 348. Sheffield: Sheffield Academic Press.

Cockburn, Cynthia. 1991. *In the Way of Women: Men's Resistance to Sex Equality in Organization.* Ithaca, N.Y.: ILR Press.

Cohen, Yehudi A. 1961. Patterns of Friendship. Pages 351–86 in *Social Structure and Personality.* Edited by Yehudi A. Cohen. New York: Holt, Rinehart & Winston.

Coleman, K. M. 1990. Fatal Charades: Roman Executions Staged as Mythological Enactments. *JRS* 80:44–73.

Collins, Adela Yarbro. 1977. The Political Perspective of the Revelation to John. *JBL* 96:241–56.

———. 1982. New Testament Perspectives: The Gospel of John. *JSOT* 22:47–53.

———. 1984. *Crisis and Catharsis: The Power of the Apocalypse.* Philadelphia: Westminster.

———. 1994. From Noble Death to Crucified Messiah. *NTS* 40:481–503.

———. 2000. Mark and His Readers: The Son of God among Greeks and Romans. *HTR* 93:85–100

Collins, John N. 1990. *Diakonia: Reinterpreting the Ancient Sources.* Oxford: Oxford University Press.

Connell, R. W. 1987. *Gender and Power: Society, the Person and Sexual Politics.* Stanford, Calif.: Stanford University Press

———. 1995. *Masculinities.* Berkeley and Los Angeles: University of California Press.

Connolly, Joy. 1998. Mastering Corruption: Constructions of Identity in Roman Oratory. Pages 130–51 in *Women and Slaves in Greco-Roman Culture: Differential*

Equations. Edited by Sandra R. Joshel and Sheila Murnaghan. New York: Routledge.

Conway, Colleen M. 1999. *Men and Women in the Fourth Gospel: Gender and Johannine Characterization*. SBLDS 167. Atlanta: Scholars Press.

———. 2003. Gender Matters in John. Pages 79–103 in vol. 2 of *A Feminist Companion to John*. Edited by Amy-Jill Levine. FCNTECW 5. Sheffield: Sheffield Academic Press.

Conzelmann, Hans. 1966. Luke's Place in the Development of Early Christianity. Pages 298–316 in *Studies in Luke-Acts: Essays Presented in Honor of Paul Schubert*. Edited by Leander Keck and J. Louis Martyn. Nashville: Abingdon.

Cooper, Kate. 1992. Insinuations of Womanly Influence: An Aspect of the Christianization of the Roman Aristocracy. *JRS* 82:150–64.

———. 1996. *The Virgin and the Bride: Idealized Womanhood in Late Antiquity*. Cambridge: Harvard University Press.

Corbeill, Anthony. 1997. Dining Deviants in Roman Political Invective. Pages 99–128 in Hallett and Skinner.

Corley, K. E., and K. J. Torjesen. 1987. Sexuality, Hierarchy, and Evangelicalism. *Theological Students Fellowship Bulletin* 10:23–27.

Cornwall, Andrea, and Nancy Lindisfarne. 1994. Introduction. Pages 1–10 in *Dislocating Masculinity: Comparative Ethnographies*. Edited by Andrea Cornwall and Nancy Lindisfarne. New York: Routledge.

Cox, Patricia. 1983. *Biography in Late Antiquity: A Quest for the Holy Man*. Berkeley and Los Angeles: University of California Press.

Creese, Gillian. 1999. *Contracting Masculinity: Gender, Class, and Race in a White-Collar Union, 1944–1994*. Oxford: Oxford University Press.

Crosby, Michael H. 1988. *House of Disciples: Church, Economics and Justice in Matthew*. Maryknoll, N.Y.: Orbis.

Cross, F. L., and E. A. Livingstone, eds. 1983. Origen. Pages 1008–10 in *The Oxford Dictionary of the Christian Church*. Rev. ed. Oxford: Oxford University Press.

Crossan, John Dominic. 1991. *The Historical Jesus: The Life of a Mediterranean Jewish Peasant*. San Francisco: Harper

Daley, Robert J. 1996. Origen. Pages 667–69 in *Encyclopedia of Early Christianity*. Edited by Everett Ferguson. New York: Garland.

D'Ambra, Eve. *Private Lives, Imperial Virtues: The Frieze of the Forum Transitorium in Rome*. Princeton: Princeton University Press.

D'Angelo, Mary Rose. 1990a. Women in Luke-Acts: A Redactional View. *JBL* 109: 441–461.

———. 1990b. Women Partners in the New Testament. *JFSR* 6: 65–86.

———. 1992a. *Abba* and "Father": Imperial Theology and the Jesus Traditions. *JBL* 111:611–30.

———. 1992b. "Theology in Mark and Q: Abba and "Father" in Context. *HTR* 85:149–74.

———. 1995. Veils, Virgins and the Tongues of Men and Angels: Women's Heads As Sexual Members in Ancient Christianity. Pages 131–64 in *Off with Her Head! The Denial of Women's Identity in Myth, Religion, and Culture*. Edited by Howard Eilberg-Schwarz and Wendy Doniger. Berkeley and Los Angeles:

University of California Press. Reprinted as pages 389–419 in *Women, Gender, Religion: A Reader*. Edited by Elizabeth A. Castelli, with assistance from Rosamond C. Rodman. New York: Palgrave, 2001.

———. 1999. (Re) Presentations of Women in the Gospel of Matthew and Luke-Acts. Pages 171–95 in *Women in Christian Origins*. Edited by Ross Shepard Kraemer and Mary Rose D'Angelo. New York: Oxford.

———. 2002. The ANHP Question in Luke-Acts: Imperial Masculinity and the Deployment of Women in the Early Second Century? Pages 46–72 in *A Feminist Companion to Luke*. Edited by Amy-Jill Levine, with Marianne Blickenstaff. FCNTECW 3. Sheffield: Sheffield Academic Press.

———. 2003a. Early Christian Sexual Politics and Roman Imperial Family Values: Rereading Christ and Culture. Pages 23–48 in vol. 6 of *The Papers of the Henry Luce III Fellows in Theology*. Edited by Christopher I. Wilkins. Pittsburgh: Association of Theological Schools.

———. 2003b. Εὐσέβεια: Roman Imperial Family Values and the Sexual Politics of 4 Maccabees and the Pastorals. *BibInt* 11:139–65.

Daniel, Constantin. 1968. Esséniens et Eunuques (Matthieu 19, 10–12). *RevQ* 6:353–90.

Davidson, James. n.d. *Courtesans and Fishcakes: The Consuming Passions of Classical Athens*. New York: HarperCollins.

Davies, Margaret. 1996a. *The Pastoral Epistles*. New Testament Guides. Sheffield: Sheffield Academic Press.

———. 1996b. *The Pastoral Epistles: I and II Timothy and Titus*. Epworth Commentaries. London: Epworth.

Davies, W. D., and Dale C. Allison Jr. 1988–97. *A Critical and Exegetical Commentary on the Gospel according to St. Matthew*. 3 vols. ICC. Edinburgh: T&T Clark.

Davis, John. 1984. The Sexual Division of Labour in the Mediterranean. Pages 17–50 in Wolf 1984.

Dean-Jones, Lesley. 1994a. Medicine: The "Proof" of Anatomy. Pages 183–215 in Fantham et al.

———. 1994b. *Women's Bodies in Classical Greek Science*. Oxford: Clarendon.

De Certeau, Michel. 1988. *The Writing of History*. Translated by Richard Howard. New York: Columbia University Press.

Dehandschutter, Boudewijn. 1995. Μηκέτι ὑδροπότει: Some Notes on the Patristic Exegesis of 1 Timothy 5:23. *LS* 20:265–70.

Delaney, Carol. 1991. *The Seed and the Soil: Gender and Cosmology in Turkish Village Society*. Berkeley and Los Angeles: University of California Press.

Derrida, Jacques. 1981. Plato's Pharmacy. Pages 61–84 in *Dissemination*. Translated by Barbara Johnson. Chicago: University of Chicago Press.

Dessen, C. S. 1995. The Figure of the Eunuch in Terence's Eunuchus. *Helios* 22:123–39.

Dewey, Arthur J. 1992. The Unkindest Cut of All? Matt 19:11–12. *Foundations and Facets Forum* 8:113–121.

Dewey, Joanna. 1992. 1 Timothy, 2 Timothy, and Titus. Pages 353–62 in *The Women's Bible Commentary*. Edited by Carol A. Newsom and Sharon H. Ringe. Louisville: Westminster John Knox.

————. 1994. The Gospel of Mark. Pages 470–509 in *A Feminist Commentary*. Vol. 2 of *Searching the Scriptures*. Edited by Elisabeth Schüssler Fiorenza. New York: Crossroad.

Dibelius, Martin, and Hans Conzelmann. 1972. *The Pastoral Epistles: A Commentary on the Pastoral Epistles*. Edited by Helmut Koester. Translated by Phillip Buttoph and Adela Yarbro. Hermeneia: Philadelphia: Fortress.

Digby, Tom, ed. 1998. *Men Doing Feminism*. New York: Routledge.

Dixon, Suzanne. 1997a. Conflict in the Roman Family. Pages 149–67 in *The Roman Family in Italy: Status, Sentiment, Space*. Edited by Beryl Rawson and Paul Weaver. Oxford: Oxford University Press.

————. 1997b. Continuity and Change in Roman Social History: Retrieving "Family Feeling(s)" from Roman Law and Literature. Pages 79–90 in *Inventing Ancient Culture: Historicism, Periodicization and the Ancient World*. Edited by Mark Golden and Peter Toohey. New York: Routledge. .

————. 1992. *The Roman Family*. Baltimore: Johns Hopkins University Press.

Donahue, John R. 1982. A Neglected Factor in the Theology of Mark. *JBL* 101: 563–94.

Doody, Margaret. 1996. *The True Story of the Novel*. New Brunswick, N.J.: Rutgers University Press.

Dover, Kenneth J. 1974. *Greek Popular Morality in the Time of Plato and Aristotle*. Berkeley and Los Angeles: University of California Press.

————. 1989. *Greek Homosexuality*. Updated and with a New Postscript. Cambridge: Harvard University Press.

Dube, Musa W. 2000. *Postcolonial Feminist Interpretation of the Bible*. St. Louis: Chalice.

Dubish, Jill. 1986. *Gender and Power in Rural Greece*. Princeton: Princeton University Press

Duke, Paul. 1985. *Irony in the Fourth Gospel*. Atlanta: John Knox.

Duling, Dennis C. 1992. Matthew's Plurisignificant "Son of David" in Social Science Perspective: Kinship, Kingship, Magic and Miracle. *BTB* 22:99–116

————. 1995. The Matthean Brotherhood and Marginal Scribal Leadership. Pages 159–82 in *Modeling Early Christianity: Social Scientific Studies of the New Testament in Its Context*. Edited by Philip F. Esler. New York: Routledge.

————. 1997. "Egalitarian" Ideology, Leadership, and Factional Conflict within the Matthean Group. *BTB* 27:124–37.

————. 1999. Matthew 18:15–17: Conflict, Confrontation, and Conflict Resolution in a "Fictive Kin" Association. *BTB* 29:4–22.

Dunn, James D. G. 1983. Let John Be John: A Gospel for Its Time. Pages 309–39 in *Das Evangelium und die Evangelien*. Edited by P. Stuhlmacher. Tubingen: Mohr Siebeck.

————. 1988. *Romans 1–8*. WBC 38a. Dallas: Word.

Dupont, Florence, and Thierry Éloi. 2001. *L'érotisme masculin dans la Rome antique*. L'Antiquité au Présent. Paris: Belin.

Dyer, Richard. 1997. *White*. New York: Routledge.

Edwards, Catharine. 1993. *The Politics of Immorality in Ancient Rome*. Cambridge: Cambridge University Press.

———. 1997. Unspeakable Performance and Prostitution in Ancient Rome. Pages 66–98 in *Roman Sexualities*. Edited by Judith P. Hallett and Marilyn B. Skinner. Princeton: Princeton University Press.

Egger, Brigitte. 1994. Women and Marriage in the Greek Novels: The Boundaries of Romance. Pages 260–80 in *Search for the Ancient Novel*. Edited by James Tatum. Baltimore: Johns Hopkins University Press.

Eilberg-Schwartz, Howard. 1994. *God's Phallus: And Other Problems for Men and Monotheism*. Boston: Beacon.

Elhstain, Jean Bethke. 1981. *Public Man, Private Woman: Women in Social and Political Thought*. Princeton: Princeton University Press.

Elliott, J. K. 1993. *The Apocryphal New Testament*. Oxford: Clarendon.

Eng, David L. 2001. *Racial Castration: Managing Masculinity in Asian America*. Durham, N.C.: Duke University Press.

Engberg-Pedersen, Troels. 2000. *Paul and the Stoics*. Louisville: Westminster John Knox.

Englesman, Joan Chamberlain. 1979. *The Feminine Dimension of the Divine*. Philadelphia: Westminster.

Epictetus. 1925. *The Discourses As Reported by Arrian, the Manual, and the Fragments*. Translated by W. A. Oldfather. 2 vols. LCL. Cambridge: Harvard University Press.

Esler, Philip F. 1997. Family Imagery and Christian Identity in Gal. 5:13 to 6:10. Pages 121–49 in Moxnes 1997.

———. 2000. "Keeping It in the Family": Culture, Kinship and Identity in I Thessalonians and Galatians. Pages 145–84 in *Families and Family Relations As Represented in Early Judaisms and Early Christianities: Texts and Fictions*. Edited by Jan W. Van Henten and Athalya Brenner. Leiden: Deo.

Eslinger, Lyle. 1987. The Wooing of the Women at the Well: Jesus, The Reader and Reader-Response Criticism. *Journal of Literature and Theology* 1:167–83.

Eusebius. 1926. *The Ecclesiastical History*. Translated by Kirsopp Lake. LCL. 1980. Cambridge: Harvard University Press.

Exum, J. Cheryl, and Stephen D. Moore, eds. 1998. *Biblical Studies/Cultural Studies: The Third Sheffield Colloquium*. JSOTSup 266; Gender, Culture, Theory 7. Sheffield: Sheffield Academic Press.

Fagan, Garrett G. 1999. *Bathing in Public in the Roman World*. Ann Arbor: University of Michigan Press.

Faludi, Susan. 1999. *Stiffed: The Betrayal of the American Man*. New York: William Morrow.

Fantham, Elaine, Helene Foley, Natalie Kampen, Sarah Pomeroy, and Alan Shapiro. 1994. *Women in the Classical World: Image and Text*. Oxford: Oxford University Press

Fatum, Lone. 1997. Brotherhood in Christ: A Gender Hermeneutical Reading of 1 Thessalonians. Pages 183–97 in Moxnes 1997.

Fitzmyer, J. A. 1993. *Romans*. AB 33. New York: Doubleday.

Fee, Gordon D. 1985. Reflections on Church Order in the Pastoral Epistles, with Further Reflections on the Hermeneutics of *Ad Hoc* Documents. *JETS* 28:141–51.

———. 1995. *Paul's Letter to the Philippians*. NICNT. Grand Rapids: Eerdmans.

Fiensy, David A. 1991. *The Social History of Palestine in the Herodian Period: The Land Is Mine.* Lewiston, N.Y.: Mellen.

Finley, M. I. 1983. *Politics in the Ancient World.* Cambridge: Cambridge University Press.

Fischler, Susan. 1998. Imperial Cult: Engendering the Cosmos. Pages 165–83 in Foxhall and Salmon 1998b.

Fitzgerald, William. 2000. *Slavery and the Roman Literary Imagination.* Roman Literature and Its Contexts. Cambridge: Cambridge University Press.

Fitzmyer, Joseph A. 1993. *Romans.* AB 33. New York: Doubleday.

Flannigan-Saint-Aubin, Arthur. 1994. The Male Body and Literary Metaphors for Masculinity. Pages 239–58 in Brod and Kaufman.

Flower, Harriet I. 2000. Damnatio Memoriae and Epigraphy. Pages 58–69 in *From Caligula to Constantine: Tyranny and Transformation in Roman Portraiture.* Edited by Eric Varner. Atlanta: Michael C. Carlos Museum.

Foucault, Michel. 1985. *The Use of Pleasure: The History of Sexuality 2.* Translated by Robert Hurley. New York: Viking.

———. 1986. *The Care of the Self: The History of Sexuality 3.* Translated by Robert Hurley. New York: Pantheon.

Foxhall, Lin. 1999. Foreign Powers: Plutarch and Discourses of Domination in Roman Greece. Pages 138–50 in Pomeroy 1999.

Foxhall, Lin, and John Salmon, eds. 1998a. *Thinking Men: Masculinity and Its Self-Representation in the Classical Tradition.* New York: Routledge.

———. 1998b. *When Men Were Men: Masculinity, Power and Identity in Classical Antiquity.* New York: Routledge.

Francis, James A. 1995. *Subversive Virtue: Asceticism and Authority in the Second-Century Pagan World.* University Park: Pennsylvania State University Press.

Frank, Georgia. 2000. *The Memory of the Eyes: Pilgrims to Living Saints in Christian Late Antiquity.* Transformation of the Classical Heritage 30. Berkeley and Los Angeles: University of California Press.

Freedman, David Noel, ed. 1992. *The Anchor Bible Dictionary.* 6 vols. New York: Doubleday.

Frontisi-Ducroux, Françoise. 1996. Eros, Desire, and the Gaze. Translated by N. Kline. Pages 81–100 in *Sexuality in Ancient Art.* Edited by Natalie Boymel Kampen. Cambridge: Cambridge University Press.

Frye, Northrop. 2000. *Anatomy of Criticism: Four Essays.* Princeton: Princeton University Press [1957].

Furnish, Victor P. 1979. *The Moral Teaching of Paul.* Nashville: Abingdon.

Gadd, C. J. 1948. *Ideas of Divine Rule in the Ancient East.* London: Oxford University Press

Galen. 1968. *On the Usefulness of Parts of the Body.* Translated by Margaret Tallmadge May. 2 vols. Ithaca, N.Y.: Cornell University Press.

Garnsey, Peter. 1970. *Social Status and Legal Privilege in the Roman Empire.* Oxford: Clarendon.

Gardiner, Judith Kegan. 2002a. Introduction. Pages 1–29 in Gardiner 2002b.

———, ed. 2002b. *Masculinity Studies and Feminist Theory: New Directions.* New York: Columbia University Press.

Garland, Robert. 1990. *The Greek Way of Life.* Ithaca, N.Y.: Cornell University Press.

Garrett, Susan R. 1999. Beloved Physician of the Soul? Luke As Advocate for Ascetic Practice. Pages 71–96 in Vaage and Wimbush.

Garrison, Daniel H. 2000. *Sexual Culture in Ancient Greece.* Norman: University of Oklahoma Press.

Geddert, Timothy J. 1989. *Watchwords: Mark 13 in Markan Eschatology.* JSNTSup 26. Sheffield: Sheffield Academic Press.

Gellius. *The Attic Nights of Aulus Gellius.* Translated by J. C. Rolfe. 3 vols. LCL. New York: Putnam's Sons.

Gilmore, David D. 1982. Anthropology of the Mediterranean Area. *Annual Review of Anthropology* 11:175–200.

———. 1987a. *Honor and Shame and the Unity of the Mediterranean.* Washington, D.C.: American Anthropological Association.

———. 1987b. Introduction: The Shame of Dishonor. Pages 2–21 in Gilmore 1987a.

———. 1990. *Manhood in the Making: Cultural Conceptions of Masculinity.* New Haven: Yale University Press.

Gilmore, Margaret and David D. 1979. "Machismo": A Psychodynamic Approach (Spain). *Journal of Psychological Anthropology* 2:281–300.

Glancy, Jennifer A. 1994. Unveiling Masculinity: The Construction of Gender in Mark 6:17–29. *BibInt* 11:34–50.

———. 1998. Text Appeal: Visual Pleasure and Biblical Studies. *Semeia* 82: 63–78.

———. 2000. Slaves and Slavery in the Matthean Parables. *JBL* 119:67–90.

Gleason, Maud W. 1990. The Semiotics of Gender: Physiognomy and Self-Fashioning in the Second Century C.E. Pages 399–402 in Halperin, Winkler, and Zeitlin.

———. 1995. *Making Men: Sophists and Self-Representation in Ancient Rome.* Princeton: Princeton University Press.

———. 1999a. Elite Male Identity in the Roman Empire. Pages 67–84 in *Life, Death and Entertainment in the Roman Empire.* Edited by D. S. Potter and D. J. Mattingly. Ann Arbor: University of Michigan Press.

———. 1999b. Truth Contests and Talking Corpses. Pages 287–313 in *Constructions of the Classical Body.* Edited by James Porter. Ann Arbor: University of Michigan Press, 1999.

Gnilka, Joachim. 1963 Die Kirche des Matthäus und die Gemeinde von Qumran. BZ 7:43–63.

Goldhill, Simon. 1995. *Foucault's Virginity: Ancient Erotic Fiction and the History of Sexuality.* Cambridge: Cambridge University Press.

———, ed. 2001. *Being Greek under Roman Rule: Cultural Identity, the Second Sophistic and the Development of Empire.* Cambridge: Cambridge University Press.

Good, Deirdre. 1998. *Jesus the Meek King.* Philadelphia: Trinity Press International.

Goux, Jean-Joseph. 1994. Luce Irigaray versus the Utopia of the Neutral Sex. Pages 175–90 in *Engaging with Irigaray: Feminist Philosophy and Modern European Thought.* Edited by Carolyn Burke, Naomi Schor, and Margaret Whitford. New York: Columbia University Press.

Graham, Susan Lochrie, and Stephen D. Moore. 1997. The Quest for the New Historicist Jesus. *BibInt* 5:438–64.

Gransden, K. W. 1984. *Virgil's "Iliad": An Essay on Epic Narrative.* Cambridge: Cambridge University Press.

Grant, Michael. 1976. *Saint Paul.* London: Weidenfeld & Nicolson.

Grant, Michael, and Rachel Kitzinger. 1988a. Introduction. Pages xxv–xxvii in vol. 3 of Grant and Kitzinger 1988b.

———, eds. 1988b. *Civilizations of the Ancient Mediterranean: Greece and Rome.* 3 vols. New York: Charles Scribner's Sons.

Gray, Rebecca. 1993. *Prophetic Figures in Late Second Temple Jewish Palestine: The Evidence from Josephus.* Oxford: Oxford University Press.

Greenblatt, Stephen. 1984. *Renaissance Self-Fashioning: From More to Shakespeare.* Chicago: University of Chicago Press.

Gundry, Robert H. 1993. *Mark: Commentary on His Apology for the Cross.* Grand Rapids: Eerdmans.

———. 1994. *Matthew: A Commentary on His Handbook for a Mixed Church under Persecution.* 2d edition. Grand Rapids: Eerdmans.

Guthrie, Donald. 1957. *The Pastoral Epistles.* TNTC. London: Tyndale.

———. 1969. *Galatians.* NCB. London: Nelson.

Hadley, D. M., ed. 1999. *Masculinity in Medieval Europe.* New York: Longman

Hagan, Kay Leigh, ed. 1992. *Women Respond to the Men's Movement: A Feminist Collection.* San Francisco: Pandora.

Hägg, Tomas. 1983. *The Novel in Antiquity.* Berkeley and Los Angeles: University of California Press.

Hagner, Donald A. 1995. *Matthew 14–28.* WBC 33b. Dallas: Word.

Hallett, Judith P. 1984. *Fathers and Daughters in Roman Society.* Princeton: Princeton University Press.

Hallett, Judith P., and Marilyn B. Skinner, eds. 1997. *Roman Sexualities.* Princeton: Princeton University Press.

Halperin, David M. 1990a. *One Hundred Years of Homosexuality: And Other Essays on Greek Love.* New Ancient World. New York: Routledge.

———. 1990b. Why Is Diotima a Woman? Platonic Eros and the Figuration of Gender. Pages 257–308 in Halperin, Winkler, and Zeitlin.

———. 1995. *Saint Foucault: Towards a Gay Hagiography.* Oxford: Oxford University Press.

Halperin, David, John Winkler, and Froma Zeitlin, eds. 1990. *Before Sexuality: The Construction of Erotic Experience in the Ancient Greek World.* Princeton: Princeton University Press.

Hansen, William, ed. 1998. *Anthology of Ancient Greek Popular Literature.* Bloomington and Indianapolis: Indiana University Press.

Hanson, Ann Ellis. 1990. The Medical Writers' Woman. Pages 309–38 in Halperin, Winkler, and Zeitlin.

———. 1999. The Roman Family. Pages 19–66 in *Life, Death and Entertainment in the Roman Empire.* Edited by D. S. Potter and D. J. Mattingly. Ann Arbor: University of Michigan Press.

Hanson, K. C. 1994. "How Honorable! How Shameful!" A Cultural Analysis of Matthew's Makarisms and Reproaches. *Semeia* 68:81–112.

Hanson, K. C., and Douglas E. Oakman. 1998. *Palestine in the Time of Jesus: Social Structures and Social Conflicts.* Minneapolis: Fortress.

Hanson, R. 1966. A Note on Origen's Self-Mutilation. *VC* 20:81–82.

Harris, William V. 2001. *Restraining Rage: The Ideology of Anger Control in Classical Antiquity.* Cambridge: Harvard University Press.

Hart, Lynda. 1998. *Between the Body and the Flesh: Performing Sadomasochism.* New York: Columbia University Press.

Hays, Richard B. 1986. Relations Natural and Unnatural: A Response to John Boswell's Exegesis of Romans 1. *JRE* 14:184–215.

Headlam Wells, Robin. 2000. *Shakespeare on Masculinity.* Cambridge: Cambridge University Press.

Hedrick, Charles. 1995. Representing Prayer in Mark and Chariton's *Chaereas and Callirhoe. PRSt* 22:239–57.

———. 1998. Conceiving the Narrative: Colors in Achilles Tatius and the Gospel of Mark. Pages 177–98 in Hock, Chance, and Perkins.

Hellerman, Joseph H. 2001. *The Ancient Church As Family.* Minneapolis: Fortress.

Henderson, Jeffrey. 1988. Greek Attitudes toward Sex. Pages 1249–63 in vol. 2 of Grant and Kitzinger 1988b.

Herzfeld, Michael. 1985. *The Poetics of Manhood: Contest and Identity in a Cretan Mountain Village.* Princeton: Princeton University Press.

Heth, William A. 1987. Unmarried "for the Sake of the Kingdom" (Matthew 19:12) in the Early Church. *Grace Theological Journal* 8:55–88.

Hill Collins, Patricia. 2000. *Black Feminist Thought: Knowledge, Consciousness, and the Politics of Empowerment.* 2d ed. New York: Routledge.

Hobbs, Angela. 2000. *Plato and the Hero: Courage, Manliness and the Personal Good.* New York: Cambridge University Press.

Hock, Ronald. 1996. Social Experience and the Beginning of Mark's Gospel. Pages 311–26 in *Reimagining Christian Origins: A Colloquium Honoring Burton Mack.* Edited by Elizabeth Castelli and Hal Taussig. Valley Forge, Pa.: Trinity International.

———. 1998. Why New Testament Scholars Should Read Ancient Novels. Pages 121–39 in Hock, Chance, and Perkins.

Hock, Ronald, J. Bradley Chance, and Judith Perkins, eds. 1998. *Ancient Fiction and Early Christian Narrative.* Atlanta: Society of Biblical Literature.

Hoffner, Harry A. 1966. Symbols for Masculinity and Femininity: Their Use in Ancient Near Eastern Sympathetic Magic Rituals. *JBL* 85:326–34.

hooks, bell. 1995. Doing It for Daddy. Pages 98–106 in Berger, Wallis, and Watson.

Hopkins, Patrick. 1992. Gender Treachery: Homophobia, Masculinity, and Threatened Identities. Pages 111–31 in *Rethinking Masculinity: Philosophical Explorations in Light of Feminism.* Edited by L. May and R. Strikwerda. Lanham: Rowman & Littlefield.

Hopwood, Keith. 1998. "All That May Become a Man": The Bandit in the Ancient Novel. Pages 195–204 in Foxhall and Salmon 1998b.

Horney, Karen. 1932. The Dread of Woman. Reprinted in Karen Horney, *Feminine Psychology.* New York: Norton, 1967.

Horowitz, Roger, ed. 2001. *Boys and Their Toys? Masculinity, Class and Technology in America.* New York: Routledge.

Horrell, David G. 2001. From ἀδελφοί to οἶκος θεοῦ: Social Transformation in Pauline Christianity. *JBL* 120:293–311.

Horrocks, Roger. 1994. *Masculinity in Crisis: Myths, Fantasies, and Realities*. New York: St. Martin's.

Horsley, Richard A. 1979. Josephus and the Bandits. *JSJ* 10:37–63.

———. 1981. Ancient Jewish Banditry and The Revolt against Rome, 66-70. *CBQ* 43:409-32.

———. 2001. *Hearing the Whole Story: The Politics of Plot in Mark's Gospel*. Louisville: Westminster John Knox.

Horsley, Richard A., and John S. Hanson. 1985. *Bandits, Prophets and Messiahs: Popular Movements at the Time of Jesus*. Minneapolis: Winston.

———. 1999. *Bandits, Prophets and Messiahs: Popular Movements at the Time of Jesus*. Harrisburg, Pa.: Trinity Press International.

Hunter, David G. 1992. The Language of Desire: Clement of Alexandria's Transformation of Ascetic Discourse. *Semeia* 57:95–111.

Iersel, Bas M. F. van 1998. *Mark: A Reader-Response Commentary*. Sheffield: Sheffield Academic Press.

Jacobs, Andrew S. 1999. A Family Affair: Marriage, Class, and Ethics in the Apocryphal Acts of the Apostles. *JECS* 7:105–38.

Janowitz, Naomi. 2001. *Magic in the Roman World: Pagans, Jews, and Christians*. London: Routledge.

Jardine, Alice, and Paul Smith, eds. 1987. *Men in Feminism*. New York: Methuen.

Jeffers, James S. 1991. *Conflict at Rome: Social Order and Hierarchy in Early Christianity*. Minneapolis: Fortress.

John Chrysostom. 1857–66. *Homilia ad Romanos* (*Homilies on Romans*). PG 60: 391–682.

Johnson, Elizabeth A. 1994. *She Who Is: The Mystery of God in Feminist Theological Discourse*. New York: Crossroad.

Johnson, Luke Timothy. 1996. *Letters to Paul's Delegates: 1 Timothy, 2 Timothy and Titus*. The New Testament in Context. Valley Forge, Pa.: Trinity Press International.

Josephus. 1927. *The Jewish War*. Translated by H. St. J. Thackeray. 2 vols. LCL. Cambridge: Cambridge University Press.

———. 1987. *The Works of Josephus: Complete and Unabridged*. Translated by William Whiston. New updated edition. Peabody, Mass.: Hendrickson.

Judge, E. A. 1968. Paul's Boasting in Relation to Contemporary Professional Practice. *ABR* 16:37–50.

Justad, Mark J. 1996. A Transvaluation of Phallic Masculinity: Writing with and through the Male Body. *Journal of Men's Studies* 4:355–74.

Justin Martyr. 1885. *The First Apology*. ANF 1:159–87.

Kahl, Brigitte. 2000. No Longer Male: Masculinity Struggles behind Galatians 3:28? *JSNT* 79:37–49.

Kaplan, Caren, Norma Alarcón, and Minoo Moallem, eds. 1999. *Between Woman and Nation*. Durham, N.C.: Duke University Press.

Kaplan, E. Ann. 1983. *Women and Film: Both Sides of the Camera*. New York: Methuen.

Keen, Sam. 1991. *Fire in the Belly: On Being a Man*. New York: Bantam.

Keener, Craig S. 1999. *A Commentary on the Gospel of Matthew*. Grand Rapids: Eerdmans.

Kelber, Werner H. 1979. *Mark's Story of Jesus*. Philadelphia: Fortress.

Kelly, J. N. P. 1968. *Early Christian Doctrines*. London: Black.

Kerner, Jürgen. 1988. *Die Ethik der Johannes-Apocalypse im Vergleich mit der des 4. Esra: Ein Beitrag zum Verhältnis von Apokalyptik und Ethik*. BZNW 94. Berlin: de Gruyter.

Kessler-Harris, A. 1982. *Out to Work*. Oxford: Oxford University Press.

Kimmel, Michael S., ed. 1995. *The Politics of Manhood: Profeminist Men Respond to the Mythopoetic Men's Movement (and the Mythopoetic Leaders Answer)*. Philadelphia: Temple University Press.

Kimmel, Michael S., and Michael Kaufman. 1994. Weekend Warriors: The New Men's Movement. Pages 259–88 in Brod and Kaufman.

Kingsbury, Jack Dean. 1989. *Conflict in Mark: Jesus, Authorities, Disciples*. Minneapolis: Fortress.

Klassen, W. 1985. The King As "Living Law," with Particular Reference to Musonius Rufus. *SR* 14:63–71.

Klauck, H.J. 1990. Brotherly Love in Plutarch and in 4 Maccabees. Pages 144–56 in *Greeks, Romans, and Christians: Essays in Honor of Abraham J. Malherbe*. Edited by David L. Balch, Everett Ferguson, and Wayne A. Meeks. Minneapolis: Fortress.

Kleiner, Diana E. E. 2000. Now You See Them, Now You Don't: The Presence and Absence of Women in Roman Art. Pages 45–57 in *From Caligula to Constantine: Tyranny and Transformation in Roman Portraiture*. Edited by Eric Varner. Atlanta: Michael C. Carlos Museum.

Knox, John. 1966. Acts and the Pauline Letter Corpus. Pages 279–87 in *Studies in Luke-Acts: Essays Presented in Honor of Paul Schubert*. Edited by Leander Keck and J. Louis Martyn. Nashville: Abingdon.

Konstan, David. 1994. *Sexual Symmetry: Love in the Ancient Novel and Related Genres*. Princeton: Princeton University Press.

———. 1998. The Invention of Fiction. Pages 121–38 in Hock, Chance, and Perkins.

Kramer, Laura, ed. 1991. *The Sociology of Gender: A Text Reader*. New York: St. Martin's.

Krenkel, Werner A. 1988. Prostitution. Pages 1291–97 in vol. 2 of Grant and Kitzinger 1988b.

Kristeva, Julia. 1982. *Powers of Horror: An Essay on Abjection*. Translated by L. S. Roudiez. New York: Columbia University Press.

Kuefler, Mathew. 2001. *The Manly Eunuch: Masculinity, Gender Ambiguity, and Christian Ideology in Late Antiquity*. Chicago: University of Chicago Press.

Lampe, Peder. 1987. *Die Stadtrömischen Christen in den ersten beiden Jahrhunderten Wissenschaftlieche Untersuchungen zum Neuen Testament 2 Reihe 18*. Tübingen: Mohr Siebeck.

Laporte, Jean. 1975. Philo in the Tradition of Biblical Wisdom Literature. Pages 103–41 in *Aspects of Wisdom in Judaism and Early Christianity*. Edited by Robert L. Wilken. Notre Dame, Ind.: University of Notre Dame Press.

Laqueur, Thomas. 1990. *Making Sex: Body and Gender from the Greeks to Freud*. Cambridge: Harvard University Press.

Lauretis, Teresa de. 1987. *Technologies of Gender*. Bloomington: Indiana University Press.

Laws, Sophie. 1988. *In the Light of the Lamb: Image, Parody, and Theology in the Apocalypse of John*. Good News Studies 31. Wilmington, Del.: Michael Glazier.

Lenski, Gerhard, E. 1966. *Power and Privilege. A Theory of Social Stratification*. Chapel Hill: University of North Carolina Press.

Lentz, John Clayton. 1993. *Luke's Portrait of Paul*. Cambridge: Cambridge University Press.

Levine, Amy-Jill. 1988. *The Social and Ethnic Dimensions of Matthean Salvation History*. SBEC 14. Lewiston, N.Y.: Mellen.

———. 1992. Matthew. Pages 252–62 in *The Women's Bible Commentary*. Edited by Carol A. Newsom and Sharon H. Ringe. Louisville: Westminster John Knox.

Leyerle, Blake. 1993. John Chrysostom on the Gaze. *JECS* 1:159–74.

Lieu, Judith. 1996. Scripture and the Feminine in John. Pages 225–40 in *Feminist Companion to the Hebrew Bible in the New Testament*. Edited by Athalya Brenner. Sheffield: Sheffield Academic Press.

Liew, Tat-siong Benny. 1999. *Politics of Parousia: Reading Mark Inter(con)textually*. Leiden: Brill.

Loraux, Nicole. 1987. *Tragic Ways of Killing a Woman*. Translated by A. Forster. Cambridge: Harvard University Press.

———. 1995. *The Experiences of Tiresias: The Feminine and the Greek Man*. Translated by Paula Wissing. Princeton: Princeton University Press.

Lorber, Judith, and Susan A. Farrell, eds. 1991. *The Social Construction of Gender*. London: Sage.

Lucian. 1936. *Lucian*. Translated by A. M. Harmon. 8 vols. LCL. New York: Macmillan.

Luz, Ulrich. 1989. *Matthew 1–7: A Continental Commentary*. Translated by Wilhelm C. Linss. Minneapolis: Augsburg.

———. 1996. The Final Judgement (Matt 25:31–46): An Exercise in "History of Influence" Exegesis. Pages 271–310 in *Treasures New and Old: Contributions to Matthean Studies*. Edited by Mark Allan Powell and David R. Bauer. Atlanta: Scholars Press.

———. 2001. *Matthew 8–20: A Continental Commentary*. Hermeneia. Translated by James E. Crouch. Minneapolis: Fortress.

Maccoby, Hyam. 1986. *The Mythmaker: Paul and the Invention of Christianity*. London: Weidenfeld & Nicolson.

MacDonald, Dennis Ronald. 1983. *The Legend and the Apostle: The Battle for Paul in Story and Canon*. Philadelphia: Westminster.

———. 1987. *There is No Male and Female: The Fate of a Dominical Saying in Paul and Gnosticism*. HDR. Philadelphia: Fortress.

———. 1998. Secrecy and Recognitions in the *Odyssey* and Mark: Where Wrede Went Wrong. Pages 139–54 in Hock, Chance, and Perkins.

———. 2000. *The Homeric Epics and the Gospel of Mark*. New Haven: Yale University Press.

MacDonald, Margaret Y. 1996. *Early Christian Women and Pagan Opinion: The Power of the Hysterical Woman*. Cambridge: Cambridge University Press.

———. 1999. Rereading Paul: Early Interpreters of Paul on Women and Gender. Pages 236–53 in *Women and Christian Origins*. Edited by Ross Shepard Kraemer and Mary Rose D'Angelo. New York: Oxford University Press.

Mack, Burton L. 1988. *A Myth of Innocence: Mark and Christian Origins.* Philadelphia: Fortress.

Maclean, Jennifer K. Berenson, and Ellen Bradshaw Aitken, trans. *Heroikos.* WGRW 1. Atlanta: Society of Biblical Literature, 2001.

MacMullen, Ramsay. 1966. *Enemies of the Roman Order: Treason, Unrest, and Alienation in the Empire.* Cambridge: Harvard University Press.

———. 1980. Women in Public in the Roman Empire. *Historia* 29:208–18.

Maier, Harold O. 1997. Staging the Gaze: Early Christian Apocalypse and Narrative Self-Representation. *HTR* 92:131–54.

Malbon, Elizabeth Struthers. 2000. *In the Company of Jesus: Characters in Mark's Gospel.* Louisville: Westminster John Knox.

Malherbe, Abraham J. 1980. Medical Imagery in the Pastoral Epistles. Pages 19–35 in *Texts and Testaments: Critical Essays on the Bible and Early Church Fathers.* Edited by W. Eugene March. San Antonio: Trinity University Press.

———. 1986. *Moral Exhortation: A Greco-Roman Sourcebook.* LEC. Philadelphia: Westminster.

———. 1994. Paulus Senex. *ResQ* 136 (4):197–207.

Malina, Bruce J. 1986. "Religion" in the World of Paul. *BTB* 16:92–101

———. 1993. *The New Testament World: Insights from Cultural Anthropology.* Rev. ed. Louisville: Westminster John Knox.

———. 2001a. *The New Testament World: Insights from Cultural Anthropology.* 3d ed. Louisville: Westminster John Knox.

———. 2001b. *The Social Gospel of Jesus. The Kingdom of God in Mediterranean Perspective.* Minneapolis: Fortress.

Malina, Bruce J., and Jerome H. Neyrey. 1988. *Calling Jesus Names: The Social Value of Labels in Matthew.* Sonoma, Calif.: Polebridge.

———. 1996. *Portraits of Paul: An Archeology of Ancient Personality.* Louisville: Westminster John Knox.

Malina, Bruce J., and Richard L. Rohrbaugh. 1992. *Social-Science Commentary on the Synoptic Gospels.* Minneapolis: Fortress.

Maloney, Linda J. 1994. The Pastoral Epistles. Pages 361–80 in *A Feminist Commentary.* Vol. 2 of *Searching the Scriptures.* Edited by Elisabeth Schüssler Fiorenza. New York: Crossroad.

Marcus, Joel. 1992. The Jewish War and the *Sitz im Leben* of Mark. *JBL* 111: 441–62.

———. 1998. *Mark 1–8: A New Translation with Introduction and Commentary.* AB 27. New York: Doubleday.

Martens, J. W. 1994. Romans 2:14–16: A Stoic Reading. *NTS* 40:55–67.

Martin, Clarice J. 1989. A Chamberlain's Journey and the Challenge of Interpretation for Liberation. *Semeia* 47:105–35.

Martin, Dale B. 1990. *Slavery As Salvation: The Metaphor of Slavery in Pauline Christianity.* New Haven: Yale University Press.

———. 1995a. *The Corinthian Body.* New Haven: Yale University Press.

———. 1995b. Heterosexism and the Interpretations of Romans 1:18–32. *BibInt* 3:332–55.

———. 1996. Arsenokoites and Malakos: Meanings and Consequences. Pages 117–136 in *Biblical Ethics and Homosexuality.* Edited by Robert L. Brawley. Louisville: Westminster John Knox.

———. 2001. Contradictions of Masculinity: Ascetic Inseminators and Menstruating Men in Greco-Roman Culture. Pages 81–108 in *Generation and Degeneration: Tropes of Reproduction in Literature and History from Antiquity to Early Modern Europe*. Edited by Valeria Finucci and Kevin Brownlee. Durham, N.C.: Duke University Press.

Martin, Ralph P. 1986. *2 Corinthians*. WBC 40. Waco, Tex.: Word.

Matera, Frank. 1982. *The Kingship of Jesus: Composition and Theology in Mark 15*. SBLDS 66. Chico, Calif.: Scholars Press.

Mattila, Sharon Lea. 1996. Wisdom, Sense Perception, Nature, and Philo's Gender Gradient. *HTR* 89:103–29.

Mayer, Tamar, ed. 2000. *Gender Ironies of Nationalism: Sexing the Nation*. New York: Routledge.

McKinlay, Judith E. 1996. *Gendering Wisdom the Host: Biblical Invitations to Eat and Drink*. Sheffield: Sheffield Academic Press.

McNeile, Alan H. 1980. *The Gospel according to St. Matthew*. Thornapple Commentaries. Grand Rapids: Baker. [Orig. 1915]

Medina, Nadia, Katie Conboy, and Sarah Stanbury, eds. 1997. *Writing on the Body: Female Embodiment and Feminist Theory*. New York: Columbia University Press.

Meeks, Wayne A. 1972. The Man From Heaven in Johannine Sectarianism. *JBL* 91:44–72.

———. 1993. *The Origins of Christian Morality: The First Two Centuries*. New Haven: Yale University Press.

Messner, Michael A. 1997. *Politics of Masculinities: Men in Movements*. The Gender Lens Series in Sociology. Thousand Oaks, Calif.: Sage.

Meye Thompson, Marianne. 2000. *The Promise of the Father: Jesus and God in the New Testament*. Louisville: Westminster John Knox.

Milbank, John, Catherine Pickstock, and Graham Ward, eds. 1999. *Radical Orthodoxy: A New Theology*. New York: Routledge.

Miles, Margaret R. 1989. *Carnal Knowing: Female Nakedness and Religious Meaning in the Christian West*. New York: Vintage.

Miola, Robert S. 1992. *Shakespeare and Classical Tragedy: The Influence of Seneca*. Oxford: Clarendon.

Modleski, Tania. 1991. *Feminism without Women: Culture and Feminism in a "Postfeminist" Age*. New York: Routledge.

Montserrat, Dominic. 1996. *Sex and Society in Greco-Roman Egypt*. London: Kegan Paul.

———. 1998. Experiencing the Male Body in Roman Egypt. Pages 153–64 in Foxhall and Salmon 1998b.

Moore, Stephen D. 1996. *God's Gym: Divine Male Bodies of the Bible*. New York: Routledge.

———. 1998a. Revolting Revelations. Pages 183–98 in *The Personal Voice in Biblical Interpretation*. Edited by Ingrid Rosa Kitzberger. London: Routledge.

———. 1998b. Ugly Thoughts: On the Face and Physique of the Historical Jesus. Pages 376–99 in Exum and Moore.

———. 2000. Colonialism/Postcolonialism. Pages 182–88 in *Handbook of Postmodern Biblical Interpretation*. Edited by A. K. M. Adam. St. Louis: Chalice.

———. 2001. *God's Beauty Parlor: And Other Queer Spaces in and around the Bible.* Stanford, Calif.: Stanford University Press.

———. Forthcoming. Revelation. In *A Postcolonial Commentary on the New Testament.* Edited by Fernando F. Segovia and R. S. Sugirtharajah. The Bible and Postcolonialism Series. Sheffield: Sheffield Academic Press.

Moore, Stephen D., and Janice Capel Anderson. 1998. Taking It Like a Man: Masculinity in 4 Maccabees. *JBL* 117:249–73.

Mowery, Robert L. 1988. God, Lord and Father: The Theology of the Gospel of Matthew. *BR* 23:24–26.

Moxnes, Halvor. 1988a. Honour and Righteousness in Romans. *JSNT* 32: 61–77.

———. 1988b. Honor, Shame and the Outside World in Paul's Letter to the Romans. Pp 207–18 in *The Social World of Formative Christianity and Judaism.* Edited by Jacob Neusner. Philadelphia: Fortress.

———. 1991. Patron-Client Relations and the New Community in Luke-Acts. Pages 241–68 in *The Social World of Luke-Acts.* Edited by Jerome Neyrey. Peabody, Mass.: Hendrickson.

———, ed. 1997. *Constructing Early Christian Families: Families As Social Reality and Metaphor.* New York: Routledge.

Mulvey, Laura. 1989. Visual Pleasure and Narrative Cinema. *Screen* 16:6–18.

Murnaghan, Sheila. 1988. How a Woman Can Be More Like a Man: The Dialogue between Ischomachus and His Wife in Xenophon's *Oeconomicus. Helios* 15:9–22.

Musurillo, H. 1972. *The Acts of the Christian Martyrs.* Oxford: Clarendon.

Myers, Ched. 1988. *Binding the Strong Man: A Political Reading of Mark's Story of Jesus.* Maryknoll, N.Y.: Orbis.

Nanos, M. *The Mystery of Romans: The Jewish Context of Paul's Letter.* Augburg Fortress.

Newton, Judith. 2002. Masculinity Studies: The Longed For Profeminist Movement for Academic Men? Pages 176–92 in Gardiner 2002b.

Neyrey, Jerome H. 1994. "What's Wrong with This Picture?" John 4, Cultural Stereotypes of Women, and Public and Private Space. *BTB* 24:77–91.

———. 1996. Luke's Social Location of Paul: Cultural Anthropology and the Status of Paul in Acts. Pages 251–79 in *History, Literature, and Society in the Book of Acts.* Edited by Ben Witherington III. Cambridge: Cambridge University Press

———. 1998a. *Honor and Shame in the Gospel of Matthew.* Louisville: Westminster John Knox.

———. 1998b. Nudity. Pages 136–42 in Pilch and Malina.

———. 1998c. Questions, Chreiai, and Challenges to Honor: The Interface of Rhetoric and Culture in Mark's Gospel. *CBQ* 60:657–81.

Neyrey, Jerome H., and Anselm C. Hagedorn. 1998. "It Was out of Envy That They Handed Jesus Over" (Mark 15:10): The Anatomy of Envy and the Gospel of Mark. *JSNT* 69:15–56.

Nineham, D. E. 1963. *Saint Mark.* Baltimore: Penguin.

Nussbaum, M. 1987. The Stoics on the Extirpation of the Passions. *Apeiron* 20: 129–77.

———. 1990. Therapeutic Arguments and Structures of Desire. *Differences* 2:46–66.

———. 1994. *The Therapy of Desire.* Princeton: Princeton.

Olyan, Saul. 1994. And with a Male You Shall Not Lie the Lying Down of a Woman. *Journal of the History of Sexuality* 5:179–206.

Ortner, Sherry, and Harriet Whitehead, eds. 1981. *Sexual Meanings: The Cultural Construction of Gender and Sexuality.* Cambridge: Cambridge University Press

Osiek, Carolyn. 1999. *The Shepherd of Hermas: A Commentary.* Hermeneia. Minneapolis: Fortress.

Parker, Holt N. 1997. The Teratogenic Grid. Pages 47–65 in Hallett and Skinner.

Parsons, Mikeal C. 1995. Hand in Hand: An Autobiographical Reflection on Luke 15. *Semeia* 72:125–52.

Parvey, Constance F. 1974. The Theology and Leadership of Women in the New Testament. Pages 139–46 in *Religion and Sexism.* Edited by Rosemary Radford Ruether. New York: Simon & Schuster.

Pelagius. 1993. *Pelagius' Commentary on Romans.* Edited by M. De Bruyn. Oxford: Oxford University Press.

Peletz, Michael. 1996. *Reason and Passion: Representations of Gender in a Malay Society.* Berkeley and Los Angeles: University of California Press.

Peristiani, J. G., ed. 1966. *Honour and Shame: The Values of Mediterranean Society.* Chicago: University of Chicago Press.

Perkins, Judith. 1995. *The Suffering Self: Pain and Narrative Self-Representation in the Early Christian Era.* New York: Routledge.

———. 1996. This World or Another? The Intertextuality of the Greek Romances, the Apocryphal Acts and Apuleius' *Metamorphoses. Semeia* 80:247–260.

Pervo, Richard I. 1994. Romancing an Oft-Neglected Stone: The Pastoral Epistles and the Epistolary Novel. *Journal of Higher Criticism* 1:25–47.

Petersen, Norman. 1993. *The Gospel of John and the Sociology of Light: Language and Characterization in the Fourth Gospel.* Valley Forge, Pa.: Trinity Press International.

Philo. 1926. *Philo in Ten Volumes and Two Supplementary Volumes.* Translated by F. H. Colson and G. H. Whitaker. LCL. Cambridge: Harvard University Press.

———. 1967. *Works.* LCL. 10 vols. Translated by F. H. Colson and G. H. Whitaker. Cambridge: Harvard University Press.

Philostratus, Flavius. 2001. *Heroikos.* Translated by J. K. Berenson MacLean and E. Bradshaw Aitken. SBLWGRW 1. Atlanta: Society of Biblical Literature.

Pilch, John J., and Bruce J. Malina, eds. 1998. *Handbook of Biblical Social Values.* Peabody, Mass.: Hendrickson.

Pippin, Tina. 1999. *Apocalyptic Bodies: The Biblical Image of the End of the World in Text and Image.* London: Routledge.

Pitre, Brant. 1999. Marginal Elites: Matt 19:12 and the Social and Political Dimensions of Becoming Eunuchs for the Kingdom of God. Paper presented in the Matthew Group at the 1999 Society of Biblical Literature Annual Meeting.

Pitt-Rivers, Julian. 1968. Honor. *IESS* 6:503–11.

———. 1977. *The Fate of Shechem or The Politics of Sex: Essays in the Anthropology of the Mediterranean.* Cambridge: Cambridge University Press

Plato. 1969. *Plato in Twelve Volumes.* Vols. 5–6. Translated by Paul Shorey. Cambridge: Harvard University Press. Cited 15 September 1997. Online: www.perseus.tufts.edu/cgi-bin/text?lookup=plat.+rep.=479c&word=eunuch.

Pliny. 1942. *Natural History*. Translated by H. Rackham. LCL. Cambridge: Harvard University Press.

Plutarch. 1949. *Moralia*. Translated by Frank Cole Babbitt. LCL. Cambridge: Harvard University Press.

———. 1952. *Plutarch's Moralia in Fifteen Volumes*. Vol. 6. Translated by W. C. Helmbold. LCL. Cambridge: Harvard University Press.

Pomata, Gianna. 1996. Blood Ties and Semen Ties: Consanguinity and Agnation in Roman Law. Pages 43–64 in *Gender, Kinship, Power: An Interdisciplinary and Comparative History*. Edited by Mary Jo Maynes et al. New York: Routledge.

Pomeroy, Sarah B. 1994. *Xenophon: Oeconomicus. A Social and Historial Commentary*. Oxford: Clarendon.

———, ed. 1999. *Plutarch's Advice to Bride and Groom and A Consolation to His Wife: English Translations, Commentary, Interpretive Essays and Bibliography*. Oxford: Oxford University Press.

Porter, David, ed. 1992. *Between Men and Feminism*. New York: Routledge.

Powell, Mark Allan. 1998. *Jesus As a Figure in History: How Modern Historians View the Man from Galilee*. Louisville: Westminster John Knox.

Quesnell, Q. 1968. Made Themselves Eunuchs for the Kingdom of Heaven (Mt. 19,12). *CBQ* 30:335–58.

Quinby, Lee. 1997. Coercive Purity: The Dangerous Promise of Apocalyptic Masculinity. Pages 154–65 in *The Year 2000: Essays on the End*. Edited by Charles B. Strozier and Michael Flynn. New York: New York University Press.

Quinn, Jerome D., and William C. Wacker. 2000. *The First and Second Letters to Timothy: A New Translation with Notes and Commentary*. Grand Rapids: Eerdmans.

Rauschenbusch, W. 1907. *Christianity and the Social Crisis*. New York: Macmillan.

Reardon, Bryan P., ed. 1989. *Collected Ancient Greek Novels*. Berkeley and Los Angeles: University of California Press.

Reid, Barbara. 1996. *Choosing the Better Part? Women in the Gospel of Luke*. Collegeville, Minn.: Liturgical Press.

Reimer, Ivoni Richter. 1995. *Women in the Acts of the Apostles: A Feminist Liberation Perspective*. Minneapolis: Fortress.

Reinhartz, Adele. 1994. Gospel of John. Pages 572–73 in *A Feminist Commentary*. Vol. 2 of *Searching the Scriptures*. Edited by Elisabeth Schüssler Fiorenza. New York: Crossroad.

———. 1999. "And the Word Was Begotten": Divine Epigenesis in the Gospel of John. *Semeia* 85:83–103.

Rhoads, David, Joanna Dewey, and Donald Michie. 1999. *Mark As Story: An Introduction to the Narrative of a Gospel*. 2d edition. Philadelphia: Fortress.

Riches, John K. 2000. *Conflicting Mythologies: Identity Formation in the Gospels of Mark and Matthew*. Edinburgh: T&T Clark.

Richlin, Amy. 1991. Zeus and Metis: Foucault, Feminism, Classics. *Helios* 18: 160–80.

———. 1992. *The Garden of Priapus: Sexuality and Aggression in Roman Humor*. Rev. ed. Oxford: Oxford University Press.

———. 1993. Not Before Homosexuality: The Materiality of the Cinaedus and the Roman Law against Love Between Men. *Journal of the History of Sexuality* 3/4:523–73.

————. 1998. Foucault's *History of Sexuality:* A Useful Theory for Women? Pages 128–70 in *Rethinking Sexuality: Foucault and Classical Antiquity.* Edited by David H. J. Larmour, Paul Allen Miller, and Charles Platter. Princeton: Princeton University Press.

Ringe, Sharon H. 1999. *Wisdom's Friends: Community and Christology in the Fourth Gospel.* Louisville: Westminster John Knox.

Robbins, Vernon K. 1991. The Social Location of the Implied Author of Luke-Acts. Pages 304–32 in *The Social World of Luke-Acts.* Edited by Jerome Neyrey. Peabody, Mass.: Hendrickson.

Robinson, James M. 1957. *The Problem of History in Mark.* London: SCM.

————, ed. 1988. *The Nag Hammadi Library in English.* San Francisco: Harper & Row.

Robinson, Sally. 2000. *Marked Men: White Masculinity in Crisis.* New York: Columbia University Press.

Rohrbaugh, Richard L. 1984. Methodological Considerations in the Debate over the Social Class Status of Early Christians. *JAAR* 52:519–46.

————. 1993. The Social Location of the Marcan Audience. *BTB* 23:114–27.

————. 1995. Legitimating Sonship—A Test of Honour: A Social-Scientific Study of Luke 4:1–30. Pages 183–97 in *Modelling Early Christianity: Social-Scientific Studies of the New Testament in Its Context.* Edited by Philip F. Esler. London: Routledge.

Rosenberg, R. 1982. *Beyond Separate Spheres.* New Haven: Yale University Press.

Rousselle, Aline. 1988. *Porneia: On Desire and the Body in Antiquity.* Translated by F. Pheasant. New York: Basil Blackwell.

Royalty, Robert M., Jr. 1988. *The Streets of Heaven: The Ideology of Wealth in the Apocalypse of John.* Macon, Ga.: Mercer University Press.

Rudd, N. 1986. *Themes in Roman Satire.* Norman: University of Oklahoma Press.

Ruether, Rosemary Radford. 1983. *Sexism and God-Talk: Toward a Feminist Theology.* Boston: Beacon [2d ed. 1993].

Ruprecht, Louis A. 1992. Mark's Tragic Vision: Gethsemane. *Religion and Literature* 24:1–25.

Russell, D. A. 1981. *Menander Rhetor.* Edited with translation and commentary by D. A. Russell and N. G. Wilson. Oxford: Oxford University Press.

Saldarini, Anthony J. 1988. *Pharisees, Scribes and Sadducees in Palestinian Society: A Sociological Approach.* Wilmington, Del.: Michael Glazier.

————. 1994. *Matthew's Christian Jewish Community.* Chicago: University of Chicago Press.

Saller, Richard P. Corporal Punishment, Authority, and Obedience in the Roman Household. Pages 144–65 in *Marriage, Divorce, and Children in Ancient Rome.* Edited by Beryl Rawson. Oxford: Clarendon.

Sallust. Translated by John C. Rolfe. LCL. Cambridge: Harvard University Press.

Sandnes, Karl Olav. 1997. Equality within Patriarchal Structures: Some New Testament Perspectives on the Christian Fellowship and a Brother or Sisterhood and a Family. Pages 150–65 in Moxnes 1997.

Santoro-L'Hoir, Francesca. 1992. *The Rhetoric of Gender Terms: "Man," "Woman," and the Portrayal of Character in Latin Prose.* Leiden: Brill.

Satlow, Michael L. 1996. "Try to Be a Man": The Rabbinic Construction of Masculinity. *HTR* 89:19–40.

Savran, David. 1998. *Taking It Like a Man: White Masculinity, Masochism, and Contemporary Culture.* Princeton: Princeton University Press.

Schaberg, Jane. 1997. Feminist Interpretations of the Infancy Narrative of Matthew. *JFSR* 13:35–62.

Schacht, Steven P., and Doris W. Ewing, eds. 1998. *Feminism and Men: Reconstructing Gender Relations.* New York: New York University Press.

Schaff, Philip, and Henry Wace. 1994. *Select Library of the Nicene and Post-Nicene Fathers of the Christian Church.* 2d series. Peabody, Mass.: Hendrickson.

Schneelmelcher, Wilhelm, ed. 1965. *Writings Relating to the Apostles; Apocalypses and Related Subjects.* Vol. 2 of *New Testament Apocrypha.* Translated by R. McL. Wilson. Philadelphia: Westminster.

Schneiders, Sandra M. 1982. Women in the Fourth Gospel and the Role of Women in the Contemporary Church. *BTB* 12:35–45.

Schoene-Harwood, Berthold. 2000. *Writing Men: Literary Masculinities from Frankenstein to the New Man.* Edinburgh: Edinburgh University Press.

Schor, Naomi A. 1992. Feminist and Gender Studies. Pages 267–87 in *Introduction to Scholarship in the Modern Languages and Literatures.* Edited by Joseph Gibaldi. 2d ed. New York: Modern Language Association of America.

Schottroff, Luise. 1995. *Lydia's Impatient Sisters: A Feminist Social History of Early Christianity.* Louisville: Westminster John Knox.

Schrenk, Gottlob. 1964. βάρος, βαρύς, βαρέω. *TDNT* 1:553–61.

Schüssler Fiorenza, Elisabeth. 1983. *In Memory of Her: A Feminist Theological Reconstruction of Christian Origins.* New York: Crossroad.

———. 1986. A Feminist Critical Interpretation for Liberation: Martha and Mary: Luke 10:38–42. *Religion and Intellectual Life* 3:21–35.

———. 1991. *Revelation: Vision of a Just World.* Proclamation. Minneapolis: Fortress.

———. 1994. *Jesus—Miriam's Child, Sophia's Prophet: Critical Issues in Feminist Christology.* New York: Continuum.

Schwalbe, Michael. 1996. *Unlocking the Iron Cage: The Men's Movement, Gender Politics, and American Culture.* Oxford: Oxford University Press.

Schweizer, Eduard. *The Good News according to Mark.* Translated by Donald H. Madvig. Atlanta: John Knox.

Scott, James C. 1977. Protest and Profanation: Agrarian Revolt and the Little Tradition. *Theory and Society* 4:1–38, 211–46.

———. 1990. *Domination and the Arts of Resistance: Hidden Transcripts.* New Haven: Yale University Press.

Scott, Martin. 1992. *Sophia and the Johannine Jesus.* Sheffield: Sheffield Academic Press.

Sedgwick, Eve Kosofsky. 1985. *Between Men: English Literature and Male Homosocial Desire.* New York: Columbia University Press [2d ed. 1992].

———. 1992. Gender Criticism. Pages 271–302 in *Redrawing the Boundaries: The Transformation of English and American Literary Studies.* Edited by Stephen Greenblatt and Giles Gunn. New York: Modern Language Association of America.

———. 1995. Gosh, Boy George, You Must Be Awfully Secure in Your Masculinity! Pages 11–20 in Berger, Wallis, and Watson.

Seeley, David. 1990. *The Noble Death: Graeco-Roman Martyrology and Paul's Concept of Salvation.* JSNTSup 28. Sheffield: Sheffield Academic Press.

———. 1993. Rulership and Service in Mark 10:41–45. *NovT* 35:234–50.

Segal, Lynne. 1990. *Slow Motion: Changing Masculinities, Changing Men.* New Brunswick: Rutgers University Press.

Seim, Turid Karlsen. 1994a. *The Double Message: Patterns of Gender in Luke-Acts.* Edinburgh: T&T Clark.

———. 1994b. Luke. Pages 185–248 in *A Feminist Commentary.* Vol. 2 of *Searching the Scriptures.* Edited by Elisabeth Schüssler Fiorenza. New York: Crossroad.

———. 1999. Children of the Resurrection: Angelic Asceticism in Luke-Acts. Pages 115–27 in Vaage and Wimbush.

Seneca. 1917. *Ad Lucilium Epistulae Morales.* Translated by Richard M. Gummere. 3 vols. LCL. Cambridge: Harvard University Press.

———. 1928–35. *Moral Essays.* Translated by John W. Basore. 3 vols. LCL. Cambridge: Harvard University Press.

Sharpe, Sue. 2000. *Uncertain Masculinities: Youth, Ethnicity, and Class in Contemporary Britain.* New York: Routledge.

Shaw, Brent. 1984. Bandits in the Roman Empire. *Past and Present* 105:5–52.

———. 1993. Tyrants, Bandits, and Kings: Personal Power in Josephus. *JJS* 44:176–204.

———. 1996. Body/Power/Identity: Passions of the Martyrs. *JECS* 4: 269–312.

Sheffield, Julian. 2001. The Father in the Gospel of Matthew. Pages 52–69 in *A Feminist Companion to Matthew.* Edited by Amy-Jill Levine, with Marianne Blickenstaff. FCNTECW 1. Sheffield: Sheffield Academic Press.

Shiner, Whitney. 1998. Creating Plot in Episodic Narrative: The *Life of Aesop* and the Gospel of Mark. Pages 155–76 in Hock, Chance, and Perkins.

Silverman, Kaja. 1992. *Male Subjectivity at the Margins.* New York: Routledge.

Skinner, Marilyn B. 1996. Zeus and Leda: The Sexuality Wars in Contemporary Classical Scholarship. *Thamyris* 3:103–23. Online: www.stoa.org/cgi-bin/ptext?doc=Stoa:text:2002.01.0006.

———. 1997. Introduction: *Quod multo fit aliter in Graecia...* Pages 3–25 in *Roman Sexualities.* Edited by Judith P. Hallett and Marilyn B. Skinner. Princeton: Princeton University Press.

Slater, Philip E. 1971. *The Glory of Hera.* Boston: Beacon.

Slater, Thomas B. 1999. *Christ and Community: A Socio-Historical Study of the Christology of Revelation.* JSNTSup 178. Sheffield: Sheffield Academic Press.

Smith, Abraham. 1999. Full of Spirit and Power: Luke's Portrait of Stephen (Acts 6:1–8:1a) As a Man of Self-Mastery. Pages 97–114 in Vaage and Wimbush.

Smith, Bruce R. 2000. *Shakespeare and Masculinity.* Oxford: Oxford University Press.

Smith, Morton. 1973. *Clement of Alexandria and the Secret Gospel of Mark.* Cambridge: Harvard University Press.

———. 1999. The Troublemakers. Pages 501–68 in *Early Roman Period.* Vol. 3 of *The Cambridge History of Judaism.* Edited by William Horbury, W. D. Davies, and John Sturdy. Cambridge: Cambridge University Press.

Smith, Paul. 1995. Eastwood Bound. Pages 77–97 in Berger, Wallis, and Watson.

Smith, Stephen H. 1995. A Divine Tragedy: Some Observations of the Dramatic Structure of Mark's Gospel. *NovT* 37:209–31.

Solomon-Godeau, Abigail. 1995. Male Trouble. Pages 69–76 in Berger, Wallis, and Watson.

Spencer, F. Scott. 1992. The Ethiopian Eunuch and His Bible: A Social Science Analysis. *BTB* 22:135–65.

Stadter, Philip A. 1999. *Philosophos kai Philandros:* Plutarch's View of Women in the Moralia and Lives. Pages 173–82 in Pomeroy 1999.

Stafford, Emma J. 1998. Masculine Values, Feminine Forms: On the Gender of Personified Abstractions. Pages 43–56 in Foxhall and Salmon 1998a.

Stecopoulous, Harry, and Michael Uebel, eds. 1997. *Race and the Subject of Masculinities.* Durham, N.C.: Duke University Press.

Stevenson, Walter. 1995. The Rise of Eunuchs in Greco-Roman Antiquity. *Journal of the History of Sexuality* 5:495–511.

Stowers, Stanley K. 1994. *Rereading of Romans: Justice Jews, and Gentiles.* New Haven: Yale University Press.

Strathern, Marilyn. 1988. *The Gender of the Gift: Problems with Women and Problems with Society in Melanesia.* Berkeley and Los Angeles: University of California Press.

Streete, Gail Corrington. 1999. Resistance and Ascesis in the Pastoral Letters. Pages 299–316 in Vaage and Wimbush.

Sugirtharajah, R. S., ed. 1998. *The Postcolonial Bible.* The Bible and Postcolonialism 1. Sheffield: Sheffield Academic Press.

Sutton, Robert F. 1981. The Interaction between Men and Women Portrayed on Attic Red-Figure Pottery. Ph.D. diss. University of North Carolina.

Swain, Simon. 1996. *Hellenism and Empire: Language, Classicism, and Power in the Greek World, AD 50–250.* Oxford: Oxford University Press.

Swancutt, Diana. 2001. *Pax Christi:* Romans As Protrepsis to Live As Kings. Ph.D. diss. Duke University.

———. Forthcoming. Sexy Stoics and the Rereading of Romans 1:18–2:16. In *A Feminist Companion to Paul.* Edited by Amy-Jill Levine. FCNTECW. Sheffield: Sheffield Academic Press.

Szewsnat, Holger. 1999. Philo and Homoeroticism: Philo's Use of GYNANDROS and Recent Work on Tribades. *JSJ* 30:140–47.

Tannehill, Robert C. 1975. Matthew 19:12: Eunuchs for the Kingdom. Pages 134–40 in *The Sword of His Mouth.* Philadelphia: Fortress.

———. 1979. The Gospel of Mark As Narrative Christology. *Semeia* 16:57–95.

Taylor, Vincent. 1996. *The Gospel according to St. Mark.* 2d ed. New York: St. Martin's.

Temporini, Hildegard. 1978. *Die Frauen am Hofe Trajans: Eun Beitrag zur Stellung der Augustae in Principat.* Berlin: de Gruyter.

Tetlow, Elizabeth M. 1980. *Women and Ministry in the New Testament.* New York: Paulist.

Thornton, Bruce S. 1997. *Eros: The Myth of Ancient Greek Sexuality.* Boulder, Colo.: Westview.

Tiger, Lionel. 1969. *Men in Groups.* London: Nelson.

Tolbert, Mary Ann. 1989. *Sowing the Gospel: Mark's World in Literary-Historical Perspective.* Minneapolis: Fortress.

———. 1995. When Resistance Becomes Repression: Mark 13:9–27 and the Politics of Location. Pages 331–36 in *Social Location and Biblical Interpretation in Global*

Perspective. Vol. 2 of *Reading from this Place*. Edited by Fernando Segovia Fernando, and Mary Ann Tolbert. Minneapolis: Fortress.

———. 2000. Gender. Pages 99–105 in *Handbook of Postmodern Biblical Interpretation*. Edited by A. K. M. Adam. St. Louis: Chalice.

Torjesen, Karen Jo. 1993. *When Women Were Priests: Women's Leadership in the Early Church and the Scandal of Their Subordination in the Rise of Christianity*. San Francisco: HarperSanFrancisco.

Traister, Bryce. 2000. Academic Viagra: The Rise of American Masculinity Studies. *American Quarterly* 52:274–304.

Treggiari, Susan. 1991. *Roman Marriage: Iusti Coniuges from the Time of Cicero to the Time of Ulpian*. Oxford: Oxford University Press.

Trigg, Wilson. 1983. *Origen: The Bible and Philosophy in the Third-Century Church*. Atlanta: John Knox.

Vaage, Leif E., and Vincent L. Wimbush, eds. 1999. *Asceticism and the New Testament*. New York: Routledge.

Van der Horst, Pieter W. 1996. Sarah's Seminal Emission: Hebrews 11:11 in the Light of Ancient Embryology. Pages 112–34 in *A Feminist Companion to the Hebrew Bible in the New Testament*. Edited by Athalya Brener. Sheffield: Sheffield Academic Press.

Vermaseren, M. J. 1966. *The Legend of Attis in Greek and Roman Art*. Leiden: Brill.

Veyne, Paul. 1978. La Famille et l'amour sous le Haut-Empire romain. *Annales E.S.C.* 3:36–63.

Villiers, Pieter G. R. de. 1996. The Vice of Conceit in 1 Timothy: A Study in the Ethics of the New Testament within Its Graeco-Roman Context. *Acta patristica et byzantina* 7:37–67.

Waetjen, Herman C. 1989. *A Reordering of Power: A Socio-Political Reading of Mark's Gospel*. Minneapolis: Fortress.

Wainwright, Elaine Mary. 1991. *Towards a Feminist Critical Reading of the Gospel according to Matthew*. Berlin: de Gruyter.

Wallace-Hadrill, Andrew. 1996. Engendering the Roman House. Pages 104–15 in *I, Claudia: Women in Ancient Rome*. Edited by Diana E. E. Kleiner and Susan B. Matheson. New Haven: Yale University Press.

Walters, Jonathan. 1991. "No More Than a Boy": The Shifting Construction of Masculinity from Ancient Greece to the Middle Ages. *Gender and History* 5:20–33.

———. 1997. Invading the Roman Body: Manliness and Impenetrability in Roman Thought. Pages 29–43 in Hallett and Skinner.

Ward, Graham. 1994. Mimesis: The Measure of Mark's Christology. *Journal of Literature and Theology* 8:1–29.

———. 1995. A Postmodern Version of Paradise. *JSOT* 65:3–12.

———. 1996. Divinity and Sexuality: Luce Irigaray and Christology. *Modern Theology* 12:221–37.

———. 1998. The Erotics of Redemption—After Karl Barth. *Theology and Sexuality* 8:52–72.

———. 1999. The Displaced Body of Jesus Christ. Pages 163–81 in *Radical Orthodoxy*. Edited by John Milbank, Catherine Pickstock, and Graham Ward. London: Routledge.

Ward, R. B. 1990. Musonius and Paul on Marriage. *NTS* 36: 281–89.

Webster, Jane S. 1998. Sophia: Engendering Wisdom in Proverbs, Ben Sira and the Wisdom of Solomon. *JSOT* 78:63–79.

Wiedemann, Thomas. 1992. *Emperors and Gladiators*. London: Routledge.

Willett (Newheart), Michael E. 1992. *Wisdom Christology in the Fourth Gospel*. San Francisco: Mellen Research University Press.

Williams, Craig A. 1998. *Roman Homosexuality: Ideologies of Masculinity in Classical Antiquity*. New York and Oxford: Oxford University Press.

Williams, Raymond. 2001. Base and Superstructure in Marxist Cultural Theory. Pages 158–78 in *The Raymond Williams Reader*. Edited by John Higgins. Malden: Blackwell.

Wills, Lawrence M. 1991. The Depiction of the Jews in Acts. *JBL* 110:651–54.

———. 1997. *The Quest for the Historical Gospel: Mark, John, and the Origins of the Gospel Genre*. London and New York: Routledge.

Winkler, John J. 1985. *Auctor and Actor: A Narratological Reading of Apuleius' Golden Ass*. Berkeley and Los Angeles: University of California Press.

———. 1990a. *The Constraints of Desire: The Anthropology of Sex and Gender in Ancient Greece*. New York: Routledge.

———. 1990b. Laying Down the Law: The Oversight of Men's Behavior in Classical Athens. Pages 171–209 in Halperin, Winkler, and Zeitlin.

Winsor, Ann Roberts. 1999a. *A King Is Bound in the Tresses: Allusions to the Song of Songs in the Fourth Gospel*. Studies in Biblical Literature 6. New York: Lang.

Winter, Bruce W. 1988. The Public Honouring of Christian Benefactors: Romans 13.3–4 and 1 Peter 2.14–15. *JSNT* 34:87–103

Wire, Antoinette Clark. 1991. Gender Roles in a Scribal Community. Pages 87–121 in *Social History of the Matthean Community: Cross-Disciplinary Approaches*. Edited by David L. Balch. Minneapolis: Fortress.

Wistrand, Magnus. 1992. *Entertainment and Violence in Ancient Rome: The Attitudes of Roman Writers of the First Century A. D.* Göteborg: Acta Universtatis Gothoburgensis.

Witherington, Ben, III. 2001. *The Gospel of Mark: A Socio-Rhetorical Commentary*. Grand Rapids: Eerdmans.

Wittig, Monique. 1983. The Point of View: Universal or Particular? *Feminist Issues* 3:63–69.

Wolf, Eric R. 1966. Kinship, Friendship, and Patron–Client Relationships in Complex Societies. Pages 3–27 in *The Social Anthropology of Complex Societies*. Edited by Michael Banton. London: Tavistock.

———, ed. 1984. *Religion, Power, and Protest in Local Communities: The Northern Shore of the Mediterranean*. New York: Mouton.

Wrede, William. 1971. *The Messianic Secret*. Translated by J. C. Greig. Greenwood: Attic [1901].

Xenophon. 1979. *Xenophon in Seven Volumes*. Translated by E. C. Merchant. Cambridge: Harvard University Press. Cited 2 February 2002. Online: www.perseus.tufts.edu/cgi- bin/ptext?lookup=Xen.+Mem.+2.3.1.

Xenophon of Ephesus. 1989. An Ephesian Tale. Translated by Graham Anderson. Pages 125–69 in Reardon.

Yanagisako, Sylvia, and Carol Delaney. 1995. Naturalizing Power. Pages 1–22 in *Naturalizing Power: Essays in Feminist Cultural Analysis*. Edited by Sylvia Yanagisako and Carol Delaney. New York: Routledge.

Young, Frances. 1994. *The Theology of the Pastoral Letters*. New Testament Theology. Cambridge: Cambridge University Press.

Young, Stephen. 1994. Being a Man: The Pursuit of Manliness in the *Shepherd of Hermas. JECS* 2:237–255.

CONTRIBUTORS

Janice Capel Anderson is Professor of Philosophy and Religious Studies at the University of Idaho. Her publications include *Matthew's Narrative Web* (Sheffield Academic Press, 1994) and "Matthew: Gender and Reading," *Semeia* 28 (reprinted in *A Feminist Companion to Matthew*). She and Stephen D. Moore have collaborated on a number of projects, including the editing of *Mark and Method: New Approaches in Biblical Studies* (Fortress, 1992). Her current interests revolve around textbooks and the discipline of biblical studies. She can be reached at jcanders@uidaho.edu.

Mary R. D'Angelo is Associate Professor in the Department of Theology at the University of Notre Dame, Indiana. She teaches New Testament and Christian Origins, specializing in religion, women, and gender in the ancient world. She is co-editor of *Women and Christian Origins* (Oxford University Press, 1999) with Ross S. Kraemer, and of *Crossroads in Christology: Essays in Honor of Ellen M. Leonard* (*Toronto Journal of Theology*, 2000) with Anne Anderson. Her articles on women, gender, imperial politics, theological language, and sexual practice in the beginnings of Christianity have appeared in collections and in such journals as the *Journal of Biblical Literature, Journal of Feminist Studies in Religion, Horizons*, and *Biblical Interpretation.* She can be reached at mdangelo@nd.edu.

David J. A. Clines is Research Professor in the Department of Biblical Studies of the University of Sheffield, England. He is editor of the ongoing *Dictionary of Classical Hebrew* and has just completed volume 2 of his commentary on Job for the Word Biblical Commentary series. As well as his involvement in matters philological and exegetical, he takes an interest in the impact of contemporary concerns, such as gender studies, on biblical criticism and hopes to produce a book on masculinity in the Bible. He can be reached at d.clines@sheffield.ac.uk.

Colleen Conway is Assistant Professor of Religion at Seton Hall University in South Orange, New Jersey. She is the author of *Men and Women in the Fourth Gospel: Gender and Johannine Characterization* (Society of Biblical Literature, 1999). Her current work involves examining constructions of masculinity in the ancient Mediterranean in relation to New Testament Christology. She can be reached at conwayco@shu.edu.

Page duBois is Professor of Classics, Comparative Literature, and Cultural Studies in the Department of Literature at the University of California, San Diego.

Her most recent books are *Trojan Horses: Saving the Classics from Conservatives* (New York University Press, 2001) and *Slaves and Other Objects* (University of Chicago Press, 2003).

Chris Frilingos is Assistant Professor in the Department of Religious Studies at Michigan State University. His book, *Spectacles of Empire: Monsters, Martyrs, and the Book of Revelation,* will be published by the University of Pennsylvania Press in 2004. He is chiefly concerned with reading early Christian texts as cultural products of the Roman Empire.

Jennifer A. Glancy is Professor of Religious Studies at Le Moyne College in Syracuse, New York. She is the author of *Slavery in Early Christianity* (Oxford University Press, 2002) and one of the co-authors of *Introduction to the Study of Religion* (Orbis, 1998). Her current research centers on the cultural conditioning of the early Christian body. She can be reached at glancy@lemoyne.edu.

Maud Gleason teaches Classics at Stanford University. She is the author of *Making Men: Sophists and Self-Presentation in Ancient Rome* (Princeton University Press, 1995). She is interested in stereotypes, cultural interfaces, and body language as well as gender (see her "Mutilated Messengers: Body Language in Josephus" in *Being Greek under Rome* [ed. S. Goldhill; Cambridge University Press, 2001]). She can be reached at maud@stanford.edu.

Seong Hee Kim is a doctoral student at Drew University, Madison, New Jersey. Her major research interest is postcolonial biblical interpretation in relation to cultural studies, feminist studies, and Asian hermeneutics.

Tat-siong Benny Liew is Associate Professor of New Testament at Chicago Theological Seminary. He is the author of *Politics of Parousia: Reading Mark Inter(con)textually* (Brill, 1999) and the guest editor of the *Semeia* volume, *The Bible in Asian America* (Society of Biblical Literature, 2002). He can be reached at bliew@ctschicago.edu.

Stephen D. Moore is Professor of New Testament at Drew University Theological School, Madison, New Jersey. His recent books include *God's Gym: Divine Male Bodies of the Bible* (Routledge, 1996) and *God's Beauty Parlor: And Other Queer Spaces in and around the Bible* (Stanford University Press, 2001). He is currently working on a further book on postcolonial studies and early Christianity. He can be reached at smoore@drew.edu.

Jerome H. Neyrey, Professor of New Testament Studies at the University of Notre Dame, Indiana, interprets the scriptures in terms of cultural and social-scientific perspective, especially honor and shame, purity and pollution, envy and limited good, the sociology of secrecy, and territoriality. He is the executive secretary for The Context Group, a network of scholars who interpret the Bible in its social and cultural context. He may be reached at neyrey.1@nd.edu.

Diana M. Swancutt is Assistant Professor of New Testament Studies at Yale Divinity School. A Pauline scholar, her interdisciplinary research examines the impact of rhetoric, politics, philosophy, gender, ethnicity, and imperialism on Pauline Christian Judaism. She is the author of "Sexy Stoics and the Rereading of Romans 1:18–2:16," in *A Feminist Companion to Paul* (Sheffield Academic Press, forthcoming), and "Paraenesis in Light of Protrepsis: Troubling the Typical Dichotomy," in *Early Christian Paraenesis in Its Ancient Context*, edited by J. M. Starr and T. Engberg-Pedersen (forthcoming). She is currently revising her Duke University dissertation, "*Pax Christi:* Romans As Protrepsis to Live As Kings," for publication. She can be reached at diana.swancutt@yale.edu.

Jeffrey Staley is Visiting Professor of Theology and Religious Studies at Seattle University in Washington. He has published widely in postcolonial and autobiographical approaches to New Testament texts, most recently co-editing with Musa Dube *John and Postcolonialism: Travel, Space, and Power* (Continuum, 2002). His current research interest focuses on early twentieth-century Methodist women's work with Chinese prostitutes and abused girls in San Francisco, California. He can be reached at staleyjl@jps.net.

Eric Thurman is a doctoral student at Drew University, Madison, New Jersey. His interests include the intersection of masculinity studies and postcolonial, queer, and feminist theories with questions of early Christian identity formation.